AF545226

CHILTON'S
REPAIR & TUNE-UP GUIDE
FAIRMONT ZEPHYR 1978-83
All models

Vice President and General Manager JOHN P. KUSHNERICK
Managing Editor KERRY A. FREEMAN, S.A.E.
Senior Editor RICHARD J. RIVELE, S.A.E.
Editor RON WEBB

CHILTON BOOK COMPANY
Radnor, Pennsylvania
19089

SAFETY NOTICE

Proper service and repair procedures are vital to the safe, reliable operation of all motor vehicles, as well as the personal safety of those performing repairs. This book outlines procedures for servicing and repairing vehicles using safe, effective methods. The procedures contain many NOTES, CAUTIONS and WARNINGS which should be followed along with standard safety procedures to eliminate the possibility of personal injury or improper service which could damage the vehicle or compromise its safety.

It is important to note that repair procedures and techniques, tools and parts for servicing motor vehicles, as well as the skill and experience of the individual performing the work vary widely. It is not possible to anticipate all of the conceivable ways or conditions under which vehicles may be serviced, or to provide cautions as to all of the possible hazards that may result. Standard and accepted safety precautions and equipment should be used when handling toxic or flammable fluids, and safety goggles or other protection should be used during cutting, grinding, chiseling, prying, or any other process that can cause material removal or projectiles.

Some procedures require the use of tools specially designed for a specific purpose. Before substituting another tool or procedure, you must be completely satisfied that neither your personal safety, nor the performance of the vehicle will be endangered.

Although information in this guide is based on industry sources and is as complete as possible at the time of publication, the possibility exists that the manufacturer made later changes which could not be included here. While striving for total accuracy, Chilton Book Company cannot assume responsibility for any errors, changes, or omissions that may occur in the compilation of this data.

PART NUMBERS

Part numbers listed in this reference are not recommendations by Chilton for any product by brand name. They are references that can be used with interchange manuals and aftermarket supplier catalogs to locate each brand supplier's discrete part number.

ACKNOWLEDGMENTS

The Chilton Book Company expresses its appreciation to the Ford Motor Company for the technical information and illustrations contained within this manual.

Ford special tools mentioned in some procedures can be ordered through your Ford dealer or directly from the Owatonna Tool Company, Owatonna, Minnesota 55060.

Published in Radnor, Pennsylvania 19089, by Chilton Book Company

Manufactured in the United States of America
34567890 210987654

Chilton's Repair & Tune-Up Guide: Fairmont and Zephyr 1978–83
ISBN 0-8019-7312-0 pbk.
Library of Congress Catalog Card No. 82-72934

CONTENTS

Quick Reference Specifications For Your Vehicle

Fill in this chart with the most commonly used specifications for your vehicle. Specifications can be found in Chapters 1 through 3 or on the tune-up decal under the hood of the vehicle.

Tune-Up

Firing Order__________

Spark Plugs:

Type Auto lite Resistor #46

Gap (in.) .050

Point Gap (in.) N/A

Dwell Angle (°)__________

Ignition Timing (°) 10 B

Vacuum (Connected/Disconnected)__________

Valve Clearance (in.)

Intake__________ Exhaust__________

Capacities

Engine Oil (qts)

With Filter Change 5 QTS.

Without Filter Change 4 QTS.

Cooling System (qts) 8.1 QTS.

Manual Transmission (pts)__________

Type__________

Automatic Transmission (pts) 14.2 pts

Type__________

Front Differential (pts)__________

Type__________

Rear Differential (pts)__________

Type__________

Transfer Case (pts)__________

Type__________

FREQUENTLY REPLACED PARTS

Use these spaces to record the part numbers of frequently replaced parts.

PCV VALVE	OIL FILTER	AIR FILTER
Manufacturer__________	Manufacturer__________	Manufacturer__________
Part No.__________	Part No. WF-1 WAL-MART	Part No. WAF-10 WAL-MART BRAND WAF-24

General Information and Maintenance

HOW TO USE THIS BOOK

Chilton's Repair & Tune-Up Guide for the Fairmont/Zephyr is intended to teach you about the inner workings of your car and save you money on its upkeep. The first two chapters contain maintenance and tune-up information and procedures. The following chapters concern themselves with the more complex systems of your car. Operating systems from engine through brakes are covered to the extent that we feel the average do-it-yourselfer should get involved. This book will not explain such things as rebuilding the differential for the simple reason that the expertise required and the investment in special tools make this task uneconomical.

We will tell you how to do many jobs (using available tools) that can save you money, give you personal satisfaction and help you avoid problems.

This book will also serve as a reference for owners who want to understand their car and/or their mechanics better. In this case, no tools at all are required.

Before removing any parts, read through the entire procedure. This will give you the overall view of what tools and supplies will be required.

The sections begin with a brief discussion of the system and what it involves, followed by adjustments, maintenance, removal and installation procedures, and repair or overhaul procedures. When repair is not considered feasible, we tell you how to remove the part and then how to install the new or rebuilt replacement. In this way, you at least save the labor costs. Backyard repair of such components as the alternator is just not practical.

Two basic mechanic's rules should be mentioned here. One, whenever the left side of the car or engine is referred to, it is meant to specify the driver's side. Conversely, the right side of the car means the passenger's side. Secondly, most screws and bolts are removed by turning counterclockwise, and tightened by turning clockwise. Safety is always the most important rule. Constantly be aware of the dangers involved in working on an automobile and take the proper precautions. Use jackstands when working under a raised vehicle. Don't smoke or allow an exposed flame to come near the battery or any part of the fuel system. Always use the proper tool and use it correctly; bruised knuckles and skinned fingers aren't a mechanic's standard equipment. Always take your time and have patience; Once you have some experience, working on your car will become an enjoyable hobby.

TOOLS AND EQUIPMENT

It would be impossible to catalog each and every tool that you may need to perform all the operations included in this book. It would also not be wise for the amateur to rush out and buy an expensive set of tools on the theory that he may need one of them at some time. The best approach is to proceed slowly, gathering together a good quality set of those tools that are used most frequently. Don't be misled by the low cost of bargain tools. It is far better to spend a little more for quality, name brand tools. Forged wrenches, 6 or 12 point sockets and fine-tooth ratchets are by far preferable to their less expensive counterparts. As any good mechanic can tell you, there are few worse experiences than trying to work on a car or truck with bad tools. Your monetary savings will be far outweighed by frustration and mangled knuckles.

Begin accumulating those tools that are used most frequently; those associated with routine maintenance and tune-up. In addition to the normal assortment of screwdrivers and pliers, you should have the following tools for routine maintenance jobs:

1. SAE and metric wrenches, sockets and combination open end/box end wrenches.
2. Jackstands—for support;
3. Oil filter wrench;
4. Oil filler spout or funnel;
5. Grease gun—for chassis lubrication;
6. Hydrometer—for checking the battery;
7. A low flat pan for draining oil;
8. Lots of rags for wiping up the inevitable mess.

In addition to the above items, there are several others that are not absolutely necessary, but are handy to have around. These include oil drying compound, a transmission funnel, and the usual supply of lubricants, antifreeze and fluids, although these can be purchased as needed. This is a basic list for routine maintenance, but only your personal needs can accurately determine your list of tools.

The second list of tools is for tune-ups. While the tools involved here are slightly more sophisticated, they need not be outrageously expensive. There are several inexpensive tachometers on the market that are every bit as good for the average mechanic as an expensive professional model. Just be sure that it works on 4, 6, and 8 cylinder engines. A basic list of tune-up equipment could include:

1. Tachometer;
2. Spark plug wrench;
3. Timing light (preferably a DC high voltage light that works from the car's battery);
4. A set of flat feeler gauges;
5. A set of round wire spark plug gauges.

In addition to these basic tools, there are several other tools and gauges you may find useful. These include:

1. A compression gauge. The screw-in type is slower to use, but eliminates the possibility of a faulty reading due to escaping pressure;
2. A manifold vacuum gauge;
3. A test light;
4. An induction meter. This is used for determining whether or not there is current in a wire. These are handy for use if a wire is broken somewhere in a wiring harness.

As a final note, you will probably find a torque wrench necessary for all but the most basic work. The beam type models are perfectly adequate, although the newer click type are more precise.

Special Tools

Normally, the use of special factory tools is avoided for repair procedures, since these are not readily available for the do-it-yourself mechanic. When it is possible to perform the job with more commonly available tools, it will be pointed out, but occasionally, a special tool was designed to perform a specific function and should be used. Before substituting another tool, you should be convinced that neither your safety nor the performance of the vehicle will be compromised.

Some special tools are available commercially from major tool manufacturers. Others for your car can be purchased from your dealer or from Owatonna Tool Co., Owatonna, Minnesota 55060.

SERVICING YOUR VEHICLE SAFELY

It is virtually impossible to anticipate all of the hazards involved with automotive maintenance and service but care and common sense will prevent most accidents.

The rules of safety for mechanics range from "don't smoke around gasoline," to "use the proper tool for the job." The trick to avoiding injuries is to develop safe work habits and take every possible precaution.

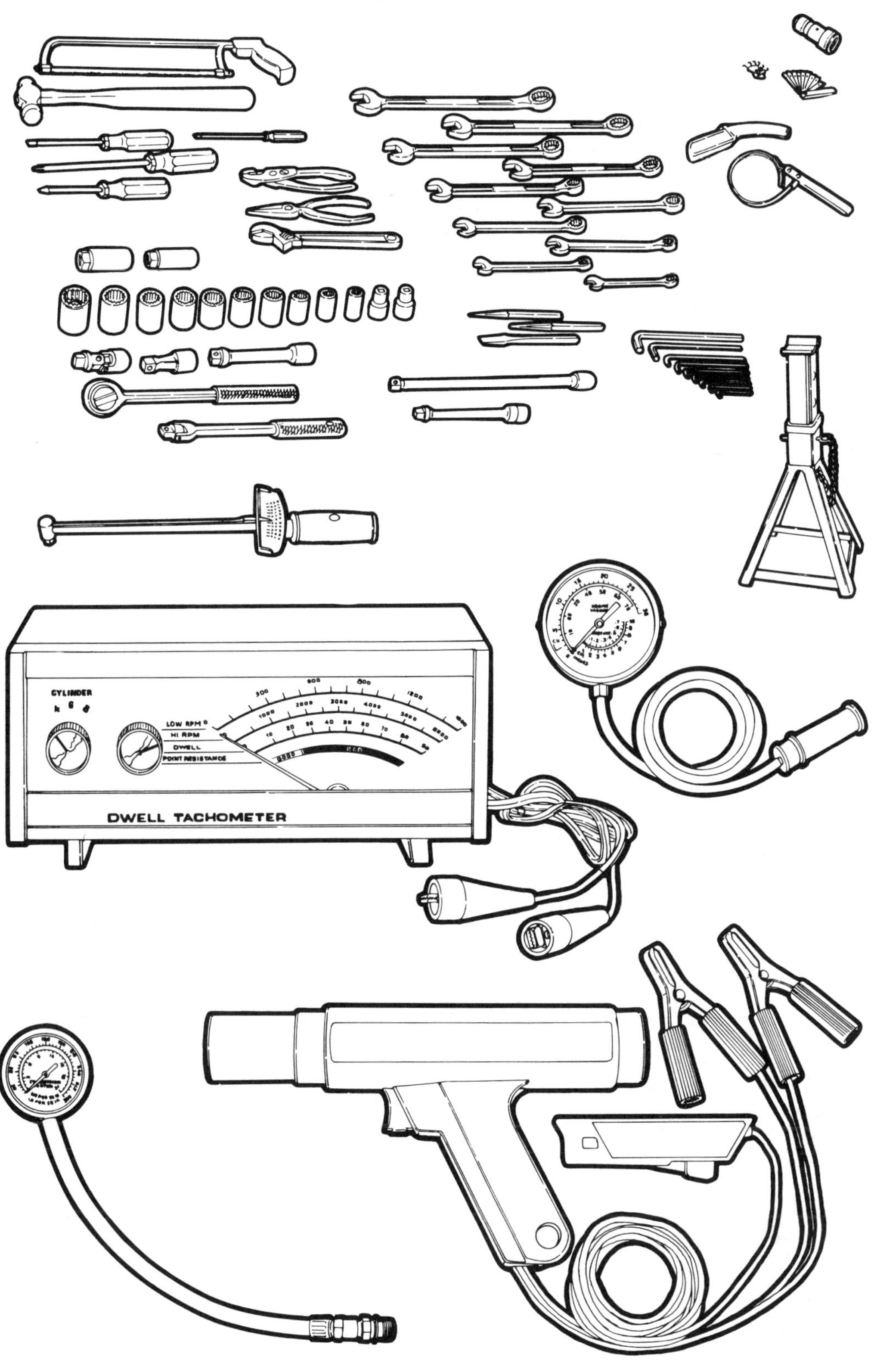

The tools and equipment shown here will handle the majority of the maintenance on a car

Do's

• Do keep a fire extinguisher and first aid kit within easy reach.

• Do wear safety glasses or goggles when cutting, drilling, grinding or prying. If you wear glasses for the sake of vision, then they should be made of hardened glass that can serve also as safety glasses, or wear safety goggles over your regular glasses.

• Do shield your eyes whenever you work aournd the battery. Batteries contain sulphuric acid; in case of contact with the eyes or skin, flush the area with water or a mixture of water and baking soda and get medical attention immediately.

• Do use safety stands for any under-car service. Jacks are for raising vehicles; safety stands are for making sure the vehicle stays raised until you want it to come down. Whenever the vehicle is raised, block the wheels remaining on the ground and set the parking brake.

• Do use adequate ventilation when working with any chemicals. Asbestos dust resulting from brake lining wear could cause cancer.

• Do disconnect the negative battery cable when working on the electrical system.

• Do follow manufacturer's directions whenever working with potentially hazardous materials. Both brake fluid and antifreeze are poisonous if taken internally.

• Do properly maintain your tools. Loose hammerheads, mushroomed punches and chisels, frayed or poorly grounded electrical cords, excessively worn screwdrivers, spread wrenches (open end), cracked sockets, slipping ratchets, or faulty droplight sockets can cause accidents.

• Do use the proper size and type of tool for the job being done.

• Do when possible, pull on a wrench handle rather than push on it, and adjust your stance to prevent a fall.

• Do be sure that adjustable wrenches are tightly adjusted on the nut or bolt and pulled so that the face is on the side of the fixed jaw.

• Do select a wrench or socket that fits the nut or bolt. The wrench or socket should sit straight, not cocked.

• Do strike squarely with a hammer; avoid glancing blows.

• Do set the parking brake and block the wheels if the work requires that the engine be running.

Don't's

• Don't run an engine in a garage or anywhere else without proper ventilation—EVER! Carbon monoxide is poisonous; it is absorbed by the body 400 times faster than oxygen; it takes a long time to leave the human body and you can build up a deadly supply of it in your system by simply breathing in a little every day. You may not realize you are slowly poisoning yourself. Always use power vents, windows, fans or open the garage doors.

• Don't work around moving parts while wearing a necktie or other loose clothing. Short sleeves are much safer than long, loose sleeves. Hard-toed shoes with neoprene soles protect your toes and give a better grip on slippery surfaces. Jewelry such as watches, fancy belt buckles, beads or body adornment of any kind is not safe while working around a car. Long hair should be hidden under a hat or cap.

• Don't use pockets for toolboxes. A fall or bump can drive a screwdriver deep into your body. Even a wiping cloth hanging from the back pocket can wrap around a spinning shaft or fan.

• Don't smoke when working around gasoline, cleaning solvent or other flammable material.

• Don't smoke when working around the battery. When the battery is being charged, it gives off explosive hydrogen gas.

• Don't use gasoline to wash your hands; there are excellent soaps available. Gasoline may contain lead, and lead can enter the body through a cut, accumulating in the body until you are very ill. Gasoline also removes all the natural oils from the skin so that bone dry hands will suck up oil and grease.

• Don't service the air conditioning system unless you are equipped with the necessary tools and training. The refrigerant, R-12, is extremely cold and when exposed to the air, will instantly freeze any surface it comes in contact with, including your eyes. Although the refrigerant is normally non-toxic, R-12 becomes a deadly poisonous gas in the presence of an open flame. One good whiff of the vapors from burning refrigerant can be fatal.

HISTORY

The Fairmont/Zephyr series, introduced in 1978, features the fuel economy and maneuverability of a compact car with the interior roominess and comfort of a mid-sized car.

Some highlights of the Fairmont/Zephyr series are: A strut-type front suspension; coil spring, four-link rear suspension; manual or power rack and pinion steering; lightweight, cast center-section rear axle; lighter front disc brake calipers and a body designed with computor analysis to provide a balance of strength and light weight.

MODEL AND SERIAL NUMBER IDENTIFICATION

Vehicle Identification Number (VIN)

The (VIN) Vehicle Identification Number for title and registration purposes is stamped on a metal tab attached to the instrument panel close to the lower windshield frame on the driver's side of the car.

A thirteen digit number is used through 1980. The first digit identifies the model year, and the fifth digit identifies the installed engine.

A seventeen digit number is used from 1981. The tenth digit identifies the model year, and the eighth digit identifies the installed engine.

13 digit VIN number

17 digit VIN number

Vehicle Certification Label

The Vehicle Certification Label is attached to the left front door lock face panel or door pillar. The Vehicle Identification Number (VIN) also appears on this label.

Engine Identification

Identification of the engine can be made by finding the letter code in the Vehicle Identi-

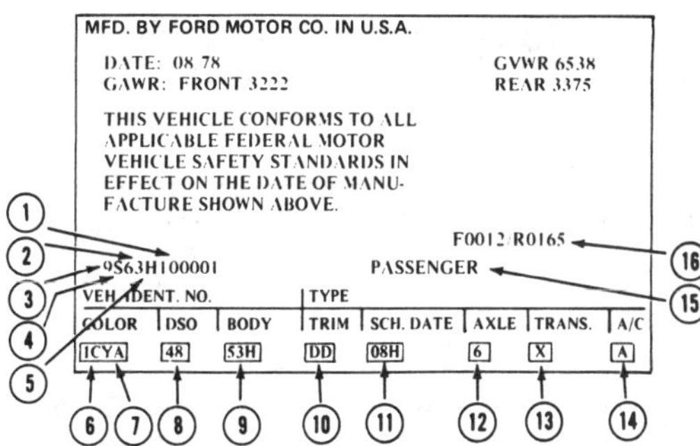

Vehicle certification number (United States)

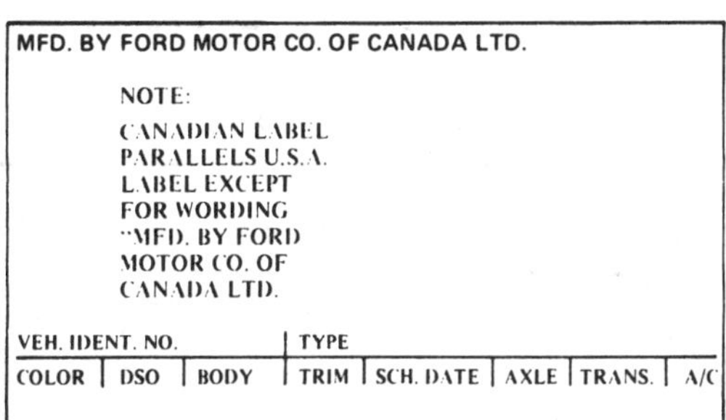

Vehicle certification label (Canada)

fication Number then referring to the engine identification chart to determine the engine type and size. An engine identification label is also attached to the engine, usually to the valve cover. The symbol codes on the identification tag not only identify the engine but are used for determining parts usage. The codes are shown in the dealer's master parts catalog to designate unique parts.

Transmission Identification

The transmission can be identified by finding the transmission code which appears on the bottom right side of the Vehicle Certification Label and referring to the transmission identification chart. There is also a transmission identification tag attached to the transmission.

ROUTINE MAINTENANCE

Air Cleaner

All engines are equipped with a dry type air cleaner mounted on top of the carburetor. The air cleaner contains a replaceable filter element and a replaceable crankcase ventilation system filter, as well as various sensors, switches and vacuum motors that control the intake air temperature. Both the air filter ele-

Body and Style Code

Vehicle	Style Code	Body Type
Fairmont	36R	2 dr. Sport Coupe
	54B	4 dr. Sedan
	66B	2 dr. Sedan
	74B	4 dr. Station Wagon
Zephyr	36R	2 dr. Sport Coupe
	54D	4 dr. Sedan
	66D	2 dr. Sedan
	74D	4 dr. Station Wagon

Engine Codes

Year	Code	Cyl.	Liters	Cubic Ins.	Carb.
1978–79	Y	4	2.3	140	2 bbl.
	T	6	3.3	200	1 bbl.
	F	8	5.0	302	2 bbl.
1980–82	A	4	2.3	140	2 bbl.
	B	6	3.3	200	1 bbl.
	D	8	4.2	255	2 bbl.
1983	A	4	2.3	140	1 bbl.
	B	6	3.3	200	1 bbl.

Transmission Codes

Code	Model	Manufacturer
1	3 Speed	Ford
6	4 Speed OD	Borg-Warner
7	4 Speed	Hummer
C	C5 Auto.	Ford
V	C3 Auto.	Ford
W	C4 Auto.	Ford

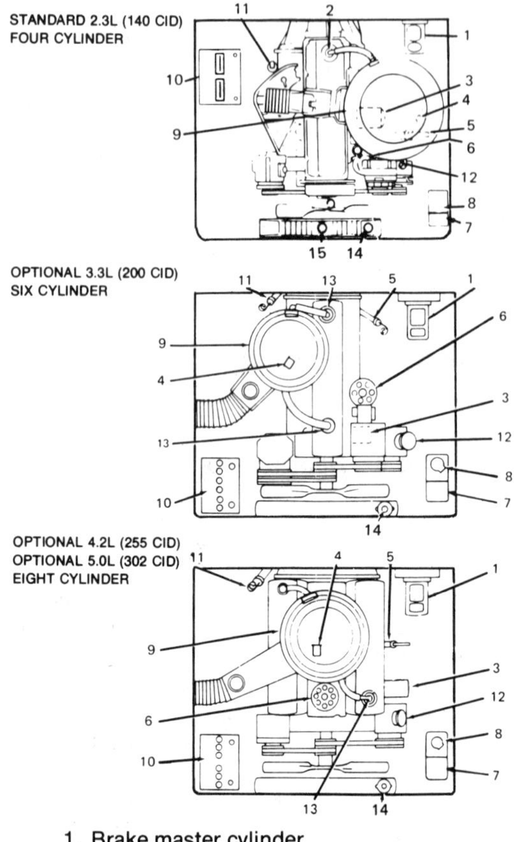

1. Brake master cylinder
2. Engine oil filler cap & PCV filter (2.3L)
3. Engine oil filter
4. Fuel filter (on carburetor)
5. Engine oil dipstick
6. Distributor
7. Coolant expansion bottle
8. Windshield washer reservoir
9. Air cleaner assembly
10. Battery
11. Automatic transmission dipstick
12. Power steering reservoir dipstick
13. PCV valve & grommet & oil filler cap (3.3L & 4.2L)
14. Radiator cap (all except 2.3L non-A/C)
15. Radiator cap (2.3L non-A/C)

Vehicle service points

ment and the crankcase ventilation filter should be changed every 30 months or 30 thousand miles. If the vehicle is operated in dusty, or severe conditions a more frequent changing of the filters may be necessary.

REPLACING THE AIR CLEANER AND PCV FILTER ELEMENTS

1. Remove the wing nut or nuts that retain the top of the air cleaner.
2. Remove the cover and gently lift the element out of the housing. Do not knock any dirt into the carburetor.
3. Pull the PCV filter out of the plastic retainer. (On some models the complete ventilation filter may have to be replaced. Remove the hose and the retaining clip from the outside body of the air cleaner. Remove and discard the filter assembly).
4. Wipe the inside of the air cleaner and the PCV filter retainer clean with a rag or soft paper towel.
5. Install a new PCV ventilation filter and a new air cleaner element.
6. Replace the air cleaner cover and install the wing nut or nuts. If more than one wing

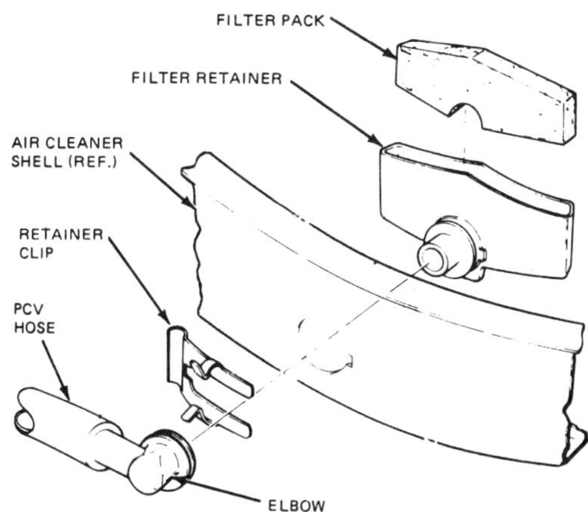

Crankcase ventilation filter in air cleaner

nut is used, be sure to check the tightness of the first ones installed after tightening the others.

PCV Valve (Positive Crankcase Ventilation)

All engines are equipped with a positive crankcase emission control system. The PCV system routes a harmful mixture of blow-by gases and condensation vapors through a modulating valve and into the intake manifold where they combine with the carburetor air/fuel mixture and are burned in the combustion chamber.

A faulty PCV valve or clogged hose can cause a rough idle and poorly performing car. Check the system at least once a year and replace the valve every 20 months or 20 thousand miles. A quick way to test the PCV valve is to free it from the grommet at the filler cap or valve cover and shake the valve. If the valve rattles it is probably all right.

If you own or can borrow an engine tachometer, a better way to test the PCV valve follows:

1. Connect a tachometer to the engine.
2. With the engine idling, remove the PCV valve from its mounting grommet.
3. Check the tachometer reading. Place a finger over the valve. Suction should be felt.
4. Check the tachometer reading again. The engine speed should have dropped at least 50 rpm. It should return to the first reading when the finger is removed from the opening.
5. If the engine does not change speed or if the change is less than 50 rpm, the hose is clogged or the PCV valve is bad. Check the hose first, if it is not clogged replace the PCV valve.

Evaporative Emission Canister

Fuel vapor emitted through the fuel vapor valve and carburetor bowl vent is stored in a carbon filled canister. There is no scheduled maintenance for the canister other than checking the hose connections periodically.

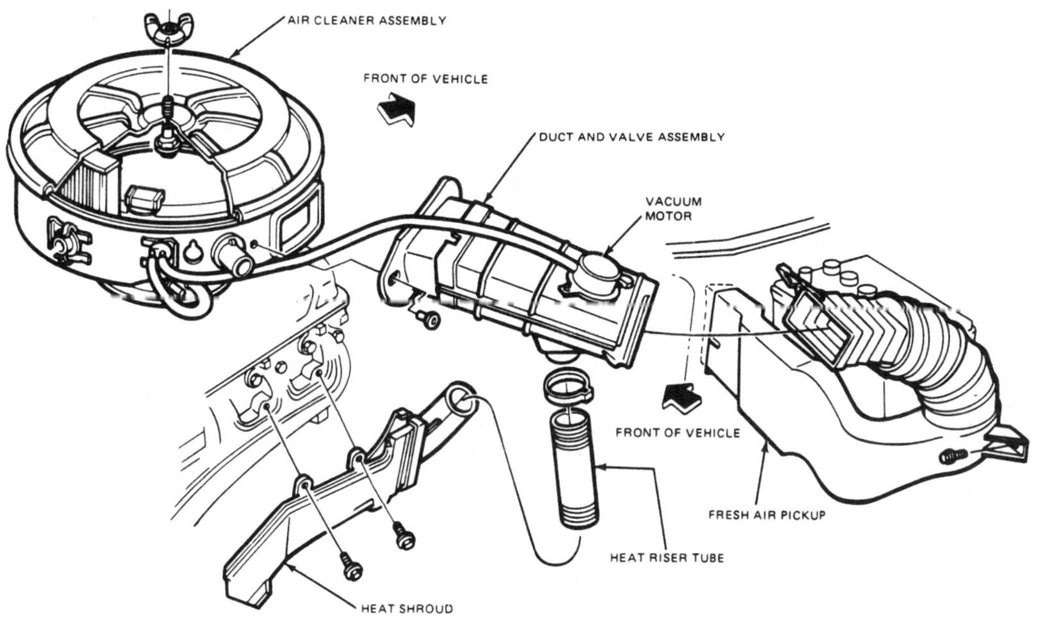

Typical air cleaner and duct system (V8 shown)

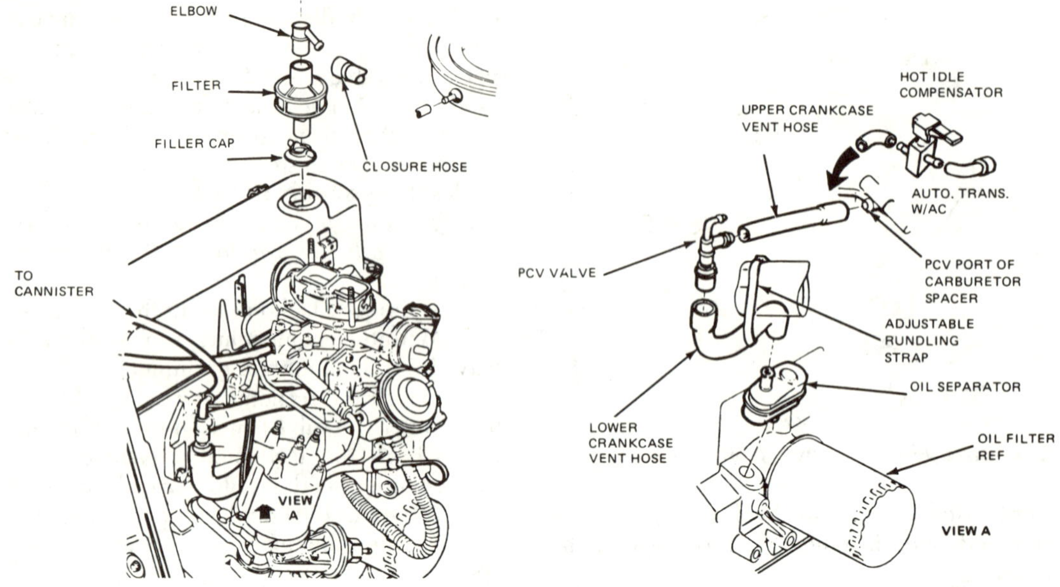

Positive crankcase ventilation system—4 cyl.

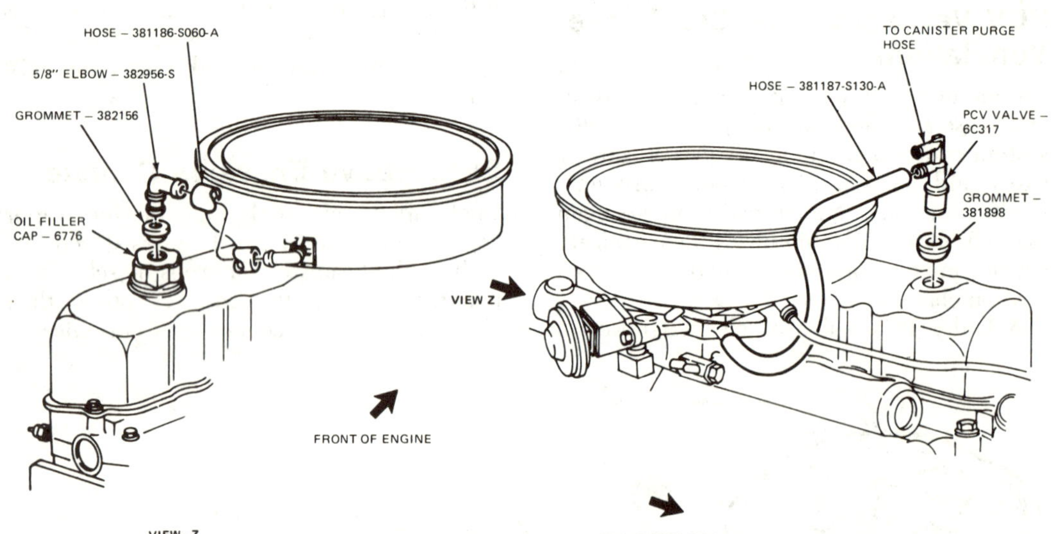

Positive crankcase ventilation system—6 cyl.

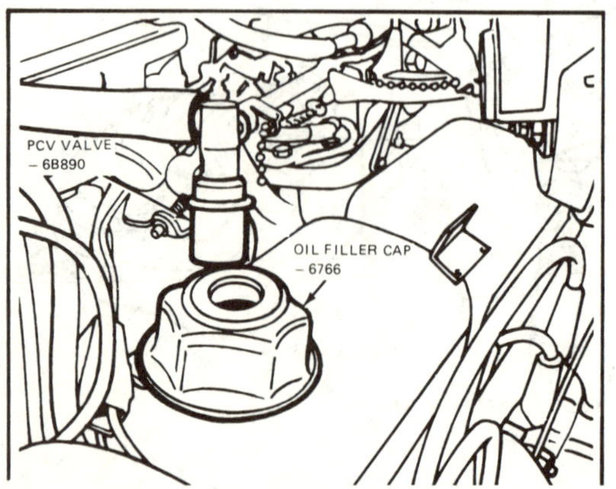

Typical crankcase ventilation system—8 cyl.

Replace the canister and/or hoses if they are damaged or cracked.

Battery

FLUID LEVEL

Check the battery electrolyte level at least once a month, or more often in hot weather or during periods of extended car operation. The level can be checked through the case on translucent polypropylene batteries; the cell caps must be removed on other models. The electrolyte level in each cell should be kept

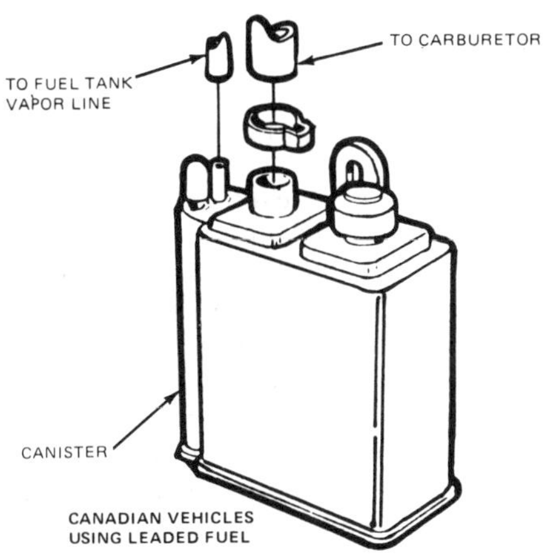

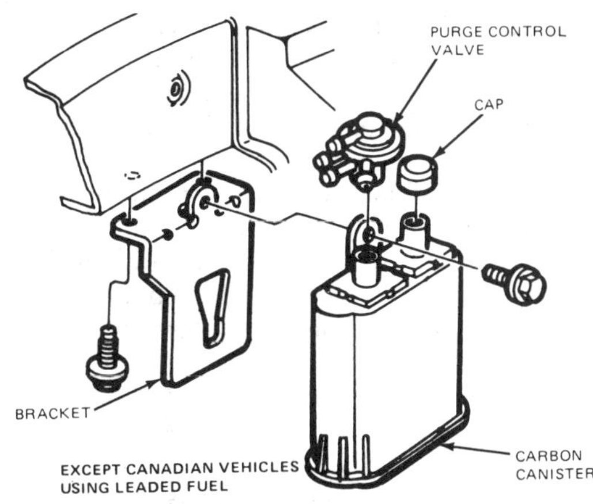

Evaporator canister (typical)

filled to the split ring inside, or the line marked on the outside of the case.

If the level is low, add water through the opening until the level is correct. Each cell is completely separate from the others, so each must be checked and filled individually.

If water is added in freezing weather, the car should be driven several miles to allow the water to mix with the electrolyte. Otherwise, the battery could freeze.

SPECIFIC GRAVITY

At least once a year, check the specific gravity of the battery. It should be between 1.20 and 1.26 at room temperature.

The specific gravity can be checked with the use of an hydrometer, an inexpensive instrument available from many sources, including auto parts stores. The hydrometer has a squeeze bulb at one end and a nozzle at the other. Battery electrolyte is sucked into the hydrometer until the float is lifted from its seat. The specific gravity is then read by noting the position of the float. Generally, if after charging, the specific gravity between any two cells varies more than 50 points (.050), the battery is bad and should be replaced.

It is not possible to check the specific gravity in this manner on sealed ("maintenance free") batteries. Instead, the indicator built into the top of the case must be relied on to display any signs of battery deterioration. If the indicator is dark, the battery can be assumed to be OK. If the indicator is light, the specific gravity is low, and the battery should be charged or replaced.

CABLES AND CLAMPS

Once a year, the battery terminals and the cable clamps should be cleaned. Loosen the clamps and remove the cables, negative cable first. On batteries with posts on top, the use of a puller specially made for the purpose is recommended. These are inexpensive, and available in auto parts stores. Side terminal battery cables are secured with a bolt.

Clean the cable clamps and the battery terminal with a wire brush, until all corrosion, grease, etc. is removed and the metal is shiny. It is especially important to clean the inside of the clamp thoroughly, since a small deposit of foreign material or oxidation will pre-

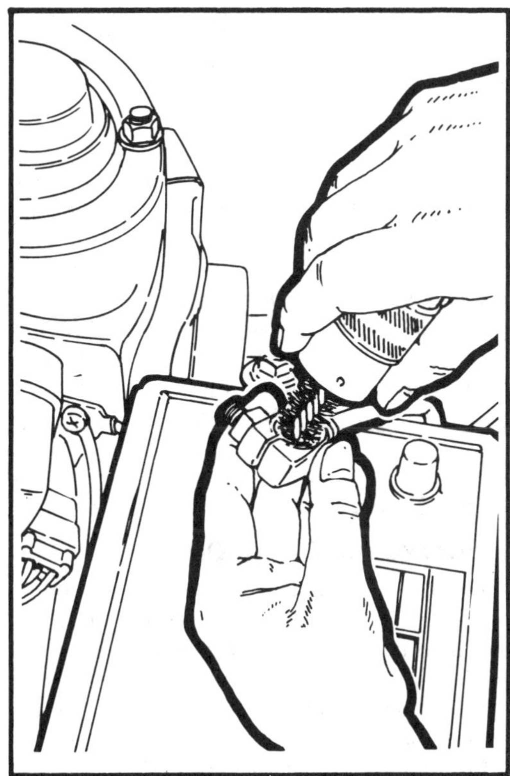

vent a sound electrical connection and inhibit either starting or charging. Special tools are available for cleaning these parts, one type for conventional batteries and another type for side terminal batteries.

Before installing the cables, loosen the battery hold-down clamp or strap, remove the battery and check the battery tray. Clear the battery tray of any debris, and check it for soundness. Rust should be wire brushed away, and the metal given a coat of anti-rust paint. Replace the battery and tighten the hold-down clamp or strap securely, but be careful not to overtighten.

After the clamps and terminals are clean, reinstall the cables, negative (ground) cable last; do not hammer on the clamps. Tighten the clamps securely, but do not distort them. Give the clamps and terminals a thin external coat of grease after installation, to retard corrosion.

Check the cables at the same time that the terminals are cleaned. If the cable insulation is cracked or broken, or if the ends are frayed, the cable should be replaced with a new cable of the same length and gauge.

NOTE: *Keep flame or sparks away from the battery; it gives off explosive hydrogen gas. Battery electrolyte contains sulphuric acid. If you should splash any on your skin or in your eyes, flush the affected area with plenty of clear water; if it lands in your eyes, get medical help immediately.*

REPLACEMENT

When it becomes necessary to replace the battery, select a battery with a rating equal to or greater than the battery originally installed. Deterioration, embrittlement and just plain aging of the battery cables, starter motor, and associated wires makes the battery's job harder in successive years. The slow increase in electrical resistance over time makes it prudent to install a new battery with a greater capacity than the old.

Drive Belts

CHECKING BELT TENSION

Check the drive belts every 6,000 miles for evidence of wear such as cracking or fraying and incorrect tension. Determine the belt tension at a point halfway between the pulleys by pressing on the belt with moderate thumb pressure. The belt should deflect about ¼ to ½ inch at this point. If the deflection is found to be too much or too little, make the necessary adjustment.

SERVICING DRIVE BELTS

Most drive belts are adjusted or replaced by loosening the mounting bolts and the pivot bracket bolt of the driven equipment. That is, the alternator, power steering pump, air pump, or the air conditioner compressor. Some pumps or alternators use an adjusting rod and nut to maintain proper belt adjustment. Some air conditioner compressor belts have an idler pulley which can pivot when the mounting bolt is loosened thus giving access to belt removal or adjustment.

If a belt breaks or shows signs of serious wear, it is a good idea to replace all other drive belts at the same time.

NOTE: *Care should be taken not to pry on the body of a power steering pump, alternator, air pump or air conditioner compressor. Always pry gently under the end frame or use the cut out if provided. Be sure to run the engine for a brief period of time after installing a new drive belt, then recheck the belt for proper tension. Readjust if necessary.*

COOLING SYSTEM

Dealing with the cooling system can be a dangerous matter unless the proper precautions are observed. It is best to check the coolant level in the radiator when the engine is cold. This is done by removing the radiator cap and seeing that the coolant is within two inches of the bottom of the filler neck. On some models the cooling system has, as one of its components, an expansion tank. If coolant is visible above the "Min" mark on the tank, the level is satisfactory. Always be certain that the filler caps on both the radiator and the expansion reservoir are tightly closed.

In the event that the coolant level must be checked when the engine is warm, place a thick rag over the radiator cap and slowly turn the cap counterclockwise until it reaches the first detent. Allow all the hot steam to escape. This will allow the pressure in the system to drop gradually, preventing an explosion of hot coolant. When the hissing noise stops, remove the cap the rest of the way.

If the coolant level is low, add equal amounts of ethylene glycol-based antifreeze and clean water. To fill the cooling system on models without an expansion tank, fill through the radiator filler neck. On models with an

How to Spot Worn V-Belts

V-Belts are vital to efficient engine operation—they drive the fan, water pump and other accessories. They require little maintenance (occasional tightening) but they will not last forever. Slipping or failure of the V-belt will lead to overheating. If your V-belt looks like any of these, it should be replaced.

Cracking or weathering

This belt has deep cracks, which cause it to flex. Too much flexing leads to heat build-up and premature failure. These cracks can be caused by using the belt on a pulley that is too small. Notched belts are available for small diameter pulleys.

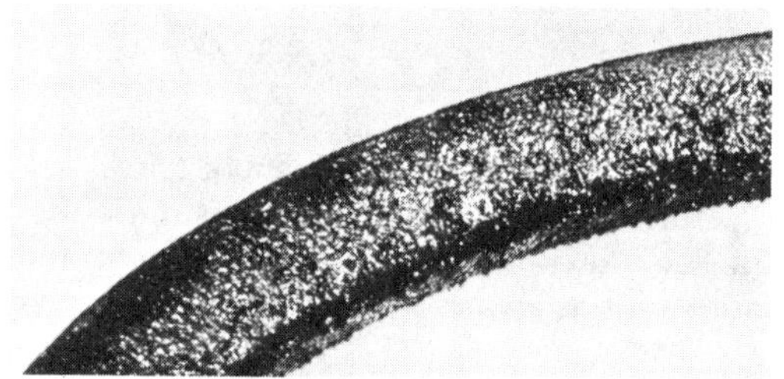

Softening (grease and oil)

Oil and grease on a belt can cause the belt's rubber compounds to soften and separate from the reinforcing cords that hold the belt together. The belt will first slip, then finally fail altogether.

Glazing

Glazing is caused by a belt that is slipping. A slipping belt can cause a run-down battery, erratic power steering, overheating or poor accessory performance. The more the belt slips, the more glazing will be built up on the surface of the belt. The more the belt is glazed, the more it will slip. If the glazing is light, tighten the belt.

Worn cover

The cover of this belt is worn off and is peeling away. The reinforcing cords will begin to wear and the belt will shortly break. When the belt cover wears in spots or has a rough jagged appearance, check the pulley grooves for roughness.

Separation

This belt is on the verge of breaking and leaving you stranded. The layers of the belt are separating and the reinforcing cords are exposed. It's just a matter of time before it breaks completely.

How to Spot Bad Hoses

Both the upper and lower radiator hoses are called upon to perform difficult jobs in an inhospitable environment. They are subject to nearly 18 psi at under hood temperatures often over 280°F., and must circulate nearly 7500 gallons of coolant an hour—3 good reasons to have good hoses.

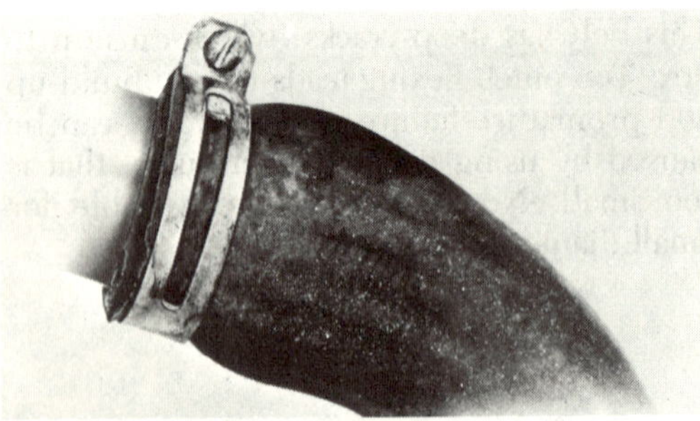

Swollen hose

A good test for any hose is to feel it for soft or spongy spots. Frequently these will appear as swollen areas of the hose. The most likely cause is oil soaking. This hose could burst at any time, when hot or under pressure.

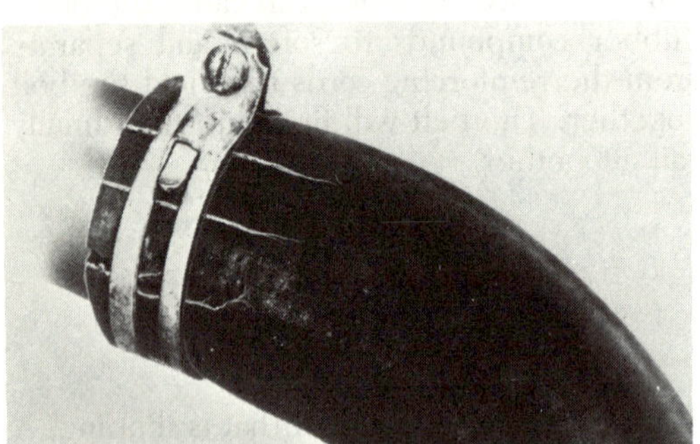

Cracked hose

Cracked hoses can usually be seen but feel the hoses to be sure they have not hardened; a prime cause of cracking. This hose has cracked down to the reinforcing cords and could split at any of the cracks.

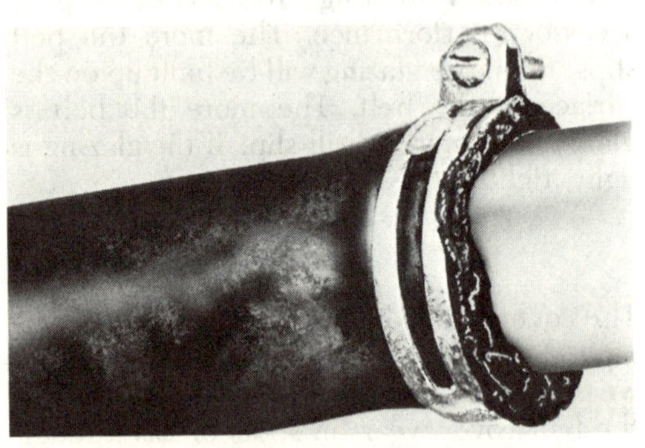

Frayed hose end (due to weak clamp)

Weakened clamps frequently are the cause of hose and cooling system failure. The connection between the pipe and hose has deteriorated enough to allow coolant to escape when the engine is hot.

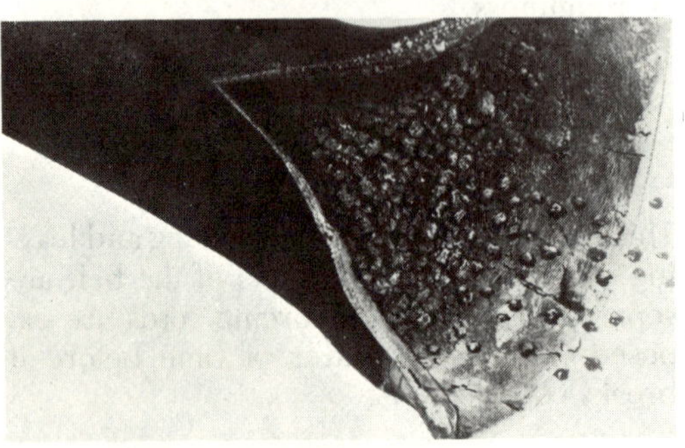

Debris in cooling system

Debris, rust and scale in the cooling system can cause the inside of a hose to weaken. This can usually be felt on the outside of the hose as soft or thinner areas.

expansion tank fill to the "max" level of the tank reservoir.

CAUTION: *Never add cold coolant to a hot engine unless the engine is running, to avoid cracking the engine block.*

The radiator hoses and clamps and the radiator cap should be checked at the same time as the coolant level. Hoses which are brittle, cracked, or swollen should be replaced. Clamps should be checked for tightness (screwdriver tight only—do not allow the clamp to cut into the hose or crush the fitting). The radiator cap gasket should be checked for any obvious tears, cracks or swelling, or any signs of incorrect seating in the radiator neck.

At least every two years, the engine coolant should be drained, the system flushed and refilled with a 50/50 mixture of fresh ethylene glycol (anti-freeze) and water. If the coolant is left in the system too long, it loses its ability to prevent rust and corrosion. If the coolant has too much water, it won't protect against freezing.

CHANGING THE COOLANT

1. Open the radiator petcock, or disconnect the lower radiator hose at the radiator outlet. Completely drain the system.

   NOTE: *Before opening the petcock, spray it with some penetrating lubricant.*

2. Close the petcock or reconnect the lower radiator hose and fill the system with clean water.
3. Add a can of quality radiator flush.
4. Idle the engine until the upper radiator hose gets hot. Make sure the dash heater control is set to hot. This lets water and radiator cleaner circulate through the heater core.
5. Drain the system again.
6. Repeat this process until the drained water is clear and free of scale.
7. Close all petcocks and connect all hoses.
8. If equipped with an expansion tank (coolant recovery system), flush the reservoir with water and leave empty.
9. Determine the capacity of your cooling system (see capacities chart). Add a 50/50 mix of antifreeze and water to provide the desired protection.
10. Run the engine to operating temperature. After operating temperature is reached, return the heater control lever to normal.
11. Stop the engine and check the coolant level. Add coolant if necessary.
12. Check the level of protection with an anti-freeze tester, replace the radiator cap and check for leaks.

Air Conditioning

SAFETY PRECAUTIONS

There are two particular hazards associated with air conditioning systems and they both relate to the refrigerant gas.

First, the refrigerant gas is an extremely cold substance. When exposed to air, it will instantly freeze any surface it comes in contact with, including your eyes. The other hazard relates to fire. Although normally non-toxic, refrigerant gas becomes highly poisonous in the presence of an open flame. One good whiff of the vapor formed by burning refrigerant can be fatal. Keep all forms of fire (including cigarettes) well clear of the air conditioning system.

Any repair work to an air conditioning system should be left to a professional. Do not, under any circumstances, attempt to loosen or tighten any fittings or perform any work other than that outlined here.

CHECKING FOR OIL LEAKS

Refrigerant leaks show up as oily areas on the various components because the compressor oil is transported around the entire system along with the refrigerant. Look for oily spots on all the hoses and lines, and especially on the hose and tubing connections. If there are oily deposits, the system may have a leak, and you should have it checked by a qualified repairman.

NOTE: *A small area of oil on the front of the compressor is normal and no cause for alarm.*

KEEP THE CONDENSER CLEAR

Periodically inspect the front of the condenser for bent fins or foreign material (dirt, bugs, leaves, etc.) If any cooling fins are bent, straighten them carefully with needlenosed pliers. You can remove any debris with a stiff bristle brush or hose.

OPERATE THE A/C SYSTEM PERIODICALLY

A lot of A/C problems can be avoided by simply running the air conditioner at least once a week, regardless of the season. Let the system run for at least 5 minutes a week (even in the winter), and you'll keep the internal parts lubricated as well as preventing the hoses from hardening.

REFRIGERANT LEVEL CHECK

There are two ways to check refrigerant level, depending on how your model is equipped.

With Sight Glass

The first order of business when checking the sight glass is to find the sight glass. It will either be in the head of the receiver/drier, or in one of the metal lines leading from the top of the receiver/drier. Once you've found it, wipe it clean and proceed as follows:

1. With the engine and the air conditioning system running, look for the flow of refrigerant through the sight glass. If the air conditioner is working properly, you'll be able to see a continuous flow of clear refrigerant through the sight glass, with perhaps an occasional bubble at very high temperatures.
2. Cycle the air conditioner on and off to make sure what you are seeing is clear refrigerant. Since the refrigerant is clear, it is possible to mistake a completely discharged system for one that is fully charged. Turn the system off and watch the sight glass. If there is refrigerant in the system, you'll see bubbles during the off cycle. If you observe no bubbles when the system is running, and the air flow from the unit in the car is delivering cold air, everything is OK.
3. If you observe bubbles in the sight glass while the system is operating, the system is low on refrigerant. Have it checked by a professional.
4. Oil streaks in the sight glass are an indication of trouble. Most of the time, if you see oil in the sight glass, it will appear as a series of streaks, although occasionally it may be a solid stream of oil. In either case, it means that part of the charge has been lost.

Without Sight Glass

On vehicles that are not equipped with sight glasses, it is necessary to feel the temperature difference in the inlet and outlet lines at the receiver/drier to gauge the refrigerant level. Use the following procedure:

1. Locate the receiver/drier. It will generally be up front near the condenser. It is shaped like a small fire extinguisher and will always have two lines connected to it. One lines goes to the expansion valve and the other goes to the condenser.
2. With the engine and the air conditioner running, hold a line in each hand and gauge their relative temperatures. If they are both the same approximate temperature, the system is correctly charged.
3. If the line from the expansion valve to the receiver/drier is a lot colder than the line from the receiver/drier to the condenser, then the system is overcharged. It should be noted that this is an extremely rare condition.
4. If the line that leads from the receiver/drier to the condenser is a lot colder than the other line, the system is undercharged.
5. If the system is undercharged or overcharged, have it checked by a professional air conditioning mechanic.

Windshield Wipers

Intense heat from the sun, snow and ice, road oils and the chemicals used in windshield washer solvents combine to deteriorate the rubber wiper refills. The refills should be replaced about twice a year or whenever the blades begin to streak or chatter.

WIPER REFILL REPLACEMENT

Normally, if the wipers are not cleaning the windshield properly, only the refill has to be replaced. The blade and arm usually require replacement only in the event of damage. It is not necessary (except on new Tridon refills) to remove the arm or the blade to replace the refill (rubber part), though you may have to position the arm higher on the glass. You can do this turning the ignition switch on and operating the wipers. When they are positioned where they are accessible, turn the ignition switch off.

There are several types of refills and your vehicle could have any kind, since aftermarket blades and arms may not use exactly the same refill as the original equipment.

One style uses a release button that is pushed down to allow the refill to slide out of the yoke jaws. The new refill slides in and locks in place. Some Trico refills are removed by locating where the metal backing strip or the refill is wider. Insert a small screwdriver blade between the frame and metal backing strip. Press down to release the refill from the retaining tab.

A second style is unlocked at one end by squeezing 2 metal tabs, and the refill is slid out of the frame jaws. When the new refill is installed, the tabs will click into place, locking the refill.

The polycarbonate type is held in place by

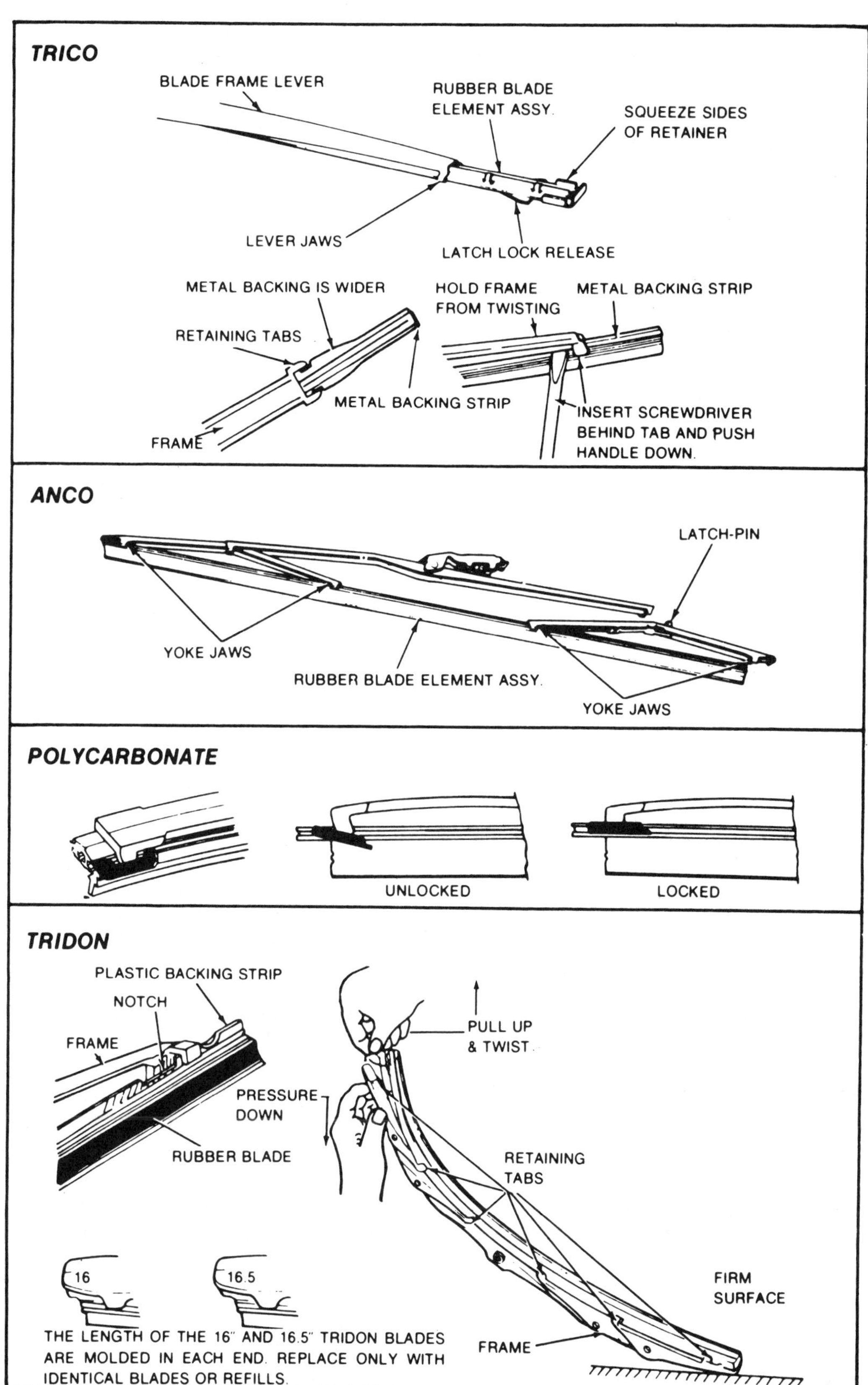

Wiper insert replacement

a locking lever that is pushed downward out of the groove in the arm to free the refill. When the new refill is installed, it will lock in place automatically.

The Tridon refill has a plastic backing strip with a notch about an inch from the end. Hold the blade (frame) on a hard surface so that the frame is tightly bowed. Grip the tip of the backing strip and pull up while twisting counterclockwise. The backing strip will snap out of the retaining tab. Do this for the remaining tabs until the refill is free of the arm. The length of these refills is molded into the end and they should be replaced with identical types.

No matter which type of refill you use, be sure that all of the frame claws engage the refill. Before operating the wipers, be sure that no part of the metal frame is contacting the windshield.

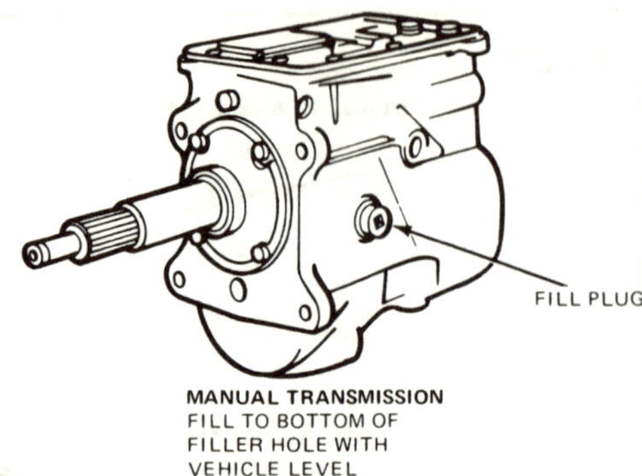

Manual transmission fill plug

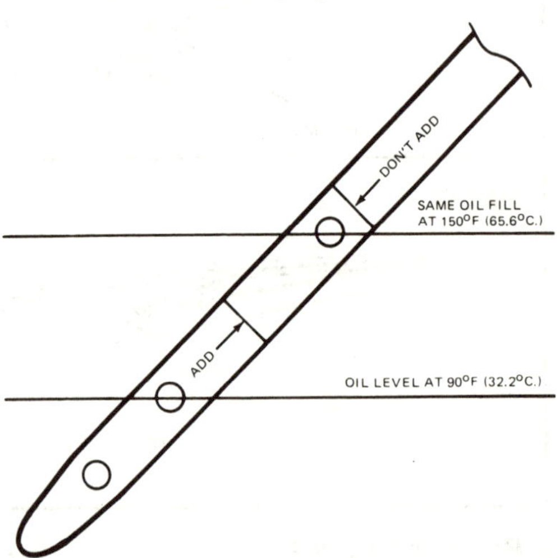

Typical fluid expansion; warm automatic transmission

FLUID LEVEL CHECKS

Engine Oil

Check the engine oil level every time you fill the gas tank. The oil level should be above the ADD mark and not above the FULL mark on the dipstick. Make sure that the dipstick is inserted into the crankcase as far as possible and that the vehicle is resting on level ground.

NOTE: *Don't check the level immediately after stopping the engine; wait a few minutes to let the oil drain back into the pan.*

V8 and six cylinder engine oil dipstick

TRANSMISSION

Manual

Before checking the lubricant level in the transmission, make sure that the vehicle is on level ground. Remove the filler plug (located on side of transmission). The level of the lubricant should be up to the bottom of the fill hole. If lubricant is not present at the bottom of the fill hole, add SAE 90 or 80 transmission lube until it reaches the proper level. A suction gun or squeeze bottle is used to fill a manual transmission with lubricant.

Automatic Transmission

The fluid level in an automatic transmission is checked when the transmission is at operating temperatures. If the vehicle has been sitting and is cold, drive it at highway speeds for at least 20 minutes to warm the transmission.

1. With the transmission in Park, the engine running at idle speed, the foot brakes applied and the vehicle resting on level ground, move the transmission gear selector through each of the gear positions, including Reverse, allowing time for the transmission to engage. Return the shift selector to the Park position and apply the parking brake. Do not turn the engine off; leave it running at idle speed.
2. Clean all dirt from around the transmission dipstick cap and the end of the filler tube.
3. Pull the dipstick out of the tube, wipe it off with a clean cloth, and push it back into the tube all the way, making sure that it seats completely.
4. Pull the dipstick out of the tube again and read the level of the fluid on the stick. The level should be between the ADD mark

and the FULL mark. If fluid must be added, add enough fluid through the tube to raise the level up to between the ADD and FULL marks. Do not overfill the transmission because this will cause foaming, loss of fluid through the vent, and malfunctioning of the transmission.

BRAKE MASTER CYLINDER

The brake master cylinder is located under the hood on the driver's side of the car.

Before removing the master cylinder reservoir cap, make sure the car is resting on level ground and clean all dirt away from the top of the master cylinder. Pry off the retaining clip. The brake fluid level should be within ¼ inch of the top of the reservoir in both sides.

If the level of the brake fluid is less than half the volume of the reservoir, check the brake hydraulic system for leaks. Leaks most commonly occur at the wheel cylinders (rear).

There is a rubber diaphragm in the top of the master cylinder cap. As the fluid level drops due to normal brake shoe wear or leakage, the diaphragm takes up the space. This prevents the loss of brake fluid out of the vent cap and contamination by dirt. After filling the master cylinder to the proper level with brake fluid, fold the rubber diaphragm up into the cap, replace the cap on the reservoir and snap the retaining clip into place. Use only Heavy Duty brake fluid meeting DOT 3 or 4 specifications.

COOLANT

The coolant level in the radiator should be checked on a monthly basis, preferably when the engine is cold. On a cold engine, the coolant level should be maintained at one inch below the filler neck on vertical flow radiators, and 2½ in. below the filler neck at the "COLD FILL" mark on crossflow radiators. On cars equipped with the Coolant Recovery System, the level is maintained at the "COLD LEVEL" mark in the translucent plastic expansion bottle. Top up as necessary with a mixture of 50% water and 50% ethylene glycol antifreeze, to ensure proper rust, freezing and boiling protection. If you have to add more than one quart at a time, check the cooling system for leaks. Also check for water in the crankcase oil, indicating a blown cylinder head gasket.

CAUTION: *Exercise extreme care when removing the cap from a hot radiator. Wait a few minutes until the engine has time to cool, then wrap a thick towel around the radiator cap and slowly turn it counterclockwise to the first stop. Step back and allow the pressure to release from the cooling system. Then, when the steam has stopped venting, press down on the cap, turn it one more stop counterclockwise and remove the cap.*

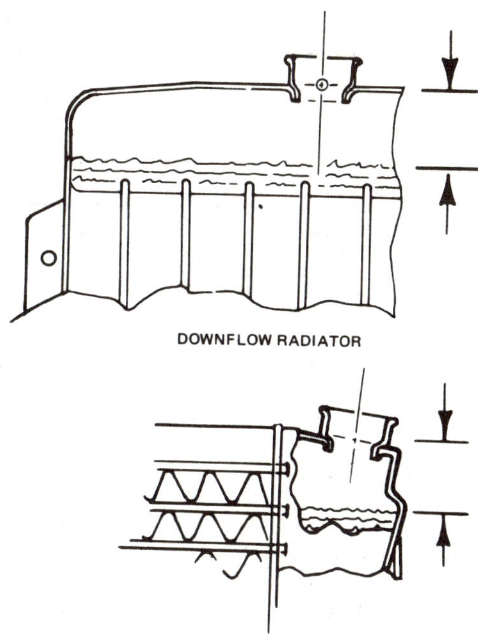

Radiator coolant levels (crossflow and downflow)

REAR AXLE FLUID

The rear axle fluid level should be checked at regular intervals (see chart). With the car standing perfectly level, apply the parking brake, set the transmission in Park or 1st gear, stop the engine and block all four wheels. Wipe all dirt and grease from the filler plug area. Use a ⅜" flex-bar, T-handle or ratchet to remove the filler plug. (Some models may require an adjustable wrench.) The fluid level must be maintained at ½ in. from the bottom of the filler plug hole.

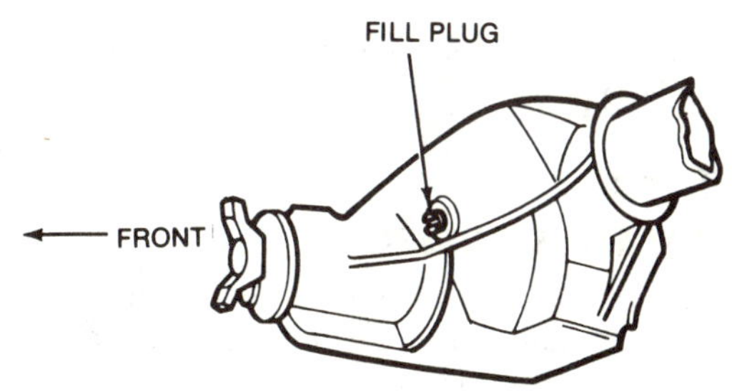

Rear axle fill plug

Capacities

Year	Model	Engine Displacement Cu In. (cc)	Engine Crankcase (qts) With Filter	Engine Crankcase (qts) Without Filter	Transmission (pts) Manual 4-spd	Transmission (pts) Automatic	Drive Axle (pts)	Gasoline Tank (gals)	Cooling System (qts) W/ AC	Cooling System (qts) W/O AC
1978	Fairmont/ Zephyr	140	5.0	4.0	2.8 ①	16	3.5 ④	16.0	9.1	8.7
		200	5.0	4.0	2.8 ①	16 ②	3.5 ④	16.0	8.9	8.7
		302	5.0	4.0	2.8	20	3.5 ④	16.0	14.1	13.5
1979–80	Fairmont/ Zephyr	140	5.0	4.0	2.8 ③	13.4	3.5 ④	14.0 ⑥	9.0	8.6
		200	5.0	4.0	2.8 ③	16 ⑦	3.5 ④	14.0 ⑥	8.1	8.1
		255	5.0	4.0	2.8 ③	20	3.5 ④	14.0 ⑥	13.5	13.4
		302 ⑤	5.0	4.0	2.8 ③	20	3.5 ④	16.0	14.1	13.5
1981–83	Fairmont/ Zephyr	140	5.0	4.0	2.8 ③	⑨	3.5 ④	14.0 ⑪	8.6 ⑩	10.2 ⑩
		200	5.0	4.0	2.8 ③	⑨	3.5 ④	16.0 ⑪	9.0 ⑩	9.0 ⑩
		255 ⑧	5.0	4.0	2.8 ③	⑨	3.5 ④	16.0 ⑪	13.4	15.2

① Three speed trans- 3.5 pints
② C4 Trans- 13.4 pints
③ 4 speed Overdrive- 4.5 pints
④ 6.75" Ring Gear- 2.5 pints
⑤ Discontinued for 1980
⑥ 1979 Models—16 gal.
⑦ C4 Trans- 14.2 pints
⑧ Discontinued for 1983
⑨ C3—16 pts
C4—19 pts
C5—22 pts
⑩ 1983; 140–10.2
200–8.4
1982; 140–10.2
200–8.1
⑪ 1982: 20 gal optional

To check the fluid level in the axle, bend a clean, straight piece of wire to a 90° angle and insert the bent end of the wire into the axle while resting it on the lower edge of the filler hole. Top up as necessary with SAE 90 hypoid gear lube, using a suction gun or kitchen baster. Install the filler plug.

POWER STEERING RESERVOIR FLUID

At the recommended intervals in the maintenance schedule, the fluid level in the power steering reservoir (if so equipped) should be checked. Run the engine until the fluid reaches operating temperature. Turn the steering wheel from lock-to-lock several times to relieve the system of any trapped air. Turn off the engine. On some models just pull out the dipstick from the rear of the reservoir, on others unscrew the cap and dipstick assembly from the reservoir. The level must be maintained between the "FULL" mark and the end of the dipstick. Top up as necessary with ATF Type F.

Tires

INFLATION PRESSURE

Tire inflation is the most ignored item of auto maintenance. Gasoline mileage can drop as much as .8% for every 1 pound per square inch (psi) of under inflation.

Two items should be a permanent fixture in every glove compartment; a tire pressure gauge and a tread depth gauge. Check the tire air pressure (including the spare) regularly with a pocket type gauge. Kicking the tires won't tell you a thing, and the gauge on the service station air hose is notoriously inaccurate.

The tire pressures recommended for your car are usually found on the face of the rear right hand door pillar or in the owners manual. Ideally, inflation pressure should be checked when the tires are cool. When the air becomes heated it expands and the pressure increases. Every 10° rise (or drop) in temperature means a difference of 1 psi, which also explains why the tire appears to lose air on a very cold night. When it is impossible to check the tires "cold," allow for pressure build-up due to heat. If the "hot" pressure exceeds the "cold" pressure by more than 15 psi, reduce your speed, load or both. Otherwise internal heat is created in the tire. When the heat approaches the temperature at which the tire was cured, during manufacture, the tread can separate from the body.

CAUTION: *Never counteract excessive pressure build-up by bleeding off air pressure (letting some air out). This will only further raise the tire operating temperature.*

Before starting a long trip with lots of luggage, you can add about 2–4 psi to the tires to make them run cooler, but never exceed the maximum inflation pressure on the side of the tire.

TREAD DEPTH

All tires made since 1968, have 8 built-in tread wear indicator bars that show up as ½" wide smooth bands across the tire when 1/16" of tread remains. The appearance of tread wear indicators means that the tires should be replaced. In fact, many states have laws prohibiting the use of tires with less than 1/16" tread.

You can check your own tread depth with an inexpensive gauge or by using a Lincoln head penny. Slip the Lincoln penny into several tread grooves. If you can see the top of Lincoln's head in 2 adjacent grooves, the tires have less than 1/16" tread left and should be replaced. You can measure snow tires in the same manner by using the "tails" side of the Lincoln penny. If you can see the top of the Lincoln memorial, it's time to replace the snow tires.

TIRE ROTATION

Tire wear can be equalized by switching the position of the tires about every 6000 miles. Including a conventional spare in the rotation pattern can give up to 20% more tire life.

CAUTION: *Do not include the new "Space Saver®" or temporary spare tires in the rotation pattern.*

There are certain exceptions to tire rotation, however. Studded snow tires should not be rotated, and radials should be kept on the same side of the car (maintain the same direction of rotation). The belts on radial tires get set in a pattern. If the direction of rotation is reversed, it can cause rough ride and vibration.

NOTE: *When radials or studded snows are taken off the car, mark them, so you can maintain the same direction of rotation.*

TIRE STORAGE

Store the tires at proper inflation pressures if they are mounted on wheels. All tires should be kept in a cool, dry place. If they are stored in the garage or basement, do not let them stand on a concrete floor; set them on strips of wood.

Fuel Filter Replacement

The fuel filter should be replaced every 12,000 miles or 12 months.

ALL (EXCEPT MODEL 2700VV CARBURETOR)

1. Remove the air cleaner.
2. Remove the spring-type clamp securing the inlet hoses to the fuel filter line. If the fuel filter is located in the line, loosen or remove the outlet hose clamps also.
3. On models so equipped unscrew the fuel filter from the carburetor.

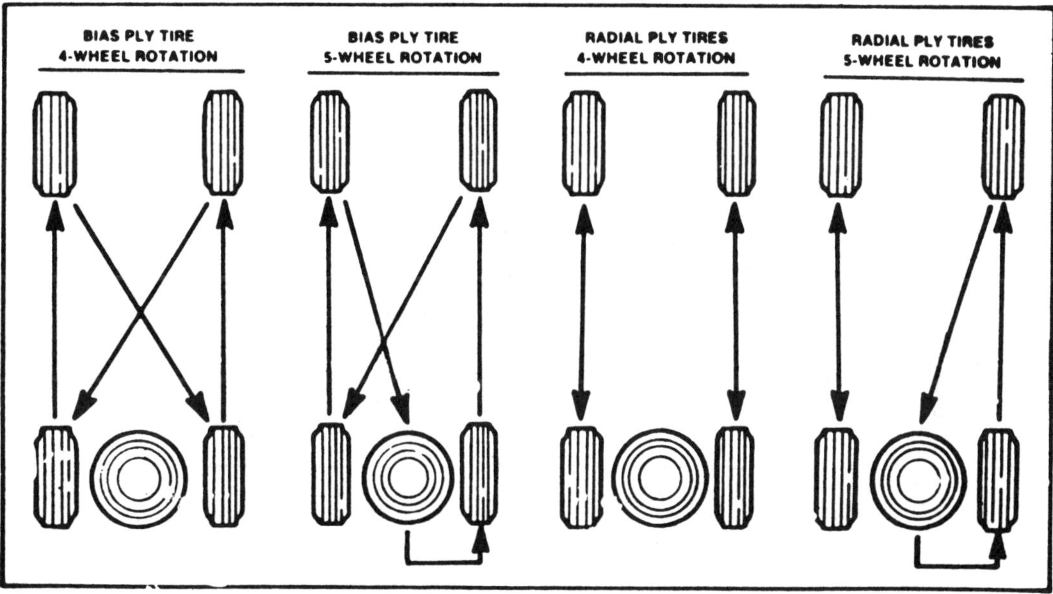

Tire rotation patterns

4. To install hand start the fuel filter into the carburetor and tighten.
5. Check the condition of the hose and clamps and replace if necessary.
6. Install the hose clamps on the fuel inlet hose and then push the hose on the fuel filter nipple. Push the fuel line into the hose.
7. Position and install the clamps and check for leaks.
8. Install the air cleaner.

MODEL 2700VV CARBURETOR

1. Remove the air cleaner.
2. Unscrew the fuel line nut from the carburetor inlet nut using a flare nut wrench.

NOTE: *To prevent kinking of the fuel line and for ease of installation loosen the fuel line nut at the fuel pump.*

3. Unscrew the inlet fitting from the carburetor and remove the fuel filter gasket and spring.
4. Install the spring, new filter, new gasket and inlet fitting into the carburetor.
5. Tighten the fuel line at the carburetor and then at the fuel pump.
6. Start the engine and check for leaks.
7. Install the air cleaner.

LUBRICATION

Oil Recommendations

When adding the oil to the crankcase or changing the oil or filter, it is important that oil of an equal quality to original be used in your car. The use of inferior oils may void your warranty. Generally speaking, oil that has been rated "SF (from 1981) or SE (prior to 1981), heavy-duty detergent" by the American Petroleum Institute will prove satisfactory.

Maintenance Interval Chart

Intervals in months or miles in thousands whichever occurs first

Operation	*1978–83*	*See Chapter*
ENGINE		
Air cleaner element replacement	30	1
Cooling system check	12	1
Coolant replacement; system draining and flushing	36	1
Crankcase breather filter replacement (in air cleaner)	30	1
Drive belts check and adjust	30	1
Evaporator control system check; inspect carbon canister	30	1
Exhaust gas recirculation system (EGR) check	15	4
Fuel filter replacement	12	1
Ignition timing adjustment	①	2
Oil change	②	1
Oil filter replacement	②, ③	1
PCV valve replacement	20	1
Spark plug replacement	30	2
CHASSIS		
Automatic transmission band adjustment	④	6
Automatic transmission fluid level check	20	1
Brake system inspection, lining replacement	30	9
Brake master cylinder reservoir fluid level check	30	1
Clutch pedal free play adjustment	10	6
Front suspension ball joints and steering linkage lubrication	30	1
Front wheel bearings cleaning, adjusting and repacking	30	9
Manual transmission fluid level check	⑤	1
Power steering pump fluid level check	15	1
Rear axle fluid level check	15	1
Steering arm stop lubrication; steering linkage inspection	15	1

①Periodic adjustment unnecessary
②8 cylinder engines—every 7.5 month/thousands miles. 4 cyl. and 6 cyl. engines every 10 months/thousands miles.
③Every oil change
④Normal service—12,000 miles, Severe (fleet) service—6,000/18,000/30,000 miles
⑤Periodic fluid level check is unnecessary

Oil Viscosity— Temperature Chart

When Outside Temperature is Consistently	*Use SAE Viscosity Number*
SINGLE GRADE OILS	
−10° F to 32° F	10W
10° F to 60° F	20W-20
32° F to 90° F	30
Above 60° F	40
MULTIGRADE OILS	
Below 32° F	5W-30*
−10° F to 90° F	10W-30
Above—10° F	10W-40
Above 10° F	20W-40
Above 20° F	20W-50

*When sustained high-speed operation is anticipated, use the next higher grade.

Oil of the SF (from 1981) or SE (prior to 1981) variety performs a multitude of functions in addition to its basic job of reducing friction of the engine's moving parts. Through a balanced formula of polymeric dispersants and metallic detergents, the oil prevents high temperature and low temperature deposits and also keeps sludge and dirt particles in suspension. Acids, particularly sulphuric acid, as well as other products of combustion of sulphur fuels, are neutralized by the oil. These acids, if permitted to concentrate, may cause corrosion and rapid wear of the internal parts of the engine.

It is important to choose an oil of the proper viscosity for climatic and operational conditions. Viscosity is an index of the oil's thickness at different temperatures. A thicker oil (higher numerical rating) is needed for high temperature operation, whereas thinner oil (lower numerical rating) is required for cold weather operation. Due to the need for an oil that embodies both these characteristics in parts of the country where there is wide temperature variation within a small period of time, multigrade oils have been developed. Basically a multigrade oil is thinner at low temperatures and thicker at high temperatures. For example, a 10W-40 oil exhibits the characteristics of a 10 weight oil when the car is first started and the oil is cold. Its lighter weight allows it to travel to the lubricating surfaces quicker and offer less resistance to starter motor cranking than, let's say, a straight 30 weight oil. But after the engine reaches operating temperature, the 10W-40 oil begins acting like a straight 40 weight oil, its heavier weight providing greater lubricating protection and less susceptibility to foaming than a straight 30 weight oil. Whatever your driving needs, the oil viscosity-temperature chart should prove useful in selecting the proper grade. The SAE viscosity rating is printed or stamped on the top of every oil container.

Fuel Recommendations

It is important that you use fuel of the proper octane rating in your car. Octane rating is based on the quantity of anti-knock compounds added to the fuel and it determines the speed at which the gas will burn. The lower the octane rating, the faster it burns. The higher the octane, the slower the fuel will burn and a greater percentage of compounds in the fuel prevent spark ping (knock), detonation and preignition (dieseling). Your car is equipped with a catalytic converter making the use of unleaded fuel mandatory.

Changing Engine Oil and Filter

The engine oil and oil filter should be changed at the recommended intervals on the maintenance schedule chart. After the engine has reached operating temperature, shut it off, firmly apply the parking brake, block the wheels, place a drip pan beneath the oil pan and remove the drain plug. Allow the engine to drain thoroughly before replacing the drain plug.

NOTE: *On some V8 engines a dual sump oil pan was used. When changing the oil both drain plugs* (front and side) *must be removed. Failure to remove both plugs can lead to an incorrect oil level reading.*

Place the drip pan beneath the oil filter. To remove the filter, turn it counterclockwise using a strap wrench. Wipe the contact surface of the new filter clean of all dirt and coat the rubber gasket with clean engine oil. Clean the mating surface of the adapter on the block. To install, hand turn the new filter clockwise until the gasket just contacts the cylinder block. Do not use a strap wrench to install. Then hand-turn the filter ½ additional turn. Unscrew the filler cap on the valve cover and fill the crankcase to the proper level on the dipstick with the recommended grade of oil. Install the cap, start the engine and operate at fast idle. Check the oil filter contact area and the drain plug for leaks.

Certain operating conditions may warrant more frequent oil changes. If the vehicle is used for short trips, where the engine does not have a chance to fully warm-up before it is shut off, water condensation and low temperature deposits may make it necessary to change the oil sooner. If the vehicle is used mostly in stop-and-go traffic, corrosive acids and high temperature deposits may necessitate shorter oil changing intervals. The shorter intervals also apply to industrial or rural areas where high concentrations of dust and other airborne particulate matter contaminate the oil. Finally, if the car is used for towing trailers, a severe load is placed on the engine causing the oil to "thin-out" sooner, making necessary the shorter oil changing intervals.

Chassis Greasing

FRONT SUSPENSION BALL JOINTS

Every 3 years or 36,000 miles, the lower ball joints must be lubricated. Fairmonts and Zephyrs are not equipped with grease fittings at the ball joints. Instead, they use plugs, one at the underside of each lower ball joint, which must be removed prior to greasing.

If you are using a jack to raise the front of the car, be sure to install jack stands, block the rear wheels and fully apply the parking brake. If the car has been parked in a temperature below 20°F for any length of time, park it in a heated garage for a half an hour or so until the ball joints loosen up enough to accept the grease. Wipe all accumulated dirt from around the ball joint lubrication plugs. Remove the plugs with a $^3/_{16}$ in. socket wrench. Install the appropriate lubrication fittings. Using a hand-operated, low pressure grease gun fitting with a rubber tip and loaded with a suitable chassis grease, force lubricant into the joint only until the joint boot begins to swell.

NOTE: *Do not force lubricant out of the rubber boot as this destroys the weather-tight seal.*

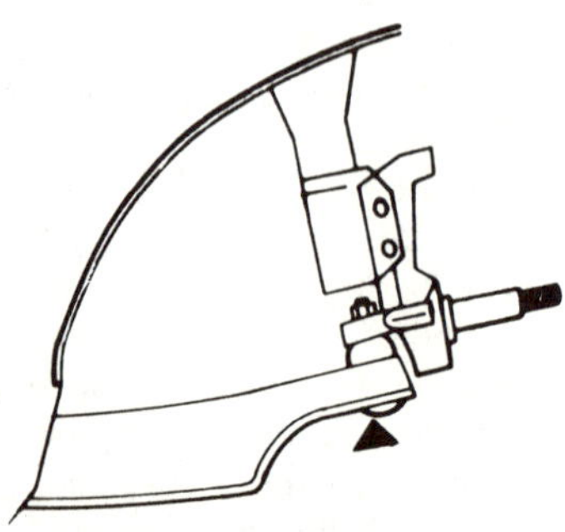
Lower ball joint lubrication points

Remove the grease fittings and install the grease plugs.

STEERING LINKAGE

At the recommended intervals in the maintenance schedule, the steering linkage must be lubricated. Grease fittings are not installed from the factory. Instead, plugs are used, which must be removed prior to lubrication. Install the appropriate lubrication fittings. The linkage may be lubricated without raising the car.

If the car has been parked in a temperature below 20°F for any length of time, park it in a heated garage for a half an hour or so until the linkage joints loosen up enough to accept the grease. Wipe all accumulated dirt from around the steering joint plugs at each tierod end. Remove the plugs with a $^3/_{16}$ in. socket wrench. Using a hand-operated, low pressure grease gun fitted with a rubber tip and loaded with suitable chassis grease, force lubricant into the holes. When grease begins to escape from the hole remove the grease fittings and insert the plugs.

STEERING ARM STOPS

At the recommended intervals in the maintenance schedule, the steering arm stops must be cleaned and lubricated. The stops are located on the inside of the steering arm and at the upturned end of the suspension strut where the strut attaches to the lower control arm. Clean all friction points and apply a suitable chassis grease as per the chassis lubrication diagram.

MANUAL TRANSMISSION AND CLUTCH LINKAGE

On models so equipped, apply a small amount of chassis grease to the pivot and friction points of the transmission and clutch linkage as per the chassis lubrication diagram.

PARKING BRAKE LINKAGE

At yearly intervals or whenever binding is noticeable in the parking brake linkage, lubricate the cable guides, levers and linkage with a suitable chassis grease.

AUTOMATIC TRANSMISSION LINKAGE

On models so equipped, apply a small amount of 10W engine oil to the kickdown and shift linkage pivot points.

Body Lubrication

At 12 month intervals, the door, hood and trunk hinges, checks, and latches should be greased with a white grease such as Lubriplate®. Also the lock cylinders should be lubricated with a few drops of graphite lubricant.

DRAIN HOLE CLEANING

The doors and rocker panels of your car are equipped with drain holes to allow water to drain out the inside of the body panels. If the drain holes become clogged with dirt, leaves, pine needles, etc., the water will remain inside the panels, causing rust. To prevent this, open the drain holes with a screwdriver. If your car is equipped with rubber dust valves instead, simply open the dust valve with your finger.

WHEEL BEARINGS

Refer to Chapter 9 for removal and installation, adjustment and repacking procedures.

PUSHING AND TOWING

If your car fails to start by jump starting and it is equipped with manual transmission, it may be push started. Cars equipped with automatic transmission cannot be push started.

NOTE: *Push starting a catalytic converter equipped car is not recommended due to possible converter damage from raw gasoline. Jump starting is recommended.*

If the bumper of the car pushing you and your car's bumper do not match perfectly, it is wise to tie an old tire either on the back of your car or on the front of the pushing car. This will avoid unnecessary trips to the body shop. To push start the car, switch the ignition to the "ON" position (not the "START" position) and depress the clutch pedal. Place the transmission in Third gear and hold the accelerator pedal about halfway down. When the car speed reaches about 10 MPH, gradually release the clutch pedal and the engine should start.

If all else fails and the car must be towed to a garage, there are a few precautions that must be observed. If the transmission and rear axle are in proper working order, the car can be towed with the rear wheels on the ground for distances under 15 miles at speeds no greater than 30 mph. If the transmission or rear is known to be damaged or if the car has to be towed over 15 miles or over 30 mph, the car must be towed with the rear wheels raised and the steering wheel locked so that the front wheels remain in the straight-ahead position.

NOTE: *If the ignition key is not available to unlock the steering and transmission lock system, it will be necessary to dolly the car under the rear wheels with the front wheels raised.*

JACKING

The Fairmont/Zephyr models are equipped with a scissors type jack which is placed under the side of the car so that it fits into the notch in the vertical rocker panel flange nearest the wheel to be changed. These jacking notches are located approximately 8 inches from the wheel opening on the rocker panel flanges.

When raising the car with the scissors jack follow these precautions: Park the car on a level spot, put the selector in P (PARK) with an automatic transmission or in reverse if your car has a manual transmission, apply the parking brake and block the front and the back of the wheel that is diagonally opposite the wheel being changed. These jacks are fine for changing a tire, but never crawl under the car when it is supported only by the scissors jack.

CAUTION: *If you're going to work beneath the car, always support it with jackstands.*

When using a floor jack the car may be lifted by positioning the jack under the center of the number two crossmember. The front, as well as either side of the rear end, may be lifted by positioning the floor jack under the rocker flange at the contact points used for the scissor jack supplied with the vehicle. To lift both sides of the rear at once, position the floor jack under the differential housing.

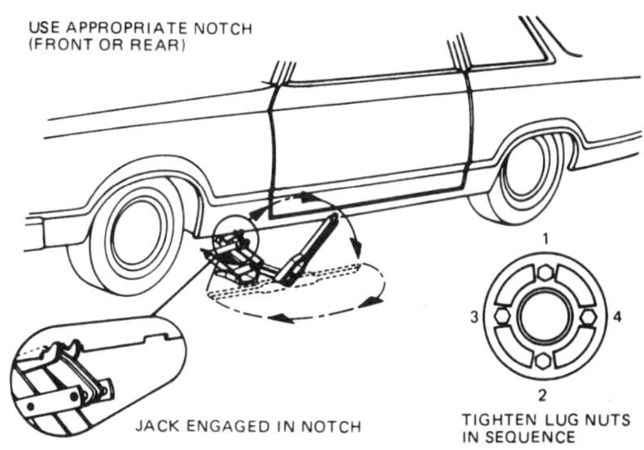

Placing the scissors jack

Jump Starting a Dead Battery

The chemical reaction in a battery produces explosive hydrogen gas. This is the safe way to jump start a dead battery, reducing the chances of an accidental spark that could cause an explosion.

Jump Starting Precautions

1. Be sure both batteries are of the same voltage.
2. Be sure both batteries are of the same polarity (have the same grounded terminal).
3. Be sure the vehicles are not touching.
4. Be sure the vent cap holes are not obstructed.
5. Do not smoke or allow sparks around the battery.
6. In cold weather, check for frozen electrolyte in the battery.
7. Do not allow electrolyte on your skin or clothing.
8. Be sure the electrolyte is not frozen.

Jump Starting Procedure

1. Determine voltages of the two batteries; they must be the same.
2. Bring the starting vehicle close (they must not touch) so that the batteries can be reached easily.
3. Turn off all accessories and both engines. Put both cars in Neutral or Park and set the handbrake.
4. Cover the cell caps with a rag—do not cover terminals.
5. If the terminals on the run-down battery are heavily corroded, clean them.
6. Identify the positive and negative posts on both batteries and connect the cables in the order shown.
7. Start the engine of the starting vehicle and run it at fast idle. Try to start the car with the dead battery. Crank it for no more than 10 seconds at a time and let it cool off for 20 seconds in between tries.
8. If it doesn't start in 3 tries, there is something else wrong.
9. Disconnect the cables in the reverse order.
10. Replace the cell covers and dispose of the rags.

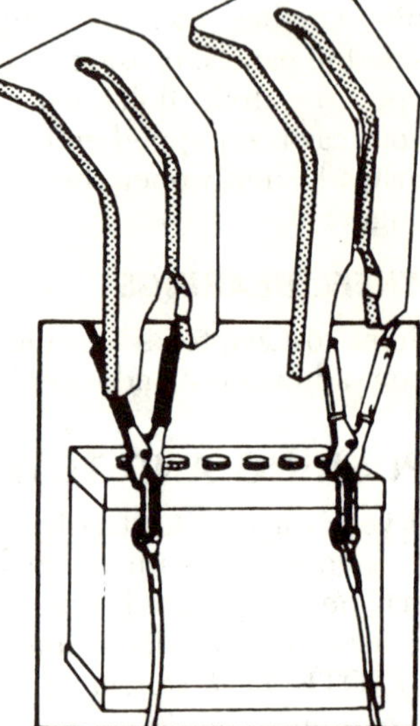

Side terminal batteries occasionally pose a problem when connecting jumper cables. There frequently isn't enough room to clamp the cables without touching sheet metal. Side terminal adaptors are available to alleviate this problem and should be removed after use.

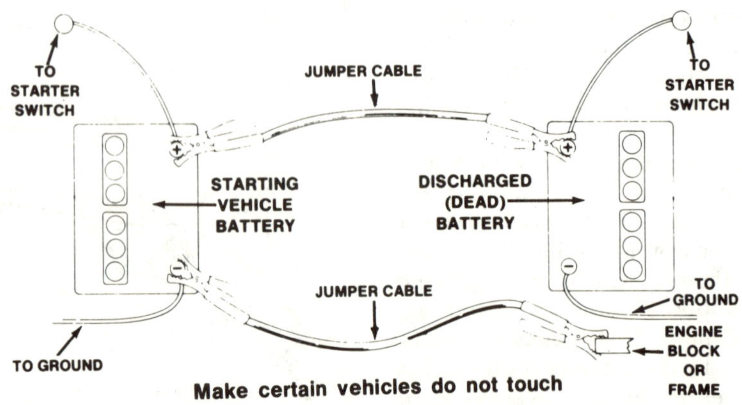

Make certain vehicles do not touch

This hook-up for negative ground cars only

Tune-Up and Performance Maintenance

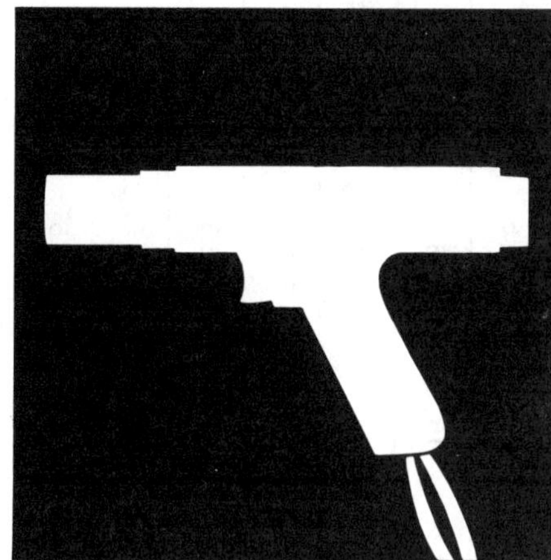

TUNE-UP PROCEDURES

The tune-up is a routine maintenance operation which is essential for the efficient and economical operation, as well as the long life of your car's engine. The interval between tune-ups is a variable factor which depends upon the way you drive your car, the conditions under which you drive it (weather, road type, etc.), and the type of engine installed in your car.

CAUTION: *When working with a running engine, make sure that there is proper ventilation. Also make sure that the transmission is in Neutral (unless otherwise specified), the parking brake is fully applied and the wheels blocked. Always keep hands, long hair, clothing, neckties and tools well clear of the hot exhaust manifold(s) and radiator. When the ignition is running, do not grasp the ignition wires, distributor cap, or coil wire, as a shock in excess of 40,000 volts may result.*

Spark Plugs

A typical spark plug consists of a metal shell surrounding a ceramic insulator. A metal electrode extends downward through the center of the insulator and protrudes a small distance. Located at the end of the plug and attached to the side of the outer metal shell is the side electrode. The side electrode bends in at a 90° angle so that its tip is even with, and parallel to, the tip of the center electrode. The distance between these two electrodes (measured in thousandths of an inch) is called the spark plug gap. The spark plug in no way produces a spark but merely provides a gap across which the current can arc. The coil produces anywhere from 20,000 to 40,000 volts which travels to the distributor where it is distributed through the spark plug wires to the spark plugs. The current passes along the center electrode and jumps the gap to the side electrode, and, in so doing, ignites the air/fuel mixture in the combustion chamber.

SPARK PLUG HEAT RANGE

Spark plug heat range is the ability of the plug to dissipate heat. The longer the insulator (or the farther it extends into the engine), the hotter the plug will operate; the shorter the insulator the cooler it will operate. A plug that absorbs little heat and remains too cool will quickly accumulate deposits of oil and carbon since it is not hot enough to burn them off. This leads to plug fouling and consequently to misfiring. A plug that absorbs too much heat will have no deposits, but, due to the excessive heat, the electrodes will burn away

Tune-Up Specifications

Year	Engine No. Cyl Displacement (cu. in.)	Spark Plugs		Distributor	Ignition Timing (deg)▲		Intake Pump Pressure (psi)	Fuel Pump Pressure (psi)	Idle Speed (rpm)▲	
		Orig Type	Gap (in.)		Man	Auto			Man	Auto
1978	4-140	AWRF-42	.034	Electronic	6B	20B	22	5.5–6.5	850	800
	6-200	BRF-82	.050	Electronic	10B	10(6)B	20	5.5–6.5	800	650
	8-350	ARF-52	.050	Electronic	10B	6(12)B	16	5.5–6.5	500	650
1979	4-140	AWSF-42	.034	Electronic	6B	20B	22	5.5–6.5	850	850(750)
	6-200	BRF-82	.034	Electronic	8B	10B	20	5.5–6.5	800	650
	8-302	ASF-52	.050	Electronic	12B	6B	16	5.5–6.5	800	600
	8-302 (Calif.)	ASF-52-6	.060	Electronic	—	6B	16	5.5–6.5	800	600
1980	4-140	AWSF-42	.035	Electronic	6B	20(12)B	22	5.5–6.5	850	750

	6-200	BSF-82	.050	Electronic	10B	10B	20	5.5–6.5	700①	550(600)
	8-255	ASF-42	.050	Electronic	8B③	8B③	16	4–6	—	EECIII
1981	4-140	AWSF-42	.034	Electronic	6B	6B	22	5.5–6.5	700	700
	6-200	BSF-92	.050	Electronic	10B	10B	20	5.5–6.5	700	700
	8-255	ASF-52	.050	Electronic	10B	10B	16	5.5–6.5	700	550
1982	4-140	AWSF-42	.034	Electronic	④	④	22	5.5–6.5	850	750
	6-200	BSF-92	.050	Electronic	—	④	20	6–8	700	600
1983	4-140	AWSF-44	.044	Electronic	④	④	22	5.5–6.5	850	800
	6-200	BSF-92	.050	Electronic	—	④	20	6–8	—	550

① 900 with air conditioning
② 700 with air conditioning
③ Calif. (EECIII)
④ Calibrations vary: refer to the underhood specifications sticker
▲Figure in parentheses are for California
NOTE: The underhood specifications sticker often reflects tune-up specification changes made in production. Sticker figures must be used if they disagree with those in this chart.

quickly and in some instances, preignition may result. Preignition takes place when plug tips get so hot that they glow sufficiently to ignite the fuel/air mixture before the actual spark occurs. This early ignition will usually cause a pinging during low speeds and heavy loads.

The general rule of thumb for choosing the correct heat range when picking a spark plug is: if most of your driving is long distance, high speed travel, use a colder plug; if most of your driving is stop and go, use a hotter plug. Original equipment plugs are compromise plugs, but most people never have occasion to change their plugs from the factory-recommended heat range.

REPLACING SPARK PLUGS

A set of spark plugs usually requires replacement after about 20,000 to 30,000 miles on cars with electronic ignition, depending on your style of driving. In normal operation, plug gap increases about 0.001 in. for every 1,000–2,500 miles. As the gap increases, the plug's voltage requirement also increases. It requires a greater voltage to jump the wider gap and about two to three times as much voltage to fire a plug at high speeds than at idle.

When you're removing spark plugs, you should work on one at a time. Don't start by removing the plug wires all at once, because unless you number them, they may become mixed up. Take a minute before you begin and number the wires with tape. The best location for numbering is near where the wires come out of the cap.

1. Twist the spark plug boot and remove the boot and wire from the plug. Do not pull on the wire itself as this will ruin the wire.

2. If possible, use a brush or rag to clean the area around the spark plug. Make sure that all the dirt is removed so that none will enter the cylinder after the plug is removed.

3. Remove the spark plug using the proper size socket. (Use a 13/16 in. for BRF plugs or 5/8 in. for AWSF and ASF plugs.) Turn the socket counterclockwise to remove the plug. Be sure to hold the socket straight on the plug to avoid breaking the plug, or rounding off the hex on the plug.

4. Once the plug is out, check it against the plugs shown in the four page color insert, "Fuel Economy & Tune Up Tips" to determine engine condition. This is crucial since plug readings are vital signs of engine condition.

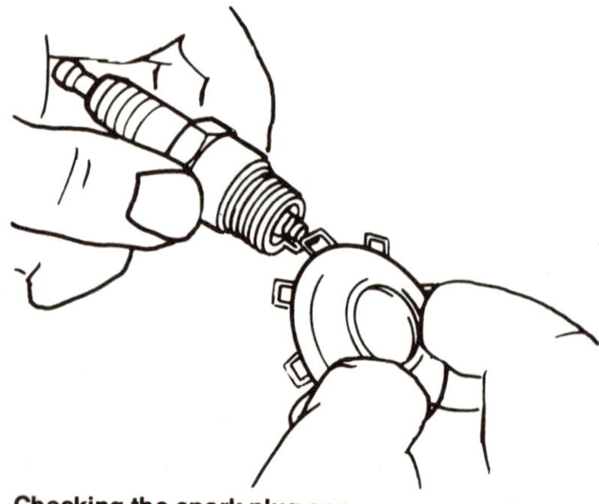

Checking the spark plug gap

5. Use a round wire feeler gauge to check the plug gap. The correct size gauge should pass through the electrode gap with a slight drag. If you're in doubt, try one size smaller and one larger. The smaller gauge should go through easily while the larger one shouldn't go through at all. If the gap is incorrect, use the electrode bending tool on the end of the gauge to adjust the gap. When adjusting the gap, always bend the side electrode. The center electrode is non-adjustable.

6. Squirt a drop of penetrating oil on the threads of the new plug and install it. Don't oil the threads too heavily. Turn the plug in clockwise by hand until it is snug.

7. When the plug is finger tight, tighten it with a wrench. If you don't have a torque wrench, tighten the plug as shown.

8. Install the plug boot firmly over the plug. Proceed to the next plug.

NOTE: *Coat the inside of each spark plug boot with silicone grease. (Motorcraft WA-10-D7AZ-19A331A, Dow Corning No. 111 or General Electric G627 are acceptable.) Failure to do so could result in a misfired plug.*

CHECKING AND REPLACING SPARK PLUG CABLES

Visually inspect the spark plug cables for burns, cuts, or breaks in the insulation. Check the spark plug boots and the nipples on the distributor cap and coil. Replace any damaged wiring. If no physical damage is obvious, the wires can be checked with an ohmmeter for excessive resistance. Nominal resistance is 5 K-ohms or less per inch of cable.

When installing a new set of spark plug cables, replace the cables one at a time so there will be no mixup. Start by replacing the longest cable first. Install the boot firmly over the spark plug. Route the wire exactly the same as the original. Insert the nipple firmly into the tower on the distributor cap. Repeat the process for each cable.

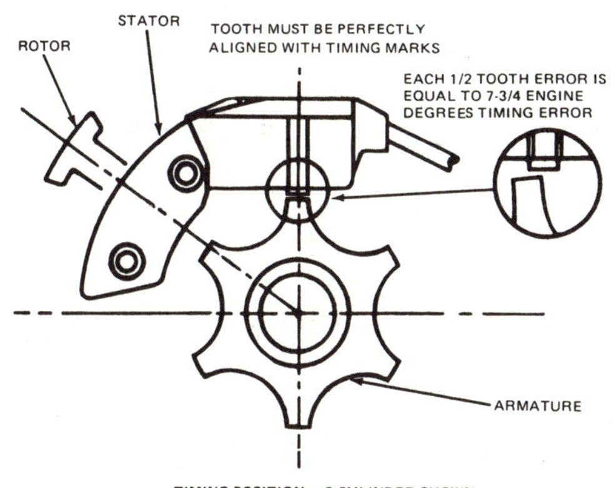

Distributor—static timing position (six cylinder, 4 cyl. similar)

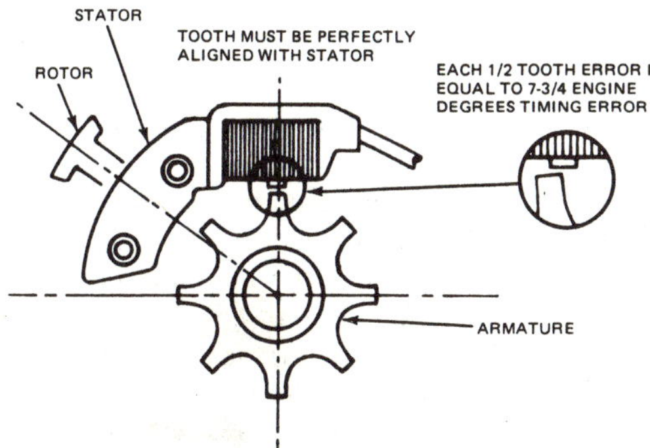

Distributor—static timing position (V8 engine)

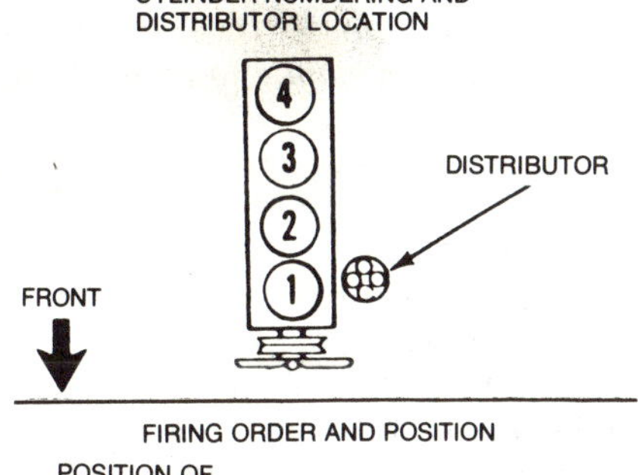

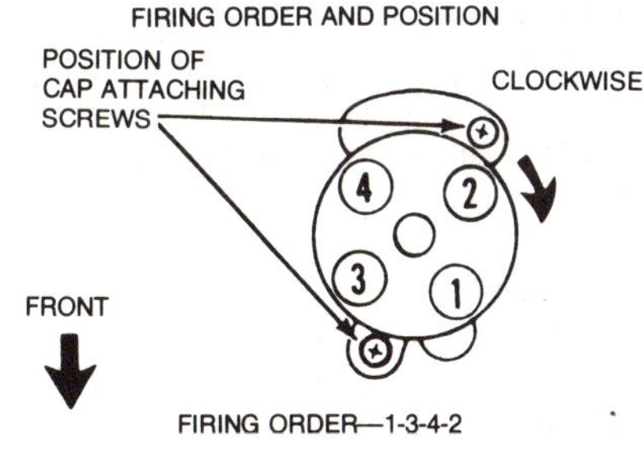

Four cylinder engine

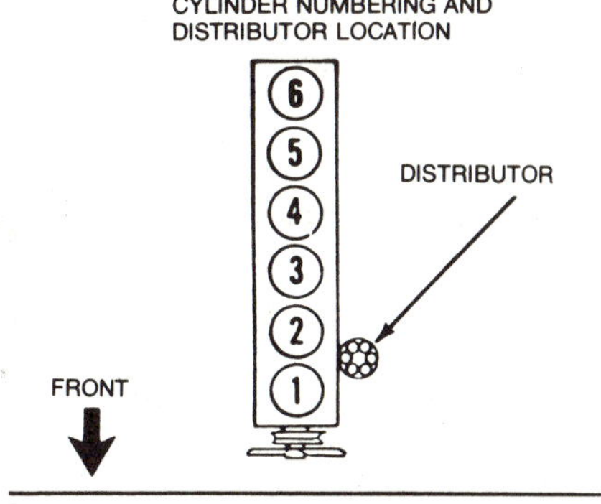

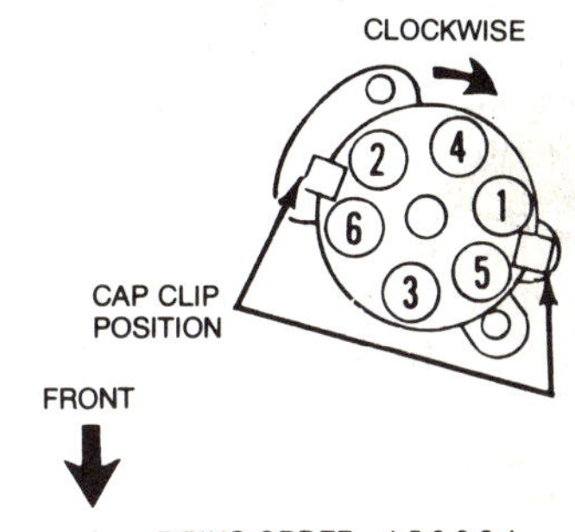

Six cylinder engine

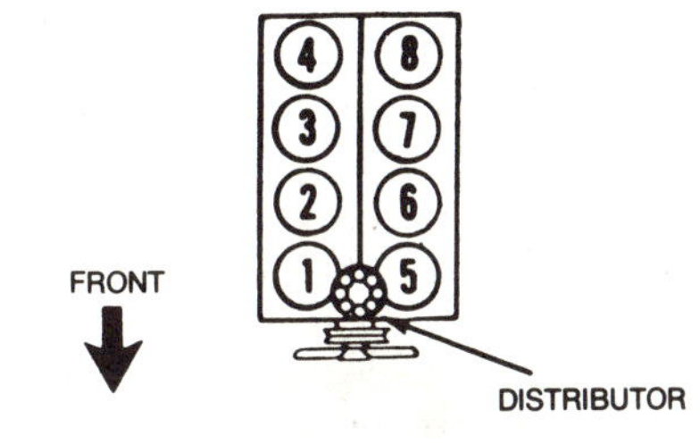

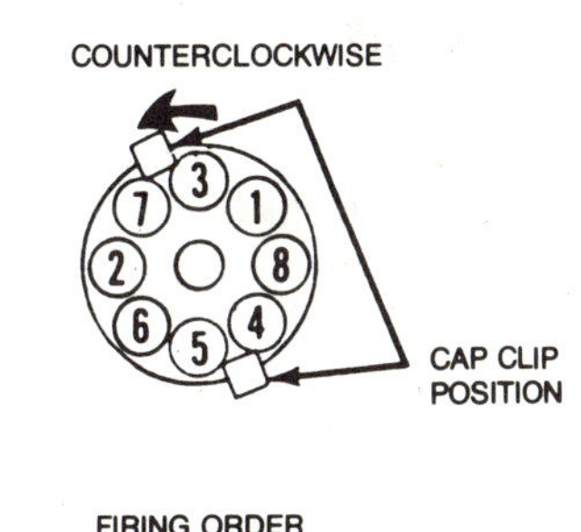

V8 engines

NOTE: *Coat the inside of each plug wire boot with silicone grease before re-installing.*

Solid-State Ignition

Standard on all Fairmonts and Zephyrs since their introduction has been the breakerless or solid-state ignition system. This is a transistorized ignition system which eliminates the breaker points and condenser, thereby eliminating a major part of a conventional tune-up. This solid-state ignition system is known as Dura-Spark. The system utilizes higher voltages—up to 42,000 volts—to allow wider spark plug gaps necessary to fire leaner fuel-air mixtures.

The dwell period is automatically controlled by the electronic module and is increased with increasing engine rpm. There is no way to adjust the dwell, which is preset.

The system features a longer spark duration, which is instrumental in firing lean and EGR diluted fuel-air mixtures. The condenser (capacitor) located within the distributor is provided for noise (static) suppression purposes *only* and is not a regularly replaced ignition system component.

Different versions of the Dura-Spark ignition system are used by Fairmont/Zephyr. The Dura-Spark I is used on all California models in 1978 and 1979, while the 49 states and Canadian versions use the Dura-Spark II. 1980 and later models use the Dura-Spark II system, except the California version of the 4.2 liter V8 which uses the Dura-Spark III System.

The basic difference between the Dura-Spark I, II and III is the coil charging current. A higher current is necessary for California cars to fire the leaner fuel/air mixtures required by the stricter emission laws.

TROUBLESHOOTING DURA-SPARK IGNITION

NOTE: *Troubleshooting of the Dura-Spark III system is not given because of the great complexity of the system. Service of the Dura-Spark III system should be referred to a qualified, professional technician.*

The symptoms of a defective component within the Dura-Spark system are exactly the same as those you would encounter in a conventional ignition system. Some of the symptoms are:

- Hard or no starting
- Rough idle

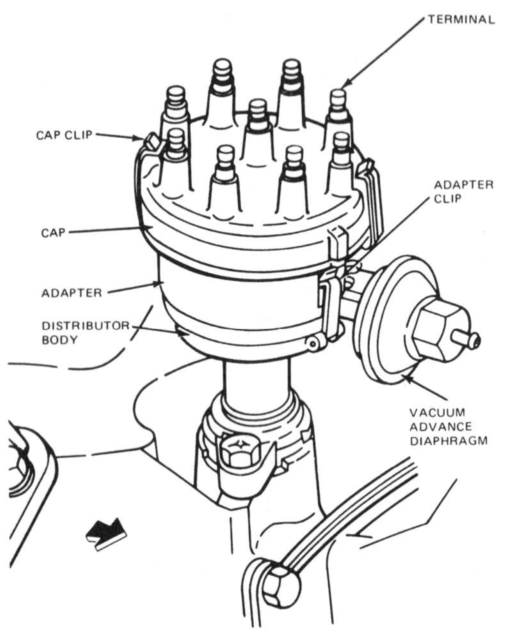

Typical distributor assembly

- Poor fuel economy
- Engine misses while under load or while accelerating.

NOTE: *Due to the sensitive nature of the Dura-Spark system and the complexity of the test procedures, it is recommended that you refer to your dealer if you suspect a problem in your electronic ignition system. The system can, of course, be tested by substituting known good components (module, stator, etc.)*

CAUTION: *If you wish to do your own troubleshooting read the next pages carefully, be sure you understand the procedures before you attempt any ignition system tests.*

OPERATION

With the ignition switch "on," the primary circuit is on and the ignition coil is energized. When the armature "spokes" approach the magnetic pickup coil assembly, they induce a voltage which tells the amplifier to turn the coil primary current off. A timing circuit in the amplifier module will turn the current on again after the coil field has collapsed. When the current is "on," it flows from the battery through the ignition switch, the primary windings of the ignition coil, and through the amplifier module circuits to ground. When the current is off, the magnetic field built up in the ignition coil is allowed to collapse, inducing a high voltage into the secondary windings of the coil. High voltage is produced each time the field is thus built up and collapsed. When Dura-Spark is used in conjunction with EEC, the EEC computer tells the Dura-Spark module when to turn the coil primary current off or on. In this case, the armature position is only a reference signal of engine timing, used by the EEC computer in combination with other reference signals to determine optimum ignition spark timing.

The high voltage flows through the coil high tension lead to the distributor cap where the rotor distributes it to one of the spark plug terminals in the distributor cap. This process is repeated for every power stroke of the engine.

Ignition system troubles are caused by a failure in the primary and/or the secondary circuit: incorrect ignition timing; or incorrect distributor advance. Circuit failures may be caused by shorts, corroded or dirty terminals, loose connections, defective wire insulation, cracked distributor cap or rotor, defective pick-up coil assembly or amplifier module, defective distributor points or fouled spark plugs.

If an engine starting or operating trouble is attributed to the ignition system, start the engine and verify the complaint. On engines that will not start, be sure that there is gasoline in the fuel tank and that fuel is reaching the carburetor. Then locate the ignition system problem using the following procedures.

DURA-SPARK I

The following Dura-Spark II troubleshooting procedures may be used on Dura-Spark I systems with a few variations. The Dura-Spark I module has internal connections which shut off the primary circuit in the run mode when the engine stalls. To perform the above troubleshooting procedures, it is necessary to by-pass these connections. However, with these connections by-passed, the current flow in the primary becomes so great that it will damage both the ignition coil and module unless a ballast resistor is installed in series with the primary circuit at the BAT terminal of the ignition coil. Such a resistor is available from Ford (Motorcraft part number DY-36). A 1.3 ohm, 100 watt wire-wound power resistor can also be used.

To install the resistor, proceed as follows.

NOTE: *The resistor will become very hot during testing.*

1. Release the BAT terminal lead from the coil by inserting a paper clip through the hole in the rear of the horseshoe coil connector and manipulating it against the locking tab in the connector until the lead comes free.
2. Insert a paper clip in the BAT terminal of the connector on the coil. Using jumper leads, connect the ballast resistor as shown.
3. Using a straight pin, pierce both the red and white leads of the module to short these two together. This will by-pass the internal connections of the module which turn off the ignition circuit when the engine is not running.

CAUTION: *Pierce the wires only AFTER the ballast resistor is in place or you could damage the ignition coil and module.*

4. With the ballast resistor and by-pass in place, proceed with the Dura-Spark II troubleshooting procedures.

DURA-SPARK II

NOTE: *Troubleshooting procedures are not given for the EEC systems because of their great complexity.*

The following procedures can be used to determine whether the ignition system is working or not. If these procedures fail to correct the problem, a full troubleshooting procedure should be performed by a qualified service department.

Preliminary Checks

1. Check the battery's state of charge and connections.
2. Inspect all wires and connections for breaks, cuts, abrasions, or burn spots. Repair as necessary.
3. Unplug all connectors one at a time and inspect for corroded or burned contacts. Repair and plug connectors back together. DO NOT remove the silicone compound in the connectors.
4. Check for loose or damaged spark plug or coil wires. A wire resistance check is given at the end of this section. If the boots or nipples are removed on 8mm ignition wires, reline the inside of each with new silicone dielectric compound (Motorcraft WA 10).

Special Tools

To perform the following tests, two special tools are needed; the ignition test jumper shown in the illustration and a modified spark plug. Use the illustration to assemble the ignition test jumper. The test jumper must be used when performing the following tests. The modified spark plug is basically a spark plug with the side electrode removed. Ford

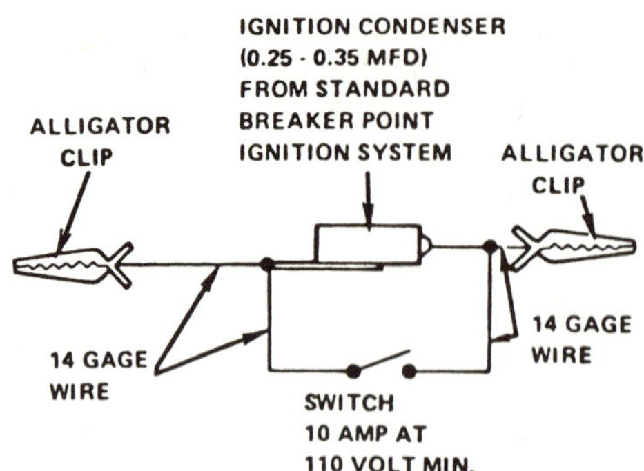

Make a special jumper wire to test the Dura Spark ignition

makes a special tool called a Spark Tester for this purpose, which besides not having a side electrode is equipped with a spring clip so that it can be grounded to engine metal. It is recommended that the Spark Tester be used as there is less chance of being shocked.

Run Mode Spark Test

NOTE: *The wire colors given here are the main colors of the wires, not the dots or hashmarks.*

STEP 1

1. Remove the distributor cap and rotor from the distributor.
2. With the ignition off, turn the engine over by hand until one of the teeth on the distributor armature aligns with the magnet in the pick-up coil.
3. Remove the coil wire from the distributor cap. Install the modified spark plug (see Special Tools, above) in the coil wire terminal and using heavy gloves and insulated pliers, hold the spark plug shell against the engine block.
4. Turn the ignition to RUN (not START) and tap the distributor body with a screwdriver handle. There should be a spark at the modified spark plug.
5. If a good spark is evident, the primary circuit is OK: perform Start Mode Spark Test. If there is no spark, proceed to Step 2.

STEP 2

1. Unplug the module connector(s) which contain(s) the green and black module leads.
2. In the harness side of the connector(s), connect the special test jumper (see Special Tools, above) between the leads which connect to the green and black leads of the module pig tails. Use paper clips on connector socket holes to make contact. Do not allow clips to ground.
3. Turn the ignition switch to RUN (not START) and close the test jumper switch. Leave closed for about 1 second, then open. Repeat several times. There should be a spark each time the switch is opened. On Dura Spark I systems, close the test switch for 10 seconds on the first cycle. After that, 1 second is adequate.
4. If there is no spark, the problem is probably in the primary circuit through the ignition switch, the coil, the green lead or the black lead, or the ground connection in the distributor: perform Step 3. If there is a spark, the primary circuit wiring and coil are probably OK. The problem is probably in the distributor pick-up, the module red wire, or the module: perform Step 6.

STEP 3

1. Disconnect the test jumper lead from the black lead and connect it to a good ground. Turn the test jumper switch on and off several times as in Step 2.
2. If there is no spark, the problem is probably in the green lead, the coil, or the coil feed circuit: perform Step 5.
3. If there is spark, the problem is probably in the black lead or the distributor ground connection: perform Step 4.

STEP 4

1. Connect an ohmmeter between the black lead and ground. With the meter on its lowest scale, there should be no measureable resistance in the circuit. If there is resistance, check the distributor ground connection and the black lead from the module. Repair as necessary, remove the ohmmeter, plug in all connections and repeat Step 1.

If there is no resistance, the primary ground wiring is OK: perform Step 6.

STEP 5

1. Disconnect the test jumper from the green lead and ground and connect it between the TACH-TEST terminal of the coil and a good ground on the engine.
2. With the ignition switch in the RUN position, turn the jumper switch on. Hold it on for about 1 second then turn it off as in Step 2. Repeat several times. There should be a spark each time the switch is turned off. If there is no spark, the problem is probably in the primary circuit running through the ignition switch to the coil BAT terminal, or in the coil itself. Check coil resistance (test given later in this section), and check the coil for

internal shorts or opens. Check the coil feed circuit for opens, shorts or high resistance. Repair as necessary, reconnect all connectors and repeat Step 1. If there is spark, the coil and its feed circuit are OK. The problem could be in the green lead between the coil and the module. Check for open or short, repair as necessary, reconnect all connectors and repeat Step 1.

STEP 6

To perform this step, a voltmeter which is not combined with a dwell meter is needed. The slight needle oscillations (½ V) you'll be looking for may not be detectable on the combined voltmeter/dwell meter unit.

1. Connect a voltmeter between the orange and purple leads on the harness side of the module connectors.

CAUTION: *On catalytic converter equipped cars, disconnect the air supply line between the Thermactor by-pass valve and the manifold before cranking the engine with the ignition off. This will prevent damage to the catalytic converter. After testing, run the engine for at least 3 minutes before reconnecting the by-pass valve, to clear excess fuel from the exhaust system.*

2. Set the voltmeter on its lowest scale and crank the engine. The meter needle should oscillate slightly (about ½ volt). If the meter does not oscillate, check the circuit through the magnetic pick-up in the distributor for open, shorts, shorts to ground and resistance. Resistance between the orange and purple leads should be 400–1000 ohms, and between each lead and ground should be more than 70,000 ohms. Repair as necessary, reconnect all connectors and repeat Step 1.

If the meter oscillates, the problem is probably in the power feed to the module (red wire) or in the module itself: proceed to Step 7.

STEP 7

1. Remove all meters and jumpers and plug in all connectors.

2. Turn the ignition switch to the RUN position and measure voltage between the battery positive terminal and engine ground. It should be 12 volts.

3. Next, measure voltage between the red lead of the module and engine ground. To make this measurement, it will be necessary to pierce the red wire with a straight pin and connect the voltmeter to the straight pin and to ground. DO NOT ALLOW THE STRAIGHT PIN TO GROUND ITSELF.

4. The two readings should be within one volt of each other. If not within one volt, the problem is in the power feed to the red lead. Check for shorts, open, or high resistance and correct as necessary. After repairs, repeat Step 1.

If the readings are within one volt, the problem is probably in the module. Replace with a good module and repeat Step 1. If this corrects the problem, reconnect the old module and repeat Step 1. If problem returns, permanently install the new module.

Start Mode Spark Test

NOTE: *The wire colors given here are the main colors of the wires, not the dots or hashmarks.*

1. Remove the coil wire from the distributor cap. Install the modified spark plug mentioned under "Special Tools", in the coil wire and ground it to engine metal either by its spring clip (Spark Tester) or by holding the spark plug shell against the engine block with insulated pliers.

NOTE: *See "CAUTION" under Step 6 of "Run Mode Spark Test".*

2. Have an assistant crank the engine using the ignition switch and check for spark. If there is good spark, the problem is probably in the distributor cap, rotor, ignition cables or spark plugs. If there is no spark, proceed to Step 3.

3. Measure the battery voltage. Next, measure the voltage at the white wire of the module while cranking the engine. To make this measurement, it will be necessary to pierce the white wire with a straight pin and connect the voltmeter to the straight pin and to ground. DO NOT ALLOW THE STRAIGHT PIN TO GROUND ITSELF. The battery voltage and the voltage at the white wire should be within 1 volt of each other. If the readings are not within 1 volt of each other, check and repair the feed through the ignition switch to the white wire. Recheck for spark (Step 1). If the readings are within 1 volt of each other, or if there is still no spark after power feed to white wire is repaired, proceed to Step 4.

4. Measure the coil BAT terminal voltage while cranking the engine. The reading should be within 1 volt of battery voltage. If the readings are not within 1 volt of each other, check and repair the feed through the ignition switch to the coil. If the readings are

within 1 volt of each other, the problem is probably in the ignition module. Substitute another module and repeat test for spark (Step 1).

SYSTEM COMPONENT TESTING

Ignition Coil Tests

The ignition coil must be diagnosed separately from the rest of the ignition system.

1. Primary resistance is measured between the two outer coil terminals. Disconnect the coil harness connector. Make sure the ignition switch is OFF. Connect an ohmmeter between the two coil terminals. Primary resistance for Dura Spark I systems should measure 0.71–0.77 ohms. Dura Spark II systems should measure 1.13–1.23 ohms.
2. Secondary resistance is measured between the BATT and center (coil wire) terminals of the coil. Disconnect the coil harness connector and the center coil wire. Make sure the ignition switch is OFF. Connect an ohmmeter between the two coil terminals. Secondary resistance should measure; 7350–8250 ohms for Dura Spark I systems and 7700–11,500 ohms for Dura Spark II.
3. If resistance tests are alright, but the coil is still suspected have the ignition coil tested on a coil tester. If the reading on the coil tester differs from the original testing, check for a defective wiring harness. If significantly different replace the ignition coil.

Resistance Wire Test

Replace the resistance wire if it doesn't show a resistance of 1.05–1.15 ohms. The resistance wire isn't used on Dura Spark I.

Spark Plug Wire Resistance

Resistance on these wires must not exceed 5,000 ohms per inch. To properly measure this, remove the wires from the plugs, and remove the distributor cap. Measure the resistance through the distributor cap at that end. Do not pierce any ignition wire for any reason. Measure only from the two ends.

Do not pull on the wires. Grasp and twist the boot to remove the wire.

Whenever the high tension wires are removed from the plugs, coil, or distributor, silicone grease must be applied inside the boot before reconnection. Use a clean small screwdriver blade to coat the entire interior surface with Ford silicone grease D7AZ-19A331-A, Dow Corning #111, or General Electric G-627.

Adjustments

The air gap between the armature and magnetic pick-up coil in the distributor is not adjustable, nor are there any adjustments for the amplifier module. Inoperative components are simply replaced. Any attempt to connect components outside the vehicle may result in component failure.

PICK-UP REPLACEMENT

Except EEC

1. Remove the distributor cap and rotor, disconnect the distributor harness plug.

   NOTE: *To remove the two-piece Dura Spark distributor cap, take off the top portion, then the rotor, then the bottom adaptor.*
2. Using a small gear puller or two screwdrivers, lift or pry the armature from the advance plate sleeve. Remove the roll pin.
3. Remove the large wire retaining clip from the base plate annular groove.

   For 1978–81 models:
4. Remove the snap-ring which secures the vacuum advance link to the pick-up assembly.
5. Remove the magnetic pick-up assembly ground screw and lift the assembly from the distributor.
6. Lift the vacuum advance arm off the post on the pick-up assembly and move it out against the distributor housing.

   For 1982–83 models:
7. Remove the ground screw which retains the ground strap.
8. Pull upward on the lead wires to remove the rubber grommet from the distributor base.
9. Remove the E-clip which retains the vacuum advance pull rod to the stator assembly.
10. Lift the pull rod off of the stator post and move the rod out against the distributor housing.
11. Remove the stator assembly. Installation—all models:
12. Place the new pick-up assembly in position over the fixed base plate and slide the wiring in position through the slot in the side of the distributor housing.
13. Install the wire snap-ring securing the pick-up assembly to the fixed base plate.
14. Position the vacuum advance arm over the post on the pick-up assembly and install the snap-ring.

15. Install the grounding screw through the tab on the wiring harness and into the fixed base plate.

16. Install the armature on the advance plate sleeve making sure that the roll pin is engaged in the matching slots.

17. Install the distributor rotor cap.

18. Connect the distributor wiring plug to the vehicle harness.

BREAKERLESS IGNITION SYSTEM TACH HOOKUP

All Fairmonts and Zephyrs have a terminal on the coil provided for connecting a tachometer. The terminal is labeled "Tach-Test" and has a small arrowhead pointing to the proper terminal. Connect the red lead (positive) to this terminal and connect the black ground lead (negative) of the dwell-tach to a good ground on the engine (e.g., thermostat housing bolt).

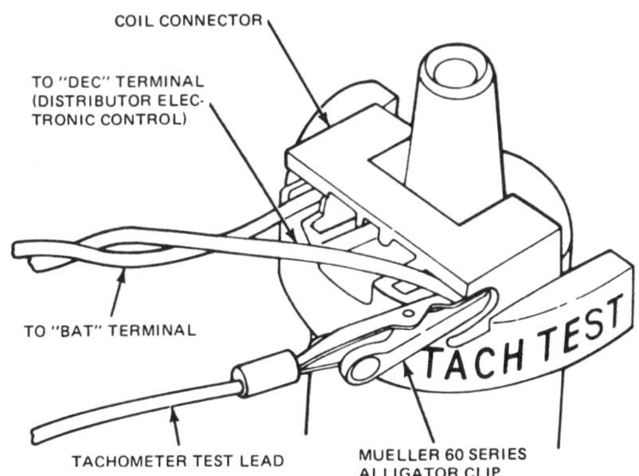

Attaching the tachometer to the coil connector

Ignition Timing

Since Fairmonts and Zephyrs have solidstate ignition, regular ignition timing adjustments are not, strictly speaking, necessary. However, it is always a good idea to check timing occasionally and a basic understanding of ignition timing is essential.

CAUTION: *On models equipped with EEC III, all ignition timing is controlled by the EEC module. Initial ignition timing is not adjustable and no attempt at adjustment should be made.*

NOTE: *Ford recommends that only timing lights of the inductive pickup variety be used; conventional timing lights may give a false reading due to the higher coilcharging currents.*

Ignition timing is the measurement in degrees of crankshaft rotation of the instant the spark plugs in the cylinders fire, in relation to the location of the piston, while the piston is on its compression stroke.

Ideally, the air-fuel mixture in the cylinder will be ignited (by the spark plug) and just beginning its rapid expansion as the piston passes top dead center (TDC) of the compression stroke. If this happens, the piston will be beginning the power stroke just as the compressed (by the movement of the piston) and ignited (by the spark plug) air-fuel mixture starts to expand. The expansion of the air-fuel mixture will then force the piston down on the power stroke and turn the crankshaft.

It takes a fraction of a second for the spark from the plug to completely ignite the mixture in the cylinder. Because of this, the spark plug must fire before the piston reaches TDC, if the mixture is to be completely ignited as the piston passes TDC. This measurement is given in degrees (of crankshaft rotation) *before* the piston reaches *top dead center* (BTDC). If the ignition timing setting for your engine is six degrees (6°) BTDC, this means that the spark plug must fire at a time when the piston for that cylinder is 6° before top dead center of its compression stroke. However, this only holds true while your engine is at idle speed.

As you accelerate from idle, the speed of your engine (rpm) increases. The increase in rpm means that the pistons are now traveling up and down much faster. Because of this, the spark plugs will have to fire even sooner if the mixture is to be completely ignited as the piston passes TDC. To accomplish this, the distributor incorporates means to advance the timing of the spark as engine speed increases.

The distributor in your car has two means of advancing the ignition timing. One is called centrifugal advance and is actuated by weights in the distributor. The other is called vacuum advance and is controlled by that large circular housing on the side of the distributor.

In addition, some distributors have a vacuum-retard mechanism which is contained in the same housing on the side of the distributor as the vacuum advance. The function of the mechanism is to retard the timing of the ignition spark under certain engine conditions. This causes more complete burning of the air-fuel mixture in the cylinder and consequently lowers exhaust emissions.

Because these mechanisms change ignition timing, it is necessary to disconnect and plug the one or two vacuum lines from the distributor when setting the basic ignition timing.

If ignition timing is set too far advanced (BTDC), the ignition and expansion of the air-fuel mixture in the cylinder will try to force the piston down the cylinder while it is still traveling upward. This causes engine "ping," a sound which resembles marbles being dropped into an empty tin can. If the ignition timing is too far retarded (after, or ATDC), the piston will have already started down on the power stroke when the air-fuel mixture ignites and expands. This will cause the piston to be forced down only a portion of its travel. This will result in poor engine performance and lack of power.

Ignition timing adjustment is checked with a timing light. This instrument is connected to the number one (no. 1) spark plug of the engine. The timing light flashes every time an electrical current is sent from the distributor, through the no. 1 spark plug wire, to the spark plug. The crankshaft pulley and the front cover of the engine are marked with a timing pointer and a timing scale. When the timing pointer is aligned with the "0" mark on the timing scale, the piston in no. 1 cylinder is at TDC of its compression stroke. With the engine running and the timing light aimed at the timing pointer and timing scale, the stroboscopic flashes from the timing light will allow you to check the ignition timing setting of the engine. The timing light flashes every time the spark plug in the no. 1 cylinder of the engine fires. Since the flash from the timing light makes the crankshaft pulley seem stationary for a moment, you will be able to read the exact position of the piston in the no. 1 cylinder on the timing scale on the front of the engine.

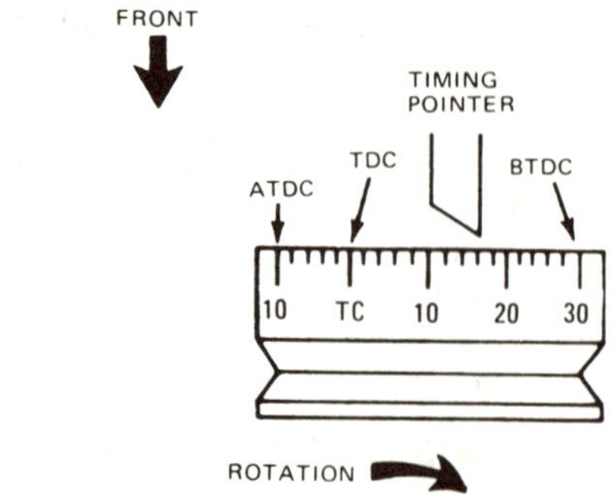

Crankshaft timing marks—4 cyl.

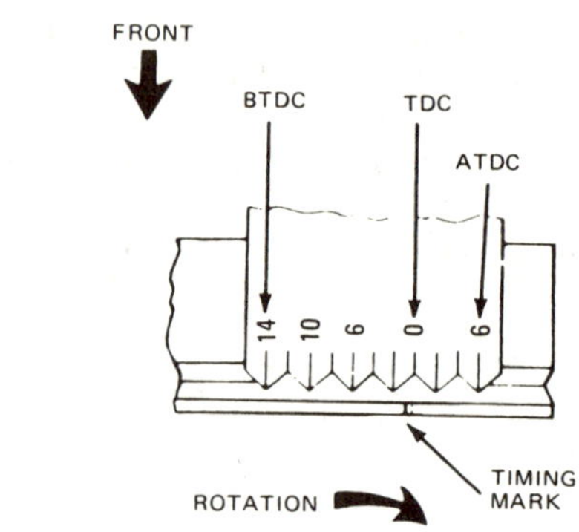

Crankshaft timing marks—6 cyl.

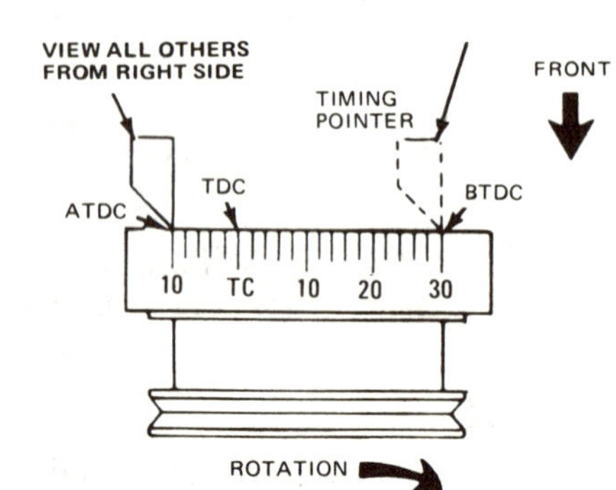

Crankshaft timing marks—V8

IGNITION TIMING ADJUSTMENT

Clean the crankshaft damper/pulley and timing pointer on the water pump housing with a solvent-soaked rag or a wire brush so that the marks can be seen. Connect a stroboscopic timing light to the no. One cylinder spark plug (see firing order illustration) and to the battery, according to the manufacturer's instructions. Scribe a mark on the crankshaft damper/pulley and on the pointer with chalk or luminescent (day glo) paint to highlight the correct timing setting. Disconnect the vacuum hose(s) at the distributor vacuum capsule and plug it (them) with a pencil, golf tee, or some other small pointed object.

Connect one lead to the "Tach Test" connection atop the ignition coil and the other wire to a good ground. Make sure all wires clear the fan. Set the idle speed to specifications. With the engine running, aim the timing light at the pointer and the marks on the damper/pulley. If the marks made with the chalk or paint coincide when the timing light flashes, the engine is timed correctly. If the marks do not coincide, stop the engine. Loosen the distributor locknut and start the engine again. While observing the timing light flashes on the markers, grasp the distributor vacuum capsule—not the distributor cap—and rotate the distributor until the marks do coincide. Stop the engine and tighten the distributor locknut, taking care not to disturb the setting. As a final check, start the engine once more to make sure that the timing marks align.

NOTE: *If necessary, readjust idle speed to specifications. The timing setting is correct only at idle speed.*

Reconnect the vacuum hose(s) to the distributor. Readjust the curb idle speed to specifications as outlined under "Idle Speed and Mixture Adjustment." Remove the timing light and tachometer from the engine.

Valve Adjustment

All Fairmont/Zephyr engines are equipped with hydraulic valve lifters or lash adjusters. Valve systems with hydraulic lifters operate with zero clearance in the valve train. There is no need of scheduled valve adjustment because of the hydraulic valve lifters ability to compensate for slack. All components of the valve train should be checked for wear if there is excessive play. If the valve train has been disassembled for any reason a preliminary valve adjustment may be necessary. Refer to the engine chapter (Chapter 3) for instruction on preliminary valve adjustment.

Carburetor

This section contains only carburetor adjustments as they normally apply to engine tune-up.

When the engine in your car is running, air-fuel mixture from the carburetor is being drawn into the engine by a partial vacuum that is created by the downward movement of the piston on the intake stroke of the four-stroke cycle of the engine. The amount of air-fuel mixture that enters the engine is controlled by throttle plate(s) in the bottom of the carburetor. When the engine is not running, the throttle plate(s) is (are) closed, completely blocking off the bottom of the carburetor from the inside of the engine. The throttle plates are connected, through the throttle linkage, to the gas pedal in the passenger compartment of the car. After you start the engine and put the transmission in gear, you depress the gas pedal to start the car moving. What you actually are doing when you depress the gas pedal is opening the throttle plate in the carburetor to admit more of the air-fuel mixture to the engine. The further you open the throttle plates in the carburetor, the higher the engine speed becomes.

As previously stated, when the engine is not running, the throttle plates in the carburetor are closed. When the engine is idling, it is necessary to open the throttle plates slightly. To prevent having to keep your foot on the gas pedal when the engine is idling, an idle speed adjusting screw was added to the carburetor. This screw has the same effect as keeping your foot slightly depressed on the gas pedal. The idle speed adjusting screw contacts a lever (the throttle lever) on the outside of the carburetor. When the screw is turned in, it opens the throttle plate on the carburetor, raising the idle speed of the engine. This screw is called the curb idle adjusting screw, and the procedures in this section will tell you how to adjust it.

In addition to the carb idle adjusting screw, most engines have a throttle solenoid. When the key is turned to "off," the engine normally stops running. However, if an engine has a high operating temperature and a high idle speed, it is possible for the temperature of the cylinder instead of the spark plug to ignite the air-fuel mixture. When this happens, the engine continues to run after the key is turned off. To solve this problem, a throttle solenoid was added to the carburetor. The solenoid is a cylinder with an adjustable plunger and an electrical lead. When the ignition key is turned to "on," the solenoid plunger extends to contact the carburetor throttle lever and raise the idle speed of the engine. When the ignition key is turned to "off," the solenoid is deenergized and the solenoid plunger falls back from the throttle lever. This allows the throttle lever to fall back and rest on the curb idle adjusting screw. This drops the engine idle speed back far enough that the engine will not run on.

Since it is difficult for the engine to draw the air-fuel mixture from the carburetor with the small amount of throttle plate opening that is present when the engine is idling, an idle mixture passage is provided in the carburetor. This passage delivers air-fuel mixture to the engine from a hole which is located in the bottom of the carburetor below the throttle plates. This idle mixture passage contains an adjusting screw which restricts the amount of air-fuel mixture that enters the engine at idle.

NOTE: *With the electric solenoid disengaged, the carburetor idle speed adjusting screw must make contact with the throttle lever to prevent the throttle plates from jamming in the throttle bore when the engine is turned off.*

IDLE SPEED AND MIXTURE ADJUSTMENTS

NOTE: *In order to limit exhaust emissions, plastic caps have been installed on the idle fuel mixture screw(s) that prevent the carburetor from being adjusted to an overly rich fuel mixture. Under no circumstances should these limiters be modified or removed. Not only is it illegal, you probably won't improve your car's performance and may even hurt it. A satisfactory idle may be obtained within the range of the limiters.*

Due to higher emission standards, idle systems have become so complex it is recommended that any idle speed adjustments be done at a qualified shop.

If the idle speed must be adjusted and you are not able to take your car to a qualified garage;

1. Start the engine and allow it to reach operating temperatures.
2. Make sure the parking brake is on and the wheels are firmly chocked. This is important since automatic transmission cars have their high idle adjusted with the transmission in drive.
3. Remove the air cleaner and make sure the choke is fully open (choke plate in vertical position). Put the air cleaner back on. Check to see that the air conditioner and other accessories are turned off.
4. If you haven't checked the timing at this point, do it now. Attach a tachometer to the engine.
5. The carburetor has two idle speeds: high idle and low idle. On automatic transmission cars, the high idle is adjusted with the transmission in drive. On V8s, the high idle speed is adjusted with the throttle solenoid activated (plugged in). The solenoid adjustment is made by turning the solenoid adjusting screw in or out, then tightening the locknut. On other models, simply turn the adjusting screw in or out. There is no locknut.
6. The low idle speed is adjusted with the throttle solenoid deactivated (unplugged). Disconnect the solenoid lead at the connector near the harness, not at the carburetor. When adjusting the low idle, the transmission should be in neutral. The adjustment is made with the curb idle adjusting screw on the carburetor. After adjusting the lower idle speed, reconnect the solenoid lead at the harness connector and open the throttle slightly by hand, allowing the solenoid plunger to extend.

NOTE: *Sometimes it is difficult to adjust the idle speed with the air cleaner installed. If you have problems, take the air cleaner off and make an approximate adjustment, keeping in mind that the reinstallation of the air cleaner will cause the idle to drop. Continue with this trial and error method until the proper idle speed is attained.*

Catalytic Converter Precautions

Most Fairmonts and Zephyrs are equipped with catalytic converters to clean up exhaust emissions after they leave the engine. Naturally, lead-free fuel must be used in order to avoid contaminating the converter and rendering it useless. However, there are other precautions which should be taken to prevent a large amount of unburned hydrocarbon from reaching the converter. Should a sufficient amount of HC reach the converter, the unit could overheat, possibly damaging the converter or nearby mechanical components. There is even the possibility that a fire could be started. Therefore, when working on your car, the following conditions should be avoided:

1. The use of fuel system cleaning agents and additives.
2. Operating the car with a closed choke or a submerged carburetor float.
3. Extended periods of engine run-on (dieseling).
4. Turning off the ignition with the car in motion.
5. Ignition or charging system failure.
6. Misfiring of one or more spark plugs.
7. Disconnecting a spark plug wire while testing for a bad wire or plug, or poor compression in one cylinder.
8. Push starting the car, especially when hot.
9. Pumping the gas pedal when attempting to start a hot engine.
10. Using leaded gasoline.

Engine and Engine Rebuilding

ENGINE ELECTRICAL

NOTE: *Refer to Chapter 2 for a description of, and troubleshooting procedures for the ignition system.*

Distributor

CAUTION: *On models equipped with EEC III ignition system. The distributor is locked into place and adjustment is never required because all timing control is handled by the EEC III module. Rotor alignment is critical with this system and any servicing should be done only by qualified mechanics.*

REMOVAL

1. Remove the air cleaner on the V8 engines.
2. On the 4-cylinder and 6-cylinder in-line engines, remove one thermactor pump mounting bolt, and the drive belt; then swing the pump to one side to allow access to the distributor. If necessary disconnect the thermactor air filter and lines.
3. Disconnect the distributor wiring connector from the vehicle wiring harness.
4. Disconnect the vacuum lines from the distributor.
5. Remove the distributor cap and wires and lay to one side. Remove the rotor and adapter then reinstall the rotor.
6. Scribe a mark on the distributor body and the cylinder block indicating the position of the rotor in the distributor and the distributor in the block. These marks will be used as guides during installation of the distributor.
7. Remove the distributor hold down bolt and clamp and lift the distributor out of the block.

NOTE: *Do not rotate the engine while the distributor is out of the block, or it will be necessary to time the engine.*

INSTALLATION

1a. If the engine was cranked (disturbed) with the distributor removed, it will now be necessary to retime the engine. If the distributor has been installed incorrectly and the engine will not start, remove the distributor from the engine and start over again. Hold the distributor close to the engine and install the cap on the distributor in its normal position. Locate the No. 1 spark plug tower on the distributor cap. Scribe a mark on the body of the distributor directly below the No. 1 spark plug wire tower on the distributor cap. Remove the distributor cap from the distributor and move the distributor and cap to one side. Remove the No. 1 spark plug and crank the engine over until the No. 1 cylinder is on its compression stroke. To accomplish this, place a wrench on the lower engine pulley and turn the engine slowly in a clockwise (4 & 6 cylinder) or counterclockwise (V8) direction until the TDC mark on the crankshaft damper aligns with the timing pointer. If you place your finger in the No. 1 spark plug hole, you will feel air escaping as the piston rises in the combustion chamber. One of the armature segments must be aligned with the stator as shown in the accompanying illustration to install the distributor. Make sure that the oil pump intermediate shaft properly engages the distributor shaft. It may be necessary to turn the engine after the distributor drive gear is partially engaged, in order to engage the oil pump intermediate shaft. Install, but do not tighten the retaining clamp and bolt. Rotate the distributor to advance the timing to a point where the armature tooth is aligned properly. Tighten the clamp.

1b. If the engine was not cranked (disturbed) when the distributor was removed, position the distributor in the block with the rotor aligned with the mark previously scribed on the distributor body and the marks on the distributor body and cylinder block in alignment. Install the distributor hold-down bolt and clamp fingertight.

2. Install the vacuum hoses and connect the ignition wire to the wiring harness.
3. Install the rotor adapter and distributor cap.
4. Install the thermactor pump and belt on the four and in-line six cylinder engines. Adjust the belt tension so that there is a ¼ inch deflection at its longest point.
5. Connect the thermactor hoses and the filter.
6. Install the air cleaner if removed and check the ignition timing.

Alternator

ALTERNATOR PRECAUTIONS

To prevent damage to the alternator and regulator, the following precautions should be taken when working with the electrical system.

1. Never reverse the battery connections.
2. Booster batteries for starting must be connected properly. See Chapter 1.
3. Disconnect the battery cables before using a fast charger; the charger has a tendency to force current through the diodes in the opposite direction for which they were designed. This burns out the diodes.
4. Never use a fast charger as a booster for starting the vehicle.
5. Never disconnect the voltage regulator while the engine is running.
6. Avoid long soldering times when replacing diodes or transistors. Prolonged heat is damaging to AC generators.
7. Do not use test lamps of more than 12 volts (V) for checking diode continuity.
8. Do not short across or ground any of the terminals on the AC generator.
9. The polarity of the battery, generator, and regulator must be matched and considered before making any electrical connections within the system.
10. Never operate the alternator on an open circuit. Make sure that all connections within the circuit are clean and tight.
11. Disconnect the battery terminals when performing any service on the electrical system. This will eliminate the possibility of accidental reversal of polarity.
12. Disconnect the battery ground cable if arc welding is to be done on any part of the car.

SIDE TERMINAL ALTERNATOR

Removal

1. Disconnect the ground cable at the battery.
2. Loosen the alternator attaching bolt and remove the adjustment arm attaching bolt. Remove the drive bolt from the pulley.
3. Remove the electrical connectors from the alternator. To remove the stator and field

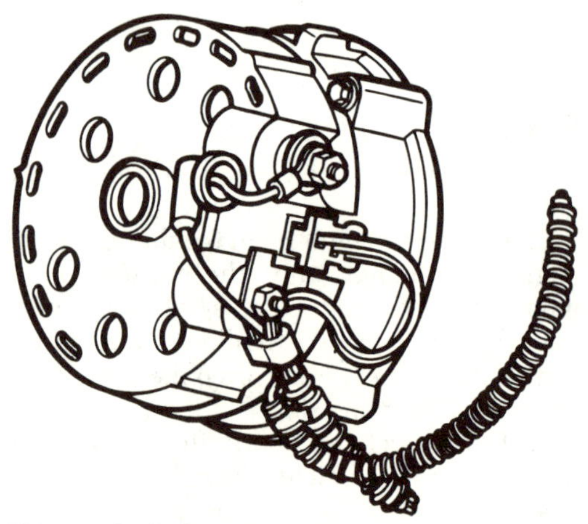

Side terminal alternator

connectors depress the lock tab and pull the connector straight off the terminals.

4. Remove the alternator attaching bolt and remove the alternator.

Installation

1. Position the alternator to the engine, and install the spacer (if used) and the alternator attaching bolt. Tighten the bolt to a snug position.
2. Install the adjustment arm attaching bolt.
3. Install the drive belt on the pulley and adjust the belt tension. Apply pressure on the alternator front housing adjusting ear and tighten the adjusting arm bolt and the alternator mounting bolt. Test the tightness of the belt by pressing it firmly with your thumb at its longest run. The deflection should be about a ¼ inch.
4. Connect the electrical connectors to the alternator.
5. Connect the battery ground cable.

REAR TERMINAL ALTERNATOR

Removal

1. Disconnect the ground cable from the battery.
2. Loosen the alternator pivot bolt and adjuster bolt and remove the drive belt.
3. Disconnect the wiring terminals from the back of the alternator. The push on type terminals should be pulled straight off the terminal to prevent damage to the terminal.
4. Remove the alternator adjuster bolt and pivot bolt and remove the alternator.

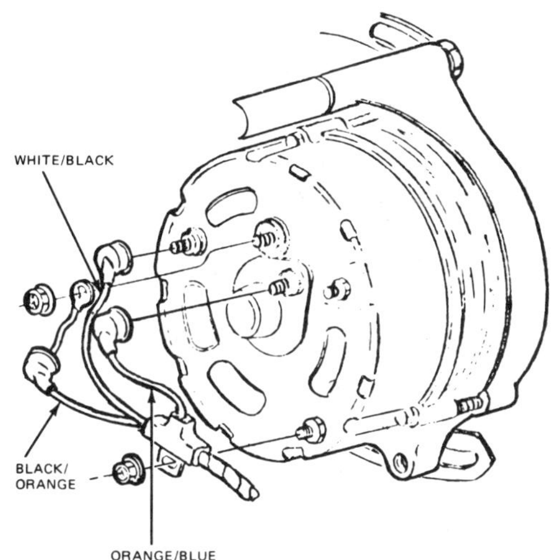

Rear terminal alternator

Installation

1. Position the alternator on the engine and install the pivot bolt and the adjuster bolt and tighten until snug.
2. Connect the wiring terminals to the back of the alternator.
3. Install the drive belt and tighten the tension until there is a ¼ inch deflection at its longest span. Apply pressure on the front housing only.
4. Tighten the adjuster bolt and connect the ground cable to the battery.

Regulator

Most of the voltage regulators used on the Fairmont and Zephyr are 100 percent solid state, consisting of transisters, diodes, and resisters. The regulators are preset and calibrated by the manufacturer. No readjustment is required or possible on these units.

REMOVAL AND INSTALLATION

1. Remove the battery ground cable.
2. Disconnect the regulator from the wiring harness.
3. Remove the regulator mounting screws and remove the regulator.
4. Installation is the reverse of removal.

Alternator/Regulator Identification

Color Code	*Amps.*	*Type*	*Regulator*
Orange	40	RT	Electronic
Green	60	RT	Electronic
Black	65	RT	Electronic
Black	70	ST	Electronic
Red	100	ST	Electronic

RT-Rear Terminal ST-Side Terminal
Field Current at 12V should be 4.0

Starting System

The function of a starting system is to crank the engine at a speed fast enough to permit the engine to start. Heavy cables, connectors, and switches are used in the starting system because of the large current required by the starter while it is cranking the engine. The amount of the resistance in the starting circuit must be kept to an absolute minimum to provide maximum current for starter operation. A discharged or damaged battery, loose or corroded connections or partially broken cables will result in slower than normal cranking speeds, and may even prevent the starter from cranking the engine.

The starting system includes an integral positive-engagement drive, battery, a remote control starter switch (part of the ignition switch), the neutral-start switch, (automatic transmission with floor shift only), the starter relay, and heavy circuit wiring.

When the ignition key is turned to the start position it actuates the starter relay, through the starter control circuit. The starter relay then connects the battery to the starter.

Starter

NOTE: *For starting system troubleshooting information refer to Chapter 11.*

REMOVAL AND INSTALLATION

4 Cylinder Engines

1. Disconnect the negative ground cable from the battery.
2. Disconnect the starter cable at the starter motor.
3. Make sure the parking brake is firmly set, block the rear wheels and raise the front of the car—support it with jackstands.
4. Remove the starter motor mounting bolts and remove the starter motor assembly.
5. To install the starter motor assembly, reverse the removal procedures.

6 Cylinder Engines

1. Disconnect the negative ground cable from the battery.
2. Remove the top starter motor mounting bolt and the exhaust pipe heat shield.
3. Disconnect the starter cable at the starter motor.
4. Make sure the parking brake is firmly set, block the rear wheels and raise the front of the car—support it with jackstands.
5. Remove the wishbone brace.
6. Remove the remaining starter mounting bolts and remove the starter motor assembly.
7. To install the starter motor assembly, reverse the removal procedures.

V8 Engines

1. Disconnect the negative ground cable from the battery.
2. Make sure the parking brake is set, block the rear wheels and raise the front of the car—support it on jackstands.
3. Remove the wishbone brace.
4. Remove the starter motor mounting bolts and remove the starter motor assembly.
5. Disconnect the starter cable from the starter motor assembly.

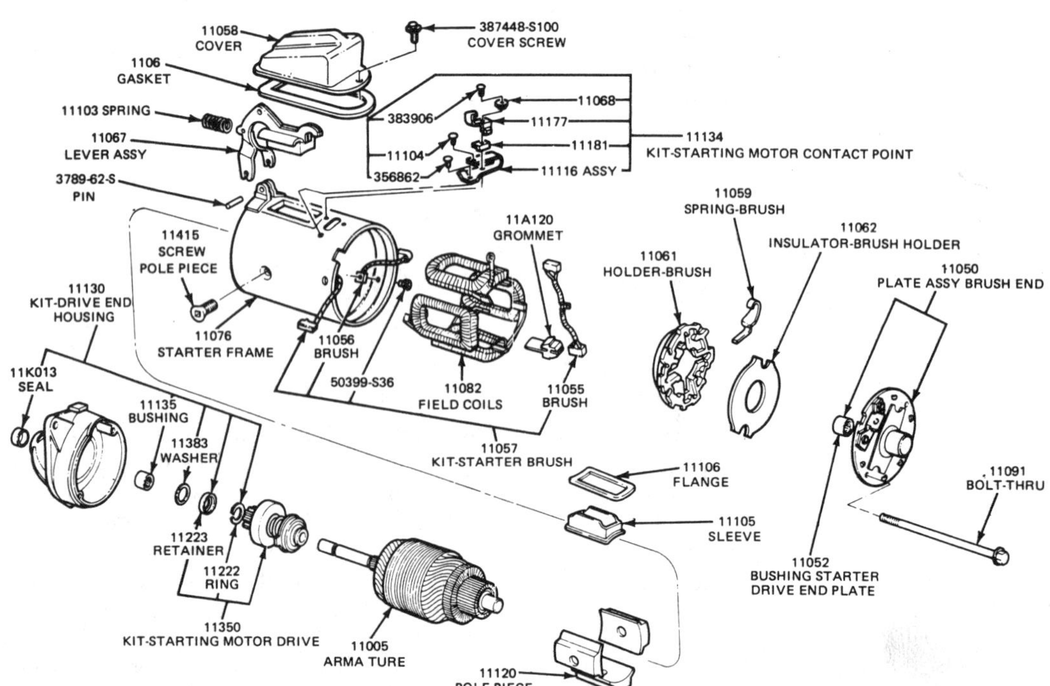

Disassembled starter (typical)

6. To install the starter motor assembly, reverse the removal procedures.

STARTER BRUSH REPLACEMENT

Replace the starter brushes when they are worn to ¼ in. Always install a complete set of new brushes.

1. Loosen and remove the brush cover band, gasket, and starter drive plunger lever cover. Remove the brushes from their holders.
2. Remove the two through-bolts from the starter frame.
3. Remove the drive end housing and the plunger lever return spring.
4. Remove the starter drive plunger lever pivot pin and lever, and remove the armature.
5. Remove the brush end plate.
6. Remove the ground brush retaining screws from the frame and remove the brushes.
7. Cut the insulated brush leads from the field coils, as close to the field connection point as possible.
8. Clean and inspect the starter motor.
9. Replace the brush end plate if the insulator between the field brush holder and the end plate is cracked or broken.
10. Position the new insulated field brushes lead on the field coil connection. Position and crimp the clip provided with the brushes to hold the brush lead to the connection. Solder the lead, clip, and connections together using rosin core solder. Use a 300-watt soldering iron.
11. Install the ground brush leads to the frame with the retaining screws.
12. Clean the commutator with 00 or 000 sandpaper.
13. Position the brush end plate to the starter frame, with the end plate boss in the frame slot.
14. Install the armature in the starter frame.
15. Install the starter drive gear plunger lever to the frame and starter drive assembly, and install the pivot pin.
16. Partially fill the drive end housing bearing bore with grease (approximately ¼ full). Position the return spring on the plunger lever, and the drive end housing to the starter frame. Install the through-bolts and tighten to specified torque (55 to 75 in. lbs). Be sure that the stop ring retainer is seated properly in the drive end housing.
17. Install the commutator brushes in the brush holders. Center the brush springs on the brushes.
18. Position the plunger lever cover and brush cover band, with its gasket, on the starter. Tighten the band retaining screw.
19. Connect the starter to a battery to check its operation.

STARTER DRIVE REPLACEMENT

1. Remove the starter from the engine.
2. Remove the brush cover band.
3. Remove the starter drive plunger lever cover.
4. Loosen the thru-bolts just enough to allow removal of the drive end housing and the starter drive plunger lever return spring.
5. Remove the pivot pin which attaches the starter drive plunger lever to the starter frame and remove the lever.
6. Remove the stop ring retainer and stop-ring from the armature shaft.
7. Remove the starter drive from the armature shaft.
8. Inspect the teeth on the starter drive. If they are excessively worn, inspect the teeth on the ring gear of the flywheel. If the teeth on the flywheel are excessively worn, the flywheel ring gear should be replaced.
9. Apply a thin coat of white grease to the armature shaft, in the area in which the starter drive operates.
10. Install the starter drive on the armature shaft and install a new stop-ring.
11. Position the starter drive plunger lever on the starter frame and install the pivot pin. *Make sure the plunger lever is properly engaged with the starter drive.*
12. Install a new stop ring retainer on the armature shaft.
13. Fill the drive end housing bearing fore ¼ full with grease.
14. Position the starter drive plunger lever return spring and the drive end housing to the starter frame.
15. Tighten the starter thru-bolts to 55–75 in. lbs.
16. Install the starter drive plunger lever cover and the brush cover band on the starter.
17. Install the starter.

Battery

REMOVAL AND INSTALLATION

1. Loosen the battery cable bolts and spread the ends of the battery cable terminals.
2. Disconnect the negative battery cable first.

3. Disconnect the positive battery cable.
4. Remove the battery hold-down.
5. Wearing heavy gloves, remove the battery from under the hood. *Be careful not to tip the battery and spill acid on yourself or the car during removal.*
6. To install, wearing heavy gloves, place the battery in its holder under the hood. *Use care not to spill the acid.*
7. Install the battery hold-down.
8. Install the positive battery cable first.
9. Install the negative battery cable.
10. Apply a *light* coating of grease to the cable ends.

ENGINE MECHANICAL

Engine

REMOVAL AND INSTALLATION

NOTE: *Tag all wires and vacuum hoses for identification to prevent confusion during installation.*

1. Scribe the hood hinge outline on the under-hood surface for reinstallation alignment. Have a helper support the front of the hood, remove the mounting bolts and the hood.
2. Position the car under the engine lift-

General Engine Specifications

Year	*Engine No. Cyl. Displacement (cu in)*	*Carburetor Type*	*Horsepower @ rpm*	*Torque @ rpm (ft. lbs.)*	*Bore x Stroke (in.)*	*Compression Ratio*	*Oil Pressure @ 2000 rpm*
1978–83	4-140	2 bbl	88 @ 4800	118 @ 2800	3.781 x 3.126	9.0:1	50
	6-200	1 bbl	94 @ 4000	158 @ 1400	3.682 x 3.126	8.5:1	30–50
	8-255	2 bbl	115 @ 3400	195 @ 2200	3.680 x 3.000	8.8:1	40–60
	8-302	2 bbl	140 @ 3600	250 @ 1800	4.000 x 3.000	8.4:1	40–65
	8-302 Cal.	2 bbl	134 @ 3600	243 @ 2200	4.000 x 3.000	8.1:1	40–65

Camshaft Specifications
(All measurements in inches)

Engine	*Journal Diameter*					*Bearing Clearance*	*Lobe Lift*		*Endplay*
	1	*2*	*3*	*4*	*5*		*Intake*	*Exhaust*	
4-140 (2.3L)	1.7713–1.7720	1.7713–1.7720	1.7713–1.7720	1.7713–1.7720	—	.001–.003	.2437	.2437	.001–.007
6-200 (3.3L)	1.8095–1.8105	1.8095–1.8105	1.8095–1.8105	1.8095–1.8105	—	.001–.003	.245	.245	.001–.007
8-255 (4.2L)	2.0805–2.0815	2.0655–2.0665	2.0505–2.0515	2.0355–2.0365	2.0205–2.0215	.001–.003	.2375	.2375	.001–.007
8-302 (5.0L)	2.0805–2.0815	2.0655–2.0665	2.0505–2.0515	2.0355–2.0365	2.0205–2.0215	.001–.003	.2375	.2474	.001–.003

Valve Specifications
(All measurements in inches)

Engine No. Cyls. Displacement (cu. in.) (L.)	Year	Seat Angle (deg.)	Face Angle (deg.)	Spring Test Pressure (lbs. @ in.)	Spring Installed Height (in.)	Stem to Guide Clearance (in.)		Stem Diameter (in.)	
						Intake	Exhaust	Intake	Exhaust
4-140 (2.3L)	1978–79	45	44	180–198 @ 1.16	1.5312–1.5938	.0010–.0027	.0015–.0032	.3416	.3411
	1980–83	45	44	159–175 @ 1.16	1.5312–1.5938	.0010–.0027	.0015–.0032	.3416	.3411
6-200 (3.3L)	1978–83	45	44	142–158 @ 1.22	1.5625–1.5938	.0008–.0025	.0010–.0027	.3100	.3098
8-255 (4.2L)	1980–82	45	44	Intake: 190–214 @ 1.36 Exhaust: 190–215 @ 1.18	Intake: 1.6719–1.7031 Exhaust: 1.5781–1.6094	.0010–.0027	.0015–.0032	.3416	.3411
8-302 (5.0L)	1978–79	45	44	Intake: 190–210 @ 1.36 Exhaust: 190–210 @ 1.20	Intake: 1.6719–1.7031 Exhaust: 1.5781–1.6094	.0010–.0027	.0015–.0032	.3416	.3411

Crankshaft and Connecting Rod Specifications

All measurements are given in inches

Engine No. Cyl. Displacement (cu in.)	Crankshaft				Connecting Rod		
	Main Bearing Journal Dia	Main Bearing Oil Clearance	Shaft End Play	Thrust on No.	Journal Diameter	Oil Clearance	Side Clearance
4-140	2.3982–2.3990	.0008–.0015	.004–.008	3	2.0464–2.0472	.0008–.0015	.0035–.0105
6-200	2.2482–2.2490	.0008–.0015	.004–.008	5	2.1232–2.1240	.0008–.0015	.0035–.0105
8-255	2.2482–2.2490	.0004–.0015	.004–.008	3	2.1228–2.1236	.0008–.0015	.010–.020
8-302	2.2482–2.2490	.0004–.0015	.004–.008	3	2.1228–2.1236	.0008–.0015	.010–.020

Ring Gap

All measurements are given in inches

Engine	Top Compression	Bottom Compression	Oil Control
4Cyl & 8 Cyl	.010–.020	.010–.020	.015–.055
6 Cyl	.008–.016	.008–.016	

Ring Side Clearance

All measurements are given in inches

Engine	Top Compression	Bottom Compression	Oil Control
All	.002–.004	.002–.004	Snug

Piston Clearance

Engine	Piston-to-Bore Clearance (in.)	
	Minimum	Maximum
4-140	.0014	.0022
6-200	.0013	.0021
8-255	.0014	.0024
8-302	.0018	.0026

ing device. Drain the coolant into a suitable container.

3. Disconnect the battery, negative cable first. Remove the battery to avoid accidental damage.

4. Disconnect all hoses to the air cleaner. Remove the air cleaner assembly and mounting brackets.

5. On four cylinder models, disconnect and remove the exhaust manifold shroud. On all engines, remove or disconnect any thermactor (air pump) parts that will interfere with the engine removal.

6. Remove the upper and lower radiator hoses. Remove all drive belts.

7. Unbolt and remove, or unbolt and move the radiator shroud back over the water pump. If your car is equipped with an automatic transmission, disconnect the two cooler lines from the radiator tank.

8. Remove the fan blades, fan spacer, pulley, radiator shroud and radiator.

9. Disconnect the heater hoses from the water pump and cylinder head/block/manifold fitting. On four cylinder models, disconnect the heater hoses from the water pump and carburetor choke fitting.

10. Disconnect the wiring to the alternator, oil pressure switch, ignition coil, temperature switch and starter motor.

NOTE: *The starter motor wiring might be easier to disconnect after the car has been jacked up and supported on jackstands.*

11. Disconnect the accelerator linkage, vacuum modulator line (automatic transmission equipped models), transmission downshift rod (automatic tansmission models), vacuum brake booster line (models equipped), EGR valve, speed control cables and connectors (if equipped).

12. Unbolt the power steering pump and air conditioner compressor with hoses connected, position out of the way and secure.

CAUTION: *If there is not enough slack in the refrigerant lines to position compressor*

Torque Specifications

All readings in ft. lbs.

Engine No. Cyl. Displacement (cu in.)	Cylinder Head Bolts	Rod Bearing Bolts	Main Bearing Bolts	Crankshaft Pulley or Damper Bolts	Flywheel to Crankshaft Bolts	Manifold	
						Intake	Exhaust
4-140	80–90	30–36	80–90	100–120	54–64	①	16–23
6-200	70–75	21–26	60–70	85–100	75–85	—	18–24
8-255, 302	65–72	19–24	60–70	70–90	75–85	24–27	18–24

① Two steps: 5–7, then 14–21

out of the way, the refrigerant in the system must be evacuated before the lines can be disconnected. See Chapter 1 for warning. Unless you are familiar with air conditioning and have the proper equipment have the system evacuated by a professional.

13. Disconnect the flexible fuel line (from the gas tank) at the fuel pump and plug the line.

14. Remove the flywheel/converter housing to engine upper mounting bolts.

NOTE: *On four cylinder engines, two 10mm x 3/8 in. studs are used to attach the upper housing to the engine. If the studs are removed, make sure they are reinstalled with the metric threads in the engine block.*

15. Raise the front of the car and safely support with jackstands. Drain the engine oil. Drain from both oil, pan plugs, if equipped, on V8 engines.

16. Disconnect the starter motor wiring, if not already disconnected. Remove the starter motor.

17. Disconnect the exhaust pipe/converter from the exhaust manifold(s). Wire the pipe(s) out of the way.

18. On cars equipped with a manual transmission, disconnect the clutch retracting spring. Disconnect the clutch equalizer shaft and arm bracket at the frame rail. Remove the clutch shaft and bracket.

19. Remove the flywheel/converter housing lower inspection cover.

20. On models equipped with an auto-

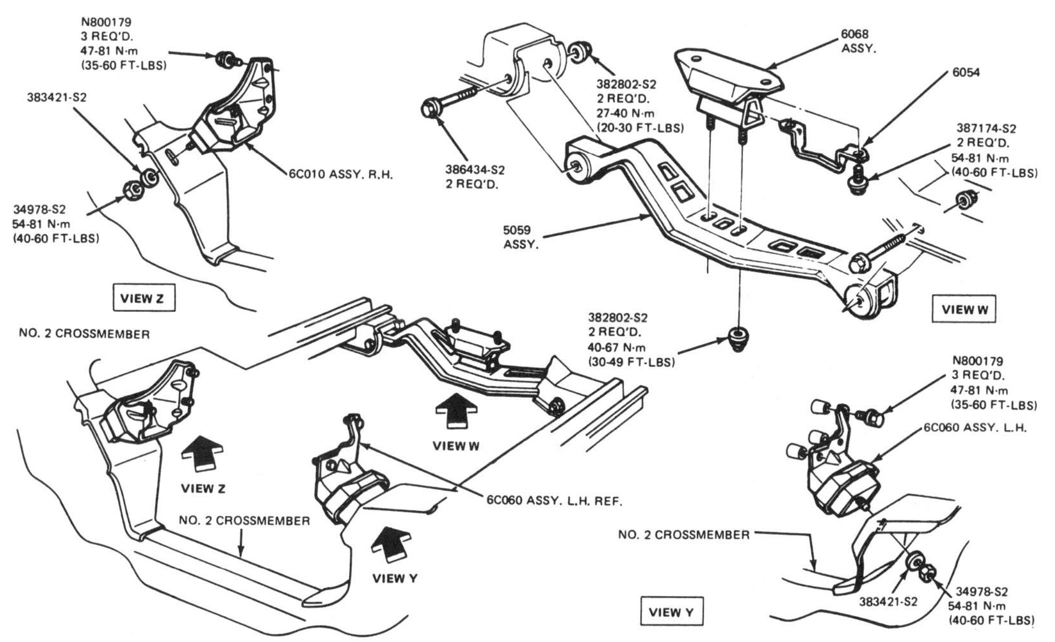

Engine supports—4 cyl.

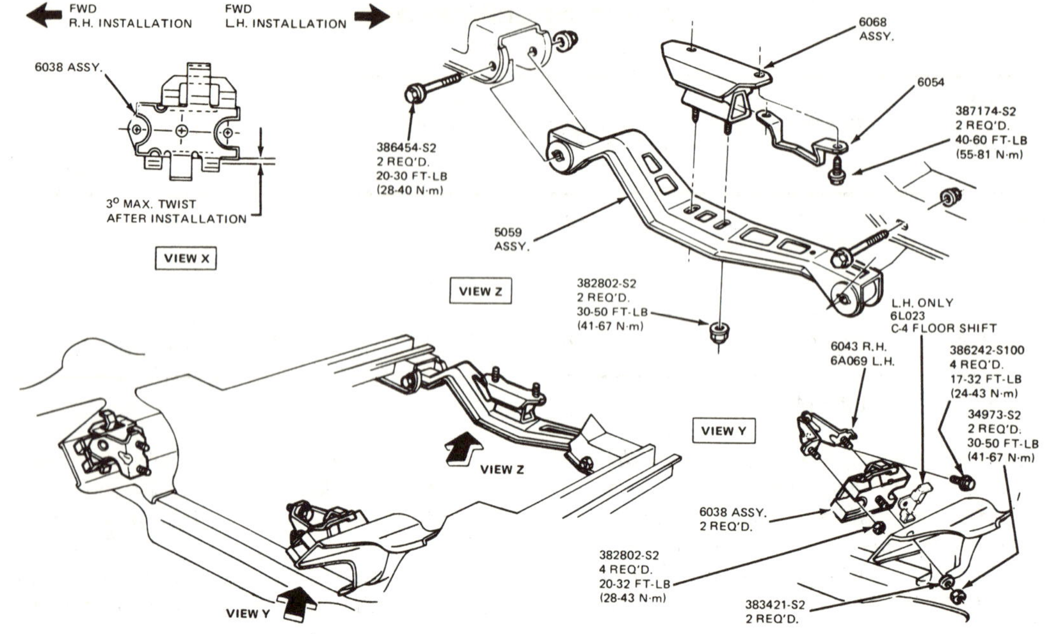

Engine supports—6 cyl.

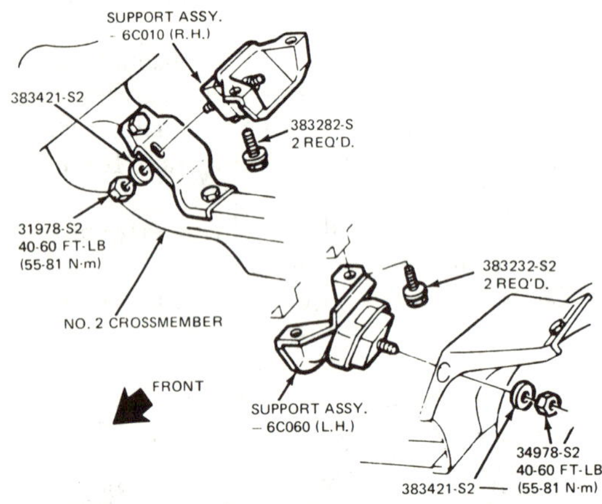

Front engine supports—V8

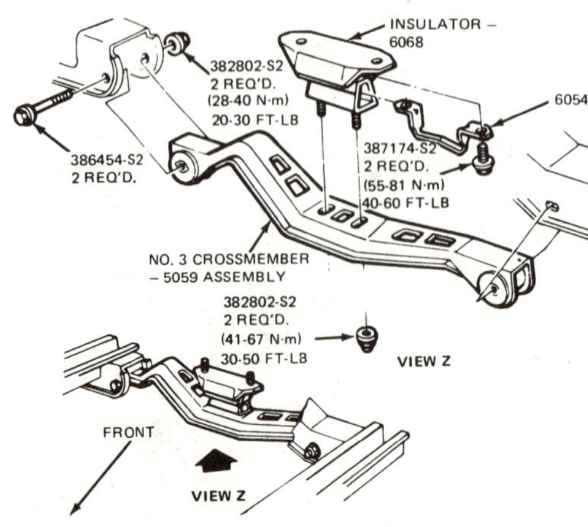

Rear engine supports—V8

matic transmission, disconnect the torque converter from the flywheel. It will be necessary to rotate the engine to gain access to the four converter mounting nuts. Use a socket on a breaker bar or ratchet to turn the engine via the crankshaft pulley center bolt. Always turn the engine in a clockwise direction.

21. Mark a converter mounting stud and the flywheel to insure balance alignment for reinstallation.

22. Disconnect the right and left front motor mount insulators at the number 2 crossmember. Remove the lower flywheel/converter housing to engine mounting bolts.

23. On automatic transmission equipped models, pry the converter slightly away from the flywheel and secure the converter to the transmission with a piece of wire or small "C" clamp on housing.

24. Lower the car from the jackstands. Support the front of the transmission on a piece of wood with a hydraulic jack.

25. Attach a lifting sling to the engine removal brackets. Connect a chain hoist and raise the engine slightly to clear the front motor mounts.

26. Carefully pull the engine forward to disengage the converter or front transmission shaft. Slowly raise the engine out of the engine compartment. Avoid bending the rear cover plate or damaging any components.

27. Secure the transmission and move the car from under hoist. Lower engine to workbench, ground or install on engine stand.

28. Installation Tips: On cars equipped with an automatic transmission, start the converter pilot into the crankshaft while aligning the marks that were made previously. Make sure the studs engage the holes in the flywheel. On manual transmission equipped cars, start the transmission mainshaft into the clutch disc. While installing the engine an adjustment of the transmission position with relation to the engine may be required. Raise transmission with the jack or lower the engine as necessary. If the converter mounting stud alignment is off, or the transmission mainshaft fails to enter the clutch disc, turn the engine in a clockwise direction (manual transmission in gear). Install the upper engine to transmission mounting bolts after the engine and transmission mate firmly together. Align engine mounting insulators with mount brackets, remove the jack from under the transmission and lower the engine into place.

29. Complete the rest of the engine installation in the reverse order of removal.

Engine/Transmission Mounts

REMOVAL AND INSTALLATION

NOTE: *Whenever self-locking nuts/bolts are used they must be replaced with new self-locking nuts/bolts. In some instances, metric fasteners are used.*

Front Mounts

1. Disconnect the negative battery cable at the battery. Jack up the front of the car and safely support with stands.
2. Remove the nut and washer that attach the front insulators to the crossmember pedestals.

NOTE: *In some cases removal of a heat shield will aid in gaining necessary clearance.*

3. Remove the fan shroud mounting screws. Raise the front of the engine using a block of wood and a hydraulic jack under the front of the oil pan.
4. When the insulator studs have cleared the mounting pedestals, remove the insulator from the engine by unbolting.
5. Install new insulator(s) and reverse the removal sequence for installation.

Transmission Mount

1. Disconnect the negative battery cable at the battery. Raise the front of the car and safely support on jackstands.
2. Place a block of wood and a hydraulic jack under the transmission.
3. On automatic transmission models; Remove the two nuts attaching the insulator to the crossmember. Raise the transmission with the jack high enough to clear the crossmember. Unbolt the insulator from the transmission.
4. On manual transmission models; Raise the jack slightly and remove the two bolts and nuts attaching the crossmember to the frame side rails. Unbolt the insulator from the crossmember and transmission.
5. Install a new insulator in the reverse order of removal.

Rocker Arm (Valve) Cover

REMOVAL AND INSTALLATION

Four Cylinder 140 Cu In. Engine
Six Cylinder 200 Cu In. Engine

1. Remove the air cleaner assembly and mounting brackets.
2. Label for identification and remove all wires and vacuum hoses interfering with valve cover removal. Remove the PCV valve with hose. Remove the accelerator control cable bracket if necessary.
3. Remove the valve cover retaining bolts. On four cylinder models, the front bolts equipped with rubber sealing washers must be installed in the same location to prevent oil leakage.
4. Remove the valve cover. Clean all old gasket material from the valve cover and cylinder head gasket surfaces.
5. Install in reverse order of removal. Use oil resistant sealing compound and a new valve cover gasket. When installing the valve cover gasket, make sure all the gasket locating tangs are engaged into the cover notches provided.

V8 Engines

NOTE: *When disconnecting wires and vacuum lines, label them for reinstallation identification.*

1. Remove the air cleaner assembly.
2. On the right side;

   a. Disconnect the automatic choke heat chamber hose from the inlet tube near the right valve cover if equipped.

b. Remove the automatic choke heat tube if equipped and remove the PCV valve and hose from the valve cover. Disconnect EGR, valve hoses.

c. Remove the thermactor bypass valve and air supply hoses as necessary to gain clearance.

d. Disconnect the spark plug wires from the plugs with a twisting pulling motion; twist and pull on the boots only, never on the wire; position the wires and mounting bracket out of the way.

e. Remove the valve cover mounting bolts; remove the valve cover.

3. On the left side;

a. Remove the spark plug wires and bracket.

b. Remove the wiring harness and any vacuum hoses from the bracket.

c. Remove the valve cover mounting bolts and the valve cover.

4. Clean all old gasket material from the valve cover and cylinder head mounting surfaces.

5. Installation is in reverse order of removal. Use oil resistant sealing compound and a new valve cover gasket. When installing the valve cover gasket, make sure all the gasket tangs are engaged into the cover notches provided.

Rocker Arm (Cam Follower) and Hydraulic Lash Adjuster

REMOVAL AND INSTALLATION

Four Cylinder 140 Cu In. Engine

NOTE: *A special tool is required to compress the lash adjuster.*

1. Remove the valve cover and associated parts as required.

2. Rotate the camshaft so that the base circle of the cam is against the cam follower you intend to remove.

3. Remove the retaining spring from the cam follower, if so equipped.

4. Using special tool T74P-6565-B or a valve spring compressor tool, collapse the lash adjuster and/or depress the valve spring, as necessary, and slide the cam follower over the lash adjuster and out from under the camshaft.

5. Install the cam follower in the reverse order of removal. Make sure that the lash adjuster is collapsed and released before rotating the cam shaft.

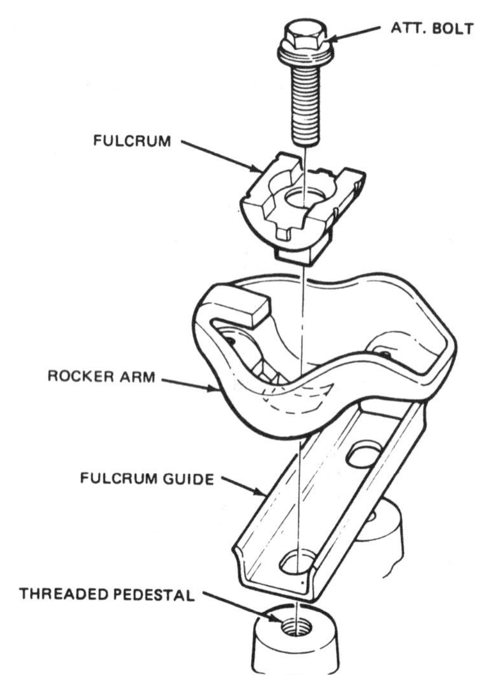

Valve rocker arms—V8 engines

Rocker Arm Shaft/Rocker Arms

REMOVAL AND INSTALLATION

6 Cylinder In-Line Engines

1. Remove the rocker arm (valve) cover (see previous section).

2. Remove the rocker arm shaft mounting bolts, two turns at a time for each bolt. Start at the ends of the rocker shaft and work toward the middle.

3. Lift the rocker arm shaft assembly from the engine. Remove the pin and washer from each end of the shaft. Slide the rocker arms, springs and supports off the shaft. Keep all parts in order or label them for position.

4. Clean and inspect all parts, replace as necessary.

5. Assemble the rocker shaft parts in reverse order of removal. Be sure the oil holes in the shaft are pointed downward. Reinstall the rocker shaft assembly on the engine.

NOTE: *Lubricate all parts with motor oil before installation.*

Clean all mounting surfaces, use a new valve cover gasket and valve cover.

V8 Engines

1. Remove the rocker arm (valve) covers (see previous section).

2. Remove the rocker arm mounting bolt, fulcrum, rocker arm and fulcrum guide. (The fulcrum guide is retained by two rocker arm

assemblies, both must be removed to free the guide).

3. Clean and inspect all parts, replace as necessary.

4. Lubricate all parts with motor oil and reinstall on engine.

5. Clean all mounting surfaces, use new valve cover gaskets and install the valve covers.

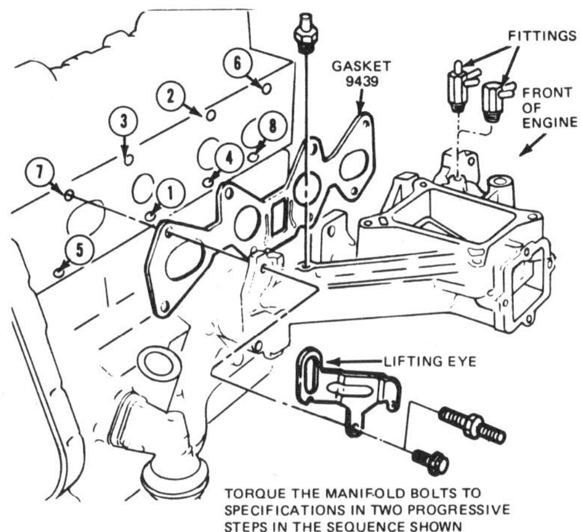

4 cyl. intake manifold installation

Intake Manifold

REMOVAL AND INSTALLATION

Four Cylinder 140 Cu In. Engine

1. Drain the cooling system.

2. Remove the air cleaner and disconnect the throttle linkage from the carburetor.

3. Disconnect the fuel and vacuum lines from the carburetor.

4. Disconnect the carburetor solenoid wire at the quick-disconnect.

5. Remove the choke water housing and thermostatic spring from the carburetor.

6. Disconnect the water outlet and crankcase ventilation hoses from the intake manifold.

7. Disconnect the deceleration valve-to-carburetor hose at the carburetor.

8. Start from each end; work toward the middle; remove the intake manifold attaching bolts and remove the manifold.

9. Clean all old gasket material from the manifold and cylinder head.

10. Apply water-resistant sealer to the intake manifold gasket and position it on the cylinder head.

11. Install the intake manifold attaching nuts. Follow the sequence given in the illustrations.

12. Connect the water and crankcase ventilation hoses to the intake manifold.

13. Connect the deceleration valve-to-carburetor hose to the carburetor.

14. Position the choke water housing and thermostatic spring on the carburetor and engage the end of the spring coil in the slot and the choke adjusting lever. Align the tab on the spring housing. Tighten the choke water housing attaching screws.

15. Connect the carburetor aolenoid wire.

16. Connect the fuel and vacuum lines to the carburetor.

17. Connect the throttle linkage to the carburetor.

18. Install the air cleaner and fill the cooling system.

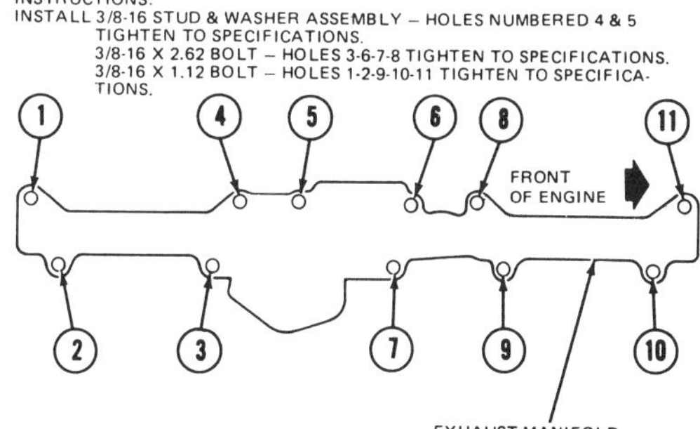

Exhaust manifold torque sequence—6 cyl.

Six Cylinder 200 Cu In. Engine

On this in-line cylinder engine the intake manifold is integral with the cylinder head and cannot be removed.

All V8 Engines

1. Drain the cooling system and disconnect the negative battery cable.

2. Disconnect the upper radiator hose and water pump by-pass hose from the thermostat housing. Disconnect the water temperature sending unit wire. Remove the heater hose from the automatic choke housing bracket and disconnect the hose from the intake manifold.

3. Remove the air cleaner. Disconnect the automatic choke heat chamber air inlet hose at the inlet tube near the right valve cover. Remove the crankcase ventilation hose and intake duct assembly. On all models so equipped, disconnect the Thermactor air hose from the check valve at the rear of the intake manifold and loosen the hose clamp at the

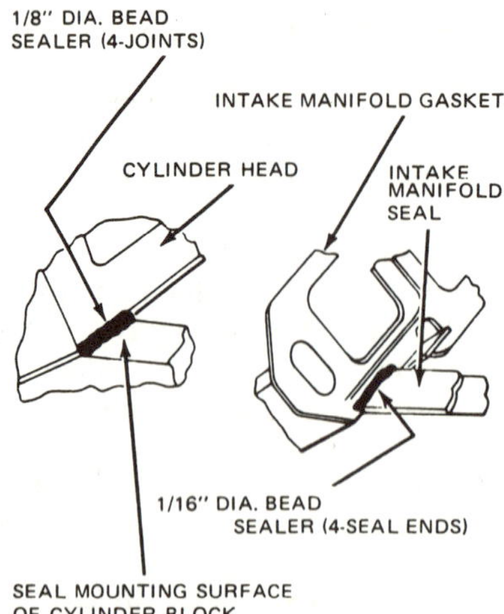

Apply a non-hardening sealer to the intake manifold

bracket. Remove the air hose and Thermactor air by-pass valve from the bracket and position it to one side.

4. Remove all carburetor linkage and automatic transmission kick-down linkage that attaches to the manifold. Disconnect the fuel line, choke heat tube, and any vacuum lines from the carburetor or intake manifold, marking them for installation.

5. Disconnect the distributor vacuum hoses from the distributor. Remove the distributor cap and mark the relative position of the rotor on the distributor housing. Disconnect the spark plug wires at the spark plugs and the primary and secondary wires from the coil. Remove the distributor hold-down bolt and remove the distributor.

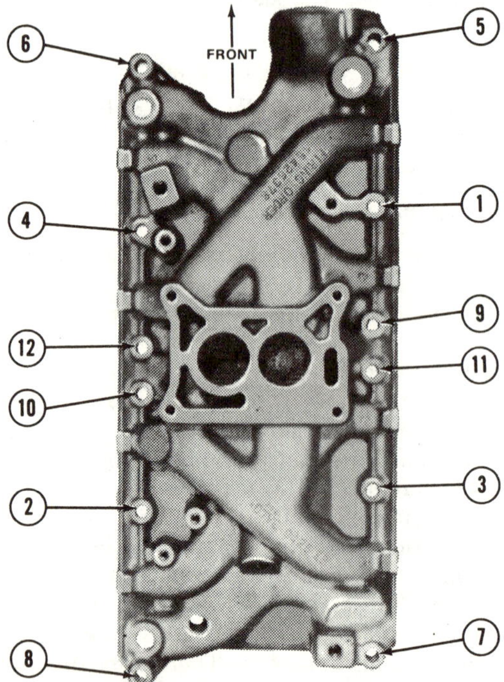

Intake manifold torque sequence—V8 engines

6. If equipped with air conditioning, remove the brackets retaining the compressor to the intake manifold.

7. Remove the manifold attaching bolts. Lift off the intake manifold and carburetor as an assembly.

NOTE: *If it is necessary to pry the manifold to loosen it from the engine, be careful not to damage any gasket sealing surfaces. Always discard all old gaskets and attaching bolt sealing washers.*

8. Clean all gasket surfaces and firmly cement new gaskets in place, using nonhardening sealer. Make sure that the gaskets interlock with the seal tabs, and that the gasket holes align with those in the cylinder heads.

9. Reverse the above procedure to install, taking care to run a finger around the seal area on the installed manifold to make sure that the seals did not slip out during installation. Finally, torque the intake manifold bolts in the proper sequence, and recheck the torque after the engine is warm.

Exhaust Manifold

NOTE: *Although, in most cases, the engine does not have exhaust manifold gaskets installed by the factory, after-mark gaskets are available from parts stores.*

REMOVAL AND INSTALLATION

Four Cylinder 140 Cu In. Engine

1. Remove the air cleaner.
2. Remove the heat shroud from the exhaust manifold.
3. Place a block of wood under the exhaust pipe and disconnect the exhaust pipe from the exhaust manifold.
4. Remove the exhaust manifold attaching nuts and remove the manifold.
5. Install a light coat of graphite grease on the exhaust manifold mating surface and position the manifold on the cylinder head.
6. Install the exhaust manifold attaching nuts and tighten them in the sequence shown in the illustration to 12–15 ft. lbs.
7. Connect the exhaust pipe to the exhaust manifold and remove the wood support from under the pipe.
8. Install the air cleaner.

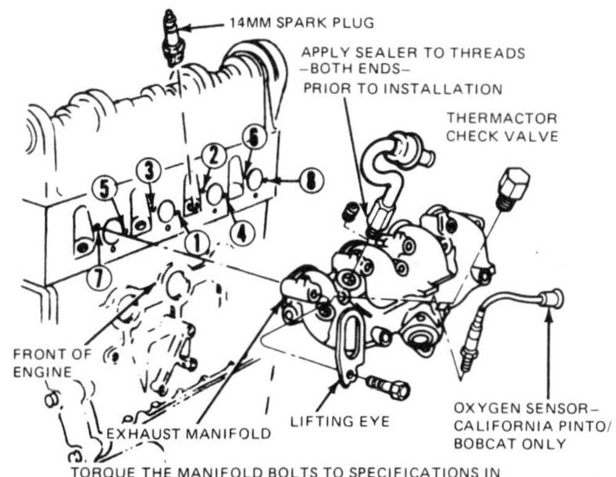

Exhaust manifold torque sequence—4 cyl.

Six Cylinder 200 Cu In. Engine

1. Remove the air cleaner and heat duct body.
2. Disconnect the muffler inlet pipe and remove the choke hot air tube from the manifold.
3. Remove the EGR tube and any other emission components which will interfere with manifold removal.
4. Bend the exhaust manifold attaching bolt lock tabs back, remove the bolts and the manifold.
5. Clean all manifold mating surfaces and place a new gasket on the muffler inlet pipe.
6. Reinstall manifold by reversing the procedure. Torque attaching bolts in sequence shown. After installation, warm the engine to operating temperature and re-torque to specifications.

All V8 Engines

1. On the right exhaust manifold, remove the air cleaner and intake duct assembly.
2. Disconnect the automatic choke heat chamber air inlet hose from the inlet tube near the right valve cover. Remove the automatic choke heat tube.
3. Remove the nuts or bolts retaining the heat stove to the exhaust manifold and remove the stove.
4. Disconnect the exhaust manifold(s) from the muffler inlet pipe(s).
5. Remove the manifold retaining bolts and washers and the manifold(s).
6. Reverse the above procedure to install, using new inlet pipe gaskets. Torque the exhaust manifold retaining bolts to specifications, in sequence from the centermost bolt outward. Start the engine and check for exhaust leaks.

Cylinder Head

REMOVAL AND INSTALLATION

4 Cylinder 140 Engine

1. Drain the cooling system.
2. Remove the air cleaner.
3. Remove the valve cover.

NOTE: *On cars with air conditioning, remove the mounting bolts and the drive belt, and position the compressor out of the way. Remove the compressor upper mounting bracket from the cylinder head.*

CAUTION: *If the compressor refrigerant lines do not have enough slack to permit repositioning of the compressor without first disconnecting the refrigerant lines, the air conditioning system will have to be evacuated by a trained air conditioning serviceman. Under no circumstances should an untrained person attempt to disconnect the air conditioning refrigerant lines.*

4. Remove the intake and exhaust manifolds from the head.
5. Remove the camshaft drive belt cover. Note the location of the belt cover attaching screws that have rubber grommets.
6. Loosen the drive belt tensioner and remove the belt.
7. Remove the water outlet elbow from the cylinder head with the hose attached.
8. Remove the cylinder head attaching bolts.

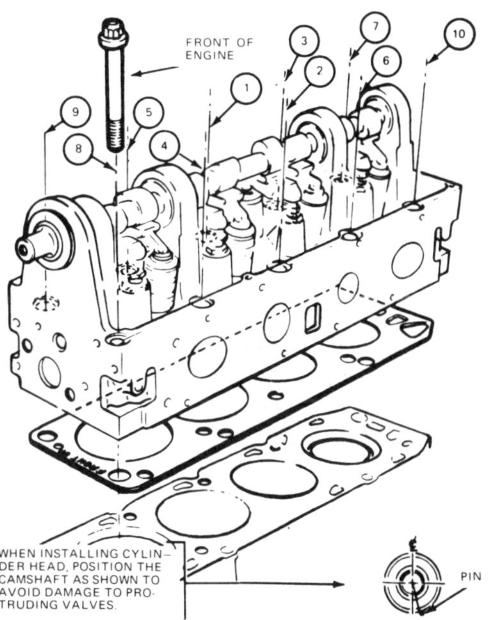

4 Cylinder—cylinder head installation

9. Remove the cylinder head from the engine.

10. Clean all gasket material and carbon from the top of the cylinder block and pistons and from the bottom of the cylinder head.

11. Position a new cylinder head gasket on the engine and place the head on the engine.

NOTE: *If you encounter difficulty in positioning the cylinder head on the engine block, it may be necessary to install guide studs in the block to correctly align the head and the block. To fabricate guide studs, obtain two new cylinder head bolts and cut their heads off with a hack saw. Install the bolts in the holes in the engine block which correspond with cylinder head bolt holes nos. 3 and 4, as identified in the cylinder head bolt tightening sequence illustration. Then, install the head gasket and head over the bolts. Install the cylinder head attaching bolts, replacing the studs with the original head bolts.*

12. Using a torque wrench, tighten the head bolts in the sequence shown in the illustration.

13. Install the camshaft drive belt.

14. Install the camshaft drive belt cover and its attaching bolts. Make sure the rubber grommets are installed on the bolts. Tighten the bolts to 6–13 ft. lbs.

15. Install the water outlet elbow and a new gasket on the engine and tighten the attaching bolts to 12–15 ft. lbs.

16. Install the intake and exhaust manifolds. See the procedures for intake and exhaust manifold installation.

17. Assemble the rest of the components in reverse order of removal.

6 Cylinder 200 Cu In. Engine

1. Drain cooling system, remove the air cleaner and disconnect the negative battery cable.

NOTE: *On cars with air conditioning, remove the mounting bolts and the drive belt, and position the compressor out of the way of the left cylinder head. Remove the compressor upper mounting bracket from the cylinder head.*

CAUTION: *If the compressor refrigerant lines do not have enough slack to permit repositioning of the compressor without first disconnecting the refrigerant lines, the air conditioning system will have to be evacuated by a trained air conditioning serviceman. Under no circumstances should an untrained person attempt to disconnect the air conditioning refrigerant lines.*

2. Disconnect exhaust pipe at the manifold end, spring the exhaust pipe down and remove the flange gasket.

3. Disconnect the fuel and vacuum lines from the carburetor. Disconnect the intake manifold line at the intake manifold.

4. Disconnect the accelerator and retracting spring at the carburetor. Disconnect the transmission kick-down linkage, if equipped.

5. Disconnect the carburetor spacer outlet line at the spacer. Disconnect the radiator upper hose and the heater hose at the water outlet elbow. Disconnect the radiator lower hose and the heater hose at the water pump.

6. Disconnect the distributor vacuum control line at the distributor. Disconnect the gas filter line on the inlet side of the filter.

7. Disconnect and label the spark plug wires and remove the plugs. Disconnect the temperature sending unit wire.

8. Remove the rocker arm cover.

9. Remove the rocker arm shaft attaching bolts and the rocker arm and shaft assembly. Remove the valve pushrods, keep them in order for installation in their original positions.

10. Remove the remaining cylinder head bolts and lift off the cylinder head. Do not pry under the cylinder head as damage to the mating surfaces can easily occur.

To help in installation of cylinder head, two 6 in. x 7/16-14 bolts with heads cut off and the head end slightly tapered and slotted, for installation and removal with a screwdriver, will reduce the possibility of damage during head replacement.

11. Clean the cylinder head and block surfaces. Be sure of flatness and no surface damage.

12. Apply cylinder head gasket sealer to both sides of the new gasket and slide the gasket down over the two guide studs in the cylinder block.

NOTE: *Apply gasket sealer only to steel shim head gaskets. Steel/asbestos composite head gaskets are to be installed without any sealer.*

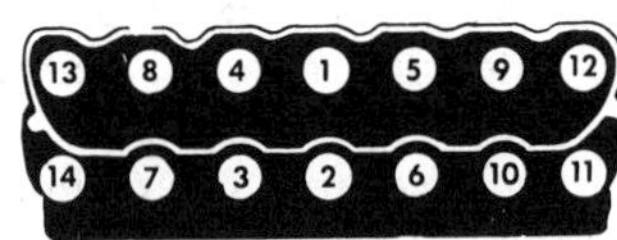

Cylinder head torque sequence—6 cyl. engine

13. Carefully lower the cylinder head over the guide studs. Place the exhaust pipe flange on the manifold studs (new gasket).

14. Coat the threads of the end bolts for the right side of the cylinder head with a small amount of water-resistant sealer. Install, but do not tighten, two head bolts at opposite ends to hold the head gasket in place. Remove the guide studs and install the remaining bolts.

15. Cylinder head torquing should proceed in three steps and in prescribed order. Tighten to 55 ft. lbs., then give them a second tightening to 65 ft. lbs. The final step is to 75 ft. lbs., at which they should remain undisturbed.

16. Lubricate both ends of the pushrods and install them in their original locations.

17. Apply lubricant to the rocker arm pads and the valve stem tips and position the rocker arm shaft assembly on the head. Be sure the oil holes in the shaft are in a down position.

18. Tighten all the rocker shaft retaining bolts to 30–35 ft. lbs. and do a preliminary valve adjustment (make sure there are no tight valve adjustments).

19. Hook up the exhaust pipe.

20. Reconnect the heater and radiator hoses.

21. Reposition the distributor vacuum line, the carburetor gas line and the intake manifold vacuum line on the engine. Hook them up to their respective connections and reconnect the battery cable to the cylinder head.

22. Connect the accelerator rod and retracting spring. Connect the choke control cable and adjust the choke. Connect the transmission kickdown linkage.

23. Reconnect the vacuum line at the distributor. Connect the fuel inlet line at the fuel filter and the intake manifold vacuum line at the vacuum pump.

24. Lightly lubricate the spark plug threads and install them. Connect spark plug wires and be sure the wires are all the way down in their sockets. Connect the temperature sending unit wire.

25. Fill the cooling system. Run the engine to stabilize all engine part temperatures.

26. Adjust engine idle speed and idle fuel-air adjustment.

27. Coat one side of a new rocker cover gasket with oil-resistant sealer. Lay the treated side of the gasket on the cover and install the cover. Be sure the gasket seals evenly all around the cylinder head.

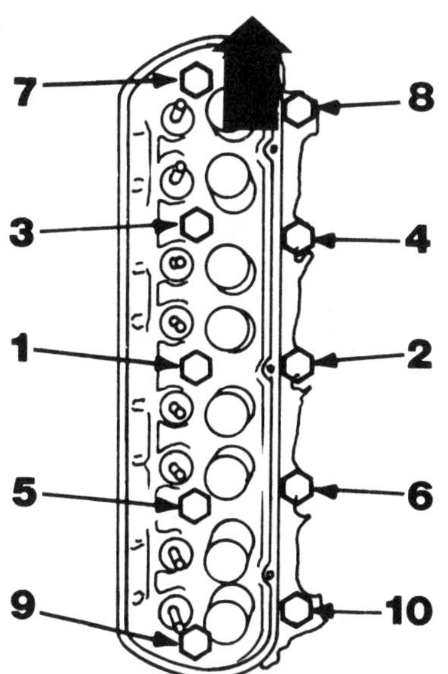

Cylinder head torque sequence—8 cyl. engines

V8 255 and 302 Cu In. Engine

1. Drain the cooling system.

2. Remove the intake manifold and the carburetor as an assembly.

3. Disconnect the spark plug wires, marking them as to placement. Position them out of the way of the cylinder head. Remove the spark plugs.

4. Disconnect the exhaust pipes at the manifolds.

5. Remove the rocker arm covers.

6. On cars with air conditioning, remove the mounting bolts and the drive belt, and position the compressor out of the way of the left cylinder head. Remove the compressor upper mounting bracket from the cylinder head.

NOTE: *If the compressor refrigerant lines do not have enough slack to permit repositioning of the compressor without first disconnecting the refrigerant lines, the air conditioning system will have to be evacuated by a trained air conditioning serviceman. Under no circumstances should an untrained person attempt to disconnect the air conditioning refrigerant lines.*

7. In order to remove the left cylinder head, on cars equipped with power steering, it may be necessary to remove the steering pump and bracket, remove the drive belt, and wire or tie the pump out of the way, but in such a way as to prevent the loss of its fluid.

8. In order to remove the right head it may be necessary to remove the alternator mounting bracket bolt and spacer, the igni-

tion coil, and the air cleaner inlet duct from the right cylinder head.

9. In order to remove the left cylinder head on a car equipped with a Thermactor air pump system, disconnect the hose from the air manifold on the left cylinder head.

10. If the right cylinder head is to be removed on a car equipped with a Thermactor system, remove the Thermactor air pump and its mounting bracket. Disconnect the hose from the air manifold on the right cylinder head.

11. Loosen the rocker arm stud nuts enough to rotate the rocker arms to the side, in order to facilitate the removal of the pushrods. Remove the pushrods in sequence, so that they may be installed in their original positions. Remove the exhaust valve stem caps, if equipped.

12. Remove the cylinder head attaching bolts, noting their positions. Lift the cylinder head off the block. Remove and discard the old cylinder head gasket. Clean all mounting surfaces.

Installation is as follows:

1. Position the new cylinder head gasket over the dowels on the block. Position new gaskets on the muffler inlet pipes at the exhaust manifold flange.

2. Position the cylinder head to the block, and install the head bolts, each in its original position. On engines on which the exhaust manifold has been removed from the head to facilitate removal, it is necessary to properly guide the exhaust manifold studs into the muffler inlet pipe flange when installing the head.

3. Step-torque the cylinder head retaining bolts first to 50 ft. lbs. then to 60 ft. lbs., and finally to the torque specification listed in the "Torque Specifications" chart. Tighten the exhaust manifold to cylinder head attaching bolts to specifications.

4. Tighten the nuts on the exhaust manifold studs at the muffler inlet flanges to 18 ft. lbs.

5. Clean and inspect the pushrods. Check the ends for nicks, grooves and wear, replace as necessary. Visually inspect the pushrods for straightness, and replace any bent ones. Do not attempt to straighten pushrods.

6. Install the pushrods in their original positions. Apply Lubriplate® or a similar product to the valve stem tips and to the pushrod guides in the cylinder head. Install the exhaust valve stem caps.

7. Apply Lubriplate® or a similar product to the fulcrum seats and sockets. Turn the rocker arms to their proper position and tighten the stud nuts enough to hold the rocker arms in position. Make sure that the lower ends of the pushrods have remained properly seared in the valve lifters. Tighten the stud nuts 17–23 ft. lbs. in the order given under Valve Adjustment.

8. Install the valve covers.

9. Install the intake manifold and carburetor, following the procedure under "Intake Manifold Installation."

10. Reinstall all other items removed.

MACHINE SHOP SERVICES

Certain rebuilding operations require special tools that may be too expensive or not feasible to buy for only occasional use. The answer to these problems is the local automotive machine shop. The machine shop can usually handle any job from drilling out and replacing a broken stud to any major rebuilding.

CYLINDER HEAD OVERHAUL

1. Remove the cylinder head(s) from the car engine (see Cylinder Head Removal and Installation). Place the head(s) on a workbench and remove any manifolds that are still connected. Remove all rocker arm retaining parts and the rocker arms, if still installed. On four cylinder engines, remove the camshaft (see Camshaft Removal).

2. Turn the cylinder head over so that the mounting surface is facing up and support evenly on wooden blocks.

3. Use a scraper and remove all of the gasket material stuck to the head mounting surface. Mount a wire carbon removal brush in an electric drill and clean away the carbon on the valves and head combustion chambers.

CAUTION: *When scraping or decarboniz-*

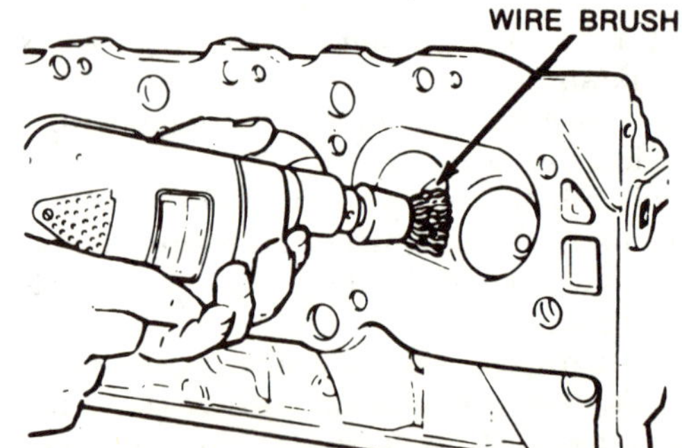

Remove carbon from the cylinder head with a wire brush and electric drill

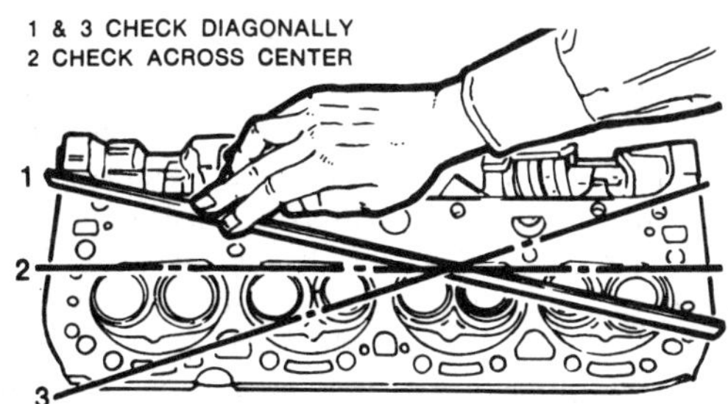

Check the cylinder head for warpage

ing the cylinder head take care not to damage or nick the gasket mounting surface.

4. Number the valve heads with a permanent felt-tip marker for cylinder location.

RESURFACING

If the cylinder head is warped, resurfacing by a machine shop, is required. Place a straight-edge across the gasket surface of the head. Using feeler gauges, determine the clearance at the center and along the length between the head and straight-edge. Measure clearance at the center and along the lengths of both diagonals. If warpage exceeds .003 inches in a six inch span, or .006 inches over the total length the cylinder head must be resurfaced. Do not grind more than .010 inch from original cylinder head gasket surface.

Valves and Springs

REMOVAL AND INSTALLATION

1. Block the head on its side, or install a pair of head-holding brackets made especially for valve removal.
2. Use a socket slightly larger than the valve stem and keepers, place the socket over the valve stem and gently hit the socket with a plastic hammer to break loose any varnish buildup.
3. Remove the valve keepers, retainer, spring shield and valve spring using a valve spring compressor (the locking C-clamp type is the easiest kind to use).
4. Put the parts in a separate container numbered for the cylinder being worked on: do not mix them with other parts removed.
5. Remove and discard the valve stem oil seal, a new seal will be used at assembly time.
6. Remove the valve from the cylinder head and place, in order, through holes punched in a stiff piece of cardboard or wooden valve holding stick. Number the cardboard or stick in case the number marked on the valve head gets rubbed off.

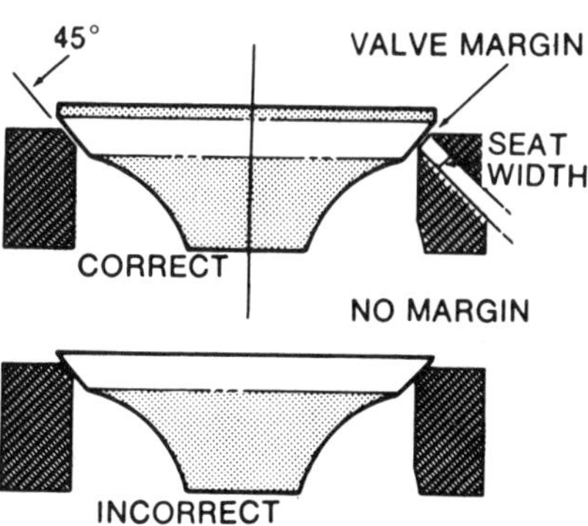

Valve seat width and centering

NOTE: *The exhaust valve stems, on some engines, are equipped with small metal caps. Take care not to loose the caps. Make sure to reinstall them at assembly time. Replace any caps that are worn.*

7. Use an electric drill and rotary wire brush to clean the intake and exhaust valve ports, combustion chamber and valve seats. In some cases, the carbon will need to be chipped away. Use a blunt pointed drift for carbon chipping, be careful around the valve seat areas.
8. Use a wire valve guide cleaning brush and safe solvent to clean the valve guides.
9. Clean the valves with a revolving wire brush. Heavy carbon deposits may be removed with the blunt drift.

NOTE: *When using a wire brush to clean carbon on the valve ports, valves etc., be sure that the deposits are actually removed, rather than burnished.*

10. Wash and clean all valve springs, keepers, retaining caps etc., in safe solvent.
11. Clean the head with a brush and some safe solvent and wipe dry.
12. Check the head for cracks. Cracks in the cylinder head usually start around an exhaust valve seat because it is the hottest part of the combustion chamber. If a crack is suspected but cannot be detected visually have the area checked with dye penetrant or other method by the machine shop.
13. After all cylinder head parts are reasonably clean check the valve stem-to-guide clearance. If a dial indicator is not on hand, a visual inspection can give you a fairly good idea if the guide, valve stem or both are worn.
14. Insert the valve into the guide until slightly away from the valve seat. Wiggle the valve sideways. A small amount of wobble is normal, excessive wobble means a worn guide or valve stem. If a dial indicator is on hand, mount the indicator so that the stem of the

valve is at 90° to the valve stem, as close to the valve guide as possible. Move the valve off the seat, and measure the valve guide-to-stem clearance by rocking the stem back and forth to actuate the dial indicator. Measure the valve stem using a micrometer and compare to specifications to determine whether stem or guide wear is causing excessive clearance.

15. The valve guide, if worn, must be repaired before the valve seats can be resurfaced. Ford supplies valves with oversize stems to fit valve guides that are reamed to oversize for repair. The machine shop will be able to handle the guide reaming for you. In some cases, if the guide is not too badly worn, knurling may be all that is required.

16. Reface, or have the valves and valve seats refaced. The valve seats should be a true 45° angle. Remove only enough material to clean up any pits or grooves. Be sure the valve seat is not too wide or narrow. Use a 60° grinding wheel to remove material from the bottom of the seat for raising and a 30° grinding wheel to remove material from the top of the seat to narrow.

17. After the valves are refaced by machine, hand lap them to the valve seat. Use valve grinding compound and a small suction cupped valve stick. Place a small amount of compound on the valve face install the valve and rotate the valve, with the stick, back and forth on the valve seat. Clean the grinding compound off and check the position of face-to-seat contact. Contact should be close to the center of the valve face. If contact is close to the top edge of the valve narrow the seat; if too close to the bottom edge, raise the seat.

18. Valves should be refaced to a true angle of 44°. Remove only enough metal to clean up the valve face or to correct runout. If the edge of a valve head, after machining, is $^{1}/_{32}$ inch or less replace the valve. The tip of the valve stem should also be dressed on the valve grinding machine, however, do not remove more than .010 inch.

19. After all valve and valve seats have been machined, check the remaining valve train parts (springs, retainers, keepers, etc.) for wear. Check the valve springs for straightness and tension.

20. Reassemble the head in the reverse order of disassembly using new valve guide seals and lubricating the valve stems. Check the valve spring installed height, shim or replace as necessary.

CHECKING VALVE SPRINGS

Place the valve spring on a flat surface next to a carpenters square. Measure the height of the spring, and rotate the spring against the edge of the square to measure distortion. If the spring height varies (by comparsion) by more than $^{1}/_{16}$ inch or if the distortion exceeds $^{1}/_{16}$ inch, replace the spring.

Have the valve springs tested for spring pressure at the installed and compressed (installed height minus valve lift) height using a valve spring tester. Springs should be within one pound, plus or minus each other. Replace springs as necessary.

VALVE SPRING INSTALLED HEIGHT

After installing the valve spring, measure the distance between the spring mounting pad and the lower edge of the spring retainer. Compare the measurement to specifications. If the installed height is incorrect, add shim washers between the spring mounting pad and the spring. Use only washers designed for valve springs; available at most parts houses.

VALVE STEM OIL SEALS

Umbrella type oil seals fitting on the valve stem over the top of the valve guide are used on the six and eight cylinder engines. The four cylinder engine uses a positive valve stem seal using a Teflon insert. Teflon seals are available for other engines but usually require valve guide machining, consult your automotive machine shop for advice on having positive valve stem oil seals installed.

When installing valve stem oil seals, ensure that a small amount of oil is able to pass the seal to lubricate the valve stems and guide walls; otherwise, excessive wear will occur.

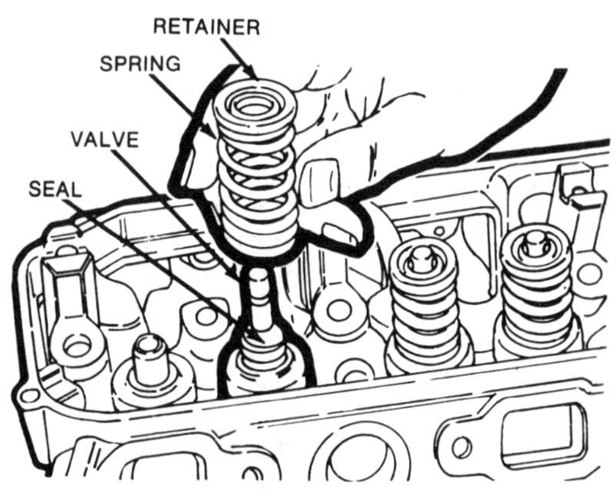

Install valve stem oil seals

VALVE SEATS

If a valve seat is damaged or burnt and cannot be serviced by refacing, it may be possible to have the seat machined and an insert installed. Consult the automotive machine shop for their advice.

VALVE GUIDES

Worn valve guides can, in most cases, be reamed to accept a valve with an oversized stem. Valve guides that are not excessively worn or distorted may, in some cases, be knurled rather than reamed. However, if the valve stem is worn reaming for an oversized valve stem is the answer since a new valve would be required.

Knurling is a process in which metal is displaced and raised, thereby reducing clearance. Knurling also produces excellent oil control. The possibility of knurling instead of reaming the valve guides should be discussed with a machinist.

HYDRAULIC VALVE CLEARANCE

The 200 cu in. six cylinder engine and the 255 and 302 cu in. engines are equipped hydraulic valve lifters. Hydraulic valve lifters operate with zero clearance in the valve train, and because of this the rocker arms are non-adjustable. The only means by which valve system clearances can be altered is by installing over or undersize pushrods; but, because of the hydraulic lifter's natural ability to compensate for slack in the valve train, all components of all the valve system should be checked for wear if there is excessive play in the system.

When a valve in the engine is in the closed position, the valve lifter is resting on the base circle of the camshaft lobe and the pushrod is in its lowest position. To remove this additional clearance from the valve train, the valve lifter expands to maintain zero clearance in the valve system. When a rocker arm is loosened or removed from the engine, the lifter expands to its fullest travel. When the rocker arm is reinstalled on the engine, the proper valve setting is obtained by tightening the rocker arm to a specified limit. But with the lifter fully expanded, if the camshaft lobe is on a high point it will require excessive torque to compress the lifter and obtain the proper setting. Because of this, when any component of the valve system has been removed, a preliminary valve adjustment procedure must be followed to ensure that when the

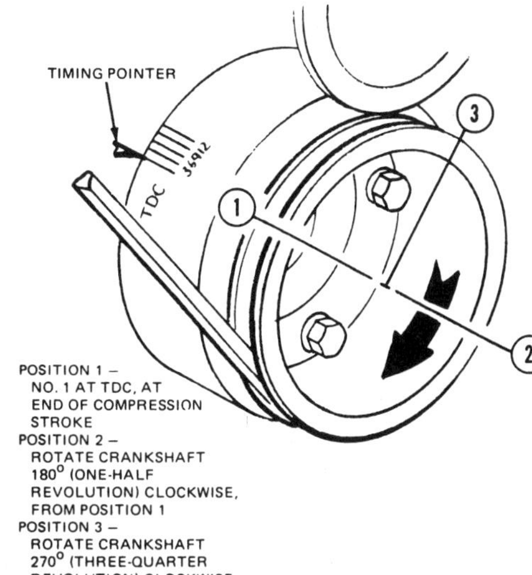

Position of crankshaft for checking and adjusting valve clearance

rocker arm is reinstalled on the engine and tightened, the camshaft lobe for that cylinder is in the low position.

To determine whether a shorter or longer push rod is necessary, make the following check:

Six Cylinder 200 Cu in. Engine

1. Connect an auxiliary starter switch in the starting circuit. Crank the engine with the ignition switch OFF until the No. 1 piston is on TDC after the compression stroke.
2. With the crankshaft in the position designated in Steps 3 and 4, position the hydraulic lifter compressor tool on the rocker arm. Slowly apply pressure to bleed down the hydraulic lifter until the plunger is completely bottomed. Take care to avoid excessive pressure that might bend the push rod. Hold the lifter in this position and check the available clearance between the rocker arm and the valve stem tip with a feeler gauge.

   If the clearance is less than specified, install an under-sized push rod. If the clearance is greater than specified, install an oversize push rod.
3. With the No. 1 piston on TDC after the compression stroke, use the procedure in Step 2, check the following valves:
   - No. 1 Intake
   - No. 1 Exhaust

- No. 2 Intake
- No. 3 Exhaust
- No. 4 Intake
- No. 5 Exhaust

4. Now rotate the crankshaft until the No. 6 piston is on TDC after the compression stroke (1 revolution of the crankshaft). By using the procedure in step 2, check the following valves:

- No. 2 Exhaust
- No. 3 Intake
- No. 4 Exhaust
- No. 5 Intake
- No. 6 Intake
- No. 6 Exhaust

5. When compressing the valve spring to remove the push rods, be sure the piston in the individual cylinder is below TDC to avoid contact between the valve and the piston. To replace a push rod, it will be necessary to remove the valve rocker arm shaft assembly. Upon replacement of a valve push rod, valve rocker arm shaft assembly or hydraulic valve lifter, the engine should not be cranked or rotated until the hydraulic lifters have had an opportunity to leak down to their normal operating position. The leak down rate can be accelerated by using the tool shown on the valve rocker arm and applying pressure in a direction to collapse the lifter.

Note: Collapsed tappet gap:

- Allowable—.085–.209
- Desired—.110–.184

V8 255, 302 Cu In. Engine

1. Connect an auxiliary starter switch in the starting circuit. Crank the engine with the ignition switch OFF until the No. 1 piston is on TDC after the compression stroke.

2. With the crankshaft in the positions designated in Steps 3, 4 and 5 position the hydraulic lifter compressor tool on the rocker arm. Slowly apply pressure to bleed down the tappet until the plunger is completely bottomed. Hold the tappet in this position and check the available clearance between the rocker arm and the valve stem tip with a feeler gauge. The feeler gauge width must not exceed ⅜ inch, in order to fit between the rails on the rocker arm. If the clearance is less than specifications, install a shorter push rod. If the clearance is greater than specifications, install a longer push rod.

3. With the No. 1 piston on TDC at the end of the compression stroke (Position No. 1 in illustration) check the following valves:

- No. 1 Intake No. 1 Exhaust
- No. 7 Intake No. 5 Exhaust
- No. 8 Intake No. 4 Exhaust

4. Rotate the crankshaft to Position No. 2 in the illustration and check the following valves:

- No. 5 Intake No. 2 Exhaust
- No. 4 Intake No. 6 Exhaust

5. Rotate the crankshaft to Position No. 3 in the illustration and check the following valves:

- No. 2 Intake No. 7 Exhaust
- No. 3 Intake No. 3 Exhaust
- No. 6 Intake No. 8 Exhaust

Note: Collapse tappet gap:

- (255 cu in.)
  Allowable—.098–.198
  Desired—.123–.173
- (302 cu in.)
  Allowable—.–.193
  Desired—.096–.163

VALVE CLEARANCE—HYDRAULIC VALVE LASH ADJUSTERS

Four Cylinder 140 Cu In. Engine

Hydraulic valve lash adjusters are used in the valve train. These units are placed at the fulcrum point of the cam followers (or rocker arms). Their action is similar to the hydraulic tappets used in push rod engines.

1. Position the camshaft so that the base circle of the lobe is facing the cam follower of the valve to be checked.

2. Using a tool shown in the illustration, slowly apply pressure to the cam follower until the lash adjuster is completely collapsed. Hold the follower in this position and insert 0.045 in. feeler gauge between the base circle of the cam and the follower.

NOTE: *The minimum gap is 0.035 in. and the maximum is 0.055 in. The desire gap is between 0.040 in. and 0.050 in.*

3. If the clearance is excessive, remove the cam follower and inspect it for damage.

4. If the cam follower seems OK measure the valve spring assembled height to be sure the valve is not sticking. See the Valve Specifications chart in this chapter.

5. If the valve spring assembled height is OK check the dimensions of the camshaft.

6. If the camshaft dimensions are OK the lash adjuster should be cleaned and tested.

7. Replace any worn parts as necessary.

NOTE: *For any repair that includes removal of the camshaft follower (rocker arm), each affected hydraulic lash adjuster must be collapsed after reinstallation of the cam-*

shaft follower, and then released. This step must be taken prior to any rotation of the camshaft.

HYDRAULIC VALVE LIFTER INSPECTION

Remove the lifters from their bores and remove any gum and varnish with safe solvent. Check the lifters for concave wear. If the bottom of the lifter is worn concave or flat, replace the lifter. Lifters are built with a convex bottom, flatness indicates wear. If a worn lifter is detected, carefully check the camshaft for wear.

To test lifter leak down, submerge the lifter in a container of kerosene. Chuck a used pushrod or its equivalent into a drill press. Position the container of kerosene so the pushrod acts on the lifter plunger. Pump the lifter with the drill press until resistance increases. Pump several more times to bleed any air from the lifter. Apply very firm, constant pressure to the lifter and observe the rate which fluid bleeds out of the lifter. If the lifter bleeds down very quickly (less than 15 seconds), the lifter should be replaced. If the time exceeds 60 seconds, the lifter is sticking and should be cleaned or replaced. If the lifter is operating properly (leak down time 15–60 seconds) and not worn, lubricate and reinstall in engine.

NOTE: *Always inspect the valve pushrods for wear, straightness and oil blockage. Damaged pushrods will cause erratic valve operation.*

Timing Cover and Chain

REMOVAL AND INSTALLATION

Six Cylinder 200 Cu In. Engine

1. Drain the cooling system and crankcase.
2. Disconnect the upper radiator hose from the intake manifold and the lower hose from the water pump. On cars with automatic transmission, disconnect the cooler lines from the radiator.
3. Remove the radiator, fan and pulley, and engine drive belts. On models with air conditioning, remove the condenser retaining bolts and position the condenser forward. *Do not disconnect the refrigerant lines.*
4. Remove the cylinder front cover retaining bolts and front oil pan bolts and gently pry the cover away from the block.
5. Remove the crankshaft pulley bolt and use a puller to remove the vibration damper.

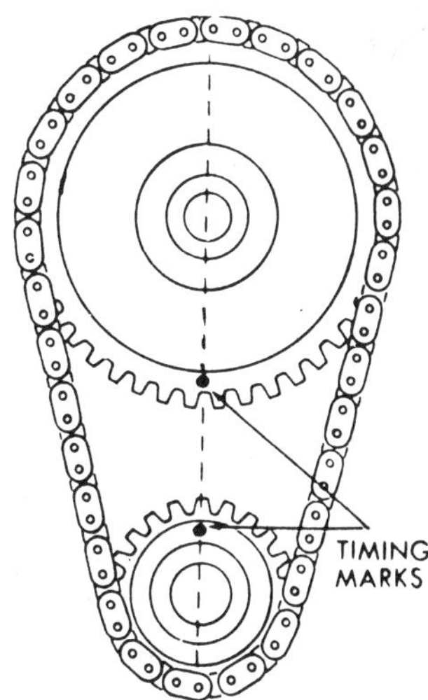

Timing mark alignment 6 and V8 engines

6. With a socket wrench of the proper size on the crankshaft pulley bolt, gently rotate the crankshaft in a clockwise direction until all slack is removed from the left side of the timing chain. Scribe a mark on the engine block parallel to the present position on the left side of the chain. Next, turn the crankshaft in a counterclockwise direction to remove all the slack from the right side of the chain. Force the left side of the chain outward with the fingers and measure the distance between the reference point and the present position of the chain. If the distance exceeds ½ inch, replace the chain and sprockets.
7. Crank the engine until the timing marks are aligned as shown in the illustration. Remove the bolt, slide sprocket and chain forward and remove as an assembly.
8. Position the sprockets and chain on the engine, making sure that the timing marks are aligned, dot to dot.
9. Reinstall the front cover, applying oil resistant sealer to the new gasket.

NOTE: *Trim away the exposed portion of the old oil pan gasket flush with front of the engine block. Cut and position the required portion of a new gasket to the oil pan, applying sealer to both sides of it.*

10. Install the fan, pulley and belts. Adjust belt tension.
11. Install the radiator, connect the radiator hoses and transmission cooling lines. If equipped with air conditioning, install the condenser.
12. Fill the crankcase and cooling system. Start the engine and check for leaks.

All V8 Engines

1. Drain cooling system, remove air cleaner and disconnect the battery.
2. Disconnect automatic transmission oil cooler lines, radiator hoses and remove the radiator.
3. Disconnect heater hose at water pump. Slide water pump by-pass hose clamp toward the pump.
4. Loosen alternator mounting bolts at the alternator. Remove the alternator support bolt at the water pump. Remove Thermactor pump on all engines so equipped. If equipped with power steering or air conditioning, unbolt the component, remove the belt, and lay the pump aside with the lines attached.
5. Remove the fan, spacer, pulley, and drive belt.
6. Drain the crankcase.
7. Remove pulley from crankshaft pulley adapter. Remove cap screw and washer from front end of crankshaft. Remove crankshaft pulley adapter with a puller.
8. Disconnect fuel pump outlet line at the pump. Remove fuel pump retaining bolts and lay the pump to the side. Remove the engine oil dipstick.
9. Remove the front cover attaching bolts.
10. Remove the crankshaft oil slinger if so equipped.
11. Check timing chain deflection, using the procedure outlined in Step 6 of the 200 cu in. six cylinder cover and chain removal.
12. Turn engine until sprocket timing marks are aligned as shown in valve timing illustration.
13. Remove crankshaft sprocket cap screw, washers, and fuel pump eccentric. Slide both sprockets and chain forward and off as an assembly.
14. Position sprockets and chain on the camshaft and crankshaft with both timing marks dot to dot on a centerline. Install fuel pump eccentric, washers and sprocket attaching bolt. Torque the sprocket attaching bolt to 40–45 ft. lbs.
15. Install crankshaft front oil slinger.
16. Clean front cover and mating surfaces of old gasket material. Install a new oil seal in the cover. Use a seal driver tool, if available.
17. Coat a new cover gasket with sealer and position it on the block.

    NOTE: *Trim away the exposed portion of the oil pan gasket flush with the cylinder block. Cut and position the required portion of a new gasket to the oil pan, applying sealer to both sides of it.*
18. Install front cover, using a crank-shaft-to-cover alignment tool. Coat the threads of the attaching bolts with sealer. Torque attaching bolts to 12–15 ft. lbs.
19. Install fuel pump, connect fuel pump outlet tube.
20. Install crankshaft pulley adapter and torque attaching bolt. Install crankshaft pulley.
21. Install water pump pulley, drive belt, spacer and fan.
22. Install alternator support bolt at the water pump. Tighten alternator mounting bolts. Adjust drive belt tension. Install Thermactor pump if so equipped.
23. Install radiator and connect all coolant and heater hoses. Connect battery cables.
24. Refill cooling system and the crankcase. Install the dipstick.
25. Start engine and operate at fast idle.
26. Check for leaks, install air cleaner. Adjust ignition timing and make all final adjustments.

Front Cover Oil Seal

REMOVAL AND INSTALLATION

Six Cylinder 200 cu in. And All V8 Engines

It is recommended to replace the cover seal any time the front cover is removed.

1. With the cover removed from the car, drive the old seal from the rear of cover with a pinpunch. Clean out the recess in the cover.
2. Coat the new seal with grease and drive it into the cover until it is fully seated. Check the seal after installation to be sure the spring is properly positioned in the seal.

Camshaft Drive Belt and Cover

Four Cylinder 140 cu in. Engine

The correct installation and adjustment of the camshaft drive belt is mandatory if the engine is to run properly. The camshaft controls the opening of the camshaft and the crankshaft. When any given piston is on the intake stroke the corresponding intake valve must be open to admit air/fuel mixture into the cylinder. When the same piston is on the compression and power strokes, both valves in that cylinder must be closed. When the piston is on the exhaust stroke, the exhaust valve for that cylinder must be open. If the opening and closing of the valves is not coordinated with the movements of the pistons, the engine will run very poorly, if at all.

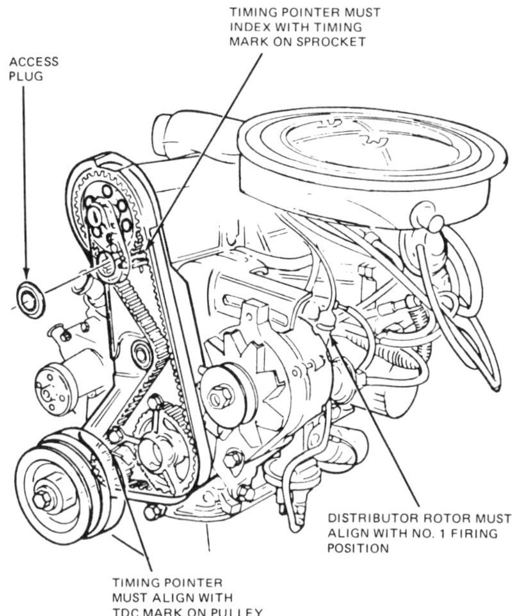

Camshaft drive train installation—4 cyl.

The camshaft drive belt also turns the engine auxiliary shaft. The distributor is driven by the engine auxiliary shaft. Since the distributor controls ignition timing, the auxiliary shaft must be coordinated with the camshaft and the crankshaft, since both valves in any given cylinder must be closed and the piston in that cylinder near the top of the compression stroke when the spark plug fires.

Due to this complex interrelationship between the camshaft, the crankshaft and the auxiliary shaft, the cogged pulleys on each component must be aligned when the camshaft drive belt is installed.

TROUBLESHOOTING

Should the camshaft drive belt jump timing by a tooth or two, the engine could still run; but very poorly. To visually check for correct timing of the crankshaft, auxiliary shaft, and the camshaft follow this procedure:

NOTE: *There is an access plug provided in the cam drive belt cover so that the camshaft timing can be checked without moving the drive belt cover.*

1. Remove the access plug.
2. Turn the crankshaft until the timing marks on the crankshaft indicate TDC.
3. Make sure that the timing mark on the camshaft drive sprocket is aligned with the pointer on the inner belt cover. Also, the rotor of the distributor must align with the No. 1 cylinder firing position.

NOTE: *Never turn the crankshaft of any of the overhead cam engines in the opposite direction of normal rotation. Backward rotation of the crankshaft may cause the timing belt to slip and alter the timing.*

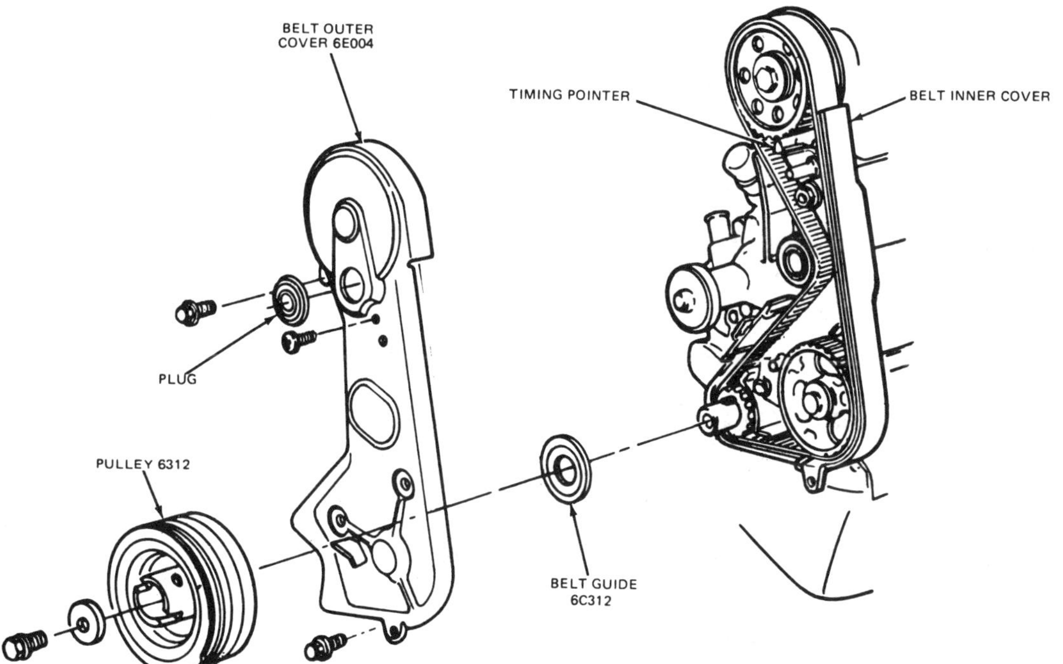

Timing belt outer cover, crankshaft belt guide and pulley installation—4 cyl. engine

REMOVAL AND INSTALLATION

1. Set the engine to TDC as described in the troubleshooting section. The crankshaft and camshaft timing marks should align with their respective pointers and the distributor rotor should point to the No. 1 plug tower.
2. Loosen the adjustment bolts on the alternator and accessories and remove the drive belts. To provide clearance for removing the camshaft belt, remove the fan and pulley.
3. Remove the belt outer cover.
4. Remove the distributor cap from the distributor and position it out of the way.
5. Loosen the belt tensioner adjustment and pivot bolts. Lever the tensioner away from the belt and retighten the adjustment bolt to hold it away.
6. Remove the crankshaft bolt and pulley. Remove the belt guide behind the pulley.
7. Remove the camshaft drive belt.
8. Install the new belt over the crankshaft pulley first, then counter-clockwise over the auxiliary shaft sprocket and the camshaft sprocket. Adjust the belt fore and aft so that it is centered on the sprockets.
9. Loosen the tensioner adjustment bolt, allowing it to spring back against the belt.
10. Rotate the crankshaft two complete turns in the normal rotation direction to remove any belt slack. Turn the crankshaft until the timing check marks are lined up. If the timing has slipped, remove the belt and repeat the procedure.
11. Tighten the tensioner adjustment bolt to 14–21 ft. lbs., and the pivot bolt to 28–40 ft. lbs.
12. Replace the belt guide and crankshaft pulley, distributor cap, belt outer cover, fan and pulley, drive belts and accessories. Adjust the accessory drive belt tension. Start the engine and check the ignition timing.

Camshaft

REMOVAL AND INSTALLATION

Four Cylinder 140 cu in. Engine

NOTE: *The following procedure covers camshaft removal and installation with the cylinder head on or off the engine. If the cylinder head has been removed start at Step 9.*

1. Drain the cooling system. Remove the air cleaner assembly and disconnect the negative battery cable.
2. Remove the spark plug wires from the plugs, disconnect the retainer from the valve cover and position the wires out of the way. Disconnect rubber vacuum lines as necessary.
3. Remove all drive belts. Remove the alternator mounting bracket-to-cylinder head mounting bolts, position bracket and alternator out of the way.
4. Disconnect and remove the upper radiator hose. Disconnect the radiator shroud.
5. Remove the fan blades and water pump pulley and fan shroud. Remove cam belt and valve covers.
6. Align engine timing marks at TDC. Remove cam drive belt.
7. Jack up the front of the car and support on jackstands. Remove the front motor mount bolts. Disconnect the lower radiator hose from the radiator. Disconnect and plug the automatic transmission cooler lines.
8. Position a piece of wood on a floor jack and raise the engine carefully as far as it will go. Place blocks of wood between the engine mounts and crossmember pedestals.
9. Remove the rocker arms as described earlier in this chapter.
10. Remove the camshaft drive gear and belt guide using a suitable puller. Remove the front oil seal with a sheet metal screw and slide hammer.
11. Remove the camshaft retainer located on the rear mounting stand by unbolting the two bolts.
12. Remove the camshaft by carefully withdrawing toward the front of the engine. Caution should be used to prevent damage to cam bearings, lobes and journals.
13. Check the camshaft journals and lobes for wear. Inspect the cam bearings, if worn (unless the proper bearing installing tool is on hand), the cylinder head must be removed for new bearings to be installed by a machine shop.
14. Cam installation is in the reverse order of removal. See following notes.

NOTE: *Coat the camshaft with heavy SF oil before sliding it into the cylinder head. Install a new front seal. Apply a coat of sealer or teflon tape to the cam drive gear bolt before installation.*

NOTE: *After any procedure requiring removal of the rocker arms, each lash adjuster must be fully collapsed after assembly, then released. This must be done before the camshaft is turned. See Valve Clearance-Hydraulic Valve Lash Adjusters.*

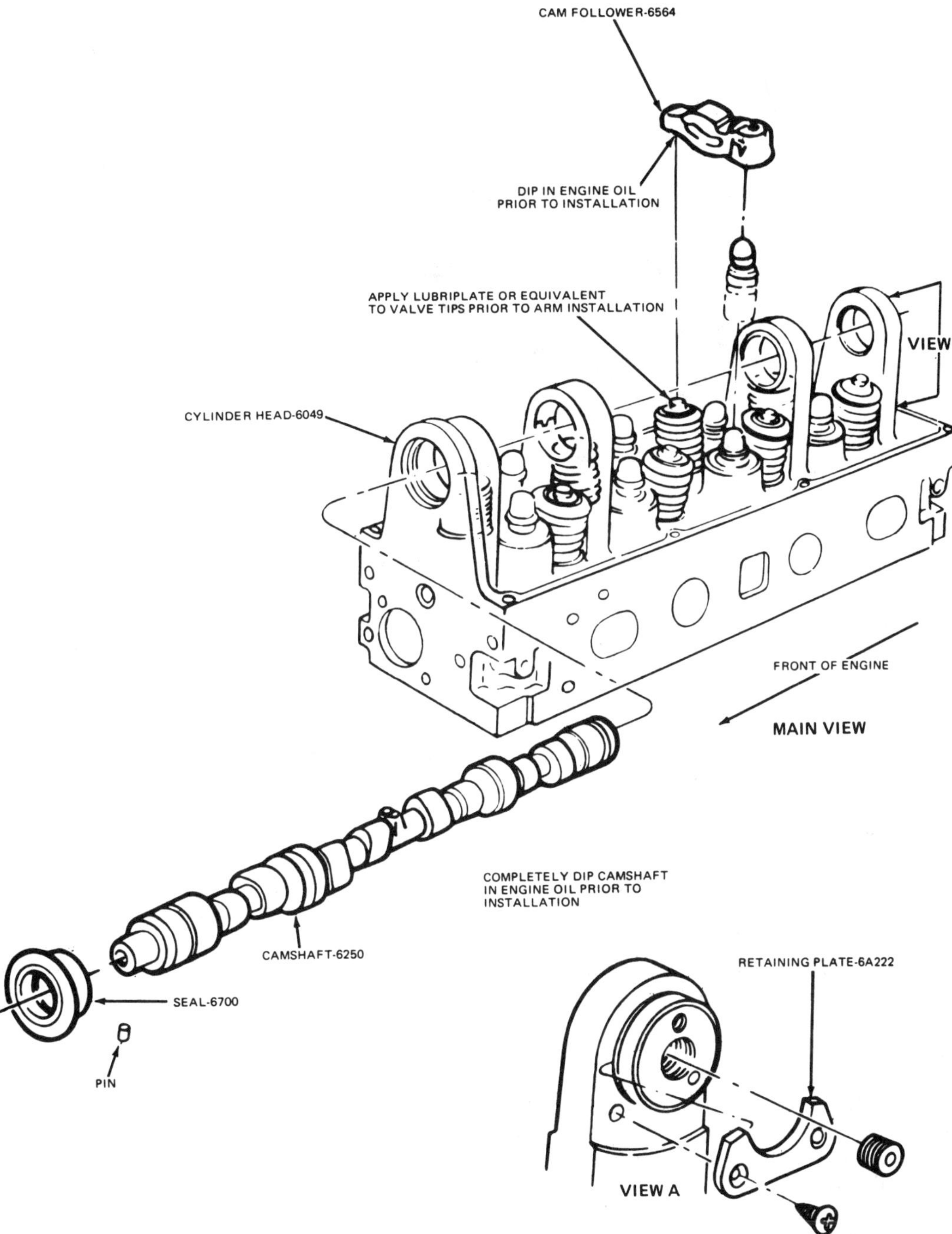

Camshaft installation—4 cyl. engine

SIX CYLINDER 200 CU IN. ENGINE

1. Remove the cylinder head.
2. Remove the cylinder front cover, timing chain and sprockets as outlined in the preceding section.
3. Disconnect and remove the grille. Remove the gravel deflector.
4. Using a magnet, remove the valve lifters and keep them in order so that they can be installed in their original positions.
5. Remove the camshaft thrust plate and remove the camshaft by pulling it from the front of the engine. Use care not to damage the camshaft lobes or journals while removing the cam from the engine.
6. Before installing the camshaft, coat the lobes with engine assembly lubricant and the

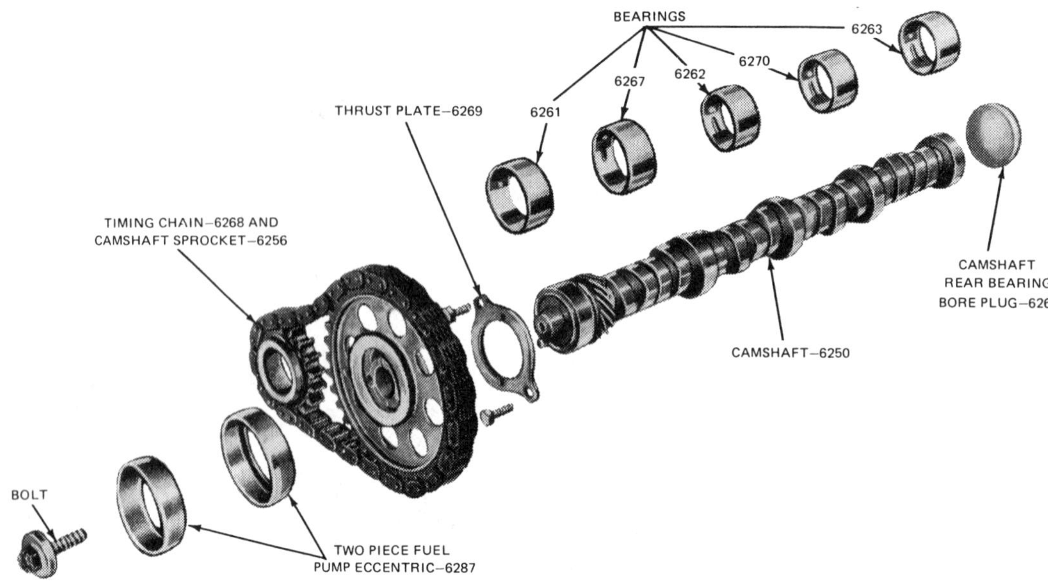

Camshaft and related parts—V8 engines

journals and all valve parts with heavy oil. Clean the oil passage at the rear of the cylinder block with compressed air.

ALL V8 ENGINES

1. Remove or reposition the radiator, A/C condenser and grille components as necessary to provide clearance to remove the camshaft.
2. Remove the cylinder front cover and timing chain as previously described in this chapter.
3. Remove the intake manifold and related parts described earlier in this chapter.
4. Remove the crankcase ventilation valve and tubes from the valve rocker covers. Remove the EGR cooler, if so equipped.
5. Remove the rocker arm covers and loosen the valve rocker arm fulcrum bolts and rotate the rocker arms to the side.
6. Remove the valve push rods and identify them so that they can be installed in their original positions.
7. Remove the valve lifters and place them in a rack so that they can be installed in their original bores.
8. Remove the camshaft thrust plate and carefully remove the camshaft by pulling toward the front of the engine. Be careful not to damage the camshaft bearings.
9. Before installing, oil the camshaft journals with heavy engine oil SF and apply Lubriplate® or equivalent to the lobes. Carefully slide the camshaft through the bearings.
10. Install the camshaft thrust plate with the groove towards the cylinder block.
11. Lubricate the lifters with heavy SF engine oil and install in their original bores.
12. Apply Lubriplate® or equivalent to the valve stem tips and each end of the push rods. Install the push rods in their original position.
13. Lubricate the rocker arms and fulcrum seats with heavy SF engine oil and position the rocker arms over the push rods.
14. Install all other parts previously removed.
15. Fill the crankcase and cooling system and adjust the timing.

CHECKING CAMSHAFT

Degrease the camshaft using safe solvent, clean all oil grooves. Visually inspect the cam lobes and bearing journals for excessive wear. If a lobe is questionable, check all lobes and journals with a micrometer.

Measure the lobes from nose to base and again at 90°. The lift is determined by subtracting the second measurement from the first. If all exhaust lobes and all intake lobes are not identical, the camshaft must be reground or replaced. Measure the bearing journals and compare to specifications. If a journal is worn there is a good chance that the cam bearings are worn too requiring replacement.

If the lobes and journals appear intact, place the front and rear cam journals in V-blocks and rest a dial indicator on the center journal. Rotate the camshaft to check for straightness, if deviation exceeds .001 inch, replace the camshaft.

Auxiliary Shaft

REMOVAL AND INSTALLATION

Four Cylinder 140 cu in. Engine

1. Remove the camshaft drive belt cover.
2. Remove the drive belt. Remove the auxiliary shaft sprocket. A puller may be necessary to remove the sprocket.
3. Remove the distributor and fuel pump.
4. Remove the auxiliary shaft cover and thrust plate.
5. Withdraw the auxiliary shaft from the block.

NOTE: *The distributor drive gear and the fuel pump eccentric on the auxiliary shaft must not be allowed to touch the auxiliary*

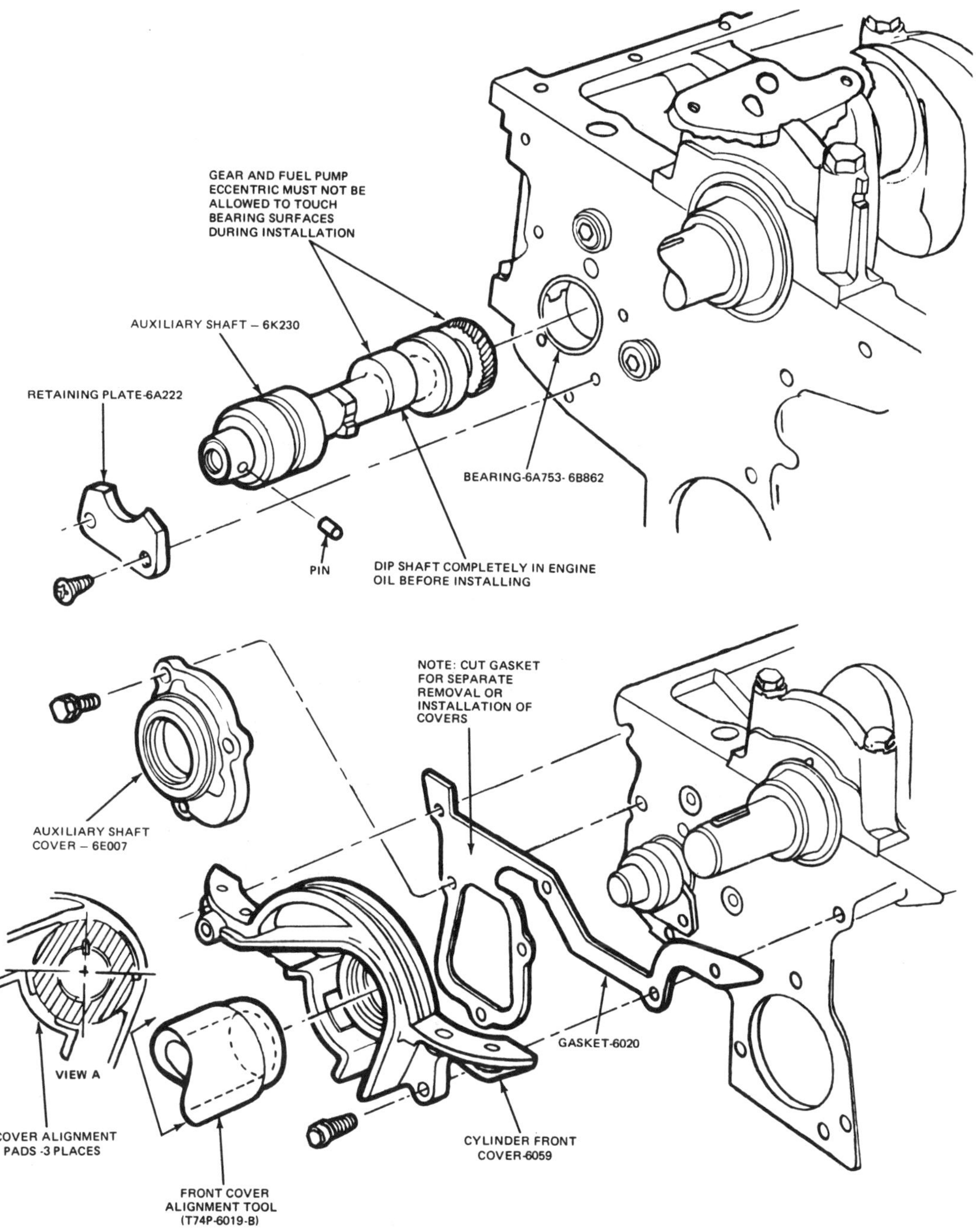

Auxiliary shaft installation—4 cyl. engine

shaft bearings during removal and installation. Completely coat the shaft with oil before sliding it into place.

6. Slide the auxiliary shaft into the housing and insert the thrust plate to hold the shaft.
7. Install a new gasket and auxiliary shaft cover.

NOTE: *The auxiliary shaft cover and cylinder front cover share a gasket. Cut off the old gasket around the cylinder cover and use half of the new gasket on the auxiliary shaft cover.*

8. Fit a new gasket into the fuel pump and install the pump.
9. Insert the distributor and install the auxiliary shaft sprocket.
10. Align the timing marks and install the drive belt.
11. Install the drive belt cover.
12. Check the ignition timing.

Pistons and Connecting Rods

REMOVAL AND INSTALLATION

NOTE: *Although, in most cases, the pistons and connecting rods can be removed from the engine (after the cylinder head and oil pan are removed) while the engine is still in the car; it is far easier to work on the engine when removed from the car.*

NOTE: *If removing pistons with the engine still installed, disconnect the radiator hoses, automatic transmission cooler lines and radiator shroud. Unbolt front mounts before jacking up the engine. Block the engine in position with wooden blocks between the mounts.*

1. Remove the engine from the car. Remove cylinder head(s), oil pan and front cover (if necessary).
2. Because the top piston ring does not travel to the very top of the cylinder bore, a ridge is built up between the end of the travel and the top of the cylinder. Pushing the piston and connecting rod assembly past the ridge is difficult and may cause damage to the piston. If new rings are installed and the ridge has not been removed, ring breakage and piston damage can occur when the ridge is encountered at engine speed.
3. Turn the crankshaft to position the piston at the bottom of the cylinder bore. Cover the top of the piston with a rag. Install a ridge reamer in the bore and follow the manufacturer's instructions to remove the ridge. Use caution, avoid cutting too deeply. Remove the rag and cuttings from the top of the piston. Remove the ridge from all cylinders.
4. Check the edges of the connecting rod and bearing cap for numbers or matchmarks, if none are present mark the rod and cap numerically and in sequence from front to back of engine. The numbers or marks not only tell which cylinder the piston came from but also helps ensure that the rod caps are installed in the correct matching position.
5. Turn the crankshaft until the connecting rod is at the bottom of travel. Remove the two attaching nuts and the bearing cap. Take two pieces of rubber tubing and cover the rod bolts to prevent crank or cylinder scoring. Use a wooden hammer handle to help push the piston and rod up and out of the cylinder. Reinstall the rod cap in proper position. Remove all pistons and connecting rods. Inspect cylinder walls and deglaze or hone as necessary.

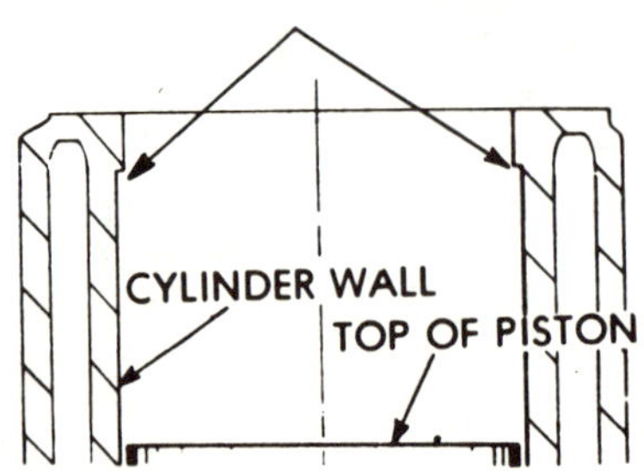

Cylinder bore ridge

Use a hammer handle to push the piston and connecting rod out of the engine

6. Installation is in the reverse order of removal. Lubricate each piston, rod bearing and cylinder wall. Install a ring compressor over the piston, position piston with mark toward front of engine and carefully install into engine. Position connecting rod with bearing insert installed over the crank journal. Install

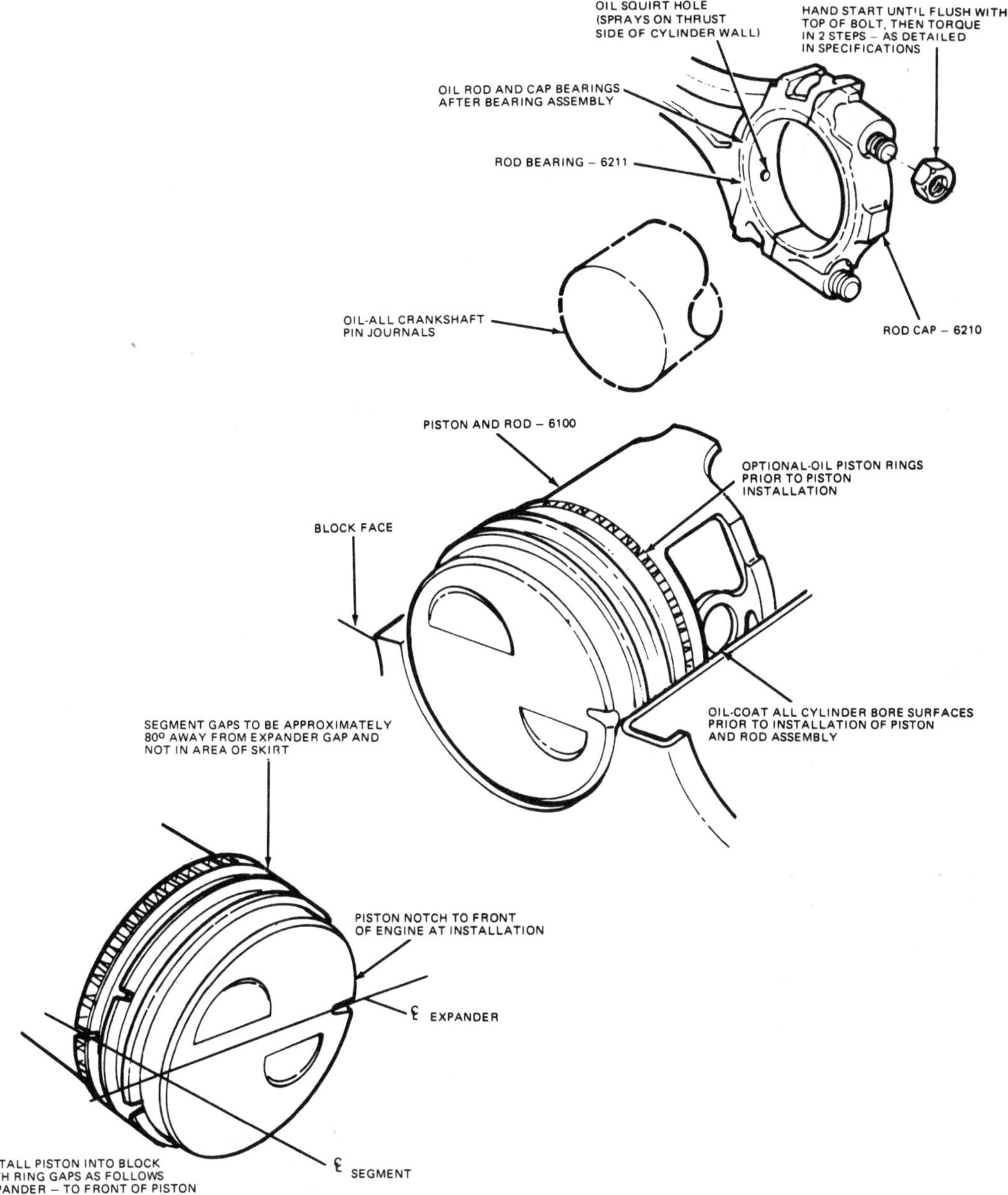

Pistons, rings and connecting rods—4 cyl. engine

the rod cap with bearing in proper position. Secure with rod nuts and torque to proper specifications. Install all rod and piston assemblies.

CLEANING AND INSPECTION

1. Use a piston ring expander and remove the rings from the piston.
2. Clean the ring grooves using an appropriate cleaning tool, exercise care to avoid cutting too deeply.
3. Clean all varnish and carbon from the piston with a safe solvent. Do not use a wire brush or caustic solution on the pistons.
4. Inspect the pistons for scuffing, scoring, cracks, pitting or excessive ring groove wear. If wear is evident, the piston must be replaced.
5. Have the piston and connecting rod assembly checked by a machine shop for correct alignment, piston pin wear and piston diameter. If the piston has "collapsed" it will have to be replaced or knurled to restore original diameter. Connecting rod bushing

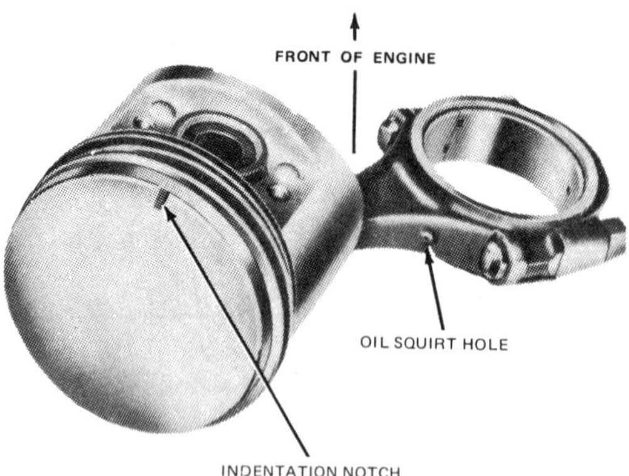

Piston installation (notch facing front) 6 cyl. engine

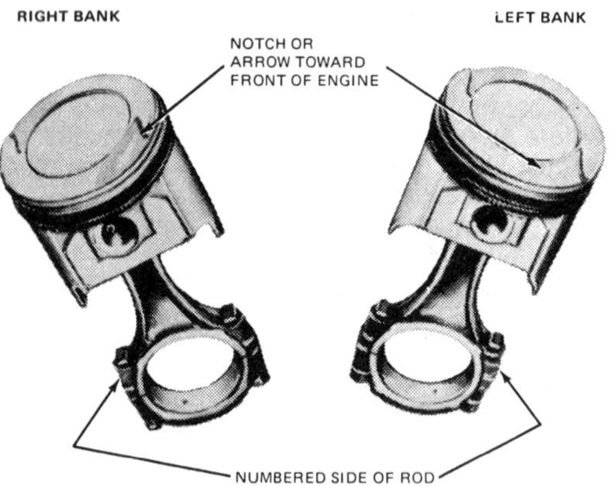

Piston and connecting rod installation—V8 engines

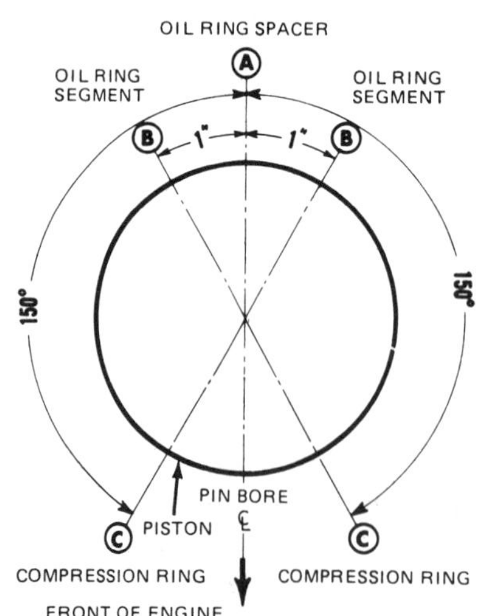

Piston ring spacing—all engines

replacement, piston pin fitting and piston changing can be handled by the machine shop.

CYLINDER BORE

1. Check the cylinder bore for wear using a telescope gauge and a micrometer, measure the cylinder bore diameter perpendicular to the piston pin at a point 2½ inches below the top of the engine block. Measure the piston skirt perpendicular to the piston pin. The difference between the two measurements is the piston clearance. If the clearance is within specifications, finish honing or glaze breaking is all that is required. If clearance is excessive a slightly oversize piston may be required. If greatly oversize, the engine will have to be bored and .010 inch or larger oversized pistons installed.

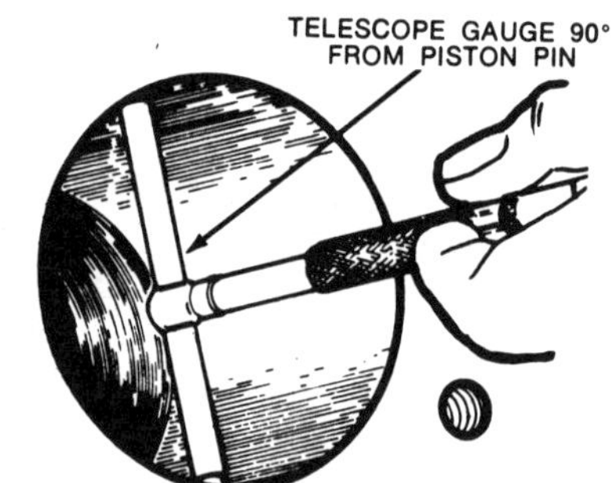

Measure the cylinder bore with a telescope gauge

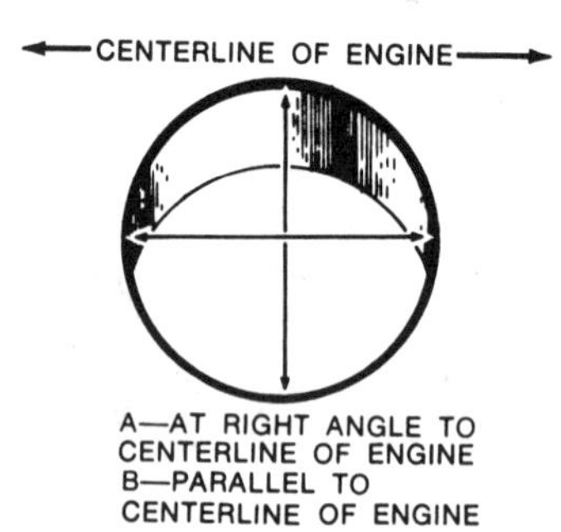

Cylinder bore measuring points

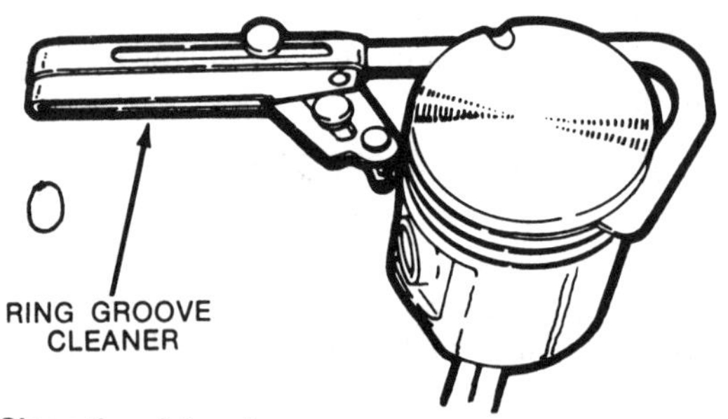

Clean the piston ring grooves

FITTING AND POSITIONING PISTON RINGS

1. Take the new piston rings and compress them, one at a time into the cylinder that they will be used in. Press the ring about one inch below the top of the cylinder block using an inverted piston.

2. Use a feeler gauge and measure the distance between the ends of the ring, this is called, measuring the ring end-gap. Compare the reading to the one called for in the specifications table. File the ends of the ring with a fine file to obtain necessary clearance.

NOTE: *If inadequate ring end-gap is utilized, ring breakage will result.*

3. Inspect the ring grooves on the piston for excessive wear or taper. If necessary have the grooves recut for use with a standard ring and spacer. The machine shop can handle the job for you. Check the ring groove by rolling the new piston ring around the groove to check for burrs or carbon deposits. If any are found, remove with a fine file. Hold the ring in the groove and measure side clearance with a feeler gauge. If clearance is excessive, spacer(s) will have to be added.

NOTE: *Always add spacers above the piston ring.*

4. Install the rings on the piston, lower ring first using a ring installing tool. Consult the instruction sheet that comes with the rings to be sure they are installed with the correct side up. A mark on the ring usually faces upward.

5. When installing oil rings; first, install the ring in the groove. Hold the ends of the ring butted together (they must not overlap) and install the bottom rail (scraper) with the end about one inch away from the butted end of the control ring. Install the top rail about one inch away from the butted end of the control but on the opposite side from the lower rail.

6. Install the two compression rings.

7. Consult the illustration for ring positioning, arrange the rings as shown, install a ring compressor and insert the piston and rod assembly into the engine.

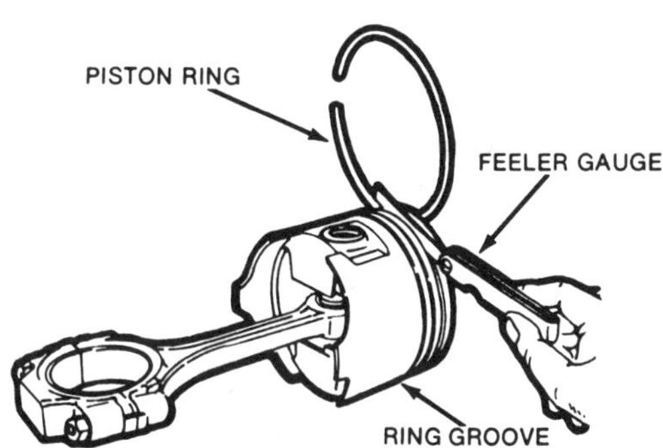

Check the piston ring side clearance

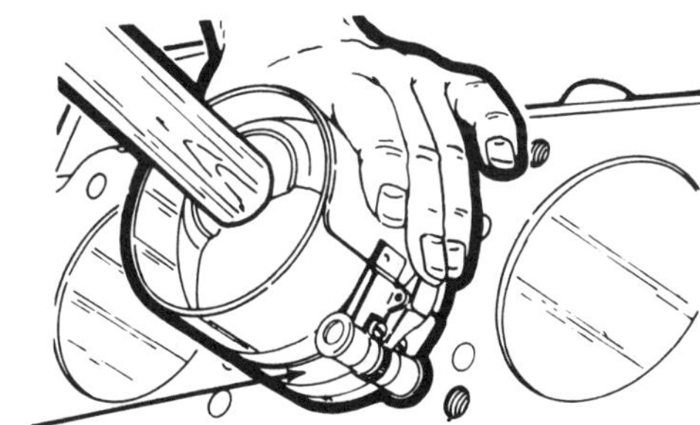

Install the piston using a ring compressor

Crankshaft and Bearings

1. Rod bearings can be installed when the pistons have been removed for servicing (rings etc.) or, in most cases, while the engine is still in the car. Bearing replacement, however, is far easier with the engine out of the car and disassembled.

2. For in car service, remove the oil pan, spark plugs and front cover if necessary. Turn the engine until the connecting rod to be serviced is at the bottom of its travel. Remove the bearing cap, place two pieces of rubber hose over the rod cap bolts and push the piston and rod assembly up the cylinder bore until enough room is gained for bearing insert removal. Take care not to push the rod assembly up too far or the top ring will engage the cylinder ridge or come out of the cylinder and require head removal for reinstallation.

3. Clean the rod journal, the connecting rod end and the bearing cap after removing the old bearing inserts. Install the new inserts in the rod and bearing cap, lubricate them with oil. Position the rod over the

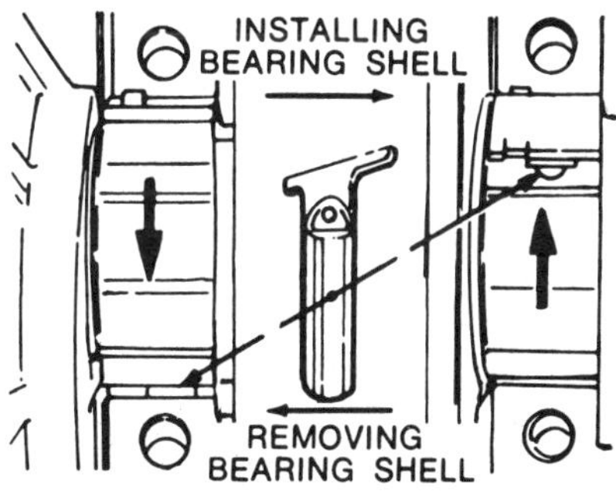

Remove or install the upper bearing insert using a roll-out pin

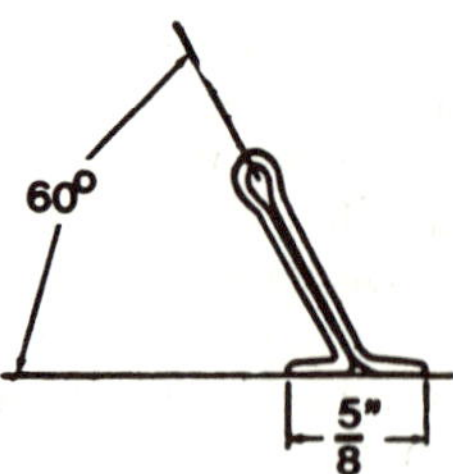

Home-made roll-out pin

crankshaft journal and install the rod cap. Make sure the cap and rod numbers match, torque the rod nuts to specifications.

4. Main bearings may be replaced while the engine is still in the car by "rolling" them out and in.

5. Special roll-out pins are available from automotive parts houses or can be fabricated from a cotter pin. The roll out pin fits in the oil hole of the main bearing journal. When the crankshaft is rotated opposite the direction of the bearing lock tab, the pin engages the end of the bearing and "rolls" out the insert.

6. Remove main bearing cap and roll out upper bearing insert. Remove insert from main bearing cap. Clean the inside of the bearing cap and crankshaft journal.

7. Lubricate and roll upper insert into position, make sure the lock tab is anchored and the insert is not "cocked". Install the lower bearing insert into the cap lubricate and install on the engine. Make sure the main bearing cap is installed facing in the correct direction and torque to specifications.

8. With the engine out of the car. Remove the intake manifold, cylinder heads, front cover, timing gears and/or chain, oil pan, oil pump and flywheel.

9. Remove the piston and rod assemblies. Remove the main bearing caps after marking them for position and direction.

10. Remove the crankshaft, bearing inserts and rear main oil seal. Clean the engine block and cap bearing saddles. Clean the crankshaft and inspect for wear. Check the bearing journals with a micrometer for out-of-round condition and to determine what size rod and main bearing inserts to install.

11. Install the main bearing upper inserts and rear main oil seal half into the engine block.

12. Lubricate the bearing inserts and the crankshaft journals. Slowly and carefully lower the crankshaft into position.

13. Install the bearing inserts and rear main seal into the bearing caps, install the caps working from the middle out. Torque cap bolts to specifications in stages, rotate the crankshaft after each torque stage.

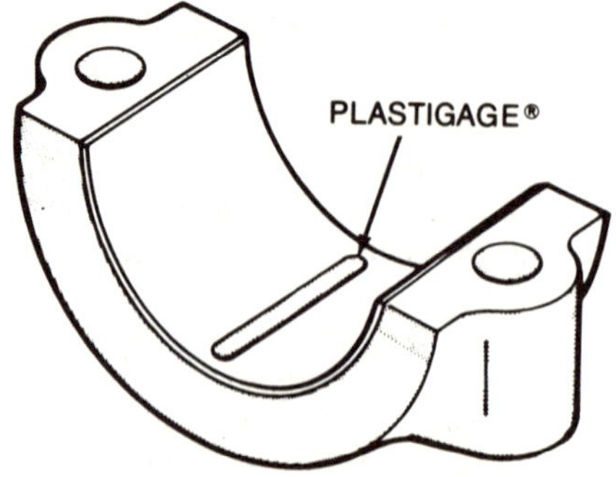

Plastigage installed on bearing shell

14. Remove bearing caps, one at a time and check the oil clearance with Plastigage®. Reinstall if clearance is within specifications. Check the crankshaft end-play, if within specifications install connecting rod and piston assemblies with new rod bearing inserts. Check connecting rod bearing oil clearance and rod side play, if correct and assemble the rest of the engine.

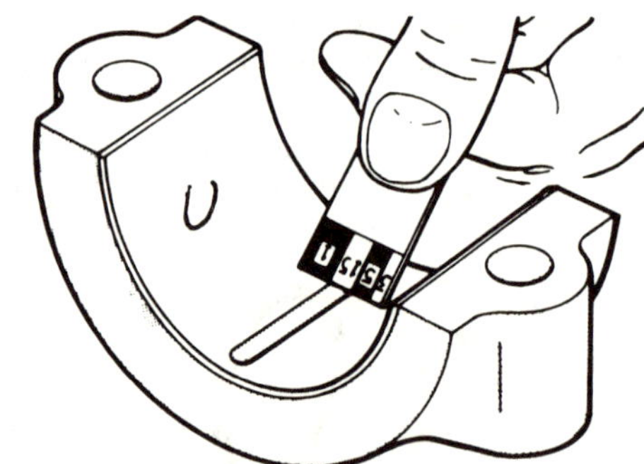

Measuring Plastigage®

BEARING OIL CLEARANCE

Remove cap from the journal to be checked. Using a clean, dry rag, thoroughly clean all oil from crankshaft journal and bearing insert.

NOTE: *Plastigage® is soluble in oil; therefore, oil on the journal or bearing could result in erroneous readings.*

Place a piece of Plastigage® along the full width of the insert, reinstall cap, and torque to specifications.

NOTE: *Specifications are given in the engine specifications earlier in this chapter.*

Remove bearing cap, and determine bearing clearance by comparing width of Plastigage® to the scale on Plastigage® envelope. Journal taper is determined by comparing width of the Plastigage® strip near its ends.

Rotate crankshaft 90° and retest, to determine journal eccentricity.

NOTE: *Do not rotate crankshaft with Plastigage® installed. If bearing insert and journal appear intact, and are within tolerances, no further main bearing service is required. If bearing or journal appear defective, cause of failure should be determined before replacement.*

CRANKSHAFT END-PLAY/CONNECTING ROD SIDE PLAY

Place a pry bar between a main bearing cap and crankshaft casting taking care not to damage any journals. Pry backward and forward measure the distance between the thrust bearing (No. 3) and crankshaft with a feeler gauge. Compare reading with specifications. If too great a clearance is determined, a main bearing with a larger thrust surface or crank machining may be required. Check with an automotive machine shop for their advice.

Connecting rod clearance between the rod and crankthrow casting can be checked with a feeler gauge. Pry the rod carefully to one side as far as possible and measure the distance on the other side of the rod.

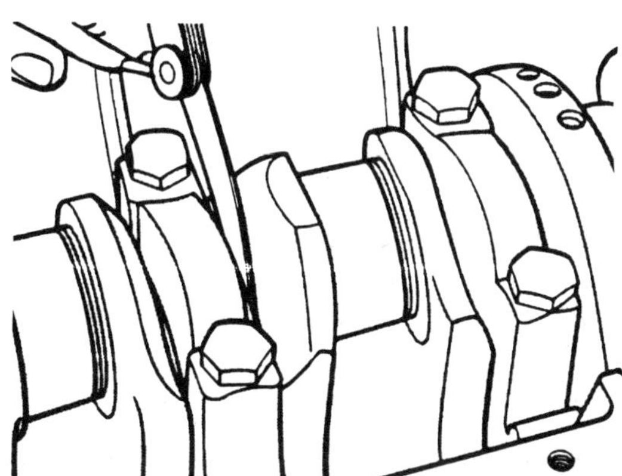

Checking the crankshaft end-play with a feeler gauge

CRANKSHAFT REPAIRS

If a journal is damaged on the crankshaft, repair is possible by having the crankshaft machined to a standard undersize.

In most cases, however, since the crankshaft must be removed from the engine, some thought should be given to replacing the damaged crankshaft with a reground shaft kit. A reground crankshaft kit contains the necessary main and rod bearings for installation. The shaft has been ground and polished to undersize specifications and will usually hold up well if installed correctly.

Oil Pan

REMOVAL AND INSTALLATION

All Engines

1. Remove the oil dipstick. Disconnect the two cooler lines at the radiator, if equipped.
2. On the four cyl. and inline six cyl., remove the two radiator top support bolts.
3. Remove the fan shroud bolts and position the shroud over the fan.
4. Raise the car and drain the oil.
5. Remove the sway bar attaching bolts and allow it to hang down.
6. Remove the steering gear to crossmember attaching bolts and allow the steering gear to rest on the frame away from the pan.
7. Disconnect the battery lead and remove the starter except on V8s.
8. Remove the engine mount bolts.
9. Raise the engine and place a 1¼ in. wooden block between the mount and chassis on each side. Use a 2 x 4 in. wood block on each side with the V8. Remove the K braces.
10. On the four and inline six only, place a jack under the transmission and raise it slightly.
11. Remove the oil pan bolts and lower the pan to the crossmember. Move the transmission cooler lines out of the way, if necessary, and remove the oil pan, rotating the crankshaft for clearance if required.
12. Clean the mounting surfaces thoroughly before installation. Coat the block and pan gasket surfaces with sealer. On the four cyl. only, the front and rear seal tabs go under the pan (side) gaskets. On all other engines, place the pan gaskets on the block first; then seal tabs go over the pan gaskets on these engines.
13. Install the pan mounting bolts. Torque the bolts from the center outwards on inline sixes and V8s. Use the torque sequences illustrated. The rest of installation is the reverse of removal.

Oil Pump

REMOVAL AND INSTALLATION

All Engines

1. Remove oil pan.
2. Remove oil pump inlet tube and screen assembly.
3. Remove oil pump attaching bolts and

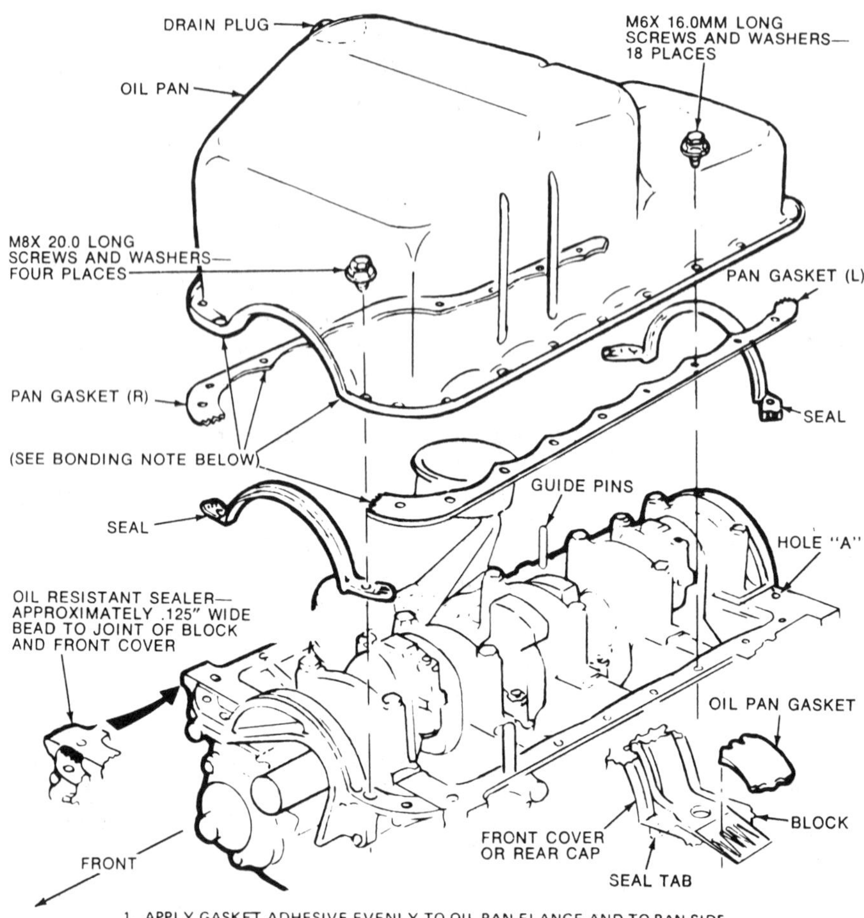

1. APPLY GASKET ADHESIVE EVENLY TO OIL PAN FLANGE AND TO PAN SIDE GASKETS. ALLOW ADHESIVE TO DRY PAST WET STAGE, THEN INSTALL GASKETS TO OIL PAN.
2. APPLY SEALER TO JOINT OF BLOCK AND FRONT COVER. INSTALL SEALS TO FRONT COVER AND REAR BEARING CAP AND PRESS SEAL TABS FIRMLY INTO BLOCK. BE SURE TO INSTALL THE REAR SEAL BEFORE THE REAR MAIN BEARING CAP SEALER HAS CURED.
3. POSITION 2 GUIDE PINS AND INSTALL THE OIL PAN. SECURE THE PAN WITH THE FOUR M8 BOLTS SHOWN ABOVE.
4. REMOVE THE GUIDE PINS AND INSTALL AND TORQUE THE EIGHTEEN M6 BOLTS, BEGINNING AT HOLE "A" AND WORKING CLOCKWISE AROUND THE PAN.

Engine oil pan bolt tightening sequence—4 cyl.

remove oil pump gasket and intermediate shaft.

4. Prime oil pump by filling inlet and outlet port with engine oil and rotating shaft of pump to distribute it.
5. Position intermediate drive shaft into distributor socket.
6. Position new gasket on pump body and insert intermediate drive shaft into pump body.
7. Install pump and intermediate shaft as an assembly.

NOTE: *Do not force pump if it does not seat readily. The drive shaft may be misaligned with the distributor shaft. To align rotate intermediate drive shaft into a new position.*

8. Install and torque oil pump attaching screws.
9. Install oil pan.

Rear Main Oil Seal

REMOVAL AND INSTALLATION

All Engines

NOTE: *The rear oil seal installed in these engines is a rubber type seal.*

1. Remove the oil pan, and, if required, the oil pump.
2. Loosen all main bearing caps allowing the crankshaft to lower slightly.

NOTE: *The crankshaft should not be allowed to drop more than* $^1/_{32}$.

3. Remove the rear main bearing cap and

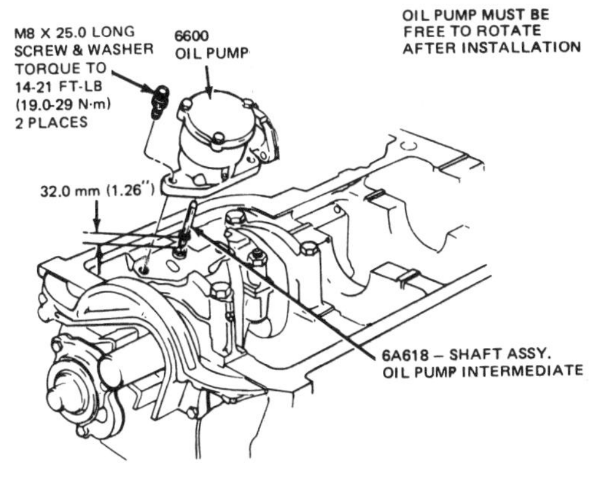

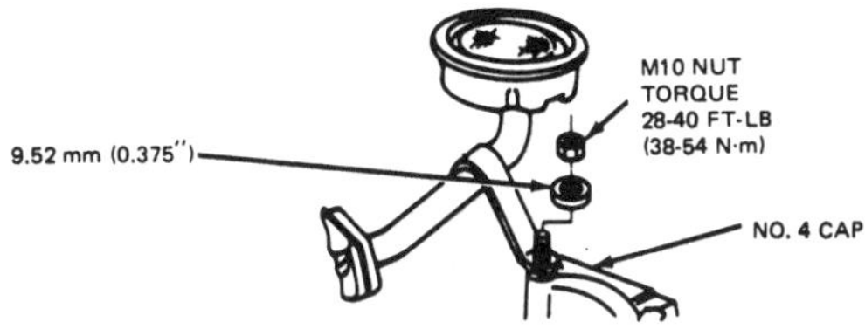

Oil pump installation—4 cyl. engine

remove the seal from the cap and block. Be very careful not to scratch the sealing surface. Remove the old seal retaining pin from the cap, if equipped. It is not used with the replacement seal.

4. Carefully clean the seal grooves in the cap and block with solvent.

5. Soak the new seal halves in clean engine oil.

6. Install the upper half of the seal in the block with the undercut side of the seal toward the front of the engine. Slide the seal around the crankshaft journal until ⅜ in. protrudes beyond the base of the block.

7. Tighten all the main bearing caps (except the rear main bearing) to specifications.

8. Install the lower seal into the rear cap, with the undercut side facing the front of the engine. Allow ⅜ in. of the seal to protrude above the surface, at the opposite end from the block seal.

9. Squeeze a $^{1}/_{16}$ in. bead of silicone sealant on the block and cap mating edges.

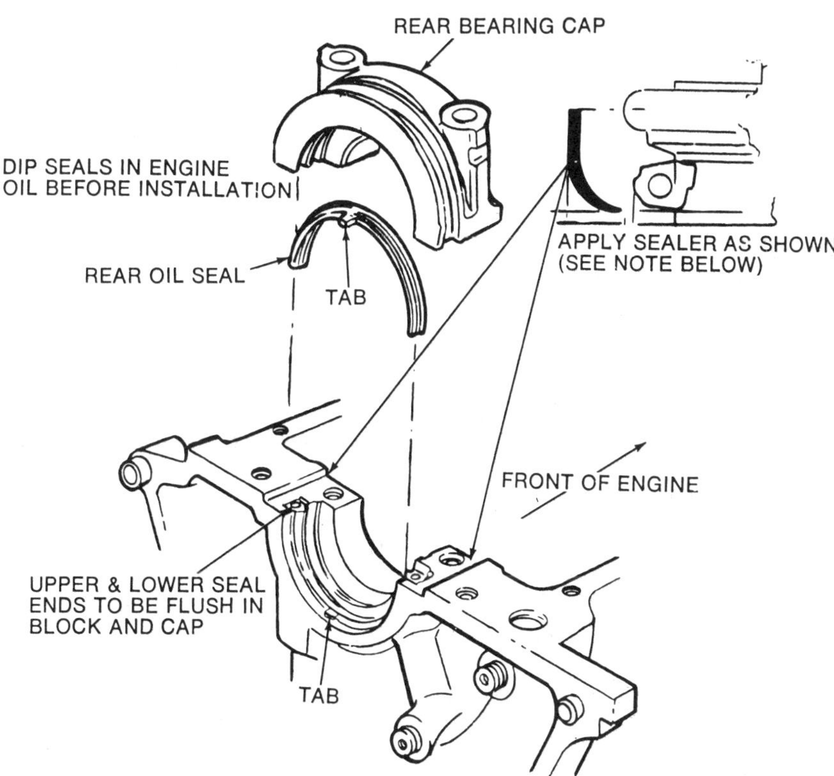

NOTE: CLEAN THE AREA WHERE SEALER IS TO BE APPLIED BEFORE INSTALLING THE SEALS. AFTER THE SEALS ARE IN PLACE, APPLY A 1/16 INCH BEAD OF SEALER AS SHOWN. *SEALER MUST NOT TOUCH SEALS*

Replacement of rear main oil seal—4 cyl.

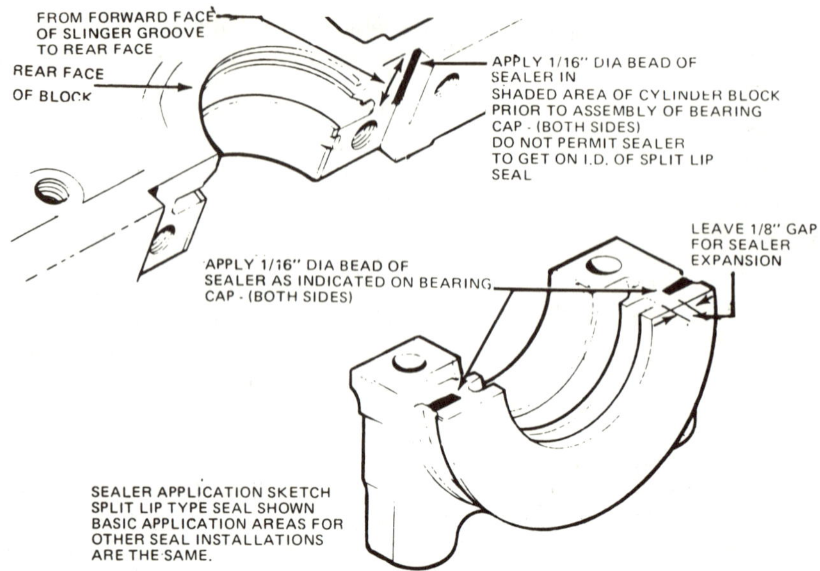

Rear main bearing cap sealer installation—6 cyl. and V8 engines

10. Install the rear cap and torque to specifications.
11. Install the oil pump and pan. Fill the crankcase with oil, start the engine, and check for leaks.

Completing the Rebuilding Process

After installing rings and bearings, complete the rebuilding process as follows:

Fill the oil pump with oil, to prevent cavitating (sucking air) on initial engine start up. Install the oil pump and the pickup tube on the engine. Coat the oil pan gasket as necessary, and install the gasket and the oil pan. Mount the flywheel and the crankshaft vibration damper or pulley on the crankshaft. NOTE: *Always use new bolts when installing the flywheel.* Inspect the clutch shaft pilot bushing in the crankshaft. If the bushing is excessively worn, remove it with an expanding puller and a slide hammer, and tap a new bushing into place.

Position the engine, cylinder head side up. Lubricate the lifters, and install them into their bores. Install the cylinder head, and torque it as specified. Insert the pushrods (where applicable), and install the rocker shaft(s) (if so equipped) or position the rocker arms on the pushrods. Adjust the valves following preliminary valve adjustment procedure.

Install the intake and exhaust manifolds, the carburetor(s), the distributor and spark plugs. Mount all accessories and install the engine in the car. Fill the radiator with coolant, and the crankcase with high quality engine oil.

Break-in Procedure

Start the engine, and allow it to run at low speed for a few minutes, while checking for leaks. Stop the engine, check the oil level, and fill as necessary. Restart the engine, and fill the cooling system to capacity. Check and adjust the ignition timing. Run the engine at low to medium speed (800–2500 rpm) for approximately ½ hour, and retorque the cylinder head bolts. Road test the car, and check again for leaks.

Repairing Damaged Threads

Several methods of repairing damaged threads are available. Heli-Coil®, Keenserts® and Microdot® are among the most widely used. All involve basically the same principle—drilling out stripped threads, tapping the hole and installing a prewound insert—making welding, plugging and oversize fasteners unnecessary.

Two types of thread repair inserts are usually supplied—a standard type for most Inch Coarse, Inch Fine, Metric Coarse and Metric Fine thread sizes and a spark plug type to fit most spark plug port sizes. Consult the individual manufacturer's catalog to determine exact applications. Typical thread repair kits will contain a selection of prewound threaded inserts, a tap (corresponding to the outside diameter threads of the insert) and an installation tool. Spark plug inserts usually differ because they require a tap equipped with pilot threads and a combined reamer/tap section. Most manufacturers also supply blister-packed thread repair inserts separately in addition to a master kit containing a variety of taps and inserts plus installation tools.

Before effecting a repair to a threaded hole, remove any snapped, broken or damaged bolts or studs. Penetrating oil can be used to free frozen threads; the offending item can be removed with locking pliers or with a screw or stud extractor. After the hole is clear, the thread can be repaired.

ENGINE COOLING

Radiator

REMOVAL AND INSTALLATION

All Models

1. Drain cooling system.
2. Disconnect upper and lower hoses at the radiator.
3. On automatic transmission-equipped cars, disconnect oil cooler lines at radiator.
4. On vehicles equipped with a fan shroud, remove the shroud retaining screws and position the shroud out of the way.
5. Remove radiator attaching bolts and lift out the radiator.
6. If a new radiator is to be installed, transfer the petcock from the old radiator to the new one. On cars equipped with automatic transmissions, transfer the fluid cooler line fittings from the old radiator to the new one.
7. Position the radiator and install, but do not tighten, the radiator support bolts. On cars equipped with automatic transmissions, connect the fluid cooler lines. Then tighten the radiator support bolts.
8. On vehicles equipped with a fan shroud, reinstall the shroud.
9. Connect the radiator hoses. Close the radiator petcock. Then fill and bleed the cooling system.
10. Start the engine and bring to operating temperature. Check for leaks.
11. On cars equipped with automatic transmissions, check the cooler lines for leaks and interference. Check transmission fluid level.

Water Pump

REMOVAL AND INSTALLATION

Four Cylinder 140 cu in. Engine

1. Drain the cooling system.
2. Disconnect the lower radiator hose and heater hose from the water pump.
3. Loosen the alternator retaining and adjusting bolt, and remove the drive belt.
4. Remove the camshaft belt cover, the fan shroud, fan and water pump pulley. It is not necessary to remove the cam belt or inner cover.
5. Remove the water pump retaining bolts and remove the pump from the engine.
6. Clean all mating surfaces and install the pump with a new gasket coated with sealer. If a new pump is being installed, transfer the heater hose fitting from the old pump.
7. Reverse the removal steps to install the pump. Refill the cooling system.

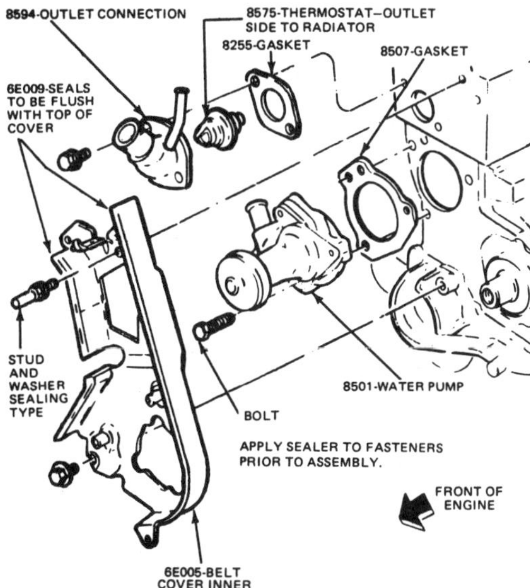

Water pump, thermostat, and inner timing bolt installation—4 cyl.

All Except Four Cylinder Engine

1. Drain cooling system.
2. Disconnect the negative battery cable.
3. On cars with power steering, remove the drive belt.
4. If the vehicle is equipped with air conditioning, remove the idler pulley bracket and air conditioner drive belt.
5. On engines with Thermactor, remove the belt.
6. Disconnect the lower radiator hose and heater hose from the water pump.

7. On cars equipped with a fan shroud, remove the retaining screws and position the shroud rearward.

8. Remove the fan and spacer from the engine, and if the car is equipped with a fan shroud, remove the fan and shroud from the engine as an assembly.

9. On cars equipped with water pump mounted alternators, loosen alternator mounting bolts, remove the alternator belt and remove the alternator adjusting arm bracket from the water pump.

10. Loosen bypass hose at water pump.

11. Remove water pump retaining screws and remove pump from engine.

12. Clean any gasket material from the pump mounting surface.

13. Remove the heater hose fitting from the old pump and install it on the new pump.

14. Coat both sides of the new gasket with a water resistant sealer, then install the pump, reversing the procedure.

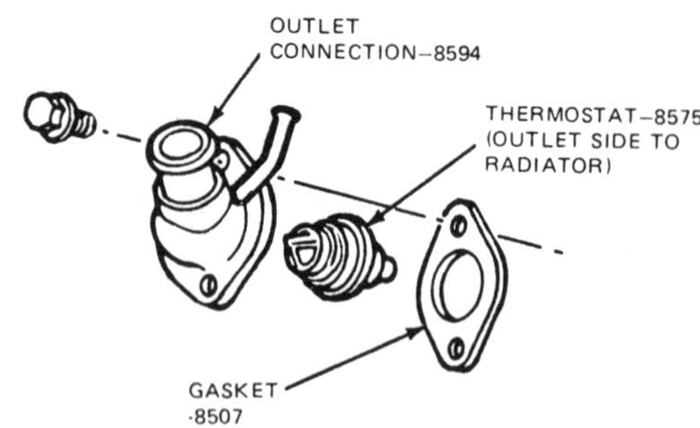

Engine thermostat and housing—4 cyl.

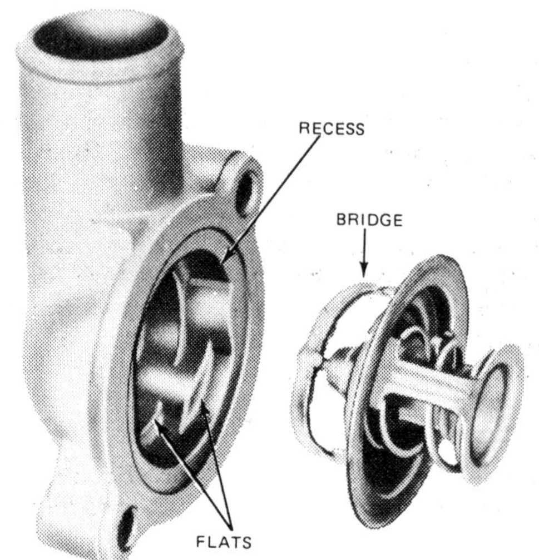

Engine thermostat and housing—6 cyl. and V8 engines

Thermostat

REMOVAL AND INSTALLATION

All Engines

1. Open the drain cock and drain the radiator so the coolant level is below the coolant outlet elbow which houses the thermostat.

2. Remove the outlet elbow retaining bolts and position the elbow sufficiently clear of the intake manifold or cylinder head to provide access to the thermostat.

3. Remove the thermostat and the gasket.

4. Clean the mating surfaces of the outlet elbow and the engine to remove all old gasket material and sealer. Coat the new gasket with water-resistant sealer and install it on the engine. Install the thermostat in the outlet elbow. The thermostat must be rotated clockwise to lock it in position.

5. Install the outlet elbow and retaining bolts in the engine. Torque the bolts to 12–15 ft. lbs.

6. Refill the radiator. Run the engine at operating temperature and check for leaks. Recheck the coolant level.

Emission Controls and Fuel System

EMISSION CONTROLS

There are three basic sources of automotive pollution in the modern internal combustion engine. They are the crankcase with its accompanying blow-by vapors, the fuel system with its evaporation of unburned gasoline and the combustion chambers with their resulting exhaust emissions. Pollution arising from the incomplete combustion of fuel generally falls into three categories: hydrocarbons (HC), carbon monoxide (CO) and oxides of nitrogen (NO_x).

Positive Crankcase Ventilation System

All Fairmonts and Zephyrs are equipped with a positive crankcase ventilation (PCV) system to control crankcase blow-by vapors. The system consists of a PCV valve and oil separator mounted on top of the valve cover or on the side of the engine block, a nonventilated oil filter cap and a pair of hoses supplying filtered intake air to the valve cover and delivering the crankcase vapors from the valve cover to the intake manifold or carburetor.

The system functions as follows: When the engine is running, a small portion of the gases which are formed in the combustion chamber leaks by the piston rings and enters the crankcase. Since these gases are under pressure, they tend to escape from the crankcase and enter the atmosphere. If these gases are allowed to remain in the crankcase for any period of time, they contaminate the engine oil and cause sludge to build up in the crankcase. If the gases are allowed to escape into the atmosphere, they pollute the air with unburned hydrocarbons. The job of the crankcase emission control equipment is to recycle these gases back into the engine combustion chamber where they are reburned.

These crankcase (blow-by) vapors are recycled in the following way: as the engine is running, clean filtered air is drawn through the air filter and into the crankcase. As the air passes through the crankcase, it picks up the combustion gases and carries them out of the crankcase through the oil separator, through the PCV valve and into the induction system. As the gases enter the intake manifold, they are drawn into the combustion chamber where they are reburned.

The most critical component in the system is the PCV valve. This valve controls the amount of gases which is recycled into the combustion chamber. At low engine speeds, the valve is partially closed, limiting the flow of gases into the intake manifold. As engine speed increases, the valve opens to admit greater quantities of the gases into the intake

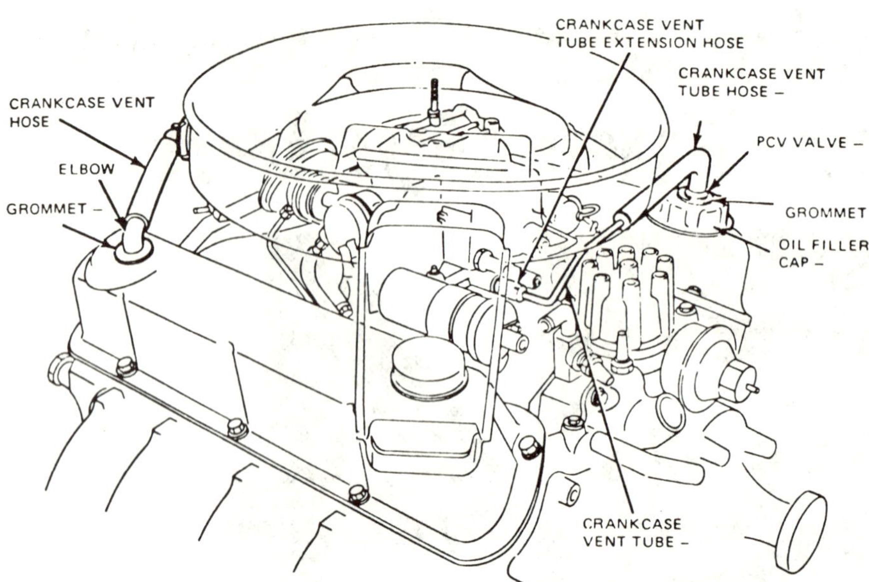

Positive crankcase ventilation system—V8 engines

manifold. If the valve should become blocked or plugged, the gases will be prevented from escaping from the crankcase by the normal route. Since these gases are under pressure, they will find their own way out of the crankcase. This alternate route is usually a weak oil seal or gasket in the engine. As the gas escapes by the gasket, it also creates an oil leak. Besides causing oil leaks, a clogged PCV valve also allows these gases to remain in the crankcase for an extended period of time, promoting the formation of sludge in the engine.

TROUBLESHOOTING

With the engine running, pull the PCV valve and hose from the oil separator. Block off the end of the valve with your finger. Engine speed should drop at least 50 rpm when the end of the valve is blocked. If engine speed does not drop at least 50 rpm, the valve is defective and should be replaced.

REMOVAL AND INSTALLATION

1. Remove the PCV system components, filler cap, PCV valve, hoses, tubes, fittings, etc. from the engine.
2. Soak the rubber ventilation hose(s) in a low volatility petroleum base solvent.
3. Clean the rubber ventilation hose(s) by passing a suitable cleaning brush through them.
4. Thoroughly wash the rubber hoses in a low volatility petroleum base solvent and dry with compressed air.
5. Thoroughly wash the crankcase breather cap, if so equipped, in a low volatility petroleum base solvent and shake dry. Do not dry with compressed air; damage to the filtering media may result.
6. Thoroughly clean tubes, fittings, connections to assure unobstructed flow of emission gases.
7. Install new PCV valve and reinstall previously removed hoses, tubes, fittings, etc. to their proper location.
8. Replace any system component that shows signs of damage, wear or deterioration as required.
9. Replace any hose or tube that cannot be cleaned satisfactorily.

Fuel Evaporative Control System

All Fairmonts and Zephyrs are equipped with a fuel evaporative control system to prevent the evaporation of unburned gasoline. This system consists of a special vacuum/pressure relief filler cap, an expansion area at the top of the fuel tank, a foam-filled vapor separator mounted on top of the fuel tank, a carbon canister which stores fuel vapors and hoses which connect this equipment. The carburetor fuel bowl vapors are retained within the fuel bowl until the engine is started, at which point they are internally vented into the engine for burning.

The rest of the system functions as follows: Change in atmospheric temperature causes

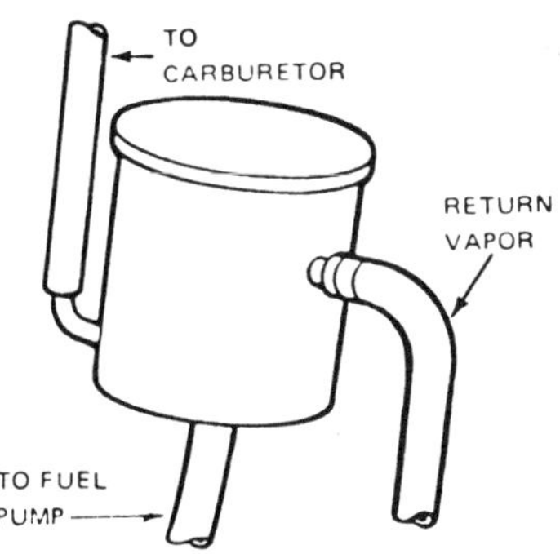

Vapor separator (typical)

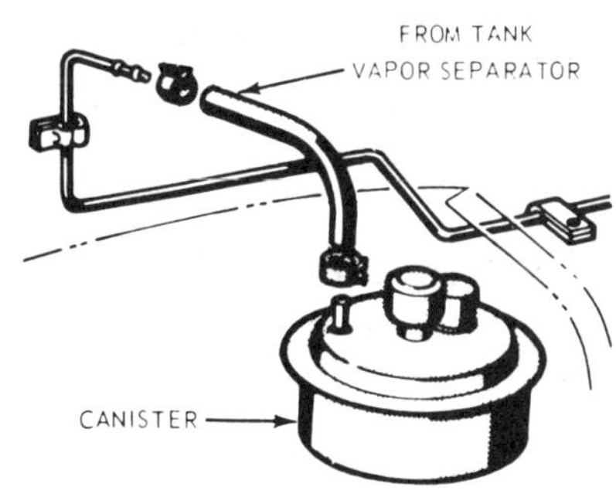

Carbon canister (typical)

the gasoline in fuel tanks to expand or contract. If this expansion and consequent vaporization take place in a conventional fuel tank, the fuel vapors escape through the filler cap or vent hose, and pollute the atmosphere. The fuel evaporative emission control system prevents this by routing the gasoline vapors to the engine, where they are burned.

As the gasoline in the fuel tank of a parked car begins to expand due to heat, the vapor that forms rises to the top of the fuel tank. The fuel tank is enlarged so that there exists an area representing 10–20% of the total fuel tank volume above the level of the fuel tank filler tube where these gases may collect. The vapors then travel upward into the vapor separator which prevents liquid gasoline from escaping from the fuel tank. The fuel vapor is then drawn through the vapor separator outlet hose, then to the charcoal canister in the engine compartment. The vapor enters the canister, passes through a charcoal filter, then exits through the canister's grated bottom. As the vapor passes through the charcoal it is cleansed, so that the air that passes out of the bottom of the canister is almost free of pollutants.

When the engine is started, vacuum from the carburetor draws fresh air into the canister. As the entering air passes through the charcoal in the canister, it picks up the hydrocarbons that were deposited there by the fuel vapors. This mixture of hydrocarbons and fresh air is then carried through a hose to the air cleaner. In the carburetor, it combines with the incoming fuel-air mixture and enters the combustion chambers of the engine, where it is burned.

To solve the problem of allowing air into the tank to replace the gasoline displaced during normal use and the problem of relieving excess pressure from the fuel tank should it reach a dangerous level, a special filler cap was devised. Under normal circumstances, this filler cap functions as a check valve, allowing air to enter the tank to replace the fuel consumed. At the same time, it prevents vapors from escaping from the cap. In case of severe pressure within the tank, the filler cap valve opens, venting the pollutants to the atmosphere.

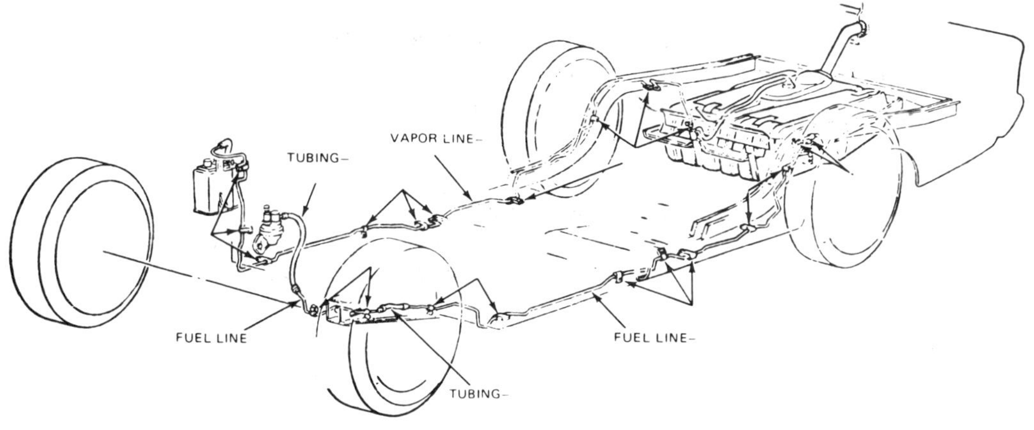

Fuel and vapor line routing (typical)

TROUBLESHOOTING & SERVICING

The only service performed on this system is the replacement of the charcoal canister.

Heated Air Intake System

The heated air intake portion of the air cleaner consists of a bimetal switch and vacuum motor and a spring-loaded temperature control door in the snorkel of the air cleaner. The temperature control door is located between the end of the air cleaner snorkel, which draws in air from the engine compartment, and the duct that carries heated air up from the exhaust manifold. When the temperature under the hood is below 90°F, the control door prevents underhood air from entering the air cleaner, allowing only heated air from the exhaust manifold to be drawn into the air cleaner. When underhood temperatures rise above 130°F, the control door blocks off heated air from the exhaust manifold and allows only cooler air to be drawn into the air cleaner.

By controlling the temperature of the engine intake air this way, exhaust emissions are lowered and fuel economy is improved. In addition, throttle plate icing is reduced and cold weather driveability is improved.

TROUBLESHOOTING

1. With the engine cold and underhood temperature below 90°F, check the position of the temperature door in the air cleaner. It should be in the up position, blocking off underhood air.
2. Immerse the air cleaner duct assembly in water after removing the air cleaner from the car. Raise the temperature to 130°F and allow the temperature to stabilize for five minutes. The temperature control door should be in the down position, blocking off heated air from the exhaust manifold.

If the temperature door does not react this way, and the door is not binding, replace the duct and valve assembly.

REPLACEMENT

1. Disconnect the vacuum hose at the vacuum motor.
2. Remove the hex-head cap screws that secure the air intake duct and valve assembly to the air cleaner.
3. Remove the duct and valve assembly from the engine.
4. Position the duct and valve assembly to the air cleaner and heat stove tube. Install the attaching cap screws.
5. Connect the vacuum line at the vacuum motor.

Dual Diaphragm Distributors

Most Fairmonts and Zephyrs are equipped with dual diaphragm distributors. The dual diaphragm is a two-chambered housing which is mounted on the side of the distributor. The outer side is a conventional vacuum advance mechanism, connected to the carburetor by a vacuum hose. The purpose of the vacuum advance unit is to advance ignition timing in response to the conditions under which the engine is operating. Vacuum advance units have been in use for many years, and their chief advantage is economical engine operation. The inner or second side of the diaphragm helps control exhaust emissions at idle and during deceleration.

This inner side of the dual diaphragm is connected by a vacuum hose to the intake manifold. When the engine is idling or decelerating, intake manifold vacuum is high and carburetor vacuum is low. Under these conditions, intake manifold vacuum, applied to the inner side of the dual diaphragm, retards ignition timing to promote more complete combustion of the fuel-air mixture in the engine combustion chambers.

TROUBLESHOOTING

1. Connect a timing light and start the engine.
2. Disconnect the vacuum hose from the

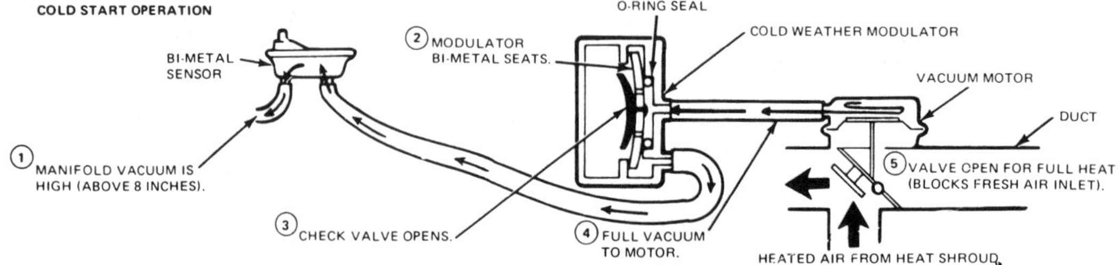

Heated air intake system

outer distributor diaphragm. Plug the line with a golf tee or pencil.

3. Shine the timing light on the lower engine pulley and observe the position of the ignition timing marks.

4. Disconnect the vacuum hose from the rear vacuum diaphragm on the distributor and hold your finger over the line.

5. Again check the ignition timing. It should be advanced beyond the reading obtained in step three. If it is not, the rear diaphragm on the distributor is defective or the vacuum hose from the intake manifold is broken.

REPLACEMENT

1. Tag the two vacuum hoses that attach to the diaphragm and disconnect them.

2. Remove the distributor cap and remove the C-clip that attaches the diaphragm arm to the breaker point mounting plate.

3. Remove the two screws that attach the diaphragm to the distributor housing and remove the diaphragm from the distributor.

4. Position the new diaphragm on the distributor and connect the hole in the diaphragm arm to the stud on the breaker point mounting plate.

5. Install the C-clip that retains the arm on the plate.

6. Install the distributor cap.

7. Install the two diaphragm attaching screws.

8. Connect the vacuum hoses to the diaphragm.

Ported Vacuum Switch (Distributor Vacuum Control Valve)

Ported vacuum switches are used to switch vacuum signals with varying engine coolant temperatures. They may have two, three or four vacuum ports and, on models equipped with catalytic converters and Thermactor systems, a set of electrical contacts. There may be as many as three or four separate ported vacuum switches, each with its own special function. PVS switches may be used to cut off exhaust gas recirculation until a predetermined engine temperature is reached, to switch vacuum signals on an ignition spark control system in order to improve cold start driveability, or to provide extra ignition advance and subsequent higher idle speed should the engine begin to overheat. They may also be used to vent Thermactor air pump air to the atmosphere under certain engine conditions, or to regulate a vacuum operated heat control in the exhaust manifold.

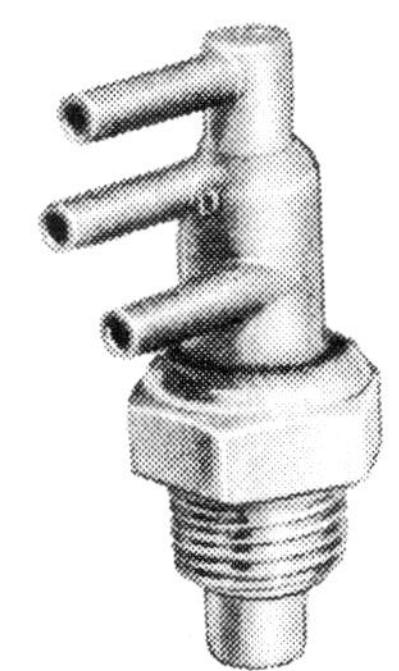

Ported vacuum switch

TROUBLESHOOTING

1. Attach a tachometer and start the engine.

2. Observe the reading on the tachometer.

3. Disconnect the hose from the intake manifold to the control valve and plug it with a golf tee or pencil.

4. Again observe the reading on the tachometer. If it has not changed, the control valve does not have an internal vacuum leak. If it does change, replace the valve.

5. Reconnect the intake manifold hose to the vacuum valve.

6. Block the front of the radiator with cardboard and have a friend watch the warning light on the instrument panel.

7. As soon as the red warning light comes on, again observe the reading on the tachometer. It should be at least 100 rpm higher than the reading obtained in step two. If it is not, replace the vacuum control valve.

8. Remove the cardboard from in front of the radiator and allow the engine to cool off before stopping the engine.

REPLACEMENT

1. Drain about one gallon (1 gal) of coolant out of the radiator.

2. Tag the vacuum hoses that attach to the control valve and disconnect them.

3. Unscrew and remove the control valve.

4. Install the new control valve.

5. Connect the vacuum hoses.

6. Fill the cooling system.

2-PORT PVS OPERATION

- Simple on-off "switch" for vacuum.
- **EGR-PVS valve** – cuts off EGR vacuum when engine is cold.

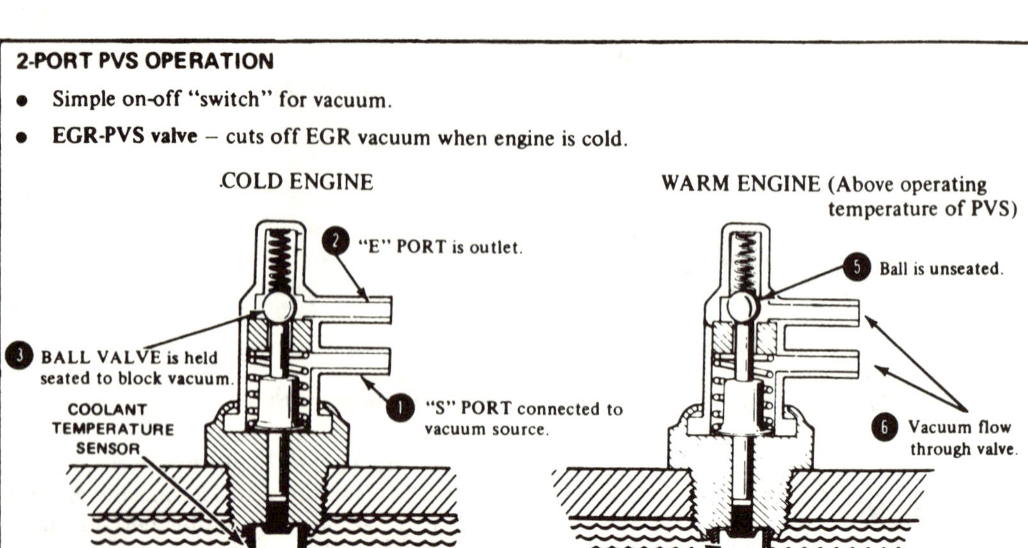

3-PORT PVS OPERATION

- **EGR/CSC** – switches EGR vacuum from EGR system to distributor advance with cold engine.
- **Cold Start Spark Advance (CSSA)** – supplies manifold vacuum to distributor below 125° F. coolant temperature.
- **Coolant Spark Control (CSC)** – cuts off distributor advance below hot engine temperature.
- **Cooling PVS** – switches advance vacuum from spark port to manifold vacuum if engine overheats.

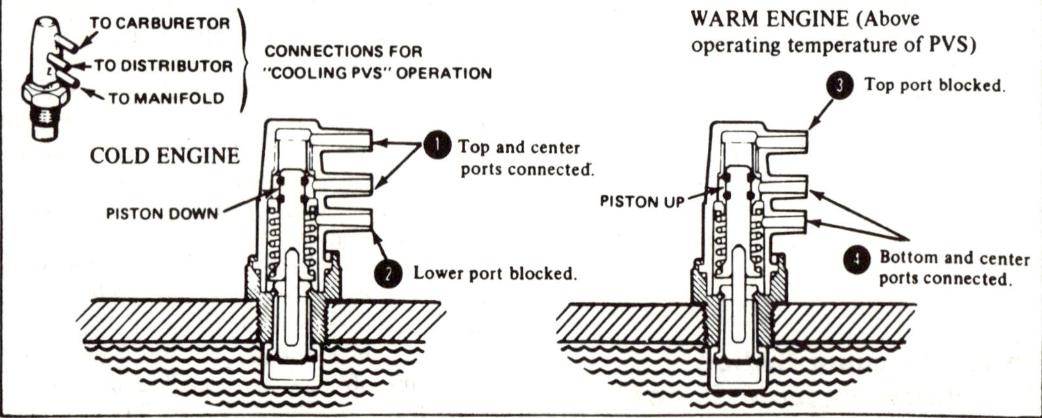

Ported vacuum switch operation

Spark Delay Valve

The spark delay valve is a plastic, spring-loaded, color-coded valve which is installed in the vacuum line to the distributor advance diaphragm. Under heavy throttle application, the valve will close, blocking normal carburetor vacuum to the distributor. After the designated period of closing time, the valve opens, restoring the carburetor vacuum to the distributor.

TROUBLESHOOTING

1. Disconnect the vacuum hose that runs from the spark delay valve to the distributor at the spark delay valve. Connect a vacuum gauge to the end of the spark delay valve from which you just disconnected the vacuum hose.
2. Start the engine and quickly raise the speed of the engine to about 2000 rpm with the transmission in Neutral. As soon as you accelerate the engine, the vacuum gauge reading should drop to zero.
3. With the engine speed held steady at about 2000 rpm, observe the time in seconds required until the vacuum gauge reading moves up to at least 6 in. Hg.
4. If the time required is less than 20 seconds, the spark delay valve is functioning properly.

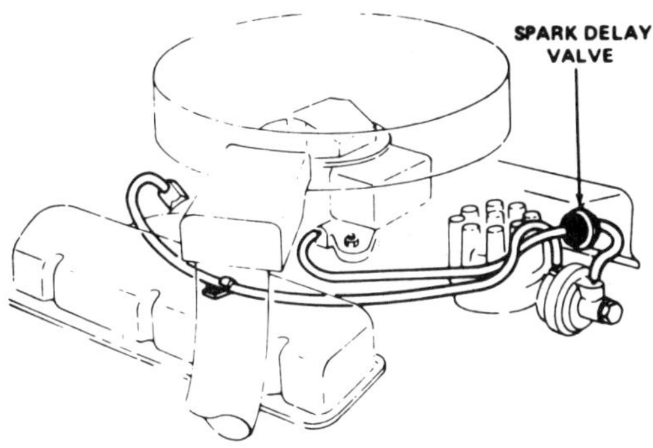

Spark delay operation

If the time required is less than two seconds, the valve is defective.

6. If the time required is more than 20 seconds, disconnect the vacuum gauge from the spark delay valve. Remove the carburetor-to-spark delay valve hose from the spark delay valve and connect the vacuum gauge to it.

Start the engine and raise the speed of the engine to about 2000 rpm. The vacuum gauge should show a reading of about 10–16 in. Hg. If it does not, there is a blockage in the carburetor vacuum port or the vacuum hose from the carburetor to the spark delay valve is plugged or broken.

REPLACEMENT

1. Locate the spark delay valve in the distributor vacuum line and disconnect it from the line.
2. Install a new spark delay valve in the line, making sure that the black end of the valve is connected to the line from the carburetor and the color coded end is connected to the line from the spark delay valve to the distributor.

Exhaust Gas Recirculation System

All Fairmonts and Zephyrs are equipped with exhaust gas recirculation (EGR) systems to control oxides of nitrogen.

On V8 engines, exhaust gases travel through the exhaust gas crossover passage in the intake manifold. A portion of these gases are diverted into a spacer which is mounted under the carburetor. The EGR control valve, which is attached to the rear of the spacer, consists of a vacuum diaphragm with an attached plunger which normally block off exhaust gases from entering the intake manifold. On four and six cylinder engines, an external tube carries exhaust manifold gases to the carburetor spacer. On all models, the EGR valve is controlled by a vacuum line from the carburetor which passes through a ported vacuum switch. The EGR ported vacuum switch provides a vacuum to the EGR valve at coolant temperature above 125°F. The vacuum diaphragm then opens the EGR valve permitting exhaust gases to flow through the carburetor spacer and enter the intake manifold where they combine with the fuel mixture and enter the combustion chambers. The exhaust gases are relatively oxygen-free, and tend to dilute the combustion charge. This lowers peak combustion temperature thereby reducing oxides of nitrogen.

EGR System Venturi Vacuum Amplifier

The EGR system also includes a venturi vacuum amplifier (VVA). The amplifier is used to boost a relatively weak venturi vacuum signal in the throat of the carburetor into a strong intake manifold vacuum signal to operate the EGR valve. By matching venturi air flow to EGR flow more closely, driveability is improved.

The amplifier features a vacuum reservoir and check valve to maintain an adequate vacuum supply regardless of variations in engine manifold vacuum. Also used in conjunction with the amplifier is a relief valve, which will cancel the output EGR vacuum signal whenever the venturi vacuum signal is equal to, or greater than, the intake manifold vacuum. Thus, the EGR valve may close at or near wide-open throttle acceleration, when maximum power is needed.

EGR/Coolant Spark Control (CSC) System

The EGR/CSC system regulates both distributor spark advance and the EGR valve operation according to coolant temperature by sequentially switching vacuum signals.

The major EGR/CSC system components are:

1. 95°F EGR-PVS valve
2. Spark Delay Valve (SDV)
3. Vacuum check valve

When the engine coolant temperature is below 82°F, the EGR-PVS valve admits carburetor EGR port vacuum (occurring at about 2,500 rpm) directly to the distributor advance diaphragm, through the one-way check valve.

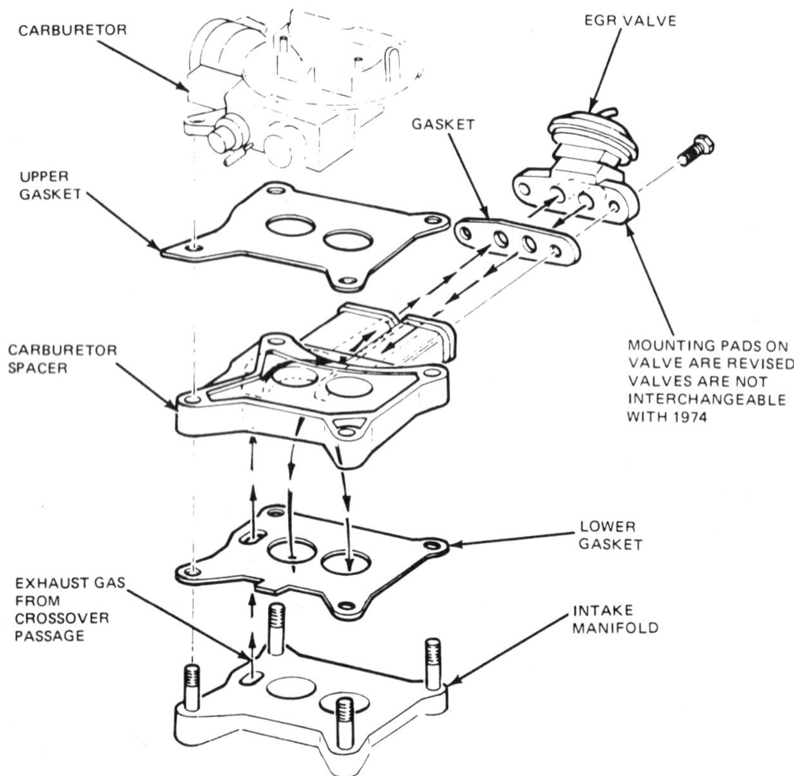

Spacer entry—EGR system

At the same time, the EGR-PVS valve shuts off carburetor EGR vacuum to the EGR valve and transmission diaphragm.

When engine coolant temperature is 95°F and above, the EGR-PVS valve is actuated and directs carburetor EGR vacuum to the EGR valve and transmission instead of the distributor. At temperatures between 82°–

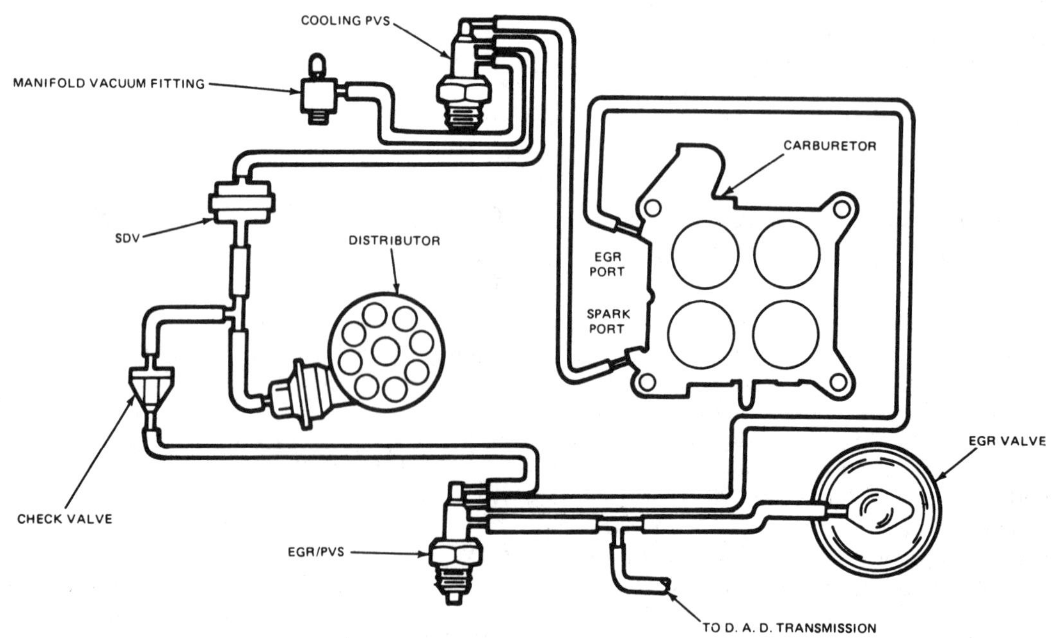

Typical EGR/CSC system

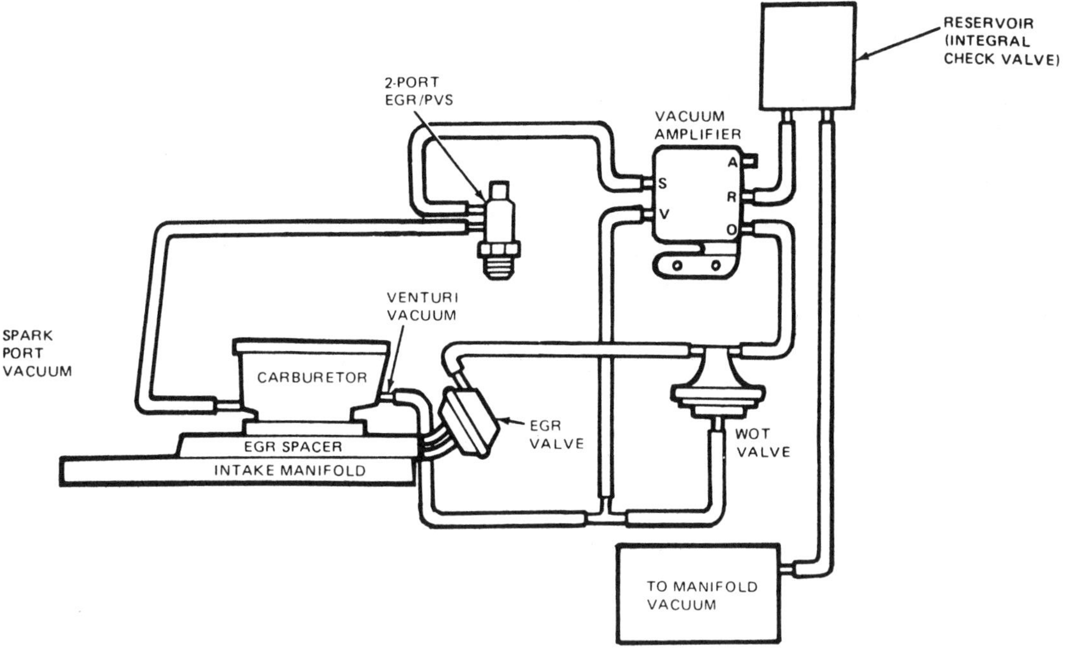

Typical system (EGR) with venturi vacuum amplifier

95°F, the EGR-PVS valve may be open, closed, or in midposition.

The SDV valve delays carburetor spark vacuum to the distributor advance diaphragm by restricting the vacuum signal through the SDV valve for a predetermined time. During normal acceleration, little or no vacuum is admitted to the distributor advance diaphragm until acceleration is completed, because of (1) the time delay of the SDV valve and (2) the rerouting of EGR port vacuum if the engine coolant temperature is 95°F or higher.

The check valve blocks off vacuum signal from the SDV to the EGR-PVS so that carburetor spark vacuum will not be dissipated when the EGR-PVS is actuated above 95°F.

Exhaust Gas Recirculation System

SYSTEM TEST

1. Allow the engine to warm up, so that the coolant temperature has reached at least 125°F.

2. Disconnect the vacuum hose which runs from the temperature cut-in valve to the EGR valve at the EGR valve end. Connect a vacuum gauge to this hose with a T-fitting.

3. Increase engine speed. Do not exceed half throttle or 3,000 rpm. The gauge should indicate a vacuum. If no vacuum is present, check the following:

a. The carburetor—look for a clogged vacuum port.

b. The vacuum hoses—including the vacuum hoses to the transmission modulator.

c. The temperature cut-in valve—if no vacuum is present at its outlet with the engine temperature above 125°F and vacuum available from the carburetor, the valve is defective.

4. If all the above tests are positive, check the EGR valve itself.

5. Connect an outside vacuum source and a vacuum gauge to the valve.

6. Apply vacuum to the EGR valve. The valve should open at 3–10 in. Hg, the engine idle speed should slow down and the idle quality should become more rough.

7. If this does not happen, i.e., the EGR valve remains closed, the EGR valve is defective and must be replaced.

8. If the valve stem moves but the idle remains the same, the valve orifice is clogged and must be cleaned.

NOTE: *If an outside vacuum source is not available, disconnect the hose which runs between the EGR valve and the temperature cut-in valve and plug the hose connections on the cut-in valve. Connect the EGR valve hose to a source of intake manifold vacuum and watch the idle. The results should be the same as in steps 6–7, above.*

Temperature Cut-In Valve EGR Ported Vacuum Switch

VALVE BENCH TEST

1. Remove the valve from the engine.
2. Connect an outside source of vacuum to the top port on the valve. Leave the bottom port vented to the atmosphere.
3. Use ice or an aerosol spray to cool the valve below 60°F.
4. Apply 20 in. Hg vacuum to the valve. The valve should hold a minimum of 19 in. Hg vacuum for 5 minutes without leaking down.
5. Leave the vacuum source connected to the valve and place it, along with a high temperature thermometer, into a nonmetallic, heat-resistant container full of water.
6. Heat the water. The vacuum in the valve should drop to zero once the temperature of the water reaches about 125°F.
7. Replace the valve if it fails either of the tests.

Vacuum Modulator Test

NOTE: *The vacuum modulator is used only with an automatic transmission.*

1. Remove the vacuum modulator from the car.
2. Connect the modulator to an outside vacuum source: a distributor tester, for example.

NOTE: *The vacuum source should be adjusted to supply 18 in. Hg, with the end of the vacuum line blocked off.*

3. Connect the vacuum line from the vacuum source to the EGR port on the vacuum modulatr.
4. The vacuum modulator should hold the 18 in. Hg reading. If it does not, then the diaphragm is leaking and must be replaced.

EGR Venturi Vacuum Amplifier System

SYSTEM TEST

The amplifiers have built-in calibrations and no external adjustments are required. If the amplifier tests reveal it is malfunctioning, replace the amplifier. All connections are located on one side of the amplifier. A vacuum connector and hose assembly is used to assure that proper connections are made at the amplifier. The amplifier is retained with a sheet-metal screw.

1. Operate the engine until normal operating temperatures are reached.
2. Before the vacuum amplifier is checked, inspect all other basic components of the EGR System (EGR valve, EGR/PVS valve, hoses, routing, etc.).
3. Check vacuum amplifier connections for proper routing and installation. If necessary, refer to the typical vacuum amplifier schematic.
4. Remove hose at EGR valve.
5. Connect vacuum gauge to EGR hose. Gauge must read in increments of at least 1 in. Hg graduation.
6. Remove hose at carburetor venturi (leave off).
7. With engine at curb idle speed, vacuum gauge reading should be within ±0.3 in. Hg of specified bias valve as shown in amplifier specifications for other than zero bias. Zero bias may read from 0 to 0.5 in. Hg. If out of specification, replace amplifier.
8. Depress accelerator and release after engine has reached 1500 to 2000 rpm. After engine has returned to idle, the vacuum must return to bias noted in step 7. If bias has changed, replace amplifier. Also, if vacuum shows a marked increase (greater than 1 in. Hg) during acceleration period, the amplifier should be replaced.
9. Hook up venturi hose at carburetor with engine at curb idle rpm. If a sizeable increase in output vacuum is observed, (more than 0.5 in. Hg above step 7), check idle speed. High idle speed could increase output vacuum due to venturi vacuum increase. See engine decal for correct idle specifications.
10. Check amplifier reservoir and connections as follows: Disconnect external reservoir hose at amplifier and AP or plug. Depress accelerator rapidly to 1500 to 2000 rpm. The vacuum should increase to 4 in. Hg or more. If out of specifications, replace amplifier.

EGR VALVE CLEANING

Remove the EGR valve for cleaning. Do not strike or pry on the valve diaphragm housing or supports, as this may damage the valve operating mechanism and/or change the valve calibration. Check orifice hole in the EGR valve body for deposits. A small hand drill of no more than 0.060-inch diameter may be used to clean the hole if plugged. Extreme care must be taken to avoid enlarging the hole or damaging the surface of the orifice plate.

Valves Which Cannot Be Disassembled

Valves which are riveted or otherwise permanently assembled should be replaced if highly contaminated; they cannot be cleaned.

Valves Which Can Be Disassembled

Separate the diaphragm section from the main mounting body. Clean the valve plates, stem, and the mounting plate, using a small power driven rotary wire brush. Take care not to damage the parts. Remove deposits between stem and valve disc by using a steel blade or shim, approximately 0.028 inch thick, in a sawing motion around the stem shoulder at both sides of the disc.

The poppet must wobble and move axially before reassembly.

Clean the cavity and passages in the main body of the valve with a power driven rotary wire brush. If the orifice plate has a hole less than 0.450 inch, it must be removed for cleaning. Remove all loosened debris, using shop compressed air. Reassemble the diaphragm section on the main body using a new gasket between them. Torque the attaching screws to specification. Clean the orifice plate and the counterbore in the valve body. Reinstall the orifice plate, using a small amount of contact cement to retain the plate in place during assembly of the valve to the carburetor spacer. Apply cement only to outer edges of the orifice plate to avoid restriction of the orifice.

EGR Supply Passages and Carburetor Spacer Cleaning

Remove the carburetor and carburetor spacer on engines so equipped. Clean the supply tube with a small power driven rotary wire brush or blast cleaning equipment. Clean the exhaust gas passages in the spacer, using a suitable wire brush and/or scraper. The machined holes in the spacer can be cleaned by using a suitable round wire brush. Hard encrusted material should be probed loose first, then brushed out. On six-cylinder engines, the external tube from the exhaust manifold must be removed and cleaned with a brush.

EGR Exhaust Gas Channel Cleanin

Clean the exhaust gas channel, where applicable, in the intake manifold, using a suitable carbon scraper. Clean the exhaust gas entry port in the intake manifold by hand, passing a suitable drill bit through the holes to auger out the deposits. Do not use a wire brush. The manifold riser bore(s) should be suitably plugged during the above action to prevent any of the residue from entering the induction system.

Thermactor System

The Thermactor emission control system makes use of a belt-driven air pump to inject fresh air into the hot exhaust stream through the engine exhaust ports. The result is the extended burning of those fumes which were not completely ignited in the combustion chamber, and the subsequent reduction of some of the hydrocarbon and carbon monoxide content of the exhaust emissions into harmless carbon dioxide and water.

The Thermactor system is composed of the following components:

1. Air supply pump (belt-driven)
2. Air bypass valve
3. Check valves
4. Air manifolds (internal or external)
5. Air supply tubes (on external manifolds only)

Air for the Thermactor system is cleaned by means of a centrifugal filter fan mounted on the air pump driveshaft. The air filter does not require a replaceable element.

To prevent excessive pressure, the air pump is equipped with a pressure relief valve which uses a replaceable plastic plug to control the pressure setting.

The Thermactor air pump has sealed bearings, which are lubricated for the life of the unit, and preset rotor vane and bearing clearances, which do not require any periodic adjustments.

The air supply from the pump is controlled by the air bypass valve, sometimes called a dump valve. During deceleration, the air bypass valve opens, momentarily diverting the air supply through a silencer and into the atmosphere, thus preventing backfires within the exhaust system.

A check valve is incorporated in the air inlet side of the air manifolds. Its purpose is to prevent exhaust gases from backing up into the Thermactor system. This valve is especially important in the event of drive belt failure and during deceleration, when the air bypass valve is dumping the air supply.

The air manifolds and air supply tubes channel the air from the Thermactor air pump

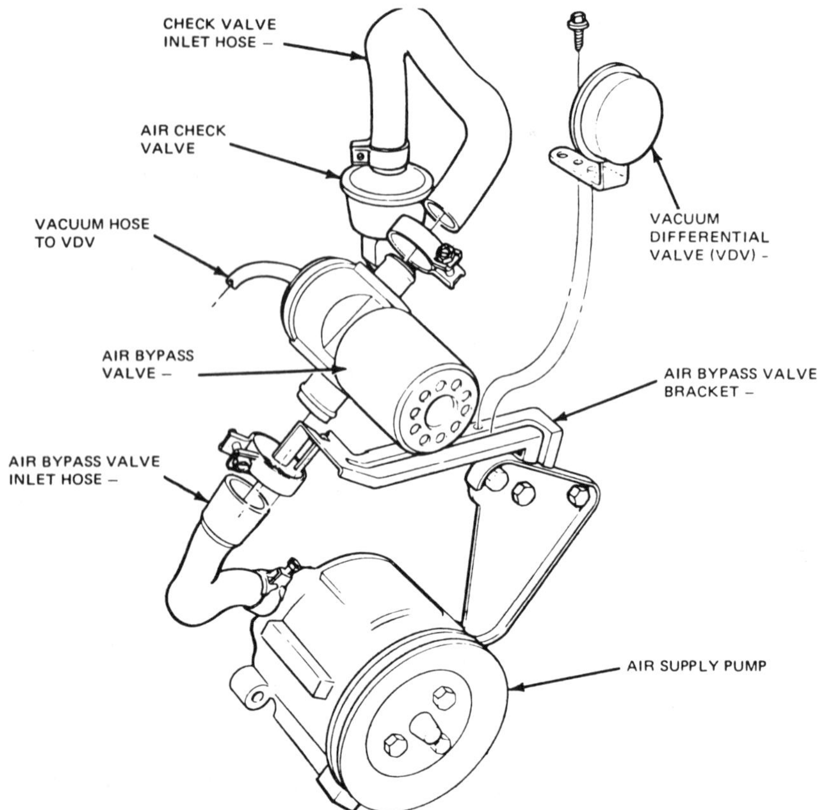

Thermactor system (typical)

into the exhaust ports of each cylinder, thus completing the cycle of the Thermactor system.

The Thermactor system used on cars with catalytic converters incorporates several components to prevent excessive converter temperatures from developing. Since the catalyst requires large quantities of oxygen to function, an air bypass valve and a vacuum differential (VDV) valve are used to control temperatures by dumping air from the Thermactor pump to the atmosphere instead of delivering it to the catalyst.

The purpose of these valves is to "dump" air during periods of vacuum failure, the rich exhaust gas condition during deceleration, prevent backfire when the exhaust gases are overly rich and provide pressure relief (due to excessive air pump volume or restriction downstream).

The air bypass valve used with catalytic converters differs from the valve used on cars without converters and can be identified by the *vacuum port on top of the valve.* The valve functions as follows: During normal operation, engine intake manifold vacuum applied through the VDV holds the valve upward, allowing Thermactor air to flow to the cylinder head(s) and blocking the vent port. When engine intake manifold vacuum rises or drops sharply (such as during acceleration or deceleration, or system blockage or failure), the VDV operates and momentarily cuts off the vacuum to the bypass valve. The spring pulls the stem down, seating the valve to cut off pump air to the exhaust manifold, and opening the dump valve at the lower end of the bypass valve to momentarily divert the pump air to the atmosphere. In the case of excess pump volume or a downstream restriction, the excess pressure will unseat the valve in the lower portion of the bypass valve and allow a partial flow of pump air to the atmosphere. At the same time, the valve in the upper part of the bypass is still unseated, allowing a partial flow of pump air to the exhaust manifold to meet system requirements.

The vacuum differential valve (VDV) controls the operation of the new bypass valve used with catalytic converter equipped systems.

The VDV is inserted in the vacuum control

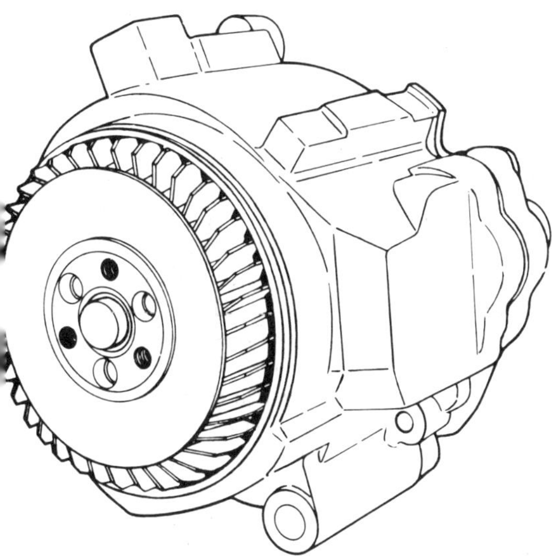

Air pump

line to the bypass valve and serves to cut off the vacuum and deenergize the bypass valve. The differential valve consists of a diaphragm connected to a dump valve that controls the vacuum to the bypass valve. During normal operation, vacuum is equalized on both sides of the diaphragm and the spring holds the dump valve closed. When sudden higher than normal vacuum is encountered, such as under deceleration conditions, vacuum is higher on the dump valve side of the diaphragm and the diaphragm operates the dump valve. As the dump valve operates, the vacuum signal to the bypass valve is diverted through the built-in filter system to atmosphere. When the vacuum bleeding through the bypass timing orifice in the VDV has equalized on both sides of the diaphragm, the diaphragm return spring once again closes the dump valve and applies vacuum to the bypass valve, which again applies pump air to the exhaust ports.

TROUBLESHOOTING THE THERMACTOR SYSTEM

Before performing an extensive diagnosis of the emission control systems, verify that all specifications on the Certification Label are met, because the following systems or components may cause symptoms that appear to be emission related.

a. Improper vacuum connections
b. Vacuum leaks
c. Ignition timing
d. Plugs, wires, cap and rotor
e. Carburetor float level
f. Carburetor main metering jets
g. Choke operation

Fabricating a Test Gauge Adapter

In order to test the three major components of a Thermactor system (air pump, check valve and bypass valve), a pressure gauge and adapter are required. The adapter can be fabricated as follows:

1. Obtain these items:
 a. ½-inch pipe tee
 b. ½-inch pipe, 2 inches long and threaded at one end
 c. ½-inch pipe plug
 d. ½-inch reducer bushing or other suitable gauge adapter
2. Apply sealer to threaded ends of pipe, plug and bushing. Assemble as shown in the illustration.
3. Drill $^{11}/_{32}$ inch (0.3437) diameter hole through center of pipe plug. Clean out chips after drilling.
4. Attach pressure gauge with ¼-psi increments to bushing or adapter.

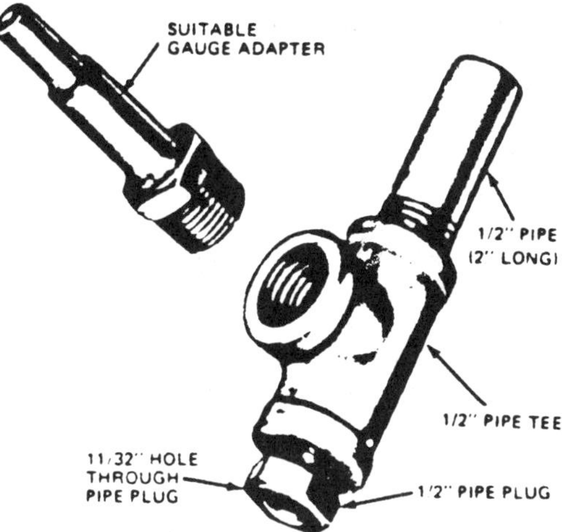

Fabricated test gauge adapter

Air Pump Tests

CAUTION: *Do not hammer on, pry, or bend the pump housing while tightening the drive belt or testing the pump.*

Belt Tension and Air Leaks

1. Before proceeding with the tests, check the pump drive belt tension to see if it is within specifications.
2. Turn the pump by hand. If it has seized, the belt will slip, producing noise. Disregard any chirping, squealing, or rolling sounds from inside the pump; these are normal when it is turned by hand.
3. Check the hoses and connections for leaks. Hissing or a blast of air is indicative of

a leak. Soapy water, applied lightly around the area in question, is a good method for detecting leaks.

Air Output Tests

1. Disconnect the air supply hose at the antibackfire valve.
2. Connect a vacuum gauge, using a suitable adapter, to the air supply hose.

NOTE: *If there are two hoses plug the second one.*

3. With the engine at normal operating temperature, increase the idle speed and watch the vacuum gauge.
4. The air flow from the pump should be steady and fall between 2–6 psi. If it is unsteady or falls below this, the pump is defective and must be replaced.

Pump Noise Diagnosis

The air pump is normally noisy; as engine speed increases, the noise of the pump will rise in pitch. The rolling sound the pump bearings make is normal; however, if this sound becomes objectionable at certain speeds, the pump is defective, and will have to be replaced.

A continual hissing sound from the air pump pressure relief valve at idle indicates a defective valve. Replace the relief valve.

If the pump rear bearing fails, a continual knocking sound will be heard. Since the rear bearing is not separately replaceable, the pump will have to be replaced as an assembly.

Check the Valve Test

1. Before starting the test, check all of the hoses and connections for leaks.
2. Detach the air supply hose(s) from the check valve(s).
3. Insert a suitable probe into the check valve and depress the plate. Release it; the plate should return to its original position against the valve seat. If binding is evident, replace the valve.
4. Repeat step 3 if two valves are used.
5. With the engine running at normal operating temperature, gradually increase its speed to 1,500 rpm. Check for exhaust gas leakage. If any is present, replace the valve assembly.

NOTE: *Vibration and flutter of the check valve at idle speed is a normal condition and does not mean that the valve should be replaced.*

Air Bypass Valve Test

1. Detach the hose, which runs from the bypass valve to the check valve, at the bypass valve hose connection.
2. Connect a tachometer to the engine. With the engine running at normal idle speed, check to see that air is flowing from the bypass valve hose connection.
3. Speed the engine up, so that it is running at 1,500–2,000 rpm. Allow the throttle to snap shut. The flow of air from the bypass valve at the check valve hose connection should stop momentarily and air should then flow from the exhaust port on the valve body or the silencer assembly.
4. Repeat step 3 several times. If the flow of air is not diverted into the atmosphere from the valve exhaust port or if it fails to stop flowing from the hose connection, check the vacuum lines and connections. If these are tight, the valve is defective and requires replacement.

COMPONENT REPLACEMENTS

Thermactor Air Pump Drive Belt Replacement and/or Adjustment

1. Loosen the air pump adjusting bolt. Loosen the air pump-to-mounting bracket bolt and push the air pump toward the cylinder block. Remove the belt.

Thermactor Air Pump

1. Disconnect the air outlet hose at the air pump.
2. Loosen the pump belt tension adjuster.
3. Disengage the drive belt.
4. Remove the mounting bolt and air pump.
5. To install, position the air pump on the mounting bracket and install the mounting bolt.
6. Place drive belt in pulleys and attach the adjusting arm to the air pump.
7. Adjust the drive belt tension to specifications and tighten the adjusting arm and mounting bolts.
8. Connect the air outlet hose to the air pump.

Thermactor Air Pump Filter Fan

1. Loosen the air pump adjusting arm bolt and mounting bracket bolt to relieve drive belt tension.
2. Remove drive pulley attaching bolts and pull drive pulley off the air pump shaft.

3. Pry the outer disc loose; then, pull off the centrifugal filter fan with slip-joint pliers.

CAUTION: *Do not attempt to remove the metal drive hub.*

4. Install a new filter fan by drawing it into position, using the pulley and bolts as an installer. Draw the fan evenly by alternately tightening the bolts, making certain that the outer edge of the fan slips into the housing.

NOTE: *A slight interference with the housing bore is normal. After a new fan is installed, it may squeal upon initial operation, until its outer diameter sealing lip has worn in, which may require 20 to 30 miles of operation.*

Thermactor Check Valve

1. Disconnect the air supply hose at the valve. (Use a 1¼-inch crowfoot wrench; the valve has standard, righthand pipe thread.)
2. Clean the threads on the air manifold adapter (air supply tube on V8 engine) with a wire brush. Do not blow compressed air through the check valve in either direction.
3. Install the check valve and tighten.
4. Connect the air supply hose.

Thermactor Air Bypass Valve

1. Disconnect the air and vacuum hoses at the air bypass valve body.
2. Position the air bypass valve and connect the respective hoses.

Suction Air System (Pulsed Air)

The suction air system is used on some models with the 200 cu. in. 6-cylinder engine. It consists of a hose which runs from the clean side of the air cleaner to the exhaust manifold. Mounted midway in the hose is a silencer and an air inlet valve. The air inlet valve acts like a check valve.

Suction in the exhaust manifold pulls air from the air cleaner. This air oxides the hydrocarbons and carbon monoxides. The inlet valve prevents backflow of the exhaust into the air cleaner.

Because there is pulsating in the exhaust, it is normal for the air inlet valve to vibrate, especially at idle. The silencer prevents these vibrations from reaching the air cleaner.

To check the system, remove the silencer and check the air inlet valve to be sure it is vibrating at idle. There should not be any backflow of exhaust out of the valve.

Catalytic Converter System

Catalytic converters are used to clean up engine exhaust emissions. Your Fairmont or Zephyr may be equipped with one or two converters. Models having only one converter, in the exhaust system, have the "Conventional Oxidation Catalyst" (COC) converter. The COC acts on two of the major pollutants-unburned hydrocarbons (HC) and carbon monoxide (CO). If the exhaust system has two converters, the first (and usually smaller) converter, called a "Three-Way Catalyst" (TWC), is designed to control oxides of nitrogen (NOx).

The TWC converter operates on the exhaust gases as they arrive from the engine. As the gases flow from the TWC to the COC converter, they mix with air from the air pump injected into a mixing chamber. This air is required for proper oxidation in the COC converter.

CAUTION: *The temperatures of the exhaust system is very high. Never work on any part of the system until it has cooled down. Use special care when working around a converter, they reach a very high temperature in a very short time.*

The continued use of leaded gas in a converter equipped car will clog the system and render the converter useless.

Feedback Carburetor Electronic Engine Control

This system actually consists of three subsystems: a two part catalytic converter, a Thermactor (air pump) system, and an electronically controlled feedback carburetor.

The converter consists of two catalytic converters in one shell. The front section is designed to control all three engine emissions (NOx, HC, and CO). The rear section acts only on HC and CO. There is a space between the two sections which serves as a mixing chamber. Air is pumped into this area by the Thermactor system to assist in the oxidation of HC and CO.

The Thermactor system is the same as that found on conventional Ford models, with the addition of a second air control valve and a second exhaust check valve.

An electronically controlled feedback carburetor (Motorcraft mode 6500 or 7200/2700) is used to precisely calibrate fuel metering. The air/fuel ratio is externally controlled and variable. There are two modes of operation: closed loop control and open loop control.

Under closed loop operation, each component in the chain is sensitive to the signals sent by the other components. This means that the carburetor mixture is being controlled by the vacuum regulator/solenoid, which is adjusted by the control unit, which is receiving signals from the oxygen sensor in the exhaust manifold, which is measuring a mixture determined by the carburetor, and so on. In this case, the feedback loop is complete. Under open loop operation, the carburetor air/fuel mixture is controlled directly by the control unit according to a predetermined setting. Open loop operation takes place when the coolant temperature is below 125°F, or when the throttle is closed, during idle or deceleration.

The control unit receives signals from the exhaust gas oxygen sensor, the throttle angle vacuum switch, and the cold temperature vacuum switch, analyzes them, and sends out commands to the vacuum solenoid/regulator, which in turn adjusts, by means of vacuum, the height of the carburetor fuel metering rod. In this way, the fuel mixture is adjusted according to conditions. The control unit also varies the transition time from rich to lean (and vice versa) according to engine rpm. The rpm signal is taken from the coil connector TACH terminal.

There are two differences between the ECU, used in 1978 and 1979, and the MCU, used in 1980 and later models. The MCU is programmable, enabling it to be used with many different engine calibrations. Additionally, the MCU controls the Thermactor solenoid valves, thus directing the air flow to the exhaust manifold, the catalytic converter mixing chamber, or the atmosphere when air flow is not needed or wanted.

Because of the complicated nature of the Ford system, special diagnostic tools are necessary for troubleshooting and repair. No attempt at testing or repair should be made unless both the Feedback Control Tester (Ford part no. T78L-50-FBC-1) and a digital volt/ohmmeter (Ford part no. T78L-50-DVOM) are available. A tachometer, vacuum gauge, hand vacuum pump and gauge, and a special throttle rpm tool are also required for diagnosis. No troubleshooting procedures will be given here, since they are supplied with the testing equipment.

FUEL SYSTEM

Mechanical Fuel Pump

The fuel pump is bolted to the left side of the engine block or front cover. It is mechanically operated by an eccentric bolted to the end of the camshaft. The pump rocker arm riding against the eccentric provides the diaphragm up and down pumping motion. The pump is not repairable and must be replaced if defective.

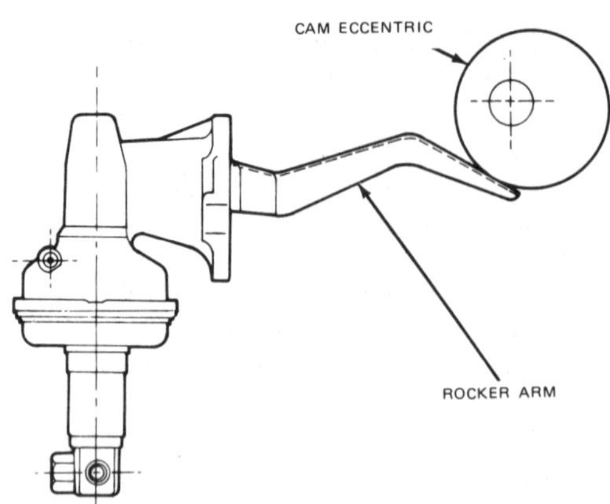

Typical fuel pump installation

TROUBLESHOOTING

The fuel pump can fail in two ways; it can fail to provide a sufficient volume of gasoline under the proper amount of pressure to the carburetor, or it can develop an internal or external leak. A quick check for an internal leak is to remove the oil dipstick and examine the oil on it. A fuel pump with an internal leak will leak fuel into the engine oil pan. If the oil on the dipstick is very thin and smells of gasoline, a defective fuel pump could be the cause.

Pressure Test

Disconnect the fuel line from the carburetor and attach a pressure tester to the end of the

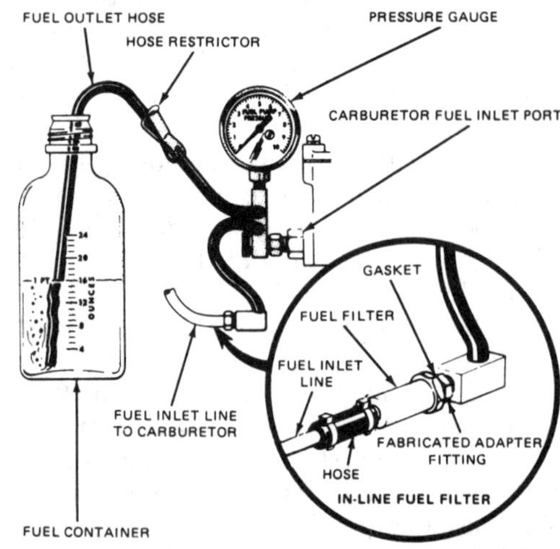

Fuel pump pressure and capacity test equipment (typical)

line. Crank the engine over and note the reading on the tester. Refer to specs in Chapter 2.

Volume Test

Disconnect the fuel line from the carburetor and insert it into a one quart container and crank the engines to the specifications listed below:

- 4 cyl. eng., one pint in 25 sec. @ idle
- 6 cyl. eng., one pint in 30 sec. @ idle
- V8 eng., one pint in 20 sec. @ idle

REPLACEMENT

1. Disconnect the fuel lines from the fuel pump and plug the inlet line from the gas tank to prevent gas leakage.
2. Remove the fuel pump retaining screws and remove the pump.
3. Remove the fuel pump actuating rod, if so equipped.
4. Clean all gasket mounting surfaces.
5. Install the fuel pump actuating rod, if so equipped.
6. Apply oil-resistant sealer to the fuel pump, position the pump on the engine and install the retaining screws.

NOTE: *Make sure that the fuel pump rocker arm is riding on the eccentric.*

7. Connect the fuel lines to the fuel pump, start the engine and check for leaks.

Carburetors

REMOVAL AND INSTALLATION

1. Remove the air cleaner.
2. Remove the throttle cable from the throttle lever.
3. Label for location identification and disconnect all vacuum lines, emission hoses, the fuel line, electrical connection and the choke heat tube at the carburetor.
4. Remove the carburetor retaining nuts and remove the carburetor.
5. Remove the carburetor mounting gasket, spacer (if equipped) and lower gasket from the intake manifold.

INSTALLATION

1. Clean all gasket mounting surfaces and place the spacer between two new gaskets and position the spacer and gaskets on the intake manifold.
2. Position the carburetor on the spacer and gasket.
3. Position and connect the choke heat tube.
4. Install the spark and EGR vacuum lines (if so equipped) before bolting the carburetor in place.
5. Install the carburetor attaching nuts to a snug position then tighten in a criss-cross pattern.
6. Connect the fuel line, throttle cable and vacuum lines.

Efficient carburetion depends greatly on careful cleaning and inspection during overhaul, since dirt, gum, water, or varnish in or on the carburetor parts are often responsible for poor performance.

Overhaul your carburetor in a clean, dust-free area. Carefully disassemble the carburetor, referring often to the exploded views. Keep all similar and lookalike parts segregated during the disassembly and cleaning to avoid accidental interchange during assembly. Make a note of all jet sizes.

When the carburetor is disassembled, wash all parts (except diaphragms, electric choke units, pump plunger, and any other plastic, leather, fiber, or rubber parts) in clean carburetor solvent. Do not leave parts in the solvent any longer than necessary to sufficiently loosen the deposits. Excessive cleaning may remove the special finish from the float bowl and choke valve bodies, leaving those parts unfit for service. Rinse all parts in clean solvent and blow them dry with compressed air or allow them to air dry. Wipe clean all cork, plastic, leather and fiber parts with a clean, lint-free cloth.

Blow out all passages and jets with compressed air and be sure that there are no restrictions or blockages. Never use wire or similar tools to clean jets, fuel passages, or air bleeds. Clean all jets and valves separately to avoid accidental interchange.

Check all parts for wear or damage. If wear or damage is found, replace the defective parts. Especially check the following:

1. Check the float needle and seat for wear. If wear is found, replace the complete assembly.
2. Check the float hinge pin for wear and the float(s) for dents or distortion. Replace the float if fuel has leaked into it.
3. Check the throttle and choke shaft bores for wear on an out-of-round condition. Damage or wear to the throttle arm, shaft, or shaft bore will often require replacement of the throttle body. These parts require a close tolerance of fit; wear may allow air leakage, which could affect starting and idling.

NOTE: *Throttle shafts and bushings are not included in overhaul kits. They can be purchased separately.*

Model 5200

Year	(9510)* Carburetor Identification	Dry Float Level (in.)	Pump Hole Setting	Choke Plate Pulldown (in.)	Fast Idle Cam Linkage (in.)	Fast Idle (rpm)	Dechoke (in.)	Choke Setting
1978	D8BE-FA D8EE-JA	0.453	2	0.236	0.118	①	0.236	2 Rich
	D8EE-DA	0.453	4	0.236	0.118	①	0.236	2 Rich
	D8BE-HA D8EE-CA, KA D8ZE-SA, RA	0.453	2	0.236	0.118	①	0.236	1 Rich
1979	D9ZE-ND	0.460	3	0.236	0.118	1800	0.236	2 Rich
	D9BE-AAA, D9BE-ABA, D9EE-AMA	0.460	2	0.236	0.118	1800	0.236	2 Rich
	D9EE-ANA, D9EE-ASA, D9EE-AYA	0.460	2	0.236	0.118	1800	0.236	1 Rich
1980	D9EE-APA, ANA	0.460	2	0.236	0.118	②	0.236	1 Rich
	EOEE-GA, RA	0.460	2	0.196	0.078	②	0.196	①
	EOEE-JA, TA	0.460	2	0.196	0.078	②	0.196	①
	EOEE-JC, TC	0.460	—	0.196	0.078	②	0.196	①
	EOEE-JD, TD	0.460	2	0.177	0.078	②	0.196	①
	EOEE-AEA, AFA	0.460	2	0.196	0.078	②	0.196	①
	EOZE-ACB	0.460	—	0.275	0.157	②	0.236	①
	EOZE-AZA	0.460	2	0.275	0.157	②	0.393	①
	EOZE-AAA	0.460	3	0.275	0.157	②	0.236	①
	EOZE-ACA	0.460	2	0.275	0.157	②	0.236	①
	EOZE-ATA	0.460	2	0.275	0.118	②	0.236	①
1981	EIZE-YA	.41–.51	2	0.200	.080	②	0.200	①
	EOEE-RB	.41–.51	2	0.200	.080	②	0.200	①
	EIZE-VA	.41–.51	2	0.200	.080	②	0.200	①
	D9EE-ANA	.41–.51	2	0.240	0.720	②	0.200	①
	D9EE-APA	.41–.51	2	0.240	0.120	②	0.200	①

Model 5200 (continued)

Year	(9510)* Carburetor Identification	Dry Float Level (in.)	Pump Hole Setting	Choke Plate Pulldown (in.)	Fast Idle Cam Linkage (in.)	Fast Idle (rpm)	Dechoke (in.)	Choke Setting
1982	E1ZE-ADB	.41–.51	3	0.275	0.240	1600	0.393	①
	E1ZE-ACA	.41–.51	2	0.200	.080	1800	0.196	①
	E1BE-RA	.41–.51	2	0.200	.080	1800	0.196	①
	E1ZE-YA	.41–.51	2	0.200	.080	2000	0.196	①
	E1ZE-VA	.41–.51	2	0.200	.080	2000	0.196	①
	E2ZE-AFA	.41–.51	2	0.236	0.118	1800	0.236	①
	E2ZE-AHA	.41–.51	2	0.236	0.118	2000	0.236	①
	E2ZE-ABA	.41–.51	2	0.236	0.118	2000	0.236	①
	E2ZE-AGA	.41–.51	2	0.236	0.118	2000	0.236	①
	E2ZE-AAA	.41–.51	2	0.236	0.118	2000	0.236	①

*Basic carburetor number
① See underhood specifications sticker

4. Inspect the idle mixture adjusting needles for burrs or grooves. Any such condition requires replacement of the needle, or you will not be able to obtain a satisfactory idle.

5. Test the accelerator pump check valves. They should pass air one way but not the other. Test for proper seating by blowing and sucking on the valve. Replace the valve if necessary. If the valve is satisfactory, wash the valve again to remove breath moisture.

6. Check the bowl cover for warped surfaces with a straightedge.

7. Closely inspect the valves and seats for wear and damage, replacing as necessary.

8. After the carburetor is assembled, check the choke valve for freedom of operation.

Carburetor overhaul kits are recommended for each overhaul. These kits contain all gaskets and new parts to replace those which deteriorate most rapidly. Failure to replace all parts supplied with the kit (especially gaskets) can result in poor performance.

Some carburetor manufacturers supply overhaul kits of three basic types: minor repair; major repair; and gasket kits. Basically, they contain the following:

Minor Repair Kits:

- All gaskets
- Float needle valve
- Volume control screw
- All diaphragms
- Spring for the pump diaphragm

Major Repair Kits:

- All jets and gaskets
- All diaphragms
- Float needle valve
- Volume control screw
- Pump ball valve
- Float
- Complete intermediate rod
- Intermediate pump lever
- Some cover hold-down screws and washers

Gasket Kits:

- All gaskets

After cleaning and checking all components, reassemble the carburetor, using new parts and referring to the exploded view. When reassembling, make sure that all screw and jets are tight in their seats, but do not overtighten as the tips will be distorted.

Tighten all screws gradually, in rotation. Do not tighten idle mixture needle valves into their seats; uneven idling will result. Always use new gaskets. Always adjust the float for correct drop and level.

5200 Carburetor Adjustment

FLOAT LEVEL ADJUSTMENT

1. Remove the air cleaner.
2. Disconnect the fuel and deceleration valve (if equipped) hoses from the carburetor.
3. Remove the small clip that attaches the choke rod to the choke plate shaft and disconnect the rod from the shaft.
4. Remove the screws that attach the upper body of the carburetor to the main body of the carburetor and carefully lift the upper body off the main body. Be careful not to tear the upper body gasket.
5. Turn the carburetor upper body upside down and measure the clearance between the bottom of each float and the bottom of the carburetor upper body. The clearance should be 0.420 in. (no. 58 drill bit).
6. If the clearance is incorrect, bend the float level adjusting tang to correct.

NOTE: *Both floats must be adjusted to the same clearance.*

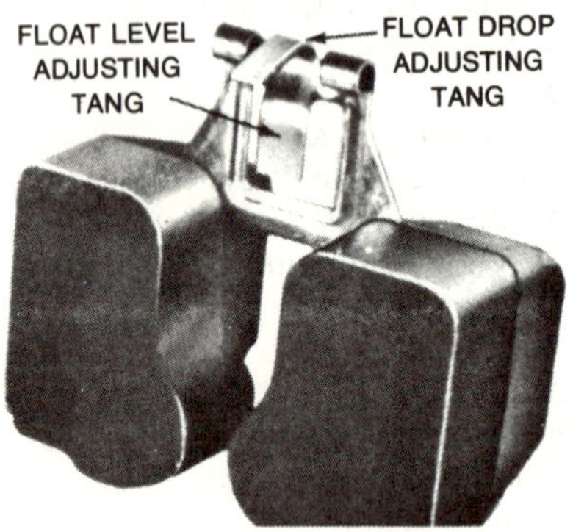

Float adjustment—5200 carburetor

7. Position the upper body and gasket of the main body of the carburetor and connect the choke rod to the choke plate lever. Install the choke rod attaching clip in the hole in the rod.
8. Install the upper body attaching screws.
9. Connect the fuel and deceleration valve hoses to the carburetor.
10. Install the air cleaner.

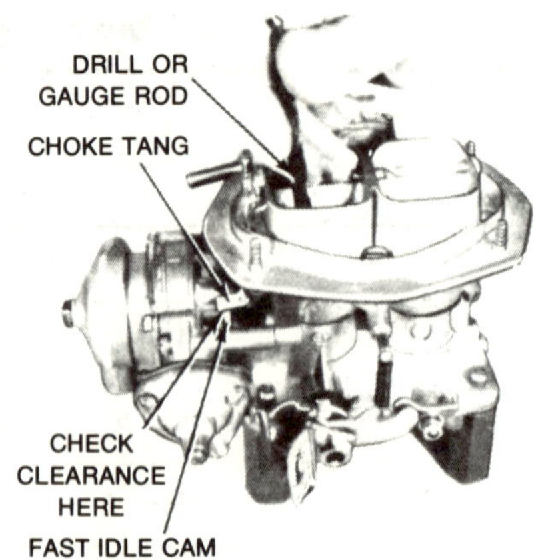

Fast idle cam adjustment—5200 carburetor

FAST IDLE CAM ADJUSTMENT

1. Insert a $^5/_{32}$ in. drill between the lower edge of the choke plate and the air horn wall.
2. With the fast idle screw held on the second step of the fast idle cam, measure the clearance between the tang of the choke lever and the arm on the fast idle cam.
3. Bend the choke lever tang to adjust it if it is not up to specification.

CHOKE PLATE PULLDOWN ADJUSTMENT

1. Remove the choke thermostatic spring cover.
2. Pull the water cover and the thermostatic spring cover assembly out of the way.
3. Set the fast idle cam on the second step.
4. Push the diaphragm stem against its stop and insert the specified gauge between the lower edge of the choke valve and the air horn wall.
5. Apply sufficient pressure to the upper edge of the choke valve to take up any slack in the choke linkage.
6. Turn the adjusting screw in or out to adjust the choke plate-to-air horn clearance.

SECONDARY THROTTLE STOP SCREW

1. Turn the secondary throttle stop screw counterclockwise until the secondary throttle plate seats in its bore.
2. Turn the screw clockwise until it touches the tab on the secondary throttle lever, then add ¼ turn.

ELECTRIC CHOKE ADJUSTMENT

For electric choke procedures refer to the 2150 carburetor section.

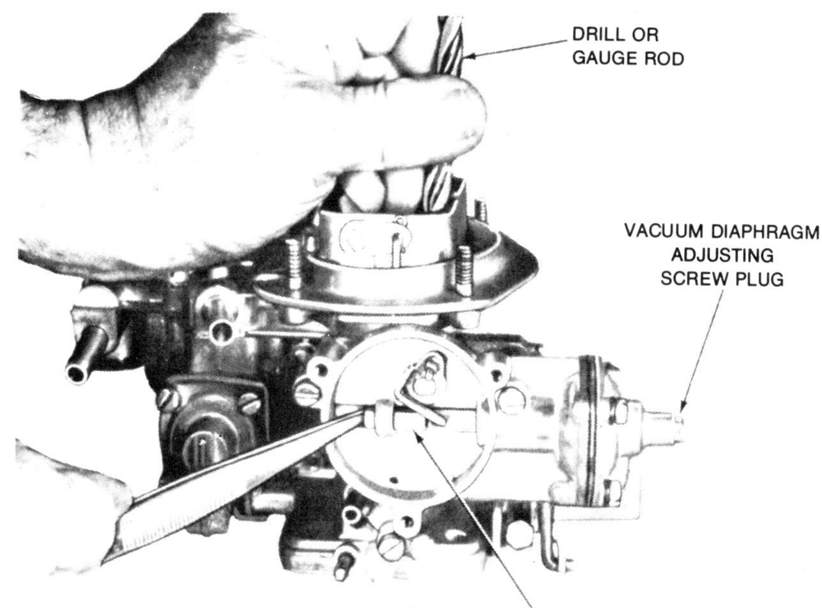

Choke pulldown adjustment—5200 carburetor

FAST IDLE SPEED ADJUSTMENT

1. Remove the air cleaner assembly and plug the vacuum line at the source of vacuum.
2. Set the parking brake and block the wheels.
3. Connect a tachometer to the engine.
4. Start the engine and warm up to normal operating temperature.
5. Reinstall any distributor vacuum lines that were removed and check the ignition timing.
6. Remove the EGR vacuum line at the valve and plug the line.
7. If applicable, remove the spark delay valve and route the primary distributor advance vacuum signal directly to the primary distributor diaphragm (advance side). If the distributor has a secondary (retard) diaphragm, leave the vacuum connection intact.
8. Disconnect and plug the fuel deceleration valve hose (if so equipped) at the carburetor connection.
9. Air conditioner, if so equipped, must be "off."
10. With the engine running at normal operating temperature and choke plate fully opened (automatic transmission in Park and manual in Neutral) set the throttle so that the fast idle adjustment screw contacts the kickdown step of the choke cam and adjust the fast idle adjusting screw to obtain the specified rpm according to vehicle specifications.
11. Set the throttle to the high step of the choke cam and allow the engine to run approximately 5 seconds.
12. Rotate the choke cam until the fast idle adjustment screw contacts the kickdown step of the choke cam. After allowing the rpm to stabilize, recheck fast idle rpm and readjust if necessary by repeating Steps 10–12 until the specified fast idle speed is obtained and can be repeated.
13. Stop the engine and install air cleaner and vacuum lines.

Overhaul-Model 5200

DISASSEMBLY

During disassembly operations, refer to the exploded view of the components which accompanies this section. Keep the parts from the different sections of the carburetor separated. Clean and inspect all components. Wash components (except the accelerating pump diaphragm and any other rubber goods) in a suitable commercial solvent. Rinse all solvent-cleaned parts in kerosene to remove traces of the cleaning solvent, then dry with compressed air.

1. Remove the float bowl cover screws and washers. Disconnect the choke rod by removing the plastic retaining bushings and remove the float bowl cover.
2. Turn the bowl cover over and remove the choke rod seal, the float hinge pin, the float, fuel inlet needle and seat with gasket.

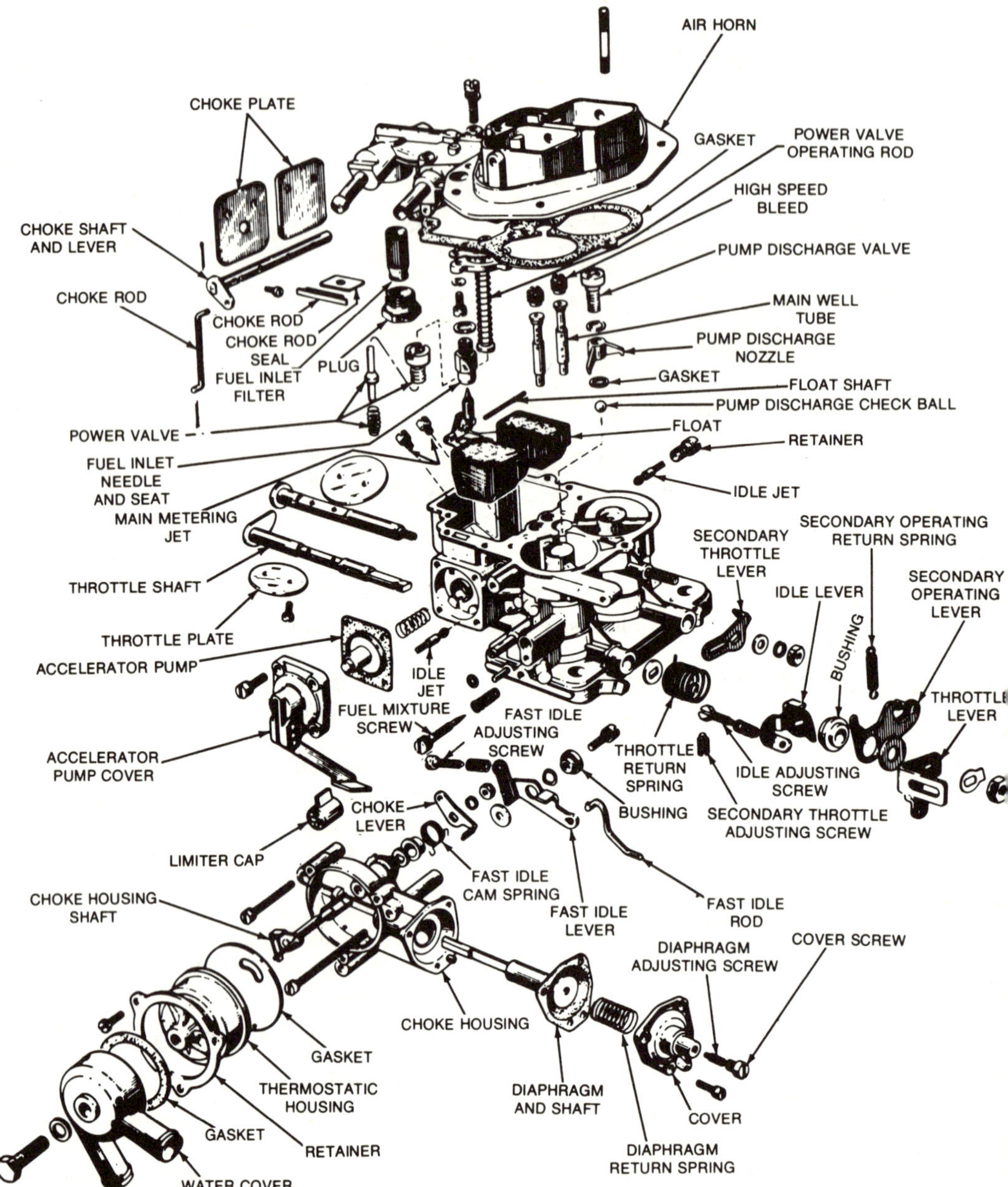

Exploded view—5200 carburetor

3. Remove the three enrichment (power) valve vacuum diaphragm screws, washers and diaphragm.

4. Remove the three vent cover/solenoid attaching screws and remove the cover.

5. Pry the vent arm pivot pin toward the fuel inlet seat and remove the pin and vent arm.

6. Remove the E-clip from the vent diaphragm stem, remove diaphragm assembly, vent spring, retainer and valve.

7. Remove the choke cover housing retaining screws; remove the ring, housing and electric heater assembly.

8. Remove the choke housing assembly mounting screws—note from where the different length screws come. Slip the housing away from the carb body and disengage the fast idle rod. Remove the O-ring gasket from the vacuum passage.

9. Remove the choke shaft nut and washer, choke lever, fast idle cam, fast idle lever screw and fast idle lever spring.

10. Remove the choke diaphragm cover

screws, the cover, return spring, diaphragm and rod assembly.

11. Remove the four accelerator pump-to-body screws and pump cover assembly. Remove the pump diaphragm and return spring.

12. From the center of the main body of the carburetor remove the accelerator pump discharge screw assembly, pump discharge nozzle and two gaskets. Cover the main body with your hand, invert it and catch the two pump discharge balls as they free the discharge passage.

13. Remove the primary high speed bleeds and main well tube and the secondary high speed bleeds and main well tube. Be sure to note the sizes of the air bleed plugs and main well tubes so they may be reinstalled in the proper position.

14. Remove the primary and secondary main metering jets. Note the different size jets and their proper locations.

15. Remove the power valve and gasket. Remove the secondary idle jet retainer and jets located on the side of the carburetor body.

16. Turn the idler limiter cap in (clockwise) to the stop. Remove the limiter cap. Count the turns required to lightly seat the idle adjustment needle. Count to the nearest $^{1}/_{16}$ turn. Remove the needle and spring.

17. Remove the secondary throttle operating lever return spring. Remove the primary throttle shaft nut, lock washer, flat washer and accelerator pump cam. Remove the idle speed screws and spring from the throttle shaft lever.

ASSEMBLY

1. Install the idle speed screw and spring. Install the accelerator pump cam, flat washer, lock washer and nut on the primary throttle shaft.

2. Install the idle mixture adjusting screw. Turn the screw in until it gently bottoms. Back out the needle screw the exact number of turns recorded when you disassembled it. Install a new limiter cap with its stop resting on the lean side of the stop on the carb body.

3. Install the idle jet and retainer assembly on the secondary side. Install the power valve gasket and power valve. Install the primary and secondary main jets, primary and secondary main well tubes and high speed bleeds.

NOTE: *Be sure they are reinstalled in the correct place.*

4. Install the two accelerator pump discharge check balls. Install the pump discharge nozzle and the two gaskets. Install the accelerator pump discharge screw.

5. Install the accelerator pump return spring, pump diaphragm and cover. Start the four pump cover screws and, holding the pump operating lever slightly opened to align the diaphragm gasket, tighten the four screws evenly.

6. Install the automatic choke diaphragm adjusting screw. Adjust the screw so that the threads are flush with the inside of the cover. Install the choke diaphragm and rod assembly, the return spring and cover. Install the cover screws and lockwashers.

7. Install the fast idle adjusting screw and spring on the fast idle arm. Install the flat spacer, fast idle arm and attaching screw. Install the choke shaft into the housing and position the fast idle cam on the housing post. Install the choke lever, lockwasher and nut.

8. Place a new O-ring washer on the vacuum passage. Install the fast idle rod with the end with one tab in the fast idle adjusting lever and the other end in the long leg of the housing. Install the retaining screws.

9. Adjust the choke plate pull down. Refer to the adjustment section of this chapter.

10. Install the electric choke heater, housing, retaining ring and attaching screws. Index the housing and tighten the screws.

NOTE: *Be sure that the choke plate is in the full closed position before installing the electric choke heater element.*

11. With fuel bowl cover inverted, install bowl vent diaphragm, vent valve, spring, retainer and E-clip. Position vent arm and install vent arm pivot pin. Install vent valve cover/solenoid with the three retaining screws and tighten them.

12. Install the needle seat and gasket. Install the power valve vacuum diaphragm. Depress the spring and install the screws and washers to finger tightness. Hold the stem so the diaphragm is horizontal and tighten the screw equally.

13. Install the float needle clip on the float tab, position the float and needle, install the needle into the seat and secure the float with the float pivot shaft.

14. Adjust the dry float setting and the float drop. Refer to the adjustment section in this chapter.

15. Install the choke rod seal. Install the choke rod and fasten it to the choke lever. Install the retaining clip.

16. Place the bowl cover gasket in position, install the choke link into position on

the choke lever and install the retaining clip.

17. Place the float bowl cover in position and install the retaining bolts. Tighten them evenly.

18. Install the throttle positioner.

Holley 6500 Feedback Carburetor

California models of the Fairmont and Zephyr using the 4 cylinder, 2.3 liter, 140 cubic inch engine may be equipped with a Feedback Engine Control system. This system requires more precise fuel metering and is equipped with the Holley/Weber 6500 Feedback carburetor.

The Holley/Weber 6500 Feedback carburetor is basically a Model 5200 carburetor that has an externally-variable auxiliary fuel metering system in place of the usual enrichment valve.

ADJUSTMENTS

Refer to the Model 5200 section.

NOTE: *If the feedback valve piston and diaphragm assembly is removed for any reason it is essential that the following procedure is followed during reassembly.*

1. Apply one drop of Loctite® 271 or equivalent to the threads of the retaining screw holes.

2. Position the feedback fuel diaphragm and piston assembly over the spring, so that the attaching holes are aligned with the tapped holes in the air horn. Make sure the diaphragm spring is properly installed with one end of the spring over the end of the adjustment screw and the other centered within the cupped washer of the diaphragm and piston assembly.

3. Install the three retaining screws and tighten to 4–5 in. lbs.

Carter YFA Adjustment

AUTOMATIC CHOKE HOUSING ADJUSTMENT

By rotating the spring housing of the automatic choke, the reaction of the choke to engine temperature can be controlled. To adjust, remove the air cleaner assembly, loosen the thermostatic spring housing retaining screws and set the spring housing to the specified index mark. After adjusting the setting, tighten the retaining screws and replace the air cleaner assembly to the carburetor.

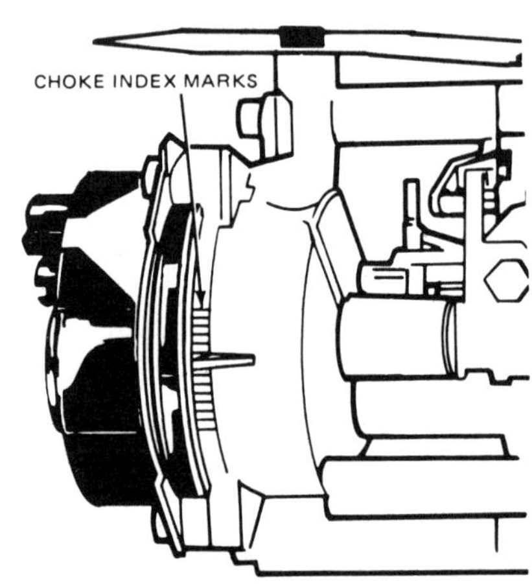

Choke housing index marks

CHOKE PLATE PULL-DOWN CLEARANCE

1. Remove the carburetor air cleaner and remove the choke thermostatic spring housing.

2. Bend a section of 0.026-inch-diameter wire at a 90° angle, approximately ⅛ inch from one end.

3. Insert the bent end of the wire gauge between the choke piston slot and the right-

Carburetor Specifications
Carter YFA

Year	*Float Level (in.)*	*Fast Idle Setting (in.)*	*Choke Plate Pulldown Clearance (in.)*	*Dechoke Clearance (minimum in.)*	*Choke Housing Adjustment*
1978	25/32	.140	.230 ①	.250	2 Rich
1979–80	25/32	.140	.260 ②	.250	1 Rich

①.200 for carb. D8DE-EA
②D9BE-RA—.180
D9DE-AA. D9DE-BA and D9DE-EA—.230

hand slot in the choke housing. Rotate the choke piston lever counterclockwise until the gauge is snug in the piston slot.

4. Exert light pressure upon the choke piston lever to hold the gauge in position. Check the specified clearance with a drill of the correct diameter between the lower edge of the choke plate and the carburetor bore.

5. Choke plate pull-down clearance may be adjusted by bending the choke piston lever as required to obtain the desired clearance. It is recommended the choke piston lever be removed prior to bending, in order to prevent distorting the piston link.

6. Install the choke thermostatic spring housing and gasket, and set the housing to the proper specification.

FLOAT LEVEL ADJUSTMENT

The float level is adjusted dry in the following manner: Remove the carburetor air horn and gasket from the carburetor. Using a gauge made to the proper dimension, invert the air horn assembly and check the clearance between the top of the float and the bottom of the air horn. Float level is ⅜ inch. When checking the float level, the air horn should be held at eye level and the float lever arm should be resting on the pin of the needle valve. Bend the float lever arm to adjust the float clearance. However, do not bend the tab at the end of the float arm, as this will prevent the float from bottoming in the fuel bowl when the bowl is empty. Using a new gasket, install the carburetor air horn.

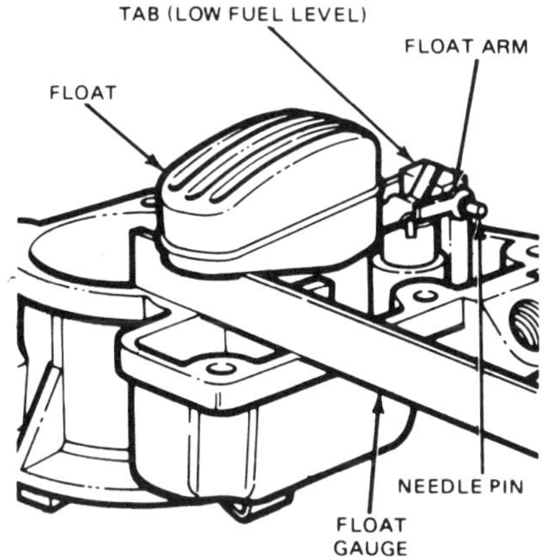

Float level adjustment—YBA carburetor

METERING ROD ADJUSTMENT

With the carburetor air horn and gasket removed from the carburetor, unscrew the idle speed adjusting screw until the throttle plate

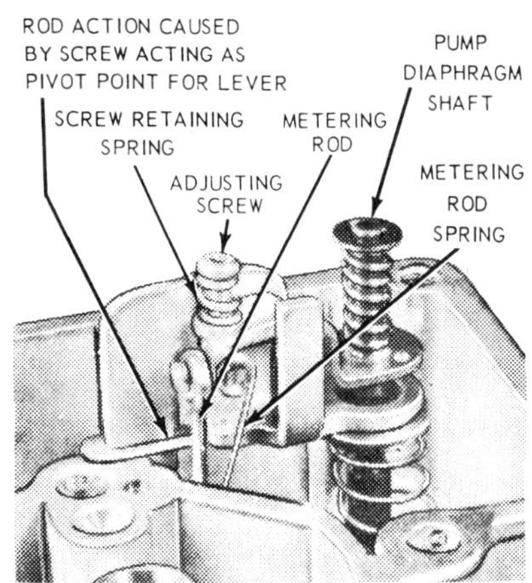

Metering rod adjustment—YBA carburetor

is tightly closed in the throttle bore. Press downward on the end of the diaphragm shaft until the metering rod arm contacts the lifter link at the diaphragm stem. With the metering rod in the preceding position, turn the rod adjustment screw (see accompanying illustration) until the metering rod just bottoms in the body casting. Turn the metering rod adjusting screw one additional turn in the clockwise direction. Install the carburetor air horn along with a new gasket.

DECHOKE CLEARANCE ADJUSTMENT

1. Remove the air cleaner.

2. Hold the throttle plate to the full open position while closing the choke plate as far as possible without forcing it. Use a drill of the proper diameter (see Specifications) to check the clearance between the choke plate and air horn.

3. To adjust, bend the arm on the choke trip lever of the throttle lever. To decrease the clearance, bend the arm downward; to increase the clearance bend the arm upward. Recheck the clearance after making the adjustment.

FAST IDLE CAM INDEX SETTING

1. Position the fast idle screw on the kick-down step of the fast idle cam against the shoulder of the high step.

2. Adjust by bending the choke plate connecting rod to obtain the specified clearance between the lower edge of the choke plate and the carburetor bore.

Overhaul—Carter YFA

DISASSEMBLY

During the disassembly operations, refer to the exploded view of components which ac-

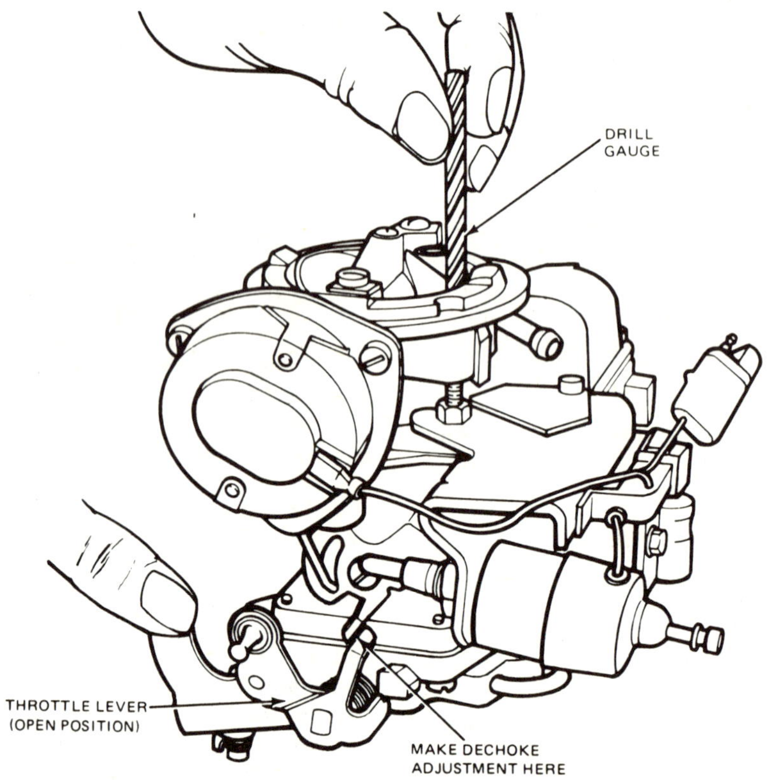

Dechoke clearance adjustment—YBA carburetor

companies this section. Separate the throttle connector rod retainer from the choke connector rod and remove the rod from the fast idle link. Remove the automatic choke components, including housing retaining screws,

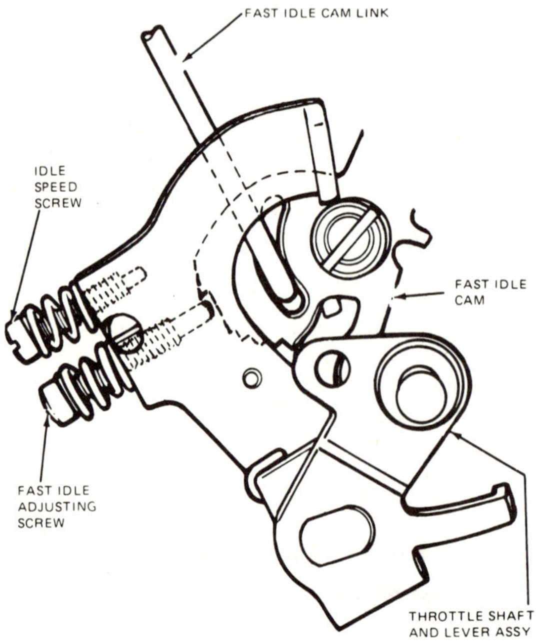

Fast idle cam setting—YBA carburetor

housing assembly, housing gasket and baffle plate, trip lever and pin assembly and fast idle link. Remove the air horn retaining screws, the dashpot and bracket, and the air horn and air horn gasket from the carburetor main body. With the air horn assembly inverted, remove the float pin and the float and lever assembly. With the air horn assembly turned upright, catch the needle pin, spring, needle and seat. Remove the float needle seat and gasket. Remove the air cleaner bracket and the choke plate retaining screws. If necessary, the ends of the screws may be filed and new screws used during assembly. Remove the choke plate. With the fast idle cam spring disengaged from the cam spring lever on the choke piston lever and shaft assembly, rotate the choke shaft and piston assembly in the counterclockwise direction until the choke piston is withdrawn from the choke piston cylinder. Remove the choke assembly from the air horn and remove the piston pin, piston, fast idle cam and spring from the piston lever and shaft assembly. With the main body casting inverted, catch the accelerating pump check needle as it falls out. With the throttle shaft arm spring disconnected, loosen the throttle shaft arm screw and remove the arm and pump connector link. Remove the re-

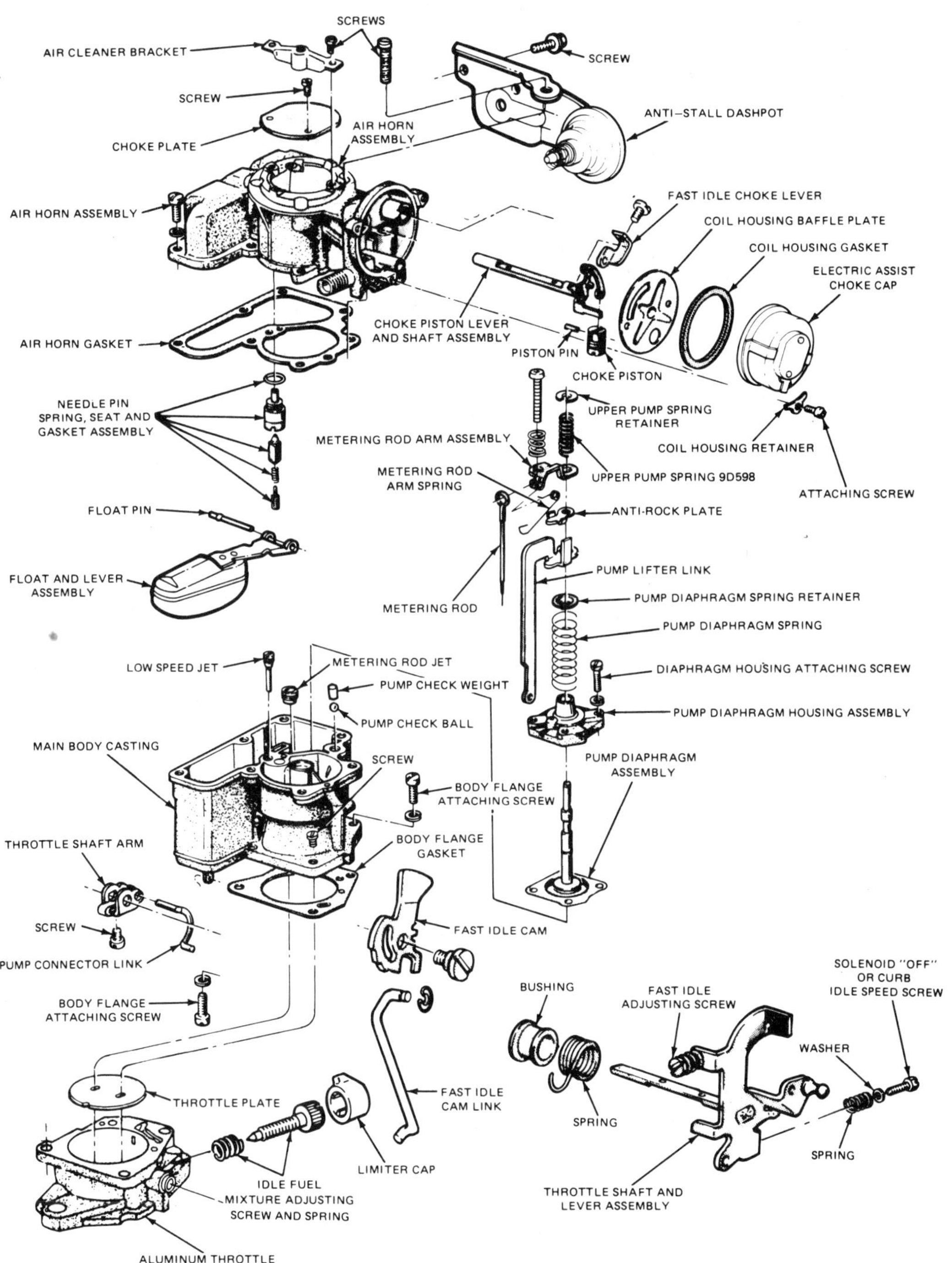

YBA system illustration (1978)

taining screws of the accelerating pump diaphragm housing and withdraw the diaphragm assembly, lifter link, metering rod and fuel bowl baffle plate as a unit. Separate the metering rod arm spring from the metering rod and remove the metering rod from the assembly. Compress the upper pump spring and remove the retainer. Lift off the upper spring and remove the metering rod arm assembly and pump lifter link from the diaphragm shaft. Compress the lower spring and remove the spring retainer, spring and pump diaphragm assembly from the housing. Use a special tool or a screwdriver of appro-

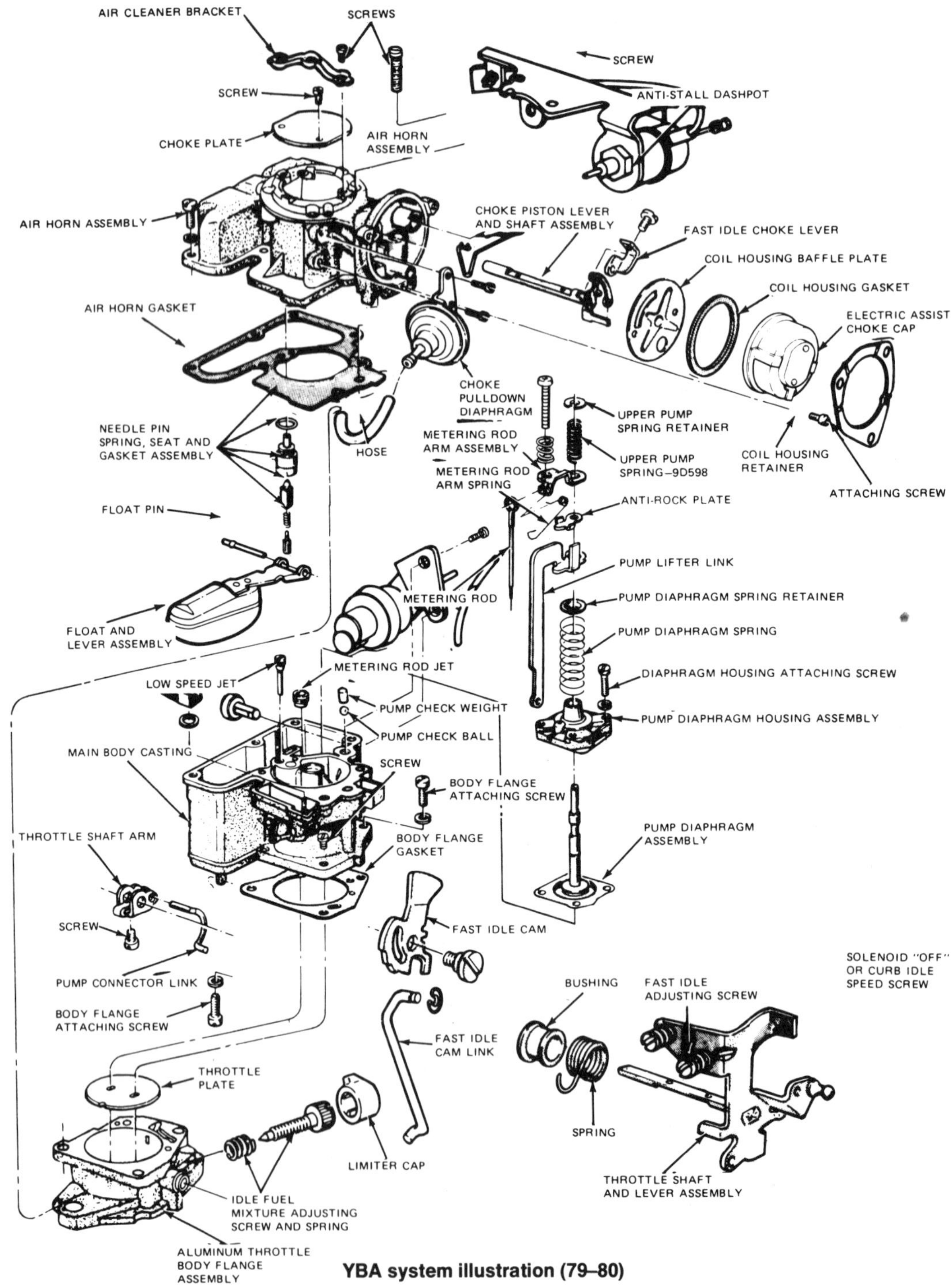

YBA system illustration (79–80)

priate size to remove the low speed jet and metering rod jet. Remove the retaining screws which attach the throttle body flange to the main body casting and separate the components. Remove the gasket between the throttle body and main body. Filing the ends if necessary, remove the screws which retain the throttle plate (use new screws during assembly) and slide the throttle shaft and lever assembly out of the throttle body flange.

NOTE: *Do not remove the idle mixture*

limiter caps or the mixture screws from the throttle body.

ASSEMBLY

Prior to assembly, clean and inspect all components. Wash all components (except the accelerating pump diaphragm and the antistall dashpot assembly) in a suitable commercial solvent. Rinse all solvent-cleaned parts in kerosene to remove traces of the cleaning solvent, then dry with compressed air. Do not use wire or drills to clean openings in the carburetor—use of such devices will enlarge the hole or passage being cleaned, thus changing the operating characteristics of the carburetor.

Install the throttle shaft and lever assembly to the throttle body flange, then position the throttle plate on its shaft so that the notch in the plate is lined up with the slotted idle port in the throttle body flange. Install the throttle plate retaining screws so that they are snug, but not tight. Move and rotate the shaft to ensure that the throttle plate does not bind in its bore and reposition the plate if necessary. Tighten the throttle plate retaining screws and stake or peen into place.

Using a new gasket, join the main body casting with the throttle body flange and evenly tighten the retaining screws. Using the proper size screwdriver or special jet tool, install the metering rod jet and low speed jet. Install the pump diaphragm to the accelerating pump diaphragm housing and position the lower spring on the diaphragm shaft and housing. Install the spring retainer, pump lifter link, metering rod arm and spring assembly, and the upper spring on the diaphragm shaft. Depress the spring and install the upper retainer. Install the metering rod to the meter rod arm as shown in the illustration accompanying the preceding section. Line up the pump diaphragm with its housing and install the retaining screws. Position the fuel bowl baffle plate on the pump assembly and line up the pump housing, pump lifter link, metering rod and baffle plate with the main body casting.

NOTE: *Be sure that the vacuum passage in the diaphragm housing is lined up with that of the main body.*

Install the assembly to the main body casting, being sure that the pump lifter link is engaged with the main body, that the baffle plate has its grooves in the main body, and that the metering rod is inserted into the metering rod jet. Install the pump housing screws so that they are snug, but not tight. Pushing down on the diaphragm shaft to compress the diaphragm, tighten the retaining screws evenly. Adjust the metering rod. Install the throttle shaft arm and pump connector link to the throttle shaft and pump lifter link. Tighten the locking screw and connect the throttle shaft arm return spring. Install the fast idle cam and spring to the choke lever and shaft assembly. Install the choke piston and pin to the choke piston lever and shaft, then disengage the cam spring from the lever and install the choke shaft assembly to the air horn. Align the piston with the cylinder, rotate the shaft assembly in the clockwise direction until the piston pin is inside the cylinder. Position the cam spring on the cam spring lever of the choke lever assembly.

NOTE: *When the cam spring is properly positioned, the tangs on the cam and the choke lever will be lined up with one in front of the other.*

With the choke plate in position on the shaft, install the retaining screws without tightening fully. As with the throttle plate, move and rotate the shaft to ensure that the plate moves freely, then tighten the screws and peen or stake to secure.

Install the needle valve seat and gasket in the air horn. Invert the air horn and install the needle, pin spring, needle pin, float and lever, the float pin. Adjust the float lever, and float pin. Adjust the float level. Install the pump check needle to the main body casting and position the air horn (with new gasket) and the antistall dashpot and bracket on the main body. Secure the dashpot bracket and evenly tighten the screws attaching the air horn to the main body. Install the choke trip lever and fast idle link to the choke housing. Be sure that the lever and link properly engage each other and the choke piston lever and shaft. Install the coil housing, gasket and baffle plate (with identification mark facing outward). The gasket should be between the baffle and the coil housing, and the thermostatic spring should engage the tang of the choke lever. Install the retainers and screws, set the housing to the proper setting, and tighten the screws. Install the air cleaner bracket and attach the throttle connector rod retainer to the fast idle link. Install the choke connector rod to the throttle lever and fast idle link. Secure the air horn to the main body and connect the connector rod retainer to the choke connector rod.

Holley Model 1946/C Carburetor Adjustments

FAST IDLE CAM ADJUSTMENT

Fast idle cam position adjustment is necessary to make sure the fast idle screw contacts the various steps of the fast idle cam at the proper time during engine warm-up. This adjustment can be made with the carburetor on the engine (with the engine off) or with the carburetor removed from the engine.

1. With the fast idle speed adjusting screw contacting the second highest step of the fast idle cam (kickdown step), move the choke plate toward the closed position with light pressure on the choke lever or choke plate.

2. Check the fast idle cam setting using the specified size gauge or drill bit between the

Holley Model 1946

Year	Part Number	Float Level (in.)	Choke Pulldown (in.)	Dechoke (in.)	Fast Idle Cam (in.)	Accelerator Pump Stroke Slot
1978–79	All	①	.026	.250	.080	#2
1980	EOBE-ALA, AMA	①	.100	.150	.070	#2
	EOEE-ANA, APA	①	.100	.150	.070	#2
	EOZE-BBA, BAA	①	.120	.150	.086	#2
	EOZE-DA, EA	①	.110	.150	.070	#2
	EOZE-FA, GA	①	.110	.150	.070	#2
	EOBE-AA, CA	①	.100	.150	.070	#2
	EOBE-ZA, AAA	①	.115	.150	.090	#1
1981	EIBE-AFA	.69	.113	.150	.082	#2
	EIBE-AKA	.69	.113	.150	.082	#2
	EOBE-CA	.69	.100	.150	.070	#2
	EOBE-AA	.69	.100	.150	.070	#2
1982	EIBE-AGA	.69	.120	.150	.086	#2
	E2BE-CA	.69	.110	.150	.078	#2
	E2BE-BA	.69	.110	.150	.078	#2
	E2BE-JA	.69	.110	.150	.078	#2
	E2BE-HA	.69	.110	.150	.078	#2
	E2BE-TA	.69	.110	.150	.078	#2
	E2BE-SA	.69	.110	.150	.078	#2

① See text

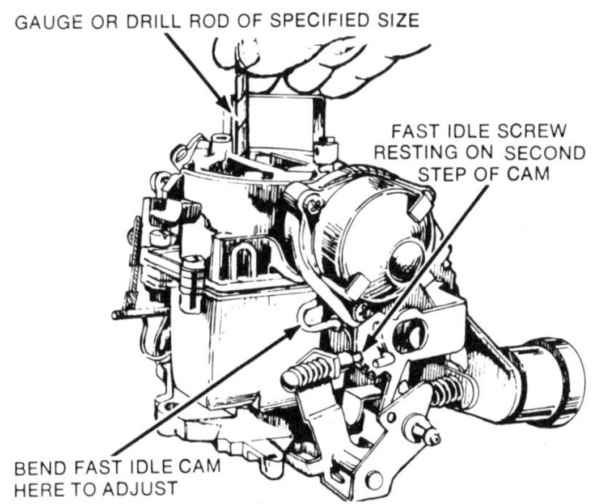

Fast idle cam position—1946/C carburetor

upper edge of the choke plate and the wall of the air horn.

3. Bend the fast idle cam link to achieve the specified setting.

NOTE: *To fabricate a convenient bending tool, file a slot in the blade of a flat screwdriver just wide enough to slip over the ⅛ inch fast idle cam link. The tool can also be used in other applications where bending a similar rod for adjustment is required.*

ACCELERATOR PUMP STROKE ADJUSTMENT

The acclerator pump stroke is pre-set at the factory and should not be adjusted to improve driveability.

DECHOKE CLEARANCE ADJUSTMENT

The dechoke feature provides a means of partially opening the choke plate during cold engine starts, even though the choke bimetal spring is holding it closed. By depressing the accelerator pedal fully, engines that may have become 'flooded' or that have stalled due to excessive choke action can be cleared. To adjust the dechoke clearance, proceed as follows:

1. With the engine off, hold the throttle in the wide open position.
2. Insert the specified size gauge or drill bit between the upper edge of the choke plate and the inner wall of the air horn.
3. With light pressure against the choke shaft lever, a slight drag should be felt as the gauge or drill bit is withdrawn.
4. To adjust, bend the tang on the throttle lever until the correct opening is obtained. The tab can be bent with a pair of pliers or other suitable bending tool. Bending the tab upward will increase the dechoke clearance.

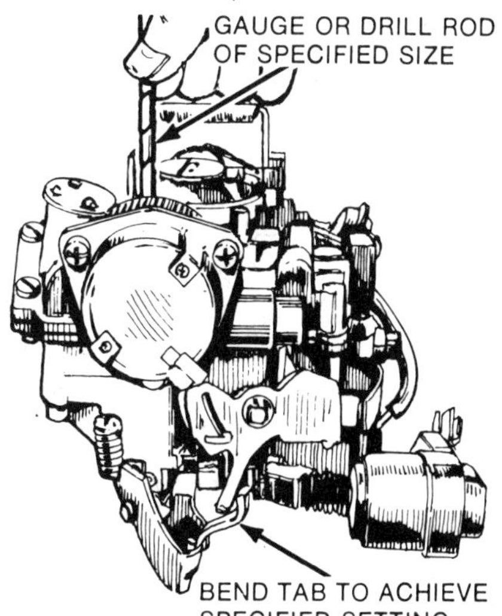

Dechoke clearance adjustment—1946/C carburetor

CHOKE PULLDOWN ADJUSTMENT

Adjust choke pulldown by bending the choke pulldown diaphragm connecting link. Use a gauge or drill bit of the specified diameter to check the clearance between the top of the choke plate and the air horn.

DASHPOT ADJUSTMENT

Adjust the dashpot by loosening the locknut and turning the dashpot in the bracket. The dashpot plunger must be fully collapsed. Use a feeler gauge to check the clearance between the plunger and the throttle pad.

EXTERNAL FUEL BOWL VENT ADJUSTMENT

Adjust the external fuel bowl vent with the carburetor installed on the engine and the ignition OFF, after having first adjusted the curb idle speed.

1. Remove the air cleaner assembly.
2. Disconnect the canister vent hose from the bowl vent tube on the air horn.
3. Attach a hand operated vacuum pump (Rotunda 21-0014 or equivalent) to the bowl vent tube, using a ⅜ inch adaptor.
4. Remove the three bowl vent cover screws located on the top of the air horn.
5. Remove the bowl vent cover gasket and spring.
6. Turn the vent adjusting screw (located on the nylon vent arm) clockwise until no more than ⅛ inch of the adjustment screw threads is visible above the vent arm.
7. While operating the hand vacuum pump, gradually turn the adjusting screw

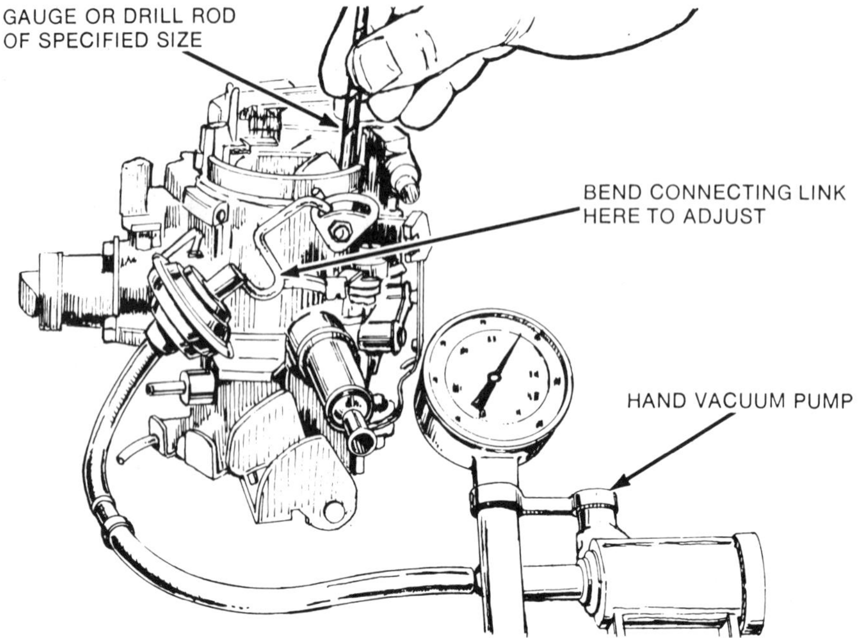

Choke pulldown adjustment—1946/C carburetor

counterclockwise ⅛ turn at a time until vacuum is indicated on the gauge, showing that the valve is closed. Release the vacuum and turn the adjusting screw ½ turn clockwise. Disconnect the hand vacuum pump and adaptor from the vent hose.

8. Reconnect the canister vent hose and install the air cleaner assembly.

FLOAT ADJUSTMENT

1. Remove the carburetor upper body (air horn) assembly.

2. With the upper body assembly removed, place a finger over the float hinge pin retainer and invert the main body. Catch the accelerator pump check ball and weight as they drop from the pump channel.

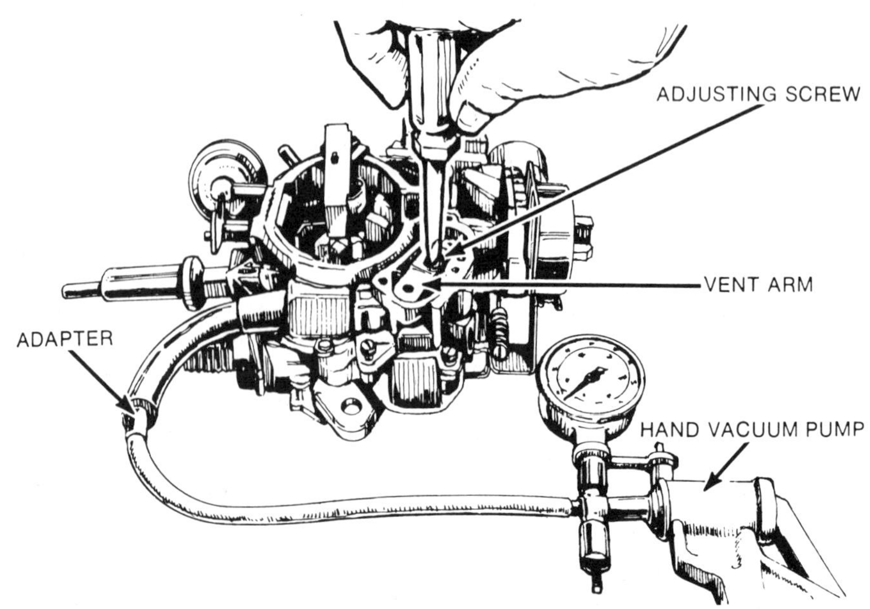

External pulldown adjustment—1946/C carburetor

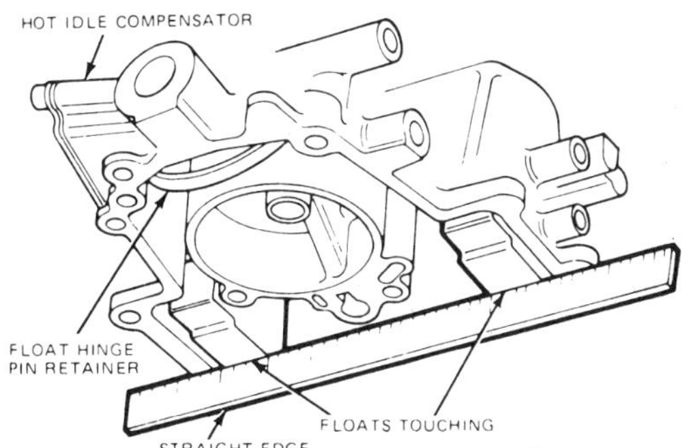

Float adjustment—1946/C carburetor

3. Using a straight edge, check the position of the floats as shown in the illustration.

- For all exc. California carburetors:

The straight edge should just touch the lowest point on the float (toe) when held as pictured.

- For California carburetors:

The straight edge should just contact the step (or heel) of the float.

4. Once the adjustment is correct, turn the main body right side up and check the float alignment. The float should move freely throughout its range without contacting the fuel bowl walls. If the float pontoons are misaligned, straighten by bending the float arms. Recheck the float level adjustment.

Overhaul-Holley 1946

DISASSEMBLY

To help prevent damage to the throttle plates, use the EGR spacer, a carburetor stand, or some bolts, held in place by nuts, as a holding device while you are working on the carburetor.

1. Remove the choke cover attaching screws, the retainer, bimetal cover and gasket.

CAUTION: *Do not put cover assembly in carb cleaner. Clean by wiping and blowing out with air.*

2. Remove the choke pulldown bracket screws (2), disconnect the vacuum hose from the carb body and remove the pulldown and linkage.

3. Remove the fuel bowl vent cover (3 screws). Remove the cover, spring and gasket from the air horn. Note the position of the spring when you remove it. Remove the bowl vent attaching screw and lift the bowl vent assembly from its seat.

CAUTION: *Do not put the bowl vent assembly in carb cleaner.*

4. Remove the fast idle cam, the choke lever retaining screw and the throttle return spring bracket. Remove the accelerator pump link, remember which slot it is located in for proper reassembly.

5. Remove the remaining air horn screws (7) and remove the air horn. Place the air horn upside down and remove the gasket. Make sure all of the gasket material is cleaned from the gasket surface.

CAUTION: *Do not scrape with a metal scraper; use a nylon or plastic scraper.*

6. A screw and a clamp attach the accelerator pump operating rod; remove them. Remove the pump spring retaining plate, rotate the pump rod and disconnect the pump drive spring and accelerator pump assembly. *Do not put the pump plunger in carb cleaner.*

7. Rotate the pump operating rod and remove the rod and grommet from the bowl cover.

8. The main well tube is not removable. Blow it out with air.

9. Remove the choke housing (3 screws).

10. Place your hand over the top of the main body and turn it upside down. The accelerator pump discharge weight and ball will be dislodged and fall in your hand. Retain them for reinstallation. Remove the fuel inlet valve and fitting, the float retainer, float shaft and float.

11. Remove the main metering jet with a jet wrench. If you do not own or cannot borrow a suitable jet wrench, a 3/8-inch deep slot screwdriver may be used.

CAUTION: *When using a screwdriver take care not to burr the edges of the main jet.*

12. Remove the enrichment valve. A tool can be made for this purpose by taking a 3/8-inch wide screwdriver and grinding a 1/1Y-inch wide by 3/8-inch deep slot in the blade. The slot will provide the necessary clearance for the enrichment valve stem.

13. Remove the hot idle compensator cover, the hot idle compensator valve, and the mounting gaskets from the main carb body.

14. Remove the three screws that attach the throttle body to the main body; separate the two parts.

Remove the low idle speed screw and the solenoid.

15. Turn the idle mixture cap on the leanest position (clockwise). The limiter cap stop should be against the throttle body. Remove the limiter cap.

16. Note the position of the idle mixture

screw slot. Slowly turn the screw in until it lightly seats, record the number of turns required. Remove the idle mixture screw.

ASSEMBLY

1. Install the idle mixture screw into the throttle body. Lightly seat it and back off the number of turns recorded when you remove it. Position the slot in the screw head at the same point as recorded when you removed the limiter cap. Install a new limiter cap, lean stop against the throttle body.

2. Install the low speed screw and solenoid. Position a new throttle body gasket on the main body and attach the throttle body. Before tightening the mounting screws, work the throttle several times to make sure it is not binding. Secure the mounting screws.

3. Install a new hot idle compensator valve gasket and the valve in the carb main body. Place the cover and gasket over the valve and secure the attaching screws.

4. Snap the small diameter end of the enrichment valve spring over the shoulder on the large end of the pin. Insert the pin into the valve body from the threaded end. Install the enrichment valve. Install the main metering jet.

5. Replace the hinge pin into the float arm and place the float into position. Install the hinge retainer and the fuel inlet valve with gasket.

6. Make dry float adjustment. Refer to the adjustment section in this chapter.

7. Install the accelerator ball and weight.

8. Install the accelerator pump operating rod and grommet on the air horn. Push the accelerator pump cup over the retaining tab on the end of the pump piston rod. Assemble the pump spring and retainer plate to the piston rod. The larger end of the spring should contact the retainer plate and seat over the shoulder.

9. While holding the accelerator pump assembly together, connect the pump operating rod through the slotted hole in the piston rod and rotate the rod so the plate can be positioned and the attaching screw installed. Tighten the attaching screw. Install the pump operating clamp and attaching screw.

10. Put a new air horn gasket in position over the alignment pin. Guide the accelerator pump cup into the pump well and the main well tube into the main well in the carb body. Align the air horn and lower it into place. Make sure the enrichment valve stem squarely contacts the enrichment valve pin.

11. Attach the air horn with seven screws.

1. Air cleaner bracket
2. Air cleaner bracket screw
3. Air horn
4. Screw
5. Choke pulldown lever
6. Choke shaft nut
7. Lockwasher
8. Choke bimetal spring cover
9. Screw
10. Choke cover retainer
11. Choke thermostatic housing locating disc
12. Choke shaft and lever assembly
13. Choke control lever
14. Screw
15. Screw
16. Choke plate
17. Accelerator pump operating rod
18. Accelerator pump rod grommet
19. Rod retaining clamp
20. Screw
21. Accelerator pump spring retaining spring
22. Screw
23. Accelerator pump piston stem
24. Accelerator pump spring
25. Accelerator pump piston cup
26. Fast idle cam link
27. Anti-diesel solenoid
28. Screw
29. Air horn gasket
30. Float-hinge retainer
31. Accelerator pump operating link
32. Retaining clip
33. Fast idle cam
34. Float assembly
35. Power valve body
36. Main metering jet
37. Power valve pin
38. Accelerator pump weight
39. Accelerator pump check ball
40. Power valve spring
41. Spring
42. Low idle (solenoid off) adjusting screw
43. Choke pulldown diaphragm assembly
44. Choke diaphragm vacuum hose
45. Fuel filter
46. Fuel inlet needle & seat assembly
47. Gasket
48. Main Body Assembly
49. Float hinge pin
50. Curb idle adjusting screw
51. Spring
52. Spring
53. Fast idle adjusting screw
54. Throttle shaft & lever assembly
55. Screw
56. Throttle plate
57. Throttle body assembly
58. Throttle body screw
59. Throttle body gasket
60. Throttle return spring bushing
61. Throttle return spring
62. Nut
63. Lock washer
64. Throttle return spring bracket

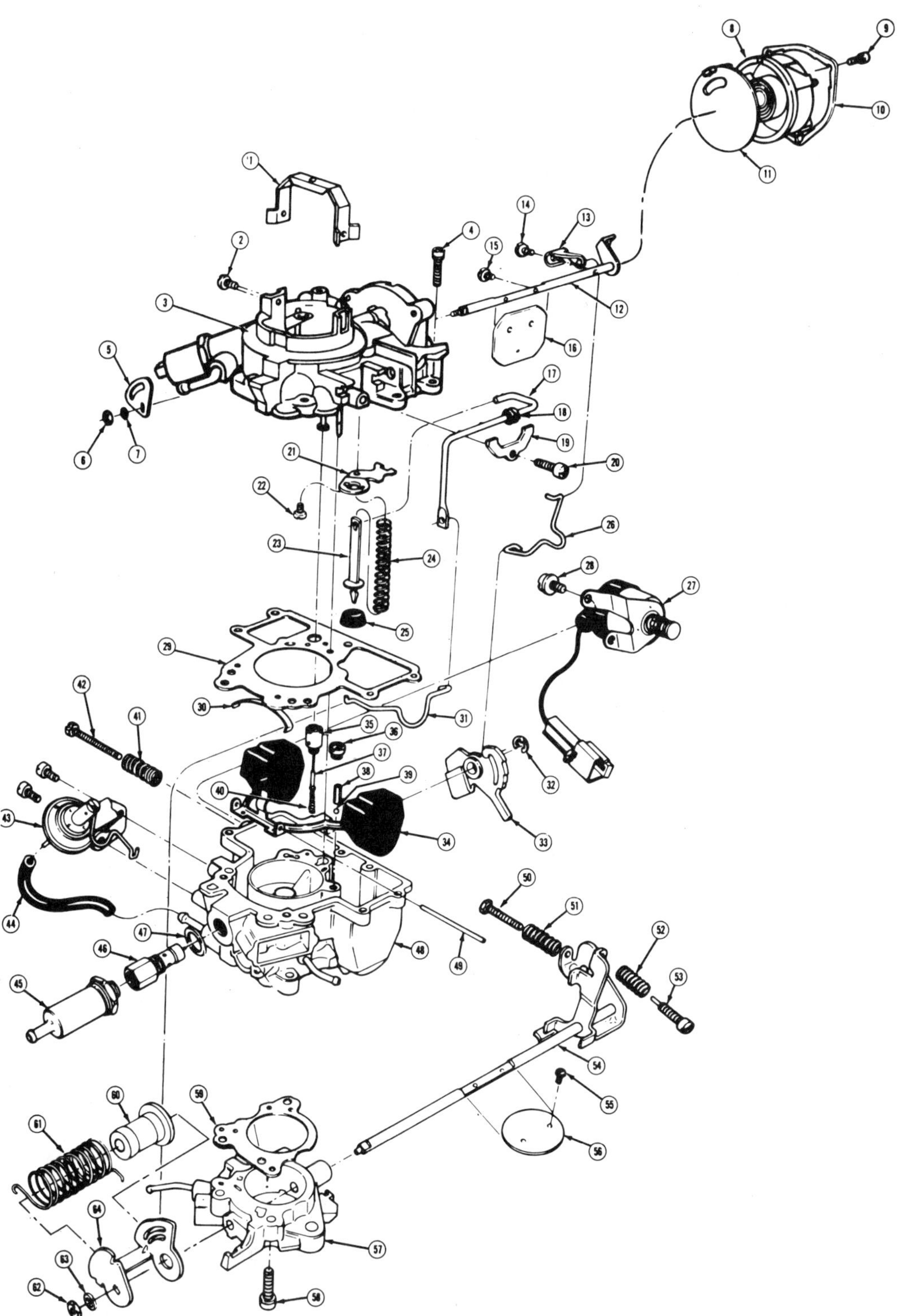

Exploded view—1946/C carburetor

Hook the accelerator pump link to the pump operating rod and the correct slot in the throttle return spring bracket. Slide the throttle return spring mounting bracket assembly over the throttle shaft ad align with the shoulders on the end of the shaft. Install the attaching nut and washer, engage the throttle return spring over the throttle stop.

12. Engage the fast idle cam link in the fast idle cam slot. Install the cam, retainer, choke control lever and screw.

13. Install the bowl vent assembly and hinge pin, secure with hinge pin screw. Place the small diameter of the bowl vent spring over the shoulder of the vent arm. Install the vent cover and gasket.

14. Connect the choke pulloff linkage, install the bracket and reconnect the vacuum line.

15. Install the bimetal choke, make sure the spring tab is engaged in the slotted choke shaft lever. Index the cover and tighten the mounting screws.

NOTE: *Be sure to use a new choke cap gasket.*

2150 2V Carburetor Adjustments

FLOAT LEVEL ADJUSTMENT—WET

1. Run the engine to normal operating temperature and stop the engine.
2. Remove the air cleaner.
3. Remove the air horn attaching screws and the carburetor identification tag. Leave the air horn and gasket in position on the carburetor main body and start the engine. Let the engine idle a few minutes, then remove the air cleaner stud and the air horn and gasket to provide access to the float assembly.
4. While the engine is idling use a standard depth scale to measure the vertical distance from the top machined surface of the carburetor main body to the level of the fuel in the fuel bowl. The measurement must be made at least a ¼ inch away from any vertical surface to assure an accurate reading. The fuel level should be measured at the point of contact of the float with the fuel. To raise the fuel level bend the flat tab contacting the fuel inlet valve upward and downward to lower it.
5. Install a new air horn gasket and install the air horn assembly.
6. Install the air cleaner anchor stud and install the air cleaner.

Float adjustment—wet (2150 carburetor)

FLOAT LEVEL ADJUSTMENT—DRY

The dry float adjustment is a preliminary fuel level adjustment only. The wet float adjustment must be made after the carburetor is mounted on the engine.

1. With the air horn removed, the air float raised and the inlet needle seated, check the distance between the top surface of the main body (gasket removed) and the surface of the float.
   a. Depress the float tab to seat the fuel inlet needle.
   b. Measure near the center of the float around ⅛ inch from the free end.
   c. Bend the tab on the float to adjust.

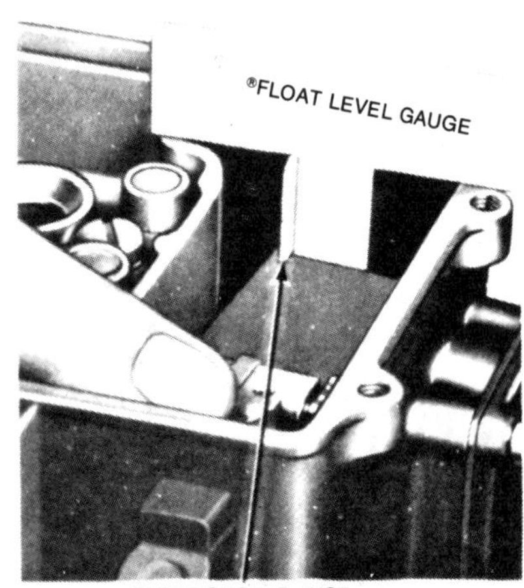

Float adjustment—dry (2150 carburetor)

ELECTRIC CHOKE

Linkage Check

1. With the engine off, remove the air cleaner and make sure that the holddown

Model 2150

Year	(9510)* Carburetor Identification	Dry Float Level (in.)	Wet Float Level (in.)	Pump Setting Hole # ①	Choke Plate Pulldown (in.)	Fast Idle Cam Linkage Clearance (in.)	Fast Idle (rpm)	Dechoke (in)	Choke Setting
1978–79	D84E-EA	7/16	13/16	2	0.110	②	⑨	—	3 Rich
	D8AE-JA	3/8	3/4	3	0.167	②	⑨	—	3 Rich
	D8BE-ACA	7/16	3/4	4	0.155	②	⑨	—	2 Rich
	D8BE-ADA	7/16	13/16	2	0.110	②	⑨	—	3 Rich
	D8BE-AEA	7/16	13/16	2	0.110	②	⑨	—	4 Rich
	D8BE-AFA	7/16	13/16	2	0.110	②	⑨	—	4 Rich
	D8BE-MB	3/8	13/16	3	0.122	②	⑨	—	Index
	D8DE-HA	19/32	13/16	3	0.157	②	⑨	—	Index
	D8KE-EA	19/32	13/16	2	0.135	②	⑨	—	3 Rich
	D8OE-BA	3/8	3/4	3	0.167	②	⑨	—	3 Rich
	D8OE-EA	19/32	13/16	2	0.136	②	⑨	—	Index
	D8OE-HA	7/16	13/16	3	0.180	②	⑨	—	2 Rich
	D8SE-CA	19/32	13/16	3	0.150	②	⑨	—	2 Rich
	D8ZE-TA	3/8	3/4	4	0.135	②	⑨	—	Index
	D8ZE-UA	3/8	3/4	4	0.135	②	⑨	—	Index
	D8WE-DA	7/16	13/16	4	0.143	②	⑨	—	1 Rich
	D8YE-AB	3/8	13/16	3	0.122	②	⑨	—	Index
	D8SE-DA, EA	7/16	13/16	3	0.147	②	⑨	—	3 Rich
	D8SE-FA, GA	3/8	13/16	3	0.147	②	⑨	—	3 Rich
1980	EO4E-PA, RA	—	13/16	2	0.104	②	③	1/4	③
	EOBE-AUA	—	13/16	3	0.116	②	③	1/4	③
	EODE-SA, TA	—	13/16	2	0.104	②	③	1/4	③
	EOKE-CA, DA	—	13/16	3	0.116	②	③	1/4	③
	EOKE-GA, HA	—	13/16	3	0.116	②	③	1/4	③

Model 2150 (continued)

Year	(9510)* Carburetor Identification	Dry Float Level (in.)	Wet Float Level (in.)	Pump Setting Hole # ①	Choke Plate Pulldown (in.)	Fast Idle Cam Linkage Clearance (in.)	Fast Idle (rpm)	Dechoke (in)	Choke Setting
1980	EOKE-JA, KA	—	13/16	3	0.116	②	③	1/4	③
	D84E-TA, UA	—	13/16	2	0.125	②	③	1/4	③
	EO4E-ADA, AEA	—	13/16	2	0.104	②	③	1/4	③
	EO4E-CA	—	13/16	2	0.104	②	③	1/4	③
	EO4E-EA, FA	—	13/16	2	0.104	②	③	1/4	③
	EO4E-JA, KA	—	13/16	2	0.137	②	③	1/4	③
	EO4E-SA, TA	—	13/16	2	0.104	②	③	1/4	③
	EO4E-VA, YA	—	13/16	2	0.104	②	③	1/4	③
	EODE-TA, VA	—	13/16	2	0.104	②	③	1/4	③
	EOSE-GA, HA	—	13/16	2	0.104	②	③	1/4	③
	EOSE-LA, MA	—	13/16	2	0.104	②	③	1/4	③
	EOSE-NA	—	13/16	2	0.104	②	③	1/4	③
	EOSE-PA	—	13/16	2	0.137	②	③	1/4	③
	EOVE-FA	—	13/16	2	0.104	②	③	1/4	③
	EOWE-BA, CA	—	13/16	2	0.137	②	③	1/4	③
	D9AE-ANA, APA	—	13/16	3	0.129	②	③	1/4	③
	D9AE-AVA, AYA	—	13/16	3	0.129	②	③	1/4	③
	EOAE-AGA	—	13/16	3	0.159	②	③	1/4	③
1981	EIKE-CA	7/16	0.810	3	0.124	②	③	0.250	③
	EIKE-EA	7/16	0.810	3	0.124	②	③	0.250	③
	EIKE-DA	7/16	0.810	3	0.124	②	③	0.250	③
	EIKE-FA	7/16	0.810	3	0.124	②	③	0.250	③
	EIWE-FA	7/16	0.810	2	0.120	②	③	0.250	③
	EIWE-EA	7/16	0.810	2	0.120	②	③	0.250	③

Model 2150 (continued)

Year	(9510)* Carburetor Identification	Dry Float Level (in.)	Wet Float Level (in.)	Pump Setting Hole # ①	Choke Plate Pulldown (in.)	Fast Idle Cam Linkage Clearance (in.)	Fast Idle (rpm)	Dechoke (in)	Choke Setting
1981	EIWE-CA	7/16	0.810	2	0.120	②	③	0.250	③
	EIWE-DA	7/16	0.810	2	0.120	②	③	0.250	③
	EIAE-YA	7/16	0.810	3	0.124	②	③	0.250	③
	EIAE-ZA	7/16	0.810	3	0.124	②	③	0.250	③
	EIAE-ADA	7/16	0.810	3	0.124	②	③	0.250	③
	EIAE-AEA	7/16	0.810	3	0.124	②	③	0.250	③
	EIAE-TA	—	0.810	2	0.104	②	③	0.250	③
	EIAE-UA	—	0.810	2	0.104	②	③	0.250	③
1982	E2BE-UA	7/16	0.810	2	0.110	②	2200	0.250	⑤
	E2BE-AAA	7/16	0.810	2	0.110	②	2200	0.250	⑤
	E2BE-VA	7/16	0.810	2	0.113	②	2200	0.250	⑤
	E2BE-ABA	7/16	0.810	2	0.113	②	2200	0.250	⑤
	E2BE-AGA	7/16	0.810	2	0.113 ④	②	2200	0.250	⑤
	E2BE-AHA	7/16	0.810	2	0.113	②	2200	0.250	⑤
	E2VE-CA	7/16	0.810	2	0.113	②	2200	0.250	⑤
	E24E-CA	7/16	0.810	2	0.110	②	1200	0.250	⑤
	E24E-DA	7/16	0.810	2	0.110	②	1200	0.250	⑤
	E24E-AA	7/16	0.810	2	0.110	②	2100	0.250	⑤
	E24E-BA	7/16	0.810	2	0.110	②	2100	0.250	⑤
	E24E-EA	7/16	0.810	2	0.110	②	③	0.250	⑤
	E24E-FA	7/16	0.810	2	0.110	②	③	0.250	⑤
	E2KE-AA	7/16	0.810	2	0.140	②	1500	0.250	⑤
	E2KE-BA	7/16	0.810	2	0.140	②	1500	0.250	⑤
	E2WE-EA	7/16	0.810	2	0.137	②	1500	0.250	⑤

Model 2150 (continued)

Year	(9510)* Carburetor Identification	Dry Float Level (in.)	Wet Float Level (in.)	Pump Setting Hole # ①	Choke Plate Pulldown (in.)	Fast Idle Cam Linkage Clearance (in.)	Fast Idle (rpm)	Dechoke (in)	Choke Setting
1982	E2WE-FA	7/16	0.810	2	0.137	②	1500	0.250	⑤
	E2DE-JA	7/16	0.810	2	0.137	②	1600	0.250	⑤
	E2DE-KA	7/16	0.810	2	0.137	②	1600	0.250	⑤
	E2DE-LA	7/16	0.810	2	0.137	②	1700	0.250	⑤
	E2DE-MA	7/16	0.810	2	0.137	②	1700	0.250	⑤
	E25E-DA	7/16	0.810	2	0.144	②	1500	0.250	⑤
	E2AE-SA	7/16	0.810	2	0.172	②	1550	0.250	⑤
	E25E-CA	7/16	0.810	2	0.137	②	1700	0.250	⑤
	E2ZE-BAA	13/32	0.780	2	0.172④	②	1400	0.250	⑤
	E2ZE-BBA	13/32	0.780	2	0.172④	②	1400	0.250	⑤

*Basic carburetor number for Ford products
① With link in inboard hole of pump lever
② Opposite "V" notch; see text
③ See underhood decal
④ ± .010"
⑤ V-notch

wingnut has not been over torqued and caused the A/C housing to interfere with the choke plate operation.

2. Make sure that the vacuum hoses, solenoid, and electrical choke wires are properly connected.

3. Check throttle system, choke plate, linkage and fast idle cam for freedom of operation.

Electrical Test

1. Disconnect the choke lead wire from the choke cap and connect a jumper wire between the choke cap terminal and the wire terminal. Start the engine.

2. Connect a test light between the connector of the choke lead wire and ground. If the light glows, current is available to the choke cap. The choke cap should be replaced. If the light does not glow, connect the test light between the alternator stator and the choke lead wire. If the light glows, replace the lead wire. If the light does not glow, the problem lies in the engine electrical circuit.

Automatic Choke Adjustment

The automatic choke has an adjustment to control its reaction to engine temperature.

1. Remove the air cleaner.

2. Remove the heater hose from the bracket (if so equipped).

3. Loosen the thermostatic spring housing clamp retaining screws.

4. Set the spring housing to the specified index mark and tighten the clamp attaching screws.

5. Replace the heater hose and air cleaner assembly.

CHOKE PLATE PULLDOWN AND FAST-IDLE CAM

The Model 2150 2V carburetor is equipped with a choke pulldown diaphragm assembly. Vacuum is metered to the diaphragm through internal passages in the carburetor, through a connecting external tube. As the vacuum bleeds through the orifices in the carburetor, the choke diaphragm pulls the choke plate to the pulldown position.

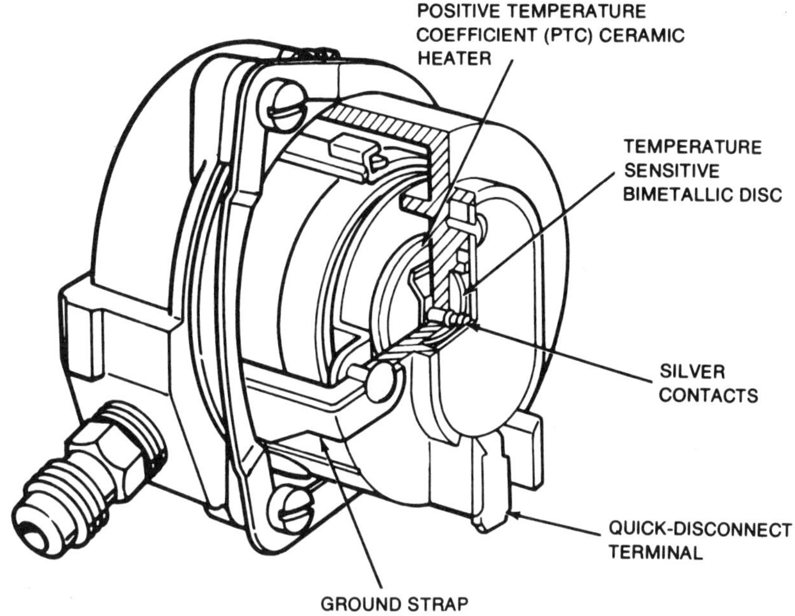

Electric assist choke—2150 carburetor

Automatic choke spring housing adjustment—2150 carburetor

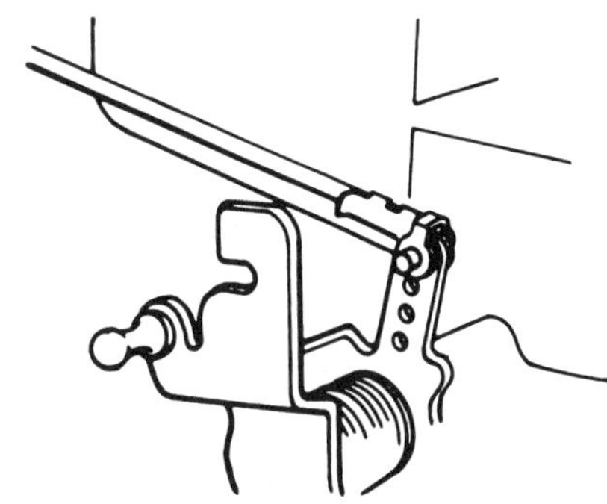
Accelerator stroke adjustment—2150 carburetor

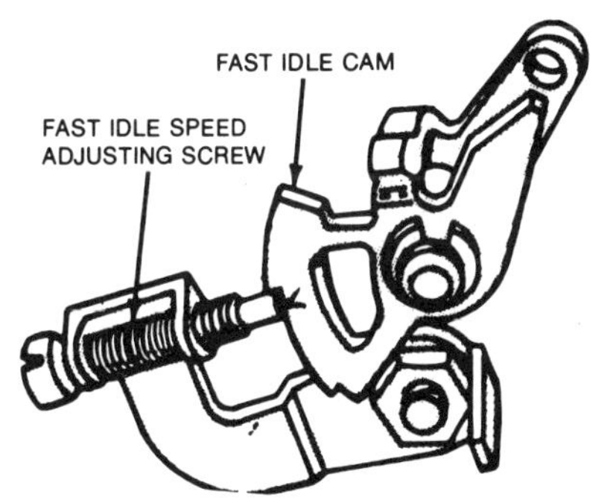

Fast idle speed adjustment—2150 carburetor

Choke Pulldown Check

1. Set the throttle on the fast idle cam top step.
2. Note the index position of the choke bimetallic cap. Loosen the retaining screws and rotate the cap 90 degrees in the rich (closing) direction.
3. Manually force the pulldown control diaphragm link in the direction of the applied vacuum or apply vacuum to the external vacuum tube to activate the pulldown motor.
4. Measure the vertical hard gauge clearance between the choke plate and the center of the carburetor air horn wall nearest the fuel bowl. Adjust the choke plate pulldown to specification by adjusting the diaphragm stop on the end of the choke pulldown diaphragm.

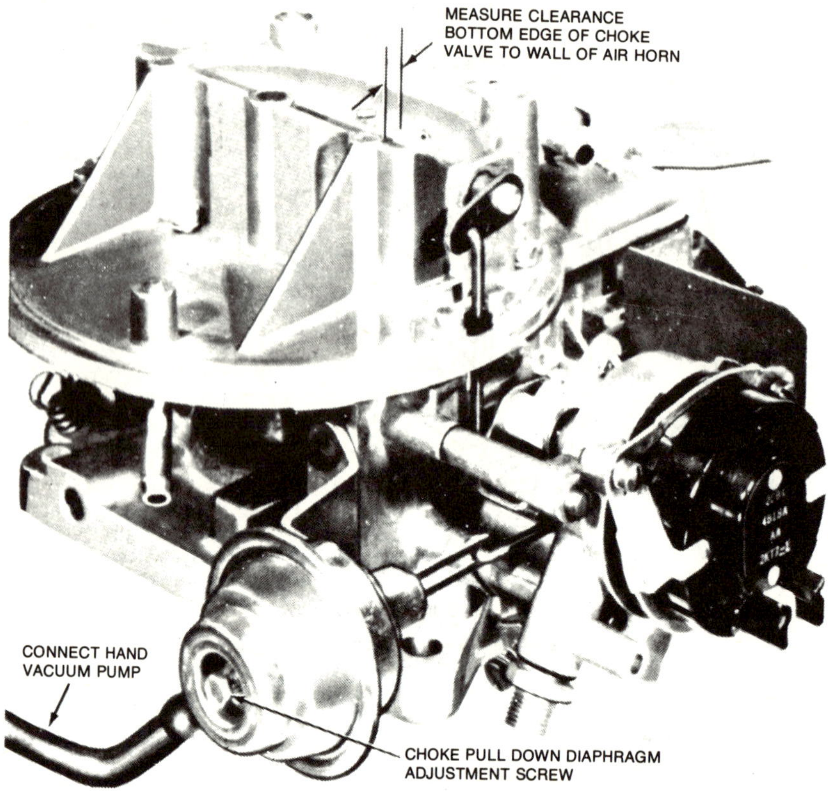

Adjusting plate pulldown—2150 carburetor

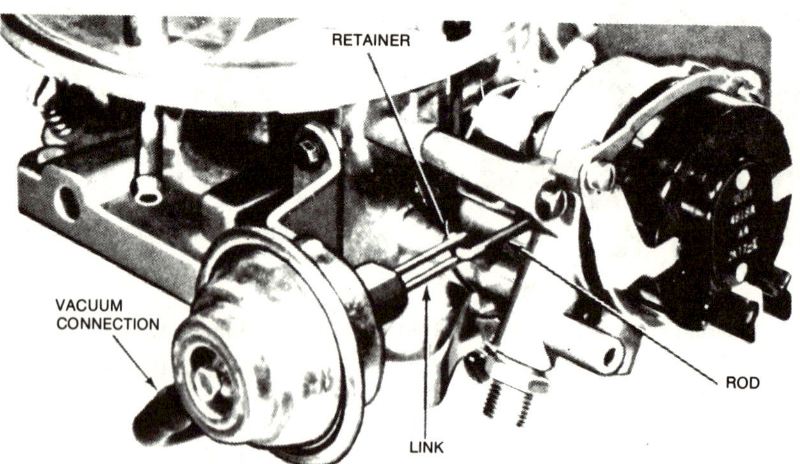

Choke pulldown diaphragm assembly—2150 carburetor

5. Set the choke bimetallic cap to specification.

Fast Idle Speed Adjustment

1. Remove the EGR vacuum line and air cleaner and plug both vacuum lines.
2. Check the ignition timing.
3. Place the transmission in Neutral and engage the parking brake.
4. Start the engine and bring to normal operation temperature.
5. Remove the spark delay valve (if so equipped) and route part throttle vacuum signal directly to advance side of distributor. If the distributor is a dual diaphragm model, leave the manifold vacuum line connected to the retard side of the distributor.
6. Set the throttle to the kickdown step on

the choke cam and make sure the adjusting screw is against the shoulder of the kickdown step.

7. Adjust the rpm to specifications.

Accelerator Pump Stroke Adjustment

The accelerator pump stroke has been preset at the factory for each particular engine and should not be readjusted. However if the rod has been changed from the specified hole it should be reset.

1. Lift up the retaining clip and release the rod.
2. Position the slip over the hole specified in the carburetor specifications chart and insert the operating rod through the clip and the overtravel lever. Snap the end of the clip over the rod to secure.

Overhaul—Model 2150

DISASSEMBLY

To facilitate working on the carburetor, and to prevent damage to the throttle plates, install carburetor legs on the base. If legs are unavailable, install four bolts (about 2¼ inches long of the correct diameter) and eight nuts on the carburetor base.

Use a separate container for the component parts of the various assemblies to facilitate cleaning, inspection and assembly.

The following is a step-by-step sequence of operations for completely overhauling the carburetor. However certain components of the carburetor can be serviced without a complete disassembly of the entire unit. For complete carburetor overhaul, follow all of the steps. To partially overhaul a carburetor or to install a new gasket kit, follow only the applicable steps.

Air Horn

1. Remove the air cleaner anchor screw.
2. Remove the automatic choke control rod retainer.
3. Remove the air horn attaching screws, lockwashers and the carburetor identification tag. Remove the air horn and air horn gasket.
4. Remove the choke control rod by loosening the screws which secure the choke shaft lever to the choke shaft. Remove the rod from the air horn. Slide the plastic dust seal out of the air horn.
5. If it is necessary to remove the choke plate, remove the staking marks on the choke plate attaching screws and remove the screws. Remove the choke plate by sliding it out of the shaft from the top of the air horn. Remove any burrs around screw holes prior to removing the choke shaft out of the air horn.

Choke Pulldown Diaphragm Assembly

1. Disconnect the choke pulldown link by removing the rod retainer and pulling the rod out of the diaphragm link slot.
2. Remove the two screws from the attaching bracket. Disconnect the vacuum supply tube and remove the pulldown diaphragm.
3. To install, position the choke pulldown diaphragm mounting bracket against the main body casting and install the two attaching screws.
4. Connect the vacuum supply tube to the correct vacuum base tube connection.
5. Insert the choke pulldown control rod through the slot in the diaphragm link. Install the retainer clip over the end of the rod in the slot.
6. Perform an automatic choke pulldown clearance and fast idle cam index setting adjustment as described at the end of this chapter.

Automatic Choke

1. Remove the fast idle cam retainer.
2. Remove the thermostatic choke spring housing retaining screws and remove the clamp, housing and gasket.
3. Remove the choke housing assembly retaining screws. If the air horn was not previously removed, remove the choke control rod retainer. Remove the choke housing assembly, gasket and the fast idle cam rod from the fast idle cam lever.
4. Remove the choke lever retaining screw and washer. Disconnect the choke control rod from the choke lever. Remove the choke lever and fast idle cam lever from the choke housing.

Main Body

1. With the use of a screwdriver, pry the float retainer from the fuel inlet seat. Remove the float, float shaft retainer and fuel inlet needle assembly. Remove the retainer and float shaft from the float lever.
2. Remove the fuel inlet needle, seat, filter screen and main jets with a jet wrench.
3. Remove the booster venturi screw (accelerator pump discharge), air distribution plate, booster venturi and metering rod assembly and gasket. Invert the main body. Let the accelerating pump discharge weight and

ball and the mechanical high speed bleed lift rod and spring fall into your hand.

4. Remove the accelerator pump operating rod from the overtravel lever to the retainer. To release the operating rod from the overtravel lever retainer, press upward on the part of the retainer which snaps over the rod. Disengage the rod from the retainer and from

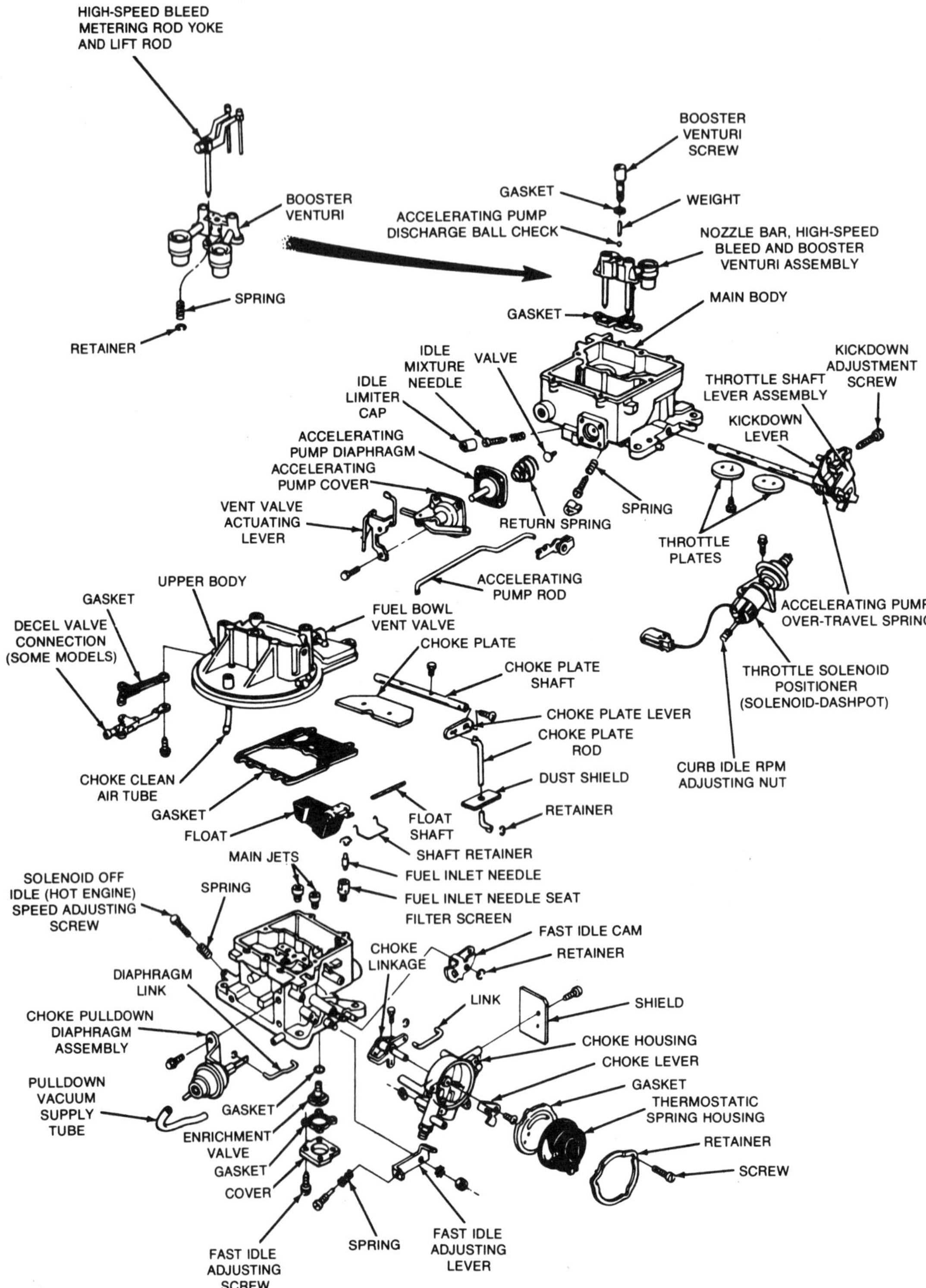

Exploded view of 2150 carburetor

the overtravel lever. Remove the rod and retainer.

5. Remove the accelerating pump cover attaching screws. Remove the accelerating pump cover, diaphragm assembly and spring.

6. If it is necessary to remove the Elastomer (power) valve, grasp it firmly and pull it out. If the Elastomer valve tip broke off during the removal, be sure to remove the tip from the fuel bowl. An Elastomer valve must be replaced whenever it has been removed from the carburetor, as it will dry out and crack.

7. Invert the main body and remove the enrichment valve with a box wrench or socket wrench. Remove the enrichment valve gasket. Discard the gasket.

8. Remove the idle fuel mixture adjusting screws (needles) and the springs. Remove the limiters from the adjusting screws.

9. If necessary, remove the nut and washer securing the fast idle adjusting lever assembly to the throttle shaft and remove the lever assembly. If necessary, remove the idle screw and the retainer from the fast idle adjusting lever.

10. Remove the anti-stall dashpot, solenoid or solenoid-dashpot (if so equipped).

11. If it is necessary to remove the throttle plates, lightly scribe the throttle plates along the throttle shaft, and mark each plate and its corresponding bore with a number or letter for proper installation.

12. Slide the throttle shaft out of the main body, making sure that you catch the mechanical high speed bleed actuator located on the throttle shaft between the throttle plates.

Clean and inspect the carburetor components.

ASSEMBLY

Make sure that all holes in new gaskets have been properly punched and that no foreign material has adhered to the gaskets. Make sure that the accelerating pump diaphragm is not torn or cut.

Main Body

1. Slide the throttle shaft assembly into the main body until it begins to enter the high speed bleed cam slot in the body.

2. Holding the cam by the edge of the point, hold it in the slot and rotate the throttle shaft until it will pass through the cam. Rotate the shaft clockwise until the throttle lever clears the boss for the TSP "off" idle speed screw. Continue inserting the shaft into the proper position, rotating as necessary to properly position the cam.

3. Refer to the lines scribed on the throttle plates and install the throttle plates in their proper location with the screws snug, but not tight. Always use new screws when installing throttle plates.

4. Close the throttle plates. Invert the main body, and hold it up to the light. Little or no light should show between the throttle plates and the throttle bores. Tap the plates lightly with a screwdriver handle to seat them. Hold the throttle plates closed and tighten and stake the attaching screws. Stake hardened screws by crimping the exposed threads with diagonal cutters.

5. If necessary, install the fast idle screw on the fast idle adjusting lever.

6. Install the anti-stall dashpot, solenoid or solenoid-dashpot (if so equipped).

7. Place the fast idle adjusting lever assembly on the throttle shaft and install the retaining washer and nut.

8. If the Elastomer power valve was removed, lubricate the tip of the new Elastomer valve and insert the tip into the accelerator pump cavity center hole. Using a pair of needlenose pliers, reach into the fuel bowl and grasp the valve tip. Pull the valve in until it seats in the pump cavity wall and cut off the tip forward of the retaining shoulder. Remove the tip of the bow.

9. Install the accelerating pump diaphragm return spring on the boss in the chamber. Insert the diaphragm assembly into position on the main body. Install the cover screws.

10. Insert the accelerating pump operating rod retainer over the specified hole in the overtravel lever. Insert the operating rod through the retainer and the hole in the overtravel lever and snap the retainer down over the rod.

11. Invert the main body. Install the enrichment valve and new gasket with a wrench. Tighten the valve securely.

12. Install the idle mixture adjusting screws (needles) and springs. Turn the needles in gently with your fingers until they just touch the seat, then back them off 1½ turns for a preliminary idle fuel mixture adjustment. Do not install the idle mixture limiters at this time. Install the enrichment valve cover and new gasket. The cover must be installed with the limiter stops on the cover in position to provide a positive stop for the tabs on the idle mixture adjusting screw limiters.

13. Install the main jets and the fuel inlet seat, filter screen, baffle and new gasket. Be sure that the correct jets are installed.

14. Install the fuel inlet needle assembly in the fuel inlet seat.

15. Slide the float shaft into the float lever. Position the float shaft retainer on the float shaft.

16. Insert the float assembly into the fuel bowl and hook the float lever tab under the fuel inlet needle assembly. Insert the float shaft into its guides at the sides of the fuel bowl.

17. With a screwdriver, position the float shaft retainer in the groove on the fuel needle inlet seat. Check the float setting.

18. Drop the accelerating pump discharge ball and weight into the passage in the main body.

19. Position the new booster assembly gasket and the booster venturi assembly in the main body. Install the air distribution plate and the accelerator pump discharge screw. Tighten the screw.

Automatic Choke

1. Position the fast idle cam lever on the thermostatic choke shaft and lever assembly. The bottom of the fast idle cam lever adjusting screw must rest against the tang on the choke lever. Insert the choke lever into the rear of the choke housing. Position the choke lever so that the hole in the lever is to the left side of the choke housing.

2. Install the fast idle cam rod on the fast idle cam lever. Place the fast idle cam on the fast idle cam rod and install the retainer. Place the choke housing vacuum pickup port to main body gasket on the choke housing flange.

3. Position the choke housing on the main body and at the same time, install the fast idle cam on the hub on the main body. Position the gasket and install the choke housing attaching screws. Install the fast idle cam retainer. Install the thermostatic spring housing.

Air Horn

1. If the choke plate shaft was removed, position the shaft in the air horn, then install the choke plate rod on the end of the choke shaft.

2. If the choke plate was removed, insert the choke plate into the choke plate shaft. Install the choke plate screws snug, but not tight. Check for proper plate fit, binding in the air horn and free rotation of the shaft by moving the plate from the closed position to the open position. If necessary, remove the choke plate and grind or file the plate edge where it is binding or scraping on the air horn wall. If the choke plate and the shaft move freely, tighten the choke plate screws while holding the choke in the fully closed position.

3. Position the main body gasket and the choke rod plastic seal on the main body. Position the air horn on the main body and gasket so that the choke plate rod fits through the seal and the opening in the main body. Insert the end of the choke plate rod into the automatic choke lever. Install the air horn attaching screws and the carburetor identification tag. Tighten the attaching screws. Install the choke plate rod retainer. Install the air cleaner anchor screw. Tighten the air cleaner anchor screw to the specified torque.

Perform all automatic choke adjustments and other carburetor functions to specifications.

Motorcraft Variable Venturi 2700VV

The design of this carburetor differs considerably from the other carburetors in the Ford lineup, an explanation of the differences in both theory and operation is presented here.

Specifications—2700 VV Carburetor

Throttle bore diameter	1$^9/_{16}$
Venturi diameter	Variable
Fuel inlet system	
Floatsetting (dry) ± $^1/_{32}$	1$^3/_{64}$
Float drop ± $^1/_{32}$	1$^{15}/_{32}$
Main metering system	
Metering rod ident.	144
Venturi valve limiter	$^{61}/_{64}$ ②
Control vacuum (in. H_2O)	5.0 ①
Spring preload vacuum (in. H_2O)	4.7
Pump system	
Internal vent	.010
Pump weight material	Aluminum
Choke system	
Bimetal identification	7-40 MF
Cap setting	Index
Fast idle cam set	1 Rich @ 3rd Step ③
Cold enrichment rod setting	.125 ± .005

①Venturi Air Bypass—6.8–7.3
Venturi Valve Diaphragm—4.6–5.1
②Limiter Setting—.38–.42
Limiter Stop Setting—.73–.77
③1 Rich/2nd Step for carb #D9ZE-LB

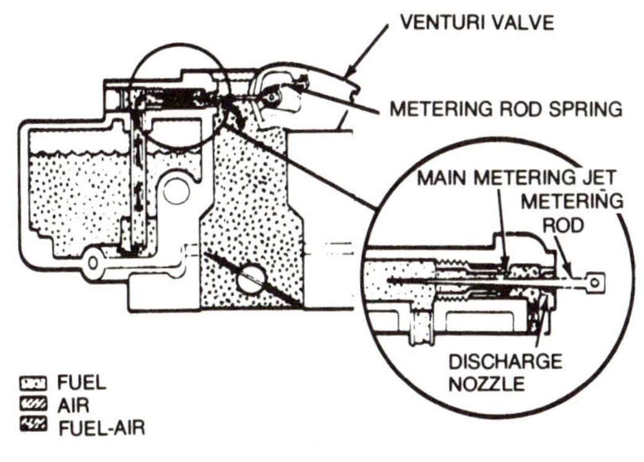

Main metering system

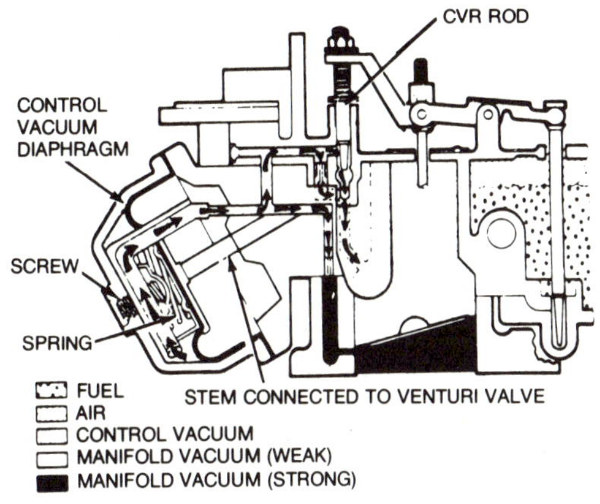

Control vacuum circuit

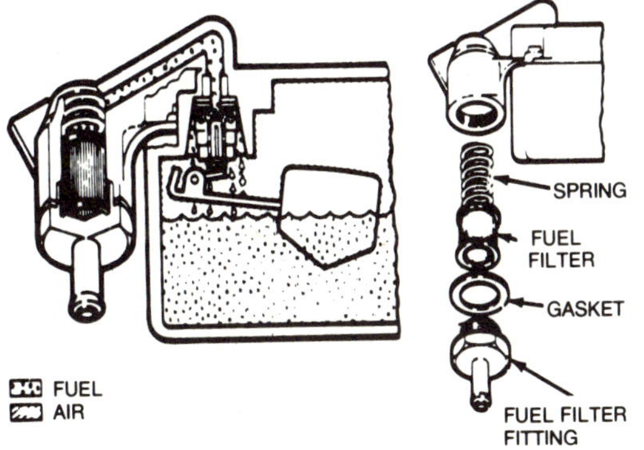

Fuel inlet system

Complete adjustment and repair instructions are also included in this section.

In exterior appearance, the variable venturi carburetor is similar to conventional carburetors and, like a conventional carburetor, it uses a normal float and fuel bowl system. However, the similarity ends there. In place of a normal choke plate and fixed area venturis, the 2700VV carburetor has a pair of small oblong castings in the top of the upper carburetor body where you would normally

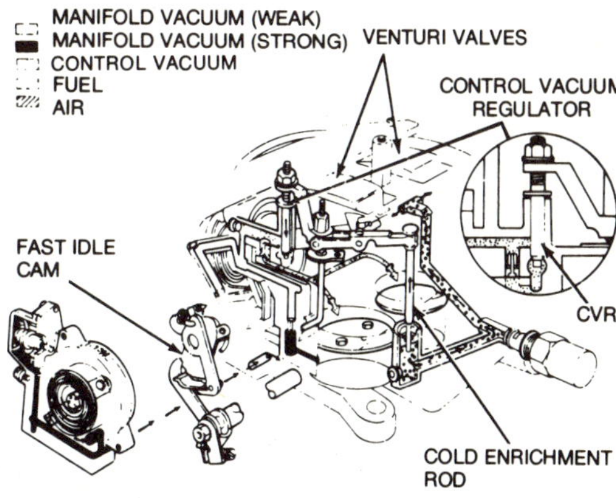

Cold enrichment system

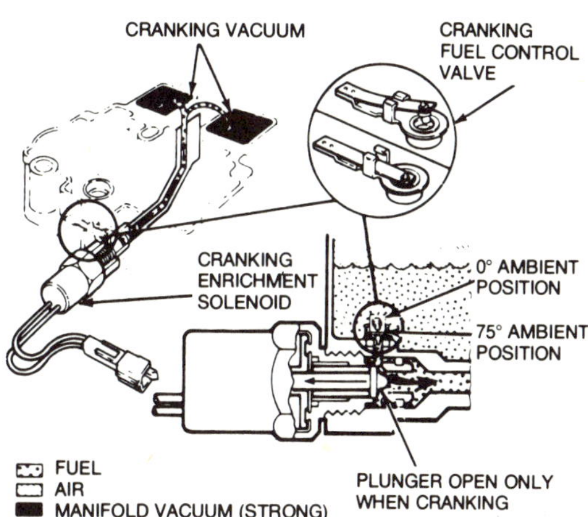

Cranking enrichment system

expect to see the choke plate. These castings slide back and forth across the top of the carburetor in response to fuel-air demands. Their movement is controlled by a springloaded diaphragm valve regulated by a vacuum signal taken below the venturis in the throttle bores. As the throttle is opened, the strength of the vacuum signal increases, opening the venturis and allowing more air to enter the carburetor.

Fuel is admitted into the venturi area by means of tapered metering rods that fit into the main jets. These rods are attached to the venturis, and, as the venturis open or close in response to air demand, the fuel needed to maintain the proper mixture increases or decreases as the metering rods slide in the jets. In comparison to a conventional carburetor with fixed venturis and a variable air supply, this system provides much more precise control of the fuel-air supply during all modes of operation. Because of the variable venturi principle, there are fewer fuel metering systems and fuel passages. The only auxiliary fuel metering systems required are an idle trim, accelerator pump (similar to a conventional carburetor), starting enrichment, and cold running enrichment.

NOTE: *Adjustment, assembly and disassembly of this carburetor require special tools for some of the operations. These tools are available from your Ford dealer. Do not attempt any operations on this carburetor without first checking to see if you need the special tools for that particular operation. The adjustment and repair procedures given here mention when and if you will need the special tools.*

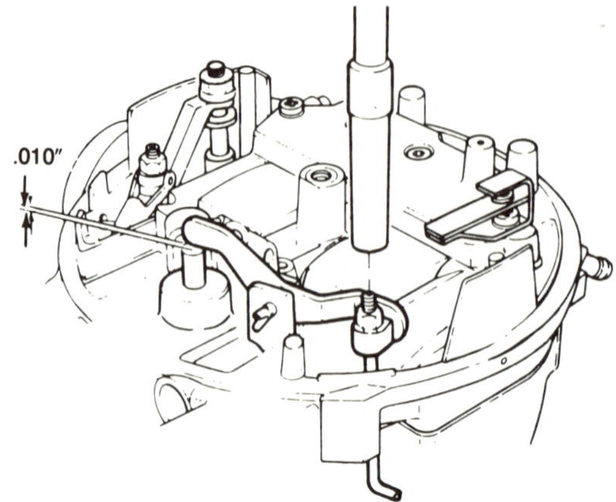

Internal vent system

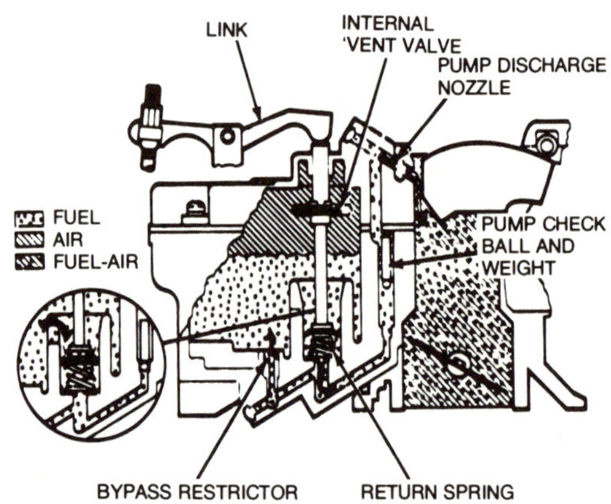

Accelerator pump system

Adjustments

Before making any adjustments with the engine running, set the parking brake and block the wheels. Make sure the engine is at normal operating temperature and that any power accessories are turned off.

CURB IDLE SPEED

Adjust the curb idle speed as you would on a conventional carburetor. Check the emission control decal under the hood for the proper idle speed.

INTERNAL VENT ADJUSTMENT

This adjustment must be checked whenever the curb idle speed is adjusted. After you have set the curb idle, place an .010 feeler gauge between the accelerator pump stem and the pump operating link. Turn the adjusting nut until there is just a slight drag when the gauge is removed.

COLD ENRICHMENT METERING ROD

NOTE: *This procedure requires special tools.*

Remove the choke cap, after noting its position so that you will be able to return it to the correct setting. Install a dial indicator with the tip of the indicator on the top of the enrichment rod and adjust the dial to zero. The cold enrichment rod is seated by installing the stator cap as a weight. After installing the cap in place of the choke cap, raise it slightly and let it drop. This should seat the cold enrichment rod. The dial indicator should still read zero. If it does not, repeat the procedure. Remove the stator cap and reinstall it in the choke cap's original position. The index mark on the stator cap should be in the same relative position as the index mark on the choke cap. The dial indicator should now read to specification. If it does not, turn the adjusting nut clockwise to increase or counterclockwise to decrease rod height. Reinstall the choke cap in its original position.

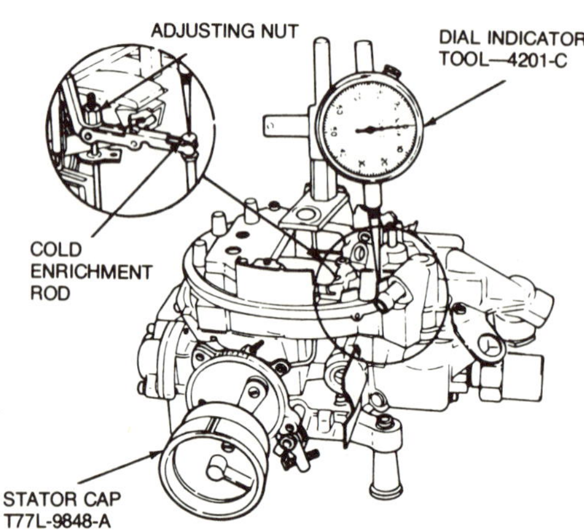

Cold enrichment metering rod adjustment

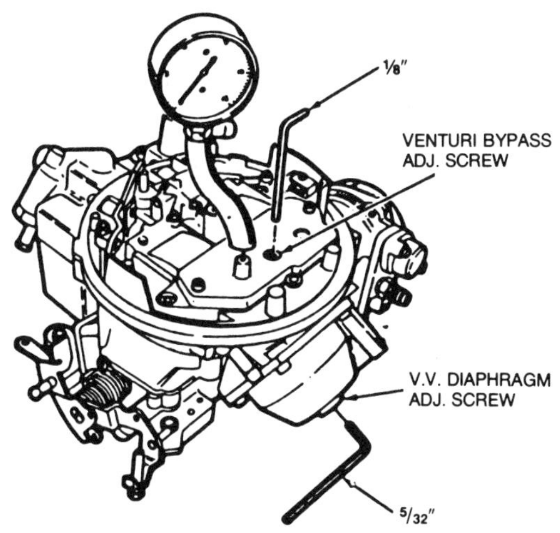

Control vacuum adjustment

CONTROL VACUUM

You will need a tachometer, a vacuum gauge and some allen wrenches for this adjustment. With the engine at curb idle and a tachometer hooked up, turn the venturi valve diaphragm adjusting screw clockwise until the valve is completely closed. Connect a vacuum gauge to the vacuum tap on the venturi valve cover. Turn the venturi bypass adjusting screw to reach the specified vacuum setting. Then turn the venturi valve diaphragm adjusting screw counterclockwise until the vacuum drops to the specified setting. In order to get the vacuum to drop, you must rev the engine once or twice. After you get the vacuum right, check and reset the curb idle if necessary.

FAST IDLE SPEED

With the engine idling, EGR disconnected and the vacuum line plugged, make sure the fast idle lever is on the specified step of the fast idle cam. Turn the fast idle adjusting screw clockwise to decrease speed.

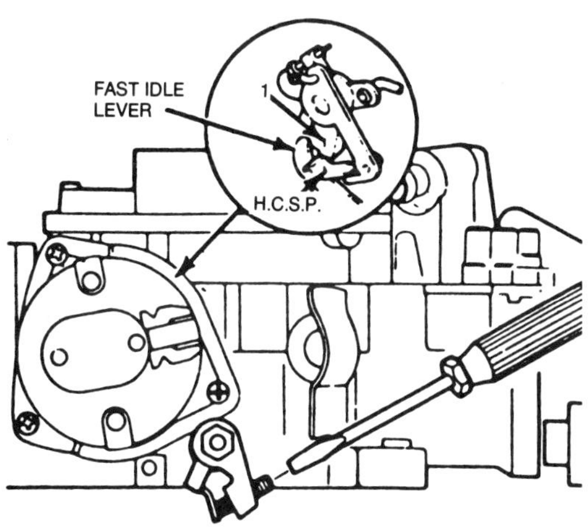

Fast idle speed adjustment

IDLE TRIM ADJUSTMENT

NOTE: *Ford states that idle trim is adjusted at the factory and not adjusted in service.*

FUEL LEVEL ADJUSTMENT

Remove the carburetor upper body. Remove the old gasket and install a new one. Fabricate a gauge to the specified dimension. Turn the upper body upside down and place the fuel level gauge on the cast surface, not on the gasket. Measure the vertical distance from the cast surface to the bottom of the float. If it needs adjustment, bend the float operating lever away from the fuel inlet needle to decrease the setting and toward the needle to increase the setting.

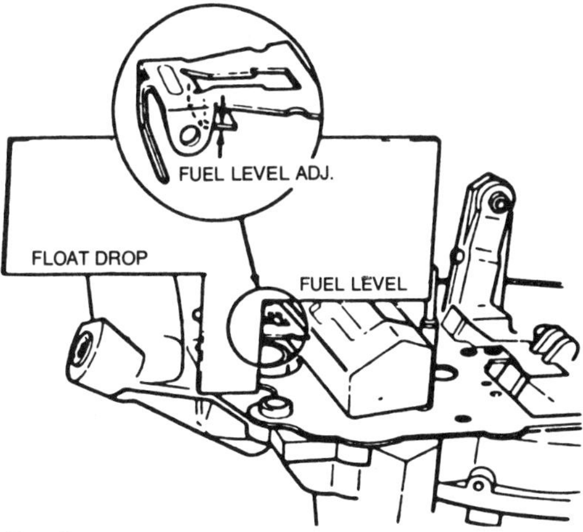

Fuel level adjustment

FLOAT DROP ADJUSTMENT

You will need to fabricate a gauge for this adjustment, also. With the upper body in the upright position, measure the distance between the cast surface of the upper body and the bottom of the float. To adjust, bend the stop tab on the float lever away from the hinge pin to increase the setting and toward the hinge pin to decrease the setting.

CONTROL VACUUM REGULATOR (CVR) ADJUSTMENT

NOTE: *The cold enrichment metering rod adjustment must be set before making this adjustment.*

Cycle the throttle to set the fast idle speed cam and then rotate the choke cap 180 de-

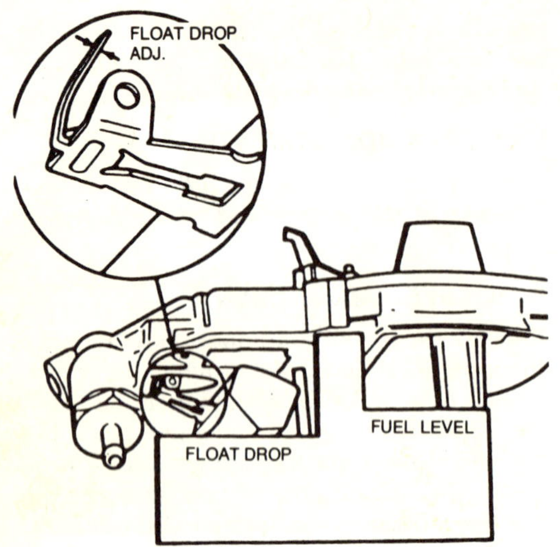

Float drop adjustment

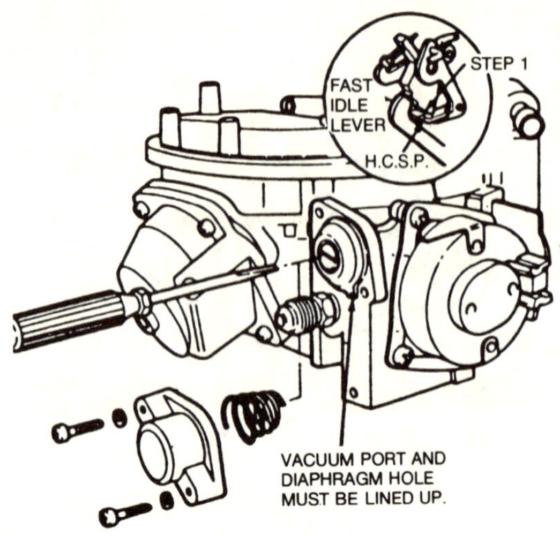

HCSP adjustment

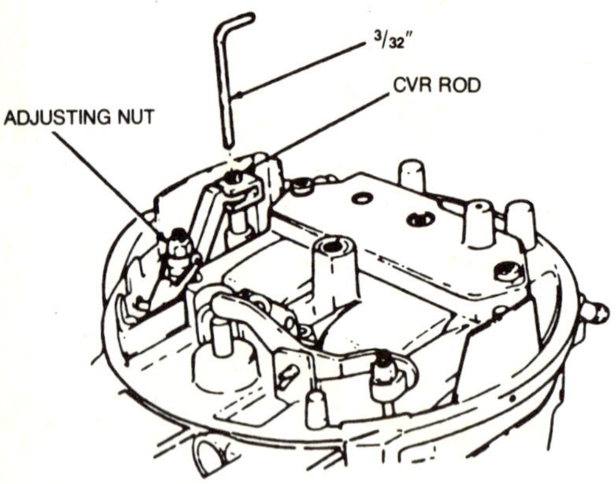

CVR adjustment

grees clockwise (rich). Press down on the CVR rod. If it moves downward, it is not seated and must be adjusted. To adjust, turn the rod clockwise until the adjusting nut just begins to rise. Then turn the adjusting screw clockwise in one-quarter turn increments until the rod is full seated (no down travel). Reset the choke cap to the original setting.

HIGH CAM SPEED POSITIONER (HCSP) ADJUSTMENT

Holding the throttle closed, place the HCSP in the corner of the specified cam step (counting the highest step as the first). Place the fast idle lever in the corner of the HCSP. Remove the diaphragm cover and turn the assembly clockwise until it just bottoms on the casting, then turn it back until the vacuum port and diaphragm hole line up. Reinstall the cover.

CHOKE LINKAGE ADJUSTMENT

There is no choke plate on the variable venturi carburetor. Therefore, no adjustments are possible or necessary.

Overhaul

It will be easier and you will avoid damaging the carburetor if you make a carburetor stand out of four bolts. The following is a step-by-step procedure. However, many components can be serviced or replaced without completely disassembling the carburetor. Read the steps over carefully before you begin and you will probably save some time.

NOTE: *Special tools are required. Also, rebuilding kits include specific procedures. Read them carefully before attempting any carburetor overhaul.*

UPPER BODY DISASSEMBLY

1. Remove the fuel inlet fitting, fuel filter, gasket and spring.
2. Remove the screws retaining the upper body assembly and remove the upper body.
3. Remove the float hinge pin and float assembly.
4. Remove the fuel inlet valve, seat and gasket.
5. Remove the accelerator pump rod and the choke control rod.
6. Remove the accelerator pump link retaining pin and the link.
7. Remove the accelerator pump swivel and the retaining nut.

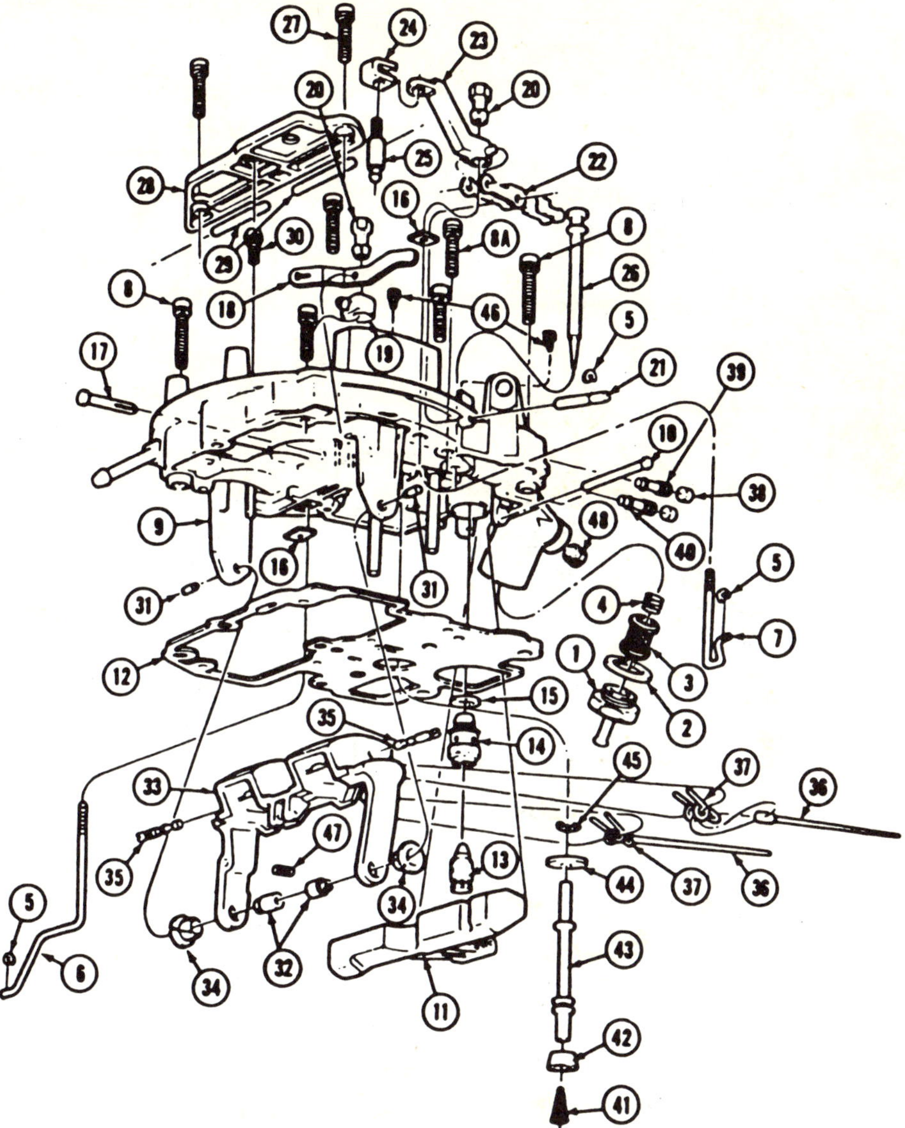

1. Fuel inlet fitting
2. Fuel inlet fitting gasket
3. Fuel filter
4. Fuel filter spring
5. Retaining E-ring
6. Accelerator pump rod
7. Choke control rod
8. Screw
8A. Screw
9. Upper body
10. Float hinge pin
11. Float assembly
12. Float bowl gasket
13. Fuel inlet valve
14. Fuel inlet seat
15. Fuel inlet seat gasket
16. Dust seal
17. Pin
18. Accelerator pump link
19. Accelerator pump swivel
20. Nut
21. Choke hinge pin
22. Cold enrichment rod lever
23. Cold enrichment rod swivel
24. Control vacuum regulator adjusting nut
25. Control vacuum regulator
26. Cold enrichment rod
27. Screw
28. Venturi valve cover plate
29. Roller bearing
30. Venturi air bypass screw
31. Venturi valve pivot plug
32. Venturi valve pivot pin
33. Venturi valve
34. Venturi valve pivot pin bushing
35. Metering rod pivot pin
36. Metering rod
37. Metering rod spring
38. Cup plug
39. Main metering jet assembly
40. O-ring
41. Accelerator pump return spring
42. Accelerator pump cup
43. Accelerator pump plunger
44. Internal vent valve
45. Retaining E-ring
46. Idle trim screw
47. Venturi valve limiter adjusting screw
48. Pipe plug

Upper body—2700VV carburetor

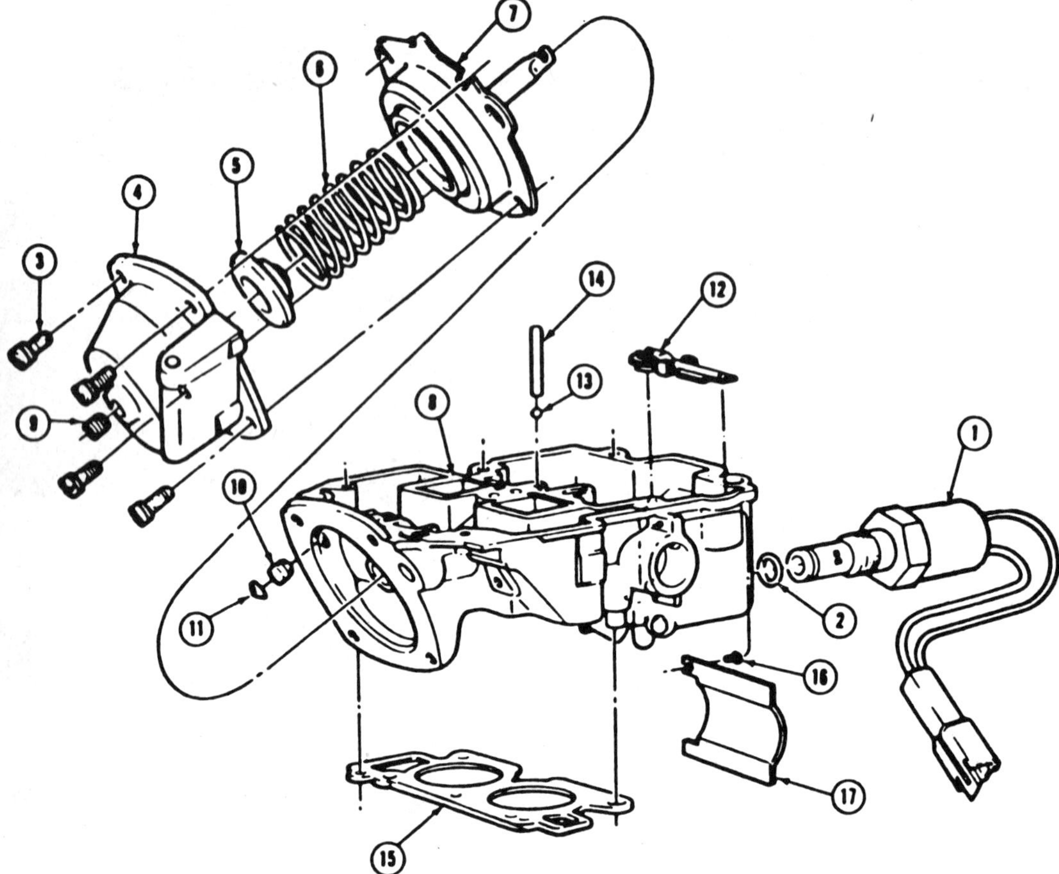

1. Cranking enrichment solenoid
2. O-ring seal
3. Screw
4. Venturi valve diaphragm cover
5. Venturi valve diaphragm spring guide
6. Venturi valve diaphragm spring
7. Venturi valve diaphragm assembly
8. Main body
9. Venturi valve adjusting screw
10. Wide open stop screw
11. Plug expansion
12. Cranking fuel control assembly
13. Accelerator pump check ball
14. Accelerator pump check ball weight
15. Throttle body gasket
16. Screw
17. Choke heat shield

Main body—2700VV carburetor

8. Remove the E-ring on the choke hinge pin and slide the pin out of the casting.

9. Remove the cold enrichment rod adjusting nut, lever and swivel; remove the control vacuum nut and regulator as an assembly.

10. Remove the cold enrichment rod.

11. Remove the venturi valve cover plate and roller bearings. Remove the venturi air bypass screw.

12. Using special tool T77P-9928-A, press the tapered plugs out of the venturi valve pivot pins.

13. Remove the venturi valve pivot pins, bushings and the venturi valve.

14. Remove the metering rod pivot pins, springs and metering rods. Be sure to mark the rods so that you know on which side they belong. Also, keep the venturi valve blocked open when working on the jets.

15. Using tool T77L-9533-B, remove the cup plugs.

16. Using tool T77L-9533-A, turn each main metering jet clockwise, counting the number of turns, until they bottom in the casting. You will need to know the number of turns when you reassemble the carburetor. Remove the jets and mark them so that you know on which side they belong. Don't lose the O-rings.

17. Remove the accelerator pump plunger assembly.

55 WAYS TO IMPROVE FUEL ECONOMY

CHILTON'S
FUEL ECONOMY & TUNE-UP TIPS

Tune-up • Spark Plug Diagnosis • Emission Controls

Fuel System • Cooling System • Tires and Wheels

General Maintenance

CHILTON'S FUEL ECONOMY & TUNE-UP TIPS

Fuel economy is important to everyone, no matter what kind of vehicle you drive. The maintenance-minded motorist can save both money and fuel using these tips and the periodic maintenance and tune-up procedures in this Repair and Tune-Up Guide.

There are more than 130,000,000 cars and trucks registered for private use in the United States. Each travels an average of 10-12,000 miles per year, and, and in total they consume close to 70 billion gallons of fuel each year. This represents nearly ⅔ of the oil imported by the United States each year. The Federal government's goal is to reduce consumption 10% by 1985. A variety of methods are either already in use or under serious consideration, and they all affect you driving and the cars you will drive. In addition to "down-sizing", the auto industry is using or investigating the use of electronic fuel delivery, electronic engine controls and alternative engines for use in smaller and lighter vehicles, among other alternatives to meet the federally mandated Corporate Average Fuel Economy (CAFE) of 27.5 mpg by 1985. The government, for its part, is considering rationing, mandatory driving curtailments and tax increases on motor vehicle fuel in an effort to reduce consumption. The government's goal of a 10% reduction could be realized — and further government regulation avoided — if every private vehicle could use just 1 less gallon of fuel per week.

How Much Can You Save?

Tests have proven that almost anyone can make at least a 10% reduction in fuel consumption through regular maintenance and tune-ups. When a major manufacturer of spark plugs sur-

TUNE-UP

1. Check the cylinder compression to be sure the engine will really benefit from a tune-up and that it is capable of producing good fuel economy. A tune-up will be wasted on an engine in poor mechanical condition.

2. Replace spark plugs regularly. New spark plugs alone can increase fuel economy 3%.

3. Be sure the spark plugs are the correct type (heat range) for your vehicle. See the Tune-Up Specifications.

Heat range refers to the spark plug's ability to conduct heat away from the firing end. It must conduct the heat away in an even pattern to avoid becoming a source of pre-ignition, yet it must also operate hot enough to burn off conductive deposits that could cause misfiring.

The heat range is usually indicated by a number on the spark plug, part of the manufacturer's designation for each individual spark plug. The numbers in bold-face indicate the heat range in each manufacturer's identification system.

Manufacturer	**Typical Designation**
AC	R **45** TS
Bosch (old)	WA **145** T30
Bosch (new)	HR **8** Y
Champion	RBL **15** Y
Fram/Autolite	41**5**
Mopar	P-**62** PR
Motorcraft	BRF-**42**
NGK	BP **5** ES-15
Nippondenso	W **16** EP
Prestolite	14GR **5** 2A

Periodically, check the spark plugs to be sure they are firing efficiently. They are excellent indicators of the internal condition of your engine.

On AC, Bosch (new), Champion, Fram/Autolite, Mopar, Motorcraft and Prestolite, a higher number indicates a hotter plug. On Bosch (old), NGK and Nippondenso, a higher number indicates a colder plug.

4. Make sure the spark plugs are properly gapped. See the Tune-Up Specifications in this book.

5. Be sure the spark plugs are firing efficiently. The illustrations on the next 2 pages show you how to "read" the firing end of the spark plug.

6. Check the ignition timing and set it to specifications. Tests show that almost all cars have incorrect ignition timing by more than 2°.

veyed over 6,000 cars nationwide, they found that a tune-up, on cars that needed one, increased fuel economy over 11%. Replacing worn plugs alone, accounted for a 3% increase. The same test also revealed that 8 out of every 10 vehicles will have some maintenance deficiency that will directly affect fuel economy, emissions or performance. Most of this mileage-robbing neglect could be prevented with regular maintenance.

Modern engines require that all of the functioning systems operate properly for maximum efficiency. A malfunction anywhere wastes fuel. You can keep your vehicle running as efficiently and economically as possible, by being aware of your vehicle's operating and performance characteristics. If your vehicle suddenly develops performance or fuel economy problems it could be due to one or more of the following:

PROBLEM	POSSIBLE CAUSE
Engine Idles Rough	Ignition timing, idle mixture, vacuum leak or something amiss in the emission control system.
Hesitates on Acceleration	Dirty carburetor or fuel filter, improper accelerator pump setting, ignition timing or fouled spark plugs.
Starts Hard or Fails to Start	Worn spark plugs, improperly set automatic choke, ice (or water) in fuel system.
Stalls Frequently	Automatic choke improperly adjusted and possible dirty air filter or fuel filter.
Performs Sluggishly	Worn spark plugs, dirty fuel or air filter, ignition timing or automatic choke out of adjustment.

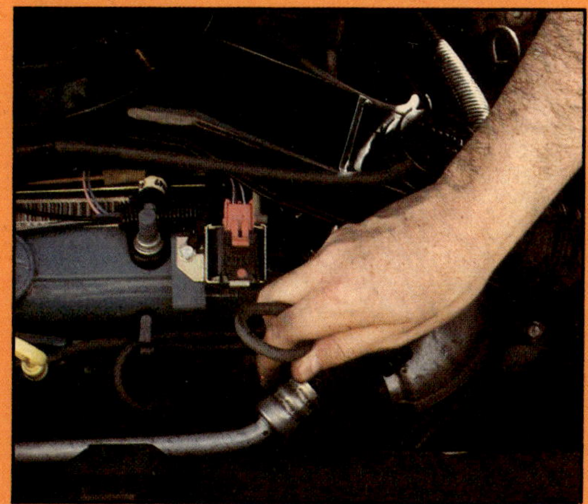

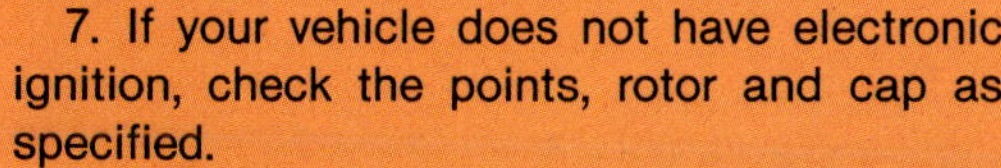

Check spark plug wires on conventional point type ignition for cracks by bending them in a loop around your finger.

Be sure that spark plug wires leading to adjacent cylinders do not run too close together. (Photo courtesy Champion Spark Plug Co.)

7. If your vehicle does not have electronic ignition, check the points, rotor and cap as specified.

8. Check the spark plug wires (used with conventional point-type ignitions) for cracks and burned or broken insulation by bending them in a loop around your finger. Cracked wires decrease fuel efficiency by failing to deliver full voltage to the spark plugs. One misfiring spark plug can cost you as much as 2 mpg.

9. Check the routing of the plug wires. Misfiring can be the result of spark plug leads to adjacent cylinders running parallel to each other and too close together. One wire tends to pick up voltage from the other causing it to fire "out of time".

10. Check all electrical and ignition circuits for voltage drop and resistance.

11. Check the distributor mechanical and/or vacuum advance mechanisms for proper functioning. The vacuum advance can be checked by twisting the distributor plate in the opposite direction of rotation. It should spring back when released.

12. Check and adjust the valve clearance on engines with mechanical lifters. The clearance should be slightly loose rather than too tight.

SPARK PLUG DIAGNOSIS

Normal

APPEARANCE: This plug is typical of one operating normally. The insulator nose varies from a light tan to grayish color with slight electrode wear. The presence of slight deposits is normal on used plugs and will have no adverse effect on engine performance. The spark plug heat range is correct for the engine and the engine is running normally.
CAUSE: Properly running engine.
RECOMMENDATION: Before reinstalling this plug, the electrodes should be cleaned and filed square. Set the gap to specifications. If the plug has been in service for more than 10-12,000 miles, the entire set should probably be replaced with a fresh set of the same heat range.

Oil Deposits

APPEARANCE: The firing end of the plug is covered with a wet, oily coating.
CAUSE: The problem is poor oil control. On high mileage engines, oil is leaking past the rings or valve guides into the combustion chamber. A common cause is also a plugged PCV valve, and a ruptured fuel pump diaphragm can also cause this condition. Oil fouled plugs such as these are often found in new or recently overhauled engines, before normal oil control is achieved, and can be cleaned and reinstalled.
RECOMMENDATION: A hotter spark plug may temporarily relieve the problem, but the engine is probably in need of work.

Incorrect Heat Range

APPEARANCE: The effects of high temperature on a spark plug are indicated by clean white, often blistered insulator. This can also be accompanied by excessive wear of the electrode, and the absence of deposits.
CAUSE: Check for the correct spark plug heat range. A plug which is too hot for the engine can result in overheating. A car operated mostly at high speeds can require a colder plug. Also check ignition timing, cooling system level, fuel mixture and leaking intake manifold.
RECOMMENDATION: If all ignition and engine adjustments are known to be correct, and no other malfunction exists, install spark plugs one heat range colder.

Photos Courtesy Fram Corporation

Carbon Deposits

APPEARANCE: Carbon fouling is easily identified by the presence of dry, soft, black, sooty deposits.
CAUSE: Changing the heat range can often lead to carbon fouling, as can prolonged slow, stop-and-start driving. If the heat range is correct, carbon fouling can be attributed to a rich fuel mixture, sticking choke, clogged air cleaner, worn breaker points, retarded timing or low compression. If only one or two plugs are carbon fouled, check for corroded or cracked wires on the affected plugs. Also look for cracks in the distributor cap between the towers of affected cylinders.
RECOMMENDATION: After the problem is corrected, these plugs can be cleaned and reinstalled if not worn severely.

MMT Fouled

APPEARANCE: Spark plugs fouled by MMT (Methycyclopentadienyl Maganese Tricarbonyl) have reddish, rusty appearance on the insulator and side electrode.
CAUSE: MMT is an anti-knock additive in gasoline used to replace lead. During the combustion process, the MMT leaves a reddish deposit on the insulator and side electrode.
RECOMMENDATION: No engine malfunction is indicated and the deposits will not affect plug performance any more than lead deposits (see Ash Deposits). MMT fouled plugs can be cleaned, regapped and reinstalled.

High Speed Glazing

APPEARANCE: Glazing appears as shiny coating on the plug, either yellow or tan in color.
CAUSE: During hard, fast acceleration, plug temperatures rise suddenly. Deposits from normal combustion have no chance to fluff-off; instead, they melt on the insulator forming an electrically conductive coating which causes misfiring.
RECOMMENDATION: Glazed plugs are not easily cleaned. They should be replaced with a fresh set of plugs of the correct heat range. If the condition recurs, using plugs with a heat range one step colder may cure the problem.

Ash (Lead) Deposits

APPEARANCE: Ash deposits are characterized by light brown or white colored deposits crusted on the side or center electrodes. In some cases it may give the plug a rusty appearance.
CAUSE: Ash deposits are normally derived from oil or fuel additives burned during normal combustion. Normally they are harmless, though excessive amounts can cause misfiring. If deposits are excessive in short mileage, the valve guides may be worn.
RECOMMENDATION: Ash-fouled plugs can be cleaned, gapped and reinstalled.

Detonation

APPEARANCE: Detonation is usually characterized by a broken plug insulator.
CAUSE: A portion of the fuel charge will begin to burn spontaneously, from the increased heat following ignition. The explosion that results applies extreme pressure to engine components, frequently damaging spark plugs and pistons.

Detonation can result by over-advanced ignition timing, inferior gasoline (low octane) lean air/fuel mixture, poor carburetion, engine lugging or an increase in compression ratio due to combustion chamber deposits or engine modification.
RECOMMENDATION: Replace the plugs after correcting the problem.

Photos Courtesy Champion Spark Plug Co.

EMISSION CONTROLS

13. Be aware of the general condition of the emission control system. It contributes to reduced pollution and should be serviced regularly to maintain efficient engine operation.

14. Check all vacuum lines for dried, cracked or brittle conditions. Something as simple as a leaking vacuum hose can cause poor performance and loss of economy.

15. Avoid tampering with the emission control system. Attempting to improve fuel econ-

FUEL SYSTEM

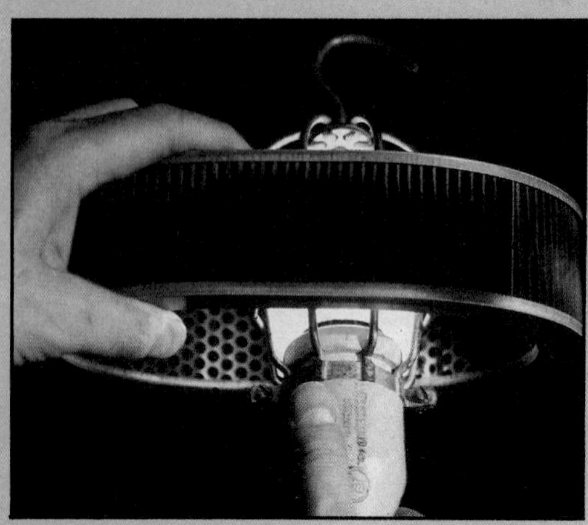

Check the air filter with a light behind it. If you can see light through the filter it can be reused.

Extremely clogged filters should be discarded and replaced with a new one.

18. Replace the air filter regularly. A dirty air filter richens the air/fuel mixture and can increase fuel consumption as much as 10%. Tests show that ⅓ of all vehicles have air filters in need of replacement.

19. Replace the fuel filter at least as often as recommended.

20. Set the idle speed and carburetor mixture to specifications.

21. Check the automatic choke. A sticking or malfunctioning choke wastes gas.

22. During the summer months, adjust the automatic choke for a leaner mixture which will produce faster engine warm-ups.

COOLING SYSTEM

29. Be sure all accessory drive belts are in good condition. Check for cracks or wear.

30. Adjust all accessory drive belts to proper tension.

31. Check all hoses for swollen areas, worn spots, or loose clamps.

32. Check coolant level in the radiator or expansion tank.

33. Be sure the thermostat is operating properly. A stuck thermostat delays engine warm-up and a cold engine uses nearly twice as much fuel as a warm engine.

34. Drain and replace the engine coolant at least as often as recommended. Rust and scale

TIRES & WHEELS

38. Check the tire pressure often with a pencil type gauge. Tests by a major tire manufacturer show that 90% of all vehicles have at least 1 tire improperly inflated. Better mileage can be achieved by over-inflating tires, but never exceed the maximum inflation pressure on the side of the tire.

39. If possible, install radial tires. Radial tires deliver as much as ½ mpg more than bias belted tires.

40. Avoid installing super-wide tires. They only create extra rolling resistance and decrease fuel mileage. Stick to the manufacturer's recommendations.

41. Have the wheels properly balanced.

omy by tampering with emission controls is more likely to worsen fuel economy than improve it. Emission control changes on modern engines are not readily reversible.

16. Clean (or replace) the EGR valve and lines as recommended.

17. Be sure that all vacuum lines and hoses are reconnected properly after working under the hood. An unconnected or misrouted vacuum line can wreak havoc with engine performance.

---

23. Check for fuel leaks at the carburetor, fuel pump, fuel lines and fuel tank. Be sure all lines and connections are tight.

24. Periodically check the tightness of the carburetor and intake manifold attaching nuts and bolts. These are a common place for vacuum leaks to occur.

25. Clean the carburetor periodically and lubricate the linkage.

26. The condition of the tailpipe can be an excellent indicator of proper engine combustion. After a long drive at highway speeds, the inside of the tailpipe should be a light grey in color. Black or soot on the insides indicates an overly rich mixture.

27. Check the fuel pump pressure. The fuel pump may be supplying more fuel than the engine needs.

28. Use the proper grade of gasoline for your engine. Don't try to compensate for knocking or "pinging" by advancing the ignition timing. This practice will only increase plug temperature and the chances of detonation or pre-ignition with relatively little performance gain.

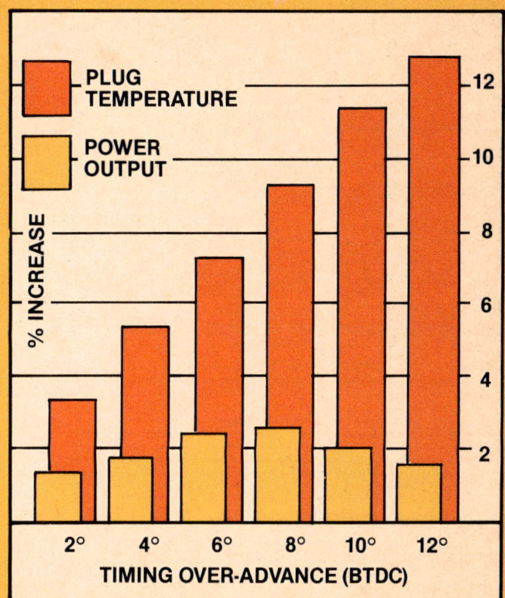

Increasing ignition timing past the specified setting results in a drastic increase in spark plug temperature with increased chance of detonation or preignition. Performance increase is considerably less. (Photo courtesy Champion Spark Plug Co.)

---

that form in the engine should be flushed out to allow the engine to operate at peak efficiency.

35. Clean the radiator of debris that can decrease cooling efficiency.

36. Install a flex-type or electric cooling fan, if you don't have a clutch type fan. Flex fans use curved plastic blades to push more air at low speeds when more cooling is needed; at high speeds the blades flatten out for less resistance. Electric fans only run when the engine temperature reaches a predetermined level.

37. Check the radiator cap for a worn or cracked gasket. If the cap does not seal properly, the cooling system will not function properly.

---

42. Be sure the front end is correctly aligned. A misaligned front end actually has wheels going in differed directions. The increased drag can reduce fuel economy by .3 mpg.

43. Correctly adjust the wheel bearings. Wheel bearings that are adjusted too tight increase rolling resistance.

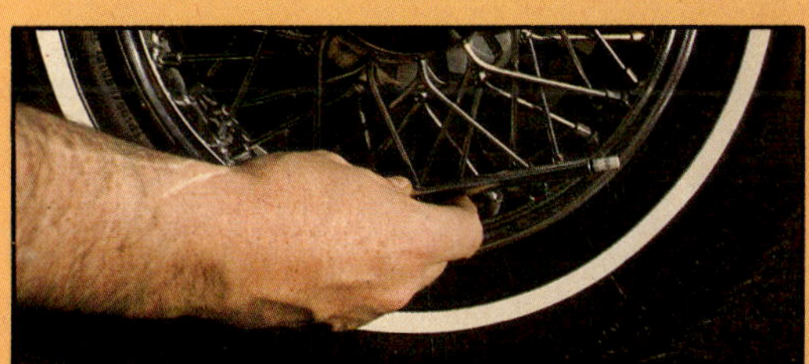

Check tire pressures regularly with a reliable pocket type gauge. Be sure to check the pressure on a cold tire.

GENERAL MAINTENANCE

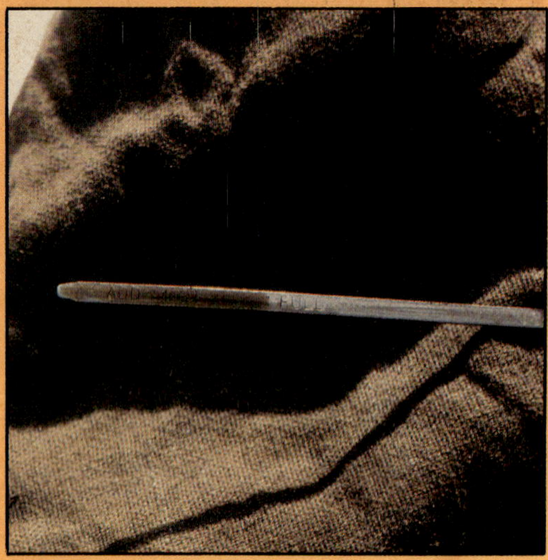

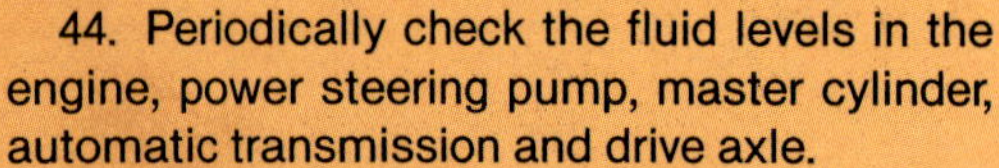

Check the fluid levels (particularly engine oil) on a regular basis. Be sure to check the oil for grit, water or other contamination.

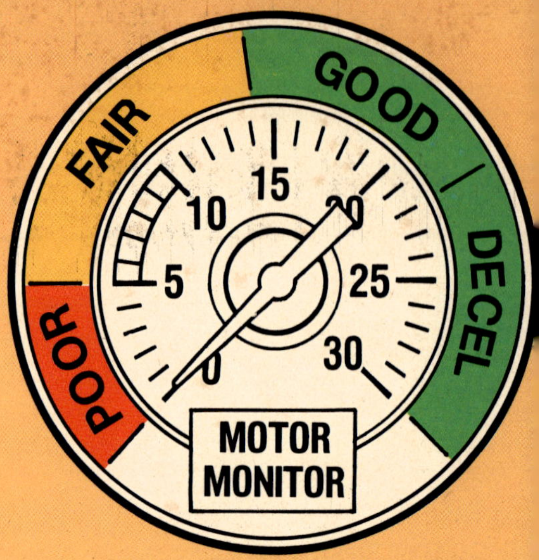

A vacuum gauge is another excellent indicator of internal engine condition and can also be installed in the dash as a mileage indicator.

44. Periodically check the fluid levels in the engine, power steering pump, master cylinder, automatic transmission and drive axle.

45. Change the oil at the recommended interval and change the filter at every oil change. Dirty oil is thick and causes extra friction between moving parts, cutting efficiency and increasing wear. A worn engine requires more frequent tune-ups and gets progressively worse fuel economy. In general, use the lightest viscosity oil for the driving conditions you will encounter.

46. Use the recommended viscosity fluids in the transmission and axle.

47. Be sure the battery is fully charged for fast starts. A slow starting engine wastes fuel.

48. Be sure battery terminals are clean and tight.

49. Check the battery electrolyte level and add distilled water if necessary.

50. Check the exhaust system for crushed pipes, blockages and leaks.

51. Adjust the brakes. Dragging brakes or brakes that are not releasing create increased drag on the engine.

52. Install a vacuum gauge or miles-per-gallon gauge. These gauges visually indicate engine vacuum in the intake manifold. High vacuum = good mileage and low vacuum = poorer mileage. The gauge can also be an excellent indicator of internal engine conditions.

53. Be sure the clutch is properly adjusted. A slipping clutch wastes fuel.

54. Check and periodically lubricate the heat control valve in the exhaust manifold. A sticking or inoperative valve prevents engine warm-up and wastes gas.

55. Keep accurate records to check fuel economy over a period of time. A sudden drop in fuel economy may signal a need for tune-up or other maintenance.

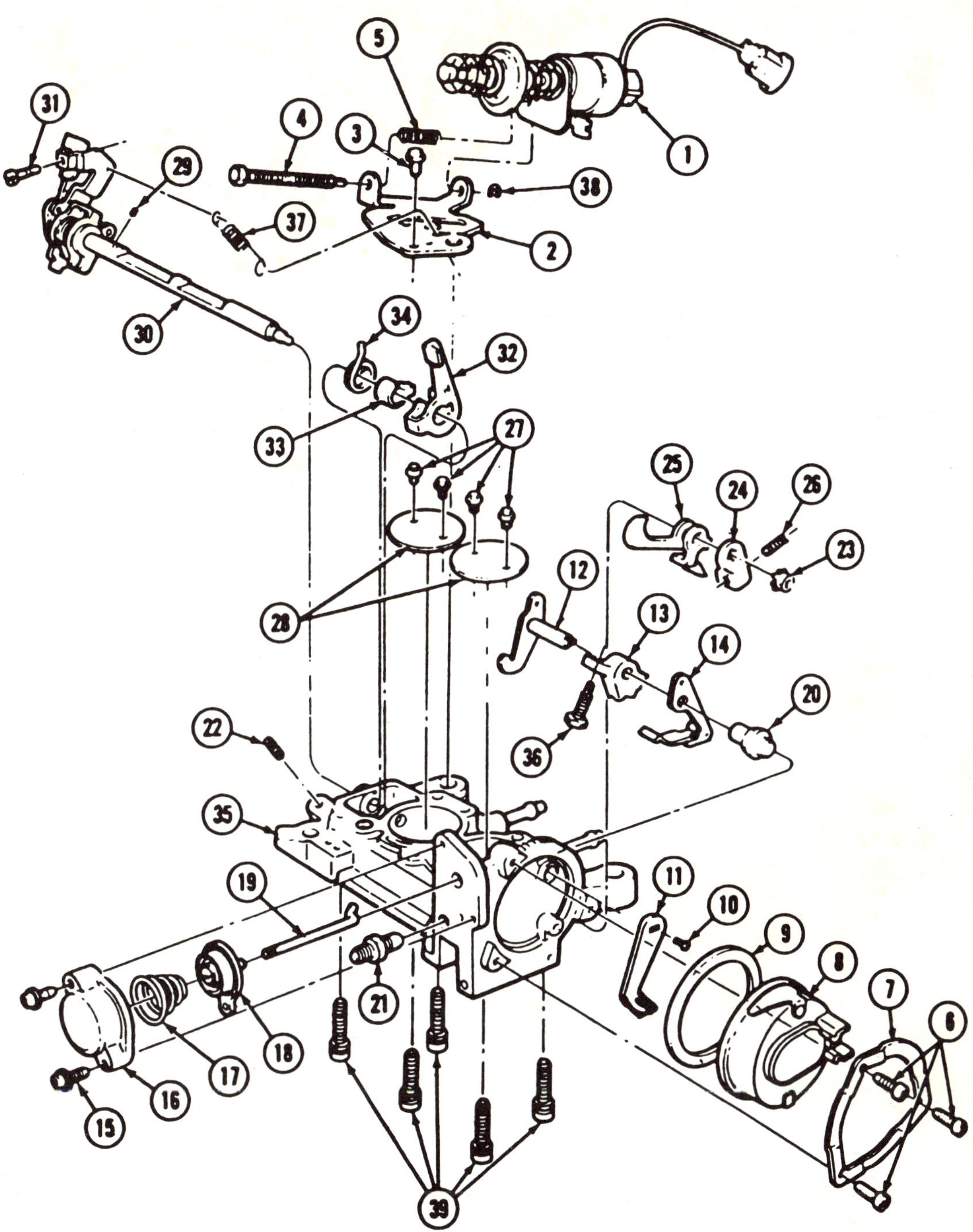

1. Throttle return control device
2. Throttle return control device bracket
3. Mounting screw
4. Adjusting screw
5. Adjusting screw spring
6. Screw
7. Choke thermostatic housing retainer
8. Choke thermostatic housing
9. Choke thermostatic housing gasket
10. Screw
11. Choke thermostatic lever
12. Choke lever and shaft assembly
13. Fast idle cam
14. High cam speed positioner assembly
15. Screw
16. High cam speed positioner diaphragm cover
17. High cam speed positioner diaphragm spring
18. High cam speed positioner diaphragm assembly
19. High cam speed positioner rod
20. Choke housing bushing

Throttle body—2700VV carburetor

18. Remove the idle trim screws. Remove the venturi valve limiter adjusting screw.
19. To assemble the upper body, reverse the order.

MAIN BODY DISASSEMBLY

1. Remove the cranking enrichment solenoid and the O-ring seal.
2. Remove the venturi valve cover, spring guide, and spring. Remove the venturi valve.
3. Remove the throttle body.
4. Remove the choke heat shield.
5. Assembly is in reverse order.

Motorcraft 7200VV Feedback Carburetor

California models of the Fairmont/Zephyr using the 255 cubic inch V8 engine are equipped with a Motorcraft 7200VV Feedback carburetor.

The Model 7200VV Feedback carburetor shares the same basic systems with the 2700VV (variable venturi) carburetor. However, the 7200VV carburetor's feedback system is controlled by an electronic engine control system (EEC III). This system provides precise control of the air/fuel ratio, thereby, improving exhaust emissions, driveability and fuel economy.

Methods of testing the 7200VV carburetor and the EEC III system are possibly beyond the resources of the do-it-yourselfer. It, therefore, is suggested that you consult your Ford dealer or a qualified repair shop for any service or repair.

Fuel Tank

REMOVAL

1. Raise the vehicle up on a hoist.
2. Drain the fuel from the tank.
3. Disconnect the fuel lines and hoses from the tank assembly.
4. Loosen the retaining straps at the adjusting bolts and remove the tank.

INSTALLATION

1. Position the fuel tank and install the retaining straps.
2. Connect all fuel lines, replacing any cracked, split, or dried out hoses.
3. Replace the fuel separator if found to be damaged or inoperative.
4. Tighten the retaining straps securely.

Chassis Electrical

HEATER

Blower Motor—Without Air Conditioning

REMOVAL AND INSTALLATION

The right side ventilator assembly must be removed for access to the blower motor and wheel.

1. Remove the retaining screw for the right register duct mounting bracket.
2. Remove the screws holding the control cable lever assembly to the instrument panel.
3. Remove the glove box liner.
4. Remove the plastic rivets securing the grille to the floor outlet, and remove the grille.
5. Remove the right register duct and register assembly:
   a. Remove the register duct bracket retaining screw on the lower edge of the instrument panel, and disengage the duct from the opening and remove through the glove box opening.
   b. Insert a thin blade under the retaining tab and pry the tab toward the louvers until the retaining tab pivot clears the hole in the register opening. Pull the register assembly end out from the housing only enough to prevent the pivot from going back into the pivot hole. Pry the other retaining tab loose and remove the register assembly from the opening.

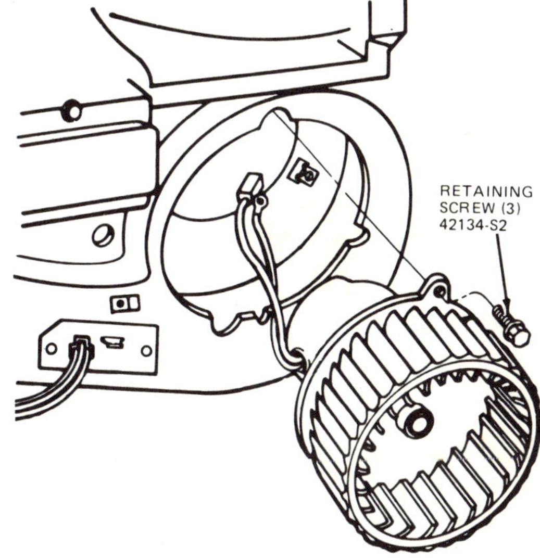

Blower motor and wheel assembly removal—without A/C

6. Remove the retaining screws securing the ventilator assembly to the blower housing. The upper right screw can be reached with a long extension through the register opening; the upper left screw can be reached through the glove box opening. The other two screws are on the bottom of the assembly.

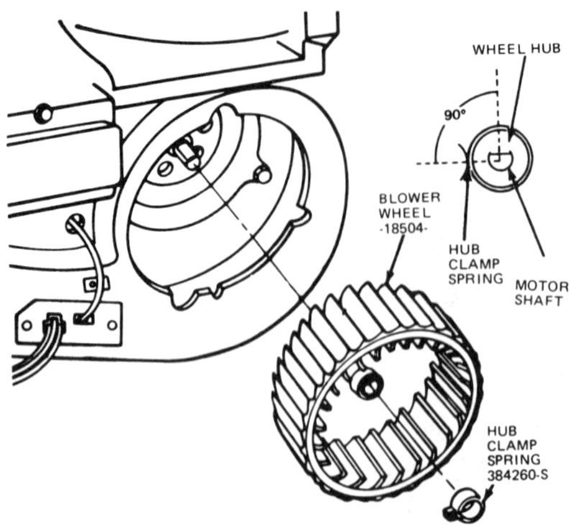

Blower motor wheel removal—without A/C

7. Slide the assembly to the right, then down and out from under the instrument panel.

8. Remove the motor lead wire connector from the register and push it back through the hole in the case. Remove the right side cowl trim panel for access, and remove the ground terminal lug retaining screw.

9. Remove the hub clamp spring from the motor shaft and remove the blower wheel.

10. Remove the blower motor bolts from the housing and remove the motor.

11. To install reverse the removal procedure.

Blower Motor—With Air Conditioning

REMOVAL AND INSTALLATION

The air inlet duct and blower housing assembly must be removed for access to the blower motor.

1. Remove the glove box liner and disconnect the hose from the vacuum motor.
2. Remove the instrument panel lower right side to cowl attaching bolt.
3. Remove the screw attaching the brace to the top of the air inlet duct.
4. Disconnect the motor wire.
5. Remove the housing lower support bracket to case nut.
6. Remove the side cowl trim panel and remove the ground wire screw.
7. Remove the attaching screw at the top of the air inlet duct.
8. Remove the air inlet duct and housing assembly down and away from the evaporator case.
9. Remove the four blower motor mounting plate screws and remove the blower motor and wheel as an assembly from the housing. Do not remove the mounting plate from the motor.
10. To install reverse the above.

Heater Core—Without Air Conditioning

REMOVAL AND INSTALLATION

It is not necessary to remove the heater case for access to the heater core.

1. Drain enough coolant from the radiator to drain the heater core.
2. Loosen the heater clamps on the engine side of the firewall and disconnect the heater hoses. Cap the heater core tubes.
3. Remove the glove box liner.
4. Remove the instrument panel-to-cowl brace retaining screws and remove the brace.
5. Move the temperature lever to warm.
6. Remove the heater core cover screws. Remove the cover through the glove box.
7. Loosen the heater case mounting nuts on the engine side of the firewall.
8. Push the heater core tubes and seal toward the interior of the car to loosen the core.
9. Remove the heater core through the glove box opening.
10. To install reverse the above.

Heater Core—With Air Conditioning

REMOVAL AND INSTALLATION

The instrument panel must be removed for access to the heater core.

1. Disconnect the battery ground cable.
2. Remove the instrument panel pad:
   a. Remove the screws attaching the instrument cluster trim panel to the pad.
   b. Remove the screw attaching the pad to the panel at each defroster opening.
   c. Remove the screws attaching the edge of the pad to the panel.
3. Remove the steering column opening cover.
4. Remove the nuts and bracket retaining the steering column to the instrument panel and lay the column against the seat.
5. Remove the instrument panel to brake pedal support screw at the column opening.
6. Remove the screws attaching the lower brace to the panel below the radio, and below the glove box.
7. Disconnect the temperature cable from the door and case bracket.

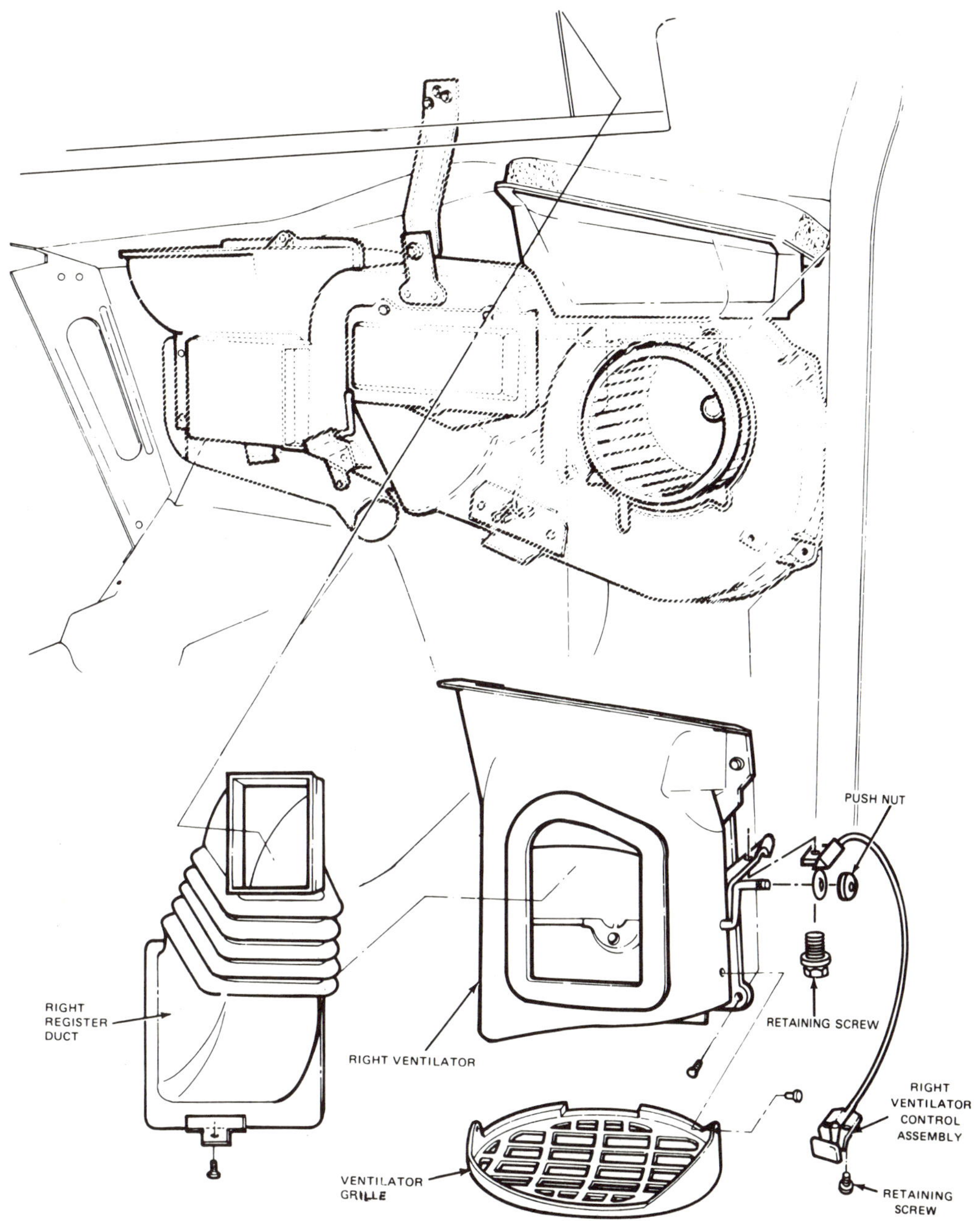

Right ventilator and register duct removal—without A/C

8. Unplug the port vacuum hose connectors at the evaporator case.

9. Disconnect the resistor wire connector and the blower feed wire.

10. Remove the screws attaching the top of the panel to the cowl. Support the panel while doing this.

11. Remove one screw at each end attaching the panel to the cowl side panels.

12. Move the panel rearward and disconnect the speedometer cable and any wires preventing the panel from lying flat on the seat.

13. Drain the coolant and disconnect the heater hoses from the heater core. Plug the core tubes.

14. Remove the nuts retaining the evaporator case to the firewall in the engine compartment.

15. Remove the case support bracket screws and air inlet duct support bracket.

16. Remove the nut retaining the bracket

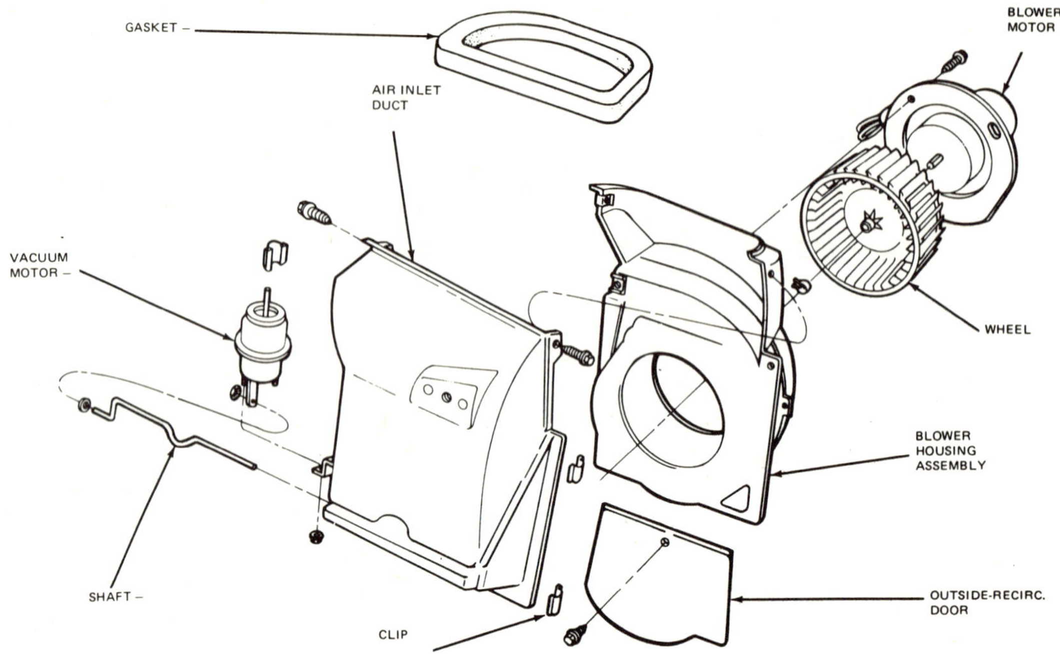

Air inlet duct and blower housing (disassembled) with A/C

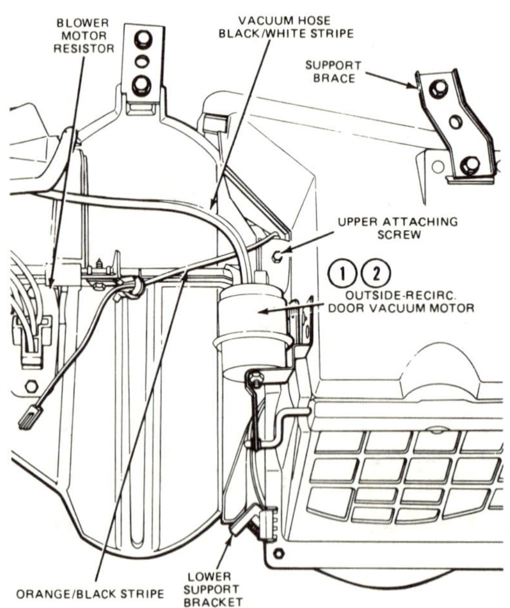

Air inlet duct and blower housing—with A/C

to the dash panel at the left side of the evaporator case, and the nut retaining the bracket below the case to the dash panel.

17. Pull the case assembly away from the panel to get to the screws retaining the heater core cover to the case.
18. Remove the cover screws and the cover.
19. Lift the heater core and seals from the evaporator case.
20. To install reverse the above.

RADIO

REMOVAL AND INSTALLATION

1. Disconnect the battery ground cable.
2. Disconnect the power lead, speaker leads and antenna lead-in-cable from the radio receiver.
3. Remove the control knobs, discs, control shaft nuts and washers.
4. Remove the ash receptacle and bracket.
5. Remove the radio rear support attaching nut.
6. Remove the instrument panel lower reinforcement.
7. Remove the heater or air conditioning floor ducts.
8. Remove the radio receiver from the bezel and the rear support, then lower the radio from the instrument panel.
9. To install reverse the above procedure.

Front Speaker (Instrument Panel)

REMOVAL AND INSTALLATION

1. Remove the instrument panel pad.
   a. Remove the three cluster panel retaining screws.
   b. Remove the four instrument panel pad retaining screws at the rear edge of the pad.

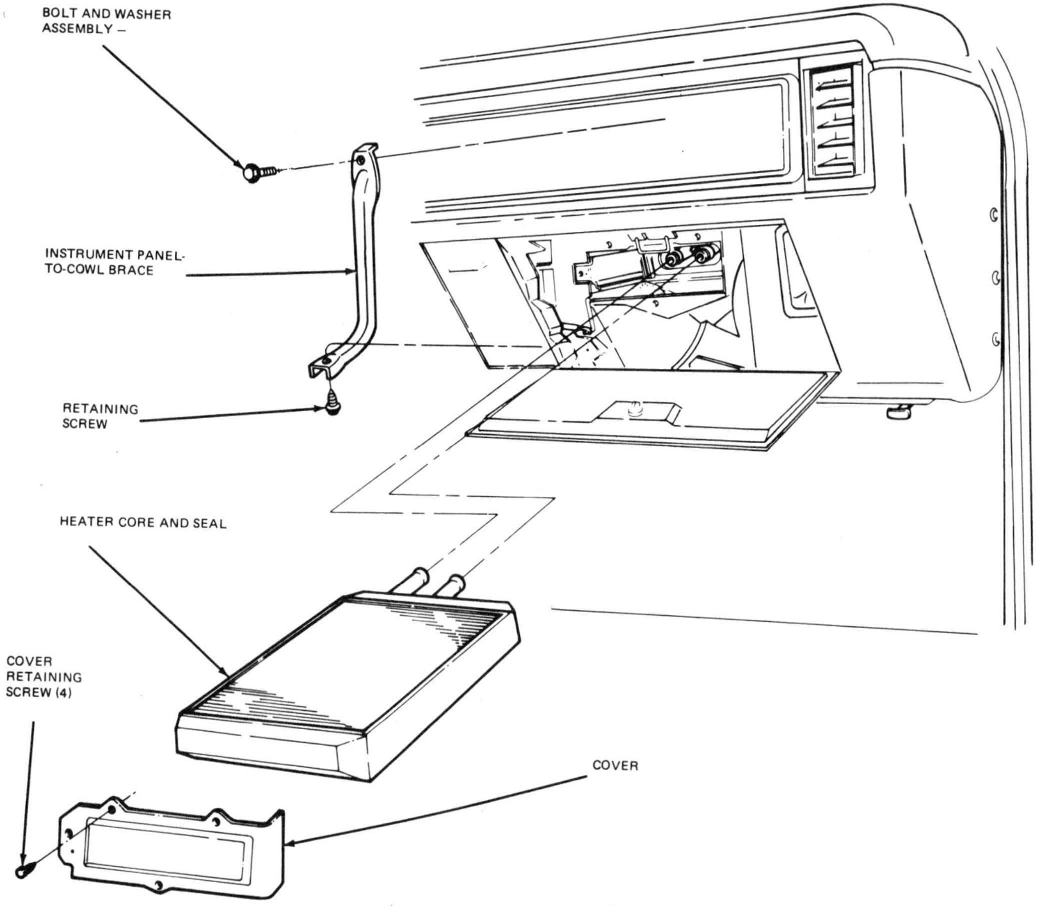

Heater core removal—without A/C

c. Remove the four instrument panel pad retaining screws in the top defroster openings, and remove the pad.

2. Remove the two speaker retaining screws, disconnect the speaker lead and remove the speaker.

3. Installation is the reverse of removal. Make sure the speaker operates properly before installing the instrument panel pad.

WINDSHIELD WIPER SYSTEM

The windshield wipers are actuated by a permanent magnet, rotary type electric motor. The two wiper arms and blades are mounted on a pivot shaft, one at each end of the windshield. The pivot shafts are connected to the motor by linkage arms and attaching clips.

Wiper Arm Assembly

REMOVAL AND INSTALLATION

1. Raise the blade end of the arm off the windshield and move the slide latch away from the pivot shaft.

2. The wiper arm should now be unlocked and can now be pulled off of the pivot shaft.

3. To install, position the auxiliary arm (if so equipped) over the pivot pin, hold it down and push the main arm head over the pivot shaft. Make sure the pivot shaft is in the park position.

4. Hold the main arm head on the pivot shaft while raising the blade end of the wiper arm and push the slide latch into the lock under the pivot shaft. Lower the blade to the windshield.

NOTE: *If the blade does not touch the windshield, the slide latch is not completely in place.*

Wiper Blade (Tridon Type)

REPLACEMENT

1. Pull up on the spring lock and pull the blade assembly from the pin.

2. To install, push the blade assembly onto the pin, so that the spring lock engages the pin.

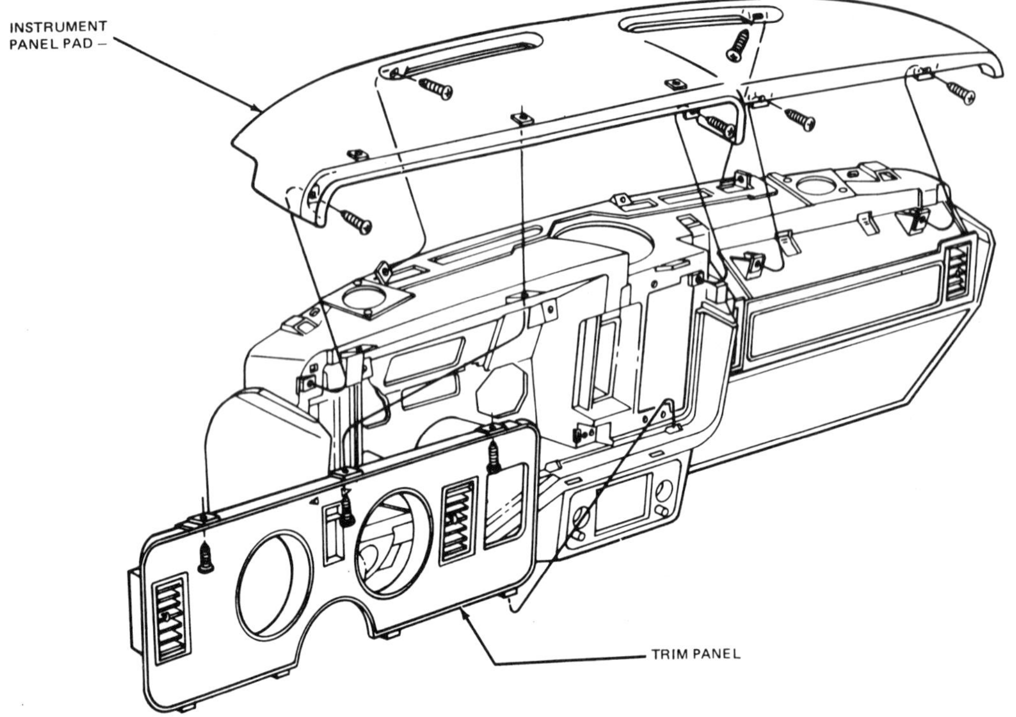

INSTRUMENT
PANEL PAD –
TRIM PANEL

Instrument panel pad removal

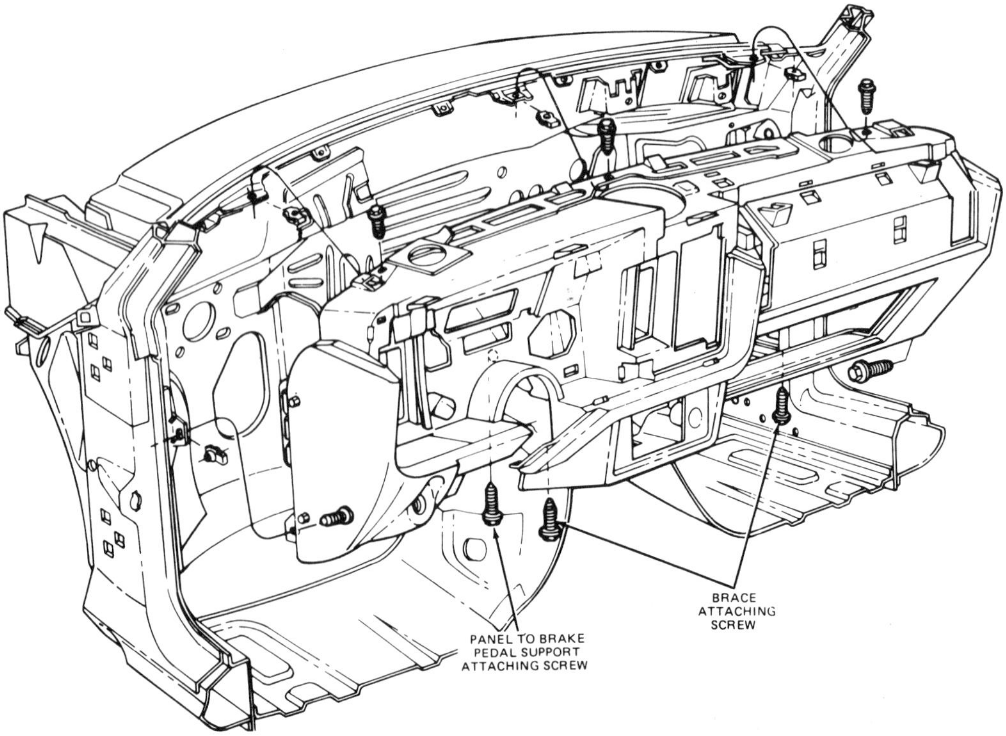

BRACE
ATTACHING
SCREW
PANEL TO BRAKE
PEDAL SUPPORT
ATTACHING SCREW

Instrument panel removal

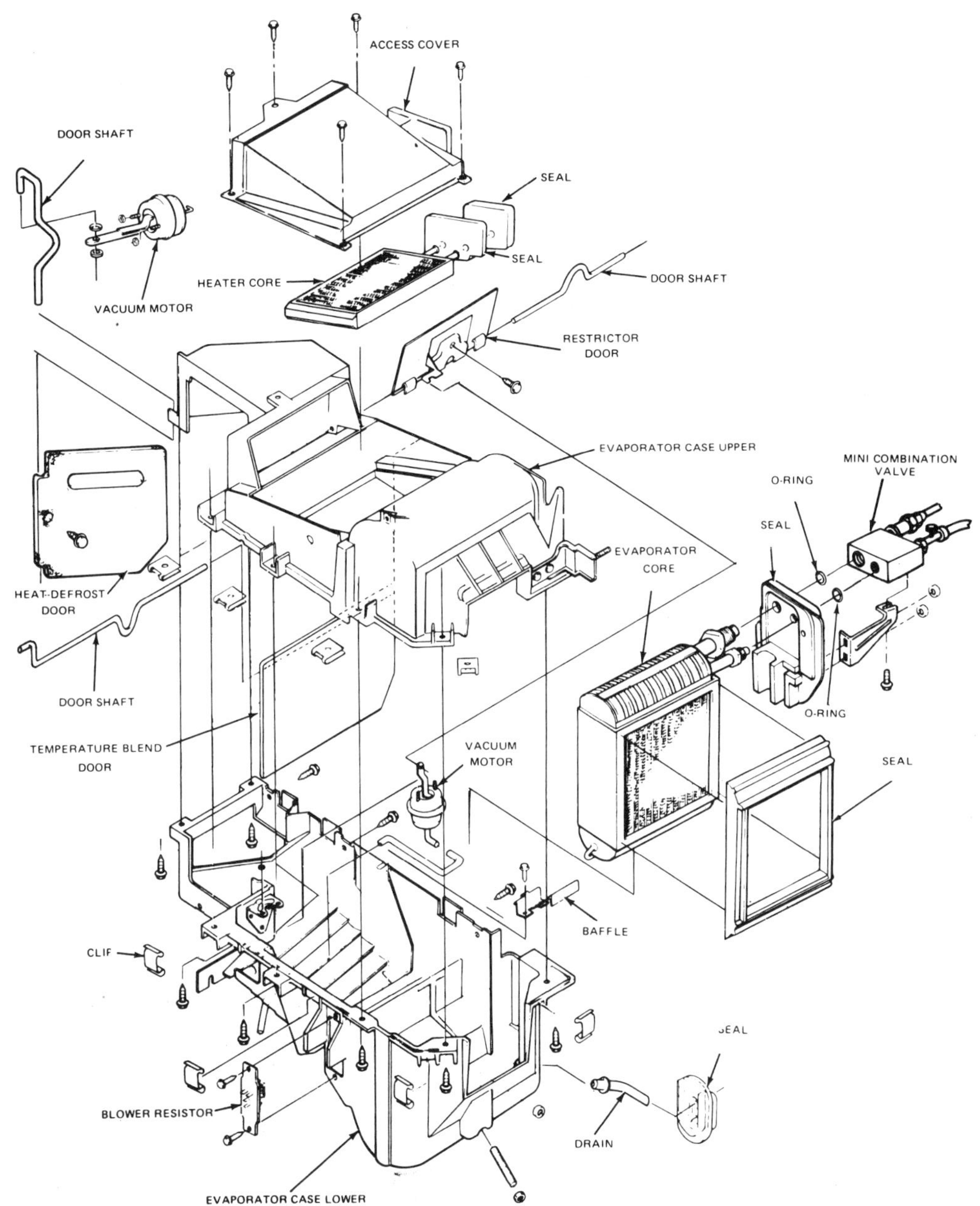

Evaporator case assembly (exploded view)

Wiper Element (Tridon)

REPLACEMENT

1. Locate a 7/16" long notch approximately one inch from the end of the plastic backing strip, which is part of the rubber blade element assembly.

2. With the wiper blade removed from the arm place the blade assembly on a firm surface with the notched end of the backing strip visible.

3. Push down on one end of the wiper assembly until the blade is tightly bowed then grasp the tip of the backing strip firmly, pulling and twisting at the same time. The backing strip will then snap out of the retaining tab on the end of the wiper frame.

4. Lift the wiper blade assembly from the surface and slide the backing strip down the frame until the notch lines up with the next retaining tab then twist slightly and the backing strip will snap out. Follow this same procedure with the remaining tabs until the element is removed.

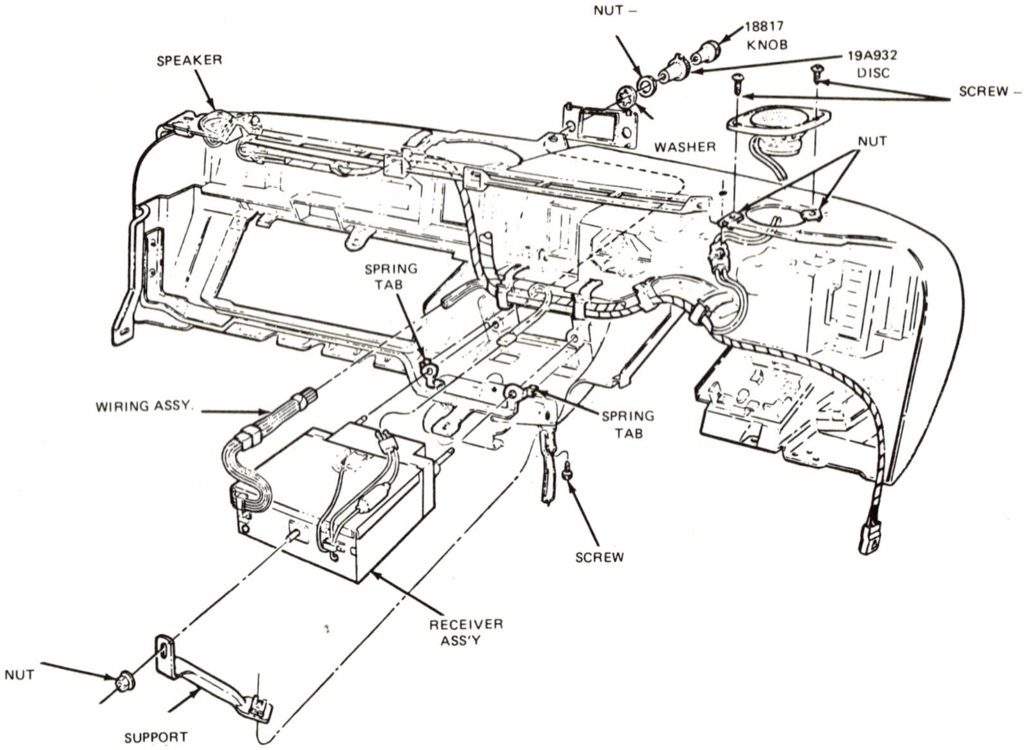

Radio installation

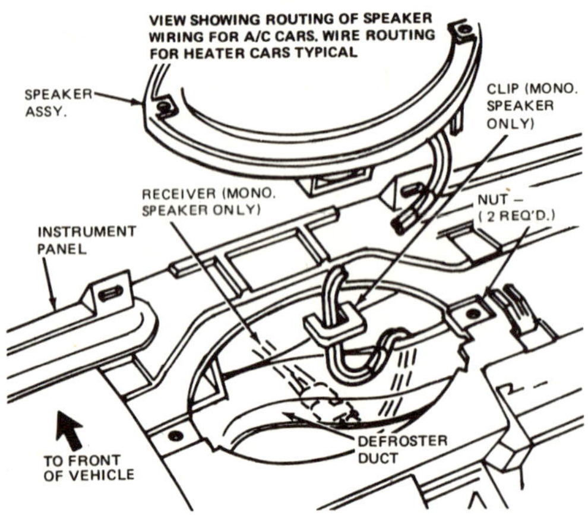

Front speaker installation

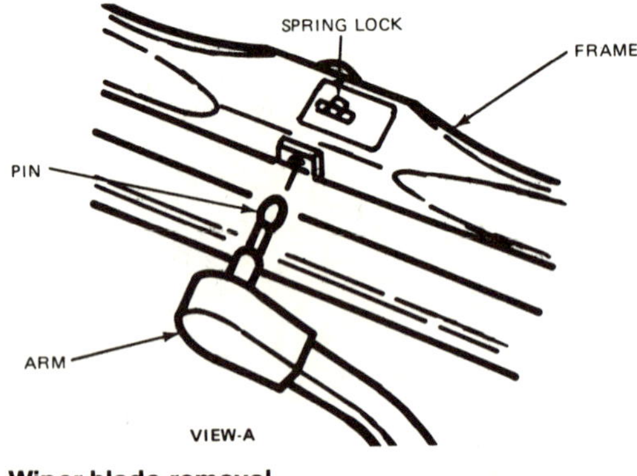

Wiper blade removal

5. To install the blade element reverse the above procedure and make sure all six tabs are locked to the backing strip.

Wiper Motor

REMOVAL AND INSTALLATION

1. Disconnect the negative (ground) cable of the battery.
2. Remove right- and left-hand wiper arm and blade assembly.
3. Remove top cowl mounting screws and remove the cowl grille.
4. Remove the link retaining clip that holds the wiper linkage to the wiper motor. Disconnect the wiper linkage from the wiper motor drive arm.
5. Disconnect the electrical connector to the wiper motor.
6. Remove the wiper motor mounting screws and remove the wiper motor.
7. Reverse to install.

CROSS SECTION
LIFT BLADE END OF ARM
AWAY FROM WINDSHIELD
RELEASE LATCH

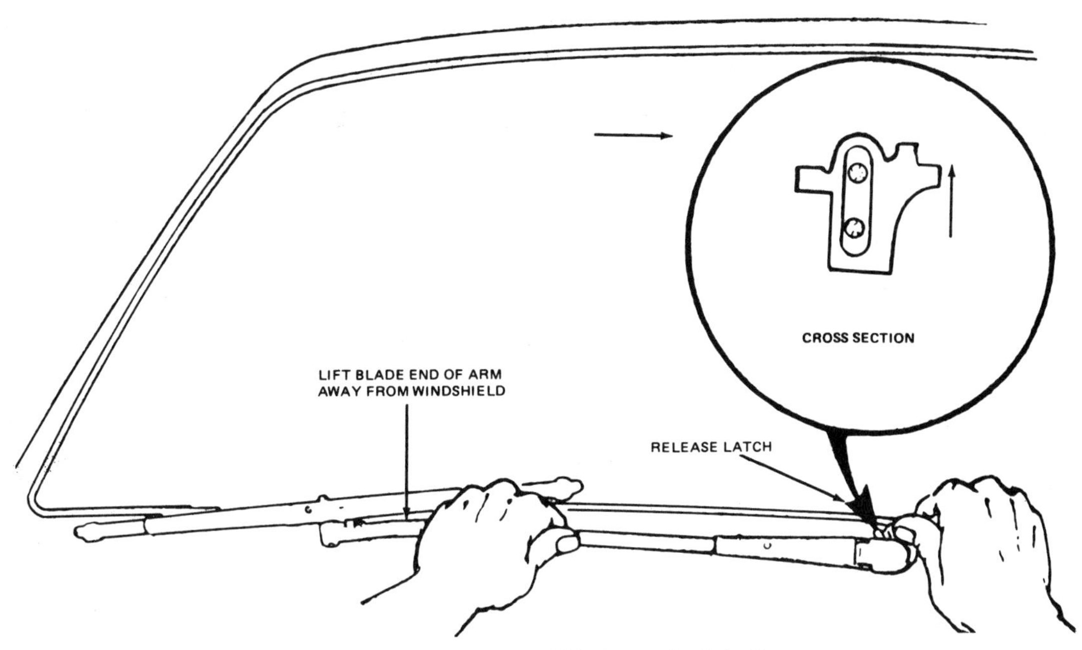

Installing wiper arm and blade on pivot shaft

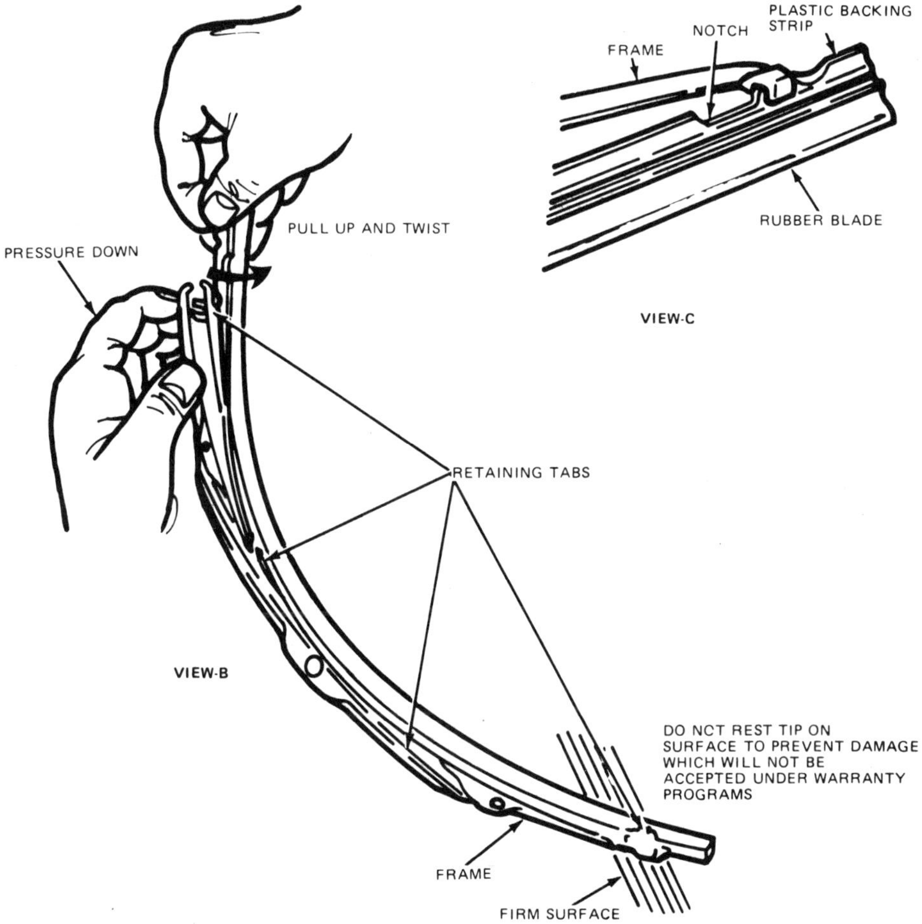

PLASTIC BACKING
STRIP
NOTCH
FRAME
RUBBER BLADE
VIEW-C
PULL UP AND TWIST
PRESSURE DOWN
RETAINING TABS
VIEW-B
DO NCT REST TIP ON
SURFACE TO PREVENT DAMAGE
WHICH WILL NOT BE
ACCEPTED UNDER WARRANTY
PROGRAMS
FRAME
FIRM SURFACE

Wiper blade insert removal

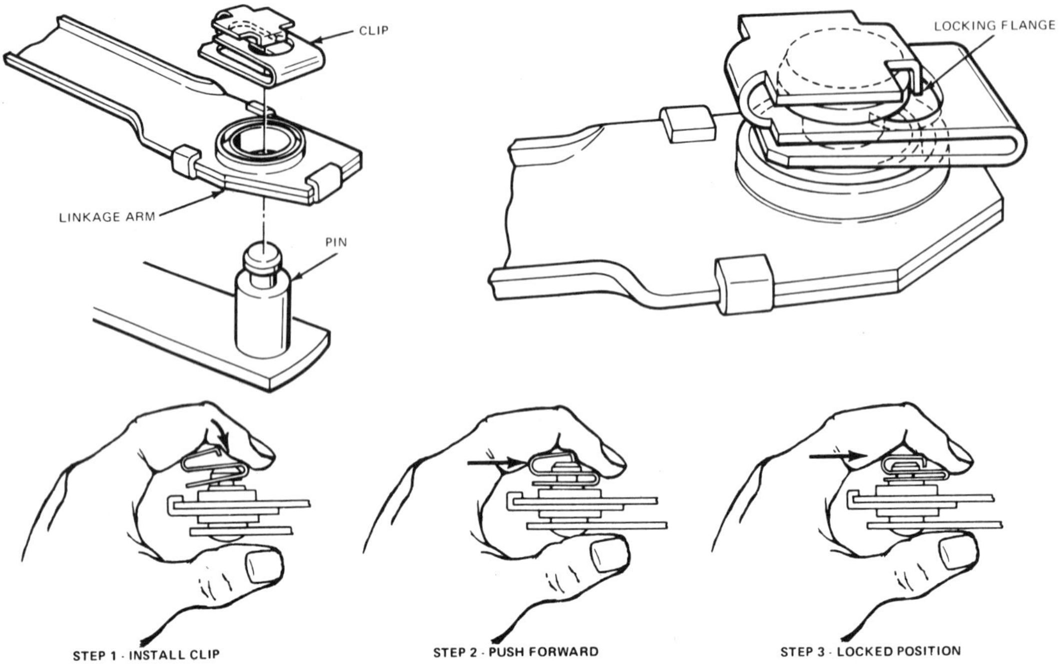

CLIP
LOCKING FLANGE
LINKAGE ARM
PIN
STEP 1 - INSTALL CLIP
STEP 2 - PUSH FORWARD
STEP 3 - LOCKED POSITION

Wiper arm connecting clips

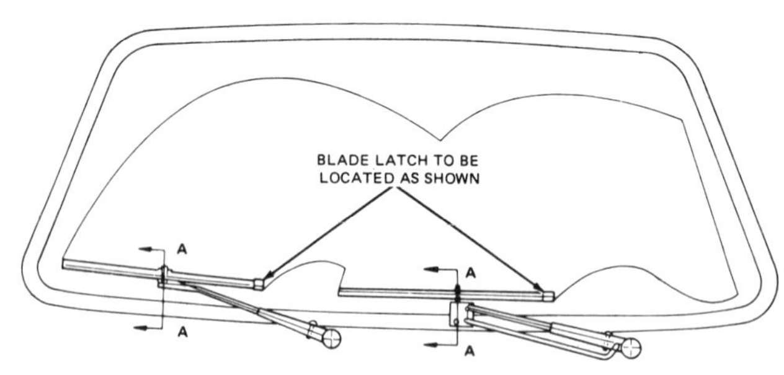

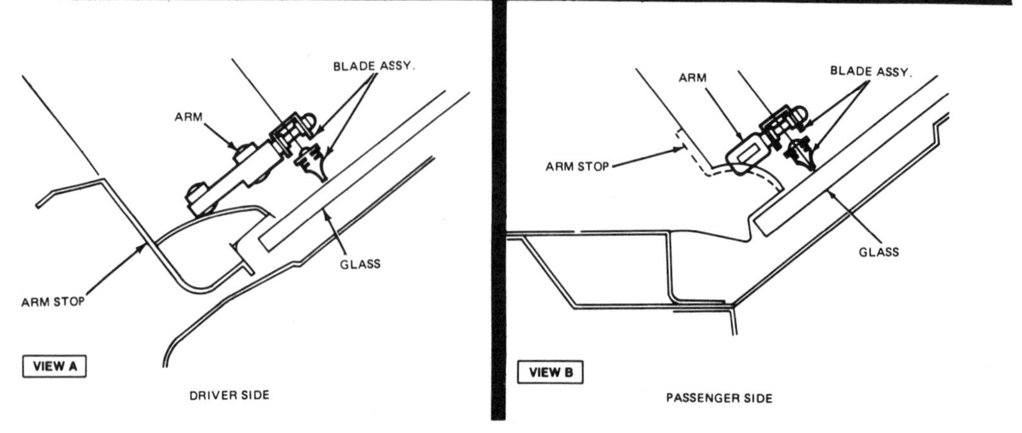

Adjusting wiper arm and blade

Pivot Shafts and Wiper Linkage

REMOVAL AND INSTALLATION

The wiper linkage is mounted below the cowl top grille. The pivot shafts and linkage assemblies are connected together with nonremoveable plastic ball joints. The left- and right-hand pivot shafts and linkage are serviced as one unit.

1. Disconnect the battery.
2. Remove the cowl top grille attaching screws and the grille.
3. Remove the clip and disconnect the linkage drive arm from the motor crank pin.
4. Remove the two bolts retaining the right pivot shaft to the cowl, and remove the large nut, washer and spacer from the left pivot shaft.
5. To install reverse the removal procedure. Before installing the blade assemblies, make sure the motor is in PARK and the blades are set to the proper dimension. See the Arm and Blade Adjustment procedure.

Arm and Blade Adjustment

1. With the arm and blade assemblies removed from pivot shafts turn on the wiper switch and allow the motor to move the pivot shafts three or four cycles, and then turn off the wiper switch. This will place the pivot shafts in the park position.
2. Install the arm and blade assemblies on the pivot shafts to the correct distance between the windshield lower moulding or weatherstrip and the blade saddle centerline.

INSTRUMENT CLUSTER

REMOVAL

1. Disconnect the battery ground cable.
2. Remove three upper retaining screws from the instrument cluster trim cover and remove the trim cover.
3. Remove the two upper and two lower screws, retaining the instrument cluster to the instrument panel.
4. Pull the cluster away from the instrument panel and reach behind the instrument cluster to disconnect the speedometer cable by pressing on the flat surface of the plastic connector (quick connect).
5. Pull the cluster further away from the instrument panel, disconnect the two cluster printed circuit connectors from their receptacles in the cluster backplate.
6. Remove the clusters.

INSTALLATION

1. Apply a $^{3}/_{16}$ inch diameter ball of silicone damping grease in the drive hole of the speedometer head.
2. Connect the cluster.
3. Connect the two cluster printed circuit connectors to their receptacles in the cluster backplate.
4. Connect the speedometer cable.
5. Install the two upper and lower screws.
6. Install the three upper retaining screws to the instrument cluster trim cover, and install the trim cover.
7. Connect the battery ground cable.

Speedometer Cable Replacement

1. Reach up behind the speedometer and depress the flat, quick disconnect tab (thumb latch), while pulling back on the cable.
2. If just the inner core is to be replaced pull the core from the casing. If the inner core is broken, raise and support the car and remove the cable-to-transmission clamp and pull the cable core from the transmission.
3. If both the cable and casing need to be replaced disconnect the cable from the speedometer head and push through the opening in the dash panel or floor pan. Raise the car on a hoist and disconnect the cable from the transmission and the retaining clips. To prevent kinking reroute the cable assembly properly. See the illustration.

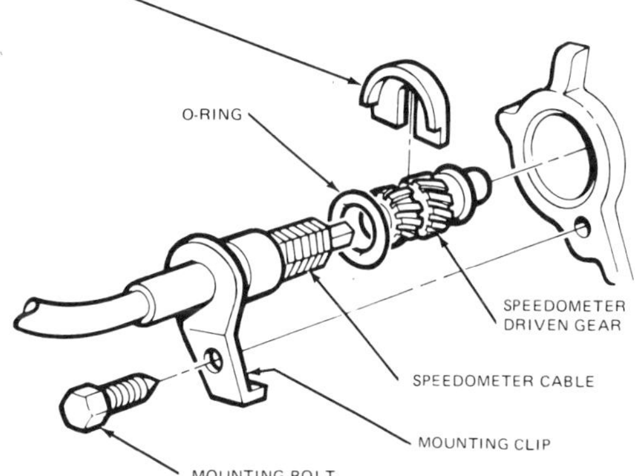

Speedometer cable to transmission mounting

Ignition Switch

Removal and Installation procedures for the ignition switch is found in Chapter 8.

LIGHTING

Headlamps

Fairmonts and Zephyrs use the two, or four headlamp system depending on the body style of the car. In 1980 and later years the four headlamp models use halogen sealed beams. The halogen sealed beams provide a whiter light while reducing the electrical load. Although the halogen sealed beams are interchangeable with the conventional sealed beams it is recommended that all headlamps on the car be of the same kind.

REMOVAL AND INSTALLATION

1. Remove the headlamp door mounting screws and remove the headlamp door.
2. Remove the four retainer ring screws and remove the retainer ring from the headlamp. Pull the headlamp bulb forward and disconnect the wiring assembly plug.
3. To install, connect the wiring plug to the new headlamp bulb and position the bulb so that the bulb tabs are in the slots.
4. Attach the bulb retaining ring to the assembly and install the screws.
5. Place the headlamp door into position and install the mounting screws.

CIRCUIT PROTECTION

Fusible Links

In addition to fuses and circuit breakers some wiring harnesses incorporate fusible links to protect the wiring.

NOTE: *Refer to the Circuit Protection Chart to find out what circuits use fusible links.*

The fusible link is a short length of special, Hypalon (high temperature) insulated wire, integral with the engine compartment wiring harness and should not be confused with standard wire. It is several wire gauges smaller than the circuit which it protects. Under no circumstances should a fuse link replacement repair be made using a length of standard wire cut from bulk stock or from another wiring harness.

To repair any blown fuse link use the following procedure:

1. Determine which circuit is damaged, its location and the cause of the open fuse link. If the damaged fuse link is one of three fed by a common No. 10 or 12 gauge feed wire, determine the specific affected circuit.

Bulb Chart

Function	*Number of Bulbs*	*Trade Number*
EXTERIOR ILLUMINATION		
Headlamps—2 lamp system	(2)	6052
Headlamps—Lo & Hi Beam	(2)	4652 ①
Headlamps—Hi Beam	(2)	4651 ①
Front Park/Turn	(2)	1157NA ②
Front Side Marker	(2)	194
Rear Tail/Stop/Turn	(2)	1157
Back-Up Light	(2)	1156
License Plate	(1)	168
Rear Side Marker	(2)	194
Tail/Stop/Turn	(2)	1157 (wgn)
Back-Up Light	(2)	1156 (wgn)
License Lamp	(1)	168
INTERIOR ILLUMINATION		
Turn Signal	(2)	194
Wipe/Wash Nomenclature	(1)	168
Fan Nomenclature	(1)	1892
Heater Control Nomenclature	(1)	161
A/C Control Nomenclature	(1)	161
Glove Compartment (opt.)	(1)	1816
Courtesy Lamp (Opt.	(2)	89
Ash Tray	(1)	1892
High Beam Indicator	(1)	194
Warning Lamps—All	(*)	194
Cluster Illumination—All*	(4)	194
Dome Lamp (Opt.)	(1)	906
Dome/Map Lamp (Opt.):		
Dome	(1)	212 ③
Map	(1)	1816
Trunk Compartment (Opt.)	(1)	89
Engine Compartment (Opt.)	(1)	89
Automatic Transmission "PRND21" Indicator (Floor shift)	(1)	1445
Electric rear window defrost	(1)	2162
RADIO LIGHTS		
Pilot (Dial Illumination)		
All except Tape Radios	(1)	1893
AM/FM Stereo Tape Radio	(2)	37 ④
Stereo Program Indicator		
AM/FM Stereo Radio	(1)	1892 ④

*Brake, engine, alt, and fasten belts.
① 1980 and later—4 head lamp system use Halogen beams:
Low Beam: H4656
High Beam: H4651
② 1980 and later—1157
Front Park—194
③ 1980 and later—912
④ 1980 and later—1893

2. Disconnect the negative battery cable.

3. Cut the damaged fuse link from the wiring harness and discard it. If the fuse link is one of three circuits fed by a single feed wire, cut it out of the harness at each splice end and discard it.

4. Identify and procure the proper fuse link and butt connectors for attaching the fuse link to the harness.

5. To repair any fuse link in a 3-link group with one feed:

a. After cutting the open link out of the harness, cut each of the remaining undamaged fuse links close to the feed wire weld.

b. Strip approximately ½ inch of insulation from the detached ends of the two good fuse links. Then insert two wire ends into one end of a butt connector and carefully push one stripped end of the replacement fuse link into the same end of the butt connector and crimp all three firmly together.

NOTE: *Care must be taken when fitting the three fuse links into the butt connector as the internal diameter is a snug fit for three wires. Make sure to use a proper crimping tool. Pliers, side cutters, etc. will not apply the proper crimp to retain the wires and withstand a pull test.*

c. After crimping the butt connector to the three fuse links, cut the weld portion from the feed wire and strip approximately ½ inch of insulation from the cut end. Insert the stripped end into the open end of the butt connector and crimp very firmly.

d. To attach the remaining end of the replacement fuse link strip approximately ½ inch of insulation from the wire end of the circuit from which the blown fuse link was removed, and firmly crimp a butt connector or equivalent to the stripped wire. Then, insert the end of the replacement link into the other end of the butt connector and crimp firmly.

e. Using rosin core solder and with a consistency of 60 percent tin and 40 percent lead, solder the connectors and the wires at the repairs and insulate with electrical tape.

6. To replace any fuse link on a single circuit in a harness, cut out the damaged portion, strip approximately ½ inch of insulation from the two wire ends and attach the appropriate replacement fuse link to the stripped wire ends with two proper size butt connectors. Solder the connectors and wires and insulate with tape.

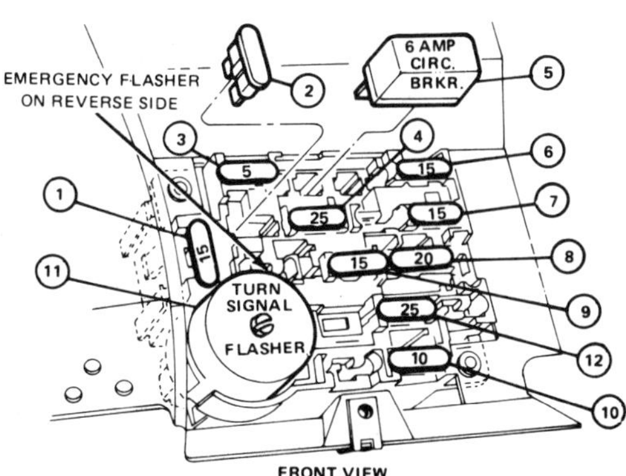

Typical fuse and circuit breaker panel

7. To repair any fuse link which has an eyelet terminal on one end such as the charging circuit, cut off the open fuse link behind the weld, strip approximately ½ inch of insulation from the cut end and attach the appropriate new eyelet fuse link to the cut stripped wire with an appropriate size butt connector. Solder the connectors and wires at the repair and insulate with tape.

8. Connect the negative battery cable to the battery and test the system for proper operation.

NOTE: *Do not mistake a resistor wire for a fuse link. The resistor wire is generally longer and has print stating "Resistor don't cut or splice."*

NOTE: *When attaching a single No. 16, 17, 18 or 20 gauge fuse link to a heavy gauge wire, always double the stripped wire end of the fuse link before inserting and crimping it into the butt connector for positive wire retention.*

Circuit Breaker

A circuit breaker is an electrical switch which breaks the circuit in case of an overload. The circuit breaker is located at the top of the fuse panel.

Fuse Panel

The fuse panel is located in the lower left portion of the instrument panel, behind a trim cover. Circuit breakers and turn signal flashers can also be located in the fuse panel. To check out or replace a fuse or circuit breaker proceed as follows:

1. Remove the two screws and remove the fuse panel trim cover.

2. Locate the blown fuse or malfunctioning circuit breaker and remove it by pulling it out of the cavity.

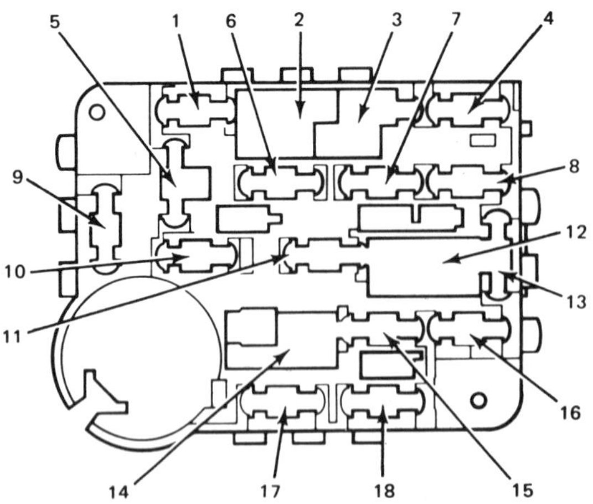

Typical fuse and circuit breaker panel (1981 and later)

3. Using the same amp rating push the fuse or circuit breaker into the panel until it seats fully.

Flasher Locations

1978 AND 1979

Turn Signal; located above and to the right of the glove box.
Hazard Warning; located above and to the left of the glove box.

1980

Turn signal; located on the front of the fuse panel-left-hand, lower corner.
Hazard Warning; back side of the fuse panel, behind the turn signal flasher.

1978 Fuse Identification

Circuit Protected	*Position*	*Size*
Ignition Feed to Engine, Warning Lamps, Seat Belt Warning Buzzer, Seat Belt Warning amp, Throttle Positiner, Emission Control Solenoid, Park Brake	1	14 Amp.
Blank	2	—
Heater A/C	3	15 Amp. 35 Amp.
Accessory, Heated Backlite Relay Coil, Rear Window Defogger, Rear Window Wiper & Washer, Turn Signal Lamps, Back-Up Lamps	4	15 Amp.
Windshield Wiper & Washer (2-Speed & Intermittent)	5	6 Amp. C.B.
Radio & Stereo Tape Player	6	7.5 Amp.
Instrument Panel Illumination, Trans. Indicator, Ash Tray, Heater, A/C & ATC Controls, Headlamp, Windshield Wiper/Washer Illumination, Radio Lamp	7	4 Amp.
Rear Wiper/Washer Motor	8	4.5 Amp. C.B.
A/C Clutch	9	15 Amp.
Courtesy Lamps, Dome, Map, Luggage Compartment, Ignition Key Warning Buzzer	10	15 Amp.
Horns, Cigar Lighter	11	20 Amp.
Emergency Flasher, Stop Lamps	12	15 Amp.

1978 Circuit Protection

Circuit Protected	*Location*	*Size*
Headlights, High Beam Indicator	Part of Headlight Switch	22 Amp. C.B.
Horn, Stoplights, Side Markers, Parking Lamps, License Plate Lamp		15 Amp.
Windshield Wiper Motor & Washer Motor	Part of Windshield Wiper Switch	6 Amp. C.B.
No. 37 Alternator	At Starter Motor Relay	14 Ga. Fuse Link
No. 80 Engine Compartment Lamp		20 Ga. Fuse Link
Liftgate Wiper/Washer (Sta. Wagon only)	Part of Wiper Switch	4 Amp. C.B.

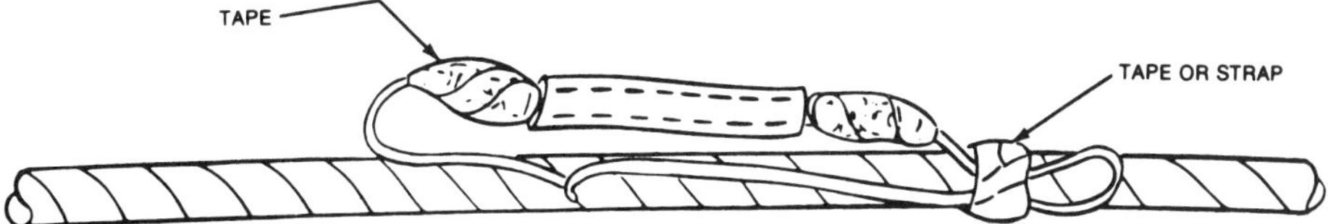

TYPICAL REPAIR USING THE SPECIAL #17 GA. (9.00" LONG-YELLOW) FUSE LINK REQUIRED FOR THE AIR/COND. CIRCUITS (2) #687E and #261A LOCATED IN THE ENGINE COMPARTMENT

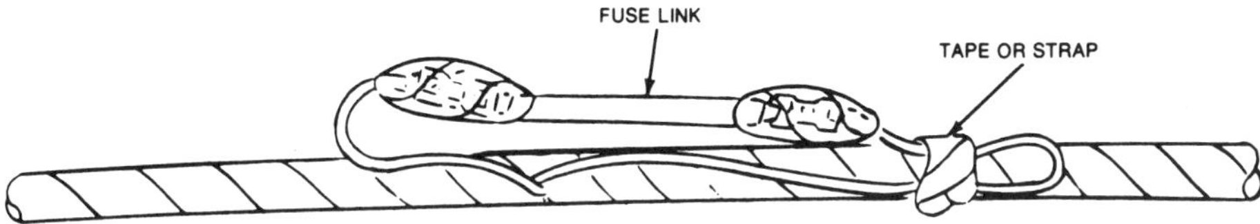

TYPICAL REPAIR FOR ANY IN-LINE FUSE LINK USING THE SPECIFIED GAUGE FUSE LINK FOR THE SPECIFIC CIRCUIT

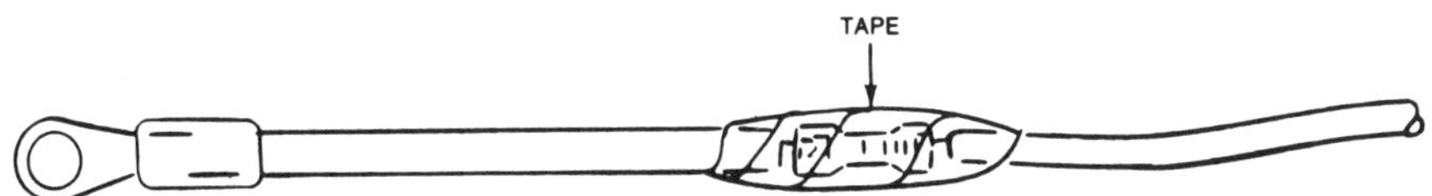

TYPICAL REPAIR USING THE EYELET TERMINAL FUSE LINK OF THE SPECIFIED GAUGE FOR ATTACHMENT TO A CIRCUIT WIRE END

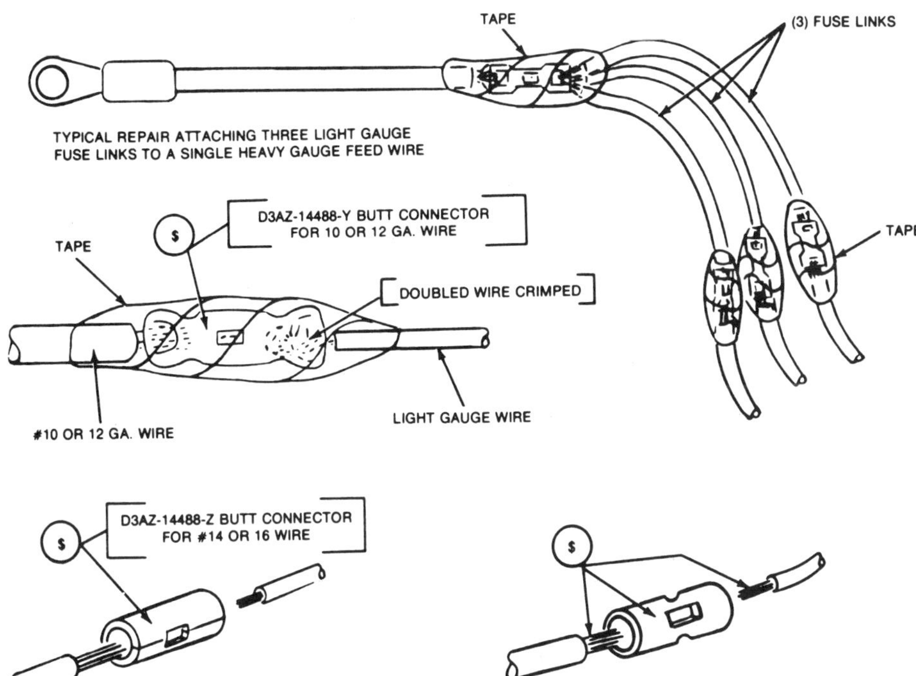

Fusible link repairs

1979 Fuse Identification

Circuit Protected	*Position*	*Size*
Ignition Feed to Engine, Warning Lamps, Seat Belt Warning Buzzer, Seat Belt Warning Lamp, Throttle Positioner, Emission Control Solenoid, Parking Brake	1	14 Amp.
Blank	2	—
Heater A/C	3	15 Amp. 35 Amp.
Turn Signal Lamps, Back-Up Lamps	4	15 Amp.
Windshield Wiper & Washer (2-Speed & Interval)	5	6 Amp. C.B.
Accessory Radio & Stereo Tape Player & Premium Sound	6	15 Amp.
Instrument Panel Illumination, Trans. Indicator Ash Tray, Heater, A/C & ATC Controls, Headlamp, Windshield Wiper/Washer Illumination, Radio Lamp	7	4 Amp.
Blank	8	—
A/C Clutch, Heated Backlite Relay Coil, Rear Window Defogger, Rear Wiper/Washer, Deck Lid Release, Power Window Safety Relay, Speed Control	9	15 Amp.
Courtesy Lamps, Dome, Map, Luggage Compartment, Ignition Key Warning Buzzer, Clock, Deluxe Belts	10	15 Amp.
Horns, Cigar Lighter	11	20 Amp.
Emergency Flasher, Stop Lamps	12	15 Amp.

1979 Circuit Protection

Circuit Protected	*Location*	*Size*
Headlights, High Beam Indicator	Part of Headlight Switch	22 Amp. C.B.
Stoplights, Side Markers, Parking Lamps, License Plate Lamp, Illum. Lamps		15 Amp.
Heated Backlite	In Engine Compartment	14 Ga. Fuse Link
No. 37 Load Circuit	In Engine Compartment	16 Ga. Fuse Link
No. 38 Load Circuit	In Engine Compartment	16 Ga. Fuse Link
No. 37 Alternator	At Starter Motor Relay	14 Ga. Fuse Link
No. 80 Engine Compartment Lamp		20 Ga. Fuse Link
Liftgate Wiper/Washer (Sta. Wagon only)	On Bracket Above Glove Box	4.5 Amp. C.B.
Power Windows & Power Door Locks & Power Seats	Attached to Starter Motor Relay	20 Amp. C.B.

1980 Fuse Identification

Circuit Protected	*Position*	*Size*
Instrument Panel Cluster and Interior Illumination, Headlamp Switch, Windshield Wiper/Washer Switch, Heater-A/C Control and Switch, Clock, Radio, PRNDL and Ashtray	1	5 Amp.
Warning Lamps—for Fuel Economy, Engine, Brakes, Fasten Seat Belts, Liftgate-Open Indicator, Emission Control Solenoid	2	10 Amp.
(Not Used)	3	Spare
Horns and Cigar Lighter	4	20 Amp.
(Not Used)	5	Spare
Electric Choke, Electric Fuel Pump (4 Amp. Fuse between resistor wire & relay)	6	20 Amp.
Courtesy Lamps—Dome, Map, Luggage Compartment, Ignition Key Warning Buzzer, Clock Feed and Glove Box	7	15 Amp.
(For Standard Car) Park, Tail and License Lamps	8	15 Amp.
(For Console Models Only)		10 Amp.
(Not Used)	9	Spare
Radio, Stereo Tape Player, Premium Sound and C.B. Radio	10	15 Amp.
Accessory—A/C Clutch, Heated Backlite Relay Coil, Rear Window Defogger, Rear Wiper/Washer, Trunk Lid Release, Power Window Safety Relay and Speed Control	11	20 Amp.
Windshield Wiper/Washer	12	6 Amp. C.B.
Stop Lamps and Emergency Warning Lamps	13	15 Amp.
Turn Signal Lamps and Back-Up Lamps	14	15 Amp.
Heater	15	15 Amp.
Air Conditioner		30 Amp.
(Not Used)	16	Spare
(Not Used)	17	Spare

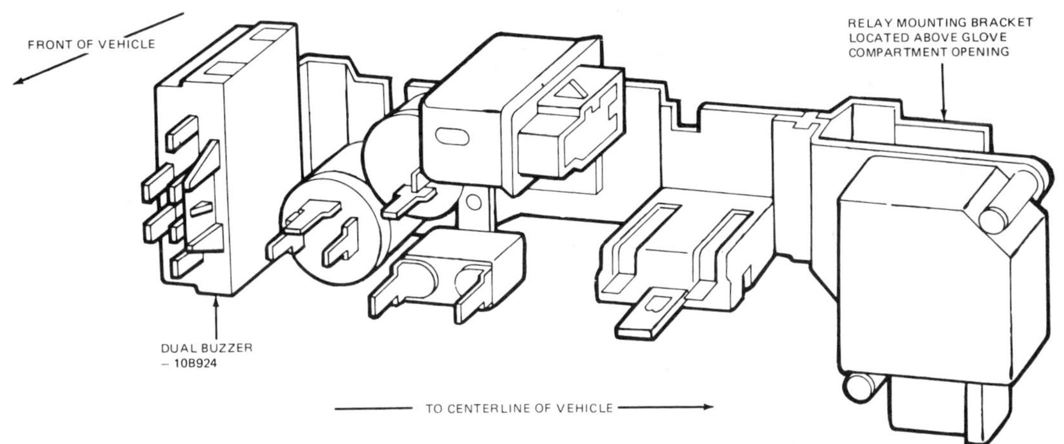

Dual buzzer installation (key and seat belt warning—typical)

1980 Circuit Protection

Circuit Protected	Location	Size
Headlights, High Beam Indicator	Part of Head-light Switch	22 Amp. C.B.
Liftgate Wiper/Washer (Station Wagon Only)	On Bracket Above Glove Box	4.5 Amp. C.B.
Power Windows and Power Door Locks and Power Seats	Attached to Starter Motor Relay	20 Amp. C.B.

Fuse Link	Location	GA
Lamp Feed	Near Voltage Regulator	16
Ignition Feed	Near Voltage Regulator	16
Charging Circuit	Near Starter Motor Relay	14
Heated Backlite and Power Door Locks	Near Starter Motor Relay	16
Engine Compartment Lamp	Near Starter Motor Relay	20
Electric Fan	Near Starter Motor Relay	20

1981–83 Fuse Identification

Circuit Protected	Position	Size
Stop Lamps, Hazard Warning Lamps	1	15 Amp.
Windshield Wiper, Windshield Washer Pump, Interval Wiper, Washer Fluid Level Indicator	2	6 Amp. C.B.
(Not Used)	3	Spare
Taillamps, Parking Lamps, Side Marker Lamps, Instrument Cluster Illumination Lamps, License Lamps	4	15 Amp.
Optional Lamp Outage System and same system as above	4	10 Amp.
Turn Signal Lamps, Back-up Lamps	5	15 Amp
A/C Clutch, Heated Backlite Relay Timer, Trunk Lid Release, Speed Control Module, Electronic Digital Clock Display, Graphic Warning Display Module, Illuminated Entry	6	20 Amp.
(Not Used)	7	Spare
Courtesy Lamps, Key Warning Buzzer, Illuminated Entry Module, Analog Clock, Tension Reliever	8	15 Amp.
Heater Blower Motor	9	15 Amp.
A/C Blower Motor	9	30 Amp.
Flash-to-Pass	10	20 Amp.
Radio, Tape Player, Premium Sound	11	15 Amp.
(Not Used)	12	Spare
Instrument Cluster Illumination Lamps, Radio, Climate Control, Ashtray Lamps	13	5 Amp.
Power Windows (2 Door)	14	20 Amp. C.B.
Power Window Relay (4 Door)	14	15 Amp.
(Not Used)	15	Spare
Horn, Front Cigar Lighter, Electronic Console Clock	16	20 Amp.
(Not Used)	17	Spare
Warning Indicator Lamps, Throttle Solenoid Positioner, Low Fuel Module, Dual Timer Buzzer, Tachometer, Engine Idle Track Relay	18	10 Amp.

1981–83 Circuit Protection

Circuit Protected	Location	Size
Windshield Wiper/Washer	Fuse Panel	6 Amp. C.B.
Headlights, High Beam Indicator	Headlight Switch	22 Amp. C.B.
Power Windows (4 Door), Power Door Locks and Power Seats	Starter Motor Relay	20 Amp. C.B.
Fuse Link	*Location*	*GA*
Lamp Feed	Near Voltage Regulator	16
Ignition Feed	Near Voltage Regulator	16
Charging Circuit	Near Starter Motor Relay	14
Heated Backlite and Power Door Locks	Near Starter Motor Relay	16
Engine Compartment Lamps	Near Starter Motor Relay	20
Electric Choke Feed	Near Master Cylinder	20
MCU Feed	Near Master Cylinder	20

NOTE: *A 15 amp. hazard warning fuse is located in a bracket above the glove box on some models.*

Warning Buzzer Locations

KEY WARNING AND SEAT BELT TIMER BUZZER

The key warning buzzer and the seat belt timer buzzer are combined into one unit. The buzzer assembly is mounted on the extreme right end of the relay panel above the glove box.

WIRING DIAGRAMS

Wiring diagrams have been left out of this book. As cars have become more complex, and available with longer and longer option lists wiring diagrams have grown in size and complexity also. It has been virtually impossible to provide a readable reproduction in a reasonable number of pages. Information on ordering wiring diagrams from the vehicle manufacturer can be found in the owners manual.

Clutch and Transmission

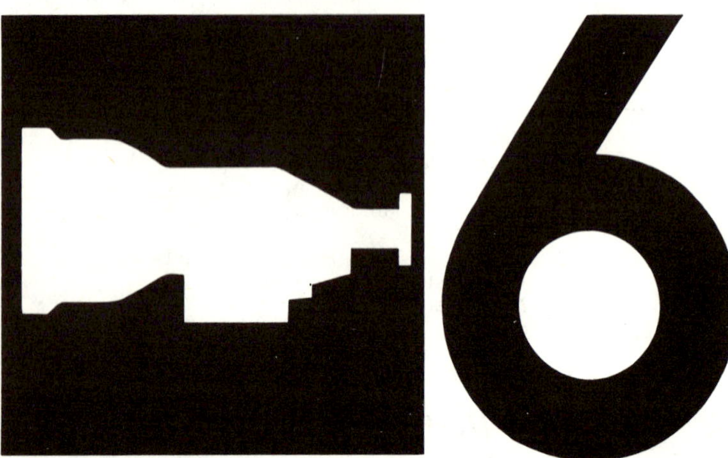

UNDERSTANDING THE MANUAL TRANSMISSION AND CLUTCH

Because of the way the gasoline engine breathes, it can produce torque, or twisting force, only within a narrow speed range. Most modern engines must turn at about 2,500 rpm to produce their peak torque. By 4,500 rpm they are producing so little torque that continued increases in engine speed produce no power increases.

The transmission and clutch are employed to vary the relationship between engine speed and the speed of the wheels so that adequate engine power can be produced under all circumstances. The clutch allows engine torque to be applied to the transmission input shaft gradually, due to mechanical slippage. The car can, consequently, be started smoothly from a full stop.

The transmission changes the ratio between the rotating speeds of the engine and the wheels by the use of gears. Three-speed or four-speed transmissions are most common. The lower gears allow full engine power to be applied to the rear wheels during acceleration at low speeds.

The clutch driven plate is a thin disc, the center of which is splined to the transmission input shaft. Both sides of the disc are covered with a layer of material which is similar to brake lining and which is capable of allowing slippage without roughness or excessive noise.

The clutch cover is bolted to the engine flywheel and incorporates a diaphragm spring which provides the pressure to engage the clutch. The cover also houses the pressure plate. The driven disc is sandwiched between the pressure plate and the smooth surface of the flywheel when the clutch pedal is released, thus forcing it to turn at the same speed as the engine crankshaft.

The transmission contains a mainshaft which passes all the way through the transmission, from the clutch to the driveshaft. This shaft is separated at one point, so that front and rear portions can turn at different speeds.

Power is transmitted by a countershaft in the lower gears and reverse. The gears of the countershaft mesh with gears on the mainshaft, allowing power to be carried from one to the other. All the countershaft gears are integral with that shaft, while several of the mainshaft gears can either rotate independently of the shaft or be locked to it. Shifting from one gear to the next causes one of the gears to be freed from rotating with the shaft, and locks another to it. Gears are locked and unlocked by internal dog clutches which slide between the center of the gear and the shaft.

Transmission Codes

Year	Code	Model	Manufacturer
1978	1	3 speed	Ford
	7	4 speed (78 ET)	Hummer (Germany)
	V	C3 Automatic	Ford
	W	C4 Automatic	Ford
1979–83	6	4 speed OD*	Ford
	7	4 speed (ET)	Hummer (Germany)
	C	C5 Automatic	Ford
	V	C3 Automatic	Ford
	W	C4 Automatic	Ford

*Overdrive in 4th gear

The forward gears usually employ synchronizers: friction members which smoothly bring gear and shaft to the same speed before the toothed dog clutches are engaged.

The clutch is operating properly if:

1. It will stall the engine when released with the vehicle held stationary.
2. The shift lever can be moved freely between first and reverse gears when the vehicle is stationary and the clutch disengaged.

A clutch pedal free-play adjustment is incorporated in the linkage. If there is 1 inch of motion before the pedal begins to release the clutch, it is adjusted properly. Inadequate free-play wears all parts of the clutch releasing mechanisms and may cause slippage. Excessive free-play may cause inadequate release and hard shifting of gears.

MANUAL TRANSMISSION

Three types of manual transmissions have been offered in the Fairmont and Zephyr. In 1978, a three-speed, or four-speed transmission (both with floor mounted shifters) were offered. 1979 and later models used either a four-speed (standard) or a four-speed overdrive (overdrive in fourth) transmission.

LINKAGE ADJUSTMENT

Three Speed Floor-Mounted Shifter

1. Place the shift lever in neutral.
2. Loosen the two shift linkage adjustment nuts, making sure the shift rods remain in the transmission shift levers.
3. Use an allen wrench as an alignment tool. Insert the alignment tool through the hole in the boot and into the shift control assembly alignment hole.
4. Tighten the adjustment nuts, making sure the slotted ends of the shift rods are over the flats of the studs on the shift control assembly.
5. Remove the alignment pin. Check to make sure the linkage operates smoothly.

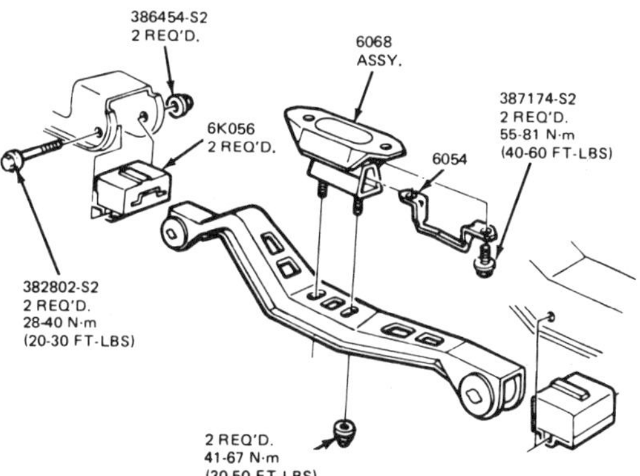

Transmission crossmember (typical 4 speed)

Four Speed Transmissions

The four speed transmissions used in your Fairmont or Zephyr are equipped with internal shift rails, having no provision for adjustment.

REMOVAL AND INSTALLATION

Three Speed and Four Speed Overdrive

REMOVAL

1a. On three speed transmissions; Remove the screws (4) that mount the shift lever boot to the floor. Remove the bolts (2) that fasten the gear shift lever to the gear shift control.

1b. On four speed overdrive transmissions; Remove the screws that hold the shift lever boot to the floor, slide the boot up the shifter shaft. Place the shift lever in neutral and remove the bolts (3) that attach the shift tower to the transmission. Remove the shift lever.

2. Disconnect the negative (ground) cable from the battery. Jack up the car and support it on jackstands.

3. Mark the drive shaft and drive flange on the differential so that the driveshaft may be reinstalled in its original position.

4. Disconnect the driveshaft at the differential and slide the front of the shaft out of the transmission extension housing. Seal the rear of the extension housing with a plastic bar, or something similar, to prevent lubricant from leaking out of the transmission.

NOTE: *If you are going to do any repairs to the transmission, drain the lubricant before transmission removal.*

5. Remove the bolt and retainer securing the speedometer cable and casing to the extension housing and remove the cable.

6. On three speed transmissions; disconnect the gear shift linkage from the shift control (2 nuts) and remove the shift control from the extension housing (3 bolts). Remove the cotter pins that retain the linkage to the shift levers and remove the linkage.

7. Remove the bolts holding the transmission to the rear support. Raise the rear of the engine enough to clear the rear crossmember. Remove the rear crossmember.

8. Support the transmission and remove the transmission mounting bolts (4). Pull the transmission to the rear until the input shaft clears the flywheel housing.

9. Lower the transmission to the floor.

NOTE: *Do not depress the clutch pedal while the transmission is removed.*

INSTALLATION

Make sure the mating surfaces of the transmission case and the flywheel housing are clean.

1. Start the input shaft through the throwout bearing and line up the splines on the input shaft to those on the clutch disc.

NOTE: *Do not allow the transmission to hang on the input shaft.*

2. Slide the transmission forward until the input shaft enters the bushing on the crankshaft and the case is against the flywheel housing. It may be necessary to wiggle the transmission slightly.

3. When the transmission is snugly against the flywheel housing and the mounting holes lined up, install and tighten the mounting bolts.

4. Raise the engine slightly and install the rear crossmember. Lower the engine, install and tighten the rear support bolts/nuts.

5. On three speed transmissions; install the shift linkage, shift control, and adjust linkage. On all transmissions, install the speedometer cable.

6. Remove the plastic bag and install the driveshaft; make sure to line up the marks.

7. Check the lubricant, add if necessary.

8. Lower car, connect the negative battery cable and install the shift lever (four speed).

MODEL ET FOUR SPEED TRANSMISSION

Removal

1. Place the gear shift lever in Neutral position.

2. Remove the attaching screws at rear of coin tray and lift to release from front hold down notch on boot retainer. Lift it over the gear shift lever boot.

3. Remove the four capscrews attaching the boot to the floor pan and move the boot upward out of the way.

4. Remove the three lever attaching bolts.

NOTE: *The attaching bolts are Metric (M8).* Remove the lever and boot asembly from the extension housing.

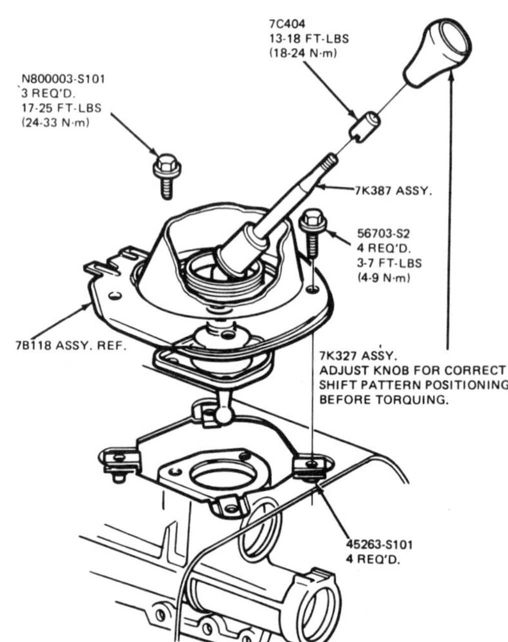

Gearshift lever installation (ET transmissions)

5. Remove the gear shift knob and locknut and slide the boot off the lever.

6. Working from under the hood, disconnect the negative (ground) cable from the battery. Remove upper bolts (or stud nuts) that attach flywheel housing to engine.

7. Raise the vehicle and support on jackstands.

8. Mark the position of the driveshaft relative to the axle companion flange. Remove the driveshaft and seal the extension housing with a plastic bag or equivalent to prevent lubricant leakage.

9. Remove the clutch release lever dust cover.

10. Disconnect the clutch release cable from the release lever.

11. Remove the starter motor attaching bolts and place the starter to one side.

12. Remove the speedometer cable attaching screw and lift the cable from the extension housing.

13. Support the rear of the engine with a jack and remove the bolts that attach the crossmember to the body.

14. Remove the bolt (or bolts) that attaches crossmember to extension housing, and remove the crossmember.

15. Lower the engine as required to permit removal of bolts that attach the flywheel housing to the engine. Slide the transmission away from the engine and from under the vehicle.

NOTE: *It may be necessary to slide the mounting bracket forward from the catalytic converter heat shield in order to move the transmission rearward far enough to remove it.*

16. Remove the cover attaching bolts and drain the lubricant into a container.

17. Remove the bolts that attach flywheel housing to transmission case and remove the housing.

Installation

1. Install a new shift rod seal in the flywheel housing (if the old seal is damaged).

2. Position flywheel housing on transmission case, and install and tighten the attaching bolts to specification.

3. Install the clutch release lever and bearing.

4. Make certain that machined surfaces of flywheel housing and engine are free of dirt and foreign material.

5. Apply lubricant to the input shaft bearing retainer. Position the flywheel housing and transmission assembly on the engine block.

NOTE: *It may be necessary to place the transmission in gear and rotate the output shaft to align the input shaft and clutch splines.*

6. Slide the flywheel housing firmly and squarely onto the locating dowels, to be sure of a positive engagement. Then, holding the flywheel housing firmly in position on the dowels, thread the attaching bolts through the hollow portion of the dowels and into the housing. Tighten the bolts to specification.

7. Install and tighten the center attaching bolts.

8. Lower the vehicle and install the two upper attaching bolts or stud nuts. Tighten to specification.

9. Make sure the shift lever insulator is in a straight downward position on the shift rail.

10. Position the shift lever in the extension housing so that the forked ends engage in the insulator properly.

11. Install the three metric attaching bolts (M8) and tighten to specifications.

12. Slide the boot over the lever and install the attaching bolts. Tighten the bolts to specifications.

13. Install the gear shift knob and adjust as shown in the illustrations.

14. Position the coin tray over the shift lever boot.

15. Secure the tray to front notch on boot retaining ring and attach at rear with screws.

16. Raise the vehicle. Raise the engine until the transmission reaches its normal position. Secure the crossmember to the body with the attaching bolts, and tighten to specification. Install the bolt that attaches crossmember to extension housing, and tighten to specification.

17. Position the catalytic converter heat shield mounting bracket to the transmission mount.

18. Remove the plastic bag, install the speedometer cable and tighten the attaching screw.

19. Position the starter, install the attaching bolts.

20. Apply grease to the ball end of the clutch release cable and connect it to the release lever. Install the clutch release fork dust cover.

21. Install the driveshaft, making sure that it is connected to the pinion flange in its original position.

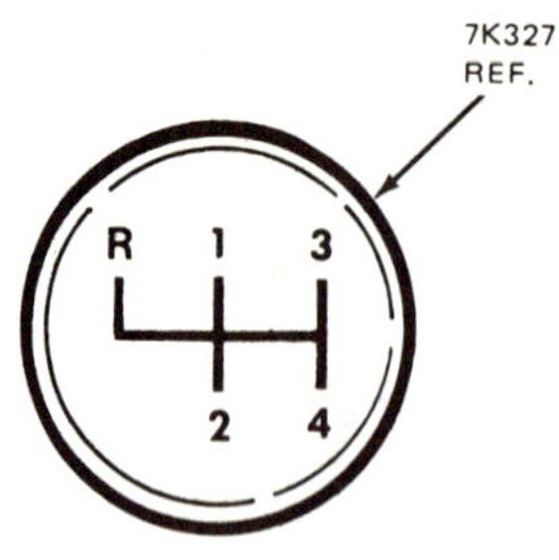

WITH LEVER IN NEUTRAL POSITION, INSTALL LOCKING NUT 7C404 UNTIL HAND TIGHT. THEN INSTALL KNOB 7K327 UNTIL HAND TIGHT. BACK KNOB OFF UNTIL SHIFT PATTERN ALIGNS WITH THE OF DRIVE LINE. TIGHTEN LOCKING NUT 13-18 FT-LBS (18-24 N·m) NO THREADS SHALL BE VISIBLE AFTER NUT HAS BEEN TIGHTENED. SHIFT PATTERN ALIGNMENT MUST BE WITHIN ±15° OF ℄ OF DRIVE LINE.

Gearshift knob installation ET transmission

22. Fill the transmission with the specified lubricant until it appears at the bottom of the filler plug hole. Install the filler plug.
23. Install the backup lamp switch and connect the wire to the switch.
24. Lower the vehicle to the ground. Install and tighten the upper flywheel housing mounting bolts. Connect the negative battery cable.
25. Check the transmission for proper operation.

Installation

1. Install a new shift rod seal in the flywheel housing (if the old seal is damaged).
2. Position flywheel housing on transmission case, and install and tighten the attaching bolts.
3. Install the clutch release lever and bearing.
4. Make certain that machined surfaces of flywheel housing and engine are free of dirt and foreign material.
5. Apply a film of C4AZ-19584-A lubricant or equivalent to the input shaft bearing retainer. Position the flywheel housing and transmission assembly on the engine block.

NOTE: *It may be necessary to place the transmission in gear and rotate the output shaft to align the input shaft and clutch splines.*

6. Slide the flywheel housing firmly and squarely onto the locating dowels, to be sure of a positive engagement. Then, holding the flywheel housing firmly in position on the dowels, thread the attaching bolts through the hollow portion of the dowels and into the housing. Tighten the bolts.
7. Install and tighten the center attaching bolts.
8. Make sure the shift lever insulator is in a straight downward position on the shift rail.
9. Position the shift lever in the extension housing so that the forked ends engage in the insulator properly.
10. Install the three metric attaching bolts (M8) and tighten to specifications.
11. Slide the boot over the lever and install the attaching bolts. Tighten the bolts to specifications.
13. Install the gear shift knob.
14. Position the coin tray over the shift lever boot.
15. Secure the tray to front notch on boot retaining ring and attach at rear with screws.
16. Raise the engine until the transmission reaches its normal position. Secure the crossmember to the body with the attaching bolts. Install the bolts that attach crossmember to extension housing, and tighten.

CLUTCH

Pedal Adjustment

NOTE: *1978 models required one and one half inch of clutch pedal free play. 1979 and 1980 models no longer have free play adjustments. The clutch release bearing is in constant contact with the clutch fingers. A clutch pedal height adjustment is required instead.*

NOTE: *Starting in 1981, a self-adjusting clutch is standard.*

4 CYL. MODELS

1. Jack up the front of the car and support on jackstands.
2. At the clutch "bell" housing, remove the return spring and the dust shield.
3. Loosen the clutch cable locknut and the adjusting nut.

4a. 1978 models; Move the clutch release lever forward until all play is removed. Hold the lever in this position until adjustment is made. Insert a .030" gauge against the release lever cable spacer. Finger tighten the nut against the gauge. Tighten the locknut. This should produce freeplay of 1½ inches.

4b. 1979 and 1980 models; To raise the pedal, turn the adjusting nut clockwise. To lower-turn counterclockwise. Adjust the pedal

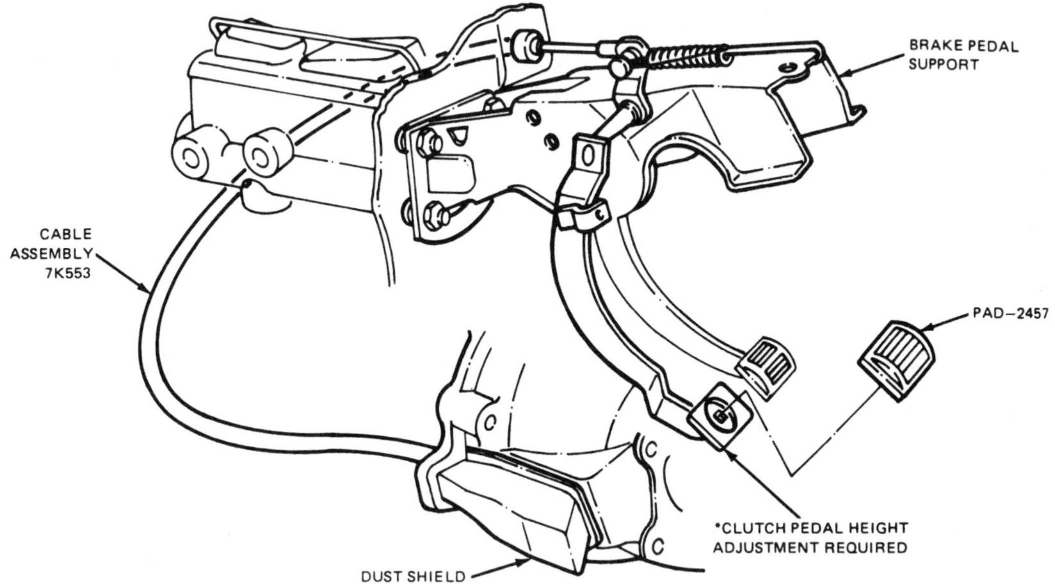

Typical clutch pedal and cable assembly

travel to 5.3 inches. (Total length of travel). Tighten the locknut.

5. Depress and release the clutch pedal several times. Recheck the freeplay or pedal travel. Readjust if necessary. To check the proper adjustment on the 1979 and 1980 models, you should be able to raise the clutch pedal (from the end of its normal return height to the pedal stop) about 2 and ¾ inches.

6. Reinstall clutch return spring and dust shield. Lower car.

6 CYL. MODELS

1. Open the hood. Find the clutch cable where it goes through dash panel. (Driver's side.) The nylon adjusting nut has a locking step built into it. The locking step fits into a rubber insulator which keeps it from moving.

2. Pull the clutch cable toward the front of the car until the adjusting nut is free from the rubber insulator. (It may be necessary to remove the clutch pedal bumper stop (78) or block the clutch release forward (79 & 80) to free the adjusting nut from the rubber insulator.

3a. 1978 models; When the adjusting nut is free, back in away from the insulator about .030 inch. Release the cable, then pull it slightly forward until all slack is taken from the clutch release lever. Turn the adjusting nut toward the rubber insulator until contact is made. Tighten until the locking tabs index in the rubber insulator. The clutch freeplay should be 1½ inches.

3b. 1979 and 1980 models; Rotate the adjusting nut until the recommended pedal travel of 5¼ inches is reached. (Adjusting nut indexed in rubber insulator).

4. Cycle the clutch pedal several times and

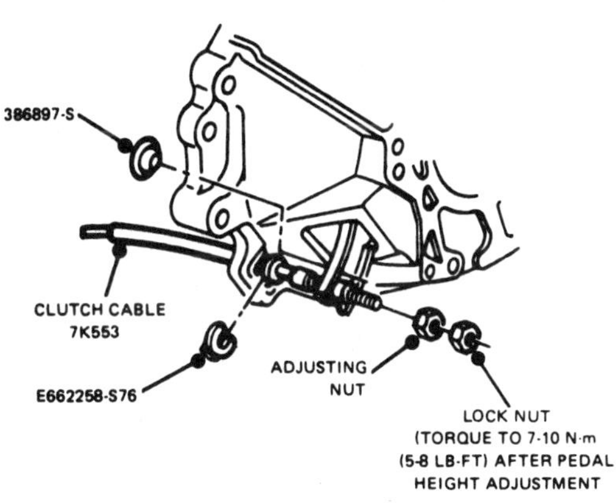

Clutch pedal adjustment—4 cyl.

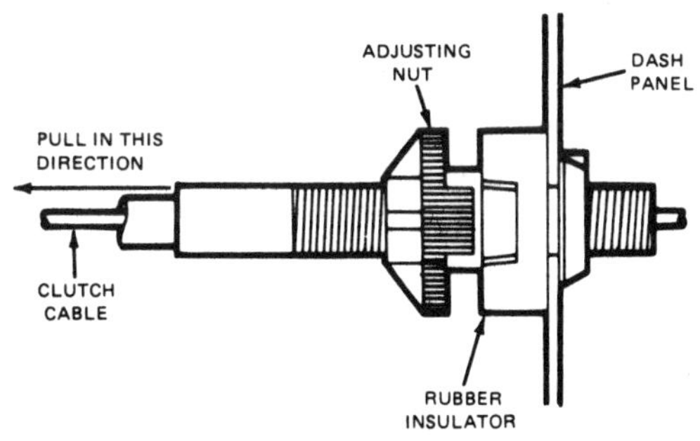

Clutch pedal adjustment—6 cyl.

check your adjustment. The freeplay on 1978 models should be 1½ inches. On 1979 and 1980 models, the pedal travel is 5¼ inches. You should be able to raise the pedal (79 and 80) about 2 and 6 inches (from normal height to pedal stop). Readjust if necessary.

SELF ADJUSTING CLUTCH

The free play in the clutch is adjusted by a built in mechanism that allows the clutch controls to be self-adjusted during normal operation.

The self-adjusting feature should be checked every 5000 miles. This is accomplished by insuring that the clutch pedal travels to the top of its upward position. Grasp the clutch pedal with your hand or put your foot under the clutch pedal, pull up on the pedal until it stops. Very little effort is required (about 10 lbs.). During the application of upward pressure, a click may be heard which means an adjustment was necessary and has been accomplished.

Clutch Cable

REMOVAL AND INSTALLATION

1. Loosen the cable adjustment or, if self adjusting, lift the clutch pedal to its upper position. Disconnect the cable from the clutch pedal or self-adjusting quadrent.
2. Disconnect the cable assembly isolator from the firewall.
3. Pull the cable through the firewall into the engine compartment. Raise the front of the car and support on jackstands.
4. Remove the dust cover from the bell housing and the rubber plug from the clutch release lever. Remove the clip retainer and cable from the bell housing.
5. Remove the clutch cable from the release lever. Remove mounting isolator from cable.
6. Install in the reverse order of removal.

Clutch Assembly

Four Cyl—140 cu in. Engine

REMOVAL

1. Disconnect negative battery cable from battery. Raise the vehicle and support on jackstands.
2. Remove the dust shield and return spring.
3. Loosen the clutch cable lock and adjusting nut. Remove rubber cable plug and disconnect the cable from the release lever.
4. Remove the retaining clip and remove the clutch cable from the flywheel housing.
5. Remove the starter electrical cable and the starter motor from the flywheel housing.
6. Remove the bolts that secure the engine rear plate to the front lower part of the flywheel housing.
7. Remove the transmission (see previous section) flywheel housing.
8. Remove the clutch release lever from the housing by pulling it through the window in the housing until the retainer spring is disengaged from the pivot. Inspect clutch release bearing and replace if required. If original bearing is reused, note orientation, mark, and install in the same position.
9. Loosen the six pressure plate cover attaching bolts evenly to release the spring tension gradually and avoid distorting the cover. If the same pressure plate and cover are to be reinstalled, mark the cover and flywheel so that the pressure plate can be reinstalled in its original position. Remove the pressure plate and clutch disc from the flywheel.

INSTALLATION

1. Install the clutch release lever if it was removed.
2. Position the clutch disc and pressure plate assembly on the flywheel. The three dowel pins on the flywheel must be properly aligned with the pressure plate. Bent, damaged or missing dowels must be replaced. Start the cover attaching bolts but do not tighten them. Avoid touching the clutch disc face, dropping parts or contaminating parts with oil or grease.
3. Align the clutch disc using the proper alignment tool inserted in the pilot bearing. Alternately tighten the cover bolts to specification. Remove the alignment tool.
4. Apply a light film of lithium base grease to (1) the outside diameter of the transmission front bearing retainer, (2) the release lever bearing fork and anti-rattle spring where they contact the release bearing hub, and (3) to the release bearing surface that contacts the pressure plate release fingers. Then, fill the grease groove of the release bearing hub with the same grease. Clean all excess grease from inside the bore of the bearing hub, otherwise, excess grease will be forced onto the spline by the transmission input shaft bearing retainer, and will contaminate the clutch disc.
5. Attach the clutch release bearing to the release lever.

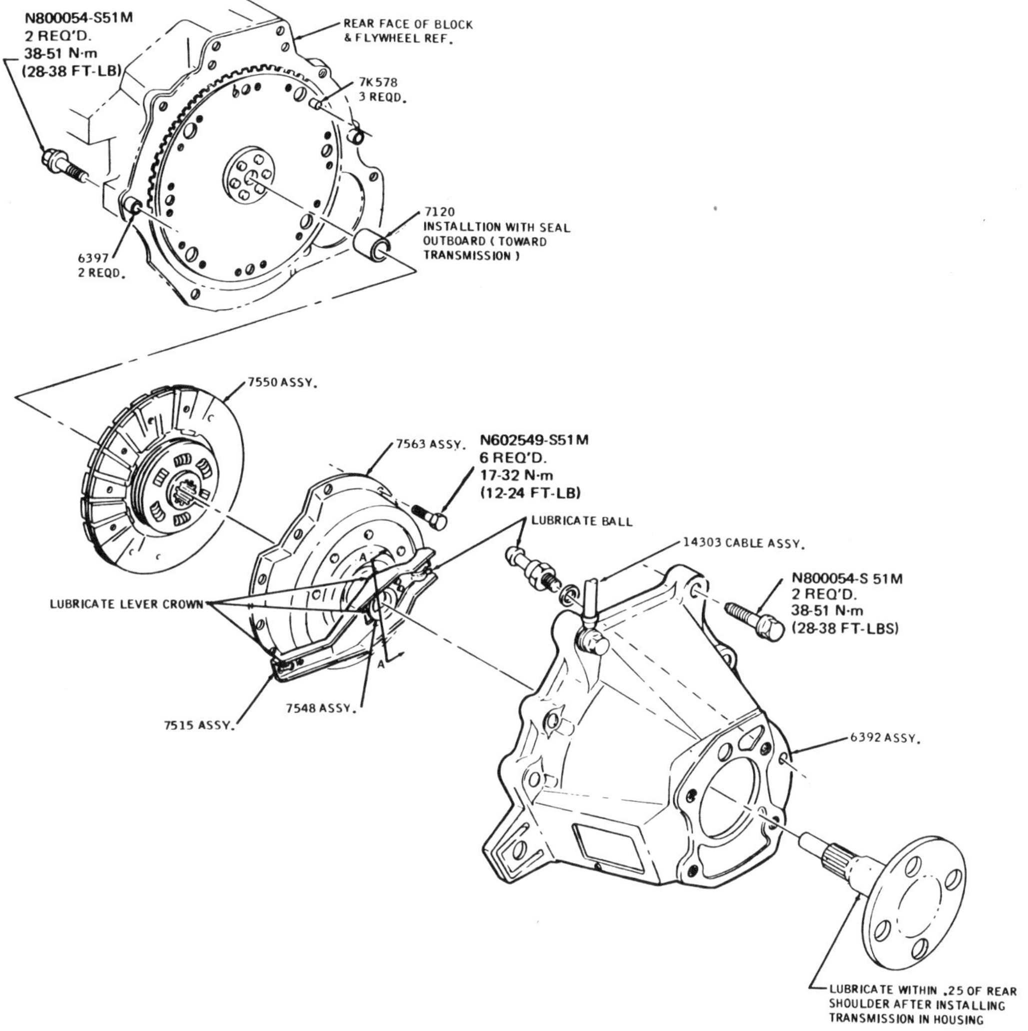

Clutch installation—4 cyl.

6. Attach the release lever and release bearing to the flywheel housing.
7. Inspect the flywheel housing dowel holes for misalignment and wear.
8. Make certain that the flywheel housing and cylinder block mounting surfaces are clean and that the dowels are in good condition.
9. Install the flywheel housing and/or the transmission.
10. Install the bolts that secure the engine rear plate to the front lower part of the flywheel housing.
11. Connect the clutch cable to the flywheel housing and connect the retaining clip.
12. Install the starter motor and starter electrical cable.
13. Connect the clutch cable and return spring to the release lever and reinstall the dust shield and return spring to the rear crossmember.
14. Adjust the clutch pedal height adjustment or freeplay.
15. Lower car and connect negative battery cable.

Six Cyl. 200 Cu In.

REMOVAL

1. Disconnect the negative battery cable from the battery. Raise the vehicle and support on jackstands.
2. Remove the transmission. (Refer to the procedure outlined earlier.)
3. Loosen the clutch adjusting nut to provide slack in the clutch cable and disengage the clutch cable from the release lever.
5. Disengage the clutch cable from the flywheel housing.

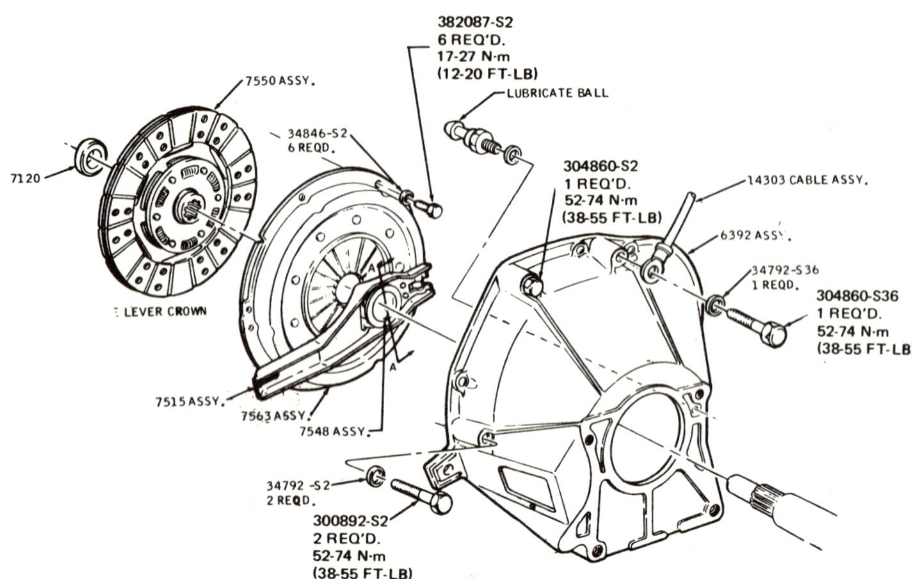

Clutch installation—6 cyl.

6. Remove the starter electrical cable; then the starter motor from the flywheel housing.

7. Remove the bolts that secure the engine rear plate to the front lower part of the flywheel housing.

8. Remove the bolts that attach the housing to the cylinder block.

9. Move the housing back just far enough to clear the pressure plate, and remove.

10. Remove the clutch release lever from the housing by pulling it through the window in the housing until the retainer spring is disengaged from the pivot.

11. Loosen the six pressure plate cover attaching bolts evenly to release the spring tension without distorting the cover. If the same pressure plate and cover assembly is to be installed after the clutch is removed, mark the cover and flywheel so that the pressure plate can be reinstalled in the same position.

12. Remove the pressure plate and clutch disc from the flywheel.

INSTALLATION

1. Install the clutch release lever.

2. Place the clutch disc pressure plate assembly in position on the flywheel. Start the cover attaching bolts to hold the pieces in place, but do not tighten them. Avoid touching the clutch disc facing, dropping the parts or contaminating them with oil or grease as clutch chatter may result.

3. Align the clutch disc using an alignment tool. To avoid distorting the pressure plate cover, alternately tighten the bolts, a few turns at a time, until they are all snug. Then, tighten the six pressure plate cover bolts to specification. Remove the alignment tool.

4. Apply a light film of lithium base grease to (1) the outside diameter of the transmission front bearing retainer, (2) both sides of the release lever fork where it contacts the release bearing spring clips and (3) to the release bearing spring surface that contacts the pressure plate release fingers. Then, fill the grease groove of the release bearing hub with the same lithium base grease. Clean all excess grease from inside the bore of the bearing hub, otherwise, excess grease will be forced onto the spline by the transmission input shaft bearing retainer, and will contaminate the clutch disc. Place the release bearing on the release lever and make certain that the flywheel housing and the cylinder block mounting surfaces are clean. Check to see that the dowels are in good condition. Position the housing on the dowels in the cylinder block. Install and alternately tighten the attaching bolts to specification.

5. Connect the clutch cable to the flywheel housing.

6. Install the starter motor and starter electrical cable.

7. Connect the clutch cable to the release lever, install the dust shield and return spring.

8. Install the transmission.

9. Adjust the clutch pedal height or freeplay. Lower car and attach the negative battery cable.

AUTOMATIC TRANSMISSION

Identification

The transmission may be identified by the code on the Vehicle Certification Label. Refer to the Transmission Code chart.

REMOVAL AND INSTALLATION

1. Disconnect the negative battery cable. Remove the fan shroud attaching bolts and position the shroud back over the fan.

NOTE: *Shroud removal, radiator hose disconnection and thermactor hose removal may be necessary, depending on engine, so damage will not occur when jacking the engine for crossmember or attaching bolt removal.*

2. Remove the upper engine-to-transmission mounting bolts (depending on engine) if they are accessible. Jack up the front and rear of the car and safely support on jackstands.
3. Drain the transmission fluid from the pan and converter.
4. Remove the exhaust pipe(s) and converter(s), if necessary, to gain clearance for transmission removal. Disconnect any sensor wiring or hose.
5. Remove the driveshaft, disconnect the transmission linkage, vacuum line, wiring harness and speedometer cable.
6. Remove the starter motor and lower converter dust shield (inspection plate) and engine brace.
7. Remove the converter-to-flywheel attaching nuts. Turn the engine by placing a wrench or socket on the crankshaft pulley nut to bring the mounting nuts in position for removal. On four cylinder engines, turn the engine in the direction of normal rotation only or the timing belt could be damaged or "jump" time.
8. Disconnect the transmission cooler lines at the transmission and remove the filler tube, if not removed when draining the transmission fluid.
9. Place a transmission jack under the transmission after disconnecting the rear motor mount from the crossmember. Raise the transmission slightly and remove the rear crossmember.
10. Take one last look to make sure everything has been disconnected from the transmission. Remove the remaining engine-to-transmission mounting bolts. On some four cylinder models it will be necessary to disconnect the motor mounts and raise the engine to reach the top engine-to-transmission mounting bolts. Use two jacks, one supporting the transmission and the other to raise the engine; use extreme caution when jacking.
11. Lower the transmission slowly until enough clearance is gained for removal. Be sure enough room is available between the fan blades and radiator and no hoses are stretched. When enough clearance has been gained, support the engine with a jack and slowly move the transmission toward the rear of the car. Be sure the converter remains on the transmission, slightly pry away from the flywheel if necessary.
12. When the transmission and converter are separated from the engine, lower and remove from under the car.
13. Installation is in the reverse order of removal. When installing, take care not to damage the flywheel, be sure the converter mounting studs are correctly aligned. The converter must rest squarely against the flywheel indicating that the converter pilot is not binding.

Torque

Engine to Transmission Bolts
C3—28–38 ft. lbs.
C4
4 and 6 Cyl. 28–38 ft. lbs.
V8 Eng. 40–50 ft. lbs.
C5—40–50 ft. lbs.
Converter to Flywheel
C3—27–49 ft. lbs.
C4—20–30 ft. lbs.
C5—40–50 ft. lbs.
Converter Drain Plug
C3—20–30 ft. lbs.
C4—17–22 ft. lbs.
C5—12–17 ft. lbs.

Transmission Fluids

1978–79	C3	Type F
	C4	Type F
1980	C3	Type F
	C4	Dexron II
1981	C3	Dexron II
	C4	Dexron II
1982–83	C3	Dexron II
	C5	Type H

PAN REPLACEMENT, FLUID AND FILTER CHANGE

1. Raise the car on a hoist or jackstands.
2. Some C4 and C5 models require that

the transmission fluid filler tube be disconnected to drain the pan; all others can be drained by loosening the pan bolts and letting the fluid drain out when the pan is lowered.

3. When the fluid has stopped draining to the level of the pan flange, remove the pan bolts starting rear and along both sides of the pan, allowing it to drop and drain gradually. Remove the pan and gasket.

4. Remove the bolts holding the filter in place, remove the filter, clean, and replace it. The filter, may be reused after cleaning it in a nondetergent solution, such as new transmission fluid.

NOTE: *The C4 filter and gasket retain the throttle pressure limit valve within the lower control valve body. The valve and its spring will drop out when the filter is removed. The valve is installed large end first into the valve body; the spring fits over the valve shaft.*

5. After completing any repairs or adjustments, install new pan gasket, and the pan on the transmission. Tighten the pan attaching bolts to 12–16 ft.

6. Install three quarts of transmission fluid through the filler tube. If the filler tube was removed to drain the transmission, install the filler tube using a new O-ring.

7. Start and run the engine for a few minutes at low idle speed, and then at the fast idle speed (about 1,200 rpm) until the normal operating temperature is reached. Do not race the engine.

8. Move the selector lever through all gear positions, then place it in the Park position. Check the fluid level and add fluid until the level is between the ADD and FULL marks on the dipstick. Do not overfill.

NOTE: *The level should be at FULL after the engine is completely warmed up. Do not overfill.*

BAND ADJUSTMENT

C3 Transmission—Front Band

NOTE: *The torque values and number of turns given in these procedures must be exactly correct to prevent transmission damage.*

1. Wipe clean the area around the adjusting screw on the side of the transmission.

2. Remove the adjusting screw locknut and discard it.

3. Install a new locknut on the adjusting screw but do not tighten it.

4. Tighten the adjusting screw to *exactly 10 ft. lbs.*

5. Back off the adjusting screw *exactly 1½ turns.*

6. Hold the adjusting screw so that it *does not turn* and tighten the adjusting screw locknut to 35–45 ft. lbs.

C4 and C5 Transmission—Intermediate Band

1. Wipe clean the area around the adjusting screw on the side of the transmission.

2. Remove the adjusting screw locknut and discard it.

3. Install a new locknut on the adjusting screw but do not tighten it yet.

4. Tighten the adjusting screw to *exactly 10 ft. lbs.*

5. Back off the adjusting screw *exactly 1¾ turns on C4 and 4¼ turns on C5.*

6. Hold the adjusting screw so that it *does not turn* and tighten the adjusting screw locknut to 35–45 ft. lbs.

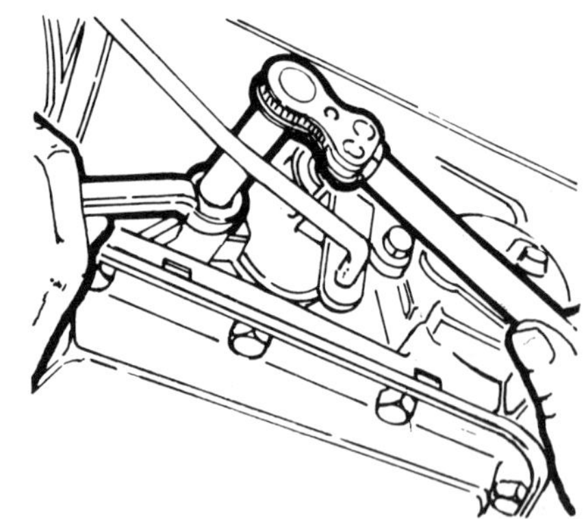

Intermediate band adjustment—C4 and C5

LOW-REVERSE BAND ADJUSTMENT

C4 and C5 Transmission

1. Wipe clean the area around the adjusting screw on the side of the transmission, near the right-rear corner.

2. Remove the adjusting screw locknut and discard it.

3. Install a new locknut on the adjusting screw but do not tighten it.

4. Tighten the adjusting screw to *exactly 10 ft. lbs.*

5. Back off the adjusting screw *exactly 3 full turns.*

6. Hold the adjusting screw so that it *does not turn* and tighten the adjusting screw to 35–45 ft. lbs.

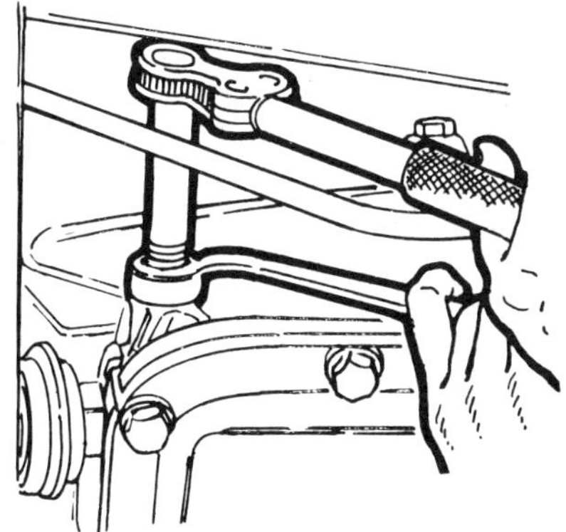

Low and reverse band adjustment—C4 and C5

NEUTRAL START SWITCH ADJUSTMENT

NOTE: *No adjustment is possible on the C3 transmission.*

C4 and C5 Transmission

1. Place the transmission selector lever in the Neutral position.
2. Raise the vehicle and support on stands. Loosen the two bolts that attach the neutral switch to the transmission.
3. Rotate the switch until a gauge pin (shank end of a no. 43 drill bit) can be inserted through the gauge pin holes in the switch. The gauge pin must be inserted a full $^{31}/_{64}$ in. into the switch, through all three holes in the switch.

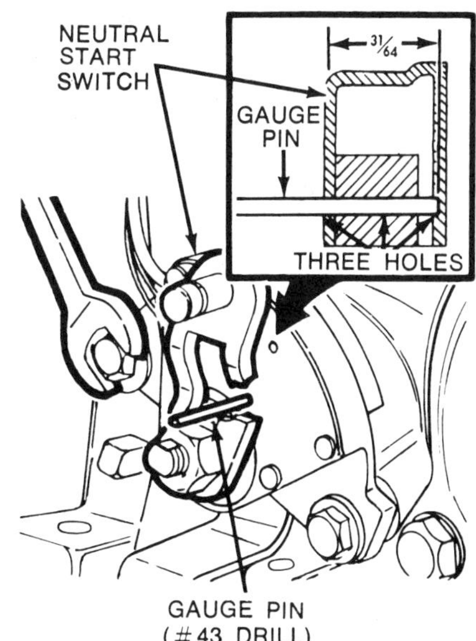

Neutral start switch adjustment—C4 and C5

4. Tighten the switch retaining bolts and remove the pin.

SHIFT LINKAGE ADJUSTMENT

1. Place the transmission shift lever in D.
2. Raise the vehicle and loosen manual lever shift rod retaining nut. Move transmission lever to D position. D is second from rear.
3. With transmission shift lever and transmission manual lever in position, tighten nut.

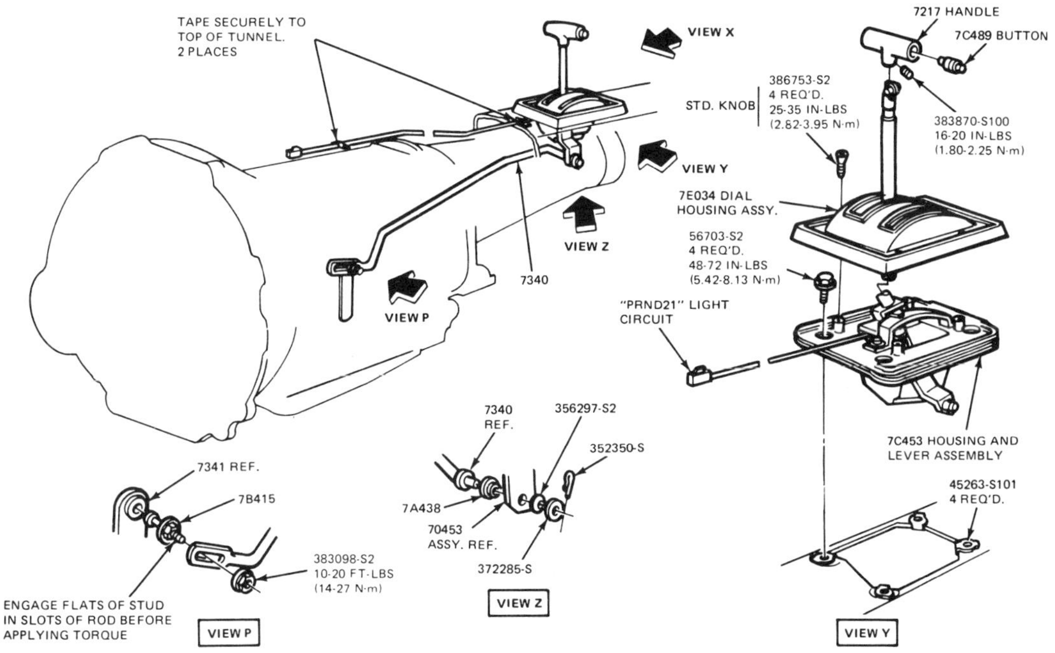

Shift linkage—all models

4. Check transmission operation for all selector lever detent positions.

DOWNSHIFT (THROTTLE) LINKAGE ADJUSTMENT

1. With the engine off, disconnect the throttle and downshift return springs, if equipped.
2. Hold the carburetor throttle lever in the wide open position against the stop.
3. Hold the transmission downshift linkage in the full downshift position against the internal stop.
4. Turn the adjustment screw on the carburetor downshift lever to obtain 0.01–0.08 in. clearance between the screw tip and the throttle shaft lever tab.
5. Release the transmission and carburetor to their normal free position.

Drive Train

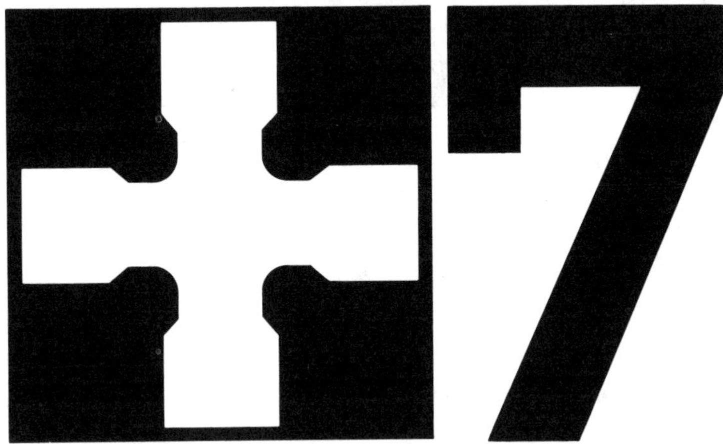

DRIVE LINE

Driveshaft and Universal Joints

The driveshaft is the means by which the power from the engine and transmission (in the front of the car) is transferred to the differential and rear axles, and finally to the rear wheels.

The driveshaft assembly incorporates two universal joints—one at each end—and a slip yoke at the front end of the assembly, which fits into the back of the transmission.

All driveshafts are balanced when installed in a car. It is, therefore, imperative that before applying undercoating to the chassis, the driveshaft and universal joint assembly be completely covered to prevent the accidental application of undercoating to their surfaces, and the subsequent loss of balance.

DRIVESHAFT REMOVAL

1. Mark the relationship of the rear driveshaft yoke and the drive pinion flange of the axle. If the original, yellow alignment marks are visible, there is no need for new marks. The purpose of this marking is to facilitate installation of the assembly in its exact original position, thereby maintaining proper balance of the driveshaft assembly.
2. Remove the four bolts or nuts which hold the rear universal joint to the pinion flange. Wrap tape around the loose bearing caps in order to prevent them from falling off the spider.
3. Pull the driveshaft toward the rear of the vehicle until the slip yoke clears the transmission housing and the seal. Plug the hole at the rear of the transmission housing or place a container under the opening to catch any fluid which might leak out.

UNIVERSAL JOINT OVERHAUL

1. Position the driveshaft assembly in a sturdy vise.
2. Remove the snap-rings which retain the bearing caps in the slip yoke (front only) and in the driveshaft (front and rear).
3. Using a large punch or an arbor press, drive one of the bearing caps in toward the center of the universal joint, which will force the opposite bearing cap out.
4. As each bearing cap is pressed or punched far enough out of the universal joint assembly so that it is accessible, grip it with a pair of pliers, and pull it from the driveshaft yoke. Then drive or press the spider in the opposite direction in order to make the opposite bearing cap accessible and pull it free with a pair of pliers. Use this procedure to remove all bearings from both universal joints.

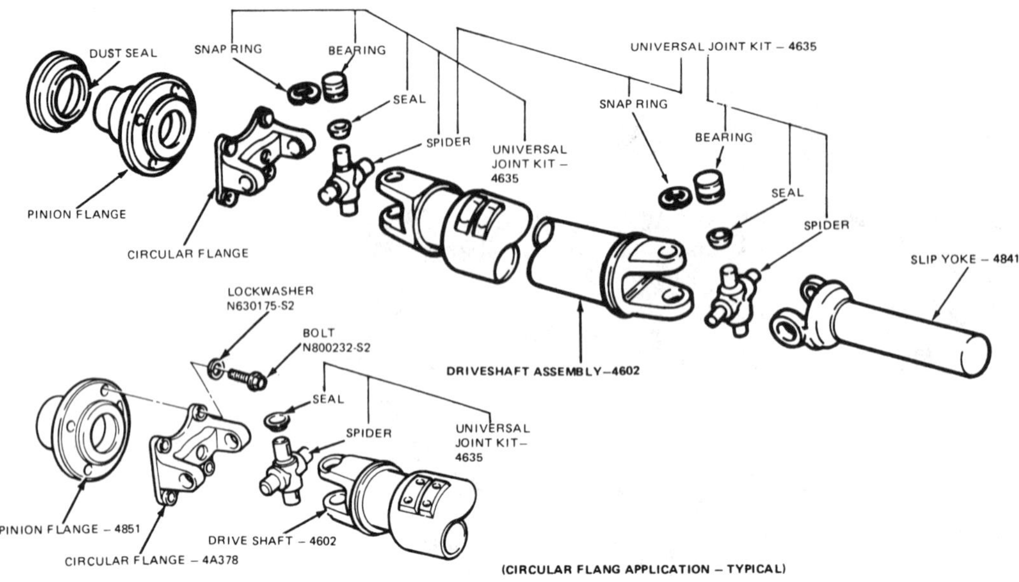

Drive shaft and U-joints (disassembled view)

5. After removing the bearings, lift the spider from the yoke.

6. Thoroughly clean all dirt and foreign matter from the yoke area on both ends of the driveshaft.

NOTE: *When installing new bearings within the yokes, it is advisable to use an arbor press. However, if this tool is not available, the bearings should be driven into position with extreme care, as a heavy jolt on the needle bearings can easily damage or misalign them, greatly shortening their life and hampering their efficiency.*

7. Start a new bearing into the yoke at the rear of the driveshaft.

8. Position a new spider in the rear yoke and press (or drive) the new bearing cap ¼ in. below the outer surface of the yoke.

9. With the bearing cap in position, install a new snap-ring.

10. Start a new bearing cap into the opposite side of the yoke.

11. Press (or drive) the bearing cap until the opposite bearing—which you have just installed—contacts the inner surface of the snap-ring.

Troubleshooting the Driveline

The Problem	*Is Caused By*	*What to Do*
Shudder as car accelerates from stop or low speed	• Loose U-joint • Defective center bearing	• Tighten U-joint or have it replaced • Have center bearing replaced
Loud clunk in driveshaft when shifting gears	• Worn U-joint	• Have U-joints replaced
Roughness or vibration at any speed	• Out-of-balance, bent or dented driveshaft • Worn U-joints • U-joint clamp bolts loose	• Have driveshaft serviced • Have U-joints serviced • Tighten U-joint clamp bolts
Squeaking noise at low speeds	• Lack of U-joint lubrication	• Lubricate U-joint; if problem persists, have U-joint serviced
Knock or clicking noise	• U-joint or driveshaft hitting frame tunnel	• Correct overloaded condition

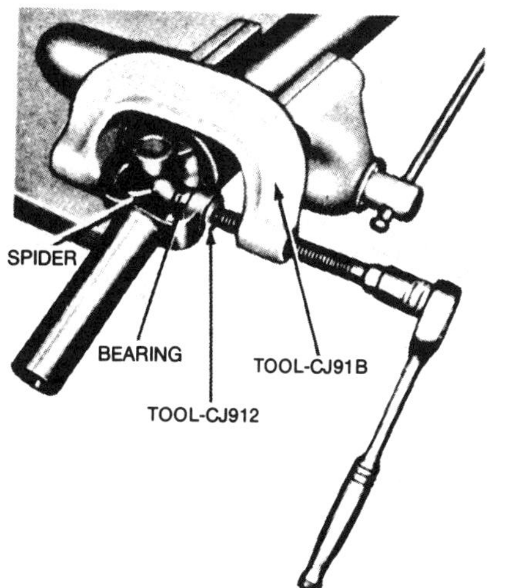

Removing bearing cap

12. Install a new snap-ring on the second bearing cap. It may be necessary to grind the surface of this second snap-ring to facilitate easy entry into its proper position.
13. Reposition the driveshaft in the vise to facilitate work on the front universal joint.
14. Install the new bearing caps, new spider, and new snap-rings in the same manner as you did for the rear universal joint.
15. Position the slip yoke on the spider. Install new bearings and snap-rings.
16. Check reassembled joints for freedom of movement. If misalignment of any part is causing a blind, a sharp rap on the side of the yoke with a brass hammer should seat the bearing needles, and provide the desired freedom of movement. Care should be exercised to firmly support the shaft end during this operation, as well as to prevent blows to the bearings themselves. Under no circumstances should a driveshaft be installed in a car if there is any bind in the universal joints.

DRIVESHAFT INSTALLATION

1. Carefully inspect the rubber seal in the end of the transmission extension housing. Replace it if it is damaged.
2. Examine the lugs on the axle pinion flange and replace the flange if the lugs are shaved or distorted.
3. Coat the yoke spline with lubricant.
4. Remove the plug which you inserted into the rear of the transmission housing.
5. Insert the yoke into the transmission housing and onto the transmission output shaft. Make sure that the yoke assembly does not bottom on the output shaft with excessive force.
6. Locate the marks which you made on the rear driveshaft yoke and the pinion flange prior to removal of the driveshaft assembly. Install the driveshaft assembly with the marks properly aligned.
7. Install the U-bolts and nuts that attach the universal joint to the pinion flange. Torque the U-bolt nuts to 8–15 ft. lbs.

Rear Axle

UNDERSTANDING REAR AXLES

The rear axle is a special type of transmission that reduces the speed of the drive from the engine and transmission and divides the power to the rear wheels. Power enters the rear axle from the driveshaft via the companion flange. The flange is mounted on the drive pinion shaft. The drive pinion shaft and gear

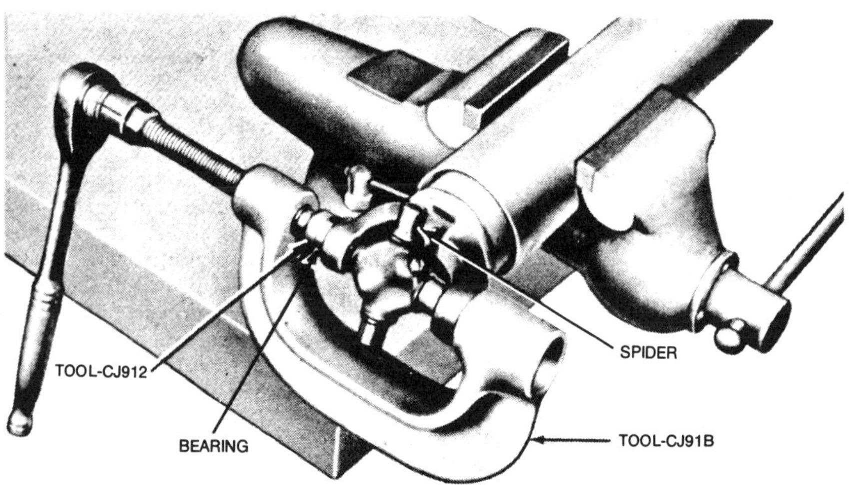

Installing bearing cap

which carry the power into the differential turn at engine speed. The gear on the end of the pinion shaft drives a large ring gear the axis of rotation of which is 90° away from that of the pinion. The pinion and gear reduce the speed and multiply the power by the gear ratio of the axle, and change the direction of rotation to turn the axle shafts which drive both wheels. The rear axle gear ratio is found by dividing the number of pinion gear teeth into the number of ring gear teeth.

The ring gear drives the differential case. The case provides the two mounting points for the ends of a pinion shaft on which are mounted two pinion gears. The pinion gears drive the two side gears, one of which is located on the inner end of each axle shaft.

By driving the axle shafts through this arrangement, the differential allows the outer drive wheel to turn faster than the inner drive wheel in a turn.

The main drive pinion and the side bearings, which bear the weight of the differential case, are shimmed to provide proper bearing preload, and to position the pinion and ring gears properly.

NOTE: *The proper adjustment of a relationship of the ring and pinion gears is critical. It should be attempted only by those with extensive equipment and/or experience.*

The rear wheels are connected to the differential assembly by axle shafts. The axle shafts are supported in the rear axle housing by bearings and are retained in the housing by bearing retainer plates which bolt to the rear brake mounting plates.

The differential assembly is mounted on two tapered bearings. These bearings are retained in the axle housing by removable bearing caps.

The drive pinion is mounted in the axle on two roller bearings.

An identification tag is attached to one of the inspection plate attaching bolts. The information on this tag must be used when ordering replacement parts.

NOTE: *Axles WER, WGX and WGZ have "C" locks, refer to the 7½" Ring Gear Axle for removal instructions.*

AXLE SHAFT AND/OR BEARING REPLACEMENT

NOTE: *On 6 ¾ inch rears, bearings should be pressed on and off the shaft with an arbor press. Unless you have access to one, it is inadvisable to attempt to perform any repair work on the axle shaft and bearing assemblies.*

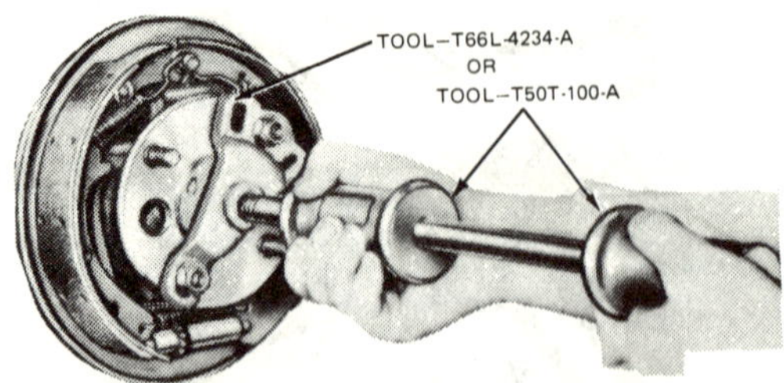

Axle shaft removal (typical)

6¾ Inch Ring Gear Axle

1. Remove the wheel, tire, and brake drum.
2. Remove the nuts holding the axle retainer plate to the backing plate.
3. Remove the retainer and install the nuts, fingertight, to prevent the brake backing plate from being dislodged.
4. Pull out the axle shaft and bearing assembly, using a slide hammer.

NOTE: *If a slide hammer is not available, the axle can sometimes be pried out using pry bars on opposing sides of the hub.*

If end-play is found to be excessive, the bearing should be replaced. Shimming the bearing is not recommended as this ignores end-play of the bearing itself and could result to improper seating of the bearing.

5. Using a chisel, nick the bearing retainer in three or four places. The retainer does not have to be cut, merely collapsed sufficiently, to allow the bearing retainer to be slid from the shaft.
6. Press off the bearing and install the new one by pressing it into position.
7. Press on the new retainer.

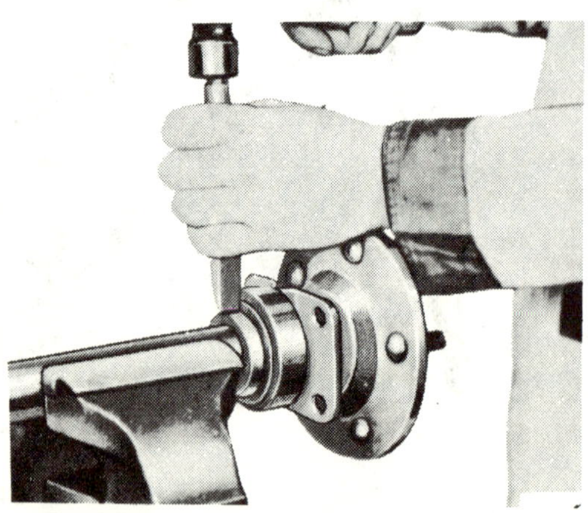
Loosening the bearing retaining ring (6¾ rear)

NOTE: *Do not attempt to press the bearing and the retainer on at the same time.*

8. Assemble the shaft and bearing in the housing, being sure that the bearing is seated properly in the housing.

9. Install the retainer, drum, wheel, and tire.

7½" Ring Gear Axle

1. Jack up and support the rear of the car.
2. Remove the wheels and tires from the brake drums.
3. Place a drain pan under the housing and drain the lubricant by loosening the housing cover.
4. Remove the nuts securing the brake drums to the axle shaft flanges and remove the drums.
5. Remove the housing cover and gasket, is used.
6. Position jackstands under the rear frame member and lower the axle housing. This is done to give easy access to the inside of the differential.
7. Working through the opening in the differential case, remove the side gear pinion shaft lockbolt and the side gear pinion shaft.
8. Push the axle shafts inward and remove the C-locks from the inner end of the axle shafts. Temporarily replace the shaft and lockbolt to retain the differential gears in position.
9. Remove the axle shafts with a slide hammer. Be sure the seal is not damaged by the splines on the axle shaft.
10. Remove the bearing and oil seal from the housing. Both the seal and bearing can be removed with a slide hammer. Two types of bearings are used on some axles, one requiring a press fit and the other a loose fit. A loose fitting bearing does not necessarily indicate excessive wear.
11. Inspect the axle shaft housing and axle shafts for burrs or other irregularities. Replace any worn or damaged parts. A light yellow color on the bearing journal of the axle shaft is normal, and does not require replacement of the axle shaft. Slight pitting and wear is also normal.
12. Lightly coat the wheel bearing rollers with axle lubricant. Install the bearings in the axle housing until the bearing seats firmly against the shoulder.
13. Wipe all lubricant from the oil seal bore, before installing the seal.
14. Inspect the original seals for wear. If necessary, these may be replaced with new seals, which are prepacked with lubricant and do not require soaking.
15. Install the oil seal.

    NOTE: *Installation of the seal without the proper tool can cause distortion and seal leakage.*

16. Remove the lockbolt and pinion shaft. Carefully slide the axle shafts into place. Be careful that you do not damage the seal with the splined end of the axle shaft. Engage the splined end of the shaft with the differential side gears.
17. Install the axle shaft C-locks on the inner end of the axle shafts and seat the C-locks in the counterbore of the differential side gears.
18. Rotate the differential pinion gears until the differential pinion shaft can be installed. Install the differential pinion shaft lockbolt. Tighten to 15–22 ft. lbs.
19. Install the brake drum on the axle shaft flange.
20. Install the wheel and tire on the brake drum and tighten the attaching nuts.
21. Clean the gasket surface of the rear housing and apply a bead of silicone sealer on the gasket surface. The bead should run inside of the bolt holes. Install the cover.
22. Raise the rear axle so that it is in the running position. Add the amount of specified lubricant to bring the lubricant level to 1¼" below the filler hole.

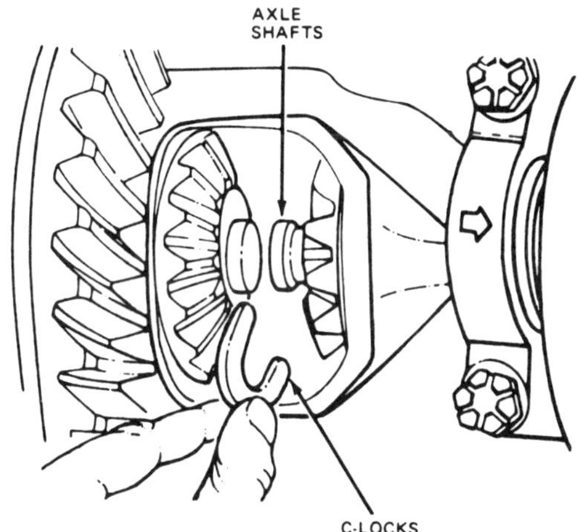

Removal and installation of C-locks (7½ rear)

AXLE SHAFT SEAL REPLACEMENT

All Models

1. Remove the axle shaft from the rear axle. See the previous procedure for details.
2. Using a two-fingered seal puller (slide hammer), remove the seal from the axle housing.

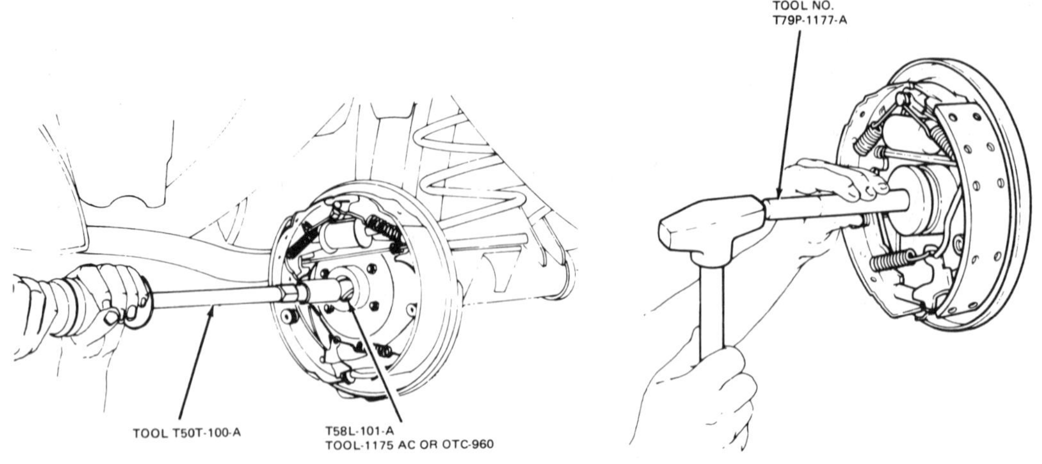

Axle seal replacement (typical)

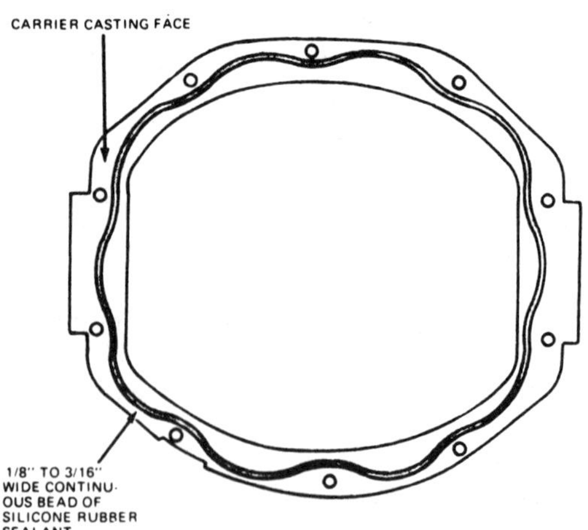

Installing sealer

3. Clean the recess in the rear axle housing from which the seal was removed.

4. Position a new seal on the housing and drive it into the housing with a seal installation tool.

5. Install the axle shaft.

Suspension and Steering

FRONT SUSPENSION

All Fairmont/Zephyr models use a modified version of the MacPherson strut front suspension. The design utilizes shock struts with coil springs mounted between the lower arm and a spring pocket in the No. 2 crossmember. The shock struts are non-repairable, and must be replaced as a unit. The ball joints lower suspension arm bushings are not separately serviced, and they also must be replaced by replacing the suspension arm as-

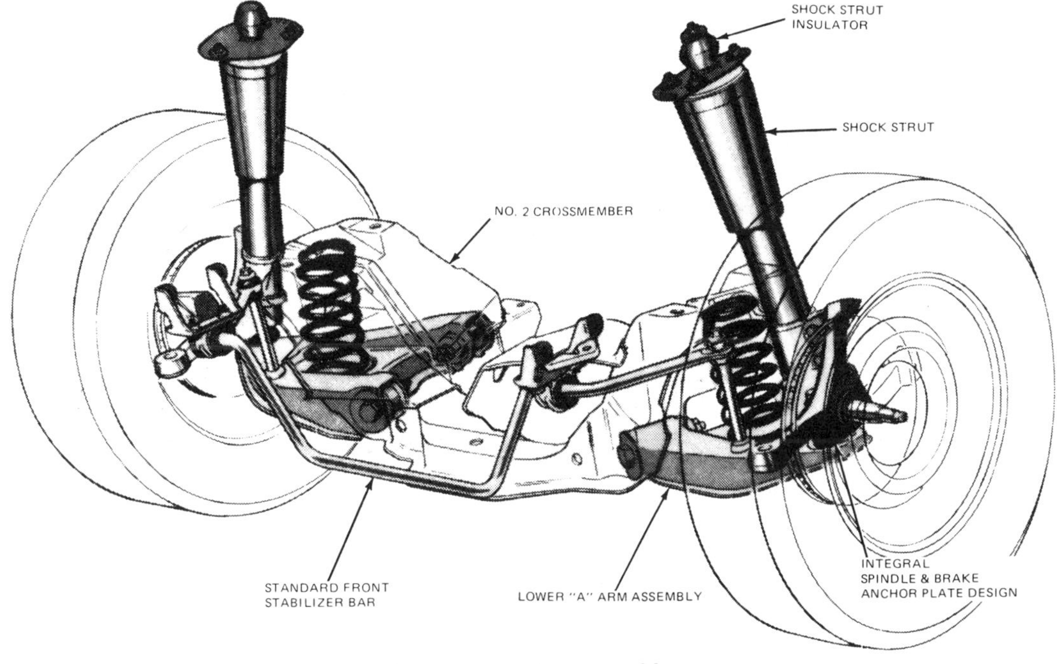

Front suspension assembly

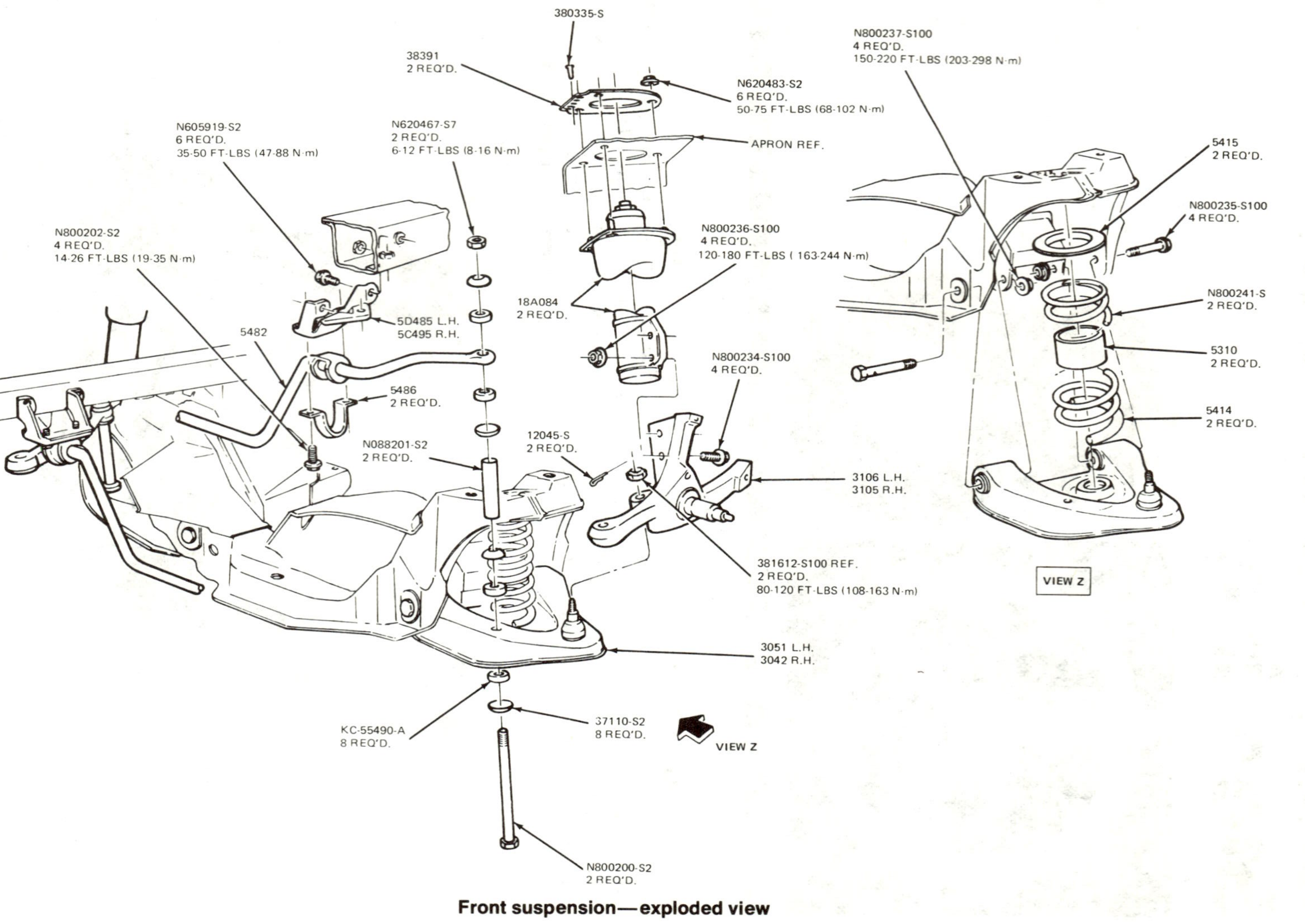

Front suspension—exploded view

sembly. The ball joint seal can be replaced separately.

Springs

NOTE: *Always use extreme caution when working with coil springs. Make sure the vehicle is supported sufficiently.*

REMOVAL

1. Raise the front of the vehicle and place safety stands under both sides of the jack pads just back of the lower arms.
2. Remove the wheel and tire assembly.
3. Disconnect the stabilizer bar link from the lower arm.
4. Remove the steering gear bolts, and move the steering gear out of the way.
5. Disconnect the tie rod from the steering spindle.
6. Using a spring compressor, install one plate with the pivot ball seat down into the coils of the spring. Rotate the plate, so that it is fully seated into the lower suspension arm spring seat.
7. Install the other plate with the pivot ball seat up into the coils of the spring. Insert the ball nut through the coils of the spring, so it rests in the upper plate.
8. Insert the compression rod into the opening in the lower arm through the lower and upper plate. Install the upper ball nut on the rod, and return the securing pin.

NOTE: *This pin can only be inserted one way into the upper ball nut because of a stepped hole design.*

9. With the upper ball nut secured turn the upper plate, so it walks up the coil until it contacts the upper spring seat.
10. Install the lower ball nut, thrust bearing and forcing nut on the compression rod.
11. Rotate the nut until the spring is compressed enough so that it is free in its seat.
12. Remove the two lower control arm pivot bolts and nuts, and disengage the lower arm from the frame crossmember and remove the spring assembly.
13. If a new spring is to be installed, mark the position of the upper and lower plates on the spring with chalk. Measure the compressed length of the spring as well as the

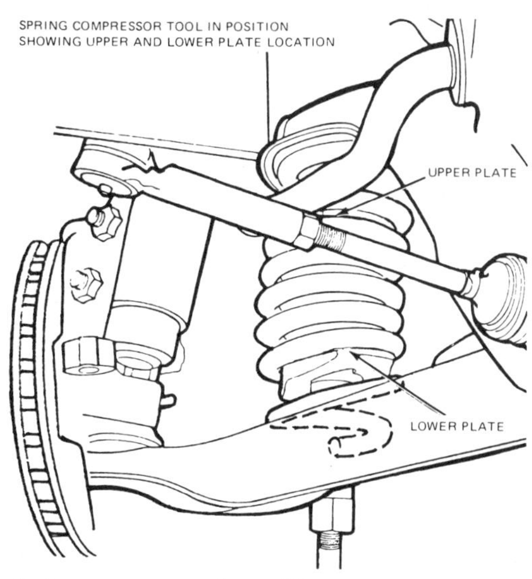

Spring compressor in position

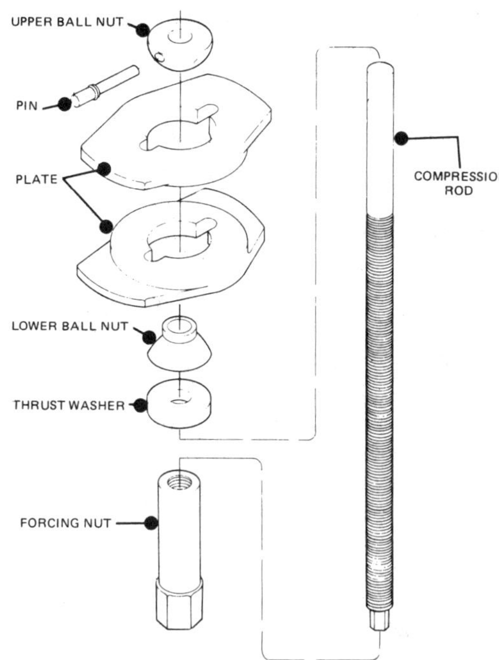

Spring compressor tool

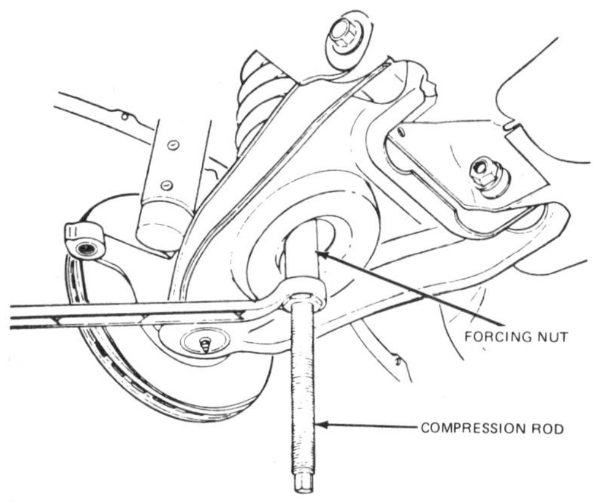

Spring compressed for removal

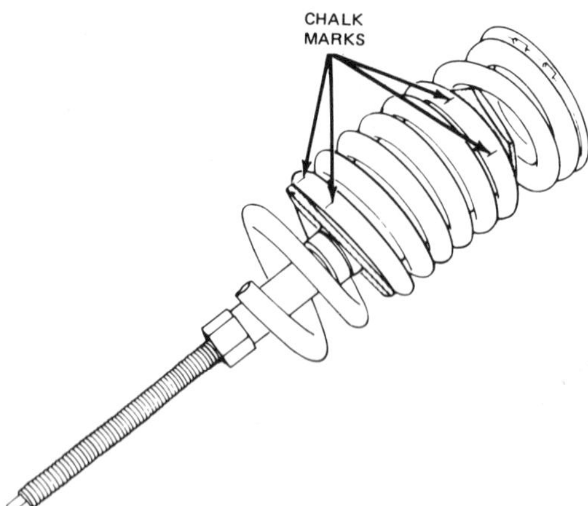

Spring removed from vehicle

amount of the spring curvature to assist in the compressing and installation of a new spring.

14. Loosen the nut to relieve spring tension, and remove the tools from the spring.

INSTALLATION

1. Assemble the spring compressor tool, and locate it in the same position as indicated in step 13 of the removal procedure.

NOTE: *Before compressing the coil spring, be sure the upper ball nut securing pin is inserted properly.*

2. Compress the coil spring until the spring height reaches the dimension in step 13.

3. Position the coil spring assembly into the lower arm.

NOTE: *Make sure that the lower end of the spring is properly positioned between the two holes in the lower arm spring pocket depression.*

4. To finish installing the coil spring reverse the removal procedure.

Ball Joints

Ball Joints are not replaceable. If the ball joints are found to be defective the lower control arm assembly must be replaced.

INSPECTION

1. Support the vehicle in normal driving position with both ball joints loaded.

2. Wipe the grease fitting and checking surface, so they are free of dirt and grease. The checking surface is the round boss into which the grease fitting is threaded.

3. The checking surface should project outside the cover. If the checking surface is inside the cover, replace the lower arm assembly.

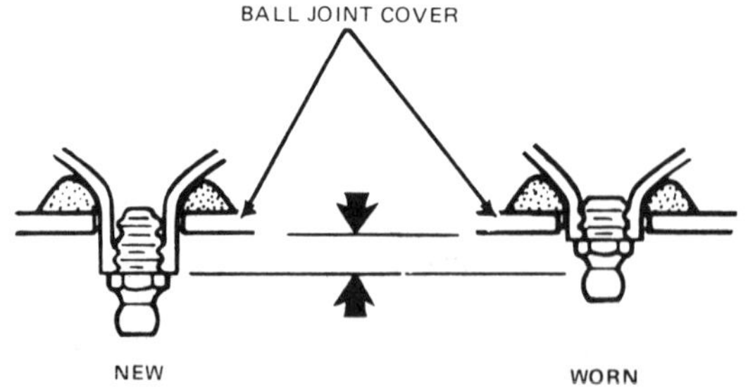

Inspection of lower ball joint

Shock Strut

REMOVAL

1. Place the ingition key in the unlocked position to permit free movement of the front wheels.

2. Working from the engine compartment remove the nut (16 mm) that attaches the strut to the upper mount. A screwdriver in the slot will hold the rod stationary while removing the nut.

NOTE: *The vehicle should not be driven while the nut is removed so make sure the car is in position for hoisting purposes.*

3. Raise the front of the vehicle by the lower control arms, and place safety stands under the frame jacking pads, rearward of the wheels.

4. Remove the tire and wheel assembly.

5. Remove the brake caliper, rotor assembly, and dust shield.

6. Remove the two lower nuts and bolts attaching the strut to the spindle.

7. Lift the strut up from the spindle to compress the rod, then pull down and remove the strut.

INSTALLATION

1. With the rod half extended, place the rod through the upper mount and hand start the mount as soon as possible.

2. Extend the strut and position into the spindle.

3. Install the two lower mounting bolts and hand start the nuts.

4. Tighten the nut that attaches the strut to the upper body mount to 60–75 ft. lbs. This can be done from inside the engine compartment.

NOTE: *Position a screwdriver in the slot to hold the rod stationary while the nut is being tightened.*

5. Remove the suspension load from the

lower control arms by lowering the hoist and tighten the lower mounting nuts to 150 ft. lbs.

6. Raise the suspension control arms and install the brake caliper, rotor assembly and dust shield.

7. Install the tire and wheel assembly.

8. Remove the safety stands and lower the vehicle.

Lower Control Arm

REMOVAL

1. Raise the front of the vehicle and position safety stands under both sides of the jack pads, just to the rear of the lower arms.

2. Remove the wheel and tire assembly.

3. Disconnect the stabilizer bar link from the lower arm.

4. Remove the disc brake caliper, rotor and dust shield.

5. Remove the steering gear bolts and position out of the way.

6. Remove the cotter pin from the ball joint stud nut, and loosen the ball joint nut one or two turns.

7. Tap the spindle sharply to relieve the stud pressure.

8. Remove the tie-rod end from the spindle. Place a floor jack under the lower arm, supporting the arm at both bushings. Remove both lower arm bolts, lower the jack and remove the coil spring as outlined earlier in the chapter.

9. Remove the ball nut and remove the arm assembly.

INSTALLATION

1. Place the new arm assembly into the spindle and tighten the ball joint nut to 100 ft. lbs. Install the cotter pin.

2. Position the coil spring in the upper spring pocket. Make sure the insulator is on top of the spring and the lower end is properly positioned between the two holes in the depression of the lower arm.

3. Carefully raise the lower arm with the floor jack until the bushings are properly positioned in the crossmember.

4. Install the lower arm bolts and nuts, finger tight only.

5. Install and tighten the steering gear bolts.

6. Connect the tie-rod end and tighten the nut to 35–47 ft. lbs.

7. Connect the stabilizer link bolt and nut and tighten to 10 ft. lbs.

8. Install the brake dust shield, rotor and caliper.

9. Install the wheel and tire assembly.

10. Remove the safety stands and lower the vehicle. After the vehicle has been lowered to the floor and at curb height, tighten the lower arm nuts to 210 ft. lbs.

Front End Alignment

On the Fairmont/Zephyr the caster and camber are set at the factory and cannot be changed. Only the toe is adjustable.

TOE ADJUSTMENT

Toe is the difference in width (distance), between the front and rear inside edges of the front tires.

1. Turn the steering wheel, from left to right, several times and center.

NOTE: *If car has power steering, start the engine before centering the steering wheel.*

2. Secure the centered steering wheel with a steering wheel holder, or any device that will keep it centered.

3. Release the tie-rod end bellows clamps so the bellows will not twist while adjustment is made. Loosen the jam nuts on the tie-rod ends. Adjust the left and right connector sleeves until each wheel has one-half of the desired toe setting.

4. After the adjustment has been made, tighten the jam nuts and secure the bellows clamps. Release the steering wheel lock and check for steering wheel center. Readjust, if necessary until steering wheel is centered and toe is within specs.

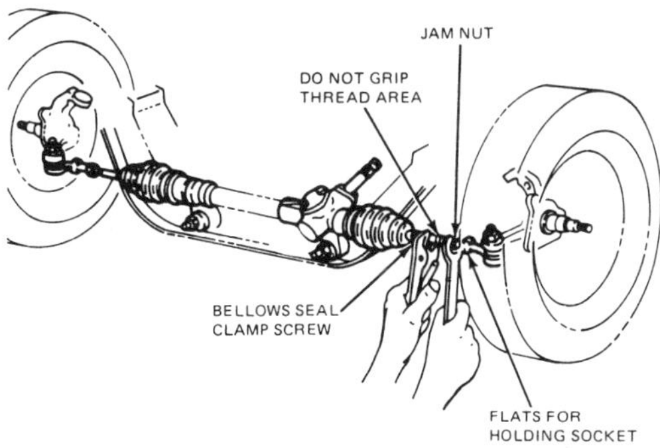

Toe adjustment

REAR SUSPENSION

The rear suspension is a four link coil spring design. The rear axle is suspended from the body by two upper arms which control side

Wheel Alignment Specifications

Year	Model	Caster Range (deg)	Caster Pref Setting (deg)	Camber Range (deg)	Camber Pref Setting (deg)	Toe-in (in.)	Steering Axis Inclin. (deg)	Wheel Pivot Ratio (deg) Inner Wheel	Wheel Pivot Ratio (deg) Outer Wheel
1978–79	Fairmont, Zephyr	①	7/8P	①	3/8P	3/16 to 7/16	—	20	19.74
1980–83	Fairmont and Zephyr (exc. station wagon)	①	1P	①	7/16P	1/16 to 5/16	15¼	—	—
	Fairmont and Zephyr station wagon	①	¾P	①	½P	1/16 to 5/16	15¼	—	—

①Caster and camber is preset and nonadjustable

② Station Wagon: N/A after 1981

to side movement and two lower arms which control forward and rearward movement. Shock absorbers are located on each side. Each coil spring is mounted between an upper seat which is welded to the body and a lower seat which is part of the lower arm assembly. The shock absorbers are attached to an upper shock bracket which is welded to the rear axle tubes.

Springs

NOTE: *Always use extreme caution when working with coil springs. Make sure the vehicle is supported sufficiently.*

REMOVAL

NOTE: *Ford recommends that if one spring requires replacement the other spring should be replaced also.*

1. Raise the vehicle and support the body at the rear body crossmember.
2. Lower the hoist until the rear shocks are fully suspended.

NOTE: *The axle must be supported by the hoist, or a transmission jack, or jack stands.*

3. Place a transmission jack under the lower arm pivot bolt and remove the bolt and nut. Lower the transmission jack slowly until the coil spring load is relieved.
4. If the vehicle is equipped with a rear

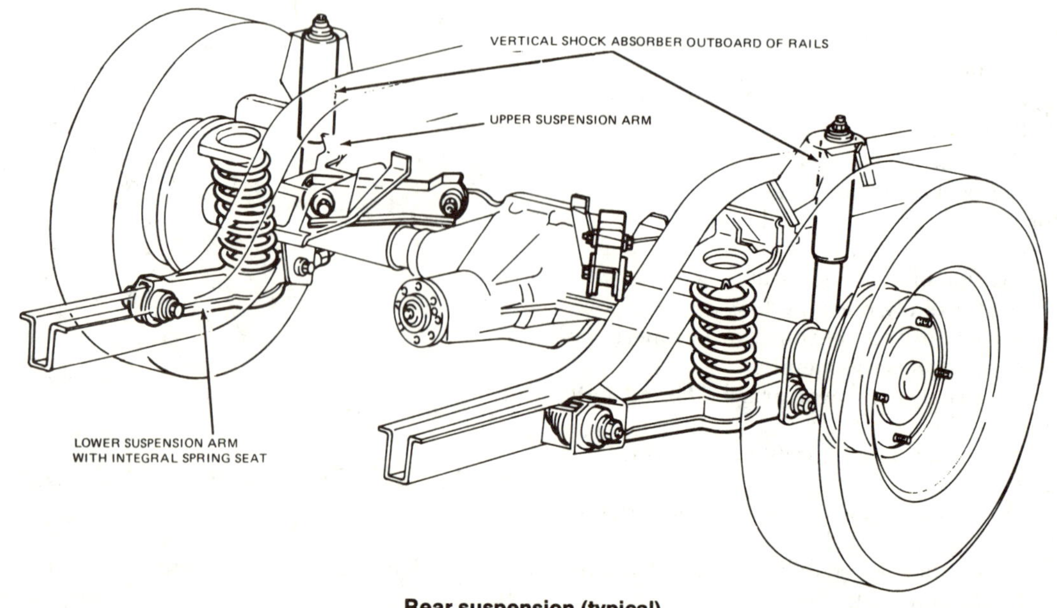

Rear suspension (typical)

stabilizer bar remove the four retaining bolts and remove the stabilizer bar.

5. Remove the coil spring and insulators from the vehicle.

INSTALLATION

1. Place the upper spring insulator into the spring seat in the body. Tape in place if necessary.

2. Place the lower spring insulator on the lower arm. Install the internal damper into the spring.

3. Position the coil spring on the lower arm spring seat. Slowly raise the transmission jack until the arm is in position. Insert a new rear pivot bolt and nut, with the nut facing outwards. Do not torque at this time.

4. Lower the transmission jack. Raise the axle to curb height. Torque the lower arm pivot bolt to 85 ft. lbs.

5. If the vehicle is equipped with a rear stabilizer bar, install it at this time. Torque the horizontal mount bolts to 35 ft. lbs. and the vertical mount bolts to 20 ft. lbs.

6. Remove the crossmember supports and lower the vehicle.

Shock Absorbers

BOUNCE TEST

Each shock absorber can be tested by bouncing the corner of the vehicle until maximum up and down movement is obtained. Release the car. It should stop bouncing in one or two bounces. Compare both front corners or both rear corners but do not compare the front to the rear. If one corner bounces longer than the other it should be inspected for damage and possibly be replaced.

REMOVAL

1. Open the trunk to gain access to the upper shock mounting.

2. Remove the rubber cap covering the shock absorber stud.

3. Remove the shock absorber attaching nut, and insulator.

4. Raise the vehicle and support the rear axle.

5. Compress the shock absorber to clear the hole in the upper shock tower.

6. Remove the lower shock absorber nut and washer from the shock mounting stud, and remove the shock absorber.

INSTALLATION

1. Expel all air from the new shock absorber by extending the shock absorber fully in its right side up position then turning it upside down and fully compressing it. Follow this procedure at least three times to expel the air.

2. Compress the shock absorber and place the lower shock mounting eye over the lower mounting stud. Install the washer and new self locking attaching nut.

3. Place the inner washer and insulator on the upper shock stud.

4. Extend the shock absorber and position the upper stud into the mounting hole.

5. Lower the vehicle and install the insulator, outer washer and nut to the upper shock stud.

6. Install the rubber cap that covers the mounting stud.

STEERING

The steering gear is of the rack and pinion type. The gear input shaft is connected to the steering shaft by means of a flexible coupling. A pinion gear, machined on the input shaft, engages the rack and rotation of the input shaft pinion causes the rack to move laterally. The system is either manual or power assisted.

The tie-rod is attached at each end of the rack joint. This allows the tie-rods to move with the front suspension. The gear is sealed at each end with rubber bellows. The manual steering gear is filled with approximately 5 oz of SAE-90 EP oil at initial assembly and checking or refilling is not required unless fluid leakage is evident or repairs become necessary.

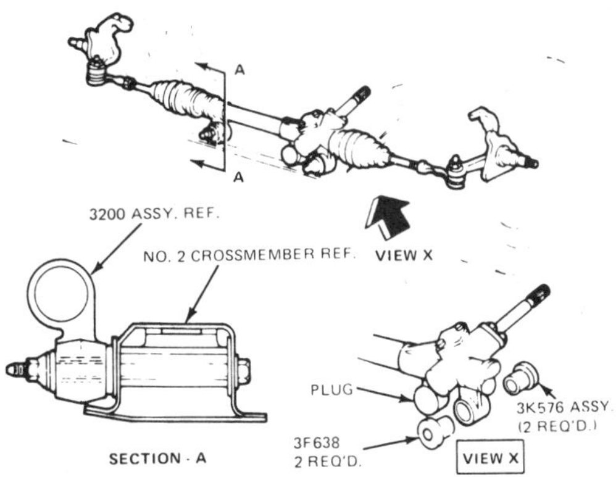

Rack and pinion steering (typical)

Couplings attaching the tie-rods are retained on the rack, are pinned, and cannot be disassembled in service. Replacement of inner tie-rods, rack, housing, or upper pinion bearing requires installation of a new steering gear assembly.

If the steering linkage, front suspension, and steering column components are in good condition, there should be no more than $^{3}/_{8}$ in. free-play in the steering wheel when measured at the rim of the wheel.

If a loud knock is heard when turning the steering wheel from lock-to-lock, the pinion bearing preload should be checked. A faint knock from the steering wheel when driving on very rough roads is normal and not an indication of a steering defect.

CAUTION: *When the front wheels of the vehicle are suspended completely off the ground, do not turn the wheels quickly or forcefully from lock to lock. This could cause a buildup of hydraulic pressure within the steering gear which could damage or blow out the bellows.*

Steering Gear

REMOVAL

1. Disconnect the negative battery cable from the battery.
2. Remove the one bolt retaining the flexible coupling to the input shaft.
3. Leave the ignition key in the ON position, and raise the vehicle support with jackstands.
4. Remove the two tie rod end retaining cotter pins and nuts. Remove the studs from the spindle arms using a "fork" or press.

NOTE: *Do not use a hammer. You might damage the spindle arms or rod studs.*

5. Support the steering gear, and remove the two nuts, insulator washers, and bolts retaining the steering gear to the No. 2 crossmember.
6. If power steering, lower the gear slightly and disconnect the pressure and return lines from the valve housing.
7. Remove the steering gear assembly from the vehicle.

INSTALLATION

1. Insert the input shaft into the flexible coupling aligning the flats and position the steering gear to the No. 2 crossmember. Connect the power steering hoses (if equipped). Install the two bolts.
2. Connect the tie rod ends to the spindle arms and install the two retaining nuts. Tighten to 40 ft. lbs. Install the two cotter pins.
3. Lower the vehicle and install the one bolt retaining the flexible coupling to the input shaft. Tighten the bolt to 30 ft. lbs.
4. Turn the ignition key to the off position.
5. Reconnect the negative battery cable.
6. Check the front end alignment (toe) and adjust if necessary.

ADJUSTMENTS

There are two adjustments which can be performed on the manual rack and pinion steering gear: support yoke-to-rack adjustment and pinion bearing preload adjustment. The steering gear assembly must be removed from the car to perform either adjustment.

The power rack and pinion steering gear provides for only one service adjustment. The adjustment is for Rack Yoke Plug Preload which may be necessary when the car wanders back and forth when the steering wheel is held firmly in position or when noises or feedback occurs in the steering. The adjustment requires special tools and should be done by qualified service personnel. The steering gear assembly requires removal for the adjustment. Removal can be done by the car owner and the assembly taken to a garage for the necessary work.

Support Yoke-to-Rack (manual)

1. Remove the steering gear from the car.
2. Mount the steering gear in a soft-jawed vise with the yoke cover up. Clean the exterior of the gear.
3. Remove the yoke cover, gasket, shims, and yoke spring. Clean the yoke cover and support thoroughly.
4. Reinstall the yoke cover on the support yoke.
5. Tighten the yoke cover until the cover just touches the yoke support.
6. Measure the clearance between the cover and support yoke flange.
7. To the clearance figure measured in Step 6, add 0.006 in.
8. Measure the thickness of the shims and gasket that were removed from under the yoke cover in Step 3.
9. Subtract the figure obtained in Step 8 from the figure obtained in Step 7. The remainder from this subtraction is the thickness of the shim that must be added under the yoke cover to obtain the correct support yoke-to-rack adjustment.

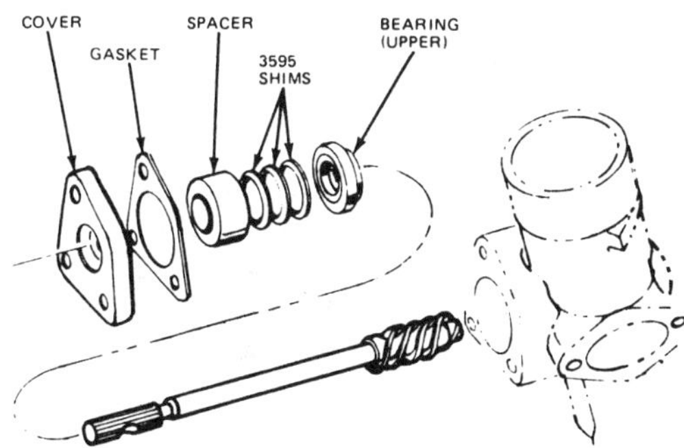

Pinion bearing cover and shim arrangement

10. Remove the yoke cover and install the yoke spring, shims, and gasket removed in Step 3, plus a shim of the correct thickness.

11. Apply sealer to the yoke cover bolts and install the yoke cover.

12. Turn the pinion shaft to ensure proper operation of the gear.

NOTE: *Return the pinion shaft to its centered position before installing it in the car.*

Pinion Bearing Preload (manual)

1. Remove the steering gear assembly from the car.
2. Mount the steering gear in a soft-jawed vise and clean the exterior of the gear.
3. Remove the pinion cover.
4. Clean the pinion flange area and remove the gasket and shims.
5. Install a new gasket and install shims until the shim pack is flush with the gasket. Check by placing a straightedge on top of the gasket and applying light pressure.
6. Remove the gasket and shims and reinstall the shims in the following order: the thinnest of the select fit shims first, followed by the other select fit shims and the 0.093 in. shim next to the cover.

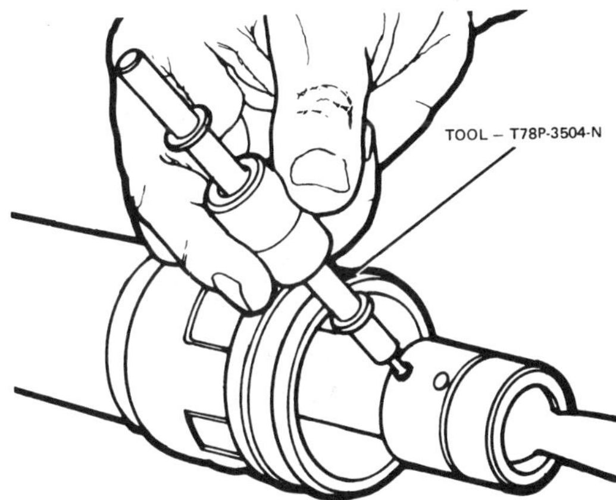

Removing the spiral pin from the ball housing

7. To the above shim pack, add a 0.005 in. shim to prelaod the bearing. Place it in the correct order in the shim pack.
8. Apply sealer to the cover attaching bolts and install the cover and gasket.

Tie Rod Articulation Effort

1. Install the hook end of a pull scale through the hole in the tie rod end stud. The effort to move the tie rod should be 1–5 pounds manual and 2–10 pounds for power.

NOTE: *Do not damage the tie rod neck.*

2. Replace the ball joint-tie rod assembly if the effort falls outside this range. Save the tie rod end for use on the new tie rod assembly.

Outer Tie Rod End

REMOVAL AND INSTALLATION

1. Loosen the wheel lug nuts. Jack up the front of the car, safely support on jackstands and remove the wheels.
2. Remove and discard the cotter pin and nut from the worn outer tie rod end.
3. Loosen the tie rod end jam nut. Disconnect the tie rod end from the steering spindle using a tie rod end puller/press.
4. Unscrew the tie rod end, counting the number of turns required for removal.
5. Install the new end in the reverse order of removal. Screw in the required number of turns, mount tie rod end and secure jam nut. Have the toe in checked.

Power Steering Pump

REMOVAL AND INSTALLATION

1. Disconnect the power steering fluid return hose and drain the fluid into a container.
2. Disconnect the pressure hose from the power steering pump fitting. Do not remove the fitting from the pump.
3. Loosen the stationary and adjusting nut and bolt, or loosen the alternator. Remove the drive belt.
4. Remove the adjusting and stationary nut and bolt or the mounting bracket bolts, and the power steering pump.
5. Install in the reverse order of removal. Fill with clean fluid, run engine and check for leaks.

CAUTION: *Do not pry against the power steering pump reservoir. The reservoir is made of fiberglass and may break.*

Steering Wheel

REMOVAL

1. On the two and three spoke wheels remove the wheel hub cover by pulling outward. On the four spoke wheels push out the emblem from the holes in backside of the steering wheel.

NOTE: *Disconnect negative battery cable from the battery.*

2. Remove and discard the steering wheel attaching nut.

3. Install a steering wheel puller on the end of the shaft and remove the wheel.

NOTE: *The use of a knock-off type steering wheel puller or the use of a hammer on*

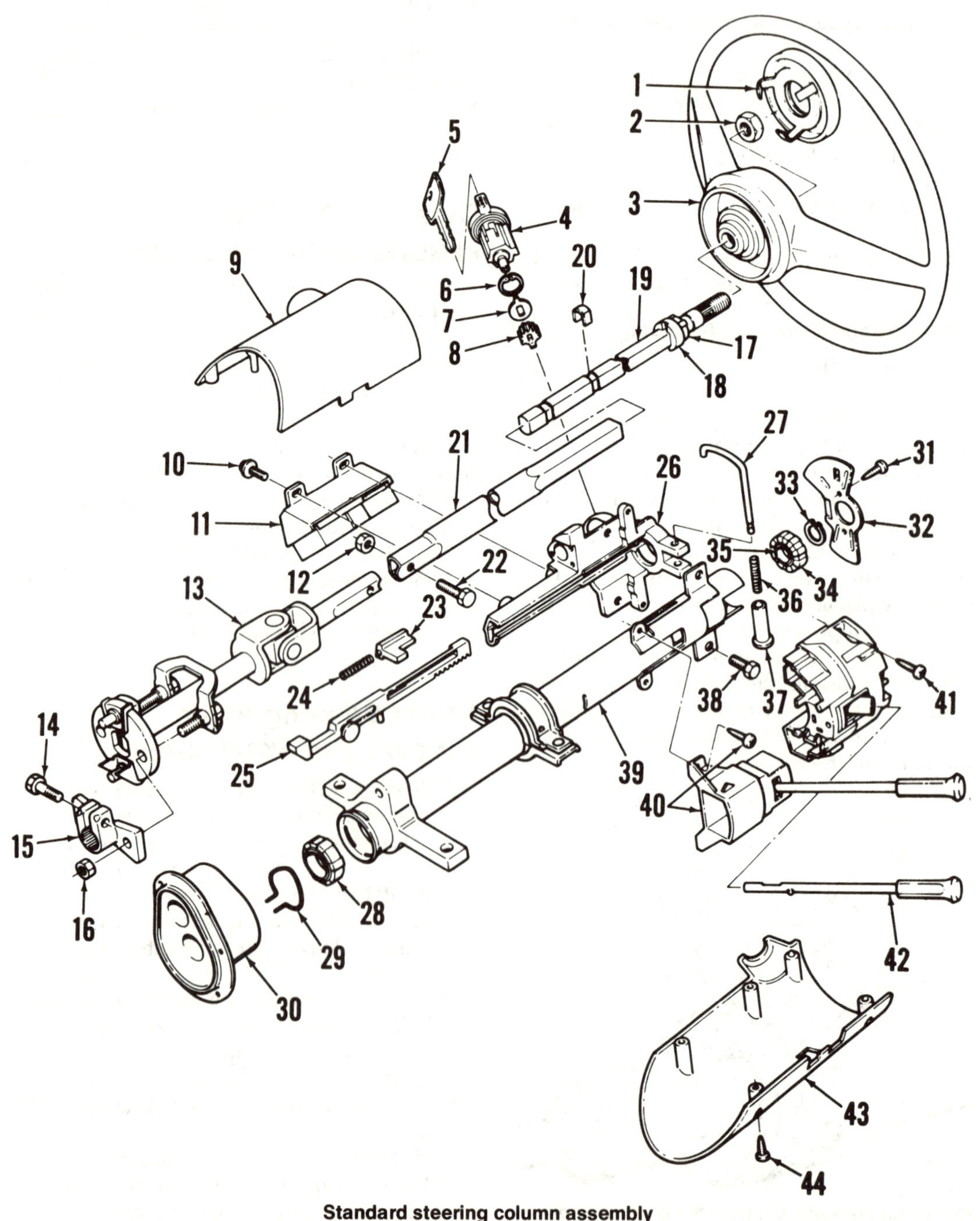

Standard steering column assembly

the steering shaft will damage the collapsible column.

INSTALLATION

1. Position the steering wheel on the end of the shaft and align the marks on the steering wheel with the marks on the shaft.
2. Install a new wheel nut and torque to 35 ft. lbs.
3. Install the hub cover to the steering wheel.

Turn Signal Switch

REMOVAL AND INSTALLATION

NOTE: *Disconnect negative battery cable from the battery.*

1. Remove the four screws retaining the steering column shroud.
2. Remove the turn signal lever by pulling and twisting straight out.
3. Peel back the foam shield. Disconnect the two electrical connectors.
4. Remove the two attaching screws and disengage the switch from the housing.
5. To install, position the switch to the housing and install the screws. Stick the foam to the switch.
6. Install the lever by aligning the key and pushing the lever fully home.
7. Install the two electrical connectors, test the switch, and install the shroud.

Ignition Switch

REMOVAL

1. Disconnect the negative battery cable.
2. Remove the steering column trim shroud by removing the self-tapping screws.
3. Disconnect the ignition switch electrical connector. Turn the key to the "lock" position (thru 1981) or the "on" position (1982 and later).
4. Drill out the "break-off head" bolts that connect the switch to the lock cylinder housing using a $1/8$ inch drill.
5. Remove the two bolts using an "easy out" tool or equivalent.
6. Disengage the ignition switch from the actuator pin.

INSTALLATION

1. Turn the key to the "lock" position (thru 1981) or the "on" position (1982 and later). When adjusting the old switch to the lock position slide the carrier to the lock position then insert a .050 inch drill bit through the switch housing and into the carrier, preventing movement of the carrier. New switches are held in place by plastic shipping pins.
2. Rotate the ignition key to the "lock" position for models through 1981 and to the "on" position for 1982 and later models.
3. Install the ignition switch on the actuator pin.
4. Install new "break-off head" bolts and tighten until the heads break off.
5. Remove the adjustment drill bit by adjusting pin.
6. Connect the electrical connector to the ignition switch.
7. Connect the negative battery cable and check to see if the ignition switch operates properly.
8. Install the steering column trim shrouds.

Brakes

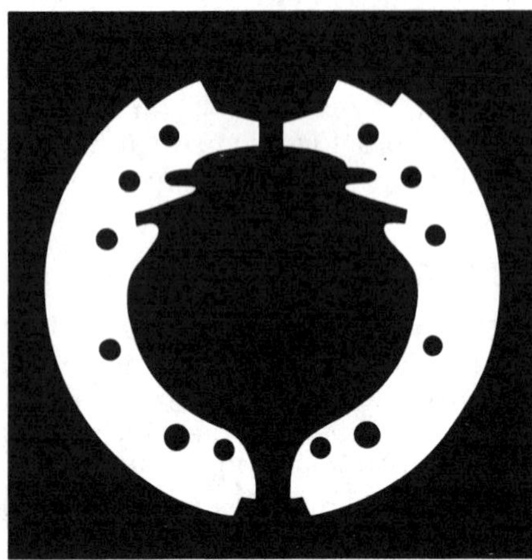

HYDRAULIC SYSTEM

The hydraulic system is compoased of the master cylinder, the brake lines, the brake control valve, and the disc calipers and rear wheel cylinders.

The master cylinder serves as a reservoir and as a pump. Brake fluid is stored in the two separate sections. The front half of the master cylinder holds the fluid that is used to activate the rear brakes. The rear half of the master cylinder holds the fluid that activates the front brakes. Since the front system is independent of the rear system, a fluid leak in one system would only cause that system to fail, allowing the other system to stop the car.

When the brake pedal is depressed, it moves a piston mounted in the bottom of the master cylinder. The movement of this piston creates hydraulic pressure in the master cylinder. This pressure is carried to the wheel cylinders and calipers by the brake lines.

On the way to the wheels, the brake fluid passes through the control valve assembly.

The brake control valve assembly may consist of a pressure differential valve, a metering valve, and a proportioning valve. These valves are housed within a single cast-iron or aluminum valve body (housing). The pressure differential and metering valves are located in the central bore of the valve body. The proportioning valve is located in a separate angular or vertical bore.

The metering valve is located in the front end of the control valve central bore between the front brake system inlet port and the front brake outlet ports. Its function is to regulate the hydraulic pressure to the front disc brakes. The metering valve location at the front end of the housing center bore provides easy accessibility to the valve bleeder rod during bleeding of the front brake system.

The brake warning light switch is mounted at the center of the valve body with the spring-loaded plunger fitting into a tapered shoulder groove in the center of the piston. With the piston in a centralized position the switch contacts remain open.

Should there be a loss of pressure in either the front or rear brake system, when the brake pedal is applied, the piston will move off center, closing the switch contacts and turning on the warning light.

After repairs are made and the brake system bled, the piston will center itself upon brake application and the switch contacts will open, turning off the warning light.

The proportioning valve regulates the rear brake system hydraulic pressure and is located between the rear brake system inlet and outlet ports.

When the brake pedal is applied, the full

rear brake fluid pressure passes through the proportioning valve to the rear brake hydraulic system until the valve split point is attained. Above the split point, the proportioning valve reduces hydraulic pressure to the rear brakes for balanced braking.

When the hydraulic pressure reaches the wheels, after the pedal has been depressed, it enters the wheel cylinders and calipers. Here it comes into contact with a piston or pistons. The hydraulic pressure causes the piston(s) to move, moving the brake shoes and pads, causing them to come into contact with the drums and rotors. Friction between the "brake shoes" and the drums/rotors causes the car to slow down. There is a relationship between the amount of pressure that is applied to the brake pedal and the amount of force which moves the brake shoes against the drums. Therefore, the harder the brake pedal is depressed, the quicker the car will stop.

Since a hydraulic system is one which operates on fluids, air is a natural enemy of the brake system. Air in the hydraulic system retards the passage of hydraulic pressure from the master cylinder to the wheels. Anytime a hydraulic component is opened or removed, the system must be bled of air to ensure proper operation. Air trapped in the hydraulic system can also cause the brake warning light to come on, even though the system has not failed. This is especially true after repairs have been performed.

The wheel cylinders used with rear drum brakes are composed of a cylinder with a polished inside bore, which is mounted on the brake shoe backing plate, two boots, two pistons, two cups, a spring, and a bleeder screw. When hydraulic pressure enters the wheel cylinder, it contacts the two cylinder cups. The cups seal the cylinder and prevent fluid from leaking out. The hydraulic pressure forces the cups outward. The cups in turn force the pistons outward. The pistons contact the brake shoes and the hydraulic pressure in the wheel cylinders overcomes the pressure of the brake springs, causing the shoes to contact the brake drum. When the brake pedal is released, the brake shoe return springs pull the brake shoes away from the drum. This forces the pistons back toward the center of the wheel cylinder. Wheel cylinders can fail in two ways; they can leak or lock up. Leaking wheel cylinders are caused either by defective cups or irregularities in the wheel cylinder bore. Frozen wheel cylinders are caused by foreign matter getting into the cylinders and preventing the pistons from sliding freely.

The calipers used on front disc brakes contain a piston, piston seal, piston dust boot, and bleeder screw. When hydraulic pressure enters the caliper, the piston is forced outward causing the disc brake pad to come into contact with the rotor. When the brakes are applied, the piston seal, mounted on the caliper housing, becomes slightly distorted in the direction of the rotor. When the brakes are released, the piston seal moves back to its normal position and, at the same time, pulls the piston back away from the brake pad. This allows the brake pads to move away from the rotor. Calipers can fail in three ways, two of these being caused by defective piston seals. When a piston seal becomes worn, it can allow brake fluid to leak out to contaminate the pad and rotor. If a piston seal becomes weak, it can fail to pull the piston away from the brake shoe when the brakes are released, allowing the brake pad to drag on the rotor when the car is being driven. If foreign material enters the caliper housing, it can prevent the piston from sliding freely, causing the brakes to stick on the rotor.

Clean, high-quality and high-temperature brake fluid is essential to the proper operation of the brake system. Always buy the highest quality brake fluid available. If the brake fluid should become contaminated, it should be drained and flushed, and the master cylinder filled with new fluid. Never reuse brake fluid. Any brake fluid that is removed from the brake system should be discarded.

Since the hydraulic system is sealed, there must be a leak somewhere is the system if the master cylinder is repeatedly low on fluid.

Master Cylinder

REMOVAL

1. Disconnect the negative battery cable.
2. Disconnect the stoplamp switch wires at the connector.
3. Remove the spring retainer and slide the stop lamp switch off the brake pedal pin just far enough to clear the end of the pin.
4. Loosen the master cylinder attaching nuts or bolts from the inside of the engine compartment and slide the master cylinder push rod, nylon washers, and bushings off the brake pedal pin.
5. Remove the brake lines from the master cylinder.
6. Remove the master cylinder attaching

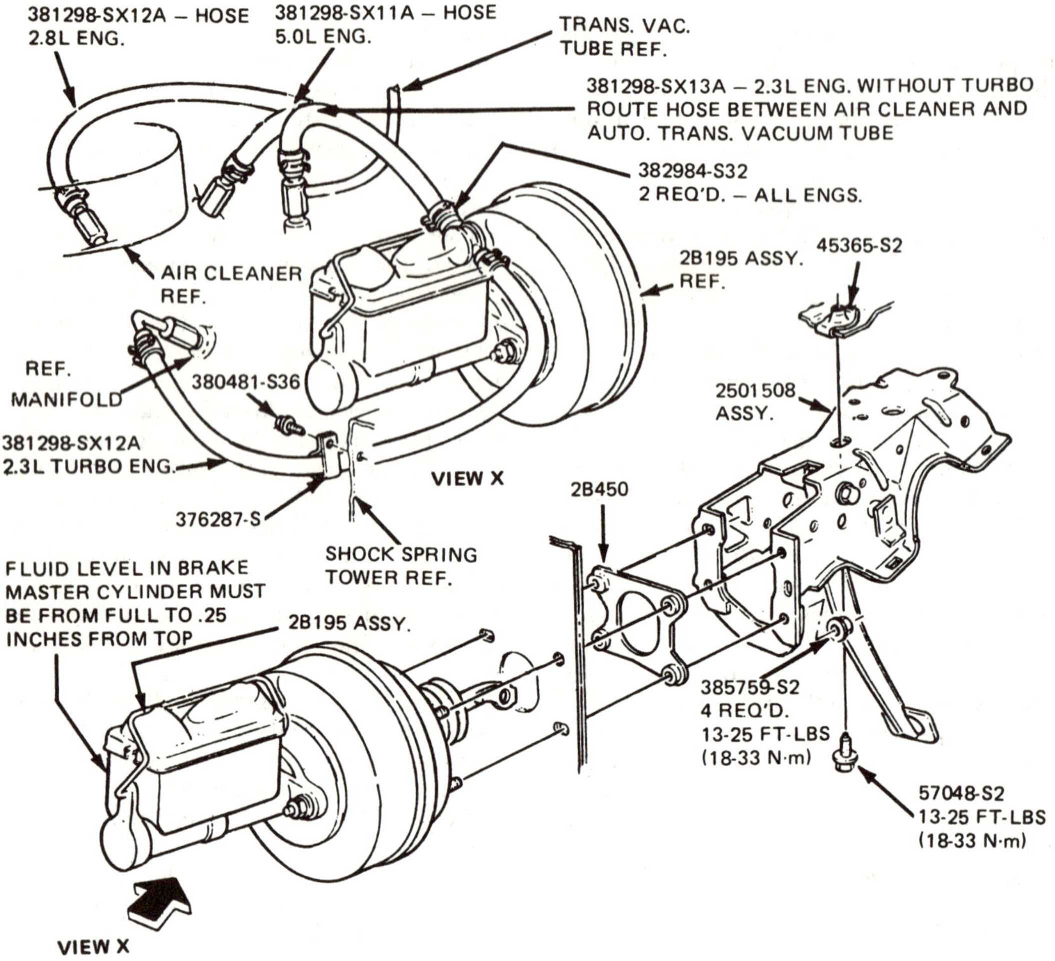

381298-SX12A – HOSE
2.8L ENG.
381298-SX11A – HOSE
5.0L ENG.
TRANS. VAC.
TUBE REF.
381298-SX13A – 2.3L ENG. WITHOUT TURBO
ROUTE HOSE BETWEEN AIR CLEANER AND
AUTO. TRANS. VACUUM TUBE
382984-S32
2 REQ'D. – ALL ENGS.
AIR CLEANER
REF.
2B195 ASSY.
REF.
45365-S2
REF.
MANIFOLD
380481-S36
2501508
ASSY.
381298-SX12A
2.3L TURBO ENG.
VIEW X
2B450
376287-S
SHOCK SPRING
TOWER REF.
FLUID LEVEL IN BRAKE
MASTER CYLINDER MUST
BE FROM FULL TO .25
INCHES FROM TOP
2B195 ASSY.
385759-S2
4 REQ'D.
13-25 FT-LBS
(18-33 N·m)
57048-S2
13-25 FT-LBS
(18-33 N·m)
VIEW X

Master cylinder installation—with power brake

bolts and remove the master cylinder from the car.

Power Brake Booster

The diaphragm power brake booster is a self-contained vacuum operated hydraulic brake unit mounted on the driver's side engine compartment panel. The brake booster and check valve can only be serviced by replacement.

OVERHAUL

1. Clean the outside of the master cylinder, and remove the cap and rubber gasket. Drain and discard the fluid that is in the master cylinder.
2. Remove the secondary piston stop bolt from the bottom of the cylinder.
3. Remove the bleeder screw from the cylinder.
4. Depress the primary piston and remove the snap-ring from the groove in the rear of the master cylinder bore.
5. Remove the primary piston and push rod from the master cylinder bore. Do not attempt to service the primary piston in any

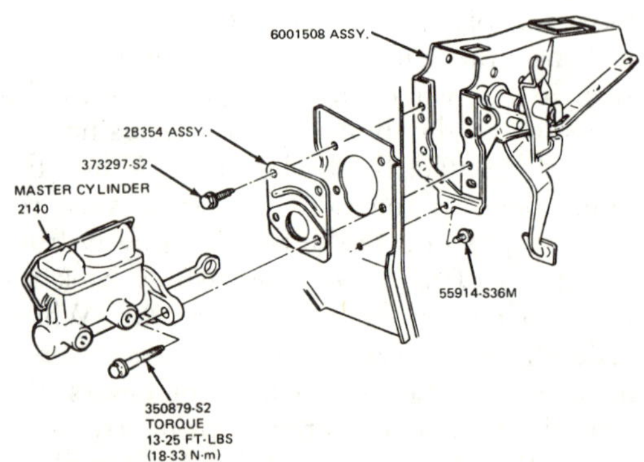

6001508 ASSY.
2B354 ASSY.
373297-S2
MASTER CYLINDER
2140
55914-S36M
350879-S2
TORQUE
13-25 FT-LBS
(18-33 N·m)

Master cylinder installation—without power brake

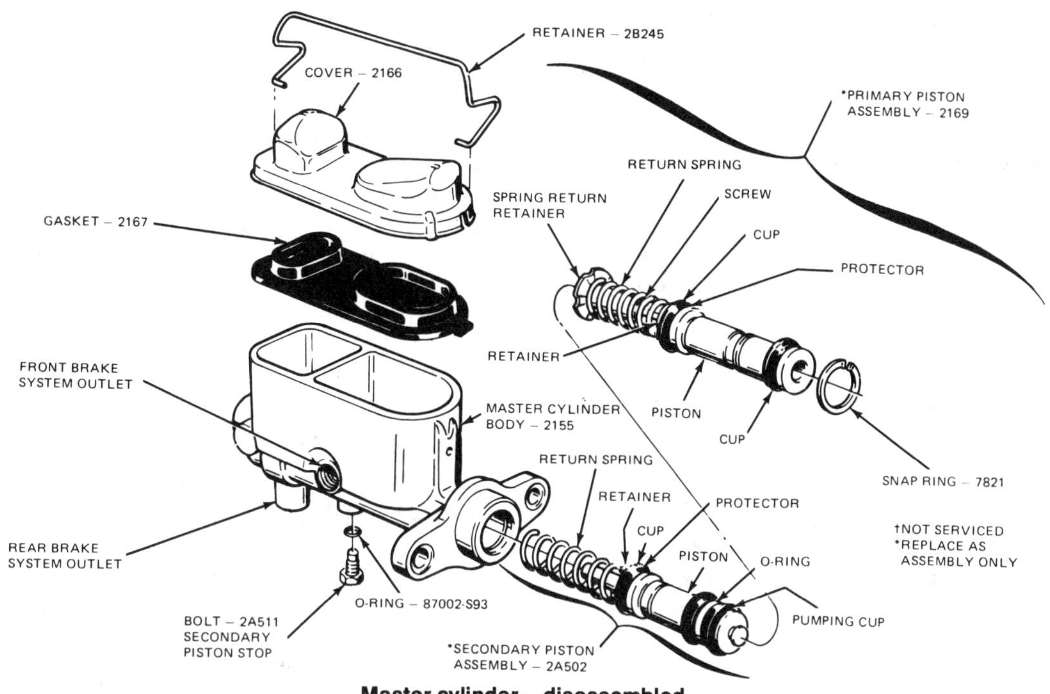

Master cylinder—disassembled

other way than removing the push rod from it. The primary piston must be replaced as an assembly.

6. Remove the secondary piston from the master cylinder.

NOTE: *Do not disassemble the master cylinder any further than this as no other parts for the master cylinder are serviced.*

7. Clean all parts in isopropyl alcohol.

8. Thoroughly inspect all parts for wear. If the primary or secondary pistons are defective, they should be replaced as an assembly. Check the master cylinder bore for scoring. The cylinder can be honed to remove surface blemishes, but no more than 0.003 in. can be removed from the cylinder walls. If in doubt, replace the master cylinder.

NOTE: *Before installing any part in the master cylinder, dip it in clean brake fluid.*

9. Install the secondary piston assembly in the master cylinder.

10. Install the primary piston assembly in the master cylinder.

11. Install the push rod, retainer, and boot, depress the piston, and install the snap-ring.

12. Install the secondary piston stop bolt and O-ring in the bottom of the master cylinder.

13. Install the bleeder screw.

14. Fill the master cylinder with new fluid, depress the push rod, and open the bleeder to remove most of the air from the master cylinder.

INSTALLATION

1. Insert the push rod and boot through the dash panel opening, and position the master cylinder on the panel.

2. Install the master cylinder retaining bolts or nuts but do not tighten them.

3. Coat the nylon bushings with light engine oil. Install the nylon washer and bushing on the brake pedal pin.

4. Position the stoplamp switch and master cylinder push rod on the brake pedal pin. Install the nylon bushing and washer and secure them with the spring retainer.

5. Connect the wires at the stoplamp switch connector.

6. Tighten the master cylinder attaching nuts or bolts and connect the brake lines to the master cylinder.

7. Fill the master cylinder with new brake fluid.

8. Bleed the dual master cylinder and the primary and secondary brake systems.

9. Centralize the pressure differential valve.

Brake Control Valve Assembly

The brake control valve assemblies may consist of a pressure differential valve, metering valve, and a proportioning valve or pressure differential and proportioning valve assembly. These valves are housed in a single aluminum or cast iron housing.

REMOVAL AND INSTALLATION

1. Disconnect the brake warning light switch wire harness connector from the warning light switch.
2. Disconnect the front brake system inlet tube and the rear system inlet tube from the brake control valve assembly.
3. Disconnect the left and right front brake outlet tubes from the brake control valve assembly.
4. Disconnect the rear system outlet tube from the brake control valve assembly.
5. Remove the control valve retaining nuts or bolts and remove the control valve.
6. To install reverse the removal procedure. Bleed the brake system and centralize the pressure differential valve.

Centralizing the Pressure Differential Valve

After any repair or bleeding of the brake system the dual brake warning light switch should be centralized.

1. Turn the ignition switch to ACC or ON position.
2. Depress the brake pedal and the piston will center itself, causing the brake warning light to go out if it was already lit.
3. Turn the ignition switch to the OFF position.
4. Check the operation of the brakes before driving.

Bleeding The Hydraulic System

NOTE: *If it is known that only one system has air in it, only that system has to be bled since the front and rear hydraulic systems are independent.*

1. Fill the master cylinder with brake fluid.
2. Install a $^3/_8$ in. box-end wrench on the bleeder screw on the right rear wheel.
3. Push a piece of small-diameter rubber tubing over the bleeder screw until it is flush against the wrench. Submerge the other end of the rubber tubing in a glass jar partially filled with clean brake fluid. Make sure the rubber tube fits on the bleeder screw snugly or you may get zapped with brake fluid when the bleeder screw is opened.
4. Have a friend apply pressure to the brake pedal. Open the bleeder screw and observe the bottle of brake fluid. If bubbles appear in the glass jar, it means there is air in the system. When your friend has pushed the pedal to the floor, immediately close the bleeder screw *before he releases the pedal.*
5. Repeat this procedure until no bubbles appear in the jar. Refill the master cylinder.
6. Repeat this procedure on the left rear, right front, and left front wheels, in that order. Periodically refill the master cylinder so it does not run dry.
7. If the brake warning light is on, depress the brake pedal firmly. If there is no air in the system, the light will go out.

FRONT DISC BRAKES

The major components of the disc brake system are the brake pads, the caliper, and the rotor (disc). The caliper is similar in function to the wheel cylinder used with drum brakes, and the rotor is similar to the brake drum used in drum brakes.

The major difference between drum brakes and disc brakes is that with drum brakes, the wheel cylinder forces the brake shoes *out* against the brake drum to stop the car, while with disc brakes, the caliper forces the brake pads *in*ward to squeeze the rotor and stop the car. The biggest advantage of disc brakes over drum brakes is that the caliper and brake pads enclose only a small portion of the rotor, leaving the rest of it exposed to outside air. This aids in rapid heat dissipation, reducing brake fade.

The disc brakes used on Fairmont/Zephyr are known as sliding caliper disc brakes. The name of this system is derived from the sliding action of the brake caliper on the anchor plate during braking. The plate-like brake rotor is attached to and mounted on the car by the front wheel hub. A brake caliper anchor plate, attached to the front wheel spindle, mounts over the top of, but does not touch, the rotor. The caliper is mounted in the middle of the large opening in the anchor plate. When the brake pedal is depressed, and hydraulic force is generated, the piston in the caliper forces the inboard brake pad inward and into contact with the brake rotor. The caliper now begins to act like a C-clamp, with the inboard shoe and the piston acting as the adjustable screw. Since there is only a small amount of clearance between the brake pads and the rotor, the inboard shoe contacts the rotor almost as soon as the brake pedal is depressed. As the brake pedal is depressed further, it increases the amount of hydraulic pressure sent to the piston in the caliper. Since the inboard shoe is already in contact with the brake rotor, it cannot be moved. As the caliper pushes on the inboard brake shoe, the increased hydraulic pressure forces the back of the caliper housing away from the back of the piston. This causes the caliper to slide inward on the anchor plate and force the outboard brake pad into contact with the rotor. Thus the name sliding caliper. This happens very quickly, so both pads contact the rotor at about the same time.

When the brakes are released, the piston seal in the caliper housing (which was stretched during brake application) returns to its normal position and, in so doing, pulls the piston back away from the brake pad. A very slight wobble in the rotor as the car begins to move pushes the brake pads back so they are not in contact with the rotor. The clearance between the pads and the rotor is very slight, but it is sufficient to prevent brake drag. The same clearance is maintained even when the brake pads wear as the car accumulates mileage and, because of this, disc brakes do not have to be adjusted.

Disc Brake Pads

INSPECTION

1. Remove the wheel and tire assembly.
2. Visually inspect the lining. If the lining is worn to within $^1/_8$ inch of the metal shoe all four shoe and lining assemblies must be replaced.
3. Visually check the caliper and hoses for leakage. If a seal is leaking, the caliper must be disassembled and new seals installed.

REMOVAL AND INSTALLATION

1. Remove about half of the fluid from the master cylinder reservoir.
2. Loosen the lug nuts and raise and support the vehicle.
3. Remove the front wheel. Be careful to avoid damage to the caliper splash shield or bleed screw.
4. Remove the caliper locating pins. Remove the caliper assembly from the integral spindle anchor plate and rotor. Remove the outer shoe from the caliper.
5. Remove the inner shoe and inspect the rotor surfaces.
6. Secure the caliper assembly with a length of wire.
7. Remove and discard the plastic bush-

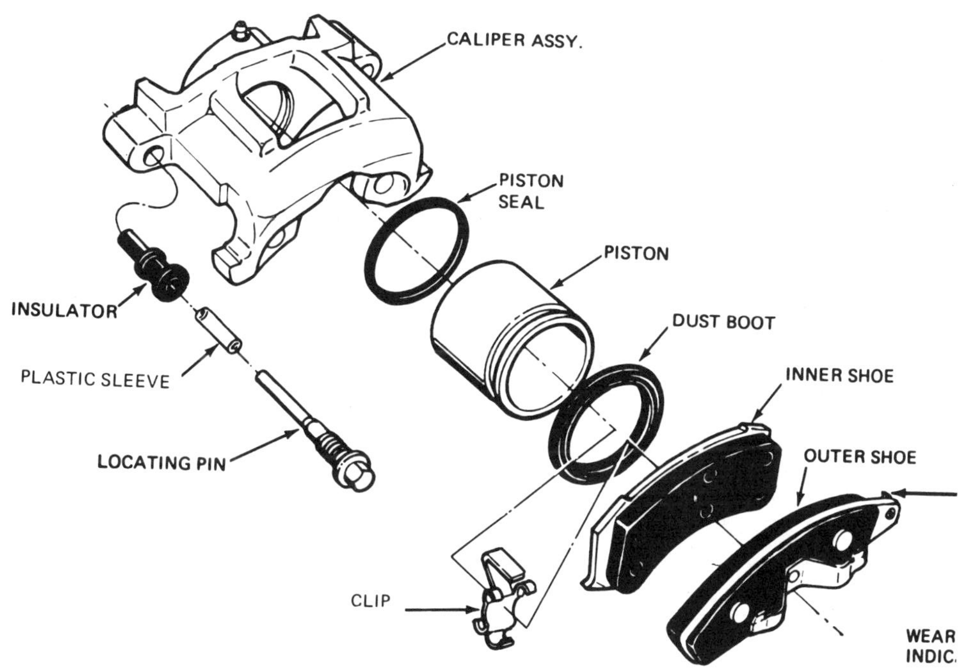

Caliper assembly—disassembled view

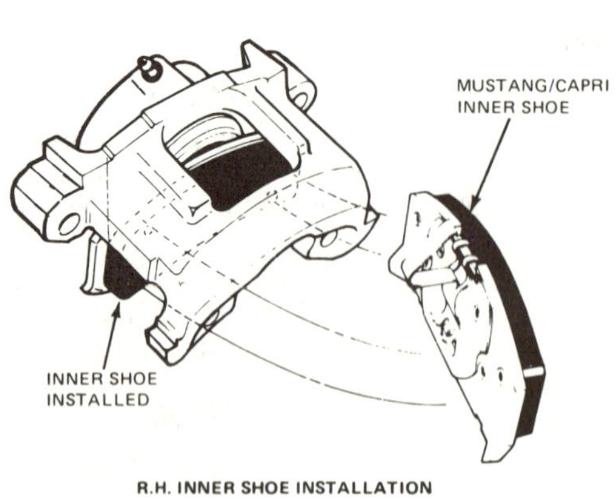

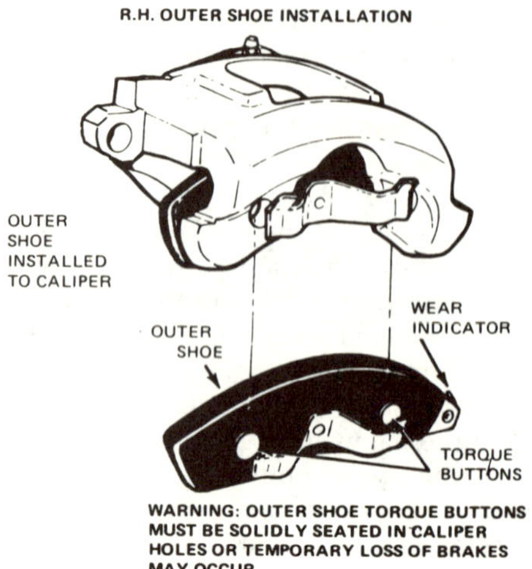

Disc brake pad installation

ings inside the caliper locating pin insulators.

8. Remove and discard the locating insulators.

9. Using a 4 inch C-clamp and a 2¾ x 1 x ¼ in. piece of wood, seat the piston in its bore.

10. Install new insulators and sleeves in the caliper housing. Both insulator flanges must straddle the housing holes and the sleeves must bottom in the insulators as well as under the upper lip.

11. Inner shoes are marked left and right. Install the proper inner shoe in the caliper. Do not bend the clips too far or they will become distorted.

12. Outer shoes are marked left and right.

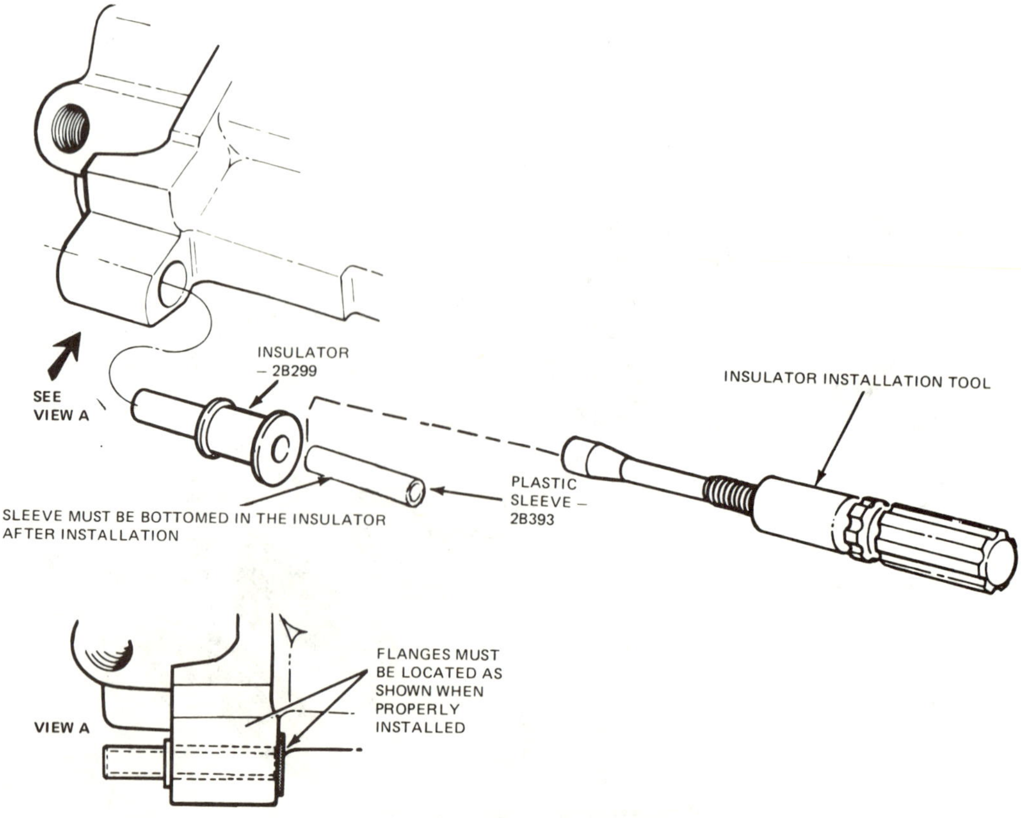

Insulator and sleeve installation

Install the proper outer shoe making sure that the clip and buttons are properly seated.

13. Refill the master cylinder.

14. Install the wheel, lower the car and test the brakes.

CALIPER OVERHAUL

1. Loosen the front wheel lug nuts.
2. Raise and support the car.
3. Remove the front wheel taking care to avoid damage to the splash shield and bleeder screw.
4. Loosen the flexible brake hose-to-brake tube fitting at the frame and remove the horseshoe type retaining clip from the hose and bracket. Remove the hose from the bracket and unscrew it from the caliper. Plug the hose to avoid contaminants from entering the brake fluid.

NOTE: *If both calipers are being removed, mark them left and right.*

5. Remove the caliper locating pins.
6. Lift the caliper from the rotor.
7. Place a wadded cloth in front of the piston and apply compressed air at the hose hole.

Never attempt to stop the piston with your hand. The piston can emerge from its bore with considerable force due to built-up air pressure.

8. Remove the dust boot and piston seal.
9. Clean all metal parts in isopropyl alcohol. Dry all parts with compressed air.
10. Coat all parts with clean brake fluid before installing. Make certain that the seal does not become twisted, and that it is firmly seated in its groove.
11. Install a new dust boot and insert the piston in its bore. Spread the dust boot over the piston as it's installed.
12. Position the caliper over the rotor with the outer shoe against the rotor braking surface to prevent pinching the boot.

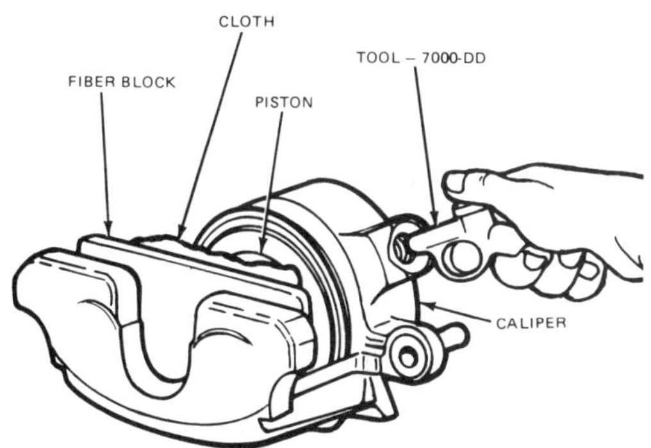

Removing the piston from the caliper

13. Connect the locating pins to the anchor plate and insulators. Be sure the locating pins are free of dirt, grease or oil.
14. Torque the locating pins to 30–40 ft. lbs.
15. Unplug the hose and install it into the caliper and torque it to 20–30 ft. lbs.

NOTE: *It is not necessary for the hose to be flush with the caliper when tightened; two or three threads may be visible when properly torqued. Do not overtorque.*

16. Connect the upper end of the hose. Tighten the fitting nut to 10–18 ft. lbs.
17. Bleed the system and center the differential valve. Fill the master cylinder to within ¼in. of the top of the reservoir.

Wheel Bearings/Hub and Rotor

REMOVAL

1. Remove the caliper assembly and temporarily secure it to the upper suspension with a piece of wire.
2. Remove the grease cap from the hub.
3. Remove the cotter key, nut retainer and adjusting nut.
4. Pull outward on the hub and rotor assembly enough to loosen the washer and outer wheel bearing.
5. Push the hub and rotor back onto the spindle and remove the washer and outer wheel bearing.
6. Slide the wheel hub and rotor assembly off the wheel spindle.

INSTALLATION

1. If the rotor is being replaced with a new one clean the surface of the rotor with carburetor degreaser.
2. If the original rotor is being installed place it on a clean, paper covered surface with the wheel studs facing upwards.
3. Working through the hole in the center of the wheel hub, tap the grease seal out of the rear of the hub with a screwdriver or drift.

NOTE: *Be careful not to damage the inner bearing while knocking out the grease seal.*

4. Remove the grease and bearing from under the rotor, and discard the grease seal.
5. Clean the inner and outer bearings and the wheel hub with a suitable solvent. Remove all old grease.
6. Thoroughly dry and wipe clean all components.
7. Clean all old grease from the spindle on the car.

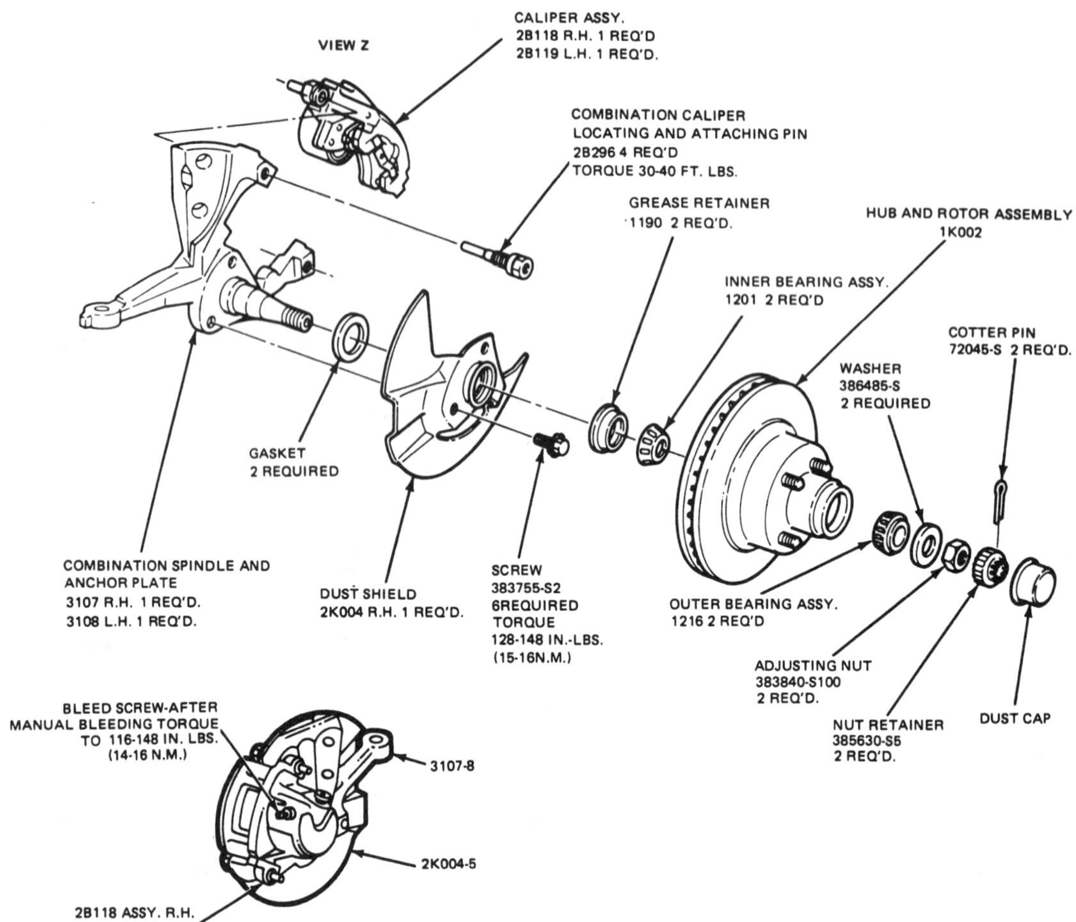

Caliper, shield and rotor assembly

8. Carefully check the bearings for any sign of scoring or other damage. If the roller bearings or bearing cages are damaged, the bearing and the corresponding bearing cup in the rotor hub must be replaced. The bearing cups must be driven out of the rotor hub to be removed. The outer bearing cup is driven out of the front of the rotor from the rear and vice versa for the inner bearing cup.

9. Whether you are reinstalling the old bearings or installing new ones, the bearings must be packed with wheel bearing grease. To do this, place a glob of grease in your left palm, then, holding one of the bearings in your right hand, drag the edge of the bearing heavily through the grease. This must be done to work as much grease as possible through the roller bearings and cage. Turn the bearing and continue to pull it through the grease until the grease is packed between the bearings and the cage all the way around the circumference of the bearing. Repeat this operation until all of the bearings are packed with grease.

10. Pack the inside of the rotor hub with a moderate amount of grease, between the bearing cups. Do not overload the hub with grease.

11. Apply a small amount of grease to the spindle.

12. Place the rotor, face down, on a protected surface and install the inner bearing.

13. Coat the lip of a new grease seal with a small amount of grease and position it on the rotor.

14. Place a block of wood on top of the grease seal and tap on the block with a hammer to install the seal. Turn the block of wood to different positions to seat it squarely in the hub.

15. Position the rotor on the spindle.

16. Install the outer bearing and washer on the spindle inside the rotor hub.

17. Install the bearing adjusting nut and

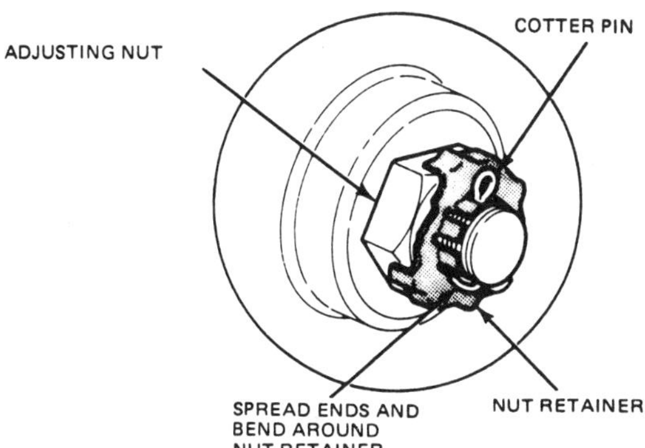

Adjusting the front wheel bearings

tighten it to 17–25 ft. lbs. while spinning the rotor. This will seat the bearing.

18. Back off the adjusting nut one half turn.
19. Tighten the adjusting nut to 10–15 in. lbs.
20. Install the nut lock on the adjusting nut so two of the slots align with the holes in the spindle.
21. Install a new cotter pin and bend the ends back so that they will not interfere with the dust cap.
22. Install the dust cap.

REAR DRUM BRAKES

All Fairmonts/Zephyrs have drum brakes on the rear wheels.

The major components of the system are the drum, the brake shoes, the brake shoe return and hold-down springs, and the automatic adjuster assembly. The rear brakes also incorporate a parking brake mechanism.

When the brake pedal is depressed, and hydraulic pressure is delivered to the wheel cylinder, the wheel cylinder expands to force the shoes against the drum. The primary shoe moves first, contacting the drum and pivoting slightly on its hold-down spring mounting pin. As the top of the primary (front) shoe contacts the drum, the bottom of the shoe moves slightly away from the drum. This movement is transferred through the adjusting screw to the secondary brake shoe, where it aids the wheel cylinder in bringing the secondary shoe in contact with the drum. Friction between the brake shoes and the drum causes the car to slow down and stop. When the brake pedal is released, the brake shoe return springs move the brakes away from the drum. If the lining on the brakes becomes contaminated or if the lining or drum becomes grooved, the engagement of the brakes and the drum will become very harsh causing the brakes to lock up and/or squeal. If the brake shoes on one wheel contact the drum before the same action occurs in the outer wheels, the brakes will pull to one side when applied.

The automatic adjuster assembly consists of a cable, cable guide, adjuster lever, automatic adjuster spring, and adjusting screw. The automatic adjuster operates only when the brakes are applied while the car is backing up. When the brakes are applied with the car moving rearward, the movement of the secondary (rear) brake shoe (the automatic adjuster is attached to this shoe) causes the adjuster cable to pull the adjusting lever upward. When the brakes are released, the automatic adjuster spring pulls the adjusting lever downward. As the lever moves downward, it contacts the star wheel on the adjusting screw and pushes it downward. This causes the adjusting screw to unscrew slightly (expand) and move the brake shoes closer to the drum. The adjusting lever then rests on the star wheel of the adjusting screw until the brakes are applied the next time the car backs up. If the brake adjustment is OK, the secondary shoe will not have to move very far to contact the drum. This limited shoe movement will not lift the adjusting lever off the star wheel, thus the brakes will not be adjusted.

The parking brake mechanism in the wheel consists of a parking brake link and lever. The link fits between the two brake shoes. The lever is attached to the parking brake cable and the secondary brake shoe. When the parking brake handle is pulled in the car, the rear brake shoes are moved into contact with the brake drums.

Inspection

1. Raise the rear of the car and support the car with safety stands. Make sure the parking brake is not on.
2. To check the rear brakes, remove the lug nuts that attach the wheels to the axle shaft and remove the tires and wheels from the car. Pull the brake drum off the axle shaft. If the brakes are adjusted too tightly to remove the drum, see step three. If you can remove the drum, see step four.
3. If the brakes are too tight to remove the drum, get under the car (make sure you have safety stands under the car to support it) and

remove the rubber plug from the bottom of the brake backing plate. Shine a flashlight into the slot in the plate. You will see the top of the adjusting screw star wheel and the adjusting lever for the automatic brake adjusting mechanism. To back off the adjusting screw, you must first insert a small, thin screwdriver or a piece of firm wire (coat hanger wire) into the adjusting slot and push the adjusting lever away from the adjusting screw. Insert a brake adjusting spoon into the slot and engage the top of the star wheel. Lift the bottom of the adjusting spoon to force the adjusting screw star wheel downward. Repeat this operation until the brake drum is free of the brake shoes and can be pulled off. See the brake adjustment procedure for an illustration.

4. Clean the brake shoes and the inside of the brake drum. There must be at least $^{1}/_{32}$ in. of brake lining above the heads of the brake shoe attaching rivets. The lining should not be cracked or contaminated with grease or brake fluid. If there is grease or brake fluid on the lining, it must be replaced and the source of the leak must be found and corrected. Brake fluid on the lining means leaking wheel cylinders. Grease on the brake lining means a leaking grease retainer (front wheels) or axle seal (rear brakes). If the lining is slightly glazed but otherwise in good condition, it can be cleaned with medium sandpaper. Lift the bottom of the wheel cylinder boots and inspect the ends of the wheel cylinders. A small amount of fluid in the end of the cylinders should be considered normal. If fluid runs out of the cylinder when the boots are lifted, however, the wheel cylinder must be rebuilt or replaced. Examine the inside of the brake drum. It should have a smooth, dull finish. If excessive brake shoe wear has caused grooves to wear in the drum, it must be machined or replaced. If the inside of the drum is slightly glazed, but otherwise in good condition, it can be cleaned with medium sandpaper.

6. If no repairs are required, install the drum and wheel. If the brake adjustment was changed to remove the drum, adjust the brakes until the drum will just fit over the brakes. After the wheel is installed it will be necessary to complete the adjustment. See the brake adjustment procedure in this chapter. If a front wheel was removed, tighten the wheel bearing adjusting nut to 17–25 ft. lbs. while spinning the wheel. This will seat the bearing. Loosen the adjusting nut ½ turn, then retighten it to 10–15 in. lbs.

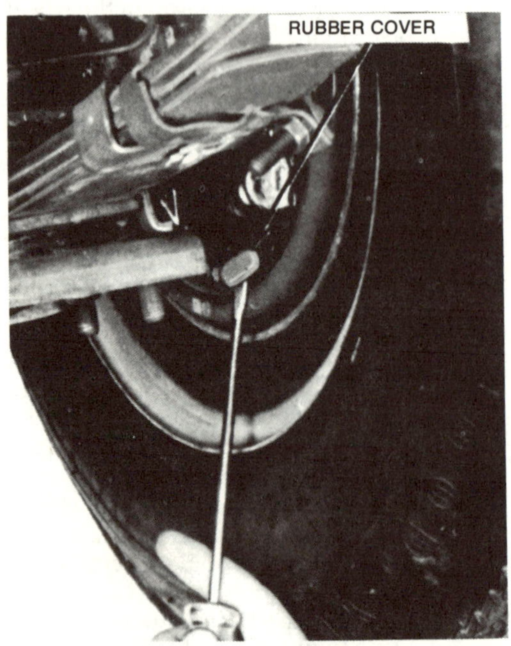

Removing the plug from the backing plate

Brake Shoe Removal

NOTE: *If you are not thoroughly familiar with the procedures involved in brake replacement, disassemble and assemble only one side at a time, leaving the other wheel intact as a reference.*

1. Remove the brake drum. See the above "Inspection" procedure.
2. Place the hollow end of a brake spring service tool (available at auto parts stores) on the brake shoe anchor pin and twist it to disengage one of the brake retracting springs. Repeat this operation to remove the other spring.

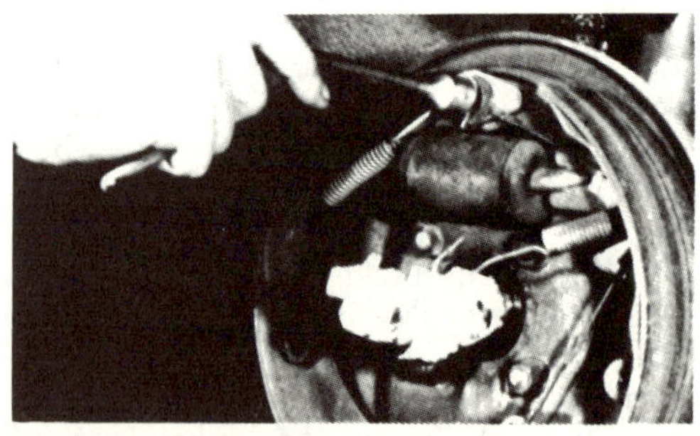

Removing the brake retracting spring

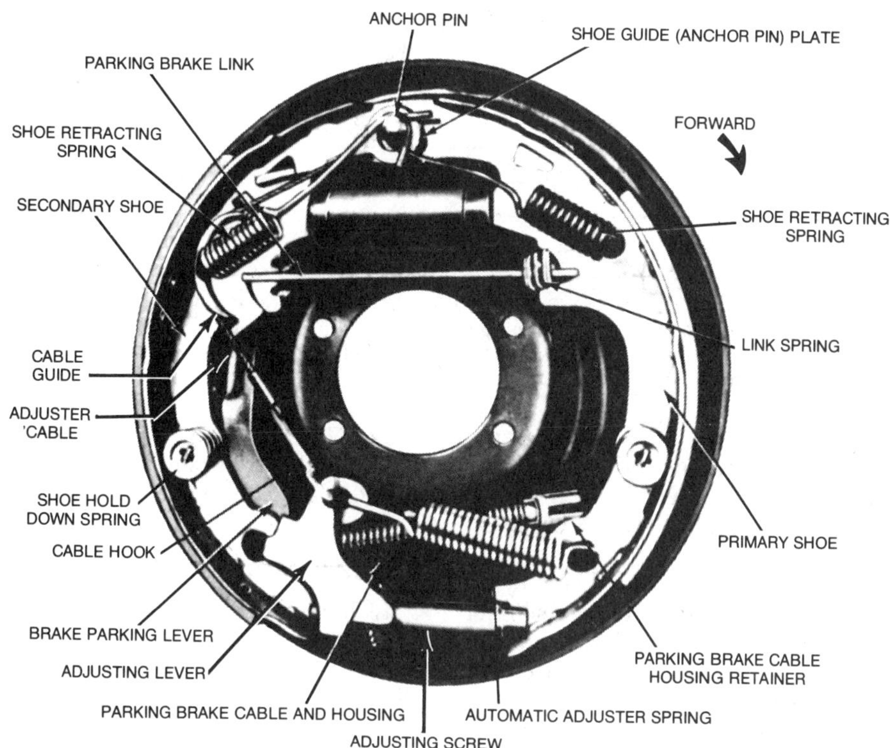

Rear brake assembly

CAUTION: *Be careful the springs do not slip off the tool during removal, as they could cause personal injury.*

3. Reach behind the brake backing plate and place a finger on the end of one of the brake hold-down spring mounting pins. Using a pair of pliers grasp the washer on the top of the hold-down spring that corresponds to the pin that you are holding. Push down on the pliers and turn them 90° to align the slot in the washer and with the head on the spring mounting pin. Remove the spring and washer and repeat this operation on the hold-down spring on the other brake shoe.

4. Place the tip of the screwdriver on the top of the brake adjusting screw and move the screwdriver upward to lift up on the brake adjusting lever. When there is enough slack in the automatic adjuster cable, disconnect the loop on the top of the cable from the anchor pin. Grasp the top of each brake shoe and move it outward to disengage it from the wheel cylinder (and parking brake link on the rear wheels). When the brake shoes are clear, lift them from the backing plate. Twist the shoes slightly and the automatic adjuster assembly will disassemble itself.

5. Grasp the end of the brake cable spring with a pair of pliers and, using the brake lever as a fulcrum, pull the end of the spring away from the lever. Disengage the cable from the brake lever.

Wheel Cylinder Overhaul

Since the travel of the pistons in the wheel cylinder changes when new brake shoes are installed, it is possible for previously good wheel cylinders to start leaking after new brakes are installed. Therefore, to save yourself the expense of having to replace new brakes that become saturated with brake fluid and the aggravation of having to take everything apart again, it is strongly recommended that wheel cylinders be rebuilt every time new brake shoes are installed. This is especially true for cars with high mileage.

1. Remove the brakes.
2. Place a bucket or some old newspapers under the brake backing plate to catch the brake fluid that will run out of the wheel cylinder.
3. Remove the boots from the ends of the wheel cylinders.
4. Push one piston toward the center of the cylinder to force the opposite piston and cup out the other end of the cylinder. Reach

Brake Specifications

All measurements given are (in.) unless noted

Year	Model	Lug Nut Torque (ft. lb.)	Master Cylinder Bore	Brake Disc: Minimum Thickness	Brake Disc: Maximum Run-Out	Brake Drum: Diameter	Brake Drum: Max Machine O/S	Max Wear Limit	Minimum Lining Thickness: Front	Minimum Lining Thickness: Rear
1978–83	A11	80–115	.875	.810	.003	①	②	③	④	⑤

① Sedans 9,000
Police, Taxi and Wagons 10,000
② Sedans 9,060
Police, Taxi and Wagons 10,060
③ Runout .007
④ Lining measures ⅛ in, above metal shoe
⑤ Lining measures ⅓ in. above rivets

in the open end of the cylinder and push the spring, cup, and piston out of the cylinder.

5. Remove the bleeder screw from the rear of the cylinder, on the back of the backing plate.

6. Inspect the inside of the wheel cylinder. If it is scored in any way, the cylinder must be honed with a wheel cylinder hone or fine emery paper, and finished with crocus cloth if emery paper is used. If the inside of the cylinder is excessively worn, the cylinder will have to be replaced, as only 0.003 in. of material can be removed from the cylinder walls. Whenever honing or cleaning wheel cylinders, keep a small amount of brake fluid in the cylinder to serve as a lubricant.

7. Clean any foreign matter from the pistons. The sides of the pistons must be smooth for the wheel cylinders to operate properly.

8. Clean the cylinder bore with alcohol and a lint-free rag. Pull the rag through the bore several times to remove all foreign matter and dry the cylinder.

9. Install the bleeder screw and the return spring in the cylinder.

10. Coat new cylinder cups with new brake fluid and install them in the cylinder. Make sure they are square in the bore or they will leak.

11. Install the pistons in the cylinder after coating them with new brake fluid.

12. Coat the insides of the boots with new brake fluid and install them on the cylinder. Install and bleed the brakes.

Wheel Cylinder Replacement

1. Remove the brake shoes.
2. Loosen the brake line on the rear of the cylinder, but do not pull the line away from the cylinder or it may bend.
3. Remove the bolts and lockwashers that attach the wheel cylinder to the backing plate and remove the cylinder.
4. Position the new wheel cylinder on the backing plate and install the cylinder attaching bolts and lockwashers.
5. Attach the metal brake line.
6. Install the brakes and bleed the brake system.

Brake Shoe Installation

1. The brake cable must be connected to the secondary brake shoe before the shoe is installed on the backing plate. To do this, first transfer the parking brake lever from the old secondary shoe to the new one. This is accomplished by spreading the bottom of the horseshoe clip and disengaging the lever. Position the lever on the new secondary shoe and install the spring washer and the hor-

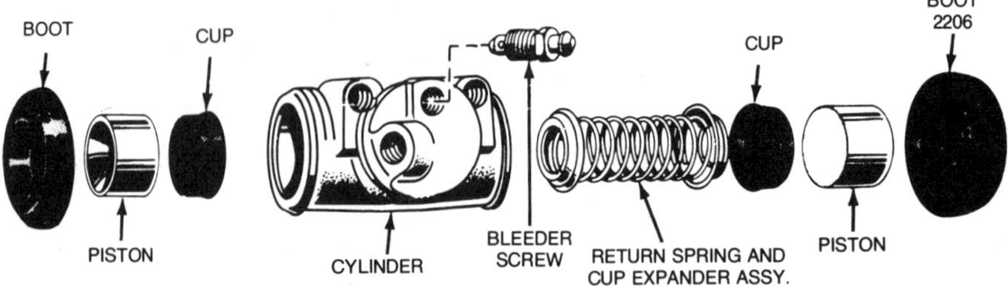

Exploded view of the rear wheel cylinder

seshoe clip. Close the bottom of the clip after installing it. Grasp the metal tip of the parking brake cable with a pair of pliers. Position a pair of side cutters on the end of the cable coil spring and, using the pliers as a fulcrum, pull the coil spring back with the side cutters. Position the cable in the parking brake lever.

2. Apply a *light* coating of high-temperature grease to the brake shoe contact points on the backing plate. Position the primary brake shoe on the front of the backing plate and install the hold-down spring and washer over the mounting pin. Install the secondary shoe on the rear of the backing plate.

3. Install the parking brake link between the notch in the primary brake shoe and the notch in the parking brake lever.

4. Install the automatic adjuster cable loop end on the anchor pin. Make sure the crimped side of the loop faces the backing plate.

5. Install the return spring in the primary brake shoe and, using the tapered end of a brake spring service tool, slide the top of the spring onto the anchor pin.

CAUTION: *Be careful the spring does not slip off the tool during installation, as it could cause personal injury.*

6. Install the automatic adjuster cable guide in the secondary brake shoe, making sure the flared hole in the cable guide is inside the hole in the brake shoe. Fit the cable into the groove in the top of the cable guide.

7. Install the secondary shoe return spring through the hole in the cable guide and the brake shoe. Using the brake spring tool, slide the top of the spring onto the anchor pin.

8. Clean the threads on the adjusting screw and apply a light coating of high-temperature grease to the threads. Screw the adjuster closed, then open it one-half turn.

9. Install the adjusting screw between the brake shoes with the star wheel nearest to the secondary shoe. Make sure the star wheel is in a position that is accessible from the adjusting slot in the backing plate.

10. Install the short hooked end of the automatic adjuster spring in the proper hole in the primary brake shoe.

11. Connect the hooked end of the automatic adjuster cable and the free end of the automatic adjuster spring in the slot in the top of the automatic adjuster lever.

12. Pull the automatic adjuster lever (the lever will pull the cable and spring with it) downward and to the left and engage the pivot hook of the lever in the hole in the secondary brake shoe.

13. Check the entire brake assembly to make sure everything is installed properly. Make sure the shoes engage the wheel cylinder properly and are flush on the anchor pin. Make sure the automatic adjuster cable is flush on the anchor pin and in the slot on the back on cable guide. Make sure the adjusting lever rests on the adjusting screw star wheel. Pull upward on the adjusting cable until the adjusting lever is free of the star wheel, then release the cable. The adjusting lever should snap back into place on the adjusting screw star wheel and turn the wheel one tooth.

14. Expand the brake adjusting screw until the brake drum will just fit over the brake shoes.

15. Install the wheel and drum and adjust the brakes. See "Brake Adjustment."

Brake Adjustment

1. Raise the car and support it with safety stands.

2. Remove the rubber plug from the adjusting slot on the backing plate.

3. Insert a brake adjusting spoon into the slot and engage the lowest tooth on the star wheel possible. Move the end of the brake spoon downward to move the star wheel upward and expand the adjusting screw. Repeat this operation until the brakes lock the wheel.

4. Insert a small screwdriver or piece of firm wire (coat hanger wire) into the adjusting slot and push the automatic adjuster lever out and free of the star wheel on the adjusting screw.

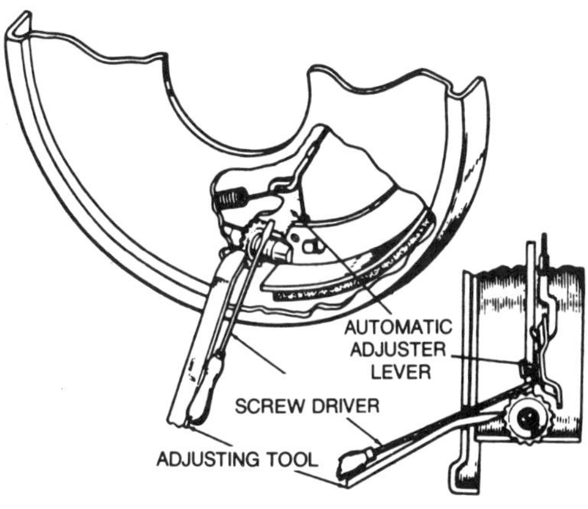

Adjusting the brakes

5. Holding the adjusting lever out of the way, engage the topmost tooth possible on the star wheel with a brake adjusting spoon. Move the end of the adjusting spoon upward to move the adjusting screw downward and contract the adjusting screw. Back the adjustment off until the wheel spins freely with a minimum of drag. Keep track of the number of turns the star wheel is backed off.

6. Repeat this operation on the other side of the car of the set (front or rear) of brakes that you are adjusting. When backing off the brakes on the other side, the star wheel must be backed off the same number of turns to prevent side-to-side brake pull.

7. Repeat this operation on the other set of brakes.

PARKING BRAKE

The parking brake on your Fairmont/Zephyr is operated by a locking foot pedal. Cables actuated by the pedal cause the rear brakes to contact the drums. The parking brake is released by pulling a T-handled control under the left side dash panel.

Cable

ADJUSTMENT

1. Release the parking brake and place the transmission control lever in the neutral position.

2. Raise the vehicle and support.

NOTE: *The rear axle must be supported so that there is weight on the rear springs.*

3. Tighten the adjusting nut against the cable equalizer (bracket that connects the cables running to the rear wheels with the front cable) until drag is felt while turning the rear wheels. Loosen the nut until all drag is released. Tighten the lock nut.

4. Check the operation of the parking brake, readjust if necessary.

REMOVAL AND INSTALLATION

1. Release the parking brake and loosen the lock and adjusting nut.

2. Raise the vehicle and support it properly.

3. Remove the rear wheel parking brake cable from the equalizer.

4. Remove the hairpin clip that attaches the conduit to the conduit bracket, and remove the retaining clip that attaches the cable to the underbody.

5. Remove the rear wheels and tires then remove the brake drums.

6. Remove the self adjuster springs, and remove the adjuster springs from the backing plates.

7. Disconnect the ends of the cables from the parking brake levers on the secondary brake shoes.

8. Compress the cable retainer prongs, and pull the cable ends from the backing plates.

9. To install reverse the above procedure and adjust the parking brake as previously described.

Body

You can repair most minor auto body damage yourself. Minor damage usually falls into one of several categories: (1) small scratches and dings in the paint that can be repaired without the use of body filler, (2) deep scratches and dents that require body filler, but do not require pulling, or hammering metal back into shape and (3) rust-out repairs. The repair sequences illustrated in this chapter are typical of these types of repairs. If you want to get involved in more complicated repairs including pulling or hammering sheet metal back into shape, you will probably need more detailed instructions. Chilton's *Minor Auto Body Repair, 2nd Edition* is a comprehensive guide to repairing auto body damage yourself.

TOOLS AND SUPPLIES

The list of tools and equipment you may need to fix minor body damage ranges from very basic hand tools to a wide assortment of specialized body tools. Most minor scratches, dings and rust holes can be fixed using an electric drill, wire wheel or grinder attachment, half-round plastic file, sanding block, various grades of sandpaper (#36, which is coarse through #600, which is fine) in both wet and dry types, auto body plastic, primer, touch-up paint, spreaders, newspaper and masking tape.

Most manufacturers of auto body repair products began supplying materials to professionals. Their knowledge of the best, most-used products has been translated into body repair kits for the do-it-yourselfer. Kits are available from a number of manufacturers and contain the necessary materials in the required amounts for the repair identified on the package.

Kits are available for a wide variety of uses, including:

- Rusted out metal
- All purpose kit for dents and holes
- Dents and deep scratches
- Fiberglass repair kit
- Epoxy kit for restyling.

Kits offer the advantage of buying what you need for the job. There is little waste and little chance of materials going bad from not being used. The same manufacturers also merchandise all of the individual products used—spreaders, dent pullers, fiberglass cloth, polyester resin, cream hardener, body filler, body files, sandpaper, sanding discs and holders, primer, spray paint, etc.

CAUTION: ***Most of the products you will be using contain harmful chemicals, so be extremely careful. Always read the complete label before opening the containers. When***

you put them away for future use, be sure they are out of children's reach!

Most auto body repair kits contain all the materials you need to do the job right in the kit. So, if you have a small rust spot or dent you want to fix, check the contents of the kit before you run out and buy any additional tools.

ALIGNING BODY PANELS

Doors

There are several methods of adjusting doors. Your vehicle will probably use one of those illustrated.

Whenever a door is removed and is to be reinstalled, you should matchmark the position of the hinges on the door pillars. The holes of the hinges and/or the hinge attaching points are usually oversize to permit alignment of doors. The striker plate is also moveable, through oversize holes, permitting up-and-down, in-and-out and fore-and-aft movement. Fore-and-aft movement is made by adding or subtracting shims from behind the striker and pillar post. The striker should be adjusted so that the door closes fully and remains closed, yet enters the lock freely.

DOOR HINGES

Don't try to cover up poor door adjustment with a striker plate adjustment. The gap on each side of the door should be equal and uniform and there should be no metal-to-metal contact as the door is opened or closed.

1. Determine which hinge bolts must be loosened to move the door in the desired direction.
2. Loosen the hinge bolt(s) just enough to allow the door to be moved with a padded pry bar.
3. Move the door a small amount and check the fit, after tightening the bolts. Be sure that there is no bind or interference with adjacent panels.
4. Repeat this until the door is properly positioned, and tighten all the bolts securely.

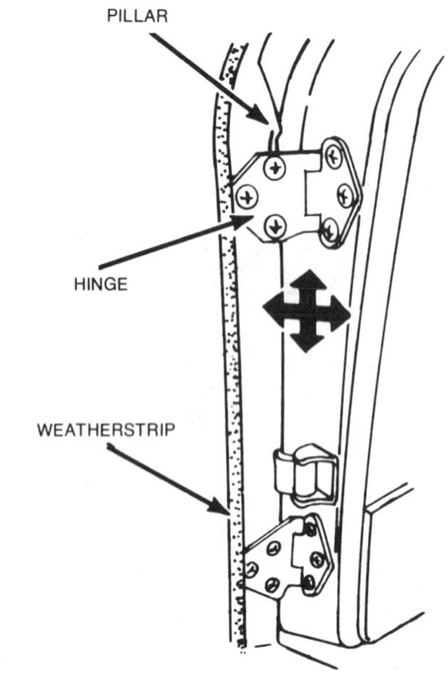

Door hinge adjustment

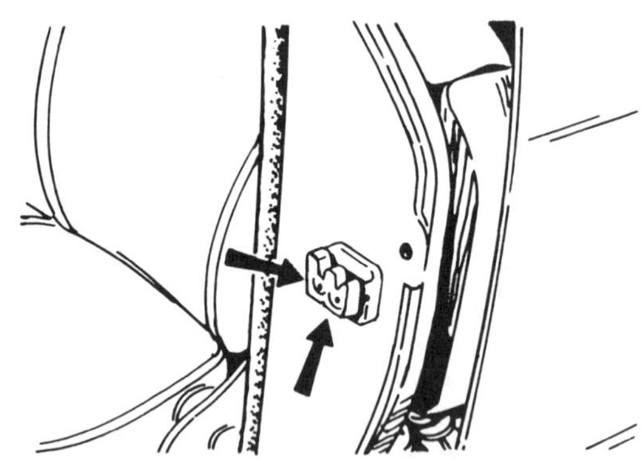
Move the door striker as indicated by arrows

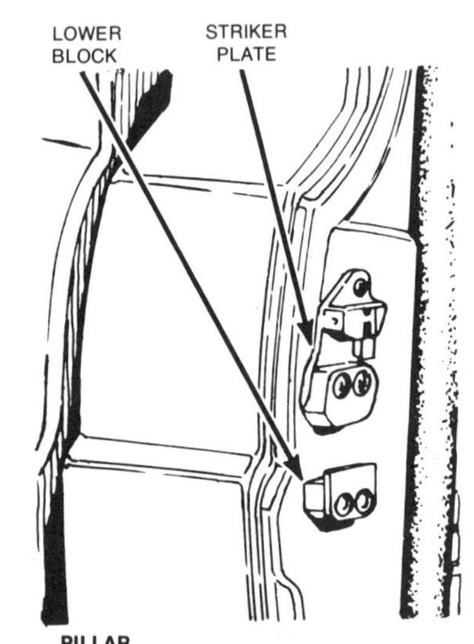

Striker plate and lower block

Hood, Trunk or Tailgate

As with doors, the outline of hinges should be scribed before removal. The hood and trunk can be aligned by loosening the hinge bolts in their slotted mounting holes and moving the hood or trunk lid as necessary.

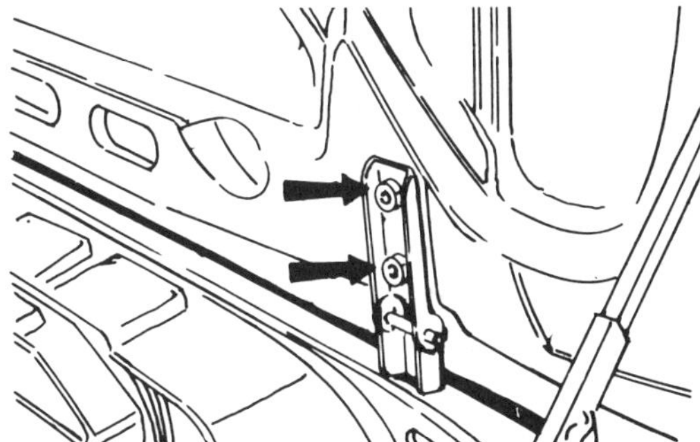

Loosen the hinge boots to permit fore-and-aft and horizontal adjustment

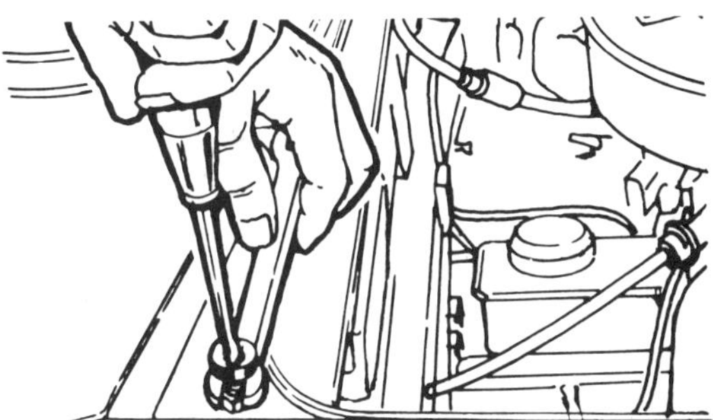

The hood is adjusted vertically by stop-screws at the front and/or rear

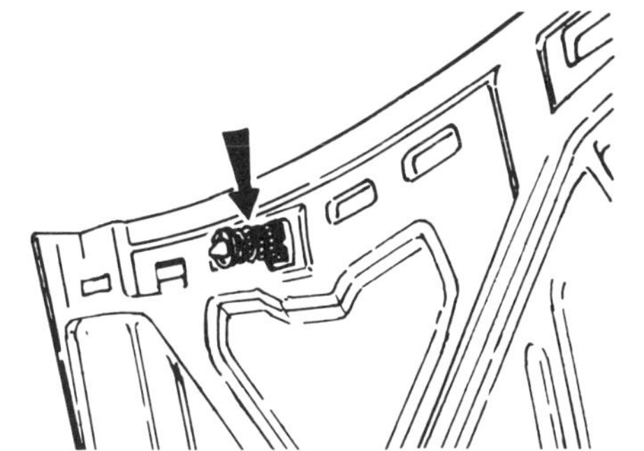

The hood pin can be adjusted for proper lock engagement

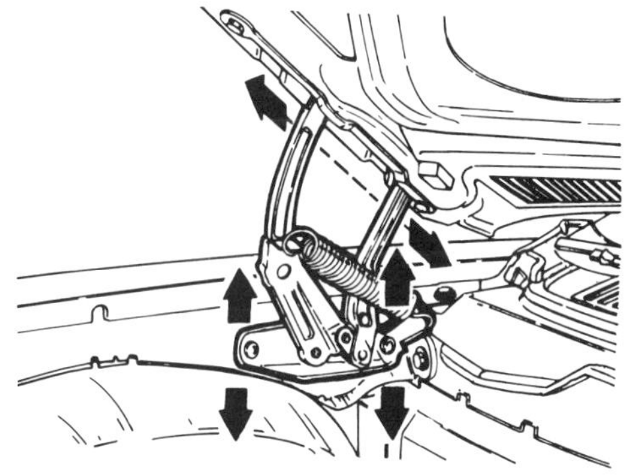

The height of the hood at the rear is adjusted by loosening the bolts that attach the hinge to the body and moving the hood up or down

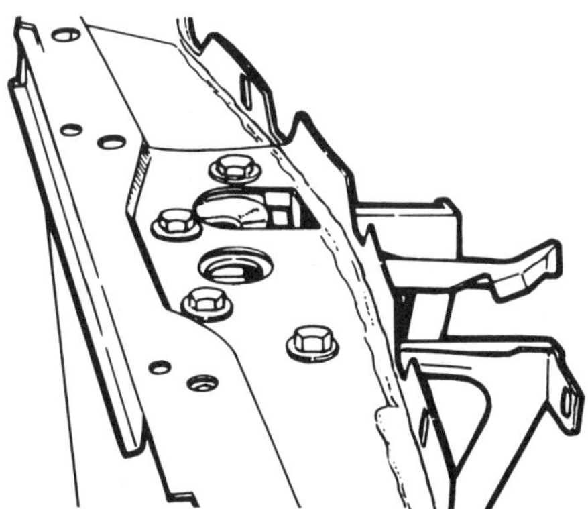

The base of the hood lock can also be repositioned slightly to give more positive lock engagement

The hood and trunk have adjustable catch locations to regulate lock engagement. Bumpers at the front and/or rear of the hood provide a vertical adjustment and the hood lockpin can be adjusted for proper engagement.

The tailgate on the station wagon can be adjusted by loosening the hinge bolts in their slotted mounting holes and moving the tailgate on its hinges. The latchplate and latch striker at the bottom of the tailgate opening can be adjusted to stop rattle. An adjustable bumper is located on each side.

RUST, UNDERCOATING, AND RUSTPROOFING

Rust

Rust is an electrochemical process. It works on ferrous metals (iron and steel) from the inside out due to exposure of unprotected surfaces to air and moisture. The possibility of rust exists practically nationwide—anywhere humidity, industrial pollution or chemical salts are present, rust can form. In coastal areas, the problem is high humidity and salt air; in snowy areas, the problem is chemical salt (de-icer) used to keep the roads clear, and in industrial areas, sulphur dioxide is present in the air from industrial pollution and is changed to sulphuric acid when it rains. The rusting process is accelerated by high temperatures, especially in snowy areas, when vehicles are driven over slushy roads and then left overnight in a heated garage.

Automotive styling also can be a contributor to rust formation. Spot welding of panels creates small pockets that trap moisture and form an environment for rust formation. Fortunately, auto manufacturers have been working hard to increase the corrosion protection of their products. Galvanized sheet metal enjoys much wider use, along with the increased use of plastic and various rust retardant coatings. Manufacturers are also designing out areas in the body where rust-forming moisture can collect.

To prevent rust, you must stop it before it gets started. On new vehicles, there are two ways to accomplish this.

First, the car or truck should be treated with a commercial rustproofing compound. There are many different brands of franchised rustproofers, but most processes involve spraying a waxy "self-healing" compound under the chassis, inside rocker panels, inside doors and fender liners and similar places where rust is likely to form. Prices for a quality rustproofing job range from \$100–\$250, depending on the area, the brand name and the size of the vehicle.

Ideally, the vehicle should be rustproofed as soon as possible following the purchase. The surfaces of the car or truck have begun to oxidize and deteriorate during shipping. In addition, the car may have sat on a dealer's lot or on a lot at the factory, and once the rust has progressed past the stage of light, powdery surface oxidation rustproofing is not likely to be worthwhile. Professional rustproofers feel that once rust has formed, rustproofing will simply seal in moisture already present. Most franchised rustproofing operations offer a 3–5 year warranty against rust-through, but will not support that warranty if the rustproofing is not applied within three months of the date of manufacture.

Undercoating should not be mistaken for rustproofing. Undercoating is a black, tar-like substance that is applied to the underside of a vehicle. Its basic function is to deaden noises that are transmitted from under the car. It simply cannot get into the crevices and seams where moisture tends to collect. In fact, it may clog up drainage holes and ventilation passages. Some undercoatings also tend to crack or peel with age and only create more moisture and corrosion attracting pockets.

The second thing you should do immediately after purchasing the car is apply a paint sealant. A sealant is a petroleum based product marketed under a wide variety of brand names. It has the same protective properties as a good wax, but bonds to the paint with a chemically inert layer that seals it from the air. If air can't get at the surface, oxidation cannot start.

The paint sealant kit consists of a base coat and a conditioning coat that should be applied every 6–8 months, depending on the manufacturer. The base coat must be applied before waxing, or the wax must first be removed.

Third, keep a garden hose handy for your car in winter. Use it a few times on nice days during the winter for underneath areas, and it will pay big dividends when spring arrives. Spraying under the fenders and other areas which even car washes don't reach will help remove road salt, dirt and other build-ups which help breed rust. Adjust the nozzle to a high-force spray. An old brush will help break up residue, permitting it to be washed away more easily.

It's a somewhat messy job, but worth it in the long run because rust often starts in those hidden areas.

At the same time, wash grime off the door sills and, more importantly, the under portions of the doors, plus the tailgate if you have a station wagon or truck. Applying a coat of wax to those areas at least once before and once during winter will help fend off rust.

When applying the wax to the under parts of the doors, you will note small drain holes. These holes often are plugged with undercoating or dirt. Make sure they are cleaned out to prevent water build-up inside the doors. A small punch or penknife will do the job.

Water from the high-pressure sprays in car washes sometimes can get into the housings for parking and taillights, so take a close look. If they contain water merely loosen the retaining screws and the water should run out.

Repairing Scratches and Small Dents

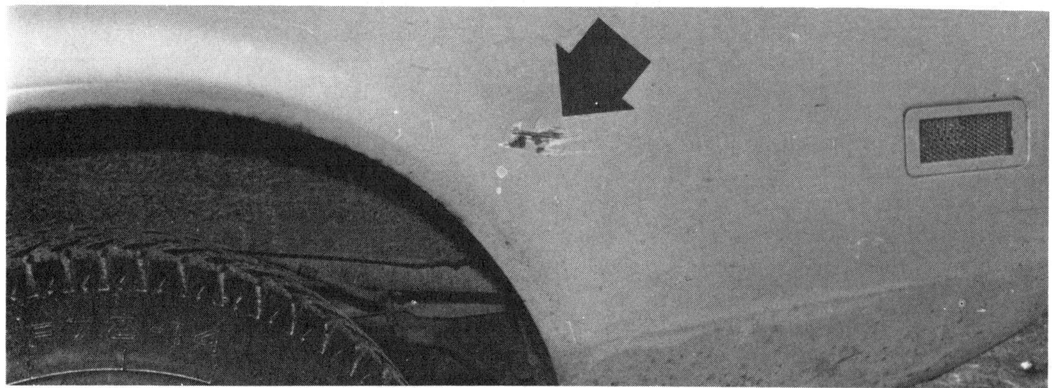

Step 1. This dent (arrow) is typical of a deep scratch or minor dent. If deep enough, the dent or scratch can be pulled out or hammered out from behind. In this case no straightening is necessary

Step 2. Using an 80-grit grinding disc on an electric drill grind the paint from the surrounding area down to bare metal. This will provide a rough surface for the body filler to grab

Step 3. The area should look like this when you're finished grinding

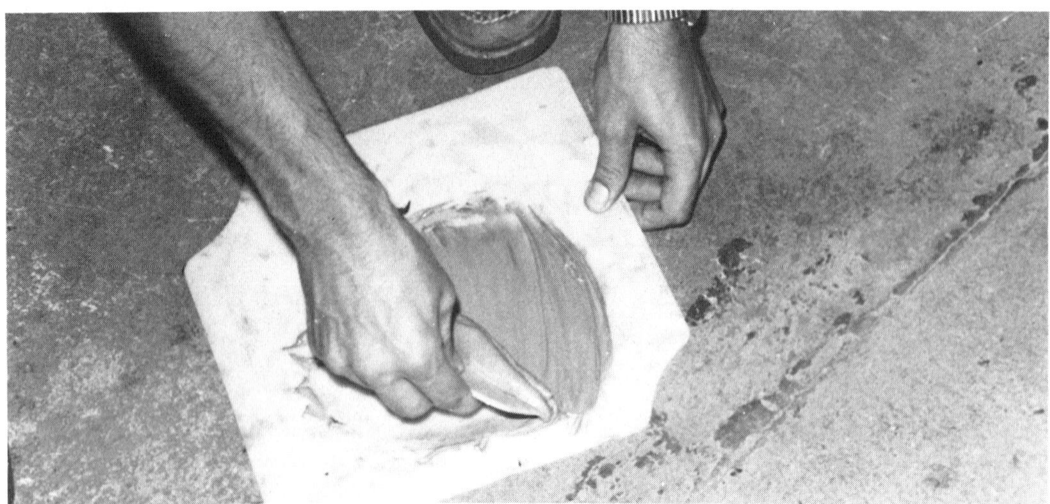

Step 4. Mix the body filler and cream hardener according to the directions

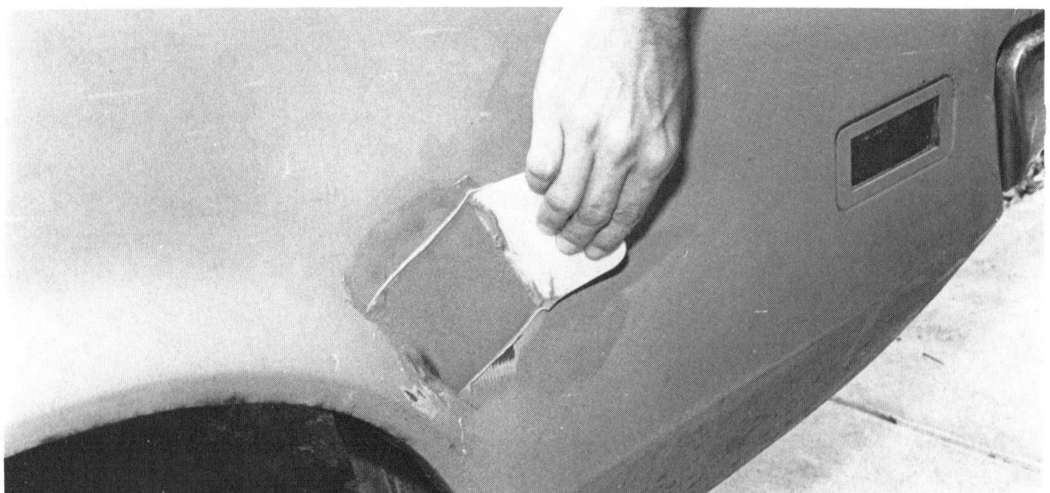

Step 5. Spread the body filler evenly over the entire area. Be sure to cover the area completely

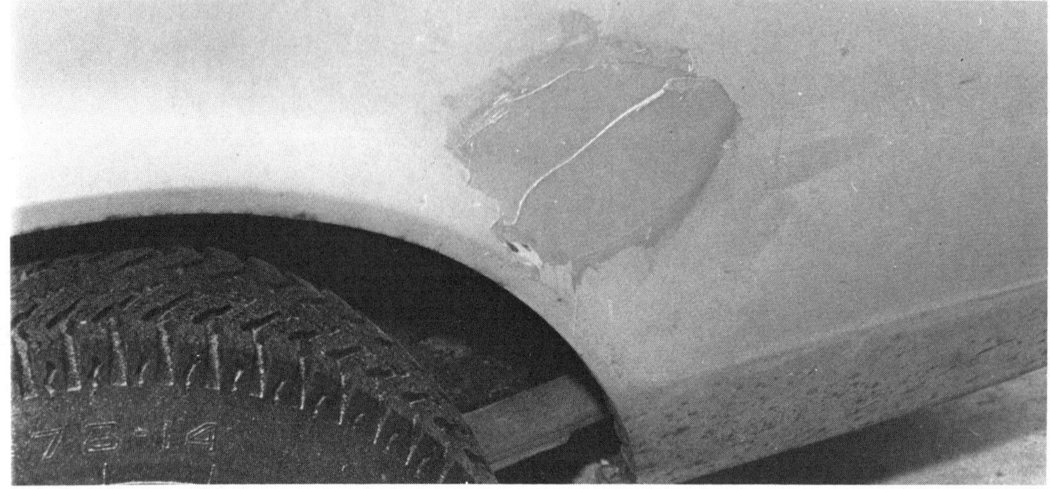

Step 6. Let the body filler dry until the surface can just be scratched with your fingernail

Step 7. Knock the high spots from the body filler with a body file

Step 8. Check frequently with the palm of your hand for high and low spots. If you wind up with low spots, you may have to apply another layer of filler

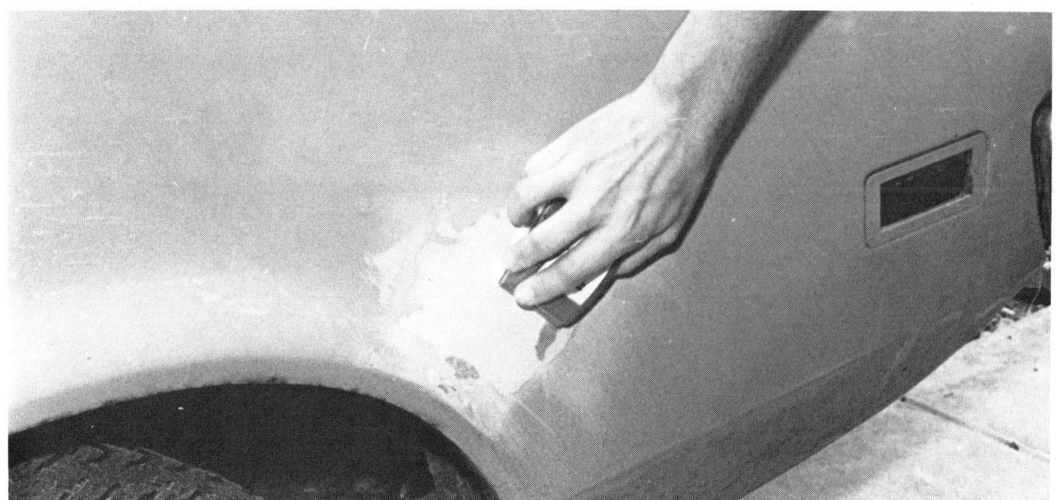

Step 9. Block sand the entire area with 320 grit paper

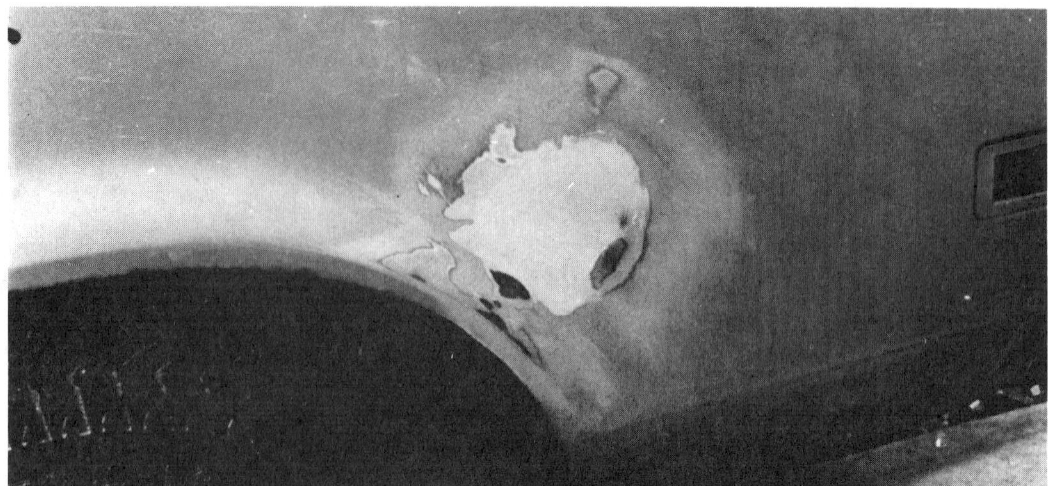

Step 10. When you're finished, the repair should look like this. Note the sand marks extending 2—3 inches out from the repaired area

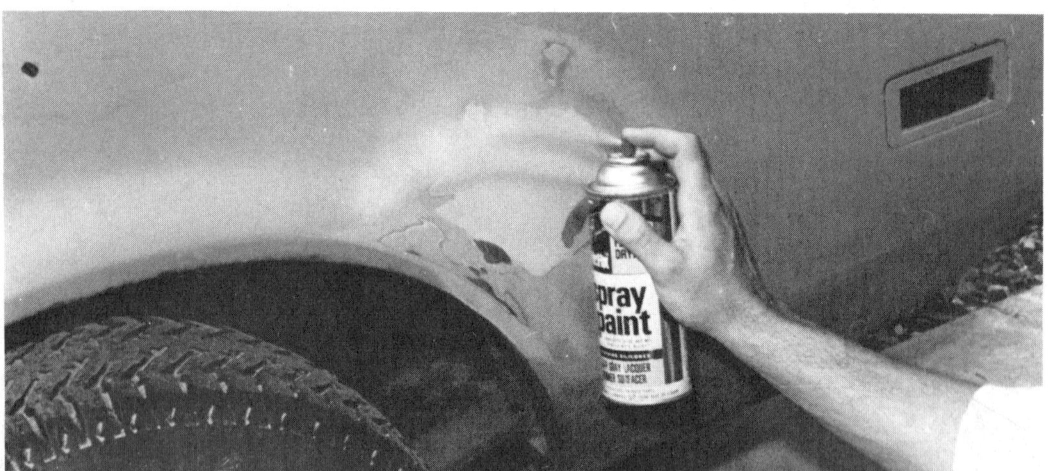

Step 11. Prime the entire area with automotive primer

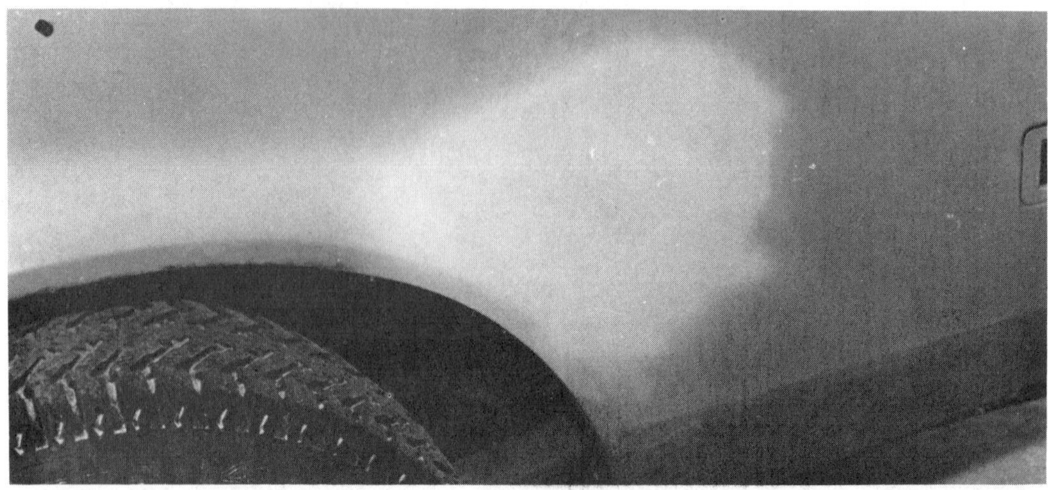

Step 12. The finished repair ready for the final paint coat. Note that the primer has covered the sanding marks (see Step 10). A repair of this size should be able to be spotpainted with good results

REPAIRING RUST HOLES

One thing you have to remember about rust: even if you grind away all the rusted metal in a panel, and repair the area with any of the kits available, *eventually* the rust will return. There are two reasons for this. One, rust is a chemical reaction that causes pressure under the repair from the inside out. That's how the blisters form. Two, the back side of the panel (and the repair) is wide open to moisture, and unpainted body filler acts like a sponge. That's why the best solution to rust problems is to remove the rusted panel and install a new one or have the rusted area cut out and a new piece of sheet metal welded in its place. The trouble with welding is the expense; sometimes it will cost more than the car or truck is worth.

One of the better solutions to do-it-yourself rust repair is the process using a fiberglass cloth repair kit (shown here). This will give a strong repair that resists cracking and moisture and is relatively easy to use. It can be used on large or small holes and also can be applied over contoured surfaces.

Step 1. Rust areas such as this are common and are easily fixed

Step 2. Grind away all traces of rust with a 24-grit grinding disc. Be sure to grind back 3—4 inches from the edge of the hole down to bare metal and be sure all traces of rust are removed

Step 3. Be sure all rust is removed from the edges of the metal. The edges must be ground back to un-rusted metal

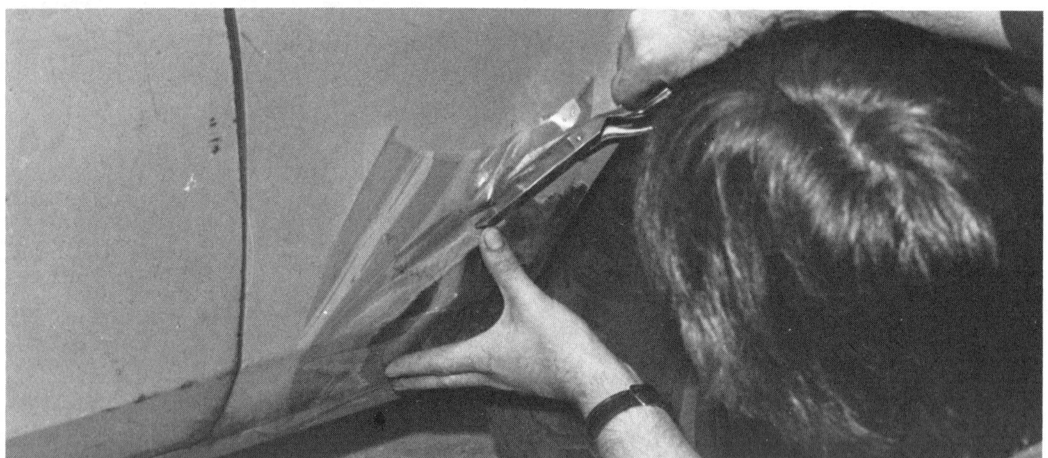

Step 4. If you are going to use release film, cut a piece about 2″ larger than the area you have sanded. Place the film over the repair and mark the sanded area on the film. Avoid any unnecessary wrinkling of the film

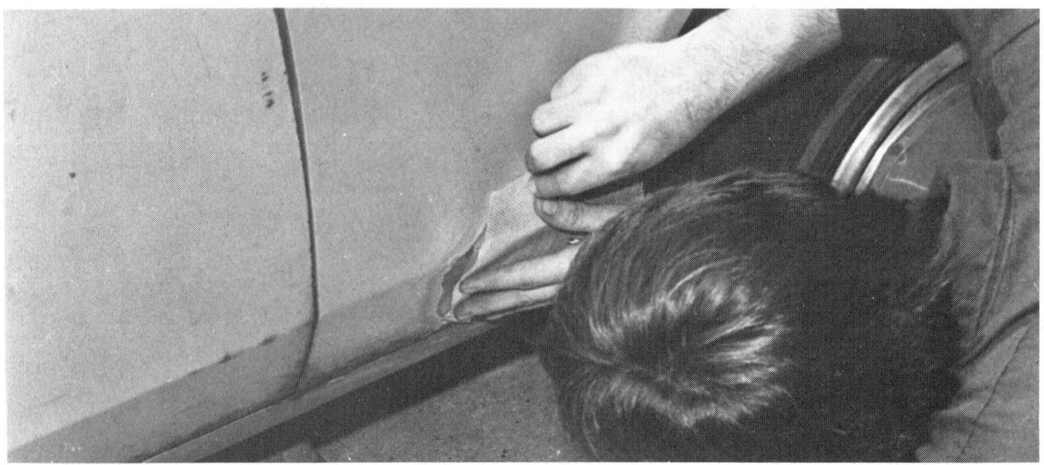

Step 5. Cut 2 pieces of fiberglass matte. One piece should be about 1″ smaller than the sanded area and the second piece should be 1″ smaller than the first. Use sharp scissors to avoid loose ends

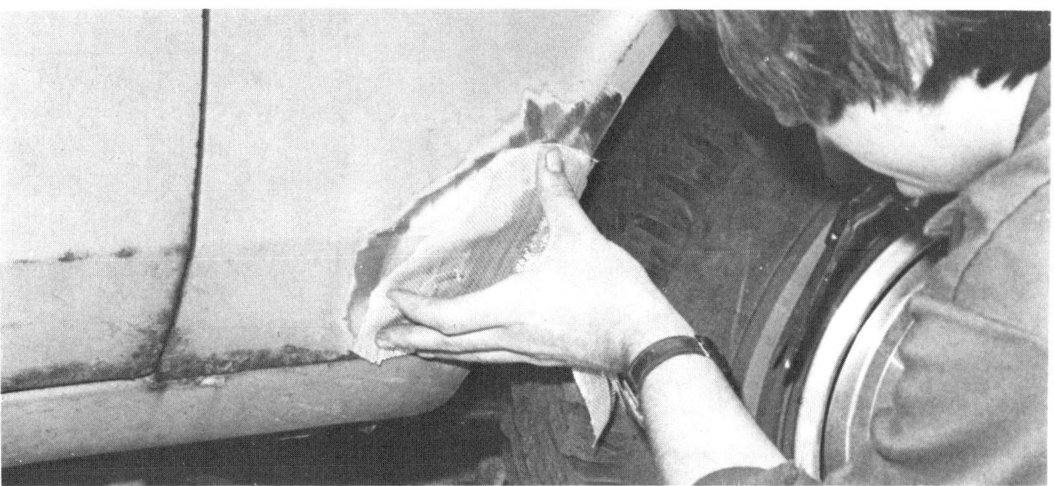

Step 6. Check the dimensions of the release film and cloth by holding them up to the repair area

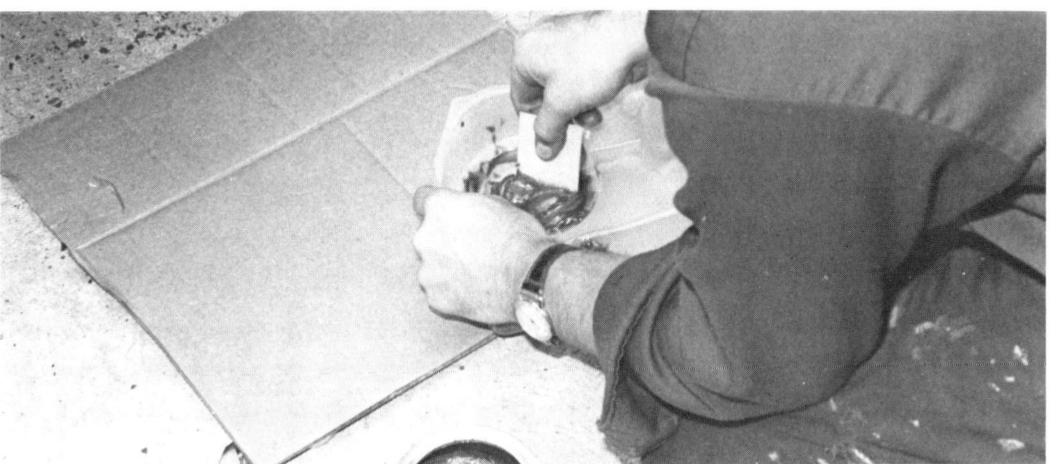

Step 7. Mix enough repair jelly and cream hardener in the mixing tray to saturate the fiberglass material or fill the repair area. Follow the directions on the container

Step 8. Lay the release sheet on a flat surface and spread an even layer of filler, large enough to cover the repair. Lay the smaller piece of fiberglass cloth in the center of the sheet and spread another layer of repair jelly over the fiberglass cloth. Repeat the operation for the larger piece of cloth. If the fiberglass cloth is not used, spread the repair jelly on the release film, concentrated in the middle of the repair

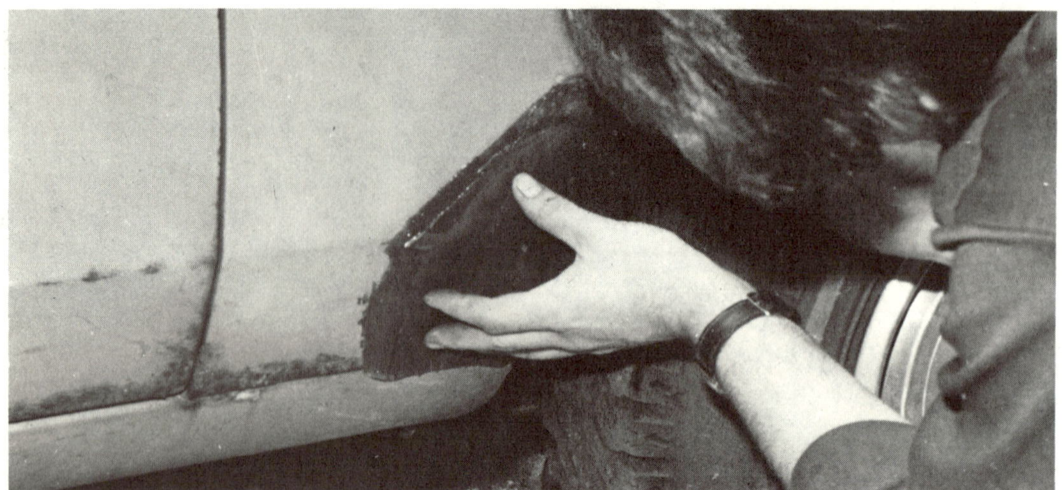

Step 9. Place the repair material over the repair area, with the release film facing outward

Step 10. Use a spreader and work from the center outward to smooth the material, following the body contours. Be sure to remove all air bubbles

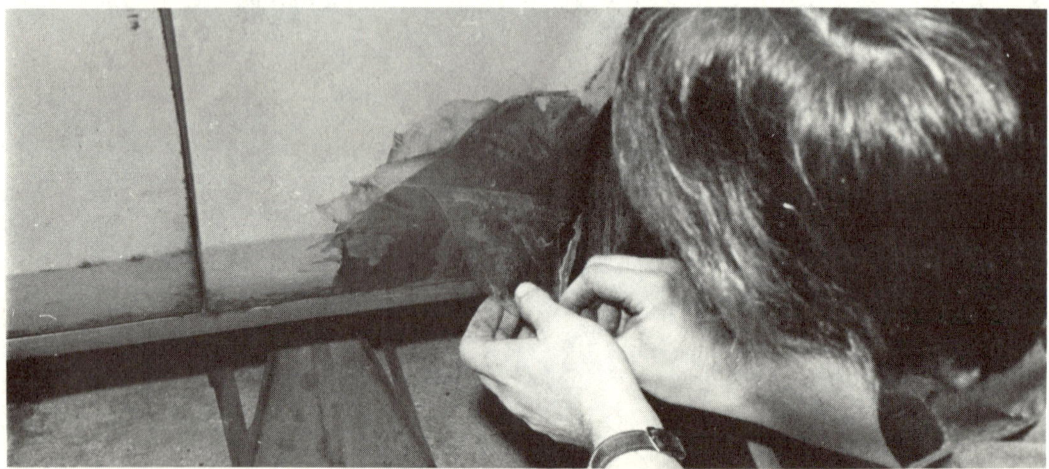

Step 11. Wait until the repair has dried tack-free and peel off the release sheet. The ideal working temperature is 65—90° F. Cooler or warmer temperatures or high humidity may require additional curing time

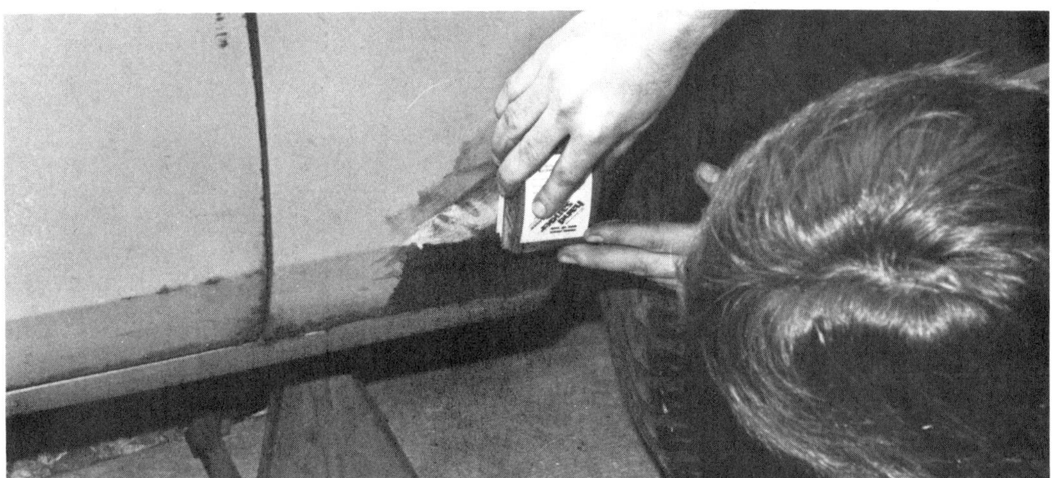

Step 12. Sand and feather-edge the entire area. The initial sanding can be done with a sanding disc on an electric drill if care is used. Finish the sanding with a block sander

Step 13. When the area is sanded smooth, mix some topcoat and hardener and apply it directly with a spreader. This will give a smooth finish and prevent the glass matte from showing through the paint

Step 14. Block sand the topcoat with finishing sandpaper

Step 15. To finish this repair, grind out the surface rust along the top edge of the rocker panel

Step 16. Mix some more repair jelly and cream hardener and apply it directly over the surface

Step 17. When it dries tack-free, block sand the surface smooth

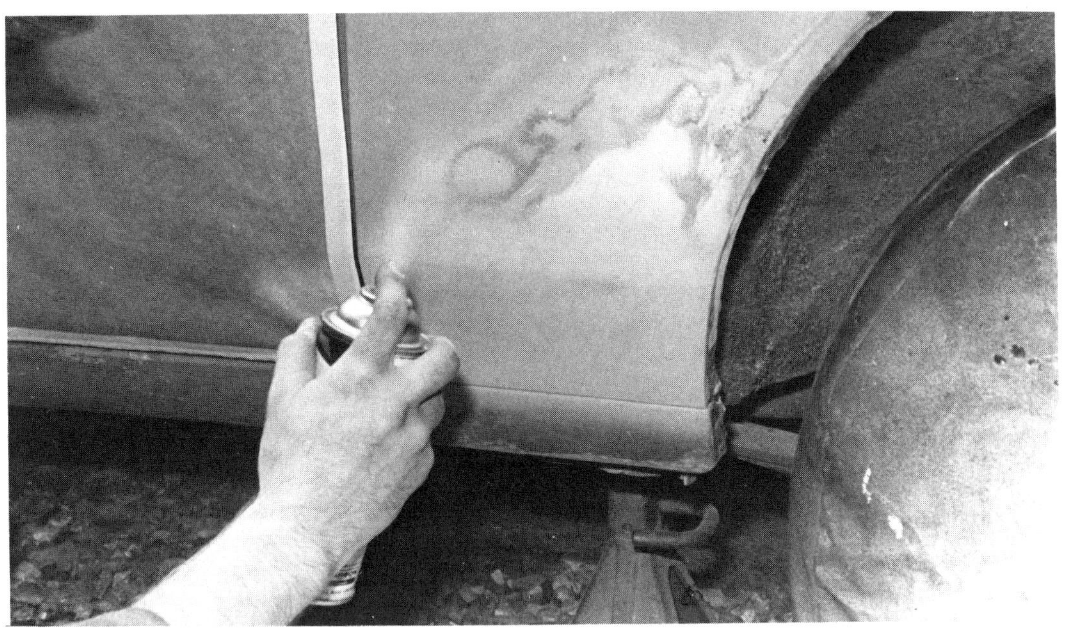

Step 18. If necessary, mask off adjacent panels and spray the entire repair with primer. You are now ready for a color coat

AUTO BODY CARE

There are hundreds—maybe thousands—of products on the market, all designed to protect or aid your car's finish in some manner. There are as many different products as there are ways to use them, but they all have one thing in common—the surface must be clean.

Washing

The primary ingredient for washing your car is water, preferably "soft" water. In many areas of the country, the local water supply is "hard" containing many minerals. The little rings or film that is left on your car's surface after it has dried is the result of "hard" water.

Since you usually can't change the local water supply, the next best thing is to dry the surface before it has a chance to dry itself.

Into the water you usually add soap. Don't use detergents or common, coarse soaps. Your car's paint never truly dries out, but is always evaporating residual oils into the air. Harsh detergents will remove these oils, causing the paint to dry faster than normal. Instead use warm water and a non-detergent soap made especially for waxed surfaces or a liquid soap made for waxed surfaces or a liquid soap made for washing dishes by hand. Other products that can be used on painted surfaces include baking soda or plain soda water for stubborn dirt.

Wash the car completely, starting at the top, and rinse it completely clean. Abrasive grit should be loaded off under water pressure; scrubbing grit off will scratch the finish. The best washing tool is a sponge, cleaning mitt or soft towel. Whichever you choose, replace it often as each tends to absorb grease and dirt.

Other ways to get a better wash include:

• Don't wash your car in the sun or when the finish is hot.

• Use water pressure to remove caked-on dirt.

• Remove tree-sap and bird effluence immediately. Such substances will eat through wax, polish and paint.

One of the best implements to dry your car is a turkish towel or an old, soft bath towel. Anything with a deep nap will hold any dirt in suspension and not grind it into the paint.

Harder cloths will only grind the grit into the paint making more scratches. Always start drying at the top, followed by the hood and trunk and sides. You'll find there's always more dirt near the rocker panels and wheelwells which will wind up on the rest of the car if you dry these areas first.

Cleaners, Waxes and Polishes

Before going any farther you should know the function of various products.

Cleaners—remove the top layer of dead pigment or paint.

Rubbing or polishing compounds—used to remove stubborn dirt, get rid of minor scratches, smooth away imperfections and partially restore badly weathered paint.

Polishes—contain no abrasives or waxes; they shine the paint by adding oils to the paint.

Waxes—are a protective coating for the polish.

CLEANERS AND COMPOUNDS

Before you apply any wax, you'll have to remove oxidation, road film and other types of pollutants that washing alone will not remove.

The paint on your car never dries completely. There are always residual oils evaporating from the paint into the air. When enough oils are present in the paint, it has a healthy shine (gloss). When too many oils evaporate the paint takes on a whitish cast known as oxidation. The idea of polishing and waxing is to keep enough oil present in the painted surface to prevent oxidation; but when it occurs, the only recourse is to remove the top layer of "dead" paint, exposing the healthy paint underneath.

Products to remove oxidation and road film are sold under a variety of generic names—polishes, cleaner, rubbing compound, cleaner/polish, polish/cleaner, self-polishing wax, pre-wax cleaner, finish restorer and many more. Regardless of name there are two types of cleaners—abrasive cleaners (sometimes called polishing or rubbing compounds) that remove oxidation by grinding away the top layer of "dead" paint, or chemical cleaners that dissolve the "dead" pigment, allowing it to be wiped away.

Abrasive cleaners, by their nature, leave thousands of minute scratches in the finish, which must be polished out later. These should only be used in extreme cases, but are usually the only thing to use on badly oxidized paint finishes. Chemical cleaners are much milder but are not strong enough for severe cases of oxidation or weathered paint.

The most popular cleaners are liquid or paste abrasive polishing and rubbing compounds. Polishing compounds have a finer abrasive grit for medium duty work. Rubbing compounds are a coarser abrasive and for heavy duty work. Unless you are familiar with how to use compounds, be very careful. Excessive rubbing with any type of compound or cleaner can grind right through the paint to primer or bare metal. Follow the directions on the container—depending on type, the cleaner may or may not be OK for your paint. For example, some cleaners are not formulated for acrylic lacquer finishes.

When a small area needs compounding or heavy polishing, it's best to do the job by hand. Some people prefer a powered buffer for large areas. Avoid cutting through the paint along styling edges on the body. Small, hand operations where the compound is applied and rubbed using cloth folded into a thick ball allow you to work in straight lines along such edges.

To avoid cutting through on the edges when using a power buffer, try masking tape. Just cover the edge with tape while using power. Then finish the job by hand with the tape removed. Even then work carefully. The paint tends to be a lot thinner along the sharp ridges stamped into the panels.

Whether compounding by machine or by hand, only work on a small area and apply the compound sparingly. If the materials are spread too thin, or allowed to sit too long, they dry out. Once dry they lose the ability to deliver a smooth, clean finish. Also, dried out polish tends to cause the buffer to stick in one spot. This in turn can burn or cut through the finish.

WAXES AND POLISHES

Your car's finish can be protected in a number of ways. A cleaner/wax or polish/cleaner followed by wax or variations of each all provide good results. The two-step approach (polish followed by wax) is probably slightly better but consumes more time and effort. Properly fed with oils, your paint should never need cleaning, but despite the best polishing job, it won't last unless it's protected with wax. Without wax, polish must be renewed at least once a month to prevent oxidation. Years ago (some still swear by it today), the best wax was made from the Brazilian palm, the Carnuba, favored for its vegetable base and high melting point. However, modern synthetic waxes are harder, which means they protect against moisture better, and chemically inert silicone is used for a long lasting protection. The only problem with silicone wax is that it penetrates all layers of paint. To repaint or touch up a panel or car protected by silicone wax, you have to completely strip the finish to avoid "fish-eyes."

Under normal conditions, silicone waxes will last 4–6 months, but you have to be careful of wax build-up from too much waxing. Too thick a coat of wax is just as bad as no wax at all; it stops the paint from breathing.

Combination cleaners/waxes have become popular lately because they remove the old layer of wax plus light oxidation, while putting on a fresh coat of wax at the same time. Some cleaners/waxes contain abrasive cleaners which require caution, although many cleaner/waxes use a chemical cleaner.

Applying Wax or Polish

You may view polishing and waxing your car as a pleasant way to spend an afternoon, or as a boring chore, but it has to be done to keep the paint on your car. Caring for the paint doesn't require special tools, but you should follow a few rules.

1. Use a good quality wax.
2. Before applying any wax or polish, be sure the surface is completely clean. Just because the car looks clean, doesn't mean it's ready for polish or wax.
3. If the finish on your car is weathered, dull, or oxidized, it will probably have to be compounded to remove the old or oxidized paint. If the paint is simply dulled from lack of care, one of the non-abrasive cleaners known as polishing compounds will do the trick. If the paint is severely scratched or really dull, you'll probably have to use a rubbing compound to prepare the finish for waxing. If you're not sure which one to use, use the polishing compound, since you can easily ruin the finish by using too strong a compound.
4. Don't apply wax, polish or compound in direct sunlight, even if the directions on the can say you can. Most waxes will not cure properly in bright sunlight and you'll probably end up with a blotchy looking finish.
5. Don't rub the wax off too soon. The result will be a wet, dull looking finish. Let the wax dry thoroughly before buffing it off.
6. A constant debate among car enthusiasts is how wax should be applied. Some maintain pastes or liquids should be applied in a circular motion, but body shop experts have long thought that this approach results in barely detectable circular abrasions, especially on cars that are waxed frequently. They advise rubbing in straight lines, especially if any kind of cleaner is involved.
7. If an applicator is not supplied with the wax, use a piece of soft cheesecloth or very soft lint-free material. The same applies to buffing the surface.

SPECIAL SURFACES

One-step combination cleaner and wax formulas shouldn't be used on many of the special surfaces which abound on cars. The one-step materials contain abrasives to achieve a clean surface under the wax top coat. The abrasives are so mild that you could clean a car every week for a couple of years without fear of rubbing through the paint. But this same level of abrasiveness might, through repeated use, damage decals used for special trim effects. This includes wide stripes, wood-grain trim and other appliques.

Painted plastics must be cleaned with care. If a cleaner is too aggressive it will cut through the paint and expose the primer. If bright trim such as polished aluminum or chrome is painted, cleaning must be performed with even greater care. If rubbing compound is being used, it will cut faster than polish.

Abrasive cleaners will dull an acrylic finish. The best way to clean these newer finishes is with a non-abrasive liquid polish. Only dirt and oxidation, not paint, will be removed.

Taking a few minutes to read the instructions on the can of polish or wax will help prevent making serious mistakes. Not all preparations will work on all surfaces. And some are intended for power application while others will only work when applied by hand.

Don't get the idea that just pouring on some polish and then hitting it with a buffer will suffice. Power equipment speeds the operation. But it also adds a measure of risk. It's very easy to damage the finish if you use the wrong methods or materials.

Caring for Chrome

Read the label on the container. Many products are formulated specifically for chrome, but others contain abrasives that will scratch the chrome finish. If it isn't recommended for chrome, don't use it.

Never use steel wool or kitchen soap pads to clean chrome. Be careful not to get chrome cleaner on paint or interior vinyl surfaces. If you do, get it off immediately.

Troubleshooting

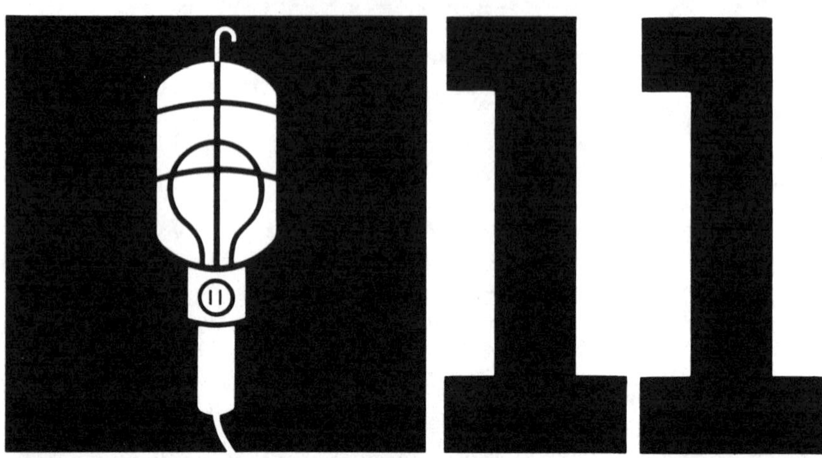

This section is designed to aid in the quick, accurate diagnosis of automotive problems. While automotive repairs can be made by many people, accurate troubleshooting is a rare skill for the amateur and professional alike.

In its simplest state, troubleshooting is an exercise in logic. It is essential to realize that an automobile is really composed of a series of systems. Some of these systems are interrelated; others are not. Automobiles operate within a framework of logical rules and physical laws, and the key to troubleshooting is a good understanding of all the automotive systems.

This section breaks the car or truck down into its component systems, allowing the problem to be isolated. The charts and diagnostic road maps list the most common problems and the most probable causes of trouble. Obviously it would be impossible to list every possible problem that could happen along with every possible cause, but it will locate MOST problems and eliminate a lot of unnecessary guesswork. The systematic format will locate problems within a given system, but, because many automotive systems are interrelated, the solution to your particular problem may be found in a number of systems on the car or truck.

USING THE TROUBLESHOOTING CHARTS

This book contains all of the specific information that the average do-it-yourself mechanic needs to repair and maintain his or her car or truck. The troubleshooting charts are designed to be used in conjunction with the specific procedures and information in the text. For instance, troubleshooting a point-type ignition system is fairly standard for all models, but you may be directed to the text to find procedures for troubleshooting an individual type of electronic ignition. You will also have to refer to the specification charts throughout the book for specifications applicable to your car or truck.

TOOLS AND EQUIPMENT

The tools illustrated in Chapter 1 (plus two more diagnostic pieces) will be adequate to troubleshoot most problems. The two other tools needed are a voltmeter and an ohmmeter. These can be purchased separately or in combination, known as a VOM meter.

In the event that other tools are required, they will be noted in the procedures.

Troubleshooting Engine Problems

See Chapters 2, 3, 4 for more information and service procedures.

Index to Systems

System	To Test	Group
Battery	Engine need not be running	1
Starting system	Engine need not be running	2
Primary electrical system	Engine need not be running	3
Secondary electrical system	Engine need not be running	4
Fuel system	Engine need not be running	5
Engine compression	Engine need not be running	6
Engine vacuum	Engine must be running	7
Secondary electrical system	Engine must be running	8
Valve train	Engine must be running	9
Exhaust system	Engine must be running	10
Cooling system	Engine must be running	11
Engine lubrication	Engine must be running	12

Index to Problems

Problem: Symptom	Begin at Specific Diagnosis, Number ___
Engine Won't Start:	
Starter doesn't turn	1.1, 2.1
Starter turns, engine doesn't	2.1
Starter turns engine very slowly	1.1, 2.4
Starter turns engine normally	3.1, 4.1
Starter turns engine very quickly	6.1
Engine fires intermittently	4.1
Engine fires consistently	5.1, 6.1
Engine Runs Poorly:	
Hard starting	3.1, 4.1, 5.1, 8.1
Rough idle	4.1, 5.1, 8.1
Stalling	3.1, 4.1, 5.1, 8.1
Engine dies at high speeds	4.1, 5.1
Hesitation (on acceleration from standing stop)	5.1, 8.1
Poor pickup	4.1, 5.1, 8.1
Lack of power	3.1, 4.1, 5.1, 8.1
Backfire through the carburetor	4.1, 8.1, 9.1
Backfire through the exhaust	4.1, 8.1, 9.1
Blue exhaust gases	6.1, 7.1
Black exhaust gases	5.1
Running on (after the ignition is shut off)	3.1, 8.1
Susceptible to moisture	4.1
Engine misfires under load	4.1, 7.1, 8.4, 9.1
Engine misfires at speed	4.1, 8.4
Engine misfires at idle	3.1, 4.1, 5.1, 7.1, 8.4

Sample Section

Test and Procedure	Results and Indications	Proceed to
4.1—Check for spark: Hold each spark plug wire approximately ¼″ from ground with gloves or a heavy, dry rag. Crank the engine and observe the spark.	→ If no spark is evident:	→ **4.2**
	→ If spark is good in some cases:	→ **4.3**
	→ If spark is good in all cases:	→ **4.6**

Specific Diagnosis

This section is arranged so that following each test, instructions are given to proceed to another, until a problem is diagnosed.

Section 1—Battery

Test and Procedure	*Results and Indications*	*Proceed to*
1.1—Inspect the battery visually for case condition (corrosion, cracks) and water level.	If case is cracked, replace battery:	**1.4**
	If the case is intact, remove corrosion with a solution of baking soda and water (**CAUTION:** ***do not get the solution into the battery***), and fill with water:	**1.2**

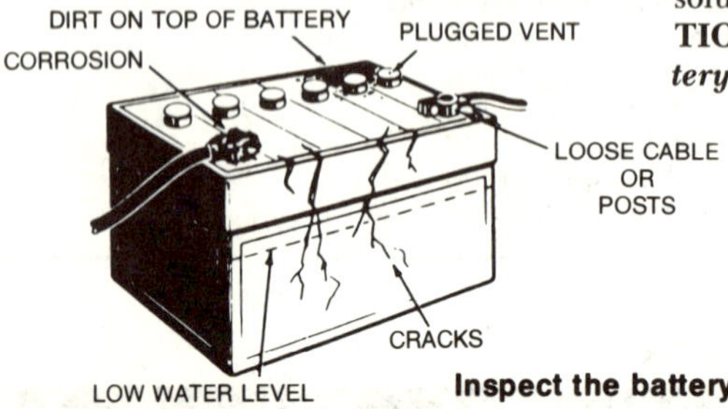

Inspect the battery case

Test and Procedure	*Results and Indications*	*Proceed to*
1.2—Check the battery cable connections: Insert a screwdriver between the battery post and the cable clamp. Turn the headlights on high beam, and observe them as the screwdriver is gently twisted to ensure good metal to metal contact.	If the lights brighten, remove and clean the clamp and post; coat the post with petroleum jelly, install and tighten the clamp:	**1.4**
	If no improvement is noted:	**1.3**

TESTING BATTERY CABLE CONNECTIONS USING A SCREWDRIVER

Test and Procedure	*Results and Indications*	*Proceed to*
1.3—Test the state of charge of the battery using an individual cell tester or hydrometer.	If indicated, charge the battery. **NOTE:** ***If no obvious reason exists for the low state of charge (i.e., battery age, prolonged storage), proceed to:***	**1.4**

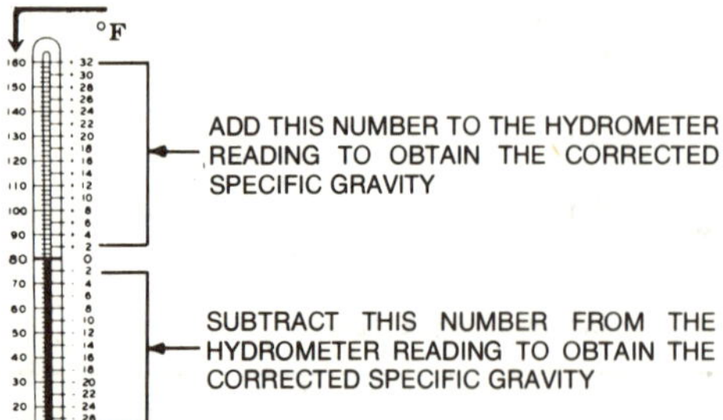

Specific Gravity (@ 80° F.)

Minimum	*Battery Charge*
1.260	100% Charged
1.230	75% Charged
1.200	50% Charged
1.170	25% Charged
1.140	Very Little Power Left
1.110	Completely Discharged

The effects of temperature on battery specific gravity (left) and amount of battery charge in relation to specific gravity (right)

Test and Procedure	*Results and Indications*	*Proceed to*
1.4—Visually inspect battery cables for cracking, bad connection to ground, or bad connection to starter.	If necessary, tighten connections or replace the cables:	**2.1**

Section 2—Starting System

See Chapter 3 for service procedures

Test and Procedure	Results and Indications	Proceed to
Note: Tests in Group 2 are performed with coil high tension lead disconnected to prevent accidental starting.		
2.1—Test the starter motor and solenoid: Connect a jumper from the battery post of the solenoid (or relay) to the starter post of the solenoid (or relay).	If starter turns the engine normally:	**2.2**
	If the starter buzzes, or turns the engine very slowly:	**2.4**
	If no response, replace the solenoid (or relay).	**3.1**
	If the starter turns, but the engine doesn't, ensure that the flywheel ring gear is intact. If the gear is undamaged, replace the starter drive.	**3.1**
2.2—Determine whether ignition override switches are functioning properly (clutch start switch, neutral safety switch), by connecting a jumper across the switch(es), and turning the ignition switch to "start".	If starter operates, adjust or replace switch:	**3.1**
	If the starter doesn't operate:	**2.3**
2.3—Check the ignition switch "start" position: Connect a 12V test lamp or voltmeter between the starter post of the solenoid (or relay) and ground. Turn the ignition switch to the "start" position, and jiggle the key.	If the lamp doesn't light or the meter needle doesn't move when the switch is turned, check the ignition switch for loose connections, cracked insulation, or broken wires. Repair or replace as necessary:	**3.1**
	If the lamp flickers or needle moves when the key is jiggled, replace the ignition switch.	**3.3**

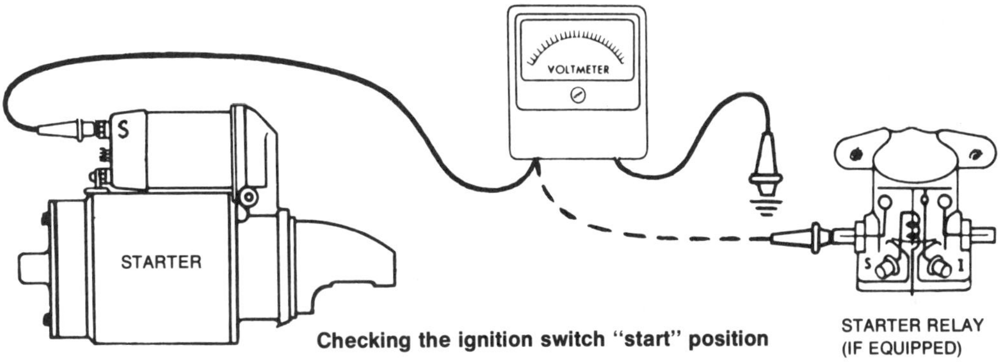

Checking the ignition switch "start" position

Test and Procedure	Results and Indications	Proceed to
2.4—Remove and bench test the starter, according to specifications in the engine electrical section.	If the starter does not meet specifications, repair or replace as needed:	**3.1**
	If the starter is operating properly:	**2.5**
2.5—Determine whether the engine can turn freely: Remove the spark plugs, and check for water in the cylinders. Check for water on the dipstick, or oil in the radiator. Attempt to turn the engine using an 18" flex drive and socket on the crankshaft pulley nut or bolt.	If the engine will turn freely only with the spark plugs out, and hydrostatic lock (water in the cylinders) is ruled out, check valve timing:	**9.2**
	If engine will not turn freely, and it is known that the clutch and transmission are free, the engine must be disassembled for further evaluation:	**Chapter 3**

Section 3—Primary Electrical System

Test and Procedure	Results and Indications	Proceed to
3.1—Check the ignition switch "on" position: Connect a jumper wire between the distributor side of the coil and ground, and a 12V test lamp between the switch side of the coil and ground. Remove the high tension lead from the coil. Turn the ignition switch on and jiggle the key.	If the lamp lights:	**3.2**
	If the lamp flickers when the key is jiggled, replace the ignition switch:	**3.3**
	If the lamp doesn't light, check for loose or open connections. If none are found, remove the ignition switch and check for continuity. If the switch is faulty, replace it:	**3.3**

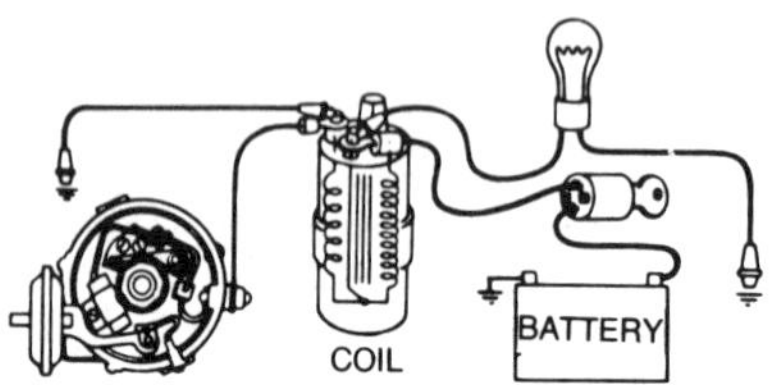

Checking the ignition switch "on" position

Test and Procedure	Results and Indications	Proceed to
3.2—Check the ballast resistor or resistance wire for an open circuit, using an ohmmeter. See Chapter 3 for specific tests.	Replace the resistor or resistance wire if the resistance is zero. **NOTE:** ***Some ignition systems have no ballast resistor.***	**3.3**

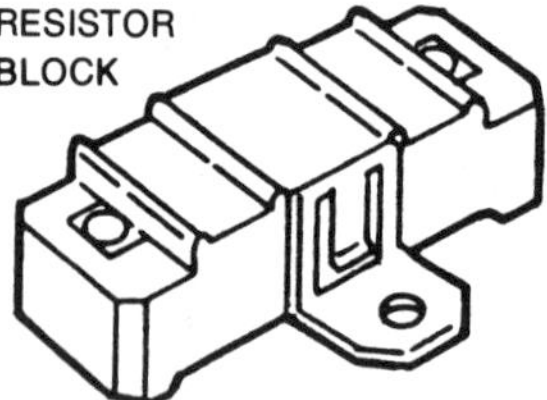

Two types of resistors

Test and Procedure	Results and Indications	Proceed to
3.3—On point-type ignition systems, visually inspect the breaker points for burning, pitting or excessive wear. Gray coloring of the point contact surfaces is normal. Rotate the crankshaft until the contact heel rests on a high point of the distributor cam and adjust the point gap to specifications. On electronic ignition models, remove the distributor cap and visually inspect the armature. Ensure that the armature pin is in place, and that the armature is on tight and rotates when the engine is cranked. Make sure there are no cracks, chips or rounded edges on the armature.	If the breaker points are intact, clean the contact surfaces with fine emery cloth, and adjust the point gap to specifications. If the points are worn, replace them. On electronic systems, replace any parts which appear defective. If condition persists:	**3.4**

Test and Procedure	Results and Indications	Proceed to
3.4—On point-type ignition systems, connect a dwell-meter between the distributor primary lead and ground. Crank the engine and observe the point dwell angle. On electronic ignition systems, conduct a stator (magnetic pickup assembly) test. See Chapter 3.	On point-type systems, adjust the dwell angle if necessary. **NOTE:** ***Increasing the point gap decreases the dwell angle and vice-versa.***	**3.6**
	If the dwell meter shows little or no reading;	**3.5**
	On electronic ignition systems, if the stator is bad, replace the stator. If the stator is good, proceed to the other tests in Chapter 3.	

Dwell is a function of point gap

Test and Procedure	Results and Indications	Proceed to
3.5—On the point-type ignition systems, check the condenser for short: connect an ohmeter across the condenser body and the pigtail lead.	If any reading other than infinite is noted, replace the condenser	**3.6**

Checking the condenser for short

Test and Procedure	Results and Indications	Proceed to
3.6—Test the coil primary resistance: On point-type ignition systems, connect an ohmmeter across the coil primary terminals, and read the resistance on the low scale. Note whether an external ballast resistor or resistance wire is used. On electronic ignition systems, test the coil primary resistance as in Chapter 3.	Point-type ignition coils utilizing ballast resistors or resistance wires should have approximately 1.0 ohms resistance. Coils with internal resistors should have approximately 4.0 ohms resistance. If values far from the above are noted, replace the coil.	**4.1**

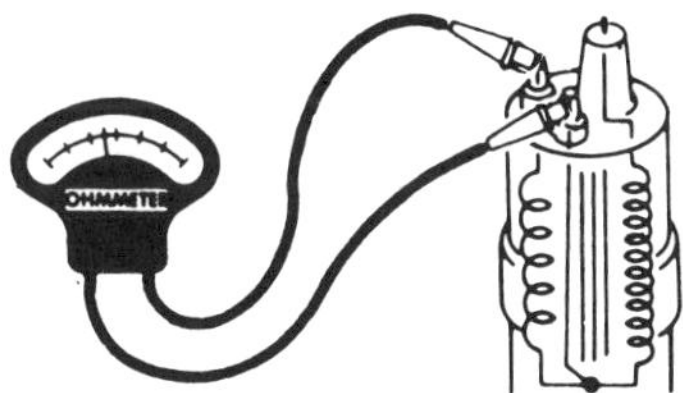

Check the coil primary resistance

Section 4—Secondary Electrical System

See Chapters 2–3 for service procedures

Test and Procedure	Results and Indications	Proceed to
4.1—Check for spark: Hold each spark plug wire approximately ¼″ from ground with gloves or a heavy, dry rag. Crank the engine, and observe the spark. 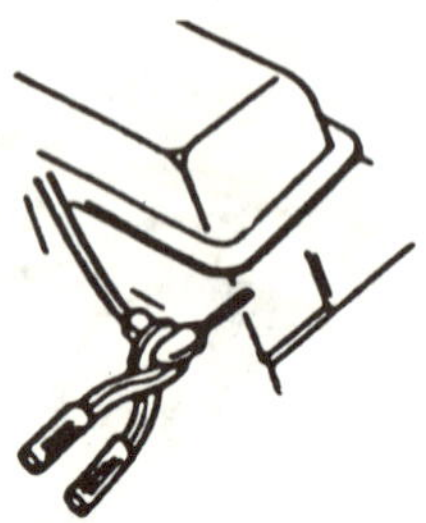 **Check for spark at the plugs**	If no spark is evident:	**4.2**
	If spark is good in some cylinders:	**4.3**
	If spark is good in all cylinders:	**4.6**
4.2—Check for spark at the coil high tension lead: Remove the coil high tension lead from the distributor and position it approximately ¼″ from ground. Crank the engine and observe spark. **CAUTION:** ***This test should not be performed on engines equipped with electronic ignition.***	If the spark is good and consistent:	**4.3**
	If the spark is good but intermittent, test the primary electrical system starting at 3.3:	**3.3**
	If the spark is weak or non-existent, replace the coil high tension lead, clean and tighten all connections and retest. If no improvement is noted:	**4.4**
4.3—Visually inspect the distributor cap and rotor for burned or corroded contacts, cracks, carbon tracks, or moisture. Also check the fit of the rotor on the distributor shaft (where applicable). 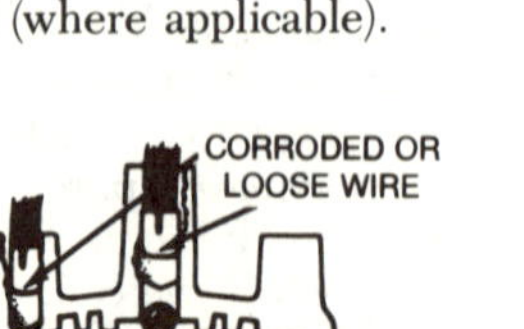 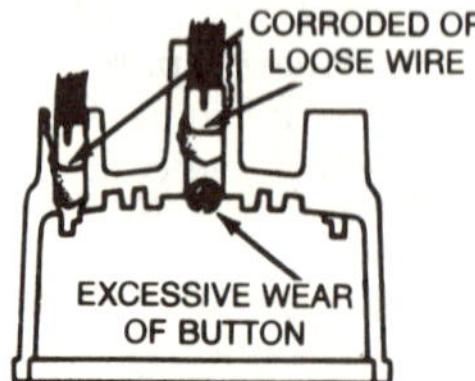 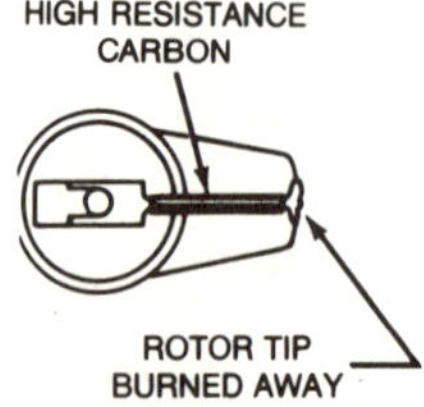 **Inspect the distributor cap and rotor**	If moisture is present, dry thoroughly, and retest per 4.1:	**4.1**
	If burned or excessively corroded contacts, cracks, or carbon tracks are noted, replace the defective part(s) and retest per 4.1:	**4.1**
	If the rotor and cap appear intact, or are only slightly corroded, clean the contacts thoroughly (including the cap towers and spark plug wire ends) and retest per 4.1: If the spark is good in all cases:	**4.6**
	If the spark is poor in all cases:	**4.5**

Test and Procedure	Results and Indications	Proceed to
4.4—Check the coil secondary resistance: On point-type systems connect an ohmmeter across the distributor side of the coil and the coil tower. Read the resistance on the high scale of the ohmmeter. On electronic ignition systems, see Chapter 3 for specific tests.	The resistance of a satisfactory coil should be between 4,000 and 10,000 ohms. If resistance is considerably higher (i.e., 40,000 ohms) replace the coil and retest per 4.1. **NOTE:** ***This does not apply to high performance coils.***	

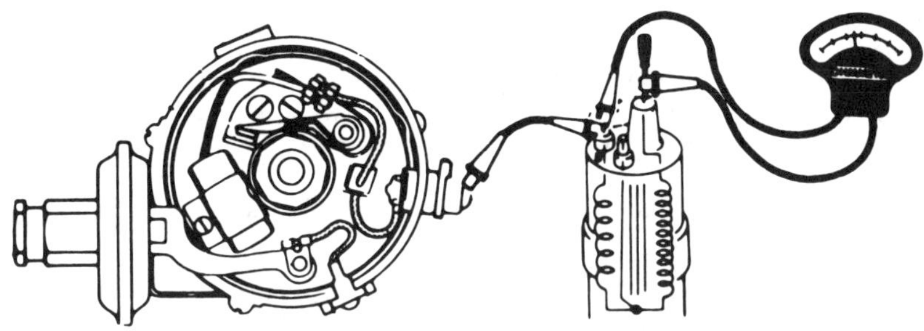

Testing the coil secondary resistance

Test and Procedure	Results and Indications	Proceed to
4.5—Visually inspect the spark plug wires for cracking or brittleness. Ensure that no two wires are positioned so as to cause induction firing (adjacent and parallel). Remove each wire, one by one, and check resistance with an ohmmeter.	Replace any cracked or brittle wires. If any of the wires are defective, replace the entire set. Replace any wires with excessive resistance (over 8000Ω per foot for suppression wire), and separate any wires that might cause induction firing.	**4.6**

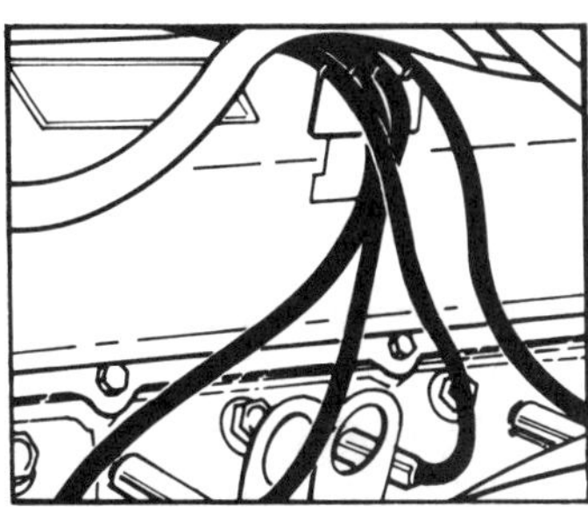

Misfiring can be the result of spark plug leads to adjacent, consecutively firing cylinders running parallel and too close together

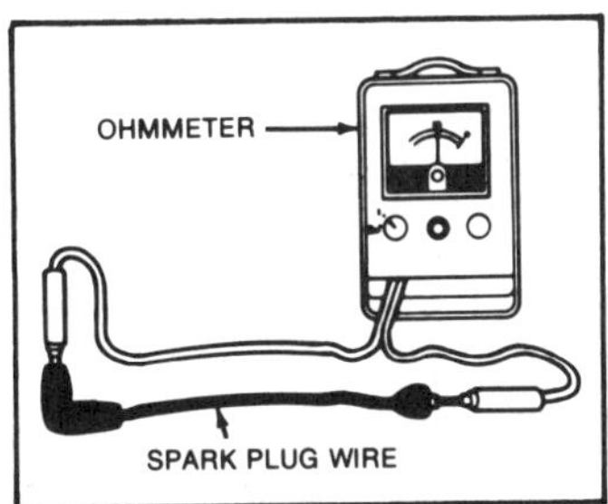

On point-type ignition systems, check the spark plug wires as shown. On electronic ignitions, do not remove the wire from the distributor cap terminal; instead, test through the cap

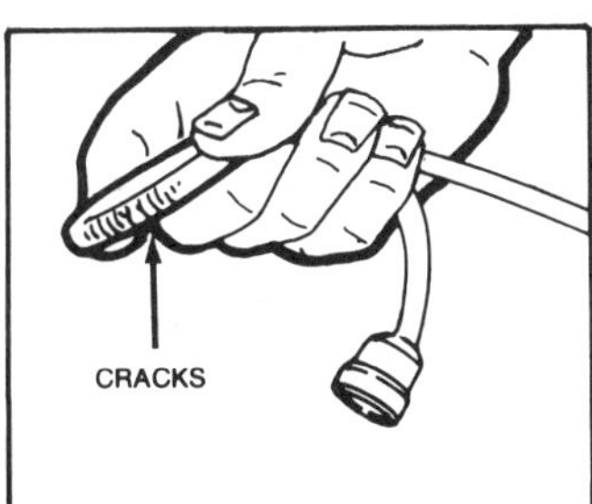

Spark plug wires can be checked visually by bending them in a loop over your finger. This will reveal any cracks, burned or broken insulation. Any wire with cracked insulation should be replaced

Test and Procedure	Results and Indications	Proceed to
4.6—Remove the spark plugs, noting the cylinders from which they were removed, and evaluate according to the color photos in the middle of this book.	See following.	**See following.**

Test and Procedure	Results and Indications	Proceed to
4.7—Examine the location of all the plugs.	The following diagrams illustrate some of the conditions that the location of plugs will reveal.	**4.8**

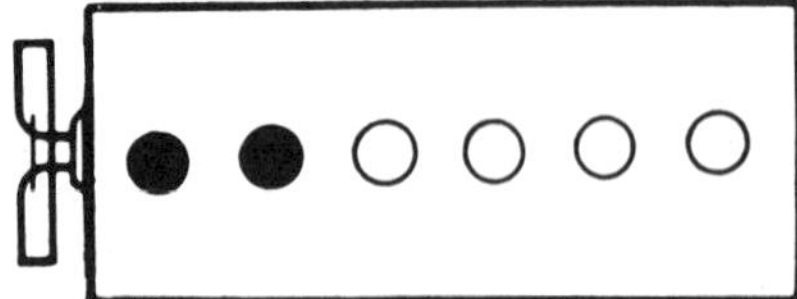

Two adjacent plugs are fouled in a 6-cylinder engine, 4-cylinder engine or either bank of a V-8. This is probably due to a blown head gasket between the two cylinders

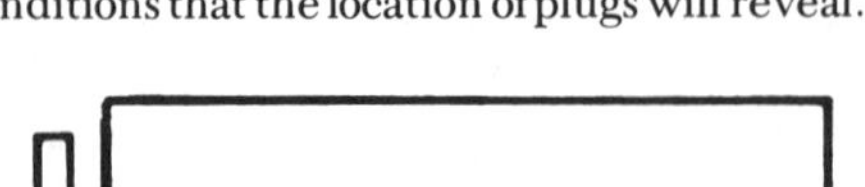

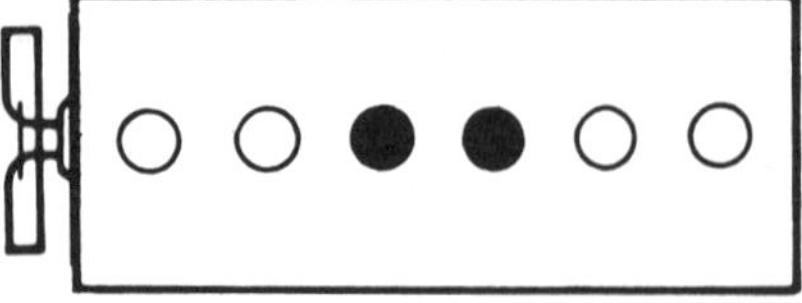

The two center plugs in a 6-cylinder engine are fouled. Raw fuel may be "boiled" out of the carburetor into the intake manifold after the engine is shut-off. Stop-start driving can also foul the center plugs, due to overly rich mixture. Proper float level, a new float needle and seat or use of an insulating spacer may help this problem

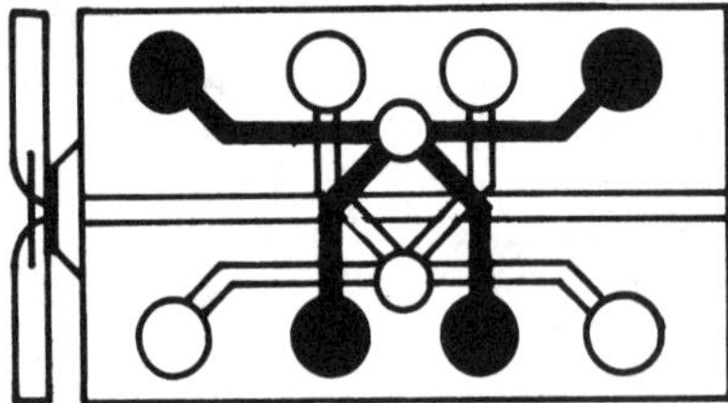

An unbalanced carburetor is indicated. Following the fuel flow on this particular design shows that the cylinders fed by the right-hand barrel are fouled from overly rich mixture, while the cylinders fed by the left-hand barrel are normal

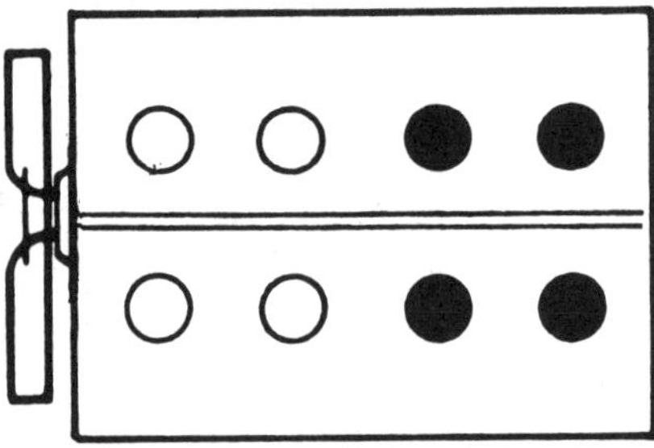

If the four rear plugs are overheated, a cooling system problem is suggested. A thorough cleaning of the cooling system may restore coolant circulation and cure the problem

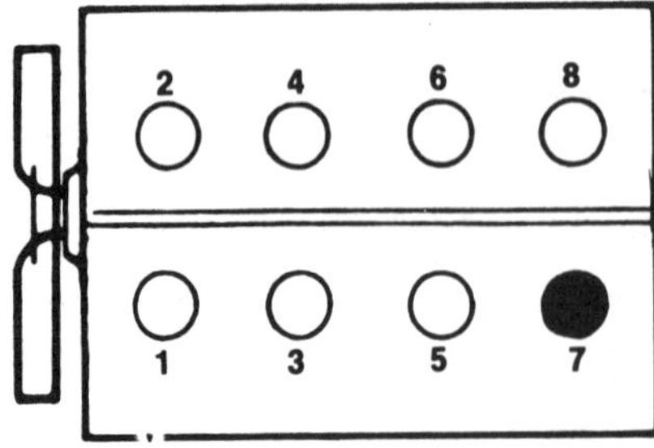

Finding one plug overheated may indicate an intake manifold leak near the affected cylinder. If the overheated plug is the second of two adjacent, consecutively firing plugs, it could be the result of ignition cross-firing. Separating the leads to these two plugs will eliminate cross-fire

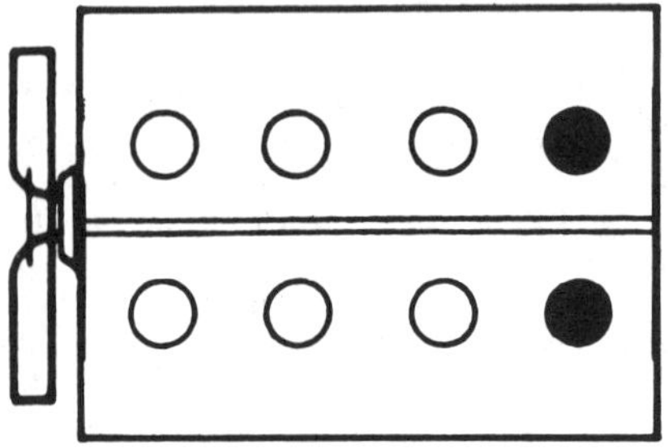

Occasionally, the two rear plugs in large, lightly used V-8's will become oil fouled. High oil consumption and smoky exhaust may also be noticed. It is probably due to plugged oil drain holes in the rear of the cylinder head, causing oil to be sucked in around the valve stems. This usually occurs in the rear cylinders first, because the engine slants that way

Test and Procedure	Results and Indications	Proceed to
4.8—Determine the static ignition timing. Using the crankshaft pulley timing marks as a guide, locate top dead center on the compression stroke of the number one cylinder.	The rotor should be pointing toward the No. 1 tower in the distributor cap, and, on electronic ignitions, the armature spoke for that cylinder should be lined up with the stator.	**4.8**
4.9—Check coil polarity: Connect a voltmeter negative lead to the coil high tension lead, and the positive lead to ground (**NOTE:** ***Reverse the hook-up for positive ground systems***). Crank the engine momentarily.	If the voltmeter reads up-scale, the polarity is correct:	**5.1**
	If the voltmeter reads down-scale, reverse the coil polarity (switch the primary leads):	**5.1**
	Checking coil polarity	

Section 5—Fuel System

See Chapter 4 for service procedures

Test and Procedure	Results and Indications	Proceed to
5.1—Determine that the air filter is functioning efficiently: Hold paper elements up to a strong light, and attempt to see light through the filter.	Clean permanent air filters in solvent (or manufacturer's recommendation), and allow to dry. Replace paper elements through which light cannot be seen:	**5.2**
5.2—Determine whether a flooding condition exists: Flooding is identified by a strong gasoline odor, and excessive gasoline present in the throttle bore(s) of the carburetor.	If flooding is not evident:	**5.3**
	If flooding is evident, permit the gasoline to dry for a few moments and restart. If flooding doesn't recur:	**5.7**
	If flooding is persistent:	**5.5**
	If the engine floods repeatedly, check the choke butterfly flap	
5.3—Check that fuel is reaching the carburetor: Detach the fuel line at the carburetor inlet. Hold the end of the line in a cup (not styrofoam), and crank the engine.	If fuel flows smoothly:	**5.7**
	If fuel doesn't flow (**NOTE:** ***Make sure that there is fuel in the tank***), or flows erratically:	**5.4**
	Check the fuel pump by disconnecting the output line (fuel pump-to-carburetor) at the carburetor and operating the starter briefly	

Test and Procedure	Results and Indications	Proceed to
5.4—Test the fuel pump: Disconnect all fuel lines from the fuel pump. Hold a finger over the input fitting, crank the engine (with electric pump, turn the ignition or pump on); and feel for suction.	If suction is evident, blow out the fuel line to the tank with low pressure compressed air until bubbling is heard from the fuel filler neck. Also blow out the carburetor fuel line (both ends disconnected):	**5.7**
	If no suction is evident, replace or repair the fuel pump: **NOTE:** ***Repeated oil fouling of the spark plugs, or a no-start condition, could be the result of a ruptured vacuum booster pump diaphragm, through which oil or gasoline is being drawn into the intake manifold (where applicable).***	**5.7**
5.5—Occasionally, small specks of dirt will clog the small jets and orifices in the carburetor. With the engine cold, hold a flat piece of wood or similar material over the carburetor, where possible, and crank the engine.	If the engine starts, but runs roughly the engine is probably not run enough. If the engine won't start:	**5.9**
5.6—Check the needle and seat: Tap the carburetor in the area of the needle and seat.	If flooding stops, a gasoline additive (e.g., Gumout) will often cure the problem:	**5.7**
	If flooding continues, check the fuel pump for excessive pressure at the carburetor (according to specifications). If the pressure is normal, the needle and seat must be removed and checked, and/or the float level adjusted:	**5.7**
5.7—Test the accelerator pump by looking into the throttle bores while operating the throttle. 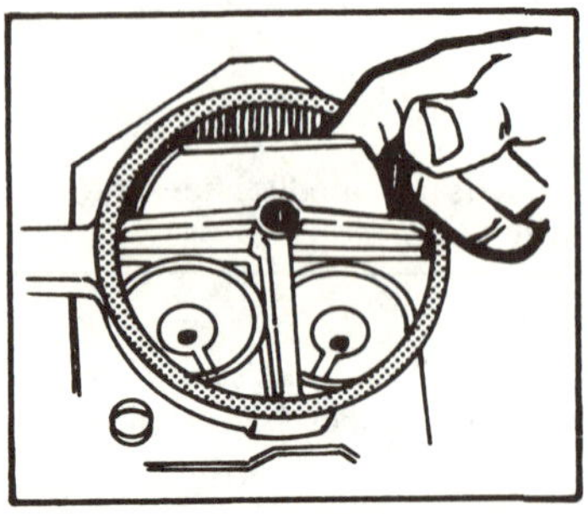 **Check for gas at the carburetor by looking down the carburetor throat while someone moves the accelerator**	If the accelerator pump appears to be operating normally:	**5.8**
	If the accelerator pump is not operating, the pump must be reconditioned. Where possible, service the pump with the carburetor(s) installed on the engine. If necessary, remove the carburetor. Prior to removal:	**5.8**
5.8—Determine whether the carburetor main fuel system is functioning: Spray a commercial starting fluid into the carburetor while attempting to start the engine.	If the engine starts, runs for a few seconds, and dies:	**5.9**
	If the engine doesn't start:	**6.1**

Test and Procedure	Results and Indications	Proceed to
5.9—Uncommon fuel system malfunctions: See below:	If the problem is solved:	6.1
	If the problem remains, remove and recondition the carburetor.	

Condition	Indication	Test	Prevailing Weather Conditions	Remedy
Vapor lock	Engine will not restart shortly after running.	Cool the components of the fuel system until the engine starts. Vapor lock can be cured faster by draping a wet cloth over a mechanical fuel pump.	Hot to very hot	Ensure that the exhaust manifold heat control valve is operating. Check with the vehicle manufacturer for the recommended solution to vapor lock on the model in question.
Carburetor icing	Engine will not idle, stalls at low speeds.	Visually inspect the throttle plate area of the throttle bores for frost.	High humidity, 32–40° F.	Ensure that the exhaust manifold heat control valve is operating, and that the intake manifold heat riser is not blocked.
Water in the fuel	Engine sputters and stalls; may not start.	Pump a small amount of fuel into a glass jar. Allow to stand, and inspect for droplets or a layer of water.	High humidity, extreme temperature changes.	For droplets, use one or two cans of commercial gas line anti-freeze. For a layer of water, the tank must be drained, and the fuel lines blown out with compressed air.

Section 6—Engine Compression

See Chapter 3 for service procedures

Test and Procedure	Results and Indications	Proceed to
6.1—Test engine compression: Remove all spark plugs. Block the throttle wide open. Insert a compression gauge into a spark plug port, crank the engine to obtain the maximum reading, and record.	If compression is within limits on all cylinders:	7.1
	If gauge reading is extremely low on all cylinders:	6.2
	If gauge reading is low on one or two cylinders: (If gauge readings are identical and low on two or more adjacent cylinders, the head gasket must be replaced.)	6.2

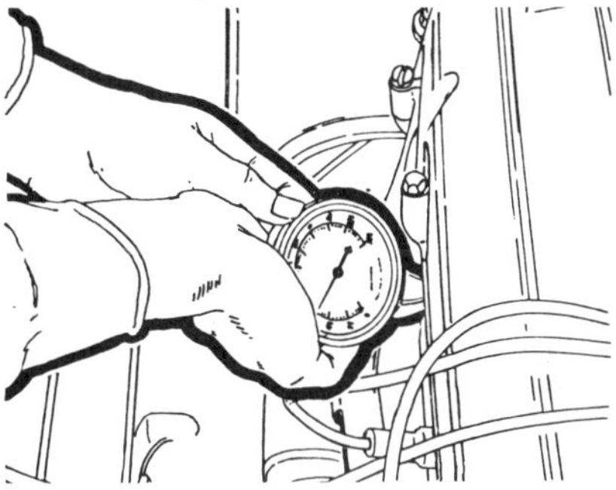

Checking compression

Test and Procedure	Results and Indications	Proceed to
6.2—Test engine compression (wet): Squirt approximately 30 cc. of engine oil into each cylinder, and retest per 6.1.	If the readings improve, worn or cracked rings or broken pistons are indicated:	See Chapter 3
	If the readings do not improve, burned or excessively carboned valves or a jumped timing chain are indicated: **NOTE:** ***A jumped timing chain is often indicated by difficult cranking.***	7.1

Section 7—Engine Vacuum

See Chapter 3 for service procedures

Test and Procedure	*Results and Indications*	*Proceed to*
7.1—Attach a vacuum gauge to the intake manifold beyond the throttle plate. Start the engine, and observe the action of the needle over the range of engine speeds.	See below.	**See below**

INDICATION: normal engine in good condition

Proceed to: 8.1

Normal engine

Gauge reading: steady, from 17–22 in./Hg.

INDICATION: sticking valves or ignition miss

Proceed to: 9.1, 8.3

Sticking valves

Gauge reading: intermittent fluctuation at idle

INDICATION: late ignition or valve timing, low compression, stuck throttle valve, leaking carburetor or manifold gasket

Proceed to: 6.1

Incorrect valve timing

Gauge reading: low (10–15 in./Hg) but steady

INDICATION: improper carburetor adjustment or minor intake leak.

Proceed to: 7.2

Carburetor requires adjustment

Gauge reading: drifting needle

INDICATION: ignition miss, blown cylinder head gasket, leaking valve or weak valve spring

Proceed to: 8.3, 6.1

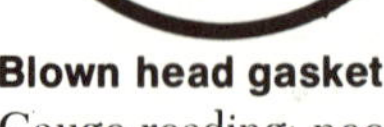

Blown head gasket

Gauge reading: needle fluctuates as engine speed increases

INDICATION: burnt valve or faulty valve clearance. Needle will fall when defective valve operates

Proceed to: 9.1

Burnt or leaking valves

Gauge reading: steady needle, but drops regularly

INDICATION: choked muffler, excessive back pressure in system

Proceed to: 10.1

Clogged exhaust system

Gauge reading: gradual drop in reading at idle

INDICATION: worn valve guides

Proceed to: 9.1

Worn valve guides

Gauge reading: needle vibrates excessively at idle, but steadies as engine speed increases

White pointer = steady gauge hand

Black pointer = fluctuating gauge hand

Test and Procedure	Results and Indications	Proceed to
7.2—Attach a vacuum gauge per 7.1, and test for an intake manifold leak. Squirt a small amount of oil around the intake manifold gaskets, carburetor gaskets, plugs and fittings. Observe the action of the vacuum gauge.	If the reading improves, replace the indicated gasket, or seal the indicated fitting or plug:	**8.1**
	If the reading remains low:	**7.3**
7.3—Test all vacuum hoses and accessories for leaks as described in 7.2. Also check the carburetor body (dashpots, automatic choke mechanism, throttle shafts) for leaks in the same manner.	If the reading improves, service or replace the offending part(s):	**8.1**
	If the reading remains low:	**6.1**

Section 8—Secondary Electrical System

See Chapter 2 for service procedures

Test and Procedure	Results and Indications	Proceed to
8.1—Remove the distributor cap and check to make sure that the rotor turns when the engine is cranked. Visually inspect the distributor components.	Clean, tighten or replace any components which appear defective.	**8.2**
8.2—Connect a timing light (per manufacturer's recommendation) and check the dynamic ignition timing. Disconnect and plug the vacuum hose(s) to the distributor if specified, start the engine, and observe the timing marks at the specified engine speed.	If the timing is not correct, adjust to specifications by rotating the distributor in the engine: (Advance timing by rotating distributor opposite normal direction of rotor rotation, retard timing by rotating distributor in same direction as rotor rotation.)	**8.3**
8.3—Check the operation of the distributor advance mechanism(s): To test the mechanical advance, disconnect the vacuum lines from the distributor advance unit and observe the timing marks with a timing light as the engine speed is increased from idle. If the mark moves smoothly, without hesitation, it may be assumed that the mechanical advance is functioning properly. To test vacuum advance and/or retard systems, alternately crimp and release the vacuum line, and observe the timing mark for movement. If movement is noted, the system is operating.	If the systems are functioning:	**8.4**
	If the systems are not functioning, remove the distributor, and test on a distributor tester:	**8.4**
8.4—Locate an ignition miss: With the engine running, remove each spark plug wire, one at a time, until one is found that doesn't cause the engine to roughen and slow down.	When the missing cylinder is identified:	**4.1**

Section 9—Valve Train

See Chapter 3 for service procedures

Test and Procedure	Results and Indications	Proceed to
9.1—Evaluate the valve train: Remove the valve cover, and ensure that the valves are adjusted to specifications. A mechanic's stethoscope may be used to aid in the diagnosis of the valve train. By pushing the probe on or near push rods or rockers, valve noise often can be isolated. A timing light also may be used to diagnose valve problems. Connect the light according to manufacturer's recommendations, and start the engine. Vary the firing moment of the light by increasing the engine speed (and therefore the ignition advance), and moving the trigger from cylinder to cylinder. Observe the movement of each valve.	Sticking valves or erratic valve train motion can be observed with the timing light. The cylinder head must be disassembled for repairs.	**See Chapter 3**
9.2—Check the valve timing: Locate top dead center of the No. 1 piston, and install a degree wheel or tape on the crankshaft pulley or damper with zero corresponding to an index mark on the engine. Rotate the crankshaft in its direction of rotation, and observe the opening of the No. 1 cylinder intake valve. The opening should correspond with the correct mark on the degree wheel according to specifications.	If the timing is not correct, the timing cover must be removed for further investigation.	**See Chapter 3**

Section 10—Exhaust System

Test and Procedure	Results and Indications	Proceed to
10.1—Determine whether the exhaust manifold heat control valve is operating: Operate the valve by hand to determine whether it is free to move. If the valve is free, run the engine to operating temperature and observe the action of the valve, to ensure that it is opening.	If the valve sticks, spray it with a suitable solvent, open and close the valve to free it, and retest.	
	If the valve functions properly:	**10.2**
	If the valve does not free, or does not operate, replace the valve:	**10.2**
10.2—Ensure that there are no exhaust restrictions: Visually inspect the exhaust system for kinks, dents, or crushing. Also note that gases are flowing freely from the tailpipe at all engine speeds, indicating no restriction in the muffler or resonator.	Replace any damaged portion of the system:	**11.1**

Section 11—Cooling System

See Chapter 3 for service procedures

Test and Procedure	Results and Indications	Proceed to
11.1—Visually inspect the fan belt for glazing, cracks, and fraying, and replace if necessary. Tighten the belt so that the longest span has approximately ½" play at its mid-point under thumb pressure (see Chapter 1).	Replace or tighten the fan belt as necessary:	**11.2**
Checking belt tension		
11.2—Check the fluid level of the cooling system.	If full or slightly low, fill as necessary:	**11.5**
	If extremely low:	**11.3**
11.3—Visually inspect the external portions of the cooling system (radiator, radiator hoses, thermostat elbow, water pump seals, heater hoses, etc.) for leaks. If none are found, pressurize the cooling system to 14–15 psi.	If cooling system holds the pressure:	**11.5**
	If cooling system loses pressure rapidly, reinspect external parts of the system for leaks under pressure. If none are found, check dipstick for coolant in crankcase. If no coolant is present, but pressure loss continues:	**11.4**
	If coolant is evident in crankcase, remove cylinder head(s), and check gasket(s). If gaskets are intact, block and cylinder head(s) should be checked for cracks or holes. If the gasket(s) is blown, replace, and purge the crankcase of coolant:	**12.6**
	NOTE: ***Occasionally, due to atmospheric and driving conditions, condensation of water can occur in the crankcase. This causes the oil to appear milky white. To remedy, run the engine until hot, and change the oil and oil filter.***	
11.4—Check for combustion leaks into the cooling system: Pressurize the cooling system as above. Start the engine, and observe the pressure gauge. If the needle fluctuates, remove each spark plug wire, one at a time, noting which cylinder(s) reduce or eliminate the fluctuation.	Cylinders which reduce or eliminate the fluctuation, when the spark plug wire is removed, are leaking into the cooling system. Replace the head gasket on the affected cylinder bank(s).	
Pressurizing the cooling system		

Test and Procedure	Results and Indications	Proceed to
11.5—Check the radiator pressure cap: Attach a radiator pressure tester to the radiator cap (wet the seal prior to installation). Quickly pump up the pressure, noting the point at which the cap releases.	If the cap releases within ± 1 psi of the specified rating, it is operating properly:	**11.6**
	If the cap releases at more than ± 1 psi of the specified rating, it should be replaced:	**11.6**

Checking radiator pressure cap

Test and Procedure	Results and Indications	Proceed to
11.6—Test the thermostat: Start the engine cold, remove the radiator cap, and insert a thermometer into the radiator. Allow the engine to idle. After a short while, there will be a sudden, rapid increase in coolant temperature. The temperature at which this sharp rise stops is the thermostat opening temperature.	If the thermostat opens at or about the specified temperature:	**11.7**
	If the temperature doesn't increase: (If the temperature increases slowly and gradually, replace the thermostat.)	**11.7**
11.7—Check the water pump: Remove the thermostat elbow and the thermostat, disconnect the coil high tension lead (to prevent starting), and crank the engine momentarily.	If coolant flows, replace the thermostat and retest per 11.6:	**11.6**
	If coolant doesn't flow, reverse flush the cooling system to alleviate any blockage that might exist. If system is not blocked, and coolant will not flow, replace the water pump.	

Section 12—Lubrication

See Chapter 3 for service procedures

Test and Procedure	Results and Indications	Proceed to
12.1—Check the oil pressure gauge or warning light: If the gauge shows low pressure, or the light is on for no obvious reason, remove the oil pressure sender. Install an accurate oil pressure gauge and run the engine momentarily.	If oil pressure builds normally, run engine for a few moments to determine that it is functioning normally, and replace the sender.	—
	If the pressure remains low:	**12.2**
	If the pressure surges:	**12.3**
	If the oil pressure is zero:	**12.3**
12.2—Visually inspect the oil: If the oil is watery or very thin, milky, or foamy, replace the oil and oil filter.	If the oil is normal:	**12.3**
	If after replacing oil the pressure remains low:	**12.3**
	If after replacing oil the pressure becomes normal:	—

Test and Procedure	Results and Indications	Proceed to
12.3—Inspect the oil pressure relief valve and spring, to ensure that it is not sticking or stuck. Remove and thoroughly clean the valve, spring, and the valve body.	If the oil pressure improves:	—
	If no improvement is noted:	**12.4**
12.4—Check to ensure that the oil pump is not cavitating (sucking air instead of oil): See that the crankcase is neither over nor underfull, and that the pickup in the sump is in the proper position and free from sludge.	Fill or drain the crankcase to the proper capacity, and clean the pickup screen in solvent if necessary. If no improvement is noted:	**12.5**
12.5—Inspect the oil pump drive and the oil pump:	If the pump drive or the oil pump appear to be defective, service as necessary and retest per 12.1:	**12.1**
	If the pump drive and pump appear to be operating normally, the engine should be disassembled to determine where blockage exists:	**See Chapter 3**
12.6—Purge the engine of ethylene glycol coolant: Completely drain the crankcase and the oil filter. Obtain a commercial butyl cellosolve base solvent, designated for this purpose, and follow the instructions precisely. Following this, install a new oil filter and refill the crankcase with the proper weight oil. The next oil and filter change should follow shortly thereafter (1000 miles).		

TROUBLESHOOTING EMISSION CONTROL SYSTEMS

See Chapter 4 for procedures applicable to individual emission control systems used on specific combinations of engine/transmission/model.

TROUBLESHOOTING THE CARBURETOR

See Chapter 4 for service procedures

Carburetor problems cannot be effectively isolated unless all other engine systems (particularly ignition and emission) are functioning properly and the engine is properly tuned.

Condition	Possible Cause
Engine cranks, but does not start	1. Improper starting procedure 2. No fuel in tank 3. Clogged fuel line or filter 4. Defective fuel pump 5. Choke valve not closing properly 6. Engine flooded 7. Choke valve not unloading 8. Throttle linkage not making full travel 9. Stuck needle or float 10. Leaking float needle or seat 11. Improper float adjustment
Engine stalls	1. Improperly adjusted idle speed or mixture **Engine hot** 2. Improperly adjusted dashpot 3. Defective or improperly adjusted solenoid 4. Incorrect fuel level in fuel bowl 5. Fuel pump pressure too high 6. Leaking float needle seat 7. Secondary throttle valve stuck open 8. Air or fuel leaks 9. Idle air bleeds plugged or missing 10. Idle passages plugged **Engine Cold** 11. Incorrectly adjusted choke 12. Improperly adjusted fast idle speed 13. Air leaks 14. Plugged idle or idle air passages 15. Stuck choke valve or binding linkage 16. Stuck secondary throttle valves 17. Engine flooding—high fuel level 18. Leaking or misaligned float
Engine hesitates on acceleration	1. Clogged fuel filter 2. Leaking fuel pump diaphragm 3. Low fuel pump pressure 4. Secondary throttle valves stuck, bent or misadjusted 5. Sticking or binding air valve 6. Defective accelerator pump 7. Vacuum leaks 8. Clogged air filter 9. Incorrect choke adjustment (engine cold)
Engine feels sluggish or flat on acceleration	1. Improperly adjusted idle speed or mixture 2. Clogged fuel filter 3. Defective accelerator pump 4. Dirty, plugged or incorrect main metering jets 5. Bent or sticking main metering rods 6. Sticking throttle valves 7. Stuck heat riser 8. Binding or stuck air valve 9. Dirty, plugged or incorrect secondary jets 10. Bent or sticking secondary metering rods. 11. Throttle body or manifold heat passages plugged 12. Improperly adjusted choke or choke vacuum break.
Carburetor floods	1. Defective fuel pump. Pressure too high. 2. Stuck choke valve 3. Dirty, worn or damaged float or needle valve/seat 4. Incorrect float/fuel level 5. Leaking float bowl

Condition	Possible Cause
Engine idles roughly and stalls	1. Incorrect idle speed 2. Clogged fuel filter 3. Dirt in fuel system or carburetor 4. Loose carburetor screws or attaching bolts 5. Broken carburetor gaskets 6. Air leaks 7. Dirty carburetor 8. Worn idle mixture needles 9. Throttle valves stuck open 10. Incorrectly adjusted float or fuel level 11. Clogged air filter
Engine runs unevenly or surges	1. Defective fuel pump 2. Dirty or clogged fuel filter 3. Plugged, loose or incorrect main metering jets or rods 4. Air leaks 5. Bent or sticking main metering rods 6. Stuck power piston 7. Incorrect float adjustment 8. Incorrect idle speed or mixture 9. Dirty or plugged idle system passages 10. Hard, brittle or broken gaskets 11. Loose attaching or mounting screws 12. Stuck or misaligned secondary throttle valves
Poor fuel economy	1. Poor driving habits 2. Stuck choke valve 3. Binding choke linkage 4. Stuck heat riser 5. Incorrect idle mixture 6. Defective accelerator pump 7. Air leaks 8. Plugged, loose or incorrect main metering jets 9. Improperly adjusted float or fuel level 10. Bent, misaligned or fuel-clogged float 11. Leaking float needle seat 12. Fuel leak 13. Accelerator pump discharge ball not seating properly 14. Incorrect main jets
Engine lacks high speed performance or power	1. Incorrect throttle linkage adjustment 2. Stuck or binding power piston 3. Defective accelerator pump 4. Air leaks 5. Incorrect float setting or fuel level 6. Dirty, plugged, worn or incorrect main metering jets or rods 7. Binding or sticking air valve 8. Brittle or cracked gaskets 9. Bent, incorrect or improperly adjusted secondary metering rods 10. Clogged fuel filter 11. Clogged air filter 12. Defective fuel pump

TROUBLESHOOTING FUEL INJECTION PROBLEMS

Each fuel injection system has its own unique components and test procedures, for which it is impossible to generalize. Refer to Chapter 4 of this Repair & Tune-Up Guide for specific test and repair procedures, if the vehicle is equipped with fuel injection.

TROUBLESHOOTING ELECTRICAL PROBLEMS

See Chapter 5 for service procedures

For any electrical system to operate, it must make a complete circuit. This simply means that the power flow from the battery must make a complete circle. When an electrical component is operating, power flows from the battery to the component, passes through the component causing it to perform its function (lighting a light bulb), and then returns to the battery through the ground of the circuit. This ground is usually (but not always) the metal part of the car or truck on which the electrical component is mounted.

Perhaps the easiest way to visualize this is to think of connecting a light bulb with two wires attached to it to the battery. If one of the two wires attached to the light bulb were attached to the negative post of the battery and the other were attached to the positive post of the battery, you would have a complete circuit. Current from the battery would flow to the light bulb, causing it to light, and return to the negative post of the battery.

The normal automotive circuit differs from this simple example in two ways. First, instead of having a return wire from the bulb to the battery, the light bulb returns the current to the battery through the chassis of the vehicle. Since the negative battery cable is attached to the chassis and the chassis is made of electrically conductive metal, the chassis of the vehicle can serve as a ground wire to complete the circuit. Secondly, most automotive circuits contain switches to turn components on and off as required.

Every complete circuit from a power source must include a component which is using the power from the power source. If you were to disconnect the light bulb from the wires and touch the two wires together (don't do this) the power supply wire to the component would be grounded before the normal ground connection for the circuit.

Because grounding a wire from a power source makes a complete circuit—less the required component to use the power—this phenomenon is called a short circuit. Common causes are: broken insulation (exposing the metal wire to a metal part of the car or truck), or a shorted switch.

Some electrical components which require a large amount of current to operate also have a relay in their circuit. Since these circuits carry a large amount of current, the thickness of the wire in the circuit (gauge size) is also greater. If this large wire were connected from the component to the control switch on the instrument panel, and then back to the component, a voltage drop would occur in the circuit. To prevent this potential drop in voltage, an electromagnetic switch (relay) is used. The large wires in the circuit are connected from the battery to one side of the relay, and from the opposite side of the relay to the component. The relay is normally open, preventing current from passing through the circuit. An additional, smaller, wire is connected from the relay to the control switch for the circuit. When the control switch is turned on, it grounds the smaller wire from the relay and completes the circuit. This closes the relay and allows current to flow from the battery to the component. The horn, headlight, and starter circuits are three which use relays.

It is possible for larger surges of current to pass through the electrical system of your car or truck. If this surge of current were to reach an electrical component, it could burn it out. To prevent this, fuses, circuit breakers or fusible links are connected into the current supply wires of most of the major electrical systems. When an electrical current of excessive power passes through the component's fuse, the fuse blows out and breaks the circuit, saving the component from destruction.

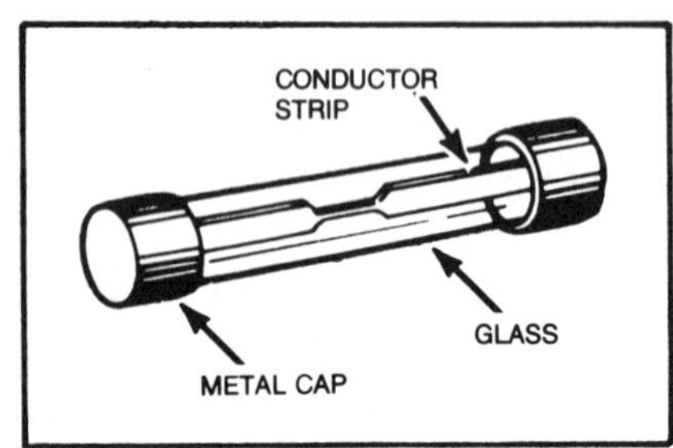

Typical automotive fuse

A circuit breaker is basically a self-repairing fuse. The circuit breaker opens the circuit the same way a fuse does. However, when either the short is removed from the circuit or the surge subsides, the circuit breaker resets itself and does not have to be replaced as a fuse does.

A fuse link is a wire that acts as a fuse. It is normally connected between the starter relay and the main wiring harness. This connection is usually under the hood. The fuse link (if installed) protects all the

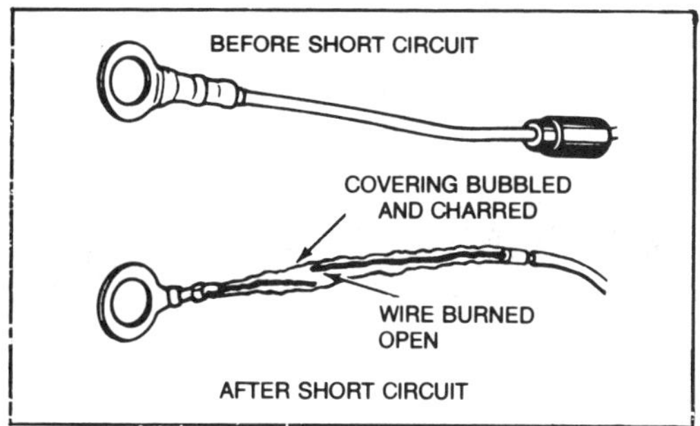

Most fusible links show a charred, melted insulation when they burn out

chassis electrical components, and is the probable cause of trouble when none of the electrical components function, unless the battery is disconnected or dead.

Electrical problems generally fall into one of three areas:

1. The component that is not functioning is not receiving current.
2. The component itself is not functioning.
3. The component is not properly grounded.

The electrical system can be checked with a test light and a jumper wire. A test light is a device that looks like a pointed screwdriver with a wire attached to it and has a light bulb in its handle. A jumper wire is a piece of insulated wire with an alligator clip attached to each end.

If a component is not working, you must follow a systematic plan to determine which of the three causes is the villain.

1. Turn on the switch that controls the inoperable component.
2. Disconnect the power supply wire from the component.
3. Attach the ground wire on the test light to a good metal ground.
4. Touch the probe end of the test light to the end of the power supply wire that was disconnected from the component. If the component is receiving current, the test light will go on.

NOTE: ***Some components work only when the ignition switch is turned on.***

If the test light does not go on, then the problem is in the circuit between the battery and the component. This includes all the switches, fuses, and relays in the system. Follow the wire that runs back to the battery. The problem is an open circuit between the battery and the component. If the fuse is blown and, when replaced, immediately blows again, there is a short circuit in the system which must be located and repaired. If there is a switch in the system, bypass it with a jumper wire. This is done by connecting one end of the jumper wire to the power supply wire into the switch and the other end of the jumper wire to the wire coming out of the switch. If the test light lights with the jumper wire installed, the switch or whatever was bypassed is defective.

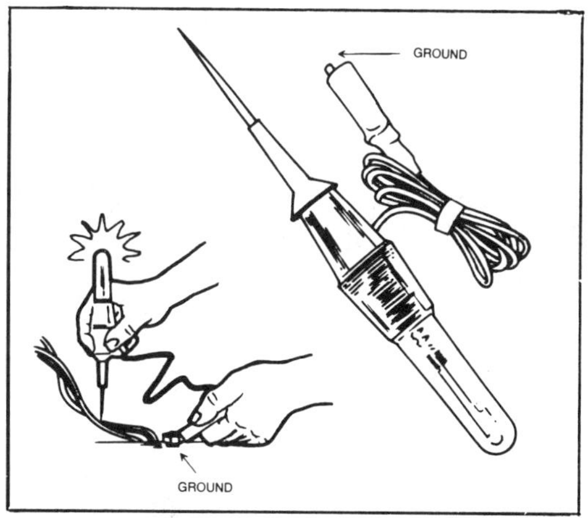

The test light will show the presence of current when touched to a hot wire and grounded at the other end

NOTE: ***Never substitute the jumper wire for the component, since it is required to use the power from the power source.***

5. If the bulb in the test light goes on, then the current is getting to the component that is not working. This eliminates the first of the three possible causes. Connect the power supply wire and connect a jumper wire from the component to a good metal ground. Do this with the switch which controls the component turned on, and also the ignition switch turned on if it is required for the component to work. If the component works with the jumper wire installed, then it has a bad ground. This is usually caused by the metal area on which the component mounts to the chassis being coated with some type of foreign matter.
6. If neither test located the source of the trouble, then the component itself is defective. Remember that for any electrical system to work, all connections must be clean and tight.

Troubleshooting Basic Turn Signal and Flasher Problems

See Chapter 5 for service procedures

Most problems in the turn signals or flasher system can be reduced to defective flashers or bulbs, which are easily replaced. Occasionally, the turn signal switch will prove defective.

F = Front   R = Rear   ● = Lights off   ○ = Lights on

Condition		Possible Cause
Turn signals light, but do not flash	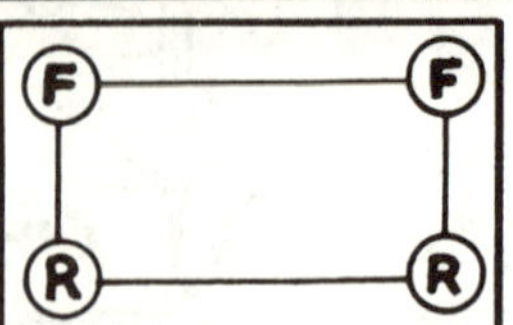	Defective flasher
No turn signals light on either side	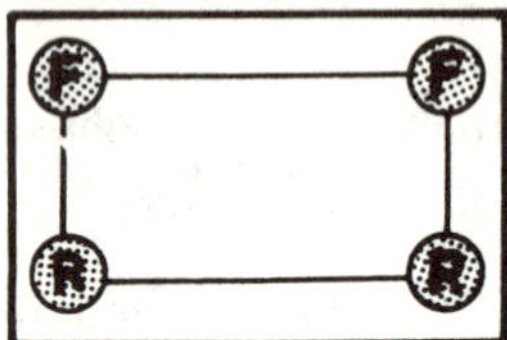	Blown fuse. Replace if defective. Defective flasher. Check by substitution. Open circuit, short circuit or poor ground.
Both turn signals on one side don't work	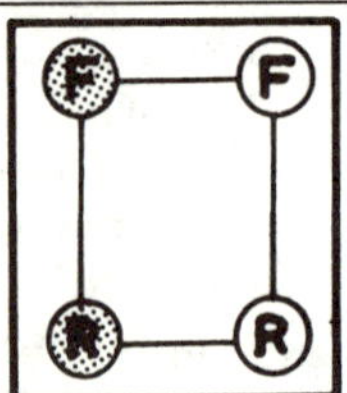	Bad bulbs. Bad ground in both (or either) housings.
One turn signal light on one side doesn't work	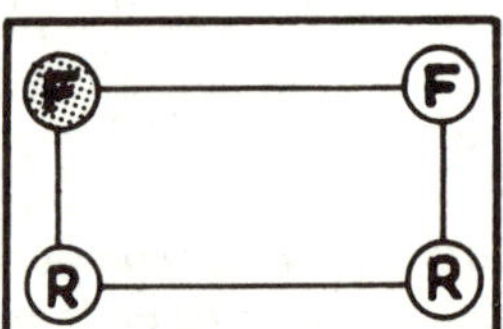	Defective bulb. Corrosion in socket. Clean contacts. Poor ground at socket.
Turn signal flashes too fast or too slowly	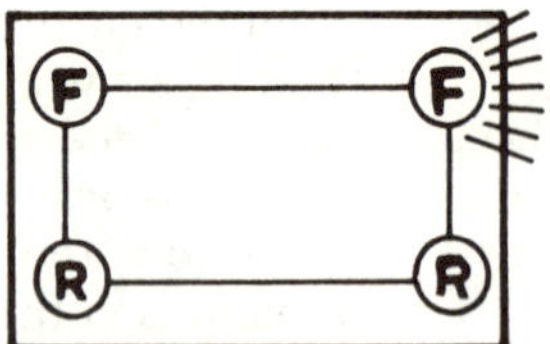	Check any bulb on the side flashing too fast. A heavy-duty bulb is probably installed in place of a regular bulb. Check the bulb flashing too slowly. A standard bulb was probably installed in place of a heavy-duty bulb. Loose connections or corrosion at the bulb socket.
Indicator lights don't work in either direction		Check if the turn signals are working. Check the dash indicator lights. Check the flasher by substitution.
One indicator light doesn't light		On systems with one dash indicator: See if the lights work on the same side. Often the filaments have been reversed in systems combining stoplights with taillights and turn signals. Check the flasher by substitution. On systems with two indicators: Check the bulbs on the same side. Check the indicator light bulb. Check the flasher by substitution.

Troubleshooting Lighting Problems

See Chapter 5 for service procedures

Condition	Possible Cause
One or more lights don't work, but others do	1. Defective bulb(s) 2. Blown fuse(s) 3. Dirty fuse clips or light sockets 4. Poor ground circuit
Lights burn out quickly	1. Incorrect voltage regulator setting or defective regulator 2. Poor battery/alternator connections
Lights go dim	1. Low/discharged battery 2. Alternator not charging 3. Corroded sockets or connections 4. Low voltage output
Lights flicker	1. Loose connection 2. Poor ground. (Run ground wire from light housing to frame) 3. Circuit breaker operating (short circuit)
Lights "flare"—Some flare is normal on acceleration—If excessive, see "Lights Burn Out Quickly"	High voltage setting
Lights glare—approaching drivers are blinded	1. Lights adjusted too high 2. Rear springs or shocks sagging 3. Rear tires soft

Troubleshooting Dash Gauge Problems

Most problems can be traced to a defective sending unit or faulty wiring. Occasionally, the gauge itself is at fault. See Chapter 5 for service procedures.

Condition	Possible Cause
COOLANT TEMPERATURE GAUGE	
Gauge reads erratically or not at all	1. Loose or dirty connections 2. Defective sending unit. 3. Defective gauge. To test a bi-metal gauge, remove the wire from the sending unit. Ground the wire for an instant. If the gauge registers, replace the sending unit. To test a magnetic gauge, disconnect the wire at the sending unit. With ignition ON gauge should register COLD. Ground the wire; gauge should register HOT.
AMMETER GAUGE—TURN HEADLIGHTS ON (DO NOT START ENGINE). NOTE REACTION	
Ammeter shows charge Ammeter shows discharge Ammeter does not move	1. Connections reversed on gauge 2. Ammeter is OK 3. Loose connections or faulty wiring 4. Defective gauge

Condition	Possible Cause
OIL PRESSURE GAUGE	
Gauge does not register or is inaccurate	1. On mechanical gauge, Bourdon tube may be bent or kinked. 2. Low oil pressure. Remove sending unit. Idle the engine briefly. If no oil flows from sending unit hole, problem is in engine. 3. Defective gauge. Remove the wire from the sending unit and ground it for an instant with the ignition ON. A good gauge will go to the top of the scale. 4. Defective wiring. Check the wiring to the gauge. If it's OK and the gauge doesn't register when grounded, replace the gauge. 5. Defective sending unit.
ALL GAUGES	
All gauges do not operate	1. Blown fuse 2. Defective instrument regulator
All gauges read low or erratically	3. Defective or dirty instrument voltage regulator
All gauges pegged	4. Loss of ground between instrument voltage regulator and frame 5. Defective instrument regulator
WARNING LIGHTS	
Light(s) do not come on when ignition is ON, but engine is not started	1. Defective bulb 2. Defective wire 3. Defective sending unit. Disconnect the wire from the sending unit and ground it. Replace the sending unit if the light comes on with the ignition ON.
Light comes on with engine running	4. Problem in individual system 5. Defective sending unit

Troubleshooting Clutch Problems

It is false economy to replace individual clutch components. The pressure plate, clutch plate and throwout bearing should be replaced as a set, and the flywheel face inspected, whenever the clutch is overhauled. See Chapter 6 for service procedures.

Condition	Possible Cause
Clutch chatter	1. Grease on driven plate (disc) facing 2. Binding clutch linkage or cable 3. Loose, damaged facings on driven plate (disc) 4. Engine mounts loose 5. Incorrect height adjustment of pressure plate release levers 6. Clutch housing or housing to transmission adapter misalignment 7. Loose driven plate hub
Clutch grabbing	1. Oil, grease on driven plate (disc) facing 2. Broken pressure plate 3. Warped or binding driven plate. Driven plate binding on clutch shaft
Clutch slips	1. Lack of lubrication in clutch linkage or cable (linkage or cable binds, causes incomplete engagement) 2. Incorrect pedal, or linkage adjustment 3. Broken pressure plate springs 4. Weak pressure plate springs 5. Grease on driven plate facings (disc)

Troubleshooting Clutch Problems (cont.)

Condition	Possible Cause
Incomplete clutch release	1. Incorrect pedal or linkage adjustment or linkage or cable binding 2. Incorrect height adjustment on pressure plate release levers 3. Loose, broken facings on driven plate (disc) 4. Bent, dished, warped driven plate caused by overheating
Grinding, whirring grating noise when pedal is depressed	1. Worn or defective throwout bearing 2. Starter drive teeth contacting flywheel ring gear teeth. Look for milled or polished teeth on ring gear.
Squeal, howl, trumpeting noise when pedal is being released (occurs during first inch to inch and one-half of pedal travel)	Pilot bushing worn or lack of lubricant. If bushing appears OK, polish bushing with emery cloth, soak lube wick in oil, lube bushing with oil, apply film of chassis grease to clutch shaft pilot hub, reassemble. NOTE: Bushing wear may be due to misalignment of clutch housing or housing to transmission adapter
Vibration or clutch pedal pulsation with clutch disengaged (pedal fully depressed)	1. Worn or defective engine transmission mounts 2. Flywheel run out. (Flywheel run out at face not to exceed 0.005") 3. Damaged or defective clutch components

Troubleshooting Manual Transmission Problems

See Chapter 6 for service procedures

Condition	Possible Cause
Transmission jumps out of gear	1. Misalignment of transmission case or clutch housing. 2. Worn pilot bearing in crankshaft. 3. Bent transmission shaft. 4. Worn high speed sliding gear. 5. Worn teeth or end-play in clutch shaft. 6. Insufficient spring tension on shifter rail plunger. 7. Bent or loose shifter fork. 8. Gears not engaging completely. 9. Loose or worn bearings on clutch shaft or mainshaft. 10. Worn gear teeth. 11. Worn or damaged detent balls.
Transmission sticks in gear	1. Clutch not releasing fully. 2. Burred or battered teeth on clutch shaft, or sliding sleeve. 3. Burred or battered transmission mainshaft. 4. Frozen synchronizing clutch. 5. Stuck shifter rail plunger. 6. Gearshift lever twisting and binding shifter rail. 7. Battered teeth on high speed sliding gear or on sleeve. 8. Improper lubrication, or lack of lubrication. 9. Corroded transmission parts. 10. Defective mainshaft pilot bearing. 11. Locked gear bearings will give same effect as stuck in gear.
Transmission gears will not synchronize	1. Binding pilot bearing on mainshaft, will synchronize in high gear only. 2. Clutch not releasing fully. 3. Detent spring weak or broken. 4. Weak or broken springs under balls in sliding gear sleeve. 5. Binding bearing on clutch shaft, or binding countershaft. 6. Binding pilot bearing in crankshaft. 7. Badly worn gear teeth. 8. Improper lubrication. 9. Constant mesh gear not turning freely on transmission mainshaft. Will synchronize in that gear only.

Condition	Possible Cause
Gears spinning when shifting into gear from neutral	1. Clutch not releasing fully. 2. In some cases an extremely light lubricant in transmission will cause gears to continue to spin for a short time after clutch is released. 3. Binding pilot bearing in crankshaft.
Transmission noisy in all gears	1. Insufficient lubricant, or improper lubricant. 2. Worn countergear bearings. 3. Worn or damaged main drive gear or countergear. 4. Damaged main drive gear or mainshaft bearings. 5. Worn or damaged countergear anti-lash plate.
Transmission noisy in neutral only	1. Damaged main drive gear bearing. 2. Damaged or loose mainshaft pilot bearing. 3. Worn or damaged countergear anti-lash plate. 4. Worn countergear bearings.
Transmission noisy in one gear only	1. Damaged or worn constant mesh gears. 2. Worn or damaged countergear bearings. 3. Damaged or worn synchronizer.
Transmission noisy in reverse only	1. Worn or damaged reverse idler gear or idler bushing. 2. Worn or damaged mainshaft reverse gear. 3. Worn or damaged reverse countergear. 4. Damaged shift mechanism.

TROUBLESHOOTING AUTOMATIC TRANSMISSION PROBLEMS

Keeping alert to changes in the operating characteristics of the transmission (changing shift points, noises, etc.) can prevent small problems from becoming large ones. If the problem cannot be traced to loose bolts, fluid level, misadjusted linkage, clogged filters or similar problems, you should probably seek professional service.

Transmission Fluid Indications

The appearance and odor of the transmission fluid can give valuable clues to the overall condition of the transmission. Always note the appearance of the fluid when you check the fluid level or change the fluid. Rub a small amount of fluid between your fingers to feel for grit and smell the fluid on the dipstick.

If the fluid appears:	It indicates:
Clear and red colored	Normal operation
Discolored (extremely dark red or brownish) or smells burned	Band or clutch pack failure, usually caused by an overheated transmission. Hauling very heavy loads with insufficient power or failure to change the fluid often result in overheating. Do not confuse this appearance with newer fluids that have a darker red color and a strong odor (though not a burned odor).
Foamy or aerated (light in color and full of bubbles)	1. The level is too high (gear train is churning oil) 2. An internal air leak (air is mixing with the fluid). Have the transmission checked professionally.
Solid residue in the fluid	Defective bands, clutch pack or bearings. Bits of band material or metal abrasives are clinging to the dipstick. Have the transmission checked professionally.
Varnish coating on the dipstick	The transmission fluid is overheating

TROUBLESHOOTING DRIVE AXLE PROBLEMS

First, determine when the noise is most noticeable.

Drive Noise: Produced under vehicle acceleration.

Coast Noise: Produced while coasting with a closed throttle.

Float Noise: Occurs while maintaining constant speed (just enough to keep speed constant) on a level road.

External Noise Elimination

It is advisable to make a thorough road test to determine whether the noise originates in the rear axle or whether it originates from the tires, engine, transmission, wheel bearings or road surface. Noise originating from other places cannot be corrected by servicing the rear axle.

ROAD NOISE

Brick or rough surfaced concrete roads produce noises that seem to come from the rear axle. Road noise is usually identical in Drive or Coast and driving on a different type of road will tell whether the road is the problem.

TIRE NOISE

Tire noise can be mistaken as rear axle noise, even though the tires on the front are at fault. Snow tread and mud tread tires or tires worn unevenly will frequently cause vibrations which seem to originate elsewhere; *temporarily, and for test purposes only,* inflate the tires to 40–50 lbs. This will significantly alter the noise produced by the tires, but will not alter noise from the rear axle. Noises from the rear axle will normally cease at speeds below 30 mph on coast, while tire noise will continue at lower tone as speed is decreased. The rear axle noise will usually change from drive conditions to coast conditions, while tire noise will not. Do not forget to lower the tire pressure to normal after the test is complete.

ENGINE/TRANSMISSION NOISE

Determine at what speed the noise is most pronounced, then stop in a quiet place. With the transmission in Neutral, run the engine through speeds corresponding to road speeds where the noise was noticed. Noises produced with the vehicle standing still are coming from the engine or transmission.

FRONT WHEEL BEARINGS

Front wheel bearing noises, sometimes confused with rear axle noises, will not change when comparing drive and coast conditions. While holding the speed steady, lightly apply the footbrake. This will often cause wheel bearing noise to lessen, as some of the weight is taken off the bearing. Front wheel bearings are easily checked by jacking up the wheels and spinning the wheels. Shaking the wheels will also determine if the wheel bearings are excessively loose.

REAR AXLE NOISES

Eliminating other possible sources can narrow the cause to the rear axle, which normally produces noise from worn gears or bearings. Gear noises tend to peak in a narrow speed range, while bearing noises will usually vary in pitch with engine speeds.

Noise Diagnosis

The Noise Is:	Most Probably Produced By:
1. Identical under Drive or Coast	Road surface, tires or front wheel bearings
2. Different depending on road surface	Road surface or tires
3. Lower as speed is lowered	Tires
4. Similar when standing or moving	Engine or transmission
5. A vibration	Unbalanced tires, rear wheel bearing, unbalanced driveshaft or worn U-joint
6. A knock or click about every two tire revolutions	Rear wheel bearing
7. Most pronounced on turns	Damaged differential gears
8. A steady low-pitched whirring or scraping, starting at low speeds	Damaged or worn pinion bearing
9. A chattering vibration on turns	Wrong differential lubricant or worn clutch plates (limited slip rear axle)
10. Noticed only in Drive, Coast or Float conditions	Worn ring gear and/or pinion gear

Troubleshooting Steering & Suspension Problems

Condition	Possible Cause
Hard steering (wheel is hard to turn)	1. Improper tire pressure 2. Loose or glazed pump drive belt 3. Low or incorrect fluid 4. Loose, bent or poorly lubricated front end parts 5. Improper front end alignment (excessive caster) 6. Bind in steering column or linkage 7. Kinked hydraulic hose 8. Air in hydraulic system 9. Low pump output or leaks in system 10. Obstruction in lines 11. Pump valves sticking or out of adjustment 12. Incorrect wheel alignment
Loose steering (too much play in steering wheel)	1. Loose wheel bearings 2. Faulty shocks 3. Worn linkage or suspension components 4. Loose steering gear mounting or linkage points 5. Steering mechanism worn or improperly adjusted 6. Valve spool improperly adjusted 7. Worn ball joints, tie-rod ends, etc.
Veers or wanders (pulls to one side with hands off steering wheel)	1. Improper tire pressure 2. Improper front end alignment 3. Dragging or improperly adjusted brakes 4. Bent frame 5. Improper rear end alignment 6. Faulty shocks or springs 7. Loose or bent front end components 8. Play in Pitman arm 9. Steering gear mountings loose 10. Loose wheel bearings 11. Binding Pitman arm 12. Spool valve sticking or improperly adjusted 13. Worn ball joints
Wheel oscillation or vibration transmitted through steering wheel	1. Low or uneven tire pressure 2. Loose wheel bearings 3. Improper front end alignment 4. Bent spindle 5. Worn, bent or broken front end components 6. Tires out of round or out of balance 7. Excessive lateral runout in disc brake rotor 8. Loose or bent shock absorber or strut
Noises (see also "Troubleshooting Drive Axle Problems")	1. Loose belts 2. Low fluid, air in system 3. Foreign matter in system 4. Improper lubrication 5. Interference or chafing in linkage 6. Steering gear mountings loose 7. Incorrect adjustment or wear in gear box 8. Faulty valves or wear in pump 9. Kinked hydraulic lines 10. Worn wheel bearings
Poor return of steering	1. Over-inflated tires 2. Improperly aligned front end (excessive caster) 3. Binding in steering column 4. No lubrication in front end 5. Steering gear adjusted too tight
Uneven tire wear (see "How To Read Tire Wear")	1. Incorrect tire pressure 2. Improperly aligned front end 3. Tires out-of-balance 4. Bent or worn suspension parts

HOW TO READ TIRE WEAR

The way your tires wear is a good indicator of other parts of the suspension. Abnormal wear patterns are often caused by the need for simple tire maintenance, or for front end alignment.

Excessive wear at the center of the tread indicates that the air pressure in the tire is consistently too high. The tire is riding on the center of the tread and wearing it prematurely. Occasionally, this wear pattern can result from outrageously wide tires on narrow rims. The cure for this is to replace either the tires or the wheels.

This type of wear usually results from consistent under-inflation. When a tire is under-inflated, there is too much contact with the road by the outer treads, which wear prematurely. When this type of wear occurs, and the tire pressure is known to be consistently correct, a bent or worn steering component or the need for wheel alignment could be indicated.

Feathering is a condition when the edge of each tread rib develops a slightly rounded edge on one side and a sharp edge on the other. By running your hand over the tire, you can usually feel the sharper edges before you'll be able to see them. The most common causes of feathering are incorrect toe-in setting or deteriorated bushings in the front suspension.

When an inner or outer rib wears faster than the rest of the tire, the need for wheel alignment is indicated. There is excessive camber in the front suspension, causing the wheel to lean too much putting excessive load on one side of the tire. Misalignment could also be due to sagging springs, worn ball joints, or worn control arm bushings. Be sure the vehicle is loaded the way it's normally driven when you have the wheels aligned.

Cups or scalloped dips appearing around the edge of the tread almost always indicate worn (sometimes bent) suspension parts. Adjustment of wheel alignment alone will seldom cure the problem. Any worn component that connects the wheel to the suspension can cause this type of wear. Occasionally, wheels that are out of balance will wear like this, but wheel imbalance usually shows up as bald spots between the outside edges and center of the tread.

Second-rib wear is usually found only in radial tires, and appears where the steel belts end in relation to the tread. It can be kept to a minimum by paying careful attention to tire pressure and frequently rotating the tires. This is often considered normal wear but excessive amounts indicate that the tires are too wide for the wheels.

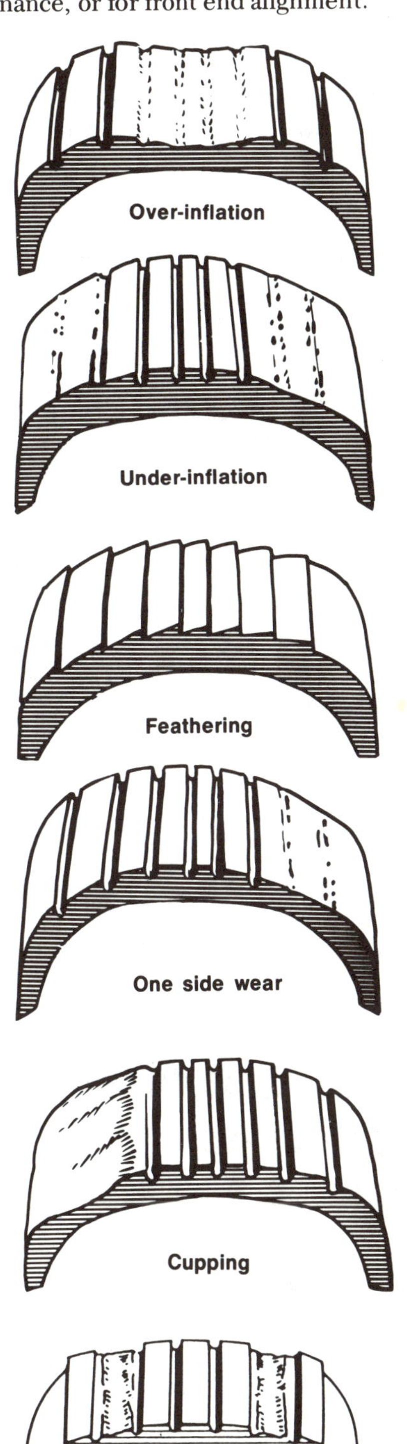

Troubleshooting Disc Brake Problems

Condition	*Possible Cause*
Noise—groan—brake noise emanating when slowly releasing brakes (creep-groan)	Not detrimental to function of disc brakes—no corrective action required. (This noise may be eliminated by slightly increasing or decreasing brake pedal efforts.)
Rattle—brake noise or rattle emanating at low speeds on rough roads, (front wheels only).	1. Shoe anti-rattle spring missing or not properly positioned. 2. Excessive clearance between shoe and caliper. 3. Soft or broken caliper seals. 4. Deformed or misaligned disc. 5. Loose caliper.
Scraping	1. Mounting bolts too long. 2. Loose wheel bearings. 3. Bent, loose, or misaligned splash shield.
Front brakes heat up during driving and fail to release	1. Operator riding brake pedal. 2. Stop light switch improperly adjusted. 3. Sticking pedal linkage. 4. Frozen or seized piston. 5. Residual pressure valve in master cylinder. 6. Power brake malfunction. 7. Proportioning valve malfunction.
Leaky brake caliper	1. Damaged or worn caliper piston seal. 2. Scores or corrosion on surface of cylinder bore.
Grabbing or uneven brake action—Brakes pull to one side	1. Causes listed under "Brakes Pull". 2. Power brake malfunction. 3. Low fluid level in master cylinder. 4. Air in hydraulic system. 5. Brake fluid, oil or grease on linings. 6. Unmatched linings. 7. Distorted brake pads. 8. Frozen or seized pistons. 9. Incorrect tire pressure. 10. Front end out of alignment. 11. Broken rear spring. 12. Brake caliper pistons sticking. 13. Restricted hose or line. 14. Caliper not in proper alignment to braking disc. 15. Stuck or malfunctioning metering valve. 16. Soft or broken caliper seals. 17. Loose caliper.
Brake pedal can be depressed without braking effect	1. Air in hydraulic system or improper bleeding procedure. 2. Leak past primary cup in master cylinder. 3. Leak in system. 4. Rear brakes out of adjustment. 5. Bleeder screw open.
Excessive pedal travel	1. Air, leak, or insufficient fluid in system or caliper. 2. Warped or excessively tapered shoe and lining assembly. 3. Excessive disc runout. 4. Rear brake adjustment required. 5. Loose wheel bearing adjustment. 6. Damaged caliper piston seal. 7. Improper brake fluid (boil). 8. Power brake malfunction. 9. Weak or soft hoses.

Troubleshooting Disc Brake Problems (cont.)

Condition	Possible Cause
Brake roughness or chatter (pedal pumping)	1. Excessive thickness variation of braking disc. 2. Excessive lateral runout of braking disc. 3. Rear brake drums out-of-round. 4. Excessive front bearing clearance.
Excessive pedal effort	1. Brake fluid, oil or grease on linings. 2. Incorrect lining. 3. Frozen or seized pistons. 4. Power brake malfunction. 5. Kinked or collapsed hose or line. 6. Stuck metering valve. 7. Scored caliper or master cylinder bore. 8. Seized caliper pistons.
Brake pedal fades (pedal travel increases with foot on brake)	1. Rough master cylinder or caliper bore. 2. Loose or broken hydraulic lines/connections. 3. Air in hydraulic system. 4. Fluid level low. 5. Weak or soft hoses. 6. Inferior quality brake shoes or fluid. 7. Worn master cylinder piston cups or seals.

Troubleshooting Drum Brakes

Condition	Possible Cause
Pedal goes to floor	1. Fluid low in reservoir. 2. Air in hydraulic system. 3. Improperly adjusted brake. 4. Leaking wheel cylinders. 5. Loose or broken brake lines. 6. Leaking or worn master cylinder. 7. Excessively worn brake lining.
Spongy brake pedal	1. Air in hydraulic system. 2. Improper brake fluid (low boiling point). 3. Excessively worn or cracked brake drums. 4. Broken pedal pivot bushing.
Brakes pulling	1. Contaminated lining. 2. Front end out of alignment. 3. Incorrect brake adjustment. 4. Unmatched brake lining. 5. Brake drums out of round. 6. Brake shoes distorted. 7. Restricted brake hose or line. 8. Broken rear spring. 9. Worn brake linings. 10. Uneven lining wear. 11. Glazed brake lining. 12. Excessive brake lining dust. 13. Heat spotted brake drums. 14. Weak brake return springs. 15. Faulty automatic adjusters. 16. Low or incorrect tire pressure.

Condition	Possible Cause
Squealing brakes	1. Glazed brake lining. 2. Saturated brake lining. 3. Weak or broken brake shoe retaining spring. 4. Broken or weak brake shoe return spring. 5. Incorrect brake lining. 6. Distorted brake shoes. 7. Bent support plate. 8. Dust in brakes or scored brake drums. 9. Linings worn below limit. 10. Uneven brake lining wear. 11. Heat spotted brake drums.
Chirping brakes	1. Out of round drum or eccentric axle flange pilot.
Dragging brakes	1. Incorrect wheel or parking brake adjustment. 2. Parking brakes engaged or improperly adjusted. 3. Weak or broken brake shoe return spring. 4. Brake pedal binding. 5. Master cylinder cup sticking. 6. Obstructed master cylinder relief port. 7. Saturated brake lining. 8. Bent or out of round brake drum. 9. Contaminated or improper brake fluid. 10. Sticking wheel cylinder pistons. 11. Driver riding brake pedal. 12. Defective proportioning valve. 13. Insufficient brake shoe lubricant.
Hard pedal	1. Brake booster inoperative. 2. Incorrect brake lining. 3. Restricted brake line or hose. 4. Frozen brake pedal linkage. 5. Stuck wheel cylinder. 6. Binding pedal linkage. 7. Faulty proportioning valve.
Wheel locks	1. Contaminated brake lining. 2. Loose or torn brake lining. 3. Wheel cylinder cups sticking. 4. Incorrect wheel bearing adjustment. 5. Faulty proportioning valve.
Brakes fade (high speed)	1. Incorrect lining. 2. Overheated brake drums. 3. Incorrect brake fluid (low boiling temperature). 4. Saturated brake lining. 5. Leak in hydraulic system. 6. Faulty automatic adjusters.
Pedal pulsates	1. Bent or out of round brake drum.
Brake chatter and shoe knock	1. Out of round brake drum. 2. Loose support plate. 3. Bent support plate. 4. Distorted brake shoes. 5. Machine grooves in contact face of brake drum (Shoe Knock). 6. Contaminated brake lining. 7. Missing or loose components. 8. Incorrect lining material. 9. Out-of-round brake drums. 10. Heat spotted or scored brake drums. 11. Out-of-balance wheels.

Troubleshooting Drum Brakes (cont.)

Condition	*Possible Cause*
Brakes do not self adjust	1. Adjuster screw frozen in thread. 2. Adjuster screw corroded at thrust washer. 3. Adjuster lever does not engage star wheel. 4. Adjuster installed on wrong wheel.
Brake light glows	1. Leak in the hydraulic system. 2. Air in the system. 3. Improperly adjusted master cylinder pushrod. 4. Uneven lining wear. 5. Failure to center combination valve or proportioning valve.

Appendix

General Conversion Table

Multiply by	To convert	To	
2.54	Inches	Centimeters	.3937
30.48	Feet	Centimeters	.0328
.914	Yards	Meters	1.094
1.609	Miles	Kilometers	.621
6.45	Square inches	Square cm.	.155
.836	Square yards	Square meters	1.196
16.39	Cubic inches	Cubic cm.	.061
28.3	Cubic feet	Liters	.0353
.4536	Pounds	Kilograms	2.2045
3.785	Gallons	Liters	.264
.068	Lbs./sq. in. (psi)	Atmospheres	14.7
.138	Foot pounds	Kg. m.	7.23
1.014	H.P. (DIN)	H.P. (SAE)	.9861
—	To obtain	From	Multiply by

Note: 1 cm. equals 10 mm.; 1 mm. equals .0394".

Conversion—Common Fractions to Decimals and Millimeters

Common Fractions	*Decimal Fractions*	*Millimeters (approx.)*	*Common Fractions*	*Decimal Fractions*	*Millimeters (approx.)*	*Common Fractions*	*Decimal Fractions*	*Millimeters (approx.)*
1/128	.008	0.20	11/32	.344	8.73	43/64	.672	17.07
1/64	.016	0.40	23/64	.359	9.13	11/16	.688	17.46
1/32	.031	0.79	3/8	.375	9.53	45/64	.703	17.86
3/64	.047	1.19	25/64	.391	9.92	23/32	.719	18.26
1/16	.063	1.59	13/32	.406	10.32	47/64	.734	18.65
5/64	.078	1.98	27/64	.422	10.72	3/4	.750	19.05
3/32	.094	2.38	7/16	.438	11.11	49/64	.766	19.45
7/64	.109	2.78	29/64	.453	11.51	25/32	.781	19.84
1/8	.125	3.18	15/32	.469	11.91	51/64	.797	20.24
9/64	.141	3.57	31/64	.484	12.30	13/16	.813	20.64
5/32	.156	3.97	1/2	.500	12.70	53/64	.828	21.03
11/64	.172	4.37	33/64	.516	13.10	27/32	.844	21.43
3/16	.188	4.76	17/32	.531	13.49	55/64	.859	21.83
13/64	.203	5.16	35/64	.547	13.89	7/8	.875	22.23
7/32	.219	5.56	9/16	.563	14.29	57/64	.891	22.62
15/64	.234	5.95	37/64	.578	14.68	29/32	.906	23.02
1/4	.250	6.35	19/32	.594	15.08	59/64	.922	23.42
17/64	.266	6.75	39/64	.609	15.48	15/16	.938	23.81
9/32	.281	7.14	5/8	.625	15.88	61/64	.953	24.21
19/64	.297	7.54	41/64	.641	16.27	31/32	.969	24.61
5/16	.313	7.94	21/32	.656	16.67	63/64	.984	25.00
21/64	.328	8.33						

Conversion—Millimeters to Decimal Inches

mm	*inches*	*mm*	*inches*	*mm*	*inches*	*mm*	*inches*	*mm*	*inches*
1	.039 370	31	1.220 470	61	2.401 570	91	3.582 670	210	8.267 700
2	.078 740	32	1.259 840	62	2.440 940	92	3.622 040	220	8.661 400
3	.118 110	33	1.299 210	63	2.480 310	93	3.661 410	230	9.055 100
4	.157 480	34	1.338 580	64	2.519 680	94	3.700 780	240	9.448 800
5	.196 850	35	1.377 949	65	2.559 050	95	3.740 150	250	9.842 500
6	.236 220	36	1.417 319	66	2.598 420	96	3.779 520	260	10.236 200
7	.275 590	37	1.456 689	67	2.637 790	97	3.818 890	270	10.629 900
8	.314 960	38	1.496 050	68	2.677 160	98	3.858 260	280	11.032 600
9	.354 330	39	1.535 430	69	2.716 530	99	3.897 630	290	11.417 300
10	.393 700	40	1.574 800	70	2.755 900	100	3.937 000	300	11.811 000
11	.433 070	41	1.614 170	71	2.795 270	105	4.133 848	310	12.204 700
12	.472 440	42	1.653 540	72	2.834 640	110	4.330 700	320	12.598 400
13	.511 810	43	1.692 910	73	2.874 010	115	4.527 550	330	12.992 100
14	.551 180	44	1.732 280	74	2.913 380	120	4.724 400	340	13.385 800
15	.590 550	45	1.771 650	75	2.952 750	125	4.921 250	350	13.779 500
16	.629 920	46	1.811 020	76	2.992 120	130	5.118 100	360	14.173 200
17	.669 290	47	1.850 390	77	3.031 490	135	5.314 950	370	14.566 900
18	.708 660	48	1.889 760	78	3.070 860	140	5.511 800	380	14.960 600
19	.748 030	49	1.929 130	79	3.110 230	145	5.708 650	390	15.354 300
20	.787 400	50	1.968 500	80	3.149 600	150	5.905 500	400	15.748 000
21	.826 770	51	2.007 870	81	3.188 970	155	6.102 350	500	19.685 000
22	.866 140	52	2.047 240	82	3.228 340	160	6.299 200	600	23.622 000
23	.905 510	53	2.086 610	83	3.267 710	165	6.496 050	700	27.559 000
24	.944 880	54	2.125 980	84	3.307 080	170	6.692 900	800	31.496 000
25	.984 250	55	2.165 350	85	3.346 450	175	6.889 750	900	35.433 000
26	1.023 620	56	2.204 720	86	3.385 820	180	7.086 600	1000	39.370 000
27	1.062 990	57	2.244 090	87	3.425 190	185	7.283 450	2000	78.740 000
28	1.102 360	58	2.283 460	88	3.464 560	190	7.480 300	3000	118.110 000
29	1.141 730	59	2.322 830	89	3.503 903	195	7.677 150	4000	157.480 000
30	1.181 100	60	2.362 200	90	3.543 300	200	7.874 000	5000	196.850 000

To change decimal millimeters to decimal inches, position the decimal point where desired on either side of the millimeter measurement shown and reset the inches decimal by the same number of digits in the same direction. For example, to convert 0.001 mm to decimal inches, reset the decimal behind the 1 mm (shown on the chart) to 0.001; change the decimal inch equivalent (0.039″ shown) to 0.000039″.

Tap Drill Sizes

National Fine or S.A.E.

Screw & Tap Size	*Threads Per Inch*	*Use Drill Number*
No. 5	44	37
No. 6	40	33
No. 8	36	29
No. 10	32	21
No. 12	28	15
1/4	28	3
5/16	24	1
3/8	24	Q
7/16	20	W
1/2	20	29/64
9/16	18	33/64
5/8	18	37/64
3/4	16	11/16
7/8	14	13/16
1 1/8	12	1 3/64
1 1/4	12	1 11/64
1 1/2	12	1 27/64

Tap Drill Sizes

National Coarse or U.S.S.

Screw & Tap Size	*Threads Per Inch*	*Use Drill Number*
No. 5	40	39
No. 6	32	36
No. 8	32	29
No. 10	24	25
No. 12	24	17
1/4	20	8
5/16	18	F
3/8	16	5/16
7/16	14	U
1/2	13	27/64
9/16	12	31/64
5/8	11	17/32
3/4	10	21/32
7/8	9	49/64
1	8	7/8
1 1/8	7	63/64
1 1/4	7	1 7/64
1 1/2	6	1 11/32

Decimal Equivalent Size of the Number Drills

Drill No.	Decimal Equivalent	Drill No.	Decimal Equivalent	Drill No.	Decimal Equivalent
80	.0135	53	.0595	26	.1470
79	.0145	52	.0635	25	.1495
78	.0160	51	.0670	24	.1520
77	.0180	50	.0700	23	.1540
76	.0200	49	.0730	22	.1570
75	.0210	48	.0760	21	.1590
74	.0225	47	.0785	20	.1610
73	.0240	46	.0810	19	.1660
72	.0250	45	.0820	18	.1695
71	.0260	44	.0860	17	.1730
70	.0280	43	.0890	16	.1770
69	.0292	42	.0935	15	.1800
68	.0310	41	.0960	14	.1820
67	.0320	40	.0980	13	.1850
66	.0330	39	.0995	12	.1890
65	.0350	38	.1015	11	.1910
64	.0360	37	.1040	10	.1935
63	.0370	36	.1065	9	.1960
62	.0380	35	.1100	8	.1990
61	.0390	34	.1110	7	.2010
60	.0400	33	.1130	6	.2040
59	.0410	32	.1160	5	.2055
58	.0420	31	.1200	4	.2090
57	.0430	30	.1285	3	.2130
56	.0465	29	.1360	2	.2210
55	.0520	28	.1405	1	.2280
54	.0550	27	.1440		

Decimal Equivalent Size of the Letter Drills

Letter Drill	Decimal Equivalent	Letter Drill	Decimal Equivalent	Letter Drill	Decimal Equivalent
A	.234	J	.277	S	.348
B	.238	K	.281	T	.358
C	.242	L	.290	U	.368
D	.246	M	.295	V	.377
E	.250	N	.302	W	.386
F	.257	O	.316	X	.397
G	.261	P	.323	Y	.404
H	.266	Q	.332	Z	.413
I	.272	R	.339		

Anti-Freeze Chart

Temperatures Shown in Degrees Fahrenheit +32 is Freezing

Cooling System Capacity Quarts	*Quarts of ETHYLENE GLYCOL Needed for Protection to Temperatures Shown Below*													
	1	*2*	*3*	*4*	*5*	*6*	*7*	*8*	*9*	*10*	*11*	*12*	*13*	*14*
10	+24°	+16°	+ 4°	−12°	−34°	−62°								
11	+25	+18	+ 8	− 6	−23	−47								
12	+26	+19	+10	0	−15	−34	−57°							
13	+27	+21	+13	+ 3	− 9	−25	−45							
14			+15	+ 6	− 5	−18	−34							
15			+16	+ 8	0	−12	−26							
16			+17	+10	+ 2	− 8	−19	−34	−52°					
17			+18	+12	+ 5	− 4	−14	−27	−42					
18			+19	+14	+ 7	0	−10	−21	−34	−50°				
19			+20	+15	+ 9	+ 2	− 7	−16	−28	−42				
20				+16	+10	+ 4	− 3	−12	−22	−34	−48°			
21				+17	+12	+ 6	0	− 9	−17	−28	−41			
22				+18	+13	+ 8	+ 2	− 6	−14	−23	−34	−47°		
23				+19	+14	+ 9	+ 4	− 3	−10	−19	−29	−40		
24				+19	+15	+10	+ 5	0	− 8	−15	−23	−34	−46°	
25				+20	+16	+12	+ 7	+ 1	− 5	−12	−20	−29	−40	−50°
26					+17	+13	+ 8	+ 3	− 3	− 9	−16	−25	−34	−44
27					+18	+14	+ 9	+ 5	− 1	− 7	−13	−21	−29	−39
28					+18	+15	+10	+ 6	+ 1	− 5	−11	−18	−25	−34
29					+19	+16	+12	+ 7	+ 2	− 3	− 8	−15	−22	−29
30					+20	+17	+13	+ 8	+ 4	− 1	− 6	−12	−18	−25

For capacities over 30 quarts divide true capacity by 3. Find quarts Anti-Freeze for the ⅓ and multiply by 3 for quarts to add.

For capacities under 10 quarts multiply true capacity by 3. Find quarts Anti-Freeze for the tripled volume and divide by 3 for quarts to add.

To Increase the Freezing Protection of Anti-Freeze Solutions Already Installed

Cooling System Capacity Quarts	*Number of Quarts of ETHYLENE GLYCOL Anti-Freeze Required to Increase Protection*													
	From +20° F. to					*From +10° F. to*					*From 0° F. to*			
	0°	*−10°*	*−20°*	*−30°*	*−40°*	*0°*	*−10°*	*−20°*	*−30°*	*−40°*	*−10°*	*−20°*	*−30°*	*−40°*
10	1¾	2¼	3	3½	3¾	¾	1½	2¼	2¾	3¼	¾	1½	2	2½
12	2	2¾	3½	4	4½	1	1¾	2½	3¼	3¾	1	1¾	2½	3¼
14	2¼	3¼	4	4¾	5½	1¼	2	3	3¾	4½	1	2	3	3½
16	2½	3½	4½	5¼	6	1¼	2½	3½	4¼	5¼	1¼	2¼	3¼	4
18	3	4	5	6	7	1½	2¾	4	5	5¾	1½	2½	3¾	4¾
20	3¼	4½	5¾	6¾	7½	1¾	3	4¼	5½	6½	1½	2¾	4¼	5¼
22	3½	5	6¼	7¼	8¼	1¾	3¼	4¾	6	7¼	1¾	3¼	4½	5½
24	4	5½	7	8	9	2	3½	5	6½	7½	1¾	3½	5	6
26	4¼	6	7½	8¾	10	2	4	5½	7	8¼	2	3¾	5½	6¾
28	4½	6¼	8	9½	10½	2¼	4¼	6	7½	9	2	4	5¾	7¼
30	5	6¾	8½	10	11½	2½	4½	6½	8	9½	2¼	4¼	6¼	7¾

Test radiator solution with proper hydrometer. Determine from the table the number of quarts of solution to be drawn off from a full cooling system and replace with undiluted anti-freeze, to give the desired increased protection. For example, to increase protection of a 22-quart cooling system containing Ethylene Glycol (permanent type) anti-freeze, from +20° F. to −20° F. will require the replacement of 6¼ quarts of solution with undiluted anti-freeze.

Index